GOD
AS THE
MYSTERY
OF THE
WORLD

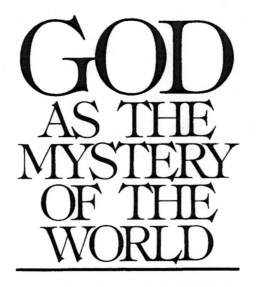

GOD
AS THE MYSTERY OF THE WORLD

*On the Foundation of the Theology
of the Crucified One
in the Dispute between Theism and Atheism*

by

EBERHARD JÜNGEL

Foreword by
R. DAVID NELSON

translated by
DARRELL L. GUDER

B L O O M S B U R Y
LONDON · NEW DELHI · NEW YORK · SYDNEY

Bloomsbury T&T Clark

An imprint of Bloomsbury Publishing Plc

50 Bedford Square   1385 Broadway
London   New York
WC1B 3DP   NY 10018
UK   USA

www.bloomsbury.com

Bloomsbury is a registered trade mark of Bloomsbury Publishing Plc

English translation first published 1983

Reprinted with a new foreword in 2014

© Wm. B. Eerdmans Publishing Company, 2014

Darrell L. Guder has asserted his right under the Copyright, Designs and
Patents Act, 1988, to be identified as Author of this work.

Translated from the Third Revised German Edtion
of *Gott als Geheimnis der Welt*,
© Eberhard Jüngel, J. C. B. Mohr (Paul Siebeck), Tübingen, 1977

British Library Cataloguing-in-Publication Data
A catalogue record for this book is available from the British Library.

ISBN: PB: 978-0-5672-6544-9
ePDF: 978-0-5676-5983-5

Library of Congress Cataloging-in-Publication Data
A catalogue record for this book is available from the Library of Congress.

Typeset by Newgen Knowledge Works (P) Ltd., Chennai, India

Contents

Foreword to the First
and Second Editions

Whether what is obvious will be understood is anything but obvious. Theology is obviously talk about God. But does it understand what it is talking about?

The studies in this book are intended in their way to aid us so that we can *say* what we are actually *talking* about when we talk *about God*. Who or what is God? Such a question may seem estranging in the context of what is obvious for theology. It interrupts the normal course of talk about God. One normally feels that he knows very well what he is talking about here, so that such an interruption appears at least superfluous. Why should yet another statement be made about what we are talking about?

It must and should be done so that our talk about God does not end up silencing him. Compared to atheistic thoughtlessness, this is the much greater danger for theology and for the Christian faith: that God will be talked to death, that he is silenced by the very words that seek to talk about him. Both what is conscious and what is unconscious, both the dumb and the garrulous silencing of God, are the result of the fact that we no longer dare to think God. Both the atheism and the theology of the modern day stand equally overshadowed by the dark clouds of the unthinkability of God. Both faith and unbelief seem to regard these shadows as their destiny. At the end of the history of metaphysics, God appears to have become unthinkable.

The attempts to think in this book are directed against that appearance. Their goal is to illumine the possibility of talk about God based on the experience of the humanity of God, and to learn to think God again on the basis of un-ambiguous talk about God. Clearly this is impossible without clarifying the appearance of the unthinkability of God as it has evolved in history. The systematic discussions are thus always linked with historical remembrances. Beyond that, the connection of systematic thinking and historical analysis should express the hermeneutical insight presupposed in this book that the perceiving and under-standing reason is thoroughly historical in its depth structure. Historical re-membrances are, however, not ends in themselves in theology. They have at least the function of protecting us from being tyrannized by the past. Thus they serve to interrupt the flow of tradition with the truth question about who or what God actually is. Whoever will permit himself this interruption will come closer to the truth.

There are two approaches in contemporary theology by which the attempt is being made to learn to think God again. The one way, pursued by Wolfhart Pannenberg with impressive consequentiality, is to think God 'God having been removed' (*remoto deo*) in order to arrive at the disclosure of the thought of God which then functions as the framework for the Christian faith's own understanding of God. The studies in this book will take the opposite approach. The thinking here pursues a path which, one might say, goes from the inside toward the outside, from the specifically Christian faith experience to a concept of God which claims universal validity. The goal of the intellectual route adopted in this book is not to demonstrate the thinkability of God on the basis of general anthropological definitions, but rather to think God and also man on the basis of the event of God's self-disclosure which leads to the experience of God, and thus to demonstrate that the Christian truth is universally valid on the basis of its inner power.

It is inherent in the nature of this content that one can go this way only by means of rather complicated thought processes—but how much more complicated were the thoughts of the great theologians of past ages! I have not shied away from this, gaining encouragement on occasion by looking at the other sciences with quite different levels of complexity, since there is certainly no lack today of popular theological books. In order to avoid any misunderstanding, I would like expressly to state that I regard this literary genre to be extremely important. The best minds are good enough for it. But since the difference from the genre of scientific theological literature is so often and apparently intentionally blurred, there is certainly reason to fear that it will only seldom be the best minds which make themselves known beyond the boundaries of their guild. A characteristic of this blurring is a certain haste with which "opus after opus is thrown at the paper"—as von Korf said of his famous "Nieswurz- und andere Sonaten" ('Sneezing Powder and Other Sonatas'). Von Korf did this while "sitting at his secure desk," whereas we recently read as the recommendation for one theological book that it had *not* been written at the desk! Be that as it may, what is beneficial for genius is probably more of a hindrance for professional and professorial work. In contemporary theology there is too much written too hastily, but there is not enough thought.

By contrast, "In thinking all things become solitary and slow."[1] That is certainly true when the goal is to expose God's thinkability out of the experience of the worthwhileness of thinking God. In this undertaking, I am conscious of my bonds to theologians of such varying approaches as Hans-Georg Geyer, Gerhard Ebeling, and Wolfhart Pannenberg, as well as not a few Catholic colleagues, although the intellectual routes taken may be different. If we, while walking those routes, would only learn to say what we are talking about when we are talking about God! Only then will we experience the dimensions of what is lost if God is silenced.

Karl Barth once critically remarked that an entire dimension, that of *mys-*

---

1. Martin Heidegger, "The Thinker as Poet," *Poetry, Language, Thought,* tr. A. Hofstadter (New York: Harper & Row, 1971), p. 9.

tery, had been lost to recent Protestantism, and also to the newer philosophy related to it.[2] But it can be gained back only through experiences with God, which when once made demand that they be told and grasped as "public mystery"—something we should not really have to hear first from Goethe as he was observing nature. The experience which is characteristic for Christian faith, that experience which allows one to think and to tell of God as the mystery of the world, is an experience with experience which is made possible by the *word of the cross.* Its particular hallmark is that in it all experiences with reality, both those past and those yet to happen, even experience itself, is to be experienced once more, because it is now encountered within the context of the possiblity of nonbeing, a possibility conquered on the cross of Jesus Christ but made thinkable by that very event. Whoever feels that he must complain about attempts to understand reality within the context of its possible nonbeing, and thus complain about speculation, mysticism, or even worse, is referred critically both to his own life experience and certainly to the neither speculative nor mystical statement of Paul according to which the God who identifies himself with the crucified Christ calls into existence what does not exist (Rom. 4:17). There is a specifically theological problem level for the discussion of the question, Why is there anything at all rather than nothing? The systematic neglect or even allegedly critical disregard of this problem level ultimately affects the concept of God. And in the end, one thinks of nothing at all when one talks about God. One finds the substitute then in the form of more or less pitiful borrowings from that oriental wisdom which does in fact have some notion of what to do with "nothingness."[3] What was once the Christian world flees now to so-called transcendental meditation instead of preparing itself, by returning to what is most authentic in it, for the composure with which a life is lived which will dare to subject itself to the mystery of nothingness.

In contrast with that, I have allowed myself to take seriously the fact that the Christian faith lives out of that particular proclamation which identifies God with the crucified man Jesus and thus differentiates between God and God. Nietzsche's polemic remark that such a God would be a 'negation of God' (*dei negatio*) has been taken up in a positive way in order to advance to a fruitful stage the controversy, now made necessary by dialectical theology, with the metaphysical tradition which dominates both theology and philosophy. Fruitful controversy is, however, something other than sweeping rejection or even defamation, as has become common in the school of dialectical theology where too easy reference is made to Pascal's (quite correct) differentiation between the God of Abraham, Isaac, and Jacob and the God of the philosophers. It is quite obvious that when this is done over a long period of time, the result is sterility. Sweeping criticism, moreover, does not change the criticized traditions, but rather permits them to expand even further under a minimally altered surface. A differentiated appreciation of our historical sources will lead, on the other hand, to an ultimately radical controversy with it.

It is to be hoped that the new treatment of the analogy problem in this

2. Karl Barth, *CD,* I/1, p. xii.
3. See, for example, the impressive book by Hoseki Shinichi Hisamatsu, *Die Fülle des Nichts; Vom Wesen des Zen; Eine systematische Erläuterung,* trs. T. Hirata and J. Fischer, ed. E. Cold (n.p., n.d.).

book will make this clear. The corresponding hermeneutical study of the problem of the speakability of God is also nourished by the material statement that God has defined himself through identification with the crucified Jesus. Thus it belongs very close to the discussion of the humanity of God which attempts to think God as the original unity of life and death for the sake of life. If this is really *thought*, then we can say what we are talking about when we talk about God. For then we can say that God is love. As love he is the mystery of the world. And through this mystery of love, man moves from the fixation of wanting to have into the freedom of being able to be. In the love which God merits being called, we are made those who are out of those who have.[4]

Basically the intent of all the studies in this book is nothing else than to exposit consequently this one statement from First John: God is love (I John 4:8). The only way to deal adequately with this statement in one's thinking is through the concept of the triune God, just as the only way to deal adequately with it in one's actions and suffering is through one's own love. Regin Prenter's suggestions along these lines[5] have encouraged me to pursue further some earlier theses (in my Barth paraphrase, *The Doctrine of the Trinity: God's Being Is in Becoming,* and in a series of shorter publications from which two were earlier versions of what is contained in this book on pp. 141ff and 314ff) with regard to the founding of the doctrine of the Trinity on faith in the crucified Son of God, and in that process to restore to the dark statement of the death of God its good christological meaning.

These thoughts on the matter, which have already been published and which have been discussed in a series of lectures, have been broadly received, although not seldom with a noteworthy silence. Not a few statements have reappeared in virtual verbatim citation in the writings of other authors. All this has encouraged me to present to the public myself how I conceive of the foundation of the doctrine of God, consisting formally in the consequent exegesis of the kerygmatic identification of God and love, because materially it should be the explication of the doctrine of the Trinity which is based on the self-identification of God with the crucified man Jesus. That I found my own thoughts (although somewhat disguised) used as *objections* to me in one book (Karl Barth had similar experiences in the same context for which he is more likely to find an explanation in heaven than I am in Tübingen!) lends the characteristics of a satirical game to the theological scene today. Perhaps that is an indication that the theological tragedies of the last ten years are finding their appropriate ending. But enough of that!

4. This fundamental anthropological proposition of the last part of this book comes close in substance to Erich Fromm's appeal to advance human existence from the basic mode of having into that of being. The remarkable book in which Fromm presents his view (*To Have or To Be* [World Perspectives, vol. 50] [New York: Harper & Row, 1976]) first came to my attention after this study went to press, so that I can only make mention of it here. But even in this reference it should not remain unsaid that in distinction from Fromm I am interested not so much in the ethical demand to exchange the existential mode of having for that of being, as I am in the indicative which makes us who have into people who are. I hope that I will have opportunity to present my points of both similarity and difference on another occasion.

5. Regin Prenter, "Der Gott, der Liebe ist; Das Verhältnis der Gotteslehre zur Christologie," *Theologische Literaturzeitung,* 96 (1971), 401ff.

What is definitely more important to me is the gratifying fact that, in spite of profound differences, there is still a mutually held awareness of the problem in the various serious movements of Protestant and Catholic theology. In my judgment this common awareness consists of the insight that Christianity is to be made understandable as a "religion" of *freedom*, and that the Christian faith is to be made understandable as a life based on the experience of *liberating freedom*. That man, as a being who is subjected to unfreedom and must constantly subject himself to unfreedom, nevertheless is destined for freedom, and that he is related to God in his unfreedom but especially in his freedom, is the fundamental conviction of any contemporary theology of importance.

But the more exact definition of the relation between God and man within the horizon of the differentiation between freedom and unfreedom reveals broad differences. Among them we find the battle about the political implications of theology. In the context of this foreword I should like to make only one remark on this: I do not regard it as appropriate and useful to the matter at hand when the political and social relevance of a theological endeavor is supposed to be demonstrated by the immediate production of the corresponding "applications and concretions." Certainly this is problematic if only because in this way the impression may easily be made that theological reflection becomes relevant only by means of such "concretions"—which in truth are mostly totally unconcrete. But whoever has eyes to read will discover in this concentration on the task of learning to think God more than enough political and social relevance of the Christian faith in the crucified God. To the person for whom the way from so-called theory to so-called practice cannot be traversed quickly enough (and I certainly do know the reasons to be given for that!), I gladly confess that it is my fear that I have not been slow enough in my thinking. Often enough, speed is desperately needed in the dimension of action. And what is unconditional is the immediate summons to action. However, the evidence of ethical immediacy to action may not be permitted to tyrannize over the stringency and consequence of the dogmatic mediation of truth. The claim of the kerygma may not do that either. There should be an end to the constant complaints about the alleged distance between dogmatic and hermeneutical studies on the one hand and social and churchly practice on the other. I could not preach without these allegedly too abstract scientific labors—and conversely, as a result of preceding scientific reflection, the sermon can be protected from its frequent transformation into apparent scientific lectures. Everything in its place and at its time!

Narrative has its own place and its special time, and as such narrative will be considered more precisely in the last section, as the basic hermeneutical feature of that kind of Evangelical talk which articulates the humanity of God. Following implicitly Karl Barth's *Church Dogmatics* and with explicit reception of the programs presented by Harald Weinrich and Johann Baptist Metz, I have attempted to present both the possibility and the necessity of a narrative theology. In so doing, I could return to my own analyses of the essence of the parables of Jesus and of metaphorical language in general. The analogy of faith has a basic narrative aspect in its structure of perception. And the humanity of God requires telling, as does any love story; to put it in Paul Gerhardt's words: ". . . Out of my rejoicing heart / will I thy deeds e'er more relate / before thy people o'er the world / until I from this life depart." But I should not fail to mention that I have not been able to decide whether it is possible to carry out narrative theology in the form of a scientific dogmatic,[6] or whether narrative theology does not rather belong to the practical expression of the church and have its *Sitz im Leben* in proclamation. But it is certainly not a matter of doubt for me that the business of argumentative theology is not an end in itself but rather takes place and must take place as a ministry of the word which tells of the identity of God and love.

The studies in this book should, in any event, be understood this way and no other way. I have set up its order 'according to the rationale of knowing' (*secundum rationem congnoscendi*), whereas the 'rationale of being' (*ratio essendi*) of the problematics under discussion would more likely invite one to begin the reading of these studies at the final section. The advantage for the reader is that he can decide more quickly whether it will be worthwhile for him to become involved in the total scope of this *study book,* which does in fact require the patience of a *studious* spirit.

In any case, my present and earlier colleagues have shown much patience in the critical review of the various manuscripts which have been written before final publication. I would like to thank the following for their many forms of assistance: Mrs. Hanne Dicke, Mrs. Christine Janowski, Mr. Eberhard Grötzinger, and Pastor Lukas Spinner. I have been pleased to entrust this book to the careful and understanding publishing art of Dr. Hans Georg Siebeck. He also encouraged me to present these studies to the public after they had been presented in constantly reworked form in lectures held since 1968 in Berlin, Zürich, Copenhagen, and Tübingen. I present them with a reminder of the epistemological maxim of Aristotle that even the most imperfect knowledge of something worth knowing is more to be striven after than the most certain knowledge of something inconsequential.

Tübingen, August 1976   EBERHARD JÜNGEL

---

6. Dietrich Ritschl's recently published sketch, " 'Story' als Rohmaterial der Theologie," *Theologische Existenz,* vol. 192, has increased my doubt even more.

Foreword to the Third Edition

When this book was presented to the public last year [1976], I doubted whether it would find interested readers in the current theological scene. For it did appear that the 'theological mode of discourse' (*modus loquendi theologicus*) to which this book subscribes had largely been forgotten and probably also repressed, if not made quite purposefully the object of suspicion. Was that a deceptive appearance? Apparently the book has found its critical readers. I have reason to add my expression of gratitude to this third edition.[1]

I have been, above all, surprised and delighted at the ecumenical echo to this study, which was even reviewed in one place under the lovely title, "Oekumene out of the Depths of Scripture."[2] It is certainly all right that especially Catholic theology should see itself challenged both positively and critically. If I am seeing things correctly, all the questions directed to my theological position can be summarized in the recommendation to return to the anthropological grounding of the thought of God, or to advance to a new and finally persuasive 'elenctic use of reason' (*usus elenchticus rationis*), the result of which should be "to demonstrate on the path of reason the boundaries of reason and the necessity of the self-surpassing of reason."[3] Man should be made understandable as the question on the basis of which the "quiddity of a possible answer," if not "its content," "is defined" or is definable.[4] The term "revelational positivism," usually used so easily and so ungraciously (cheap un-grace!), has not been called on here, and I appreciate that. But the objections of the very respectable critics maintain that, in spite of the effort to overcome theologically the ugly chasm between "the God of Abraham, Isaac, and Jacob" and the "God of the philosophers," the possibilities of reason have not been fully exhausted, those possi-

---

1. I am happy to note here my proximity to the Descartes interpretation of Julius Harms, "Sein und Zeit bei Cartesius," *Neue Zeitschrift für systematische Theologie*, 18 (1976), 277-94, and Christian Link, *Subjektivität und Wahrheit; Die Grundlegung der neuzeitlichen Metaphysik durch Descartes* (Stuttgart: Klett-Cotta, 1978).

2. Albert Brandenburg, "Oekumene aus der Tiefe der Schrift; Die Gotteslehre als letzter Orientierungspunkt für alle theologischen Positionen," *Rheinischer Merkur*, 33 (May 26, 1978), nr. 21, p. 29.

3. Thus Walter Kasper, "Abschied vom Gott der Philosophen," *Evangelische Kommentare*, 10 (1977), 622.

4. Thus Heinrich Fries, "Gott als Geheimnis der Welt; zum neuesten Werk von Eberhard Jüngel," *Herder Korrespondenz*, 31 (1977), 529.

bilities which would permit the validation of those presuppositions of the Christian faith which illumine its necessity.

In point of fact I have not done that, and for good reason. The entire book sought to make plausible this good reason for not pushing the desire to provide a rational ground too far and letting it have its effect in the wrong place. For too much, not too little(!), speaks for the reasonableness of God's revelation and of faith in him for it to be rational to provide a rational foundation for that reasonableness. The scandal which the word of the cross is for the wisdom of the world is not to be found in the fact that it is not reasonable enough. That explains why I regard the question-answer model in which man is asserted to be the question to which talk about God is supposed to answer as inappropriate. This model fails to recognize the center of the Christian faith whose necessity it still wants to prove, namely, that God *has* spoken definitively, that *God has become man*—and what is there the answer and the question? If *that* is supposed to be capable of seriously being believed, then any rational grounding which precedes faith arrives too late and in a fashion which disqualifies the entire undertaking. In a colloquium with my Catholic colleague in Tübingen, Walter Kasper, and his colleagues, we agreed that theological thinking lives both materially and formally out of the past statements of the New Testament which bear the future in themselves and thus are neither capable of nor require any rational grounding. That theology which is concerned about its reasonableness would do well to be reminded by "the philosopher" (and not only be reminded!) that 'to have to find a proof for the unknown but not for other things' is the downfall of the 'unlettered.' Both the school of philosophy and the school of Scripture will help *against that*.

Tübingen, October 1978   EBERHARD JÜNGEL

Foreword to the English Text

R. David Nelson

Gott als Geheimnis der Welt, Darrell Guder's translation of which is found below, is Eberhard Jüngel's most enduring and significant work, and is widely regarded as one of the great masterpieces of twentieth century Christian theological literature. It is a momentous intellectual feat, a sprawling but meticulously plotted analysis of a theme of perennial interest to the church and academic theology, namely, the question of the nature and functions of responsible human thought and speech about God. The volume, too, has justifiably earned notoriety for the opacity of its language and the intricacy of its argumentation, and is especially challenging for readers searching for an accessible entryway into the thought of its author. Nevertheless, it is a work of profound and lasting theological wisdom, and those who approach it with patience, discernment, and at least a modest level of competency in the issues of the modern Western intellectual tradition will be rewarded richly.

A meager foreword, of course, is hardly the place in which to cultivate virtues of comprehensive reading such as patience, discernment, and competency. Jüngel himself has urged that patience is passion that perseveres.[1] The wisdom literature of the Old Testament, which offers a window into the ethics of daily life in the Second Temple period, persistently locates discernment at the far end of many years of experience, practice, and self-reflection. And competency in any subject is the profit of love's long labor. Indeed, in order to really "get" *Gott als Geheimnis der Welt*—and this is true of any work of literature, theological or otherwise, that is worth getting—one must, as it were, *live with it*, at least for a little while: read it through inquisitively, once, twice, maybe even three times; audit Jüngel's cross-references, and read up on the themes that lie in the background; think hard, beyond the printed page, over its architectonic and the tenability of its argument; etc. To be quite sure, such an approach to *any* text will transcend the interests of all of its readers. And yet many works, including the present volume, resist easy perusal, becoming transparent only upon earnest, careful, and thoughtful study. This being the case, these opening words are not so much an

---

1. See Eberhard Jüngel, "Gottes Geduld—Geduld der Liebe," in *Wertlose Wahrheit—Zur Identität und Relevanz des christlichen Glaubens. Theologische Erörterungen III*, 2. Auflage (Tübingen: Mohr Siebeck, 2003), pp. 183–93.

introductory summary of Jüngel's opus as they are an *invitation* to it. At one pivot in the text, Jüngel insists that any theology worth its salt is a *theologia viatorum*, a theology of the wayfarers, of pilgrims. In precisely that spirit, we invite readers of this reissue of *Gott als Geheimnis der Welt* to hit the road!

Theology as Word-Event

The first German printing of *Gott als Geheimnis der Welt* appeared in 1977[2], fifteen years after the initial release of *Paulus und Jesus*, an edition of Jüngel's doctoral dissertation and also his first major work.[3] These two monographs book-end an extremely productive period of research and writing during which time Jüngel published two additional book-length studies (*Gottes Sein ist im Werden*[4] and *Tod*[5]), several large essays released as pamphlets (perhaps the most notable of which are *Zum Ursprung der Analogie bei Parmenides und Heraklit*[6], *Was ist ein Sakrament?* (with Karl Rahner)[7], and *Metapher* (with Paul Ricoeur)[8], two collections of sermons, and numerous shorter articles. The prodigiousness of this output is especially remarkable when we consider the fact that he spent most of the decade of the 1960s ascending academic ranks and relocating accordingly, before finally settling down at the University of Tübingen in 1969, where he would remain, serving in various capacities in the faculty of Protestant theology, until his retirement in 2003. The texts composed on the fly during Jüngel's early period set the tone, style, and commitments that distinguish his literary career from those of his contemporaries.

We find emerging in this period a vision of Christian theology that follows the trajectory of Anselm of Canterbury's much-celebrated locution *fides quarens*

---

2. Jüngel, *Gott als Geheimnis der Welt. Zur Begründung der Theologie des Gekreuzigten im Streit zwischen Theismus und Atheismus* (Tübingen: J. C. B. Mohr [Paul Siebeck], 1977).

3. Jüngel, *Paulus und Jesus. Eine Untersuchung zur Präzisierung der Frage nach dem Ursprung der Christologie*, Hermeneutische Untersuchungen zur Theologie 2, hgs. Gerhard Ebeling, Ernst Fuchs, and Manfred Mezger (Tübingen: J. C. B. Mohr [Paul Siebeck], 1962).

4. Jüngel, *Gottes Sein ist im Werden. Verantwortliche Rede vom Sein Gottes bei Karl Barth. Eine Paraphrase* (Tübingen: J. C. B. Mohr [Paul Siebeck], 1965). English translation: *God's Being is in Becoming: The Trinitarian Being of God in the Theology of Karl Barth*, trans. John B. Webster (London & New York: Bloomsbury T&T Clark, 2014).

5. Jüngel, *Tod*, Themen der Theologie 8 (Stuttgart & Berlin: Kreuz-Verlag, 1971). English translation: *Death: The Riddle and the Mystery*, trans. Iain & Ute Nicol (Philadelphia: Westminster Press, 1974).

6. Jüngel, *Zum Ursprung der Analogie bei Parmenides und Heraklit* (Berlin: de Gruyter, 1964).

7. Eberhard Jüngel and Karl Rahner, *Was ist ein Sakrament? Verstöße zur Verständigung*, Ökumenische Forschungen. Ergänzende Abteilung. Kleine ökumenische Schriften 6 (Freiburg: Herder, 1971).

8. Eberhard Jüngel and Paul Ricœur, *Metapher. Zur Hermeneutik religiöser Sprache*, Evangelische Theologie: Sonderheft (München: Kaiser Verlag, 1974). The English translation of Jüngel's contribution appears as: "Metaphorical Truth: Reflections on the theological relevance of metaphor as a contribution to the hermeneutics of narrative theology," in *Theological Essays I*, ed. John B. Webster (Edinburgh: T&T Clark, 1989): pp. 16–71.

intellectum—faith seeking understanding. For Jüngel, God has disclosed himself in the world *sub contrario*, in the humanity of Jesus Christ and especially in the humiliation and crucifixion of this man, and, precisely in doing so, has established the intellectual and linguistic conditions necessary for true thought and speech of God. Hence, by *faith* in Jesus Christ alone, theological thinking and speaking become possible, and not *vice versa*. Put another way, Christian theology faithfully pursues its tasks and goals and, indeed, is even worth the effort, only as *theological* theology, that is, as thought and speech oriented toward the *prior* actions of God in electing, creating, and redeeming humanity.

This description of theology as theological is, again, conspicuous in the texts that mark the period leading up to the publication of *Gott als Geheimnis der Welt*. The results are often breathtaking, as, for example, the essay in which he sketches a *theological* theological reading of the question of whether Christian theology should be considered a science alongside the other university disciplines,[9] or his monograph on death in the course of which he parses the existential, social, and metaphysical significances of dying in preparation for an account of death interpreted in light of the gospel,[10] or his extensive engagement with Barth's doctrine of God set within the context of a contemporaneous debate concerning the relation of the Christian confession of God as Father, Son, and Holy Spirit to the doctrine of election.[11] We discover in such paradigmatic pieces a rhetorical and stylistic panache that is well suited for communicating Jüngel's commitment to a theological agenda for theology. He typically commences a reflection by setting forth a problem to be resolved, and then both deconstructing and exacerbating the dilemma in order to expose its theological dimension(s). He then devotes his attention to addressing themes *dogmatically* by positing a tension between thought held sway by the gospel and other "ordinary" modes of human reasoning. The heart of an exemplary piece by our author consists of a sustained commentary upon the extent to which Christianity's peculiar mode of God-talk impacts theology's understanding of the matter(s) at hand. Toward this end, Jüngel engages source materials flexibly rather than exegetically, extracting concepts and assertions on the basis of their usefulness in demonstrating the priority of revealed theology. From beginning to end—and such structural language is deliberately vague, as his writings rarely contain standard introductory and conclusory devices, a quintessential Jüngel work is bereft of expendable prose and thus almost never flatfooted. Rather, the rhetoric is lean muscle; functional, but also powerful and persuasive, and always motivated by the aim of reiterating a theological theology for contemporary Christianity.

A few additional words on the (to extend the metaphor) *athleticism* of Jüngel's prose may be helpful to readers encountering him for the first time in these pages.

---

9. Jüngel, "Das Verhältnis der theologischen Dizsziplinen untereinander," in *Unterwegs zur Sache. Theologische Erörterungen I*, 3. Auflage (Tübingen: Mohr Siebeck, 2000): pp. 34–59.

10. Jüngel, *Tod.*

11. Jüngel, *Gottes Sein ist im Werden.*

The abruptness of Jüngel's style and the subtlety of his method can potentially result in an exasperating reading experience. He is quite fond of spinning neologisms and engaging in other forms of creative wordplay. In the German originals, his syntax is somehow simultaneously complex and poetic, the latter a characteristic that, unfortunately, tends to get lost in translation. Indeed, Jüngel's works are notoriously difficult to render into proper, fluid English, mainly because the German language itself—its instrumentality in bringing to peculiar expression the history, culture, and intellectual tradition shared by its native users (a possibility constitutive of any language vis-à-vis its practitioners)—features so prominently in his literary career. Moreover, Jüngel appears to set extraordinarily high expectations upon his reader, and thus only rarely furnishes contextual information for the sake of the uninitiated. He does not at all produce "textbook" theology, but, on the contrary, assumes that his reader is either quite at home in the intellectual environment surrounding the issue(s) at hand, or perfectly capable of reduplicating the scenery by appealing to outside resources. Perhaps most unnervingly, Jüngel rarely concludes a piece having exhaustively or even satisfactorily resolved any of the dilemmas addressed in the course of the text. He tends to raise new questions while answering others, to fray strings of thought just as he is tying up loose ends. And, finally, it is crucial to note here that, as a general rule, his discourse is hardly linear, though by no means haphazard. Rather, not unlike Barth's oeuvre, the center of Jüngel's theology, and thus also the feature at the heart of his written work, is God's self-revelation in Jesus Christ, and other theological motifs are affixed to theology's witness to Jesus Christ like spokes on a wheel.[12] By consequence of all of these features, the architecture of Jüngel's theology, though impeccably designed, resists easy diagramming. Put another way: he doesn't systematize his theology, he preaches it. Its latent potency resides in its persuasive capacity to grab the attention with and to sway the mind toward Jesus Christ as the mystery of the world.

This brief foray into the rhetoric and style that marks Jüngel's published work leads us right back to the overwhelmingly *theological* temperament of his theology, though now we may hone in on a particular feature that is decisive for an appreciation of the present text, both structurally and materially. As we commented, beginning in *Paulus und Jesus* and culminating in the present volume (though still very much in the foreground in subsequent works), Jüngel is preoccupied with the question of the relation between the revelatory word of God and the human language spoken in correspondence to it. In particular, he invests an enormous amount of energy toward articulating a sophisticated ontology of

---

12. The nod here is to George Hunsinger's study, *How to Read Karl Barth: The Shape of His Theology* (New York and Oxford: Oxford University Press, 1991). While Barth's full literary yield dwarfs that produced by Jüngel, the works of both theologians reflect an internal logic according to which the various themes of theology are positioned subsequently to theology's role of reiterating the gospel of Jesus Christ. See also Paul DeHart's excellent though early essay, "Eberhard Jüngel on the Structure of Theology," in *Theological Studies* 57 (1986): pp. 46–64, esp. pp. 56–9.

language that stresses the event character of those words conscripted by God in communicating his self-revelation in Jesus Christ. Jüngel's preferred locution for encapsulating this phenomenon is *word-event*, a phrase used with great frequency by his *Doktorvater*, Ernst Fuchs, and resonant of a style of post-Ritschlian Lutheran thought oriented to the existential aspects of Christianity.[13] Accordingly, whenever God commandeers human language in order to disclose himself in the event of the word, his coming to speech interrupts the ordinary, referential function of discourse and brings to the occurrence of speech possibilities that transcend the very boundaries of language. The living word of God, that is, makes the human word capable of much more than its functions of denomination and signification. In the event of God's advent in and as the word, human language explodes with power and meaning, for it communicates *Jesus Christ* himself. And in this event, the hearer is human being *in becoming*, for the interruptive word confronts whoever it addresses with *true* humanity, namely, the humanity of God in Jesus Christ. The eschatological speech of the gospel points the hearer toward the *telos* of God's reconciling and sanctifying work, and thus, concomitantly, to humanity's journey toward finding its perfect rest, *as human*, in him.

It is not difficult to grasp why, within Jüngel's *theological* theological account of the intersection of the word of God and human words, the word-events of scripture and sermon are especially important.[14] God arrives in language whenever the word of the cross is spoken; the Old and New Testaments are the recorded testimony of God's arrival in speech, and God comes again to the world whenever and wherever this word is preached according to scripture's testimony. Furthermore, while he never really clarifies precisely how the idea of word-event applies to scriptural and sermonic *textual* forms, that is, to the *written* word, Jüngel includes such first order texts within the analogical-linguistic structure that, he proposes, characterizes God's relation to the world. To be sure, the suggestion that the sermon, especially in its textual form, is ingredient to this relation is a move that will likely meet with suspicion by those inclined to restrict talk of the word of God to

---

13. For overviews of the developments in philosophical and theological hermeneutics behind Jüngel's own analyses, we direct the reader to two excellent studies: James M. Robinson, *Language, Hermeneutic, and History: Theology after Barth and Bultmann* (Eugene, OR: Cascade, 2008), especially pp. 69–137; and Werner G. Jeanrond, *Theological Hermeneutics: Development and Significance* (New York: Crossroad, 1991), pp. 120–58. See also my own brief comments on Jüngel's location along the trajectory of *Lutheran* engagements with these issues in R. David Nelson, *The Interruptive Word: Eberhard Jüngel on the Sacramental Structure of God's Relation to the World*, T&T Clark Studies in Systematic Theology 24, eds. John Webster, Ian A. McFarland, and Ivor Davidson (London: Bloomsbury T&T Clark, 2013), pp. 2–7.

14. See the entirety of *Paulus und Jesus*, during the course of which Jüngel contends that Jesus's own proclamation, the witnesses to which constitute the New Testament gospels, and the early Christian kerygma, documented in Paul's letters and the writings of the latter New Testament, were word-events in the occurrences of which the kingdom of God came to the world in coming to speech. Subsequent to these original kerygmatic occurrences, the church's proclamation of the gospel reiterates this event of arrival. Jüngel never departs from this high view of the sermon as connected to Jesus's preaching and incipient Christian proclamation.

Jesus Christ as the incarnate word, to scripture as the written word, and, perhaps, to tradition as the word's abiding diachronicity in the church. But the description of the sermon as, somehow, a prophetic-linguistic mode of God's eschatological presence in the world was hardly uncommon among those theologians whose thought shaped the intellectual milieu of Jüngel's early career—Barth, Bultmann, Käsemann, Ebeling, and Fuchs, to name only a few.

In any event, just here a camel's nose appears through the tent flap. If a preached sermon, in both its oral and textual forms, participates in the word-shaped structure of God's relation to the world, what about a *theological text* that is sermonic in form and content? Can and does God conscript theological language—the church's secondary reflection upon God's self-revelation in Jesus Christ—such that God can be found in the contingent and often faltering and sometimes even clumsy words of the theologian? We are compelled to raise such hazardous questions because Jüngel's program for theology, especially as we encounter it in the texts from this early period, at least hints at an affirmative answer. We must stress that he never fully explicates the point so as to construct a satisfactory statement on the matter. Nor does he ever claim the category of word-event for any or all of his own theological works (and neither do we do so here!). But the question is worth considering since it embosses *both* the possibilities *and* the problems of Jüngel's hermeneutical moves, and sheds sight upon the implications of such moves for the rhetoric, methods, and obligations of theological discourse. And it brings us right to the threshold of *Gott als Geheimnis der Welt*, which is, unquestionably, Jüngel's most thoroughgoing exercise in *sermonic* theological theology.

Toward the Heart of the Matter

That we are, in fact, confronted by such a theology in *Gott als Geheimnis der Welt* is apparent almost immediately. Jüngel launches his argument by offering some rather brusque comments on the problems of thinking and speaking God in modernity, in doing so identifying those aspects of the tradition from which he desires to depart and setting the stage for his own countermove, which, we discover, is an approach to theological thought and speech that prioritizes the revelation of God's humanity in Jesus Christ. Those who skim his brief preliminary remarks risk overlooking a feature of considerable importance for understanding the entirety of the volume. In the first subsection of the introduction to the text, Jüngel calls into question the legitimacy of, as he encapsulates it, the "traditional hermeneutics of signification," which, according to his reading, is itself a theological gloss on the Aristotelian distinction of form and content.[15] His argument, to which we have already alluded, goes something like this: the Western tradition, following Augustine's following of Aristotle, supposes that reality consists of signs and things signified. A language, for chief instance, is a system

---

15. This point is especially clear in Jüngel's remarks in *Paulus und Jesus* on modern parable interpretation (pp. 87–139, especially pp. 92–8).

of signs—words—organized according to flexible syntactical and grammatical rules such that its user is empowered with the capacity to grasp the reality that lies, ineluctably, externally to occurrences of speech. So far, Jüngel concedes, so good. But what happens when the "thing" allegedly signified by human words is *God*? The hermeneutic of the sign, Jüngel contends, collapses whenever God is identified as the *res significata*, for it allows church and theology to speak of God, but only in such a way that God remains remote from the word, a thing absent to the speech that putatively signifies him. Jüngel is worried, then, that the Western tradition is committed to a hermeneutical program according to which God cannot be truly encountered in speech and thought. God remains, as it were, ineffable and incogitable in human God-talk and God-thought.

For all intents and purposes, *Gott als Geheimnis der Welt* consists of an outright hermeneutical counterproposal to this tradition, so read. For Jüngel, precisely because the hermeneutics of signification posits an ontological gap between the sign and the thing signified, it is unsuitable for the task assigned to it when employed for the purpose of theological speaking and thinking. Consequently, he argues in the course of our text that something altogether different and new happens in revelation, in *God's* word. Normal human discourse, marked as it is by the structural correspondences of sign and thing, knowledge and object, form and content, etc., does not suffice as a vessel for communicating a word that corresponds to God, and must therefore be broken, or interrupted, whenever God conscripts human language for the sake of his self-communication. God, that is, is the primal *speaker* in our God-talk, who, in speaking, explodes the limits and capacities of our language with new possibilities. God comes to speech in and as the superfluity of meaning occurring in the word about him, which, when heard in faith, is capable of speaking new life to the hearer. In just this sense, God, in Jüngel's idiom, is *more than necessary*. God, in perfect freedom vis-à-vis worldly necessity, comes to the world in a word of sheer self- and life-giving love. So it is not the case that theology must simply discard the hermeneutics of the sign. Rather, Jüngel proposes that theological theology must juxtapose with the Augustinian semiotics a hermeneutic of event in order to demonstrate how the word of God behaves in comparison to the ordinary usages of the words of human language.

Jüngel weaves together his reading of this hermeneutical dilemma and its proposed solution with a critique of both classical and modern metaphysical doctrines of God. This segment of the book's argument unfolds in the course of the second chapter of the text, and the trajectory of the analysis, though it appears labyrinthine, is, in fact, crafted with great care. Jüngel begins by demonstrating that the so-called "Death of God" theology, a movement that had succeeded in inspiring a surprising degree of public fanfare in the 1960s, emerged as a result of one of modern thought's legitimate insights, namely, that the metaphysical tradition assigns to God a location 'over' the creaturely economy, and, precisely so, on an ontological plane unreachable via any avenues of creaturely mediation. Nietzsche's madman, personifying one of modernity's most notable responses to this metaphysical concept of deity, concludes that God has been effectively displaced, since a God located above—i.e. *beyond*—the world would necessarily transcend all of the categories and concepts of human thought and the words of human language. Interestingly, Jüngel wastes hardly a breath discussing the proponents and primary sources associated with the "Death of God" theology, using, as it were, merely the movement's name and Nietzschean background as bare furniture for subsequent analyses of, in turn, Bonhoeffer, Hegel, and (briefly) Feuerbach. It is a brilliant gambit that somehow works, and does so *because of*, rather than in spite of, the anachronistic arrangement of his interlocutors. According to Jüngel's exegesis, Bonhoeffer and Hegel read the modern problem of the death of God *Christologically*, asserting, albeit in very different ways, that, in the death of Jesus Christ, God has taken up into his own being the absence of being. The consequence of this move for both theologians, Jüngel shows, is a non-religious (Bonhoeffer) or atheistic (Hegel) reorientation of theological thought and speech, for the death of God in the death of Jesus Christ is, by logic, the death of Western metaphysics—i.e. of a philosophical, though frequently baptized, concept of God. It is Feuerbach who, oddly, becomes both a hero and a foil in Jüngel's tale precisely because he dared push back against his forebear Hegel by asserting that the entire edifice of Christian thought and practice collapses if it is defined as the identity of faith and unbelief, of God and death, of theology and its negation.

Contending that modern theology has not sufficiently answered Feuerbach's legitimate protest against Hegel's Christological idea of the death of God, Jüngel now turns to advance his own proposal, his demonstration of which composes three large chapters covering the final three-fourths of the book's pages. Contra Feuerbach and going beyond Hegel's insight, Jüngel urges that the thesis of the being of God as the unity of life and death in Jesus Christ provides Christian theology with a genuine opportunity both to overturn metaphysical theism and to rebut the admissible claims of modern atheism. Arguing that God's existence is identical to his essence, he proposes that the death of Jesus Christ is, from eternity (however that might be conceived), the very event of God's self-differentiation as Father and Son in the power of the Holy Spirit. Consequently, it is only God's identification with this dead man that can serve as the basis for theological modes of thinking that corresponds to truth. Otherwise, theology drifts into speculation and props up the transcendent God of the philosophers, reducing theological discourse to abject apophaticism which leads, in due course, to the cul-de-sac of atheism (Chapter III). Moreover, theology's God-talk parallels theological God-thought, insofar as theology can truly speak of God and thus commence its unique mode of discourse only by narrating the story of God's decision to be God only by and in his identification with the Crucified Christ. Such a story, when proclaimed, is the world's mystery, an interruptive event of language that confounds all creaturely values and notions of truth and beauty, precisely by introducing the impossible possibility of the creator's unity with non-being (Chapter IV). And such a vision for theological theology entails a radical reorientation of traditional trinitarian concepts. For a doctrine of God that begins and ends with God's going out from and coming back to himself in the crucified and resurrected one must include God's intimate, ontological involvement with creaturely time—with history, and never otherwise (Chapter V).

We can hardly do justice in this foreword to the many nuances of this staggering argument, and will therefore conclude this section by making some general observations. First, we reiterate for the reader that the heart of *Gott als Geheimnis der Welt* is a hermeneutical response to what is, inevitably, a hermeneutical dilemma. Not surprisingly, then, Jüngel is persistently occupied in the main portion of the text with the problem of the relation of God's word and human words, always describing the former as the crisis of the latter that occurs in the event of revelation. For Jüngel, thought and speech of God are only possible on the basis of the new hermeneutical situation that emerges when God comes to the world in the word.

Second, we do well to note that, in German, the titles of the three final chapters suggest some form of symmetry, a rhetorical feature that is somewhat diminished in translation: *Zur Denkbarkeit Gottes, Zur Sagbarkeit Gottes, Zur Menschlichkeit Gottes*. However, the argument, again, is not linear, but a working around the spokes of the wheel in order to highlight the wheel's center, namely, the humanity of God—including and especially his death—in Jesus Christ. This being the case, we suggest that it is not necessary to read these three chapters in their given order. On the contrary, the best strategy for new readers may in fact be to begin this portion, having worked through the introduction and chapter two, with the book's final chapter, "On the Humanity of God," for there Jüngel both employs and modifies the tradition's trinitarian language for God in order to identify the implications of the incarnation for the doctrine of God. This material is helpful to have in mind when working through the earlier chapters on God's conceivability and utterability. In any case, we do well to stress the caveat that the "wheels within wheels" structure of Jüngel's argument in our text demands flexibility and creativity on the part of his readers.

Finally, the circularity of *Gott als Geheimnis der Welt* is a reminder that we should not, especially when wandering upon the expansive plateau of the argument, expect to find the text in its entirety behaving as an exhaustive, organized summary of the Christian faith in the course of which every "i" is dotted and "t" crossed. Nor should we go thumbing through the pages in search of "Jüngel's doctrine of _____," as if the volume provided textbook definitions of various theologoumena. Our point is this: quite a lot goes missing in *Gott als Geheimnis der Welt*. It is, as we have show, a text written to address a specific nexus of issues, and Jüngel is very selective in employing doctrines and concepts toward a solution. Consequently, many alternative moves are simply not considered. This is not say that the book should be exalted to a status beyond criticism for its failure to articulate certain classical themes of Christian theology. On the contrary, we should indeed ask how Jüngel's account of God's *Denkbarkeit*, *Sagbarkeit*, and *Menschlichkeit* may have appeared had he a more robust pneumatology, or ecclesiology, or doctrine of creation, etc. Still, we should not allow

what is lacking to distract us too much from what we actually find in the course
of the analysis.

Theologia viatorum

There is plenty more that can and should be said about the text before us. But
the preceding remarks will suffice, we hope, to equip readers of this reissue to
recognize some of the basic rhetorical conventions and theological commitments
that stand out in *Gott als Geheimnis der Welt*.

   We close by recalling Jüngel insistence that responsible Christian theology is
always a *theologia viatorum*, a theology for those on the way, for faithful pilgrims, for the members of the *ecclesia pressa*, the church marching forward in
time toward the coming eschatological kingdom. If this is true, at least two things
follow, the first of which has been the dominant theme of this opening commentary, namely, that Christian theology is, as Jüngel reminds us, ineluctably
theological, oriented to the priority of God's going out from and returning to
himself in the event of the word. At the same time, a *theologia viatorum*, at least
as Jüngel describes it, is *restless*. Ceaselessly pursuing God's revelatory word,
such a theology is never truly arriving, but always questioning, always exegeting,
always open to the surprises it might uncover. In short, a theological theology, a
theologia viatorum, is, as Jüngel might put it, a *theology in becoming*.

Pentecost
2014

Translator's Preface

It has been both a challenge and an honor to translate Prof. Eberhard Jüngel's highly significant and widely acclaimed work, GOTT ALS GEHEIMNIS DER WELT. As he comments in his own preface, this work requires the "patience of a studious spirit"; the language itself is a paradigm of the thought processes through which Prof. Jüngel leads his reader. It has been my goal to capture the content and the intellectual architecture of his thought in this translation, to render his treatise in English which is both lucid and as true as possible to the original.

For the sake of the English student, all bibliographical citations have been researched and are cited in an English translation if available. All other foreign language citations, primarily Greek and Latin, have also been rendered in English and often provided in the original language as well (the Greek is transliterated). The indices are based upon those of the German edition. Very few abbreviations have been used, and they are listed below. Works have usually been cited in full the first time the title appears in a section, and if necessary, with a brief summary of the title when later referred to within the same section.

I would like to thank the editorial staff of the Wm. B. Eerdmans Publishing Company for their patient and encouraging spirit; I very much respect the integrity of these publishers and their commitment to a high quality of publication. I am grateful to Dr. Ingolf U. Dalferth, Assistant to Prof. Jüngel in the Seminar for Evangelical Theology of the University of Tübingen, for his help at several points, particularly in matters bibliographical. Prof. Owen Cramer of Colorado College, Colorado Springs, provided invaluable help in rendering those Latin and Greek passages which could not be found in English editions into English. The Tutt Library of Colorado College and its industrious staff (particularly at the interlibrary loan desk!) merit particular thanks for their continually gracious help, without which the bibliographical research could not have been completed.

I would like to express my special thanks to William Lee, now of the Institute of Youth Ministries of Fuller Theological Seminary and Young Life, for his meticulous research and editing which resulted in the annotations of both the English editions and the complete bibliographical data for all German works cited in the book; every scholar who uses the book will echo my thanks!

Finally, I am grateful to my colleagues in Young Life for their understanding and encouragement during this project. My wife Judy has lived with this project since just after our marriage, and has thoughtfully and sensitively supported me through every stage of the translation; I am deeply grateful to her and for her!

Ash Wednesday, 1983   DARRELL L. GUDER

Abbreviations

ANF	*The Ante-Nicene Fathers*, ed. Roberts and Donaldson (Buffalo: The Christian Literature Publishing Company, 1884-86).
CD	Karl Barth, *Church Dogmatics*, eds. G. W. Bromiley and T. F. Torrance (Edinburgh: T. & T. Clark, 1936-69; New York: Scribner, 1955-62).
ET	English translation.
LCC	*Library of Christian Classics*, eds. J. Baillie, J. T. McNeill, and H. P. van Dusen (Philadelphia: Westminster Press, 1953ff).
n.d.	No date of publication.
n.p.	No publisher.
NPNF	*Nicene and Post-Nicene Fathers*, ed. P. Schaff (1st series; Grand Rapids: Eerdmans, 1956 [1887ff]; 2nd series; New York: The Christian Literature Company, 1890ff).
STh	Thomas Aquinas, *Summa Theologica*, tr. Fathers of the English Dominican Province (3 vols.; New York: Benziger Press, 1947-48).
TR	Translator.
WA	*Weimarer Ausgabe*, the standard German edition of Luther's works.

GOD
AS THE
MYSTERY
OF THE
WORLD

CHAPTER I

Introduction

SECTION 1: The Definition of the Problem

Often, and in many ways, talk about God has been an embarrassment for the human spirit. Today, at the end of a long history of talk about God, this embarrassment appears to have become a dead-end street. Not only do we not know how one ought to talk about God, but beyond that, the question is raised whether one can talk about him at all, or whether, if one can, one ought to do so. The word "God" was at one time an exact and significant term. However, it now threatens to become a more and more inappropriate word. Outside of a certain narrowly defined religious context, it is seldom made use of anymore with any seriousness. Should it nevertheless be mentioned, painful embarrassment results immediately.

Theology encounters a similar sense of embarrassment today in the field of the sciences when it undertakes to make God understandable as a generally significant word and to endow talk about him with a function relevant to the world. Within the horizon of contemporary scientific thought, God appears at best as a quotation. Science has no need of him, neither as a ground of its own legitimation nor as a reference to the ground of legitimation for that which science itself cannot legitimize. There is no sense in which science needs God. In fact, it is not even permissible for it to have need of him if it wants to be science in accordance with its contemporary understanding of itself. Thus, it not only does not talk about God, it does not even refrain from doing so. It excludes him. In excluding him, it is then atheistic. For the atheism of science, according to a famous statement of Rudolf Bultmann, can "not consist in a denial of the reality of God. It would be equally atheistic if, as science, it affirmed that reality."[1] It would appear, then, that God has no place in our thought and thus has no place in our language. He does not occur, has no *topos* (place, position). That is how it appears. And this appearance is the reason for the embarrassment which God calls forth when, in spite of that, he is encountered as a word in our language. It would seem to be agreed that we are living in an age of the verbal placelessness of God. This placelessness finds its counterpart in the increasing

1. Rudolf Bultmann, "What Does It Mean to Speak of God?", in *Faith and Understanding*, I, tr. L. P. Smith (New York: Harper & Row, 1969), 54.

3

inability to think God and the speechlessness of theology, which is only poorly concealed in its opposite. Theology is thus in a bad state.

This is the way in which a consideration of God as the mystery of the world must probably begin today, if one does not want to forego from the outset being in tune with the times. One must first of all strike up a theological lamentation and declare that the endeavor is almost impossible (but still only "almost") to which he then, remarkably enough, intends to devote his industry, power, and reason. If he does not say this, then he faces from the outset the danger of thinking out of synchronization with the spirit of the time, so that his contemporaries raise their eyebrows and turn away from that which they are supposed to be invited or challenged to think about. A mournful tone dominates contemporary theology, which appears to have taken the true statement in Ecclesiastes 1:18, "For in much wisdom is much vexation," and turned it upside down so that the motto "In much vexation is much wisdom" presents itself as the description of a truly wise theology.

In what follows, the attempt at thought is to be made in opposition to the theological lamentation just described. However, this is not to dispute in any way that the fundamental theoretical and practical changes of our so-called modern age have defined the contemporary awareness of the problem in a way which is especially unsettling for theology. One simply cannot ignore the fact that the dubiousness of talk about God has intensified in the course of what has been called the Second Enlightenment. A theologically responsible use of the word "God" which fails to come to terms with this dubiousness is difficult to conceive of. Nevertheless, this dubiousness need not lead to a state of theological mourning. Such aporias (situations of doubt or dubiousness), if they are really thought through, are still an appropriate way to intensify not only the awareness of the problem but also the possibilities for the further development of a science. Where the difficulties grow, the possibilities also increase. It would appear, then, to be appropriate to work through this basic aporia, which has emerged in the modern age around all talk about God, as an opportunity for more theological theology, if this phrase be allowed.

The following studies are devoted to this intention; in them, the problem of the grounding of the Christian doctrine of God is to be discussed in the dispute between theism and atheism. Since the order of thought belongs to the process of thought, the sequence of these considerations will have to justify itself. The design of these studies will appear either as successful or a failure only at the end of the discussion. However, it would be wise to make some remarks about the structure of the work as a whole. The way in which I intend to do this is to present some considerations which will lead into the essential problem, which then will be the subject of what follows.

1. The word "God" is supposed to be discussed. What does it connote? Does it still signify anything at all?

The traditional hermeneutics of signification tended to decide such questions by dealing with the word "God" as a *sign*. Its assumption was that words are essentially signs. As such, they *mean* something, namely, that which they signify. The critical question which must immediately be posed is this: Is the linguistic relevance of the word exhausted with its sign function? Are the words of language merely signs for something else? We will pursue this question further by considering what words are understood to be when they are taken linguistically as signs and only signs. In this, we shall orient ourselves on some statements of Augustine, who has become the dominant figure in theology with regard to hermeneutics.

What is a sign? The opposite of a thing? A mere label? A reference to something else?

The whistle of a marmot, for example, is a sign. It means something. Similar to the pealing of church bells, it has the function of drawing one's attention to something. The whistle is a signal. As such, it refers to something else. Thus one is tempted to deprive the sign of any autonomous value, any meaning of its own. It appears only to represent. Its own being is exhausted in its function of presenting something else. As the representative of something else, the sign appears to exist solely for the sake of that something else. The sign then means only something which for its part is distinguished from the sign itself.

Yet every sign has a being beyond its sign function. For example, the whistle can be physically measured. The physically measured being of the whistle is, however, something which exists independently of its sign function. Whoever drives against the traffic light notices very quickly that this sign is more than just a sign. The old sign theory, as it can be found, for example, in Augustine's *On Christian Doctrine*,[2] thus distinguished between signs (*signa*) and things (*res*), but understood the *signa* as *res*, although as inauthentic *res*, namely, as signifying things (*res significantes*), which in their 'signifying' (*significare*) relate to certain 'signified things' (*res significatae*). In all this, a 'signified thing' (*res significata*) can for its part signify another 'thing' (*res*), so that the signified thing can also become a sign, a signifying thing.

But there are then those things which signify nothing, which mean nothing else but which are meaningful only in and of themselves, and that is all. They do not refer to anything else, no longer refer away from themselves, but hold us firmly to themselves. They invite us to pause there because they are meaningful in and of themselves. These 'things' (*res*) which do not represent anything else except themselves are, according to Augustine, the *eternal* conditions or facts, the 'eternal things' (*res aeternae*). Man is supposed to and is permitted to 'enjoy' (*frui*) them. "Enjoy" means here to continue to find joy in these objects of pleasure, 'to cling to' them (*inhaerere*). The 'signs' (*signa*), on the other hand, are the temporal things, the *temporalia*, which are never to be enjoyed but only to be used (*uti*), although they certainly are enjoyable. The 'signifying things' (*res significantes*) are only objects for use and nothing more. But the 'signified things' (*res significatae*), which no longer signify anything

---

2. See on what follows: Augustine, *On Christian Doctrine, NPNF,* 1st ser., vol. II, bk. I, ch. 2/2, p. 523. For a more precise understanding, the following essays are helpful: R. Lorenz, "Die Wissenschaftslehre Augustins," *Zeitschrift für Kirchengeschichte,* 67 (1955/56), 29ff and 213ff; G. Ebeling, "Der hermeneutische Ort der Gotteslehre bei Petrus Lombardus und Thomas von Aquin," in *Wort und Glaube II; Beiträge zur Fundamentaltheologie und zur Lehre von Gott* (Tübingen: Mohr [Siebeck], 1969), pp. 209ff. On the meaning of the Augustinian sign theory for the doctrine of the sacraments, see my essay "Das Sakrament—Was ist das?", in E. Jüngel and K. Rahner, *Was ist ein Sakrament?; Vorstösse zur Verständigung* (Freiburg/Basel/Wien: Herder, 1971), pp. 11ff.

else, are those true objects of enjoyment. And only they are such. This distinction between that which is to be enjoyed and that which is to be used was, according to Augustine, constitutive for the good order of being. Thus the very epitome of sin was that man confused the two. Man's sin consists of the fact that he enjoys what he ought only to use. Thus he becomes entangled in the mortality of the *temporalia* ('temporal things') and threatens to perish with the mortal (to enjoy means *inhaerere,* 'to cling to'!).

What is important for our discussion of the word "God" in this context is that the eternal and authentic 'things' *(res)* can be reached only through the *mediation of 'signs' (signa)*. This is true of the whole process of living[3] and especially of thought. Without earthly signs we cannot think the eternal, just as we cannot think of scientific objects without scientific signs. *Res per signa discuntur*: 'things are learned and comprehended through signs.'

This happens in that the signs address the senses and what is signified penetrates through the senses as the content of thought into consciousness *(in cognitationem)*. Signs lead therefore to thinking. They always provide *something* to be thought, which is precisely what they signify. Signs provide that which is signified for our thinking in that they allow it to penetrate via the senses into consciousness. The consciousness imagines what the signs present to it, that which they represent. Thinking means then in this context "to internalize representations," "to appropriate ideas."

In all this, *words* have a very special and decisive function among all the possible signs. Augustine regards them as one of those signs with which people purposefully provide themselves something to think about. Words thus belong to the category of 'given signs' *(signa data)*, which Augustine distinguishes from 'natural signs' *(signa naturalia)*. Whereas natural signs arise without any particular intent (as, e.g., animal tracks), given signs are signals by means of which living beings communicate their thoughts or feelings to each other.

'Given signs' *(signa data)*, which are what humans use in order to arrive at understanding, can relate to all the human senses, but they address primarily the sense of hearing (the *sensus aurium*), sometimes the sense of sight (the *sensus oculorum*), but seldom the other senses. For that reason, the words which encounter the sense of hearing are those signs which have priority for the human person. The 'words' *(verba)* possess 'among men' *(inter homines)* the 'preeminence of signification' *(principatus significandi)*. The word is thus the most significant sign for the function of signifying. That does not lead to the conclusion, however, that signification exhausts the essence of the word. Nonetheless, the word has often been taken only as a sign, and language understood only in terms of its communicative function.

If one deals with the word "God" as a mere sign, then we resolve the question about what this word means or if it means anything at all by examining whether this word signifies something and what it might then signify. Does the word "God" correspond as a *signum* to a 'signified thing' *(res significata)*? Does it mean something? To put it another way: Can something be conceived of in

3. Seen against the hermeneutical background of the doctrine of signs, one can understand why the sacraments, understood as signs which mediate eternal grace effectually, could become theologically the central point of the Christian life in the Catholic Church.

connection with the word "God"? Does the word "God" lead to some kind of thought? Does the word "God" bring some thought content into 'consciousness' (*cogitatio*)? And if so, which content? Or is the word "God" just a meaningless assemblage of letters?

In order to answer these questions, one must first examine how the word "God" is *normally used*. For the "meaning of a word is its use in the language."[4] Usually the usage of a word is perceived both through its syntactic relationship to other words and through the situation in which it is used. What words mean is revealed in the context of other words or on the basis of a situation which replaces the function of other words.

That context of words giving meanings which is our first focus is the sentence. ". . . it is only in the context of a proposition that words have any meaning."[5] If one examines customary language usage in this sense, then it is soon discovered that the word "God" appears to signify something unsurpassable or perhaps an unsurpassable Something: God can do everything. God decides everything. God effects everything. God is everything, has always been all in all. Yet, God is still "more" than "all." There is nothing so great that God is not greater. There is nothing so definitive that it could not still be made into a problem by God. God himself is indefinable: "God cannot be defined."[6] That is because he is the ultimate and highest instance, even in a logical sense. He is the surpassing of the superlative, the 'most perfect being' (*ens perfectissimum*) in the sense of a 'perfection entirely perfected' (*perfectio omnino perfecta*). In every regard, God is perfect, and the temporal component certainly should be heard here: God can always look back on himself in a perfect sense; his being is free of becoming. Formulated in the dimension of thought and related to it, God is accordingly "that than which nothing greater can be conceived."[7] For that reason, one calls on him when in distress, one appeals to his name in court, one thanks him for good and perfect gifts. If the word "God" provides something for our thinking, then it would appear to be a being which is absolutely superior to everything else which is. Accordingly, the philosophical description of what is signified by the word "God" as we find it, for instance, in Anselm of Canterbury is ". . . one Nature which is the highest of all existing beings. . . ."[8] That means that God is *over everything*, and thus he is *above us*, he is *absolutely superior* to us. That is the only way in which he can be considered.

The 'thing signified' (*res significata*) by "God" would then also have to

---

4. Ludwig Wittgenstein, *Philosophical Investigations*, tr. G. E. M. Anscombe (New York: Macmillan, 1968³), p. 20ᵉ.

5. Gottlob Frege, *The Foundations of Arithmetic; a logico-mathematical Enquiry into the Concept of the Number*, tr. J. L. Austin (Evanston, IL: Northwestern University Press, 1968² [1959¹]), p. 73ᵉ. Modern linguistics has appropriated this fundamental proposition: "One only refers as part of the performance of an illocutionary act, and the grammatical clothing of an illocutionary act is the complete sentence"; J. R. Searle, *Speech Acts; an Essay in the philosophy of language* (London: Cambridge University Press, 1970), p. 25.

6. See Thomas Aquinas, *The Summa Contra Gentiles*, tr. English Dominican Fathers (London: Burns, Oates & Washbourne, 1924), vol. I, ch. 25, p. 61.

7. See Anselm, "Proslogion," chs. II and III, in *St. Anselm; Basic Writings*, tr. S. N. Deane (LaSalle, IL: Open Court Publishing Company, 1962), pp. 7-9.

8. Anselm, "Monologium," ch. I, in *op. cit.*, p. 37.

be absolutely superior to human *thinking* and *comprehending*. And that is the reason why "God is not capable of definition." What the word "God" provides for our *thinking* is then basically impossible to think through, cannot be grasped by thinking, and thus can be grasped only as something incomprehensible. At least, that is implied by a broad tradition with its language usage, a tradition which theology has largely followed in its dogmatic formulations. Augustine classically stated this approach. His famous proposition was as follows: "We are speaking of God; it shouldn't surprise you if you do not comprehend it! If you were to comprehend him, it would not be God." Augustine thus prefers, with regard to God, a "pious confession of ignorance" over a "foolhardy presentation of knowledge." For "to approach God a little with the spirit is great happiness, but it is totally impossible to comprehend him."[9] According to John Chrysostom, it is blasphemous hybris to want to comprehend God.[10] And the theologian called Dionysius the Pseudo-Areopagite concludes that the divine in its originality is above all knowledge: "We approach Deity in its concealment only after we have set aside all thinking."[11]

This tradition, which dared to speak of God only as the Incomprehensible due to his absolute superiority, confronts theology with the problem of the *thinkability* of God. For the sign "God" belongs as a 'thing' (*res*) to the 'temporalities' (*temporalia*), whereas the being of God signalized by this sign is absolutely other than and beyond the entire world whose existence is defined by space and time; "other, totally other from everything else."[12] Because of his absolute transcendence and superiority, God can neither be captured by our speech nor conceived of by our thought.

But if God is thinkable only as the Unthinkable, must not then our thinking ultimately resign when it turns to God? Must not the thought of God, as a thought which basically is thinking something unthinkable, necessarily end with

9. Augustine, *Sermo* 117, iii, 5, in Migne, *Patrologia Latina*, XXXVIII, 663: "We speak of God, what wonder if you do not understand? For if you understand, it is not God. Let there be a pious confession of ignorance rather than a rash profession of knowledge. To touch God to some extent with the mind is a great blessing, but to comprehend him is entirely impossible."

10. See the third discourse, *De Incomprehensibile*, in Migne, *Patrologia Graeca*, XLVIII, 714: "He who meddles with his nature commits hybris."

R. Otto devoted an essay to this thought and its broader setting, in which he sought to establish thematically that the incomprehensibility of God is "matter of honor to Christian theology"; "Chrysostomus über das Unbegreifliche in Gott," in *Aufsätze, das Numinose betreffend* (Gotha: Klotz, 1923, 1929[4]), pp. 1-10; see esp. pp. 2 and 8. An English translation is available, but this section is not included; see *Religious Essays; A Supplement to 'The Idea of the Holy,'* tr. B. Lunn (London: Oxford University Press, 1931).

11. "On the Divine Names and the Mystical Theology" (*Translations of Christian Literature*, ser. 1), tr. C. E. Rolt (New York: Macmillan, 1920), II/7, p. 74: "All divine things . . . are known only by their communications. Their ultimate nature, which they possess in their own original being, is beyond Mind and beyond all Being and Knowledge. . . . while that Mystery Itself we strive to apprehend by casting aside all the activities of our mind . . ." (my literal translation in the text—TR).

12. See R. Otto, "The Wholly Other as the 'Aliud Valde' with Augustine," in *Religious Essays. . . . , op. cit.*, pp. 92ff, speaking of Augustine, *Confessions*, bk. VII, ch. 10, in *NPNF*, 1st ser., I, 109f.

resignation? And has not the history of thought about God not arrived at this final resignation?

Such resignation would affect not only thought. It has practical consequences. How should the Christian faith *act* if it is no longer able to think God and thus no longer understands itself as *faith*? How can godless activity founded on its own freedom be positively certain of its freedom and happy with it if the freedom of godlessness is born out of resignation? For their own sakes, both atheism and faith cannot be satisfied with this, but rather, if they understand themselves properly, they must resist the idea that the attempts to think God and thus the history of the thought of God should perish now in resignation. Such resistance, however, is meaningful only by thinking in a way which contradicts the traditional approach to thinking God and proceeds toward a new way to think God, carefully and yet decisively. It must be careful because it must respect the elements of truth in the traditional thought of God, "No one has ever seen God" (John 1:18a). Decisively, in that in view of this very truth it must emphasize fully that God himself has made himself accessible: ". . . the only Son, who is in the bosom of the Father, he has made him known" (John 1:18b).

2. A theological countermovement against the tradition just described will have to oppose the traditional thought of God, which was obligated to think of God as the unthinkable, with the attempt to think of God and of thought itself in a new way. This cannot be merely an issue of an absolutely new beginning, however, but rather of a step forward which emerges from the debate with the tradition. We must in fact emphatically warn against the common contemporary arrogance with regard to the tradition, and especially against the wholesale rejection of the traditional thought of God. Usually the object of such criticism is nothing more than a dreadful caricature. There is very little to be learned from such criticism. Conversely, the common disparagement today of tradition should not hold us back from attempting an objective debate with the decisive thoughts of the past, in order to emerge from such a debate with new questions and perhaps with new answers. Only the person who will risk returning to paths long trodden will really find new paths.[13]

The attempt at confronting theologically the history of the thought of God as it moves toward resignation, in order to learn to think God in a new way, will have to query again the *linguistic* meaning and function of the word "God." Is the word "God" really understandable only as a sign? Is it correct to say that the word in general is only a 'sign' (*signum*) through which a 'signified thing' (*res significata*) enters our consciousness? Is it correct to say that words only represent and that thinking means no more than imagining and comprehending?

Certainly it is true that thinking is dependent on imagined ideas and concepts. And it is correct to say that a word must mean something if it is supposed to be used in a sensible fashion. To that extent, every sensibly used word has its appropriate sign function, a denominating function. A word, in syntactical connection with other words, refers to something. We can call this referential sign character the signal function of the word.

13. See Martin Heidegger, *Unterwegs zur Sprache* (1959), p. 99: "The enduring element of thought is the way. And the ways of thought conceal within themselves the mystery that we can walk on them both forward and backward, that even the way backward is what first leads us forward."

The question now, however, is whether that to which the word refers must itself exist *beyond* the word, *outside* of the language context in which it is "found." Is the thing which is interpreted by the word itself fundamentally speechless? Does the word fundamentally signalize something which is beyond language? Or is it not at least partially possible that the thing, about which words are spoken, is not what it is without the word? Is there some existing thing which exists only or chiefly in the word event? It would not have to be true of everything, every object, that it exists through or in the word event. It could well be an unallowable poetic exaggeration to say, "I learned then sadly to desist: Where words default, no things exist."[14] We must carefully consider whether words really are always mere representatives of something else which itself is wordless. The tradition which viewed words as mere 'signs' (*signa*) itself allowed for *one sign* which also effected the presence of what was signified, namely, the sacrament. The sacraments (of the new covenant) were regarded by Peter Lombard, who took up and modified the Augustinian theory of signs, as signs which themselves "offer that which becomes effective in a helpful way in the receiver."[15] Luther refers to this tradition (without agreeing with it) by speaking of the sacraments as 'efficacious signs of grace' (*efficatia signa gratiae*).[16]

However, we encounter a theory of signs which ascribes to the sign more than a signifying function not only in the doctrine of the sacraments. Poetry and vernacular language can provide helpful clues. For example, in a poem it is possible that the thing talked about is actually taking place. To be sure, the words here are also 'signs' (*signa*). But they do not necessarily signalize something which is absent in relation to the sign. Under certain circumstances, words can allow something to happen which is present in the words or with them or through them. The sign function of the word would be in such an instance only one and possibly not even the decisive function of language. When the judge utters a judgment, then while he speaks the event happens which the language expresses. Or when the priest says to a believer, "I absolve thee," then absolution takes place. Or if one person says to another, "I love you," "I believe you," "I contemn you"—then these are not just pieces of information, signals, but what one might call *acts of inclusion*. The person addressed in such a case is included in the word event. This can easily be illustrated with the use of invective. If one Swabian says to another, *"Halbdackel"* ("half a dachshund" or "stupider than a dog"), then he is impugning the being of that individual. That does not happen through the word but in the very event of the word. The invective spoken against me repudiates my being by coming too close to me, in a sense, by intervening between me and myself. Invective thus gathers together the existence of the person addressed around itself. If it really hits me, then it penetrates deeply into me and has a profound effect on me. If the word were only a sign, a denominating, then the person who was cursed could respond, "Wrong signification!" But normally the person addressed reacts in another way.

14. Stefan George, "The Word," in *Stefan George: Poems*, tr. Olga Marx (Carol North Valhope) and Ernst Morwitz (New York: Pantheon Books, Inc., 1943), p. 239.
15. See G. Ebeling, *op. cit.*, p. 217.
16. Martin Luther, "A Prelude on the Babylonian Captivity of the Church," in *Three Treatises* (Philadelphia: The Muhlenberg Press, 1947), pp. 131f.

He becomes worked up. Why? It is because the word includes the person in its meaning and thus approaches him *too closely*. The act of speaking does not result in something different from itself; instead, its effect consists of the fact that the person addressed and the result of what is said are both drawn into the act of speaking.[17] In such an instance, words are not the signs for absent things, namely, absent in relation to the sign, but are signs of present things, namely, contents which are present in the word; to use Luther's language, they are 'notes of a present thing' (*notae praesentis rei*).

In this sense we can regard the word "God" as a 'note of the presence of a thing' whereby we have not yet arrived at any agreement about the relation between presence and absence. Accordingly, the 'signified thing' (*res significata*) signalized through this word, God himself, is not the question at all "in the usual sense of a content distinct from the word itself—a sort of speechless thing that has to be brought into the language by being named, that is, designated by a vocable. On the contrary, it is here a question of God himself as Word."[18] That which the word "God" signalizes can be found only *in* the word, more precisely, in the fact that certain words confront a person in a way at least hermeneutically comparable to the experience of invective.

Therefore, language has still other functions than that of signifying. One of its essential functions is that of *address*. From the perspective of the hermeneutics of signification, the address character of language is understood only as a means to an end. Of course, the signal once sent is supposed to be received. It should address someone. But the receiving of the signal, according to this theory, is a means to an end. In contrast to this, we would emphasize that the address function of language, even though address can at times be merely a means to an end, is no less inherent to the essence of language than the signal character. It is the address character of language which first makes it humane.

The word of address affects not only the consciousness of the person addressed but his whole being. To be sure, address can deteriorate into mere input into one's consciousness. Yet, even a word of greeting is really more than just a communication penetrating the consciousness. There are acts of speaking through which that which is said is actually ascribed to the person being addressed. Beyond that, there are acts of speaking through which the person addressed is, so to speak, drawn into the spoken word by means of what is said. Language does certainly have the function of uniting people with that which is

---

17. Linguistically speaking, we are dealing here not only with a "perlocutionary act" in Austin's sense, but rather with a perlocutionary-*attractive* act, whose 'goal' (*telos*) is not outside of the act but rather effected by it and included in the act. This is comparable with the entelechic structure of 'action' (*praxis*) in distinction from 'making' (*poiēsis*) in Aristotle. According to Aristotle (*Ethica Nicomachea*, tr. W. D. Ross, in *The Works of Aristotle*, ed. W. D. Ross [Oxford: Oxford University Press, 1954], IX, vi.5, 1140b, 6ff), making (*poiēsis*) has its goal outside the act of making. The house stands when the building of the house is finished. But the action which intends good (*praxis*), on the other hand, bears its goal in itself: "For while making has an end other than itself, action cannot; for good action itself is its end." Aristotle ascribes the necessary view for the good action, which is its own goal, primarily to the experts in "managing households or states" ("domestic economy" and "political science") (1140b, 10f).

18. G. Ebeling, *God and Word*, tr. J. W. Leitch (Philadelphia: Fortress Press, 1967), p. 28.

being talked about, uniting them in such a way that not only through the word something penetrates the person's consciousness (*in cogitationem*), but that the entire person is drawn out of himself in the process. Such acts of speaking which permit a person to be drawn out of himself are what we would call *language events*, to borrow from Ernst Fuchs.[19]

In the language event, more is happening than merely communication from one consciousness to another. In the language event, the being of some content is expressed in language in such a way that it addresses the being of a person and summons that person out of himself through the word which addresses him, and in the word which addresses him that person is brought to himself or perhaps divorced from himself. In the language event what happens is that a person is drawn together into the word and there, 'outside of himself' (*extra se*), he comes to himself in the other word.

If one then considers what the word "God" connotes within the horizon of this language function, then the word "God" will certainly be regarded not only as a 'sign' (*signum*) by means of which an idea enters consciousness or a thing is conceptualized. As a 'note of the presence of a thing' (*nota praesentia rei*), the word "God" in syntactical connection with other words and in relation to a concrete situation *can* become something like a language event which brings God and the addressed person together lingually and thus really. If God and a person do come together in the word event in such a way that they *are* in the word, then God can no longer be thought of only as the one who exists *over us,* and he must no longer be thought of as the Inconceivable. In the event of the word, he is in our midst, as the one who draws us into this event. And because he communicates and discloses himself in the word event, just as persons can communicate and disclose themselves in their words, God becomes *thinkable* on the basis of his speakability. The way God is to be thought is then dependent on the kind of speakability which is his.

3. The problem of the thinkability of God leads back to the problem of the speakability of God. To this point, we have been led in our thinking by general hermeneutical considerations. The special character of Christian theology now intensifies our insight into the essential priority of the problem of the speakability of God over the problem of the thinkability of God. For Christian theology can use the word "God" meaningfully only in a context which is defined by the understanding of the human person Jesus. Whatever the word "God" is to mean for our thinking is determined, for the Christian faith, in Jesus. Faith understands and confesses him as the word of God. According to the Johannine prologue (John 1:1), he is the word which was with God at the beginning. Through him, according to Hebrews (1:2), God has *spoken* to us *definitively.* Whoever wants to understand Jesus, whoever truly wants to understand the crucified man Jesus in the context of Easter faith, must conceive of God himself as the one who speaks. What does it mean to understand God as the one who speaks?

The New Testament usage to which we have alluded (John 1:1; Heb. 1:2) makes clear that God, according to this tradition's understanding, not only speaks

---

19. Ernst Fuchs, "Das Sprachereignis in der Verkündigung Jesu, in der Theologie des Paulus und im Ostergeschehen," in *Zum hermeneutischen Problem in der Theologie; Die existentiale Interpretation, Gesammelte Aufsätze* (Tübingen: J. C. B. Mohr [Paul Siebeck], 1965²), I, 281ff.

in order to communicate something; rather, he speaks in order to communicate himself and thus to make possible fellowship with himself and to provide a way to participate in his own being. It is in the power of the word that he raises the dead, according to Romans 4:17, and he calls what is not into being. As the word he becomes flesh (John 1:14) and dwells among us in order to communicate himself. In his word, God goes out of himself. As such, he is the one who speaks, who expresses himself, who states his being. In speaking he shares and communicates himself.

Since Christian theology understands God himself, for the sake of Jesus, in this sense as the one who speaks, as the word, it ascribes to the word "God" a function of announcing God himself, but solely on the basis of the word of God.[20] The traditional language of Christianity insists, therefore, on the fact that we must *have said to us* what the word "God" should be thought to mean. The presupposition is that ultimately only the speaking God himself can say what the word "God" should provide us to think about. Theology comprehends this whole subject with the category of revelation.[21]

We have understood that God is one who speaks and as such one who expresses himself as an assertion which is inseparably tied to faith in Jesus. Hebrews, like Romans 1:2, relates Old Testament talk about God (as God speaking through prophets) to Jesus. This expresses the fact that in the person Jesus is revealed what God as the one who speaks is all about. The humanity of this person is extremely relevant to the meaning of the word "God," according to the New Testament view. This is true not just of the life but especially of the death of this person. Therefore, when we attempt to think of God as the one who communicates and expresses himself in the person Jesus, then we must always remember that this man was *crucified,* that he was killed in the name of God's law. For responsible Christian usage of the word "God," the Crucified One is virtually the real definition of what is meant with the word "God." Christian theology is therefore fundamentally the theology of the Crucified One.[22]

20. Whoever or whatever Peter Handke is cannot be grasped without attending to the fact that Peter Handke is one who speaks, and thus not without appreciation of the words which Peter Handke has produced.

21. We shall deal at another place with the recently raised criticism that theological thought which takes this approach is a "pretentious irrationalism of mere ('kerygmatic') assurances" (see W. Pannenberg, *The Idea of God and Human Freedom,* tr. R. A. Wilson [Philadelphia: Westminster, 1973], p. viii).

22. I have repeatedly referred to the relevance of Jesus' death for the concept of God in other contexts and called for a grounding of the Christian doctrine of God, especially as doctrine of the Trinity, in a 'theology of the Crucified One' (*theologia crucifixi*). We are still waiting for an answer to that call, although on various fronts attempts have been made in that direction. The most notable attempt of this kind is, in my opinion, the short work by Heribert Mühlen, *Die Veränderlichkeit Gottes als Horizont einer zukünftigen Christologie; Auf dem Wege zu einer Kreuzestheologie in Auseinandersetzung mit der altkirchlichen Christologie* (Muenster: Aschendorff, 1969). See, in addition, Hans Küng, *Menschwerdung Gottes; Eine Einführung in Hegels theologisches Denken als Prolegomena zu einer künftigen Christologie* (Freiburg/Basel/Vienna: Herder, 1970); Jürgen Moltmann, *The Crucified God; The Cross of Christ as the Foundation and Criticism of Christian Theology,* trs. R. A. Wilson and J. Bowden (New York: Harper & Row, 1974); Walter Kasper, *Jesus the Christ,* tr. V. Green (New York: Paulist Press, 1976).

These studies are an attempt at a 'theology of the Crucified One' (*theologia crucifixi*), or at least an attempt at an explication of its approach. From the formal and hermeneutical perspective, a theology of the Crucified One must confront the problems of the thinkability and speakability of God. From the material and dogmatic perspective, talk about God which is oriented to the crucified man Jesus must understand God's deity on the basis of his humanity revealed in Jesus. Thus we must deal with problems which emerge in the context of the questions of God's thinkability, God's speakability, and God's humanity.

These studies, arranged accordingly, are therefore preceded by a discussion which is intended to provide something like a statement of purpose, the "epistemological interest" which guides this entire set of studies. On the one hand, our discussion must deal with the problem of contemporary atheism because the question of the thinkability of God can be dealt with seriously today only from that perspective. In doing this, the question must remain open as to whether the problem can be resolved within the context of modern atheism, or whether this context itself must not be changed or even left behind. On the other hand, the problem of the speakability of God, and certainly of the humanity of God, can be discussed only in constant reference to the possibility of an understanding of God which proves itself in the death of Jesus. Our opening discussion should draw attention at once to the importance of the death of Jesus for talk about God. Both problem areas meet in the setting of the dark statement of the death of God. An analysis of the various points which touch each other in talk of the death of God will thus occupy the first part of these studies.

SECTION 2. Is God Necessary?

1. What is the meaning of God-talk in an age in which man has made himself the measure of all things? To say that man is the measure of all things is still a rather daring assertion, but it has been made from very early on.[1] It can be assented to or rejected. That man makes himself the measure of all things is, on the other hand, a statement which characterizes the very nature of the modern age. It cannot be rejected. What makes man modern is his making himself the measure of all things. The fundamental problems of the so-called modern age are, to that extent, all primarily anthropological problems. We understand the modern age as that age in which man newly discovers himself to be the point of relationship for all that exists.

The scientific discoveries of the modern age admittedly appear to contradict this. The discoveries of Nicolaus Copernicus and Galileo Galilei, which have fundamentally defined the modern age, have removed man from the center of the universe on the basis of the calculated laws for the movements of the heavens. Giovanni Pico della Mirandola, in his discourse *De dignitate hominis* (finally finished in 1486), had assigned man his place "at the center of the world" (*in*

1. See the Protagoras quotation in Plato, "Theaetetus," in *The Dialogues of Plato*, tr. B. Jowett, 2 vols. (New York: Random House, 1937), II, 152, p. 153.

mundi meditullio),[2] but as Friedrich Nietzsche aptly put it, "since Copernicus man has been rolling from the center into x."[3] Together with his earth, man no longer stood at the center of the universe. And when man once shifts away from the center of the universe he can move in any direction at will. To what extent, then, can the assertion be made that man is making himself the measure of all things and that the basic problems of the modern age are all anthropological problems?

The answer must be this: For that very reason. In order properly to appreciate what has happened, we must remember that medieval man had not moved himself into the center of the universe. Rather, he found himself there as an assumed matter of course. As the image of God, man knew that he was at the center of the universe because God had determined that it was to be that way. It was not the consequence of being moved away from the center of the universe that man, "rolling from the center into x," simply let himself continue to roll. Rather, he began to regain his lost heritage, in order to possess it. Until now, he had merely been *in* the center. Now he was making himself *into* the center. Once ejected from this central position through the scientific discovery of the laws of the heavenly movements, did not man have to fend for himself, in order not to be lost in arbitrariness or end up on an eternal crooked path?

It has been correctly noted that that "which makes Copernicus the protagonist of the modern age, . . . can best be formulated negatively": "Reason, through a model instance, had uncovered the mechanism of its illusions and errors. It had found an instrument which could be applied again and again to new areas of knowledge: it was the instrument of inquiry directed at the position of the questioning, experiencing, and researching human person."[4] What would be more plausible than that man would apply this instrument to himself, so that, in order to know himself, he would make his fundamental positionlessness a

2. Pico della Mirandola, *Oration on the Dignity of Man*, tr. A. Robert Caponigri (Chicago: Henry Regnery Company, 1956), p. 3. In the 'Oratio,' God ascribes to man an existence in the *middle* of the world, so that, existing there without limits, he can define himself and survey everything from this middle point in order to recognize it more easily. Being in the middle of everything, man has been made by God neither as a heavenly nor as an earthly being, so that he is free to develop the form which he has chosen for himself. It should be possible for him to degenerate into an inferior state (*in inferiora*) as well as to regenerate into a superior state (*in superiora*). See *ibid.*: "I have placed you at the very center of the world, so that from that vantage point you may with greater ease glance round about you on all that the world contains. We have made you a creature neither of heaven nor of earth, neither mortal nor immortal, in order that you may, as the free ['arbitrary,' *arbitrarius*—TR] and proud shaper of your own being, fashion yourself in the form you may prefer. It will be in your power to descend to the lower, brutish forms ['inferior state,' *in inferiora*—TR] of life; you will be able, through your own decision, to rise again to the superior orders whose life is divine." The use of the term "arbitrary" ("free") makes this text terminologically virtually a classic reference for the understanding of man which Luther was combatting in his thesis on the bondage of the will.

3. F. Nietzsche, *Nachgelassene Fragmente (Herbst 1885 bis Herbst 1886), Werke, Kritische Gesamtausgabe,* eds. G. Colli and M. Montinari (Berlin, New York: Walter De Gruyter, 1974), VIII/1, p. 125.

4. H. Blumenberg, "Kopernikus und das Pathos der Vernunft," *Evangelische Kommentare,* 6 (1973), 463.

theme and thus begin to rely totally and only on himself? Ejected from the center of the universe, man had to secure himself by himself. After he had lost the objectivity of his centralized existential position through the discoveries of science, he had to secure his subjectivity and rebuild the entire universe anew on that basis, if he did not want to end up in endless uncertainty. In this sense, he became the point of reference for everything that exists. This happened in exemplary fashion in the Cartesian discovery of *"cogito sum"* (I think/I am), and in the securing of all existence, built upon it, through the human ego. With this discovery the anthropological orientation of all modern problems was given, also and chiefly of the theological ones.

This anthropological orientation was expressed most clearly, if not necessarily most appropriately, in the modern thought of German idealism. It sounds like the antithesis to the idea that man has rolled from the center when Schelling says of this man, "He alone is a central being and should thus remain in the center. All things are created in him, just as God only assumes nature and connects himself with it through man."[5] But what sounds like an antithesis to the idea of man rolling away from the center and to the Copernican discovery which is expressed in that idea is in truth its most logical implication. Man making himself the measure of all things no longer understands himself to be 'at the center of the world' (*in mundi meditullio*) because of his being in the image of God. If God is related to nature only through man who makes himself the measure of all things, then the threat is that God will become the image of man and will remain central only in that way. In any event, this is where the specifically theological and basic aporia of the modern age arose, in that all problems of the age are locked into a basically anthropological orientation.

This basic theological aporia of the modern age is expressed anthropologically in our experience that man can be human without God. Man no longer has the criterion for his own necessity and reality in God; rather, he understands himself on the basis of himself, whether accidentally or necessarily. And for this reason he raises the question, Is God necessary?

The problem connected with this question is primarily present today in theology. It defines theology comprehensively. Theology cannot avoid becoming involved with this question, even if it becomes the source for the most difficult problems for it. For we live in an age in which the extraordinarily exciting discovery that God has to prove that he is God *in and through man* has become a generally accepted assumption and thus cannot be ignored or neglected by theology. Theology, too, is confronted with the question, Is God necessary?

Whoever has to pose the question that way, whoever has to question the necessity of God, has really already answered the question negatively. Thus, the modern discovery implies a thesis that God is within the world's horizon, or God is *not necessary in any worldly sense*. To be sure, this had to be discovered first. But once it was discovered, this truth has been received and accepted with a suspicious alacrity. For its part, theology, with a certain understandable delay, has been at the point of adopting this truth. Why should it not do so, if it is really true?

5. F. W. J. Schelling, *Philosophische Untersuchungen über das Wesen der menschlichen Freiheit und die damit zusammenhängenden Gegenstände, Sämmtliche Werke*, ed. K. F. A. Schelling (Stuttgart and Augsburg: J. G. Cotta, 1860), I/7, p. 411.

In distinction from other theological endeavors which certainly have perceived the problem we have described,[6] the following investigations will proceed on the basis that theology is, in fact, being confronted with a truth when the

6. Reference here should be made, above all, to the respectable attempts made by Wolfhart Pannenberg to demonstrate the worldly necessity of God on an anthropological basis. One must remember that Pannenberg has revised his argumentation several times and argues differently in his newest publications from his 1962 monograph *What Is Man?; Contemporary Anthropology in Theological Perspective*, tr. D. A. Priebe (Philadelphia: Fortress Press, 1970). At that time Pannenberg, in agreement with Max Scheler and in debate with Arnold Gehlen on the structure of human drives, concluded that man had an infinite dependence, in which he "presupposes a being beyond everything finite, a vis-a-vis upon which he is dependent," for which "our language uses the word 'God'. . . ." "The word can be used in a meaningful way only if it means the entity toward which man's boundless dependence is directed. Otherwise it becomes an empty word" (*ibid.*, p. 10). This is not intended to be "any theoretical proof for the existence of God" (p. 11), and is not that. But it is something like a demonstration of the worldly necessity of a supra-worldly God for man, and it is intended to be that. For "what the environment is for animals, God is for man. God is the goal in which alone his striving can find rest and his destiny be fulfilled" (p. 13). In his newer works, Pannenberg argues in a more differentiated way. His thesis of the infinite dependence of man on God is now modified through the attention he gives to man's modern experience of freedom. Here again, reference is made to "the elevation of man above the finite content of human experience to the idea of infinite reality which sustains everything finite, including man himself," which is "an essential of man's being, so that one is not really considering man if one ignores this dimension." This is regarded as the necessary condition so that what is said about God can make the "claim to intellectual veracity" ("Anthropology and the Question of God," *The Idea of God and Human Freedom*, tr. R. A. Wilson [Philadelphia: Westminster Press, 1973], p. 89). Still, he thinks it necessary to remark that "God is conceivable as the basis of human freedom, and no longer as its negation" (*ibid.*, p. 93). If God is thought of at all anymore as "a being beyond everything finite, a vis-a-vis upon which he is dependent," then it is more as the vis-a-vis of man's dependence on freedom. "But the basis of freedom cannot be a being that already exists, but only a reality which reveals to freedom its future, the coming God" (*ibid.*)
Pannenberg's methodological procedure conceals, in my opinion, difficulties which make it advisable to take another approach to reach his goal, which is the anthropological demonstrability of the claim connected with the word "God" within the boundaries of the world. It does not seem compelling to me that the "claim to intellectual veracity" is better dealt with by assuming that the anthropological relevance of talk about God is first to be demonstrated 'apart from God' (*remoto deo*). Rather it appears to me that this is the very way to tread on "the ground of atheist theory," a procedure for which "theology pays a high price," according to Pannenberg (p. 88). Does this procedure, which makes the necessity of God plausible by first analyzing human existence without God, take seriously enough the fact that God, like man, should be thought of *from the context of freedom*? Although I fully affirm his purpose, I still have serious reservations with regard to the approach, precisely because of Pannenberg's concern for the intellectual veracity of theological work. Certainly Pannenberg knows the boundaries of his procedure. "General anthropological consideration can never take us further than the assertion that when man's being is fully aware, man is conscious that he is dependent on a reality which surpasses and sustains everything finite, and in this sense is a divine reality" (p. 95). But aside from the fact that it is always rather awkward to have to declare that a large number of one's contemporaries are asleep (people who certainly would be regarded as intellectually alert!), in order to prevent one's own thesis from appearing improbable, it simply is not clear in this thesis why one should not begin with the claim made on man by the divine reality. Pannenberg states aptly and well, "The reality of God, on which man is dependent in the structure of his subjectivity, is encountered only where, in the context of his world, he receives himself as a gift in the experience of freedom" (p. 96). God, then, is first encountered where he allows himself to be experienced as the one who gives. That is precisely what I call revelation.

worldly nonnecessity of God is asserted. The important thing then is how this truth achieves recognition within theology, or rather, how theology appropriates this truth. It is possible to acknowledge the insight that God is not necessary in a worldly sense either with a sense of resentment or a sense of resignation, theologically speaking. In both cases, an alien truth is being appropriated. It will then remain an alien element in theology and as such will dominate theology in a nontheological way. The consequence of such an appropriation of the insight into the worldly nonnecessity of God will consist ultimately of the fact that this insight is accepted but theologically is not worked through. Basically, then, there is the same relationship to that truth as is found in those theological endeavors which defame this truth as the lie of the modern spirit of the age and then in antithesis to it postulate and assert the worldly necessity of God with even greater emphasis. In both situations, what is lacking is the theological processing of the discovery.

In contrast to that, I will risk the assertion that the discovery of the worldly nonnecessity of God on the part of theology can not only be processed in a genuinely theological way but can also be identified as a genuinely theological discovery. This latter claim is made, of course, not in order to raise claims to historical priority or something like that, but to summon theology to remember the genuinely theological character of this truth.

Perhaps an historical reflection at this point will be helpful. A favorite way of formulating the thesis of the worldly nonnecessity of God is to state that man lives secularly and must live secularly, as though there were no God, *"etsi deus non daretur"* ('as though God were not a given'). The argument continues: the natural orders of the world would still possess their irrevocable general validity if there were no God. Independent of a relationship to God the structures of existence would have to be recognizable as the proper order of being. In consequence, God would be dismissed as a moral, political, and scientific "working hypothesis." Via Dietrich Bonhoeffer, the motto *"etsi deus non daretur"* achieved currency among theologians as the trademark of modernity. For his part, Bonhoeffer was guided by the analyses of modernity of, for example, Wilhelm Dilthey and Ernst Cassirer. Following their approach, he appealed for the argument that modern man had to live his life as the mastering of the world 'even if there were no God' to the famous proposition from the prolegomena to the three books *De jure belli ac pacis* by Hugo Grotius. According to him, the natural law which arises from the human drive for community and which thus can be termed the 'law of human nature' (*ius humanae naturae*) would still be valid if one were *to assume (an assumption which could not be made without committing the greatest sin) that there were no God or that he were not concerned with human affairs*: ". . . even if we should concede that which cannot be conceded without the utmost wickedness, that there is no God, or that the affairs of men are of no concern to him."[7] In terms of its original intentions and

7. Hugo Grotius, *The Law of War and Peace*, tr. Francis W. Kelsey (Indianapolis, New York: The Bobbs-Merrill Company, Inc., 1925), Prolegomena (11), p. 13. For Bonhoeffer, see *Letters and Papers from Prison*, ed. E. Bethge, tr. R. H. Fuller (New York: Macmillan, 1972), pp. 360f. On Grotius, see E. Cassirer, *The Philosophy of the Enlightenment*, trs. Fritz C. A. Koelln and James P. Pettegrove (Princeton, NJ: Princeton University Press, 1951), p. 240, and W. Schweitzer, *Der entmythologisierte Staat; Studien zur Revision der evangelischen Ethik des Politischen* (Gütersloh: Gütersloher

structure, this argument is neither untheological nor even antitheological in its orientation. And if it is to be regarded as specifically modern, then the modern age had already begun during the Middle Ages. For this argument can be traced back to the Middle Ages, and when properly understood it is a praise of the Creator in view of his successful creation (Gen. 1:31), which was accomplished so well that its good order has been maintained even, under some circumstances, without the Creator and the Lord of the world. In this sense the proposition that God is not necessary in the world is completely understandable *theologically*. Therefore, theology will have to do something different from what is normally done today with this view, which is based on an originally theological insight, and which has become a fundamental assumption of the modern age.

The thesis of the worldly nonnecessity of God must then be made understandable as not only a statement about the world or man in his world, but also as a statement about God himself. Only when that has been done, has it been worked through in a genuinely theological way. As an expression of a fundamental assumption of the modern age, the thesis of the worldly nonnecessity of God is initially a statement about man and his world. As such, it is really not yet a statement about God in any sense. However, before we attempt to read this thesis as a statement about God, we must turn to one historical objection.

The thesis of the worldly nonnecessity of God does not stand abruptly at the beginning of the modern age. It was already anticipated in the High Middle Ages and then emerges in the course of the modern age as a decisive factor. At the beginning of the modern age, however, there was one more outspoken proof for the necessity of God. The modern age did, after all, really begin with Descartes and his proof of the necessity of God for human self-certainty. For Descartes' new metaphysical approach to the establishment of all certainty in the self-certainty of the ego, God was indispensable. Thus God was proven to be a necessary being. This could lead to the objection that the thesis of the worldly nonnecessity of God is not specifically modern at all. In response to that we would emphasize that, in this process of guaranteeing the *ego cogito* ('I think; therefore I am') through the being of God, which is fundamental for the modern age, we recognize the precondition for the possibility of a completely new and quite radical disputation of the necessity of God for man.[8] This proof of the necessity of God is the midwife of modern atheism. The decision about any form of atheism is always made through the understanding of God which it is combatting and which makes its opposition to God possible. No atheism simply falls from heaven. Specifically modern atheism could be said to arise from an ascension, which is the self-establishment of the "I think" in the thought of God, an approach which attacks the ramparts of heaven. Once God has been made a theme in the context of man's self-establishment and thus declared nec-

---

Verlagshaus G. Mohn, 1968), p. 145, n. 2. The suggestion that Bonhoeffer may have been referring to W. Dilthey's book, *Weltanschauung und Analyse des Menschen seit Renaissance und Reformation,* in *Gesammelte Schriften,* 15 vols. (Leipzig: Teubner, 1914-58), II (1914), 280, has been substantiated by E. Feil, "Der Einfluss Wilhelm Diltheys auf Dietrich Bonhoeffers 'Widerstand und Ergebung'," *Evangelische Theologie,* 29 (1969), 662ff and especially 668. In Bonhoeffer the Grotius text is taken as one of many documentations for the thesis that God had been done away with as a working hypothesis. I hope at some time to be able to provide a more precise consideration of the history of the term *"etsi deus non daretur."*

8. On this, see section 9 below.

essary, it is not far to the next step, which is to question the necessity of God. All that is required is that man expressly think the thought that humans define the horizon of their existence themselves, as rational beings, and then the worldly necessity of an extra-worldly being is revealed to be a dialectical illusion. With the "deduction and explanation of the dialectical illusion" we then discover that "when I regard this supreme being, which, relatively to the world, was absolutely (unconditionally) necessary, as a thing *per se* . . . I find it impossible to represent this necessity in or by any conception, and it exists merely in my own mind, as the formal condition of thought, but not as a material and hypostatic condition of existence."[9]

Moreover, the concept of God as a necessary being becomes questionable at that point where man, grounding himself in his "I think," discovers the autonomy of his practical reason and the basic process of freedom in his "I will." This freedom does not harmonize with the concept of God as a necessary being. Schelling expressed it when he described the genesis of the concept "of a being which exists necessarily," and then sought to explain "with what power it descends on man's consciousness and deprives him of all freedom. It is a concept against which all thought loses its freedom."[10] Both theoretically and practically, the transformation of the assertion of the necessity of God into the experience of the worldly nonnecessity of God was going on—and in the process, the modern age emerged![11] This transformation process has by no means reached its end.[12]

2. As a statement about man in his world, discourse about the worldly nonnecessity of God means this: man can be human without God. There is no doubt that man can do that. He can live without experiencing God. He can speak, hear, think, and act without speaking about God, without perceiving God, without thinking of God, without working for him. And he can do all of that very well and with great responsibility. The human person can well live without God, can listen attentively, think acutely, act responsibly. The examples of the opposite, unavoidable and horrible as they are, and so easily and widely observable, do not have their basic reason necessarily in the godlessness of the various actions. But at the same time, we would never seek to dispute that, on the contrary, the struggle against poor living conditions, unbearable dissipation, ruinous thinking, and irresponsible actions can certainly be motivated by the certainty that God exists. Nor can we dispute that all this can and should be undertaken by man even without God.

Man can be human without God. One can! Once this discovery is made, the temptation is immediately there to postulate from the *possibility* of human

9. I. Kant, *The Critique of Pure Reason*, tr. J. M. D. Meiklejohn (*Everyman's Library*, 909) (London: J. M. Dent & Sons, 1950), pp. 358 and 361.

10. F. W. J. Schelling, *Zur Geschichte der neueren Philosophie; Münchener Vorlesungen*, in *Sämmtliche Werke*, ed. K. F. A. Schelling (Stuttgart and Augsburg: J. G. Cotta, 1860), I/10, p. 19.

11. It is certainly no coincidence that German Idealism's dispute with Kant's philosophy regarding his attempt to think through the necessity of God in a new way and to understand it thus remained an episode.

12. See M. Welker, *Der Vorgang Autonomie; Philosophische Beiträge zur Einsicht in theologischer Rezeption und Kritik* (Neukirchen-Vluyn: Neukirchener Verlag, 1975).

existence without God to the *necessity* of humanity without God and thus to a godless human race. Must not the human person *will* to do what he *can* do, at least to the extent that thereby the consequence is excluded that he would become inhuman? Must he not then, if he can be godless in a humane way, not also want to be godless? To be sure, the principle stands that 'being does not necessarily follow from potency' (*a posse ad esse non valet consequentia*). However, for the 'human condition' (*sub conditione humana*), is not the dictum binding that 'the potential to will something renders it an obligation' (*a posse ad velle valet obligatio*)?

If "the spirit of the modern age" should try to force the stringency of this 'potential to will,' which logically is not enforceable, then theology would certainly have to resist the spirit of the modern age with compromise in this regard—which obviously would not mean that the modern spirit should not be reversed but that it should be overcome in favor of an even newer spirit. One must not overemphasize the 'particles of truth' (*particula veri*) in the conclusion of the necessity of human godlessness based on its possibility. The stringency of the conclusion which deduces from the possibility of being human without God the necessity of being human without God is based on the fact that the assumption of the worldly necessity of God (an assumption contested by the view that without God one can be human) implies a certain understanding of God which is destroyed by this very assumption. This must now be explained in greater detail.

The assertion of the worldly necessity of God appeared to presuppose a decision about what God is thought to be. The God who is necessary in the world is always conceived of as *God the Lord*. And it appeared that there was general agreement as to what a lord is. God's lordship was discussed in the sense of his exercise of omnipotence. The God who is necessary in the world was understood as the almighty Lord whose love and mercy appear to be fundamentally secondary and subsidiary to his claim to lordship. This is the earthly way of thinking of a lord: first he has all power and then perhaps he can be merciful—but then again, perhaps not. God's lordliness and lordship are thought of in the same general way. He is mighty, able, and free to love or not to love. "I will be gracious to whom I will be gracious, and will show mercy on whom I will show mercy" (Exod. 33:19) is the classic biblical text, which is quickly cited and can easily be expanded with other 'proof texts' (*dicta probantia*).

Certainly we are not contesting the fact that mercy and love are always acts of freedom and *to that extent* of power. He who acts in freedom is truly mighty. On the other hand, one must not conclude that freedom or power is superior to love, while the love of God becomes a secondary attribute. The thesis of the worldly nonnecessity of God is directed precisely against this view of God according to which God, as the almighty Lord who can be differentiated from his love, is necessary in the world. Because God was an overpowering word which dominated human life and thought, the discovery that one could be godless was connected easily with an obligation to want to be godless. This led then to the task of liberating life and thought from the dominating power of the claim which was made with the word "God." The ability to exist without God meant, based on the premise of this concept of God, the desire to exist against God. Thought then logically had to contest that God was 'that than which nothing greater could be thought' in order to liberate itself in this battle and arrive at freedom of thought. The course of thought then began to motivate people to refrain from hearing the claim to lordship expressed by the word "God."

Even the theologian will pursue this whole process not without some sympathetic understanding. And the presumption cannot be ignored that the claim to lordship of the word "God," when it emerges as a threat to the freedom of thought, can scarcely be said to have defined relevantly in a theological sense the essence of God. This presumption brings this process of the modern discovery of the worldly nonnecessity of God to the actual task of working it through in a *genuinely theological* way. To say that *God is the Lord* is understood in this presumption as a claim which stands in the most precise agreement with the statement *"God is love."* Thus, godly power and godly love are related to one another neither through subordination nor dialectically. Rather, God's mightiness is understood as the power of his love. Only love is almighty. Then God's lordship is to be understood as the rule of his mercy and God's law is accordingly the law of his grace.

3. Based on this theological insight, the necessity then emerges to make a critical differentiation between *God himself*—understood thus!—and the *anthropological valuation* which the word "God" naturally claims to hold. When the desire to be human without God once emerged, that did not mean that the anthropological function which the (misunderstood) word "God" had exercised until then simply disappeared. Instead, we must now critically see that if "God" *could* be an all-dominating word, then man must be ascribed the passivity of absolute dependence as a natural capacity[13]—and it is irrelevant what he is, pretends to be, or desires to be dependent on. We would then have to ask whether relating this passive capacity to an active God, that is, the identification of this almighty lordship on which man is supposed to be absolutely dependent with *God,* is not the concealed expression of the elementary anthropological fact that man exists in absolute dependence on *man* because men want to dominate men totally. This theological differentiation between God himself and the anthropological valuation ascribed to the God who is thought to be necessary would then reveal that the point claimed by the word "God," until the discovery of the worldly nonnecessity of God, is a fundamental point of anthropological conflict. One would then have to demonstrate convincingly that this absorption of "theology" into anthropology would represent a demonstration of man as a person in conflict who cannot resolve this conflict with himself but must simply endure it.

If theology does not accept the discovery of the worldly nonnecessity of God as an alien element but realizes it for theological reasons, then theology has a basic contribution to make to the illumination of modern man's self-under-

---

13. It would be helpful to point out that these considerations are *not* to be understood as a discussion with Schleiermacher's interpretation of piety as the feeling of absolute dependence. Schleiermacher's concept of absolute dependence implies the concept of freedom and thus is already an attempt to overcome the understanding of God which we are criticizing here. Whether the term "dependence"—even in Schleiermacher's precise definition—is a fortunate one terminologically to express the interaction of God's lordship and being the child of God may be doubted. The debate, necessary as it is, with Schleiermacher must begin with the interpretation of the concept of absolute dependence at its best.

standing. That contribution would be seen in theology's helping toward a deeper insight into the fact that mankind, in contesting the secular necessity of God, has not erased the anthropological function which until now had been the function of a God. Theology could contribute to a transformation of this function by revealing that the tendency toward total dominion over people is an original tendency toward the deification of domination and the enslavement of mankind. Further, theology could encourage the humaneness of modern man by resisting the illusion that man could do away with the dominion itself as it removes the tendency toward the deification of might. The fundamental conflicts of human existence will not be resolved by doing away with the content of conflict. That would mean that man would have to be done away with. The fundamental conflicts of human existence are dealt with in that one endures the content of conflict. With regard to the relation of dependence and domination, this would mean that not every form of domination must be discredited as inhuman but rather that one should examine the deficiencies present in what is usually practiced as domination. The deficiency in poorly practiced domination arises from the temptation, which is given with domination itself, to want to dominate *alone*. Domination endangers itself to the degree that the will to constant exaggeration of domination arises from it. The word "God" could well serve for that kind of will. By contrast, theologically appropriate definition of the dominion of God would produce the insight that domination and service by no means must be related to each other paradoxically and that domination does not necessarily imply the enslavement of others.

These are all what one might call the *indirect* consequences of the theological discovery or attempt to work through theologically the truth that man can be human without God, so that God is not necessary in the world. Utterances along this line do reflect this discovery again in the context of statements about man and his world and are to that degree a contribution to a better self-understanding on the part of modern man. However, it is the fundamental task of theology to probe the question about what it means for the relationship of God to man and for man's corresponding relationship to God if God is not necessary in the world. Until now we have examined what is *negated*, both with regard to God and to man's relationship to God, when the assertion of the worldly nonnecessity of God is made. Much more important is the question about what is *confirmed* in regard to God, and man's relationship to God, when this assertion is made. After all, the biblical texts speak of God because they have something affirmative to say about his relationship to man and man's relationship to God. Therefore, our question must be this: If the necessity of God within the horizons of the world has lost its evidentiality, then what evidence must be rendered to God within the horizon of the human experience of the world so that one can and must speak of God? What claim can the word "God" still make?

4. The statement that God is not necessary within the world can be comprehended as a genuinely theological discovery only if in the process God does not become something capricious. It will be theology's task to insist that the antithesis to necessity understood as nonnecessity is not bridged by resorting to capriciousness.

Obviously, one cannot simply equate capriciousness with contingency (accidence). Capricious means, "this or that way," and thus, "less than necessary."

That which is capricious is thus regarded as unessential. One would distinguish
from capriciousness that accidence which is beyond the alternative of "thus and
no other way" and "this or that way." The contingent cannot be deduced, cannot
be based on something else. But that is certainly no reason to equate it with the
unessentiality of the capricious. Tradition does assert the capriciousness of the
contingent (accidental). These lines are characteristic:

> "Become essential, Man! When the world fails at last,
> Accident falls away, but Essence, that stands fast." [14]

Here, accidence is understood as the opposite of necessity. And necessity
alone is regarded as essential. In contrast to it, accidence is unessential. Ultimately, it disappears. However, that proposition is to be contested. Theologically
it cannot be maintained that only that which is necessary is essential. Accidence
also has its essence, and the contingent is also essential. That which happens
contingently must not necessarily be less than necessary, or become capriciousness, merely because it is not necessary. It can also be *more than necessary.*

If the assertion of the worldly nonnecessity of God is not to lead God into
capriciousness, then the affirmation made by the assertion of the nonnecessity
of God must mean that God is more than necessary in the world. And that is the
thesis which will be advanced here: *God is more than necessary.* The logical
difficulty of the proposed formula "more than necessary" is not denied.[15] But
it may be an appropriate way to draw attention to the uniqueness of God, which
cannot so easily be fit into the logic of modality.

Obviously, "more than necessary" is not to be understood as a quantitative
expansion of necessity. The formula does not mean "necessary and more than
necessary," but "not necessary *because* more than necessary." The constant presupposition here is that the *worldly* necessity of God is meant and thus being
contested. An assertion of *absolute* necessity which was abstracted from worldly
necessity would be a concept which denied itself, as Immanuel Kant has shown;
to this we will return.[16] If God, from the world's perspective, is more than
necessary, then to assert the absolute necessity of God based on a concept of
God *without* the world is at best to play logical games. Of course, such games
are constantly motivated by the analogy to the necessary being which may be
meaningfully expressed based on that which does exist in the world. However,

---

14. Angelus Silesius, *Selections from "The Cherubinic Wanderer,"* tr. J. E.
Crawford Flitch (Westport, Connecticut: Hyperion Press, Inc., 1932), p. 166 (II, 30).

15. Statements made by Schelling demonstrate that the admittedly unusual and
logically difficult formula "more than necessary" can be justified philosophically in connection with the name "God." In discussion with Descartes and his proof of the necessary
existence of God, he asks, "If God and a necessarily existing being are identical concepts,
then to what extent is he *more* than just that?" (*op. cit.,* I/10, p. 17). According to
Schelling, "that which exists necessarily" must be regarded "also as that which exists
blindly" (*ibid.,* p. 20). "The mere concept of necessary existence would thus not lead
to the living but rather to the dead God," whereas the living God "can transform his
necessary being himself into an accidental, namely, into a self-established being, so that
. . . necessity would always be the basis for that self-established being without the effective real being of God having merely to be that necessary being" (*ibid.,* p. 22).

16. See below, pp. 40f.

that does not lead to a more meaningful statement about a worldless necessity of God. The phrase "more than necessary in the world" can therefore certainly be abbreviated to read "more than necessary."[17]

Necessity, therefore, is a category which does not reach too high for God but which does not reach as far as God. The proposition "God is necessary" is a poor proposition. It is not worthy of God. This must be explained in greater detail. Differentiations in the concept of necessity must be attended to so that the admittedly awkward logical assertion that God is more than necessary can be explained and its meaning adequately interpreted.

Necessity is regarded as a mode of being. For an existing thing, necessity means "this way and no other way." The most rigorous definition is still Aristotle's definition of 'necessity' as "that which cannot be otherwise. . . ."[18] The decision about "that which cannot be otherwise" will always be made by *some other one,* however.[19] It is important to note that the adequate reason for the existence of something which exists, whether it be a tangible thing or a noetic thing, always resides on the same level as its consequence. If there were no existing thing outside of it, then there would be no such entity as a necessarily existing thing. Of course, the structure of the concept "necessity" is not something of which one is always aware in normal language usage. For that reason, it will be useful to review the various aspects in the usage of the term "necessary." What does 'necessary' mean?

Following Nicolai Hartmann[20] one can distinguish the following meanings of the term "necessary" in normal usage:

(a) Necessary is that which is needed for a certain purpose, the indispensable condition or prerequisite for an appearance or an effect to take place. Necessity is constituted here through the dependence of a result on the required condition for its taking place. To that extent it is true then that "the condition is not really necessary here, . . . it could also not be present, but then the intended result would not happen."[21] If the result is present, however, then the condition is necessarily also given. The condition is thus *necessary* for something else and thus necessary itself only when the other thing exists.

(b) That which is fatefully unavoidable or predetermined is necessary. The assumption made in presupposing such necessity is that everything which happens is intended to happen the way it does and what does not happen was not intended to happen. "This concept of necessity is teleologically based, its struc-

---

17. The assertion that God is absolutely necessary simply cannot be restated in the form of a strict proof, regardless of the dignity of the ontological proof of the existence of God, and every attempt to do so can only lead from the first premise, via the second premise, to a divine smile.
18. Aristotle, "Metaphysica," in *The Works of Aristotle,* tr. W. D. Ross (Oxford: Clarendon Press, 1954), VIII, Δ, 5, 1915a, 34f.
19. This corresponds to the fact that in logic the apodictic judgments which express logical necessity, distinguished from problematic and assertorial judgments, are ascribed their apodictic nature only with regard to the form of their conditionedness, that is, in the form of "if—then."
20. Nicolai Hartmann, *Möglichkeit und Wirklichkeit* (Berlin: De Gruyter, 1966³), pp. 37ff.
21. *Ibid.,* p. 37.

tural schematic is final determination, as the determination of the entire course of the world in general."[22]

(c) That which is factually unavoidable but fundamentally (in the case of different behavior) avoidable or changeable is necessary. If one had known that. . . , and if one could have done what one wanted, then. . . . But since one did not know it and since one was not able to do it, it had to happen as it did. This means: ". . . since the conditions were such and such, there was no other possible result. . . . The concept of the unavoidable thus formulated is based on the schematic of causal determination." The causal process is regarded as "certainly guidable, for it is not bound to any goals. Whoever has the power to intervene in it can direct it. Its necessity is merely that of consequence."[23]

These meanings of necessity found in the normal usage of language require further scientific explanation. To do that, we shall seek out that which is common to all three definitions of necessity.

That which is common to the three definitions described is that necessity always emerges solely as a peculiarity of a context but never as an isolated entity. Necessity is a relational concept. Something is necessary only in relationship to something else. It is only in relationship to something else, whether it is "ideal" or "real," that one can assert of an entity that it must be this and nothing else, or that it must exist at all and cannot not exist. An existing something can be demonstrated as unable to be something else only in relationship to something else; only in such a context can one prove that something is "that which cannot be otherwise." Thus, Nicolai Hartmann proceeded to distinguish four philosophically essential meanings of the necessarily existent, to which a fifth form of necessity must be added:

(a) Logical necessity: It "means the conditional yet in its conditionedness indisputable and irremovable validity [!] of one thing on the basis of another."[24] The relational form of logical necessity is that of "if . . . then."

(b) Cognitive necessity: This must be dealt with separately because our knowledge is not identical with the existence of something existent which is to be known—against the tradition which has become dominant since Parmenides.[25] In fact, according to Hartmann, that which exists is as such completely indifferent to our knowledge of it. The knowledge of a reason (rational grounding) is to be distinguished from the fact that an existent something has its rational basis. The cognitive necessity means "that one not only knows what something is or that it is but also why it is that way and why it is at all." It includes "not only the knowledge of the thing itself but also the knowledge of the reason for the thing,"[26] on the basis of which the knowledge of something receives its necessity and with which then the known thing is captured in its necessity—the chief goal of all knowledge. The necessity as relationality here is the groundedness of something known in the knowledge of some other knowable thing.

22. *Ibid.*, p. 38.
23. *Ibid.*
24. *Ibid.*
25. ". . . for the same thing can be thought and can exist"; Parmenides, Fragment III, in Leonardo Tarán, *Parmenides* (Princeton, NJ: Princeton University Press, 1965), p. 41.
26. N. Hartmann, *op. cit.,* p. 39.

(c) Essential necessity (inner necessity): This means that which inheres in a thing on the basis of the (ideal) structure of that thing. Something is essentially necessary which, on the basis of the essence of an existent something, cannot be separated from it "under any circumstances, in any case, however special or 'accidental'. . . . This necessity is the strict opposite to that which is 'accidental' (that which is a matter of chance as far as the essence of something is concerned). . . . It has the structure of 'real, possible, present existence' (*hyparchein*), that is, of relation,"[27] whereby the reason for the existence of essentially necessary properties (*proprietates essentiales*) is given in the essence of that existent thing. The thing itself must not be necessary itself, just as in logical necessity the first premises and in cognitive necessity the recognizable reason for that which is known to be necessary are themselves not necessary.

(d) Real necessity (outer necessity): This means the determination of a really existing thing by something else, whereby the nexus of determination can be that of causality but must not necessarily be so. There are other reasons on the basis of which a thing is "thus and not other" than only that of an effect following its earlier cause. But there must be *reasons* for it. "For this necessity also has the form of a relation; that reality is only necessary 'on the basis of something'. And since the series of reasons neither stretches back into infinity nor can return into itself, there must be first reasons which are in reality accidental."[28]

(e) I add to all this a fifth form of necessity which one could call *hermeneutical* necessity. It consists of the fact that I, in order to understand something *as* itself, must resort to some other thing which first constitutes this hermeneutical "*as.*" In this sense, the child makes the mother a mother. I have to resort to the child in order to understand the mother as mother. The child is necessary for the understanding of the mother as mother, although the child must necessarily have a mother.[29] This hermeneutical necessity overlaps partially with cognitive necessity, essential necessity, and real necessity.

In all instances of necessity, we are dealing with a relational structure, which grounds necessity in something else. In addition, in all forms of necessity we are dealing with a relationship of that which necessarily exists to something else that exists, which for its part must not necessarily exist. Necessity does not exclude a *relationship back to something accidental*, so that the groundedness of something does not necessarily lead to an infinite series of reasons, a grounding without end.

The metaphysical tradition of Kant did, of course, insist that the backward relationship inherent in necessity did make an ultimate reason necessary, and that was not just as an heuristic principle of reason. Thus, it asserted that there was an ultimate adequate ground as a necessary existent. Hegel, in conscious contradiction of Kant, again asserted expressly the being of "that which is absolutely

---

27. *Ibid.*
28. *Ibid.*, p. 40.
29. In the realm of theology Ernst Fuchs, following Martin Heidegger, has consistently drawn attention to this hermeneutical form of necessary existence. He is concerned with the temporal implications of this relationship in which something later is necessary for something earlier. See, for example, E. Fuchs, *Marburger Hermeneutik* (Tübingen: J. C. B. Mohr, 1968), pp. 194f.

necessary," which in its "absolute necessity" is not dependent on anything. "The absolutely Necessary is only because it *is*, and has otherwise neither condition nor ground." To that extent, it is "simple immediacy or pure being." In that, as it has always grounded itself, it is simultaneously "simple intro-reflection"— "it is, *because* it is"—, "Absolute Necessity" is for Hegel not only *"pure Essence"* but also *"pure being."* [30] Through his definition of "absolute necessity" Hegel attempts to preserve the relational structure of the concept of "necessity" by seeing the relation within "absolute necessity." Accordingly, "absolute necessity" versus others, or even "pure being" versus "pure essence," appears as accidental. "But this Contingency is rather Absolute necessity; it is the Essence of these free Actualities which are necessary in themselves." Thus Hegel calls "absolute necessity" "blind" and describes its contingently defined essence as "that which shuns the light" because "absolute Necessity" is "founded purely" on itself. It requires the special event that the essence of absolute necessity must "burst out . . . and reveal" in the "necessary actualities" "what *it* is and what *they* are." [31]

Hegel's concept of "absolute necessity" shows clearly the kind of difficulties one encounters when one tries to deal adequately with the relational structure of necessary existence and still wants to assert the existence of an "absolute necessity" which is not dependent on something else. On the other hand, Hegel's interpretation of "absolute necessity" points out clearly the elements which characterize an existence which surpasses the concept of necessity. The issue, first, is the groundlessness of this existence, which nonetheless does not allow this existence to be regarded as arbitrary. Then, the issue is the event character of this existence which allows it to be understood in its accidence which surpasses necessity. Finally, the issue is the freedom of this existence which makes it necessary to understand this existence as one which is "breaking out of itself," an existence which is revealing itself.

We take up these elements for the definition of the formula "more than necessary" without justifying the concept of "absolute necessity" itself.[32] However, the explication of what "more than necessary" means in relationship to that which is necessary must be discussed. For that which is "more than necessary"

---

30. G. W. F. Hegel, *The Science of Logic,* trs. W. H. Johnston and L. G. Struthers (*The Muirhead Library of Philosophy*) (New York: The Macmillan Company, 1961), II, 185.

On the general interpretation of this context, see Harald Knudsen, *Gottesbeweise im Deutschen Idealismus; Die modaltheoretische Begründung des Absoluten, dargestellt an Kant, Hegel, und Weisse* (Berlin/New York: de Gruyter, 1972), pp. 160-67.

Hegel's dialectic of absolute necessity as the grounding for the freedom of subjectivity is dealt with by Wolfhart Pannenberg in his instructive lecture, "The Significance of Christianity in the Philosophy of Hegel," *The Idea of God and Human Freedom,* tr. R. A. Wilson (Philadelphia: Westminster, 1973), pp. 144-77, especially pp. 171ff.

In addition, we find something like a parody of Hegel's concept of absolute necessity when we read the comment on life's being grounded on itself made by the Silesian Swan: "One thing is clear to me at every point: / Life is the way it is! / And even if it were something else, / It still would agree with itself, / so that one then would have to say: / Life is the way it is" (see Gerhart H. Mostar, pseud. Gerhart Herrmann, *Frederike Kempner, der schlesische Schwan; Das Genie der unfreiwilligen Komik* (1974[6]), p. 123.

31. Hegel, *op. cit.,* pp. 185f.

32. We do not need to deal with the question as to how in Hegel the ontological concept of "absolute necessity" is related to the concept of God.

has a point of relationship in that which is necessary. We will have to orient ourselves to the concept of necessity if we want to explain the formula "more than necessary" as a meaningful way of stating something. I will attempt to do that by turning to the proposition of the adequate reason, which takes into consideration the concept of necessity, and I will especially deal with the *question* raised by this proposition.

The proposition of the adequate reason is regarded as a fundamental proposition, as a principle or an axiom. It is known as the 'principle of sufficient reason' ('why should it be rather than not be?'; *principium rationis sufficientis — cur potius sit quam non sit*). Leibniz calls it "the great principle"[33] or the 'received axiom' (*axioma receptum*).[34] The principle states "that nothing takes place without sufficient reason,"[35] "there is nothing without a reason, and there is no effect without a cause."[36] What does that mean?

Leibniz explains: ". . . that is to say that nothing happens without its being possible for one who has enough knowledge of things to give a reason sufficient to determine why it is thus and not otherwise."[37] Leibniz's principle of the sufficient ground requires (as a 'principle of rendering reason'—*principium reddendae rationis*) expressly a ground for *every* entity: 'nothing is without a reason.' That means that a ground for all the grounds is called for, so that Leibniz postulates a "final reason of things" (*"ultima ratio rerum"*), for which the word "God" is used. God is supposed to be the name for the "final reason of things," which as such is the "necessary being" (*"Ens necessarium"*), the absolutely necessary Existing One.[38]

If God is understood in this sense as necessary, namely, as the 'necessary

33. G. W. Leibniz, "Principles of Nature and of Grace, Founded on Reason," in *Leibniz: Philosophical Writings*, tr. M. Morris (*Everyman's Library*) (New York: Dutton, 1968), nr. 7, p. 25.

34. G. W. Leibniz, *Primae veritates*, in *Opuscules et fragments inédits de Leibniz; Extraits des manuscrits de la Bibliothèque royale de Hanovre*, par L. Couturat (Paris: F. Alkan [=Hildesheim: Georg Olms], 1903 [=1961]), pp. 518ff; GT: G. W. Leibniz, *Fragmente zur Logik*, tr. and ed. F. Schmidt (Berlin: Akademie Verlag, 1960), pp. 434ff.

35. G. W. Leibniz, "Principles of Nature and of Grace," in *op. cit.*, p. 25.

36. G. W. Leibniz, *Primae veritates*, in *op. cit.*, p. 519.

37. G. W. Leibniz, "Principles of Nature and of Grace," in *op. cit.*, pp. 25f.

38. *Ibid.*; G. Leibniz, *Specimen inventorum de admirandis naturae Generalis arcanis*, in *Die philosophischen Schriften*, ed. C. J. Gerhardt (Hildesheim: Georg Olms, 1965 [repr. of Berlin, 1890]), VII, 309f; see on that Martin Heidegger, *Der Satz vom Grund* (Pfullingen: Gunther Neske Verlag, 1957), p. 53. Heidegger's assertion is misleading, "that the proposition of the ground as a proposition was first discovered by Leibniz in the seventeenth century" (p. 51). Heidegger states, "It took centuries until the proposition of the ground was expressed *as a proposition* in its short version" (*nihil est sine ratione*; nothing without a ground). But I read in the *Rhetorica* of Aristotle ". . . that if the *cause* is present, the *effect* is present, and if absent, absent. For by proving the cause you at once prove the effect and conversely nothing can exist without its cause" (Aristotle, *Rhetorica*, tr. W. R. Roberts, *The Works of Aristotle*, ed. W. D. Ross [Oxford: Clarendon Press, 1952], XI, ii.23, 1400a, 30-32). And in Lucretius, *Of the Nature of Things*, tr. William Ellery Leonard (New York: E. P. Dutton and Company, Inc., 1950), I, ll. 148-57, p. 8, we read that the 'principle' of the observation and explanation of nature (*"naturae species ratioque"*) concludes that no thing arises out of itself in some divine fashion (*"nullam rem e nihilo gigni divinitus umquam"*). And thus, "Nothing from nothing ever yet was born." A part of the background in the tradition for this could be the well-known prohibition of the goddess in Parmenides (Fragment VIII, 7f [*op. cit.*, p. 85]): "Not from non-Being shall I allow you to say or to think."

being' in the sense of the 'last reason of things,' then we are confronted with a whole bundle of necessities. This bundle of necessities involves the first two of the three commonly used meanings of necessity discussed above, to the extent that this view understands God, on the one hand, as the indispensable condition for the being of all that exists and, on the other hand, understands all that exists as determined by grounds which have their final ground, their *ultima ratio,* in God. At the same time, we are dealing here with an hermeneutical necessity. For, according to this view, God is necessary in order to understand the world as world.

In the thesis, "God is not necessary in the world," we are dealing with the disputation of the necessity of God both in the sense of hermeneutical necessity and in those common usage meanings of necessity. The thesis, "God is more than necessary," is thus interested only in the proposition about the ground with regard to the question implied in it. The question contained in the proposition of adequate cause is this: *why this way and not otherwise*? The being (existence) of that which is this way and thus not otherwise is, for the time being, presupposed.

Yet the question, "why this way and not otherwise?", is ultimately and unavoidably directed to this presupposed being (existence) which is ascribed to things. With regard to the existence of things one must ask, "why this way and not otherwise?" Why *is* the thing that is? The antithesis which is contrasted with being is nonbeing. Thus we must ask, Why is that which is, and why is it not? And since this question applies not only to specific things but to everything which exists, we must ask generally, Why is there existence at all and not nothing instead? That is the question which the proposition of sufficient cause ultimately raises. Whoever wants to arrive at the cause of things must ask about the cause of their being in view of the possibility of their nonbeing. Leibniz then continues directly after the citation above: "This principle having been laid down, the first question we are entitled to ask will be: *Why is there something rather than nothing?* For 'nothing' is simpler and easier than 'something.' "[39]

The proposition of the adequate reason raises then the question about the advantage (*plustot, potius,* 'rather than') of existence over against nonexistence. This question, contained in the proposition of the adequate reason, seeks to probe the advantage of existence over nonexistence, to investigate it thoroughly. To accomplish that, however, nonexistence must now be dealt with as the opposite possibility to existence. If no reason for the advantage of existence over nonexistence can be found, then man is confronted with two things: the fundamental issue of the adequate reason, and now the possibility of nonexistence as a possibility which threatens not only man but everything which is. Thus a possibility becomes relevant which as such can no longer be excluded by even the purest causal nexus. The possibility of nonexistence brings existing man before a *qualitatively* other dimension than the provision of an adequate reason for the existence of what is. The *question* as to why there is anything existing at all and not rather nothing cannot be answered on the level at which the existent is explained by the existent. Instead, it places everything which exists as such in question and thus puts the questioner in a qualitatively new, other, and incom-

39. G. W. Leibniz, "Principles of Nature and of Grace, Founded on Reason," in *loc. cit.,* p. 26.

parable situation. The question contained in the proposition of the adequate reason inquires fundamentally beyond the grounding of that which exists in other existing things, in that it seeks to understand all that exists in view of the possibility of nothingness. The possibility of nonexistence does not rest at the same level as that which exists and its adequate reason. It is therefore understandable that the question about why anything exists at all, rather than nothing existing, has been established as the basic question of philosophy.

It is well known that Schelling designated this question as the basic issue which springs forth from the being of man: "He himself, man, drives me to the last despairing question: why does anything exist at all? Why is there not nothingness. . .? If I cannot answer this last question, then everything else sinks for me into the abyss of bottomless nothingness."[40] Scheler understood the uniqueness of human existence, an existence which sets itself apart from the context of all worldly existence, as characterized by the discovery of the "possibility of an 'absolute nothingness'," and in that sense he formulated the basic metaphysical question in this way: "Why is there a world as such, and why and how do I exist?"[41] Heidegger, in dealing with Leibniz's idea of the "Proposition of the Reason" and Kant's localization of the "problem of the reason" in the "realm of transcendence," went beyond the questions, "Why thus and not otherwise?", and "Why this and not that?", and said that the actual question of metaphysics was rather: "Why is there anything at all and not nothing?"[42] In his essay "What is Metaphysics?" he transforms this question into the variant, "Why is there any Being at all—why not far rather Nothing?" (a remarkable variation of Leibniz's "Why is there something rather than nothing?"), and in doing so, he writes Nothing with a capital letter,[43] in order to designate man as the being which is held out into Nothing, which in projecting itself into Nothing beyond existing basically permits that which exists as a whole to come to itself.[44] Setting aside for a moment the great distance between them, we find a similar statement in Jaspers: "Based on the experience of nothingness, actually first set in motion by this marginal experience, I entrust myself, believing anew, to the vast reaches in the illumination of all forms of that which encloses me, that I am and in that I find myself."[45] Of the theologians, Tillich interpreted the Parmenidean proposition that "being is and nonbeing is not" as the expression of the "original fact" "that there is *something* and not *nothing*."[46] This basic fact grasps consciousness as an "ontological shock" in that it implies the possibility of nonex-

40. F. W. J. Schelling, *Philosophie der Offenbarung*, in *Sämmtliche Werke*, ed. K. F. A. Schelling (Stuttgart and Augsburg: J. G. Cotta, 1858), II/3, pp. 7f.

41. Max Scheler, *Man's Place in Nature*, tr. Hans Meyerhoff (New York: Noonday, 1961), p. 89; compare Max Scheler, *On the Eternal in Man*, tr. Bernard Noble (London: SCM Press, 1960), pp. 98f.

42. Martin Heidegger, *The Essence of Reasons*, tr. Terrence Malick (Evanston: Northwestern University Press, 1969), pp. 115 and 123ff.

43. "What is Metaphysics?", in *Existence and Being*, trs. R. F. C. Hull and A. Crick (Chicago: H. Regnery Company, 1949), pp. 380 and 359f.

44. *Ibid.*, p. 377.

45. Karl Jaspers, *Der philosophische Glaube* (Fischer Bücherei, 249) (München: Fischer Bücherei, 1958), p. 249.

46. Paul Tillich, *Systematic Theology*, 2 vols. (Chicago: University of Chicago Press, 1951), I, 110.

istence. In this ontological shock, "the negative side of the mystery of being—its abysmal element—is experienced. 'Shock' points to a state of mind in which the mind is thrown out of its normal balance, shaken in its structure. Reason reaches its boundary line, is thrown back upon itself, and then is driven again to its extreme situation. This experience of ontological shock is expressed in the cognitive function by the basic philosophical question. . . : Why is there something? Why not nothing?"[47] According to Tillich, the counterpart to the shock of nonexistence, within the consciousness, is the stigma of mortality on the level of events: "There is a stigma that appears on everything, the stigma of finitude, of implicit and inescapable nonbeing."[48] That shock and this stigma belong, as negative conditions, constitutively to revelation and to the miracle which mediates it; they are the negative side of the ecstasy of consciousness. The question inherent in the proposition of the ground, in Tillich's thought, bears not only the significance of a logically introduced querying of being, but also the power of an event which rudely interrupts the whole context of life.

Accordingly, we are not entering new territory when we make the point that with the question about the ground of the non-nonbeing of that which exists, nonbeing now appears to man as a possibility. It is a possibility which allows him to have a qualitatively new experience over against the experience of that which exists. In this new experience, all that has been experienced until now under the aspect of its nothingness is experienced once more. The new quality of this experience makes it impossible to align it with other experiences. Rather, it is related to those experiences from which it differs in that "old becomes new." Human existence experiences itself when it confronts the possibility of not being in a qualitatively other way than in all those experiences which it has within the context of existence. In view of the possibility of nonbeing, man has a qualitatively new experience with his being. I call it *an experience with experience*,[49] because in it not only every experience already had, but experience itself is experienced anew.

5. However, this experience with experience is twofold within itself. It can take shape as *anxiety* and would then be a fundamental jeopardizing of being. It has been understood as the fundamental and basic experience in this sense from Schelling to Heidegger. The experience with experience which emerges from the encounter with nonbeing can also take shape as gratitude. This happens whenever being is experienced as something out of nothingness and as such preserved from it, as something which is gifted to be, as creation. The twofold character and ambivalence of this experience of the nonbeing of experience is something which absolutely cannot be led to decision based on itself. It is of the essence of the experience with the experience that *transitions* from the basic experience of anxiety based on nonbeing to the basic experience of thankfulness based on the joy of being, as well as the *simultaneity* of both basic experiences,

47. *Ibid.*, p. 113.
48. *Ibid.*, p. 116.
49. On this expression, see Gerhard Ebeling, "Die Klage über das Erfahrungs-defizit in der Theologie als Frage nach ihrer Sache," *Wort und Glaube III; Beiträge zur Fundamendaltheologie, Soteriologie, und Ekklesiologie* (Tübingen: Mohr [Siebeck], 1975), p. 22; Eberhard Jüngel, *Unterwegs zur Sache; Theologische Bemerkungen* (München: C. Kaiser, 1972), p. 8.

take place. If, then, a decision should take place which is unambiguous, which resolves the ambivalence in favor of an irreversible experience of the affirmation of being and sets aside this twofold character, then what has happened is precisely what theologically merits being called a *miracle*. It is a miraculous experience, one not deducible from experiences already had, when his existence, and not only his own existence, is disclosed to man as something brought forth out of nothing and preserved from nothingness. Such a miraculous experience is not just an experience *with* nothingness—that is what man is preserved from—but an experience *in view* of nothingness, with that which man has always and always will experience. It cannot be induced, but, like a miracle, is possible only as the result of an event which is called in theology the *revelation of God*.

When God reveals himself, then man experiences his existence and the being of his world as a being which has been plucked from nothingness. To that extent, man has already experienced God himself as a being which is not necessary but more than necessary. For, in the experience of being preserved from nothingness in such a way that gratitude results, God is experienced as the Being who disposes over being and nonbeing. Such a Being, however, which disposes over being and nonbeing, cannot be conceived of as dependent on some other being, even if it is not to be conceived of by excluding this contradiction. But that is precisely what would have happened if God were supposed to be asserted as necessary. God would be grounded then in the being of some other being, or in the being of being as such. However, a being which disposes over being and nonbeing can have no ground outside of itself. This means: God has no ground. If God is the one who disposes over being and nonbeing (and thus the one who distinguishes between being and nonbeing), then there is no degree of necessity which can be postulated of him. As groundless being, God is not necessary and yet more than necessary.

If one still wanted to postulate for God the highest and absolute necessity, then it could not be distinguished from absolute accidence, and then one would have to do as Hegel did, and postulate that the essence of "absolute necessity" is pure accidence. The expression chosen instead, "more than necessary," to the extent that it rejects necessity and yet not its opposite, which is the affirmation of the arbitrariness of a "this way or possibly that way," is an expression which only implies what is at stake, but implies the issue in a better way than a concept of absolute necessity which conceals the nonnecessity of God.

Talk about God has its fundamental position at that point where in the experience of the existing one the difference between being and nonbeing becomes relevant, where being or nonbeing is the question. This leads to the insight that the God who is conceived of in the contradiction of being and nonbeing explodes the entire concept of one who grounds, one who is the reason (as a phenomenon necessarily on the same level as that which is grounded). The question, "Why is there anything at all and not nothing?", cannot be answered with logical necessity by giving a reason. It is *not necessary*, when one experiences one's own being and that of the world in view of the possibility of nonbeing, to arrive at talk about God. Here, too, God is not necessary. Against Leibniz and the metaphysical tradition, this is the meaning of our proposition that God is groundless. The fact that something exists at all and not nothing is in and of itself ambivalent and does not exclude that that which exists could be destroyed by nothing. Thus the question, "Why is there anything at all and not nothing," leads to that dimension within which the question of God is raised, but it does not lead to God as the necessary ground. The experience of possible nonbeing can also summon up anxiety and nothing else. Anxiety is not to be understood as a deficit, but rather as something positive, as concern for that which exists. Man is not less human when he perseveres in that anxiety than when he is definitively removed from it.[50] In a definitive way, however, man cannot remove himself from this anxiety. Definitively he can only *be removed* from it. And if man is definitively removed from his anxiety about nonbeing, then God has been at work and is experienced as the one who *always was* at work, so that one can only look after him (Exod. 33:23), and can only recognize the *posteriora dei* ('hinder parts of God').[51] If God is experienced in this sense as the one who distinguishes between being and not being and who decides in favor of being, then this experience for its part cannot be grounded out of the context of the one who exists. God does not come from the context of the world—not even as the result of basic trust (*Urvertrauen*)!—but rather always from God himself! Therefore, to use the language of theology, God is experienced only on the basis of self-revelation. *God comes from God.* If God reveals himself as the one who distinguishes between being and not being and decides in favor of being, then he cannot be placed within the category of the necessary. As Thomas Aquinas neatly puts it, God is "above the order of the necessary and the contingent, just as he is above all created being."[52] God is more than necessary.

6.   This insight at which we have arrived has its consequences for talk about God within the horizons of contemporary thought. They are to be expressed in three fundamental propositions. Put in its shortest form, the anthropological and theological truth of the contemporary discovery of the nonnecessity of God is as follows:

(a) Man and his world are interesting for their own sake.

(b) Even more so, God is interesting for his own sake.

(c) God makes man, who is interesting for his own sake, interesting in a new way.

The necessary as necessary is always thematic or interesting for the sake of something else. Whatever is more than necessary is interesting for its own sake, even though not everything which is interesting for its own sake must then be more than necessary, "above the order of the necessary and the contingent." This is all the more true of the one who decides between being and not being.

The fact that God, although he is the one who decides between being and

50. It is useful to note that definitive removal from anxiety does not mean that this anxiety is destroyed. It is reworked fundamentally and can become concern and caring.

51. Luther, in the Heidelberg Disputation (Thesis 20), with reference to Exodus 33:18ff, focused the possibility of correct theology on the recognition of the "hinder parts of God," the *posteriora dei,* and restricted this "to mean the passion and the cross"; *Luther: Early Theological Works* (in *Library of Christian Classics,* vol. 16), ed. and tr. James Atkinson (Philadelphia: Westminster Press, 1962), pp. 278 and 290f, and on that, Paul Althaus, *The Theology of Martin Luther,* tr. Robert C. Schultz (Philadelphia: Fortress Press, 1966, 1975³), pp. 25ff; Gerhard Ebeling, *Luther: An Introduction to his Thought,* tr. R. A. Wilson (Philadelphia: Fortress Press, 1970), pp. 226ff.

52. Thomas Aquinas, *De Malo,* q. 16, a. 7, ad 15.

not being, nevertheless is not just *above* this contradiction between being and not being but is God *in the midst* of this contradiction, is the point of *Christian* talk about God, which now goes beyond what we have said until now. When we refer to the word of the cross as the criterion for talk about God, we will then be pointing out all the more plainly the contemporary aporia in the traditional concept of God. We had expressed our call for the theological examination of the contemporary aporia of the word "God." In recognizing the worldly groundlessness of God, this theological examination has advanced so far that the discovery of the worldly nonnecessity of God can now be identified as a genuinely theological truth. When this identification takes place, then, of course, the basic theological aporia of a theology oriented on the cross of Jesus Christ becomes plain behind the contemporary aporia of the word "God."

SECTION 3. The Basic Theological Uncertainty (Aporia) of Christian Talk about God

What now follows consists of a theological countermovement to what was expounded with the thesis of the worldly nonnecessity of God. That this is really not a contradiction is something which the discussion itself will reveal.

1. The statement, "God comes from God," is the *positive* formulation of the discovery that God is not necessary in a worldly sense, that God is groundless in the worldly sense. "God comes from God" means, negatively formulated, that God stands under no conditions of any kind. The customary expression of this is the concept Unconditionalness. God is unconditioned. For this reason, God has even been defined as "The Unconditioned." However, such a definition places theological thought in the danger of losing itself in the abstractions of a concept rather than rising to concreteness through thinking abstractions. False abstractness deprives that which is "generally valid" of its relatedness to the concrete and thus to validity. The Unconditioned is in this sense an inappropriately abstract category, because it is much too ambivalent to be able to speak for itself.[1] Only after we have established the positive formula, "God comes from God," can the category of the unconditional be interpreted in a relatively adequate way.

Something abrupt or sudden can also be unconditional—for example, the "big bang" out of which the world might have emerged. The "big bang" and any event which ever happened abruptly are unconditional not only in the sense of independence from something else but further in the sense of complete lack of motivation. Unconditionalness can also be understood in the sense of unmotivatedness. Whoever conceives of God in this way thinks of him as a being who is defined by nothing else, and easily thinks of his unconditionalness as unmotivated and unmotivatable *arbitrariness*. "The Unconditioned" is then accord-

---

1. See M. Kähler's reservations about attempts to think of God as "the unconditioned and unconditional" and to identify him with the "highest being" (*Die Wissenschaft der christlichen Lehre von dem evangelischen Grundartikel aus im Abrisse dargestellt* [Erlangen: Deichert, 1905[3], p. 165; repr. Neukirchen: Verlag des Erziehungsvereins, 1966]). According to Kähler, faith presupposes instead "that God has the capacity in conscious self-definition to condition himself," so that it is possible to speak relevantly of the "personality of God" (*ibid.*, p. 167).

ingly understood as a *numen* ('divinity'), as *mysterium tremendum* ('tremendous mystery' or 'fearful mystery'). The majesty of God is compared then in a fatal way with the majesty of a tyrant. When, in opposition to that, we state that "God comes from God," then we mean, at the very least, that God *is motivated by God*. This expresses the idea that the being of God is not an indeterminate event, which suddenly releases itself, so to speak, but rather an event which *determines* itself. God determines himself. In this twofold sense, God is the event of self-determination, God is self-determination taking place.

The theological category for this ontological matter is called *freedom*. Freedom is always self-determination. For that reason, Luther said that freedom was the only predicate of being which could legitimately be asserted of God. Because only God can determine himself, 'free will' (*liberum arbitrium*) is for Luther a predicate of God.[2] By contrast, Luther asserted that he could know and conceive of a free person only as a *freed* or *liberated* person. It has been objected to Luther's thesis of the 'enslaved will of man' (*servum arbitrium hominis*) both then and now that God is being magnified at the cost of man. However, this objection only appears to be a valid one.

Freedom has two sides: (a) self-determination as the opposite of alien determination, but also (b) self-determination as the opposite of indeterminateness (arbitrariness). Freedom understood without the goal of determinateness would be an impermissible abstraction. The will to determination is what makes self-determination, makes freedom something concrete. Thus freedom is something other than a state of free suspension which has no bonds or obligations. Faithfulness is constitutive of freedom. God, the free God, is the very opposite of something like an eternal state of suspension.[3] God determines himself. Only as one who is determined on the basis of his self-determination is God a concrete reality. As the faithful God he is the free God.

If the proposition, "God comes from God," implies freedom as *self-determination*, freedom as will to the determinateness of one's own being, then we must ask what God determines himself to be. If God comes from God, then *where* does he come *to*?

The traditional answer to this question would be that he comes to himself. God comes to himself when he comes from himself. Obviously the proposition threatens to become nothing else than a cheap tautology. Christian tradition has excluded this appearance of cheap tautology with the trinitarian dogma. The doctrine of the Trinity conceives of this as a real event, as a history of the divine being: that God comes from himself to himself. The word "come" is taken seriously here to the extent that it interprets God's being as an event from God to God, an event in which God is not only his own derivation but also his future. Although the doctrine of the Trinity originally arose as a confession of the man Jesus as true God, it is remarkable that this eternal event in the theological tradition has not been understood on the basis of the being of this man

---

2. See Martin Luther, *Luther and Erasmus: Free Will and Salvation* (in *Library of Christian Classics*, vol. 17), eds. and trs. P. Watson and E. G. Rupp (Philadelphia: Westminster Press, 1969), p. 141: "It follows now that free choice is plainly a divine term, and can be properly applied to none but the Divine Majesty alone."
3. In this regard, the thinking of W. Weischedel about a "philosophical theology" which is possible today is to be especially contradicted.

who died on the cross. That God became *man* was for the classical trinitarian doctrine not the constitutively determining event for the trinitarian being of God, although it then derived from that event as a further consequence of the basic thought. One could think God as God without having thought of the Crucified One as God. The death of Jesus concerned the concept of deity, the divine nature, as little as the life of this man was significant for the concept of divine being. According to this view, God comes to himself even apart from Jesus. God's freedom, therefore, was conceived of without his concrete self-determination.

Here again we find in Luther a completely opposite view. He sought to know God solely in Jesus, the Crucified, in a theocentric application of the Pauline concentration on the Crucified One (I Cor. 2:2). In the Heidelberg Disputation he says, "in Christ crucified is true theology and the knowledge of God."[4] Luther was exegetically consequent enough to give the only possible biblical answer to the question, What does God determine himself for? God determines himself for the human existence of the man Jesus, in order to be *God* in and with this man. Thus the Christian faith, as he puts it later in the commentary on Galatians, can speak of no other God than the 'incarnate God' and the 'human God' (*deus incarnatus, deus humanus*).[5] It is from this insight that we shall proceed.

A doctrine of God oriented to the man Jesus must then develop two avenues of thought: God does indeed come from God and only from God, and he is determined by nobody and nothing other than by himself; however, he determines himself to be God not without man. That is the sense of the New Testament statements about the preexistence of the Son of God identified with Jesus. As the tradition correctly asserts, God comes from himself to himself without outside help. But God comes to himself in accordance with his own self-determination in such a way that he comes to man and only thus does man come to himself. God comes from God, but he does not want to come to himself without us. God comes to God, but with man. Thus, God's humanity belongs to his divinity. This is what theology must finally begin to learn.

In doing so, it will have to exclude a misunderstanding of its task. The task of thinking God in such a way that he is conceived of as coming to himself and simultaneously coming to man cannot be meant in such a way that God is thought of as dependent on the existence of man.[6] The final result of our thought cannot be that ultimately man is necessary for God. That God does not want to

---

4. *Luther: Early Theological Works* (in *Library of Christian Classics*, vol. 16), ed. and tr. James Atkinson (Philadelphia: Westminster Press, 1962), Thesis XX, p. 291.

5. Compare Martin Luther, *A Commentary on St. Paul's Epistle to the Galatians*, ed. P. S. Watson (Westwood, NJ: Fleming H. Revell Company, 1953), p. 44.

6. Of course, this misunderstanding could easily be disposed of by saying that God could come to himself without coming to man, that, in fact, he is God by virtue of the fact that he has always come to himself without man and the world. But I regard this argument as godless. It conceives of the freedom of God as mere self-possession and restricts the sovereignty of God, conceived of as the absolute having of being, to God himself, in that it sets aside the selflessness of love from this sovereignty and allows freedom to be derived from it as a distinct and secondary factor. Basically the studies presented here are nothing other than a concerted attack on the godlessness of this argument.

come to himself without man does not make man the consummation of God. God perfects or consummates himself. But it may and must be said that God does not want to perfect himself without man. God's coming to himself must be understood as an act of freedom, in which God gives himself a future in such a way that he disposes over his future and thus over himself. That God does not desire to come to himself without man is to be understood in such a way that God has definitively decided about his future. This can be compared with the decision of a loving person who does not want to be able to come to himself, based on the decision of love, without his beloved one, and thus is not able to desire to come to himself without the beloved. This comparison is more than a comparison. It is possible only because God is love himself, and this disposing over one's own being inheres in love.

A further misunderstanding must also be set aside. If God does not desire to come to himself without man, then one could draw the conclusion, which is what we are trying to dispute, that God is ontologically necessary for man. This conclusion certainly recommends itself if the deity of God is supposed to imply humanity, fully apart from the necessity of a creator for the being of a creature. There is certainly to be no theological doubt of the fact that man is God's *creature*; and if a creature is to be conceived of as a creature, then it is necessary to think of a *creator*. However, theology must consider that man as creature is not the product of creative arbitrariness. A theology of creation which does not lead this possibility *ad absurdum* does not deserve the name. Man can be thought of only as the creature of a creator who is not conceived of as arbitrary when the being of this man who is to be created moves the being of the creating God inwardly. Talk about the humanity which belongs to the divinity of God should express this, together with faith in the "personal unity" of the eternal word with the man Jesus. That God *creates* as his counterpart man is the execution of his self-determination, according to which God does not desire to come to himself without man. This self-determination, if it really is a decision of *love* which desires to come to itself with another one and only with that one, implies the *freedom* of God and man as opposites of each other. If God has created man as the one elected *for love,* then man is what he is *for his own sake*. For one is loved only for his own sake or not at all. In this regard, the difference between God and man is in the fact that God can *create* what then as something created is *loved* by its creator for its own sake, whereas man, although his love is creative in a certain sense, does not first create what he loves. If then man is the one elected for love, he is what he is in a relationship to God which is determined by freedom. This relationship could only be diminished by any talk of the necessity of God for man. Love bursts apart the relationship of necessity by surpassing it.

If God unconditionally concerns us, then the reason is not just that God comes from God but rather much more and much more centrally that God does not desire to come to himself without man. As such, he is more than necessary.

Since tradition has largely been unable to think in this fashion, it is necessary for us to criticize this tradition. In such criticism the basic contemporary uncertainty about the word "God" is transformed into a basic theological uncertainty about talk about God which is oriented to Jesus the Crucified. Theological critique is materially the orientation of theology to the 'word of the cross' as the 'word' (*logos*) which is constitutive for all talk about God, and this orientation must constantly be renewed. The word of the cross is really what presents theology with its actual problems. The word of the cross then also makes plain what is the actual uncertainty or aporia of the theological tradition.

That the Christian faith does its reflective thought with the language of the metaphysical tradition is not really what is so aporetical. Faith must speak with the language of the world if it does not want to become dumb. Therefore, beginning with the age of early Christendom it had to speak the language of metaphysics as the language of thought at that time if it did not want to deteriorate into thoughtlessness. But the danger was certainly present that in so doing it would fall under the *dictatorship* of metaphysics, rather than using its language *critically*. As far as the concept of God is concerned, the history of European Christianity until now has fallen prey to this danger in one regard. It has considered itself capable of thinking of God in his being as God without thinking of him simultaneously as the Crucified. A characteristic indication of that is the constantly recurring attempts ever since early church Christology to conceive of the death of the Crucified One as an event which only affected the "true man" but not the "true God." The *perfection* of God required by the law of metaphysics forbade imagining God as suffering or even thinking of him together with one who was dead. This prohibition and its alleged reason are seen, however, from the perspective of the word of the cross, to be the basic aporia into which European theology has blundered.

2. The basic uncertainty or aporia which is confronted by the word of the cross in its substance can be briefly summarized with the concept of the *absolute nature* of God.[7] This basic aporia is already present in the context of the biblical texts, of course, and not just in the context of contemporary formulation of the Christian faith. That Jesus Christ "was crucified in weakness, but lives by the power of God" (II Cor. 13:4) seems to characterize the death of Jesus as a specifically human weakness which is then opposed directly to the absoluteness of divine life. Even in the New Testament, then, God and the death of Jesus seem to be related to each other only as antitheses. Even the apostle Paul, whose thinking like no other's was based on the Crucified One, does not seem to "be consequent" in this regard. More careful exegesis would be able to show that this appearance is deceptive. Yet such statements by the apostle indicate the difficulty of the problem. Faith in the Crucified One *as* true God and the theological consequences of this faith do not merge easily and without difficulty.

Theologians of the early church, and then chiefly Luther, Hegel, and the theologians who followed them, have seen and sought to resolve the aporia which emerges here. However, the appearance of simple contradiction between

---

7. Thus Eugen Biser, "Der Atheismus als Problem der Theologie; Überlegungen zu einer theologischen Aporetik," in *Glaube als Verpflichtung: Horizontale und vertikale Strukturen des christlichen Glaubens; Festschrift für J. Hasenfuss zum 70. Geburtstag* (München: Schöningh, 1971), pp. 49ff, who ascribes to the aporia of the absoluteness of God that of the contingency of the world and that of the mediation of God and man. The work of Eugen Biser borders closely on my studies here and elsewhere. The differences, however, will not remain concealed to the interested reader and will perhaps stimulate him to formulate his own thought beyond the contemporary stance of the so-called controversial-theology debate.

God's life and the death of Jesus has, in the history of theology and generally in spite of remarkable opposing positions, established itself and been broadly accepted as valid. In the theological understanding of the resurrection of Jesus from the dead it becomes rather plain as a rule that no one has really sought to *think* of the Crucified One as God. The death of Jesus, generally speaking, has had little significance for the concept of God. Not only in the metaphysical tradition but in the Christian as well, the concept of divine being has been so dominated by the thought of absoluteness that to think of the christological identity of God with the crucified Jesus at best could lead only to a paradox which bursts all thought apart. That God's being does not contradict itself in the crucified man Jesus, but rather harmonizes with itself, was at most stated but certainly not thought through. It was the older Karl Barth who, in this regard, dared to pursue resolutely the path which had been opened up by Luther and Hegel—the theological public has largely failed to notice this. The style of the dispute about the resurrection of Jesus is the best proof of the fact that the axiom of the absoluteness of God still broadly dominates theology, and at times this is not even sensed to be an aporia at all.

On the other hand, we observe that in attempts at theological and philosophical thought which are critically beholden to the modern consciousness of truth, there is generally a very pronounced sensibility toward the problems which are given with the absoluteness of God. The aporetic consciousness noted here is rooted, however, not so much in the theological problem as in the basic attitude of modern thought. For the axiom of the absoluteness of God which modern thought first had completely accepted from tradition gradually awakened more and more opposition on the part of man, who felt his freedom threatened by such an absolute being.

Modern man has his own awareness of freedom. Even if he lacks that freedom, he has with great difficulty gained an awareness of the right to that freedom, not least through the self-criticism of his theoretical and practical reason. This intellectual right to freedom has been at least partially realized politically and as such is constantly subject to jeopardy; man devotes great if not always successful efforts to realizing it, and it is hoped that he will continue to do so; it is, however, fundamentally placed in question by the concept of a God who is absolutely superior to man. Modern man especially is allergic to a God who can only be thought of absolutistically. This distinguishes him from his medieval fathers. Whereas the absoluteness of God was in an earlier age the guarantor of the coherence of the world and human societies, it now appears to modern man to be a power which paralyzes human responsibility for the world and society.

The unbearable character of what appears to be an unavoidable absolutistic concept of God, the entire aporia of the apparent absolute necessity of an absolute being—all this was illuminated by Immanuel Kant with reference to the inner structure of the concept of God when he wrote: "We cannot bear, nor can we rid ourselves of the thought, that a being, which we regard as the greatest of all possible existences, should *say to himself*: I am from eternity to eternity;

beside me there is nothing, except that which exists by my will; *but whence then am I?"*[8]

A God who cannot answer the question about his own derivation because there is nothing outside of himself which is not there except by his will places himself in question with this question: "But where do I come from then?" The thought of the absoluteness of God has ended in a cul-de-sac.

3. Further, this aporia of the idea of the absoluteness of God has its own historical paradox. Reason, which must think of the absoluteness of God and yet cannot bear it, becomes practical as the awareness of one's own *freedom,* yet this modern awareness of freedom became possible historically through the Reformation's insistence on the absoluteness of God's claims over against all earthly claims. Karl Marx, following Hegel, formulated it pointedly: "Germany's[9] *revolutionary* past is . . . the *Reformation.* As the revolution then began in the brain of the *monk,* so now it begins in the brain of the *philosopher. Luther,* we grant, overcame bondage out of *devotion* by replacing it by bondage out of *conviction.* He shattered faith in authority because he restored the authority of faith."[10] There is indeed a remarkable continuity between the Wittenberg of the Reformation and the Paris of the Revolution, between the newly asserted justification of the godless by faith alone and the proclamation of human rights, between the freedom of the Christian man and the freedom of the human race, between the emphasis on the deity of God and the abolition of God which was ordered in Paris in November 1793 but then was reversed on May 8, 1794, through the acknowledgment of a highest being.

Once one is aware of this paradox, then the question must be raised whether the Reformation's doctrine of justification did not imply very different consequences for our understanding of God than the passing on of the absoluteness axiom which probably belonged more to the nominalistic background of Luther's thought. *Luther's* Christology in its antischolastic and anti-Zwinglian

8. I. Kant, *Critique of Pure Reason,* tr. J. M. D. Meiklejohn (*Everyman's Library,* 909) (London: J. M. Dent & Sons Ltd., 1950), p. 357. The statement is supposed to express the aporia of the concept of "unconditioned necessity, which, as the ultimate support and stay of all existing things, is an indispensable requirement of the mind," and yet "is an abyss on the verge of which human reason trembles in dismay" (*ibid.*). E. Biser, *op. cit.,* p. 28, has pointed out that this fictional monologue of God was taken by Kant almost entirely from his early work "Der einzig mögliche Beweisgrund . . ." and put in *The Critique of Pure Reason.* In the earlier work (*Werke in Sechs Bänden,* ed. W. Weischedel [Wiesbaden: Insel-Verlag, 1960], I, 724 [A 180]), the question "but whence then am I?" is lacking, although it is what makes the entire thought so unbearable. Accordingly, this thought is here "the noblest of all" whereas in *The Critique of Pure Reason* it signifies the "true abyss for human reason."

9. For Hegel, the Reformation was not simply the revolutionary past of Germany; rather he thought that in the *French Revolution* "in another form they completed the Reformation that Luther began" (G. W. F. Hegel, *Lectures on the History of Philosophy,* 3 vols., trs. E. S. Haldane and F. H. Simson [New York: Humanities Press, 1963], III, 398).

10. Karl Marx, "Contribution to the Critique of Hegel's Philosophy of Right," in K. Marx and F. Engels, *On Religion* (Moscow: Foreign Languages Publishing House, 1957), pp. 50f.

thrust[11] certainly contains enough explosive material. It was at least a pervasive misunderstanding of Luther's distinction between the revealed and concealed God which prevented the further development of Luther's christological approach into a concept of God which is appropriate to it. Thus the absoluteness axiom as a model for the understanding of God was preserved, with the result that every critique of the axiom of absoluteness must also be directed at the concept of God. Together with the absoluteness axiom, God was put into question.

4. Sensitivity to the aporia which then resulted is expressed in the dark statement about the death of God. There is no other phrase which so appropriately indicates the basic theological aporia of Christian talk about God in the modern age because it also reminds us of the innermost problem of a theology of the Crucified One. However, a dispute about the true meaning of the proposition that God is dead must then follow. This is all the more necessary because a so-called "God-is-dead theology" assumes that it can overcome the *aporia* indicated by the phrase "God is dead" only by rejecting not only the axiom of absoluteness but also God.

The origin of the idea of the death of God shows how the axiom of absoluteness in theology can be surmounted in favor of a Christian concept of God. Nietzsche, who was polemically sensitive to the unique character of the Christian faith, made this point in his fashion. *"God on the Cross*—does no one yet understand the terrible ulterior motive of this symbol?"[12] If one wants to understand the "thoughts in the background of this symbol," then one cannot evade learning to distinguish between a meaningful and an absurd use of language about the death of God.

---

11. See chiefly "Vom Abendmahl Christi. Bekenntnis," *WA*, 26, 261ff. On that, see R. Schwarz, "Gott ist Mensch," *Zeitschrift für Theologie und Kirche*, 63 (1966), 289ff, and E. Jüngel, "Vom Tod des lebendigen Gottes," in *Unterwegs zur Sache; Theologische Bemerkungen* (München: C. Kaiser, 1972), pp. 105ff.

12. F. Nietzsche, "The Antichrist," in *The Complete Works of Friedrich Nietzsche* (New York: Macmillan Company, 1911), vol. 16 (*The Twilight of the Idols*), nr. 51, pp. 204ff.

CHAPTER II

Talk about the Death of God
as an Expression of the Uncertainty
of Modern Thinking about God

There is adequate reason today for a discussion of the significance and absurdity of talk about the death of God, particularly when one wants to think using more or less precise terms. "Death of God" can mean almost anything! In view of the generous usage which is made of the words "God" and "death" and of their syntactical connection today, a philosophical mind could well see reason to rescue the terms for the sake of the phenomena. Furthermore, for a self-critical theology which does not cut itself off from the present day, there is today a material necessity to discuss the significance and absurdity of talk about the death of God. After metaphysics had perfected itself as the philosophy of *the* death of God, there has been for some time something like a "theology *after* the death of God." This cannot well be ignored.

SECTION 4. The Significance and the Absurdity of Talk about the Death of God

1. During my studies the philosophical talk about the death of God fascinated us, especially what we came to know through Friedrich Nietzsche. Jean Paul's vision, the first bouquet of his *Siebenkäs*: the "talk of the dead Christ down from the world building, saying that there is no God," accompanied our study of theology as the other possibility, rejected by faith but certainly perceived by reason. And theology consisted also for us of constantly rejecting in our thinking the possibility of atheism which faith already rejected. In doing this, we learned that atheism can be rejected only if one overcomes theism, which is the presupposition of modern metaphysics and its disputation. In its intention to overcome theism, theology came together with that particular philosophy which was interesting to us at that time. Our theological teachers were in their way emphatic critics of theism in theology.

This has almost been forgotten today. It may be useful to be reminded of that fact. To the degree that German theology today criticizes theism, it is a theology in the school of "dialectical theology." Of course, the opposition between Friedrich Gogarten and Karl Barth effected a polarity in the process.

Certainly it is not an accident that in the theological work of the Gogarten student, Dorothee Sölle, the critique of theism has been made a theme of the experience of the history of thought,[1] so that this critique has been elevated to the level of a theological axiom in its historical uniqueness. At the same time, theological work instructed by Karl Barth saw the actual radicality of the criticism of theism as grounded in the Christian faith itself,[2] and thus knew that it was obligated to arrive at a new formulation of the concept of God.[3] Whether in the one instance or the other, the statement about the "death of God" was a substantive partner in dialogue for theology. Then it became a fad. Not a few theologians who began to be somewhat embarrassed about their actual task now used the statement as a kind of fig leaf in order to conceal the nudity of their theology behind it. The motto "God is dead" can be used to make theological thinking unbelievably simple. The serious involvement with the problems raised by the idea of the death of God is then seriously jeopardized. A theology which participates in criticism of theism has much reason to counter the absurd and irresponsible use of the statement through a discussion of the meaning of talk about the death of God. The best possibility for countering the irresponsible and absurd use of this phrase is still that of working through its actual meaning.

2. The discussion of the significance of talk about the death of God leads to the substantive center of theology. The decisive question is this: Can theology appropriately talk about the death of God without ceasing to be theology? On the other hand, one must ask with equal emphasis whether theology which avoids

1. See above all Dorothee Sölle, *Christ the Representative; an Essay in Theology after the Death of God*, tr. David Lewis (Philadelphia: Fortress Press, 1967).

2. In this sense I criticized, before any "theology after the death of God," H. Gollwitzer's phrase "God is in and for himself" (*The Existence of God as Confessed by Faith*, tr. J. W. Leitch [Philadelphia: Westminster Press, 1965], p. 217) from the perspective of the antimetaphysically oriented trinitarian doctrine of Karl Barth (*The Doctrine of the Trinity: God's Being is in Becoming*, tr. H. Harris [Grand Rapids: Wm. B. Eerdmans, 1976]). On Barth, see also my lecture, ". . . keine Menschenlosigkeit Gottes . . . Zur Theologie Karl Barths zwischen Theismus und Atheismus," *Evangelische Theologie*, 31 (1971), 376ff.

3. Wolfhart Pannenberg asserted, "The present-day tendency to argue away and exclude the idea of God in Protestant theology must be understood as a consequence of the movement which began with the rejection of 'natural' knowledge of God, and with it of all philosophical theology" ("Speaking about God in the Face of Atheist Criticism," *The Idea of God and Human Freedom*, tr. R. A. Wilson [Philadelphia: Westminster, 1973], p. 101). This statement cannot be upheld in its crudeness for the very reason that as a "result" of that approach the attempt was made to arrive at a "far-reaching reformulation of the idea of God," something to which theology is obliged, according to Pannenberg (*ibid.*, p. 107). The differences on method should not becloud the view of the common factors which have arisen with regard to the matter at hand. That with "Barth and his followers" (p. 100), "the postulate that in the case of Christianity we have something quite different, not a human religion but a divine revelation, could only appear to be a bare assertion—and what is more a completely human assertion" (p. 101), is too undifferentiated a statement in view of Barth's concept of religion. It is also a somewhat confusing statement, as far as the accusation about "bare" and "completely human" assertion is concerned, since I am quite unable to understand how one could propound the idea that "Christianity [is] a divine revelation" in any other way than through completely human and bare assertions. Perhaps there is an intention to conceal the nudity of the bare assertion with the emperor's new clothes. That does not exclude something like a "theology of the religions," an undertaking for which Karl Barth provided orally his own systematic approach during the last year of his life.

talk about the death of God can still be theology. It could well be—and much indicates that this is so—that theology is put in question not so much by the proclamation of the death of God as by the industrious ignoring of the problem contained in that proclamation. It must be feared in general that theology is not perishing at the bastions of unbelief but as a result of its own sleepiness. The symptoms of drowsy theology can easily be observed in our day. Whenever theology awakens from its historical twilight zone, it develops an all the more excited hectic activity and grasps at anything which appears remotely relevant in order to regain the course which it lost while sleeping. Thus, one can grasp for the dark statement "God is dead" without even beginning to perceive its actual problems. In spite of all the hectic activity, one remains asleep. On the other hand, an alert theology—"The waking have one world in common"[4]— shares the problems (not the fads) of the world without compromising for that reason its own theological questions. Theology's own questions—those are the variants of that one single problem which we *are* ourselves, that is, which we are *before* God. Within the perspective of this problem those other problems arise for theology which we *create* when we begin to process the world. Only to the extent that the problem which we are before God is dealt with do the problems of the world attain theological relevance. For that reason, the biblical texts confront us with the world only to the degree that they confront us with ourselves. They do this by confronting us with God. Talk about God, however, finds its *Sitz im Leben* not only in the problem which we are. One would also talk about God if man were an unproblematic being. But that is not what he is now. Therefore, the word "God" is not an unproblematic word now.

Theological consideration of the significance of talk about the death of God must attend to both aspects. Its attention is directed to the problems of the world which are indicated in such talk, that is, the problems which have arisen in our history, or at least in the history of thought. In the process, theology is primarily interested in the problem concealed in such talk, the problem of what we are ourselves before God and with which we are confronted through the biblical texts. Regard must be given to the indissoluble relationship of the two complexes. Such a study must thus have both an historical and a dogmatic orientation.

We may also state what such a study is *not* intended to accomplish. We do not intend to provide an apologetic for Christianity. We are occupied with the talk about the death of God because of the theological relevance of the problem concealed in such talk, but not for apologetic reasons: neither in the sense that theology's case should be defended against the claims of such talk, nor in the sense that we might want to make theology interesting—again—with this dark statement. Theology is either interesting on its own, or not at all.

SECTION 5. The Twofold Source of Talk about the Death of God

1. The proposition that God is dead is a dark statement. And it will remain dark as long as it is not understood in terms of its origin. In order to understand

4. Heraclitus, B 89 (W 15), in Philip Wheelwright, *Heraclitus* (Princeton, NJ: Princeton University Press, 1959), p. 20.

its origin, we must examine the period of time in which it was asserted. One of the particular characteristics of this proposition is that it was not always germane. Its time emerged. The truth concealed in this dark statement cannot be understood as independent from the events of history. It can be grasped only as an historical truth, that is, through understanding what has taken place in the history of those particular traditions in which such a statement became possible. Whoever thinks he is able to understand talk about the death of God as possible at any time or as a statement which ought to be possible at any time has not understood it at all. For "time is long, but that which is true takes place."[1]

Mythology, to be sure, speaks of the dying of gods. Pascal is probably referring to that when he cites Plutarch, "Great Pan is dead."[2] Ch.-M. des Granges comments, "Pan, through a false etymology, symbolized the great All; it was thus the death of paganism which this voice announced."[3] Be that as it may, the dark statement about the death of God speaks of the death of paganism as little as it speaks of the dying of the gods. Even the "primitive German statement, All gods must die," in which Nietzsche asserted that he believed,[4] probably has

1. F. Hölderlin, "Mnemosyne" (2. Fassung), *Sämtliche Werke (Kleine Stuttgarter Ausgabe*), ed. F. Beissner (Stuttgart: W. Kohlhammer Verlag, 1951), II, 195.

2. B. Pascal, *Pascal's Pensées*, nr. 695, in *Great Books of the Western World*, tr. W. F. Trotter, ed. R. M. Hutchins (Chicago: Encyclopaedia Britannica, Inc., 1952), XXXIII, 302.

3. B. Pascal, *Pensées*, Introduction et notes par Ch.-M. des Granges (Paris: Éditions Garnier Frères, 1955), p. 340, n. 127. The report passed on by Plutarch (Moralia 419 B-E, "The Obsolescence of Oracles") in *Plutarch's Moralia* (tr. F. C. Babbitt [Cambridge, Mass.: Harvard University Press, 1936], V, 401-3) states that on a ship traveling from Greece to Italy, near the islands Paxos and Propaxos, suddenly a voice was heard from the islands which commanded the boatsman Thamus to announce in the area of Palodes, "Great Pan is dead." Eusebius recounted the same story two centuries later and referred it to the end of the demons which Christ had accomplished (*Praeparatio evangelica*, V, 17, 6-8, in *Die griechischen christlichen Schriftsteller der ersten Jahrhunderte* [Berlin: Deutsche Akademie der Wissenschaften, 1954-56], vol. 43, I, 253, 16ff).

But later Christian interpretations were not satisfied with that and related the event to the death of Jesus Christ on the cross—either in the sense that his death caused the death of Satan understood as Pan, or in the contrary sense that in the proclamation of the death of the great Pan the death of the Savior himself was announced (the word *Pan* was interpreted in the sense of pan-deity, or else the shepherd office of both Pan and Christ was referred to). During the Enlightenment the christological interpretations were doubted again. See the study by G. A. Gerhard, "Der Tod des grossen Pan," *Sitzungsberichte der Heidelberger Akademie der Wissenschaften, Philosophisch-Historische Klasse* (1915), VI, 5. Abhandlung. Then in German Idealism, the christological interpretation returned. F. W. J. Schelling (*Philosophie der Offenbarung, Sämmtliche Werke*, ed. K. F. A. Schelling [Stuttgart and Augsburg: J. G. Cotta, 1858], II/4, p. 240) does reject the direct identification of the deceased great Pan with the Crucified One "as more edifying than relevant," but still wants to allow for a christological application: "If we want to concede some significance to the story, then the great Pan who has died is the blind cosmic principle itself, which rules throughout the entire period of paganism. It did not finally expire until the death of Christ. In Christ, the great Pan too died. The death of Christ, in which he set aside the power of all extra-divine cosmic forces as such was the common end of paganism and Judaism, which itself was subject still to cosmic elements."

4. F. Nietzsche, "Aus den Aufzeichnungen zur Geburt der Tragödie" (1870), *Die Unschuld des Werden*, I, *Der Nachlass*, ed. A. Bäumler (*Kröners Taschenbuch Ausgabe*, 82) (Stuttgart: Alfred Kroener Verlag, 1956), p. 3. See E. Biser, *"Gott ist tot"; Nietzsches Destruktion des christlichen Bewusstseins* (München: Kösel Verlag, 1962), pp. 11ff.

only a biographical relationship to the death of God which Nietzsche proclaimed as man's noblest deed.[5] The statement "God is dead" stands for itself as an *historical truth*. It announces what Nietzsche called the "most important of more recent events."[6] Hegel, too, refers to an historical phenomenon when he speaks of ". . . the infinite grief [which] only existed historically in the formative process of culture[;] it existed as the feeling that 'God himself is dead,' upon which the religion of more recent times rests," and when he wants to understand this grief "as a moment of the supreme idea."[7]

If we want to illuminate the darkness of this statement about the death of God, then we will have to throw light on the historical origin of what is stated in this word. This includes a consideration of the possibility of conceiving the death of God with our minds. How did the unusual thought that God were dead become historically possible?

2. When we consider the possibility of thinking of the death of God, we must ask not only about the negation which takes place in this thought but also about the one who is being negated in this thought, that is, about the God who is thought to be dead and about the thought given to him until that point. The origin of the concept of the death of God must be sought in the thought of God which was pursued through to its conclusion in the thought of the death of God.

The origin of the dark statement about the death of God is at least twofold. In both Hegel and Nietzsche, although in varying ways, it becomes clear that the thought which is expressed in this statement has both a metaphysical and a genuinely Christian origin. Both origins must be differentiated methodically, although in their consequences they permeate each other. It also becomes clear that the metaphysical and the Christian origin of this thought have been passed on in Christian theology itself. That is why it is not surprising that *either* in connection with the apparently anti-metaphysical concept of the death of God it is also asserted that "the belief in the Christian God has become unworthy of belief,"[8] *or* in connection with the theological justification of talk about the death of God such talk is won back for metaphysics and thus the metaphysical idea of God is elevated, for which Ludwig Feuerbach thought he had to level accusations at Hegel.[9]

3. In what follows, I am making the otherwise well-tested assumption that metaphysics was acting in terms of its inner necessity when it traced the thought of God to its end,[10] but that to think seriously of the *death* of God without the

5. F. Nietzsche, *The Joyful Wisdom* (in *The Complete Works of Friedrich Nietzsche*, vol. 10), tr. Thomas Common, ed. Dr. O. Levy (Edinburgh, London: The Darien Press, 1910), nr. 343 and nr. 125, pp. 275f and 167ff.

6. *Ibid.*, nr. 343: "What our Cheerfulness Signifies," p. 275.

7. G. W. F. Hegel, *Faith and Knowledge*, trs. W. Cerf and H. S. Harris (Albany: State University of New York Press, 1977), p. 190.

8. F. Nietzsche, *The Joyful Wisdom*, nr. 343, p. 275.

9. Ludwig Feuerbach, "Principles of the Philosophy of the Future," in *The Fiery Brook: Selected Writings of Ludwig Feuerbach*, tr. Z. Hanfi (Garden City, NY: Doubleday, 1972), pp. 204ff.

10. Martin Heidegger, "Nietzsches Wort 'Gott ist tot'," in *Holzwege* (Frankfurt: V. Klostermann, 1963⁴), pp. 193ff.

Christian faith was totally impossible.[11] Thus, in dealing with the thought of the death of God, we will have to ask about its necessity in the metaphysical concept of God and about its possibility in Christian faith in God. In doing so, we give proper attention to the practical intermixture of metaphysics and Christianity. Further, we must ask carefully whether (a) the thought of the death of God brings both metaphysics and Christianity to their end in the same way so that, because they both have reached their end, we would say that metaphysics and Christianity were identical forever after, or (b) the thought of the death of God forces metaphysics and Christianity to separate from each other in such a way that a Christian theology becomes possible which, although not simply free of metaphysics, still would be free in its relationship to metaphysics.

Metaphysics assigns God the place of his being fundamentally and exclusively *over us*, even when it speaks of "God in us" who then, in us, elevates us beyond ourselves. That which is superior to everything else has its place over us. Death, on the other hand, works under us. Whoever dies cannot be absolutely superior. If one assigns to God both the place over us, as the place of his being, and at the same time assigns death to him, it would appear that one has torn the being of God apart. The thought of God appears then to have destroyed itself.

Christian faith must then ask if God's place is fundamentally and exclusively over us. Does not the divine "Father in heaven" over us have a "divine Son" who in the mode of being of a man was among us as one of us? And does not the divine Spirit belong to the relationship of God the Father and God the Son, the Spirit who works faith in us so that the *one* divine being in his three-foldness (*trinity*) is, according to his being, never over us but always in our midst? Is the Christian faith allowed to emplace God firmly over us? Does not "over us" in this context, namely, as the designation of an absolutely superior place, really mean: everywhere and nowhere?[12]

The decision about the relationship of Christianity and metaphysics, the decision about the possibility of the free usage of the metaphysical tradition by Christian theology, the decision about the freedom of theology is made in the response to the question: Where is God? That a possible departure of Christian theology from metaphysics still cannot lead simply to a "metaphysics-free" theology will not be concealed from a critical and self-critical theological awareness. For even in the case that thought might go beyond metaphysics by simply leaving it to itself,[13] it will preserve its freedom only when it does not refuse to

11. E. Jüngel, "Vom Tod des lebendigen Gottes," in *Unterwegs zur Sache; Theologische Bemerkungen* (München: C. Kaiser, 1972), pp. 105ff; and "Das dunkle Wort vom 'Tode Gottes'," *Evangelische Kommentare*, 2 (1969), 133ff and 198ff, now in *Von Zeit zu Zeit, Betrachtungen zu den Festzeiten im Kirchenjahr* (München: Kaiser, 1976), pp. 15ff.

12. On this question, see the argumentation in Anselm's *Monologium* on the "highest of all existing beings" (*St. Anselm; Basic Writings*, tr. S. N. Deane [LaSalle, IL: Open Court Publishing Company, 1962]): "It exists in every place and at every time" (ch. XX, p. 72); "it exists in no place and time" (ch. XXI, p. 73); "How it exists in every place and time, and in none" (ch. XXII, p. 78).

13. Martin Heidegger self-critically demanded this recently in his book *On Time and Being*, tr. Joan Stambaugh (New York: Harper & Row, 1972), p. 24: "To think Being without beings means: to think Being without regard to metaphysics. Yet a regard for metaphysics still prevails even in the intention to overcome metaphysics. Therefore, our task is to cease all overcoming, and leave metaphysics to itself."

make use of the metaphysical tradition critically. If the answers of metaphysics may be suspect, its questions certainly must not be. And the asking of a question does not mean that the phenomenon which may be abused in the question has been completely dealt with. Theology's dispute with metaphysics for the sake of a free theology must direct itself still to at least the answers, questions, and inquiries of the metaphysical tradition. But it must do so in such a way that theology gains for itself the freedom of a completely *ambivalent* relationship to this tradition. In the sense of such an ambivalence it is important that Christianity take leave of metaphysics. This happens with regard to the God-question by asking where God is.

SECTION 6. Where Is God?

Since the beginning of the philosophy which has formulated the basic stance of metaphysics, the question of God was the first and for a long time the only question it raised. Now, at the end of metaphysics, an end which many serious thinkers regard as having arrived for good reasons, the question of God is a secondary issue—and that is the criterion for the fact that the end of metaphysics has come. If he is at all interesting, then he is such among other things. And if one asks about God, then the question, in distinction from the classic metaphysical tradition, is no more about whether God is and who or what God is, but rather: Where is God? In this question, "Where is God?", the old questions which dealt with the being and the existence of God have been summarized in a new and unique way. Whether there is a God *at all* and *what* a God is, are decided for contemporary man by answering this question: *Where* can God be encountered and *where* can he be addressed as God? "Where is God gone?", Nietzsche's madman asks[1] and expresses thus the fact that God is no longer at the place where he belongs as God, namely, completely above, in order from there to make it possible to distinguish between Above and Below and thus to set up an hierarchy of values. If God is no longer above and thus no longer a God, then necessarily the question emerges as to whether it is even possible to distinguish any more between Above and Below, whether everything has not become directionless, disoriented, free of values. "Where is God gone? . . . Whither do we move? Away from all suns? Do we not dash on unceasingly? Backwards, sideways, forwards, in all directions? Is there still an above and below? Do we not stray, as through infinite nothingness?"[2] The contemporary question, "Where is God?", is the expression of the experience that can no longer grasp God as the description of something which is completely above and thus preserves orientation by differentiating between Above and Below. The unique character of this modern query about God can be drawn out in an especially fruitful way when we confront it with the question, "Where is God?", a question which is also heard in the Bible. In doing so, we are noting the difference in the way the question is put.

1. Friedrich Nietzsche, *The Joyful Wisdom*, in *The Complete Works of Friedrich Nietzsche*, vol. X, tr. Thomas Common, ed. Dr. O. Levy (Edinburgh, London: The Darien Press, 1920), nr. 125, pp. 167f.
2. *Ibid.*

a. The Biblical Question

1. The question about where God is, is found in the Bible primarily in the Old Testament. There it has only marginally to do with atheism, if at all. The statement, "There is no God," which could be read as a possible answer to the question, "Where is God?", is an answer reserved for fools in the Old Testament (Ps. 14:1). "Fools" are those people who were regarded as disgraceful because they did not take God seriously in their hearts and felt that they could make it through life better that way. For the faith of Israel, that is foolishness because ultimately it is proven to be untenable. The fools who say "there is no God" are by no means stupid individuals but rather those who are too clever. Their talk will prove to be foolish at the end because then it will be seen to be untenable. Then they are the stupid ones. And God laughs at them.

The actual *Sitz im Leben* which can be stated for the biblical question about where God is has little to do with the problem of atheism. The biblical question, "Where is God?", finds its proper *Sitz im Leben* in the struggle for the *right* God. The struggle for the right God, which constantly accompanies the faith of Israel, does imply a dimension within which the issue in ultimate radicality is the being or nonbeing of God. For in the struggle for the right God, the deity of God is the issue, that is, the question of the essence of God. But if the essence of God is disputed, then so is his existence, even if only implicitly and not consciously. In every serious debate about the right God, the essence of God is linked up with the existence of the deity as the basic issue. This dogmatic insight, which can be formulated in this way only in our modern age, should not drown out the special character of the biblical question.

2. The biblical question "Where is God?" is meant as an *argumentative question* to *provoke* those addressed. Those addressed are usually one person or a group of people. Very severe testing had to take place before the faith of Israel came to the point that it addressed this question to God himself, in order to struggle with God about God. At first, the debate about the right God goes on between people who attack each other with this question, "Where is now *thy* God?" This almost scornful question, when spoken by a pagan, was motivated by the existential distress of Israel or one of its members, according to the Old Testament witness. "There you see what you have with your God! Where is he then?" The question focuses sharply on the negated presence of God. It is to be heard as an hypothetical challenge. A true God would not discredit himself by allowing the misery of his worshipers to happen. The opponents of his adherents mock not only their misery but their God. They challenge his presence hypothetically—just as, in the New Testament, the claim that Jesus is the Son of God is challenged as the mockers pass by the cross (compare Matt. 27:39-44 with Ps. 42:4, 11; 79:10; 115:2; Jon. 2:17). The question turned against Israel and Israel's God finds its counterpart in the mouth of Israel as well: we find it in Elijah's scornful address against the priests of Baal on Mt. Carmel (1 Kings 18:27). Just as in the Psalms the person praying calls out for Yahweh's effective presence so that the pagans cannot mock him with the question "Where is thy God?", the priests of Baal on Carmel must hear Elijah scornfully cry, "Cry aloud, for he is a god; either he is musing, or he has gone aside, or he is on a journey, or perhaps he is asleep and must be awakened."

3. Whether said by Israel or turned against Israel, such utterances are not a questioning of the existence of a god in general, but rather always "thy God" or "your God" who is questioned by other people, who are by no means godless themselves. This scorn is directed against a God who is already claimed through a personal relationship, as well as against the person who knows that God has laid a claim on him. What is being questioned is not the existence of the deity in general but a specific relationship with God. We could say that the certainty of God which Israel has, or conversely the certainty of God of the worshipers of Baal, is what is to be led *ad absurdum* through the scorn and mocking. *One side's* certainty of God is questioning the *other side's* certainty. However, a fundamental lack of certainty with regard to God does not place in question something like the *certainty of God in general*.

It would also be false to impose this understanding on the internal testing of one's own faith in the God who alone should be the object of one's faith, a testing which emerges out of one's own heart. To be sure, the *presence* of the God of faith may be radically removed from faith. But the faith tested in such a way could not then state that in this experience the very *being* of his God had been put in question. If God is not present, then he is concealed, absent. But once absent, he certainly is not now nothing, but rather the hidden God, who as hidden still is the only true God, who is the only one in whom faith is to be put. Right faith cries with its questions for the right God. This is the meaning of the quotation from Psalm 22 on the lips of the dying Jesus. "My God, my God, what hast thou forsaken me" (Mark 15:34) is the most agonizing variant of the biblical question "Where is God?"

b. The Modern Question

1. Modern man formulates the question in a completely different way:[3] Where is God? Today anyone could ask that question. It could be the question of the atheist who is not asking about God at all anymore. For it is the justification of his not asking anymore—although it is a justification which is not admitted in his not asking the question. It could, however, just as well be the question of the person crying out to God from the depths of despair, or also the quiet question of the person who speaks of God from isolated heights with apparently no confusion about him. Not only hostility toward God but also intensive piety could express itself today by rephrasing the 139th Psalm, which actually praises the omnipresence of God, in this way: "If I ascend to heaven, thou art *not* there! If I make my bed in Sheol, thou art *not* there! If I take the wings of the morning and dwell in the uttermost parts of the sea, even there thy hand shall *not* lead me, and thy right hand shall *not* hold me. . . ." Where is God?

The question has gained special urgency ever since man has begun to demand *certainty* in a special way. But it appears that the demand for certainty about God forces one further and further into uncertainty. There seems to be a

---

3. Different with regard to the position of the "fools," with regard to the challenge which polemicizes against the God of the others, *and* with regard to the testing of faith through the absence of God.

peculiar correlation at work between the human requirement for certainty and the removal of God to the realm of uncertainty, so that the existence of the deity, which was certainly not uncertain earlier, becomes all the more questionable the more man seeks to gain security for himself. The striving for assured certainty seems to devour the certainness of divine being. This apparent phenomenon is strengthened within the dimension of the contemporary experience of the world.

2. In contemporary metaphysics the question "Where is God?" has a unique and unmistakable characteristic. It consists of the confrontation with the possibility "that there might be no God." This peculiarity of the modern question, which guides current talk about God, can be understood only when it is considered against the backdrop of modern world experience in which the human ego progressively gives the world ever greater weight and at the same time can find ever less meaning in it. The question "Where is God?" derives from the experience of an overimportance of the world, and this in turn is explained on the basis of the massive changes to which the world has been subjected as man has progressed from the mere *working* of the created world to something more like the *production* of the world. One could aptly describe the modern age as the period in which the transition is taking place from the utilization of the natural world through the processing or working of it to the replacement of nature as it is more and more used up through construction and the production of an artificial world. This step from the working of the world by *homo faber* to the production of the world has led to the serious disturbance of the once well-ordered relationship of God experience, world experience, and self experience. Earlier, God was experienced as eternally enduring, the world by contrast as temporal, and man as a being between God and the world which participates both in the eternal and in the temporal aspects. Ever since its initiation, the modern world tends to become more and more what man makes of it, and God is methodically set aside. The world forces itself into God's place, as the world of man.

That means, then, that modern man can no longer distance himself from the contradictions and nihilisms around him, perhaps by deducing that they come from the nihilistic nature of a passing world. Rather, modern man is responsible for "his" world. That is how he experiences himself. He experiences thus his failure, his guilt, and even his misfortune as the worldly consequences of his own actions. Man casts his shadow on the world, and it falls back on him from the world monstrously enlarged. The more the world becomes the object of human processing and production, the more it is alienated in its naturalness by human history. That is the very reason for the accession of an excessive amount of significance for the world, significance which it really does not have but rather is given to it by man as he processes and changes the world. Man burdens the world with himself, and thus the world becomes too weighty.

The experience of an overweighted world is thus the experience of a world burdened with the subjectivity of man. The transformation of a created "natural" world into a world made by man, which permits ever less distinction between "natural" and "artificial," results in the world's being perceived almost solely as the mirror of human activity. Politics, understood as the epitome of what people do with and make out of the world, becomes fate, to use a phrase directed by Napoleon to Goethe.[4] Further, and conversely, the world's contradictions now become identifiable as self-contradictions of human nature, which make the incontestable responsibility of man now for his world and thus the world itself appear as futile. Man discovers the contradictions and the meaninglessness around him deeply rooted within himself, and thus for him the world which is so overly weighted with his own subjectivity moves perilously close to the edge of futility into which it threatens to fall—and because the world is his responsibility, he will be responsible for that fall.

In this historical situation, the question of God is changing more and more into a specifically modern *theodicy question*. For this apparently most radical of all questions about God, which is also the most remarkable of questions, exercises at least the function of relieving man of himself in view of his own inability to withstand the total responsibility for the world which he has undertaken. That inability is made all the more intensive by the fact that man no longer may or can surrender his responsibility for the world. In view of the experience of such weakness which corresponds to the experience of meaninglessness, absurdity, and irreparable injustice; in view of all the questions man can't answer (although without an answer he threatens to despair for his very being); in view of the experience of the futility of a world burdened with human subjectivity, which conceals all these questions in itself—in view of all this, the question about God is raised again, but in such a way that one cannot find God within the complex of all that for which man would like to make God responsible. Man, for his own relief, would like to find peace, and yet he cannot find the one in whom alone he might find that peace. For between him and God, all of the experiences of futility interpose themselves, and they make it impossible for him to find God. "Father, where art thou? . . . O Father! Father! Where is that boundless breast of thine that I may rest upon it?", is the expression of this in "The dead Christ proclaims that there is no God,"[5] which should be read as a prelude to the twentieth century. Vis-à-vis nothingness, one does not ask who or what God is but rather *where* God is. Yet this most concrete of all questions about God is directed toward the indefinite. Actually, God himself should be the one to receive this question, in order to be challenged by it himself. But that intent of the question is withdrawn even before it is expressed. For it appears that God is nowhere. One asks a question about someone whom one no longer knows.

3. Probably the final question of metaphysics about God derives from this theodicy problematic. God was sued. Together with the question "Where is God?" arose the most indefinite way of asking about God, which nonetheless remained the most concrete: indefinite in that it had no one to address the question to from whom an answer could be expected; concrete because the where-question queries much more concretely than any other question. As the

4. See J. W. von Goethe, "Unterredung mit Napoleon, 1808, September," *Autobiographische Einzelheiten, Goethe's Werke*, 14 vols. (Hamburg: Christian Wegner Verlag, 1963³), vol. 10, 546, 10ff (see also Albert Bielschowsky, *The Life of Goethe*, tr. W. A. Cooper, 3 vols. [New York: Putnam's Sons, 1907], II, 412).
    5. Jean Paul (Johann Paul Friedrich Richter), *Flower, Fruit, and Thorn Pieces; or the Wedded Life, Death, and Marriage of Firmian Stanislaus Siebenkaes*, tr. A. Ewing (London: George Bell & Sons, 1892), bk. II, ch. VII, "The dead Christ proclaims that there is no God," pp. 263f.

most indefinite way of asking about God, the question "Where is God?" belongs
to the end of metaphysics, which answers the question with the dark statement
about the death of God. As the most concrete way to ask about God, the question
"Where is God?" is the basic question of Christian faith, which may perhaps
illuminate the dark statement of the death of God. The question could be read
by Christian theology and by philosophy as the unspoken mystery of the new
age, which is itself already aging. It would still be such a mystery even if the
reason given for not speaking it were that one regarded it as superfluous to ask
where God is.

    4. "Where is God gone?" is the question asked by Nietzsche's madman.[6]
The question assumes that God is not present. Whatever is not there does not
have a nameable Where, is not to be found in its place or in any other place at
all. What has a place to be but is not there is noticed. To human reason it
appears to be displaced. But with regard to the displacement of an only relative
atopon ('placeless thing'), reason does not capitulate. Instead, it will be challenged by such a thing. What is simply absent from the place where it belongs
or appears to belong, which is not in *its* place, can be replaced from this its
displacement through reason. Reason is provoked and leads from head-shaking
astonishment to deeper thought.[7] However, that which has *no* place at all but
still is supposed to *be* provokes at best the indifferent shrug of one's shoulders
rather than head-shaking astonishment. It is more than noticeable in the sphere
of that which is noticed: it falls outside the pale. That which has no place at all
does not even appear to reason as something displaced, so that reason could go
to work putting it back in its place; it appears as absolute foolishness. That
which has no place has, according to the rules of thought, no definable being.
It cannot be determined. Does God have no place at all? Does he disappear into
the realm of the indeterminate? Is he everywhere—or nowhere? The indeterminate can be localized neither as present nor as absent. Is God then neither
present nor absent?

    Presence and absence are determinations of that which exists, which refer
to this existence always in relationship to human existence. If I say of God that
he is present or absent, then I am not just saying "he is," but rather I am thinking
of his being as related to me either positively or negatively. He is either this way
or that way. As long as the question about the Where of God can be answered
with the *alternative* reference either to his presence *or* his absence, then God's
being has not been put into question radically. However, the question "Where
is God?" has not been placed in its ultimate radicality either. This happens only
when the answer to it can no longer be sought in the alternative of *present* or
absent.

    If then, with the metaphysical tradition, God's being has been thought of
as pure reality which excludes every possibility from its self and conditions all

    6. See F. Nietzsche, *The Joyful Wisdom, op. cit.*, nr. 125, pp. 167f.
    7. See Plato, "Theaetetus," in *The Dialogues of Plato*, tr. B. Jowett, 2 vols. (New
York: Random House, 1937), II, 155; p. 157: ". . . for wonder is the feeling of a
philosopher, and philosophy begins in wonder."
    And Aristotle, "Metaphysica," in *The Works of Aristotle*, tr. W. D. Ross (Oxford:
Clarendon Press, 1954), VIII, A.2, 982b, 12ff: "For it is owing to their wonder (*thaumazein*) that men both now and at first began to philosophize."

other reality, in other words, if God has been asserted to be the "absolute necessity," then the negation of his presence is much more than just the affirmation of his absence. Here, God himself is negated along with his absence, and the distinction between presence and absence becomes senseless with reference to God. That appears to be exactly the case today. The modern atheist appears to be unable to deal either with talk about God's presence or talk about his absence. In this, he has at least a little in common with the Christian faith, since the alternative of presence and absence with reference to God contradicts the Christian concept of God and the experience of faith which accords with it. Faith cannot speak of God's presence without conceiving at the same time of God's absence, just as it has never been certain of God's presence without experiencing his hiddenness.

Thus, in the unspoken mystery of the modern age which is to be read in the question "Where is God?", there resound two contrary possibilities for settling the long history of man with God. *Either* beyond the alternative of the presence or absence of God only the nonbeing of God can be thought of. Then, in point of fact, this question becomes the most superfluous of all queries, and human talk about God is materially at an end. All further talk about God could only be senseless chatter. *Or* this question can be led to a positive answer which for its part is beyond the alternative of presence or absence. Then the question about the Where of God is certainly to be seen as an hermeneutically fundamental question. Theology proceeds on the basis of this prejudice. The hermeneutic urgency of this question results for theology from the loss of the unquestioned certainty with which traditionally God has been spoken of. Beyond the alternative of the presence or absence, the decision must be made as to whether this question itself is absolutely superfluous or else indispensable: Where is God? And that will then be the decision on the meaning of talk about the death of God.

SECTION 7. Talk about the Death of God as the Theological Answer to the Question: Where Is God?

The usage of the concept of the death of God in contemporary theological literature leaves the impression that this dark proposition, after having been at home primarily in philosophy, is now entering Christian theology in order possibly to seal its end finally. But this appearance is deceptive. In fact, talk about the death of God is not entering theology for the first time in our century; rather, it is returning home to theology.

Talk about the death of God was not at all alien to Christian theology originally. The fathers of the ancient church could talk about it, and Martin Luther virtually demanded that it was necessary to speak of the death of God, using, of course, very precise presuppositions. The statement "God has died" was not originally the province of philosophy but of theology. Then it became alien to theology.

The history of the alienation between theology and talk about the death of God began primarily with the intellectual accomplishments of Georg Wilhelm Friedrich Hegel. This happened paradoxically in his attempt to reconcile philosophy with the theological meaning of the philosophically intolerable thought of the death of God, which was the negation of the absolute. In doing so, Hegel was seeking to take up the atheistic tendencies of the age in which he lived and to work through them positively, and this is what gives his dealing with the idea of the death of God its special significance. That Hegel's massive accomplishment was almost immediately misunderstood is no excuse for the scandalous fact that there are contemporary thinkers who would have us believe that they could appeal to Hegel for their theologically senseless use of the idea of the death of God. For that reason alone it would be useful to sketch briefly Hegel's discourse on the death of God.

Hegel, at the beginning of the last century, tried with his talk about the death of God to assert a theological proposition as the "world spirit's" truth consciousness. Conversely, the attempt has been made in our century, by use of the fragmentary thought of Dietrich Bonhoeffer, to draw the "truth-consciousness" of the "world spirit" into theology, so that religionlessness might be exposed as an element of theological truth. In doing this, Bonhoeffer could build on Karl Barth's critique of religion; but going beyond that, he proposed that the atheistic thought of the nonbeing of God should be so worked through theologically that the Christian faith could receive elements of truth from atheistic religionlessness and work them into the Christian concept of God. To that extent, Bonhoeffer prepared the way for the return home to theology of talk about the death of God. This is true of both the theologically meaningful and the theologically meaningless use of the idea of the death of God in contemporary literature. It is thus appropriate to recall the well-known thoughts in Bonhoeffer's letters in order to point out the decisive turning point which led to the return home to theology of talk about the death of God. It will have to remain an open question whether Bonhoeffer would have been interested in the return of the idea of the death of God, which certainly, against Hegel's intention, had emigrated from theology to philosophy, was then used against Christianity, and ultimately found its classic antitheological meaning in its usage by Friedrich Nietzsche.

It is, however, indisputable that through Hegel's philosophical interpretation of the theological proposition "God is dead," the historical possibility, and through Bonhoeffer's concept of "nonreligious interpretation" of the Christian faith, the theological possibility, arose to answer both negatively and positively the modern question "Where is God?" with discourse on the death of God. Hegel and Bonhoeffer represent, although in very different ways, such an original connection of a genuinely secular and a genuinely theological attitude toward the problem of God, that a theology which is seeking new possibilities for responsible talk about God and responsible interaction with the world may well dare to learn from both of them. Certainly the voices of other thinkers should not be ignored, all of whom have molded in their various ways and according to their abilities the situation in which we have to do theology today. Obviously one must always expressly state what it is for which one is indebted to the masters. For this reason we will limit ourselves to a consideration of Hegel and Bonhoeffer.

For reasons of method, we will begin with a discussion of Bonhoeffer's thought, which quite directly determines our present situation, and then proceed from his thought to a requestioning of Hegel's use of the concept of the death of God.

a. Bonhoeffer's Contribution to the Return of "Death of God" Talk to Theology

The return of talk about the death of God to theology, which is going on currently, was prepared if not initiated in the remarks Dietrich Bonhoeffer wrote down in prison.[1] It is no accident that the proponents of God-is-dead theology in all the world appeal to him. However, a clear distinction must be made between the special intellectual achievement of Bonhoeffer and the thoughts of those who appeal to him. The chief element of this distinction is that Bonhoeffer did not take modern atheism to be a reason to remove God from contemporary thought, but rather conversely took modern atheism as an opportunity to investigate anew a Christian concept of God in critical interaction with the theological tradition. Bonhoeffer, writing in prison, was thus sharing in the problems as seen by the young Hegel—and this is what we shall seek to show.

The working through of modern atheism and the effort to arrive at a Christian concept of God are for Bonhoeffer two tasks which belong extremely close together. That means—and here we see also a certain analogy to Hegel— that God cannot be thought of as God without simultaneously considering the world and its historical situation. The historical situation of the world is seen by Bonhoeffer not just as the location of the *thought* of God, but also as the location of the divine *being*. It is the location of God himself. To that extent, the situation of modern atheism instructs faith to think *God as God*. God's own nature becomes a theme when the nature of the atheistic modern day is comprehended.

On the other hand, modern atheism is the very attempt to think the world *without* God. Theology is thus confronted with what appears to be the profoundly paradoxical task of thinking out God not only without the world but rather out of an historical situation of the world which makes it necessary to think of the world without God. However the apparent paradox must be resolved, the task must be seen to be at least in principle soluble if theology is to be a meaningful undertaking of any kind anymore. How then should this be done: to think God without the world which, for its part, is to be thought without God? To what extent does God's deity imply the world if the worldliness of the world excludes God expressly? This question has characterized the problematic situation rather adequately, that situation in which the well-known notes by Bonhoeffer were written and are to be understood. I will relate the important thoughts for our discussion briefly. They are found in the writings from Bonhoeffer's imprisonment which were published posthumously under the title *Letters and Papers from Prison*.

1. Bonhoeffer first explains the situation of the modern period and its atheism by thinking through the historical genesis of this situation. In this, he

---

1. In substance, Martin Buber's idea of the darkness of God belongs at this point. It is the integrative component of a philosophy of religion which consciously avoids the center of the New Testament—the saving death of Jesus Christ. If at this point Buber's concept of the darkness of God is not dealt with further, then it is for the reason that factually it has scarcely had any influence on the return to theology of talk about the death of God.

sees the cultural and the scientific developments, if the distinction may be made, as two parallel tendencies whose present results force theology to a "nonreligious interpretation of the biblical concepts." For the purpose of the development which determines the modern age is the *autonomy* of man and the *independence* of the world with respect to God. The situation which results is defined by the irrelevance of religion. "Now again a few thoughts on our theme . . . the nonreligious interpretation of the biblical concepts. . . . With regard to history: there is *one* great development which leads to the autonomy of the world. In theology first of all Herbert of Cherbury, who asserted the sufficiency of reason for religious knowledge. In morality, Montaigne and Bodin, who set up rules of life in the place of commandments. In politics, Macchiavelli, who separated politics from general morality and established the doctrine of the state's reason. Later, and different from him in content, but still in conformity with him in regard to the autonomy of human society H. Grotius, who set up his natural law as the law of nations, which was valid 'even if God did not exist.'[2] Finally the philosophical bottom line: on one hand we have the deism of Descartes, who holds that the world is a mechanism, running by itself with no interference from God; and on the other hand the pantheism of Spinoza, who says that God is nature. In the last resort Kant is a deist, and Fichte and Hegel are pantheists. Everywhere the thinking is directed towards the autonomy of man and the world."[3]

Bonhoeffer sees this cultural development toward the autonomy of man paralleled by the development in the natural sciences, to the extent that it intends to think of the world as resting completely in itself. The decisive thing for this development is the "heretical" doctrine of the infinity of the world which was presented by Nicholas of Cusa and Giordano Bruno. The concept of an infinite world cannot be thought in connection with the concept of God, unless it is done so in Spinoza's sense that everything is in God and everything which happens happens solely through the laws of the infinite nature of God.[4] Bonhoeffer knows, of course, that modern physics again doubts the infinity of the world, but refers to the fact that it is by no means returning to earlier ideas of the finitude of the world. However the world may be thought of, albeit no longer as finite, it "rests in itself 'even if there were no God.' "[5]

The result of this "development leading to the autonomy of the world," which human reason has made possible, is the removal of God as a working hypothesis for the understanding of the world. "God as a working hypothesis in morals, politics, or science, has been surmounted and abolished; and the same thing has happened in philosophy and religion (Feuerbach!). For the sake of intellectual honesty, that working hypothesis should be dropped, or as far as

2. Grotius of course presupposes the agreement of divine law and natural law as a given. See above, pp. 18f.

3. Dietrich Bonhoeffer, *Letters and Papers from Prison*, ed. E. Bethge, tr. R. H. Fuller (New York: Macmillan, 1972), p. 359.

4. B. Spinoza, *Ethics*, in *Chief Works*, 2 vols., tr. R. H. M. Elwes (New York: Dover Publications, 1955), II, part I, prop. XV, p. 49: "Whatsoever is, is in God, and without God nothing can be, or be conceived."

It was thus no accident that the young Schleiermacher, in deference to Spinoza, spoke of God and the world in the concept of the perception of the universal as the perception of the infinite in the finite.

5. Bonhoeffer, *op. cit.*, p. 359.

possible eliminated. A scientist or physician who sets out to edify is a hybrid."[6] For he would represent in one person both progress toward a "world come of age" and the regression to an immature world.

Thus Bonhoeffer regards it as impossible to reverse the development of the world to its maturity. Any return to the reception of a working hypothesis outside of the world in order to explain the world, any return to God as a working hypothesis, would be a "counsel of despair," "a death leap back into the Middle Ages." "There is no such way—at any rate not if it means deliberately abandoning our mental integrity; the only way is that of Matt. 18:3, i.e. through repentance, through *ultimate* honesty."[7] But it is a part of this honesty that we "recognize that we have to live in the world—'even if there were no God.' And this is just what we do recognize" as penitents, which is "before God! God himself compels us to recognize it. So our coming of age leads us to a true recognition of our situation before God. God would have us know that we must live as men who manage our lives without him. The God who is with us is the God who forsakes us (Mark 25:34)! The God who lets us live in the world without the working hypothesis of God is the God before whom we stand continually. Before God and with God we live without God."[8]

In the cited sentences we see first of all what one might call the cognitively critical basic tendency of the secular understanding of the world. With honest sobriety, Bonhoeffer pointed out the historical status quo over against which there can be no reproduction of the *status quo ante* ('previous status quo'): the world lives without God. And as world it is understood through the fact that one lets it live as world without God.

2. However, Bonhoeffer did not just point out this status quo. At the same time, he interpreted it. The honesty which compels us to recognize the status quo is for him "ultimate honesty." And for Bonhoeffer ultimate honesty is honesty before God. He calls it *repentance*. "Even if there were no God"—that can be carried out as the methodological consciousness of worldly explanation and scientific research with no problem, simply by going on to the task at hand and leaving behind a thoroughly dispensable, even obstructive premise once and for all. In the process, the presupposition of the absence of God is not at the basis of one's thought, but rather the removal of the presupposition, that is, the setting aside of the premise "God." The concept "even if there were no God"—in contrast to its original meaning!—is not a presupposition to be thought about by a "mature world," but is the expression of a now removed false presupposition. This false presupposition was that of the worldly necessity of God.

The statement "even if there were no God" does not delineate a new presupposition for one's thinking, but rather the removal of a presupposition which is not to be used for one's thinking under any circumstances. The problem which is given with the statement is not considered. But that is what Bonhoeffer does do. He thinks the truth, which is concealed in the problem expressed by this phrase. And thus he is thinking *theologically*. Bonhoeffer understands this "even if there were no God," whose function is to set aside a presupposition of

6. *Ibid.*, p. 360.
7. *Ibid.*
8. *Ibid.*

thought, as the absence of God which becomes the presupposition of the mature world: "God himself compels us to recognize it. So our coming of age leads us to a true recognition of our situation before God. . . . The God who lets us live in the world without the working hypothesis of God is the God before whom we stand continually. Before God and with God we live without God."[9] One could not put more sharply the insight into the nonnecessity of God, over against which it would be anachronistic to seek to prove to the world "that it cannot live without the tutelage of 'God.' "[10] Put positively, this insight means this: "We are to find God in what we know, not in what we don't know; God wants us to realize his presence, not in unsolved problems but in those that are solved."[11]

3. Now it is characteristic and of the greatest theological relevance that Bonhoeffer immediately traces this theological interpretation of the historical status quo further to a reflection which considers the being of God itself. In the context of the historical analysis we encounter a *christological* reflection which seeks to assert the biblical understanding of God in the setting of our historical world understanding: "God allows himself to be pushed out of the world on to the cross. He is weak and powerless in the world, and that is precisely the way, the only way, in which he is with us and helps us. Matthew 8:17 makes it quite clear that Christ helps us, not by virtue of his omnipotence, but by virtue of his weakness and suffering."[12]

This christological reflection is the background of his theological interpretation of the historical status quo in which we have to live and to explain the world "even if there were no God." That "God himself compels us to this knowledge" is not simply a paradoxical assertion. The crucifixion of Jesus is the actual element of persuasion in the knowledge that we must live and know in a world "even if there were no God." The actual persuasive factor in this knowledge is effective in the suffering of God, in the powerlessness and weakness of God. To recognize in the suffering and powerlessness of God that which salvifically convicts us and to allow the persuasive factor of this knowledge to be established there—that is a *religionless* understanding of God for Bonhoeffer. For the death of Jesus Christ on the cross is the event in which God allows himself to be pushed out of the world. This event forces us theologically to live "even if there were no God," and forces us theologically to recognize that we must live this way if we want to be honest not only in regard to the world but also before God.

"Here is the decisive difference between Christianity and all religions. Man's religiosity makes him look in his distress to the power of God(!) in the world: God is the *deus ex machina*. The Bible directs man to God's powerlessness and suffering; only the suffering God can help. To that extent we may say that the development toward the world's coming of age outlined above, which has done away with a false conception of God, opens up a way of seeing the God of the Bible, who wins *power* and space in the world by his *weakness*. This will

9. *Ibid.*, p. 360.
10. *Ibid.*, p. 326.
11. *Ibid.*, p. 311.
12. *Ibid.*, pp. 360f. Following the summary statement in Matthew 8:16, "and [he] healed all who were ill," we read "to make good the prophecy of Isaiah: 'He took away our illnesses and lifted our diseases from us.' "

probably be the starting-point for our 'secular interpretation'."[13] And further: "When we speak of God in a 'non-religious' way, we must speak of him in such a way that the godlessness of the world is not in some way concealed, but rather revealed, and thus exposed to an unexpected light. The world that has come of age is more godless, and perhaps for that very reason nearer to God, than the world before its coming of age."[14]

Bonhoeffer feels that all of this is "put so terribly clumsily and badly."[15] In a poem[16] this "terribly clumsy" content is formulated in such a way that in fact the death of God is spoken of:

Men go to God when they are sore bestead,
Pray to him for succour, for his peace, for bread,
For mercy for them sick, sinning, or dead;
All men do so, Christian and unbelieving.

Men go to God when he is sore bestead,
Find him poor and scorned, without shelter or bread,
Whelmed under weight of the wicked, the weak, the dead;
Christians stand by God in his hour of grieving.

God goes to every man when sore bestead,
Feeds body and spirit with his bread;
For Christians, pagans alike he hangs dead,
And both alike forgiving.

4. We said that Bonhoeffer demanded that God not be thought of without the world which, for its part, is to be thought of without God. Now the paradox is resolved in that "not thinking God without the world" means to think God as *the one who lets himself be pushed out of the world* and thus the one *who relates himself to the world.* To let oneself be pushed out, to depart, to go away, are all something other than a total lack of relationship. This can actually signify the most intensive relationship. The relationship established by departure must not necessarily be negative either. It can even imply an intensification. Thus, for example, the departure of the Johannine Christ is what first makes it possible to approach him properly.

God is therefore thought as God and not without the world when God so understood allows the worldliness of the world without God to be thought. The reason for the theological necessity to think God in this way is given both by the world which factually exists "even if there were no God" and by the nature of the God who reveals himself in the crucified Christ. With his fragmentary thoughts, Bonhoeffer achieved no less than to teach us to think of the world which exists "even if there were no God" *coram deo* ('in the presence of God'), and *he did so* by teaching us to understand the God who exists in the crucified Christ as the *deus coram mundo* ('God who is present in the world'). God exists *coram mundo* ('as a worldly presence') in that he bears the world on the cross,

13. *Ibid.*, p. 361 (my italics).
14. *Ibid.*, p. 362.
15. *Ibid.*
16. *Ibid.*, pp. 348f.

as the world which will not bear him. That is the *gospel* which allows the world to exist in the dimensions of the law of its own reality "even if there were no God."[17]

With this approach at interpreting the godlessness of the world christologically and making it fruitful for the concept of God, Bonhoeffer established a fundamental concept for the Christian faith in God, a concept which should be developed further. The statement that God lets himself "be pushed out of the world" is oriented to the cross and thus is to be understood soteriologically. But beyond that, it contains a profound insight into the ontological character of the divine being. For if God lets "himself be pushed out of the world" and bears the world on the cross as the world which will not bear him, then the being of God is in fact to be thought of as a being which explodes the alternative of presence and absence. This has its consequences. If God existed only in the sense of worldly presence, then he would be conceived of as a massive superlative of worldly presence, even if this presence were thought of fundamentally as superiority to the world and thus as worldly omnipresence. If God is conceived of thus, then Augustine's proposition is true, "If thou comprehendest, then it is not God."[18] But if God is present as the one who is absent in the world, if absence is not simply the alternative opposite to the presence of God, then what Bonhoeffer presented as the interpretation of the cross event actually expresses in focused soteriological fashion the ontological characteristics of the divine being.

This characteristic can be illustrated analogously by reference to human existence. It is also true of human presence *mutatis mutandis* that a certain kind of removedness belongs to its presence. This is connected to the ontological determination of man for freedom. There is inherent in freedom a reality which is full of possibility. As a being of possibility, man transcends his reality at any given time, so that he is simultaneously present as well as removed. That man, further, is removed not only from others but also from himself is what distinguishes him from the being of God—which with regard to the inter-involvement of presence and absence is analogous to him.[19]

When the interconnection of presence and absence has been established as constitutive for the relationship of God to the world, then at least thetically the fixation of God as an extra-mundane "above us" is contradicted as much as is an easy understanding of divine omnipresence. The metaphysical theory of

17. On this problem, see my theses: "Säkularisierung—Theologische Anmerkungen zum Begriff einer weltlichen Welt," in *Christliche Freiheit—im Dienst am Menschen; Martin Niemöller zum 80. Geburtstag* (Frankfurt am Main: O. Lembeck, 1972), pp. 163ff.
18. See above, p. 8, n. 9.
19. W. Pannenberg, "Speaking about God in the Face of Atheist Criticism," *The Idea of God and Human Freedom*, tr. R. A. Wilson (Philadelphia: Westminster, 1973), p. 112, using the combination of 'presence' (*Vorhandensein*) and 'concealment' (*Verborgensein*), described the same idea, and he focused the whole thing on the concept of personal being: "But the personality of God becomes relevant in a new way to the question of a reality which is not an existent being: a person is the opposite of an existent being. Human beings are persons by the very fact that they are not wholly and completely existent for us in their reality, but are characterized by freedom, and as a result remain concealed and beyond control in the totality of their existence," Of. course, they are all the more present when they in freedom disclose themselves.

the worldly omnipresence of a God who is above everything and nowhere corresponds much too much to the fixation of God as a supra-worldly "above us." The faith that the "Father in heaven" above us was among us through the crucified Son of God and in the Holy Spirit is united with the Son not only for himself but as one absent is present with us and that as the one who "lets himself be pushed out of the world" *comes to the world*—this faith grants to the theologoumenon of the omnipresence of God a meaning which reconstructs it entirely. This happens in that God's omnipresence is to be understood now on the basis of his very presence on the cross of Jesus and not without a christologically established removal of God. The concept of the omnipresence of God must pass through the eye of the needle of the properly understood concept of the death of God.

5. Bonhoeffer decisively molded the theological situation of the present day. The alleged consequences which have been drawn from his last utterances must be the responsibility of the individual interpreter.[20] Every theology is responsible for itself even if it is nourished by historical possibilities which preceded it. Another possibility of theological thought which defines the theological situation of the present day is the philosophical theology of G. W. F. Hegel, which often comes very close to Bonhoeffer's thought. Apart from the possibilities worked through by Hegel the entire theology of the twentieth century is scarcely conceivable. Nevertheless it can hardly be said that these possibilities had been adequately perceived or even researched. Hegel's discussion of the death of God deserves substantive theological attention.

b. Hegel's Mediation between the Atheistic Modern Feeling and the Christian Truth of the Death of God

It is of a significance not to be underestimated that the first philosophical interpretations of talk of the death of God known to us neither deny nor forget the theological origin of this expression, but rather make it very plain. It was Georg Friedrich Wilhelm Hegel who introduced talk of the death of God into philosophy and in doing so was well aware of the fact that he was using a theological expression. This must be borne in mind if one wants to probe the foundations of modern atheism. It is important that the pointedly anti-Christian use of the phrase "God is dead" to describe what Friedrich Nietzsche called the "most important of more recent events"[21] would scarcely be conceivable without Hegel's mediation between the originally Christian meaning of this phrase and the possibility of reading into it the atheistic feeling of the "modern age," as Hegel put it. What Nietzsche was thinking when he proclaimed the death of God had become thinkable because Hegel interpreted the spirit of his age with a

20. Helmut Thielicke has correctly pointed out that Bonhoeffer's persuasively developed thesis of the nonnecessity of God still needs to be worked through in its *"positive consequences"* and that this thesis is still too unclear in "its negative passus" to be insured against "all kinds of escapades" on the part of its interpreters. Thielicke asks, "How in a *positive* sense does God become experienceable anew in the changed modern situation?" ("Was meint das Word 'Gott'?; Ueber Relevanz und Verbindlichkeit des Theos in der Theologie," *Studium Generale*, 23 [1970], 96). That is precisely the issue.

21. F. Nietzsche, "What Our Cheerfulness Signifies," in *The Joyful Wisdom, op. cit.*, nr. 343, p. 275.

christological proposition and then in the spirit of his age interpreted this christological proposition. What now follows is not intended to be more than a
"report" on the relevant texts and cannot replace philosophical interpretation but
at best stimulate it.[22]

1. The phrase "God is dead" received its philosophical significance in the
concluding sentence of Hegel's essay "Faith and Knowledge or the Reflective
Philosophy of Subjectivity, in the Completeness of its Forms, as Kantian, Ja-
cobite, and Fichtian Philosophy," which appeared in the *Kritischer Journal der
Philosophie* in 1802. Hegel only indirectly reveals that the issue here is a christological proposition. But he knows it. Phrases like "speculative Good Friday"
imply it. Later, in the "Lectures on the Philosophy of Religion" delivered in
Berlin a number of times between 1821 and 1831, Hegel expressly tells his
listeners that the sentence "God himself is dead" is a quotation from the Protestant hymnbook: " 'God himself is dead,' as it is said in a Lutheran hymn."[23]

This "Lutheran hymn" is not, incidentally, a "hymn by Luther," as often
incorrectly asserted.[24] Rather it is the second verse, written by Johannes Rist
around 1641, for a chorale by a Catholic poet documented in Würzburg in 1628
and entitled "O Traurigkeit, O Herzeleid" ('O Sorrow, O Suffering'). Whereas
the Catholic hymn sings of the liturgical ceremony of the entombment of Christ
in the form of the host, Rist was thinking of the burying of the man from
Nazareth when he wrote: "O great distress! / God himself lies dead. / On the
cross he died, / and by doing so he has won for us the realm of heaven."

The sentence "God himself lies dead" was known and debated as a pronounced expression of Lutheran theology; it was so controversial that, for example, the Dortmund hymnbook replaced it with the less objectionable "The
Lord is dead." At the theological faculties, learned disputations were conducted
about the dogmatic correctness of the chorale,[25] and these disputations picked
up on the tradition of early church discussions. It was Tertullian who said that
it was the faith of Christians that God had died and nevertheless still lived

22. See H. Küng, *Menschwerdung Gottes; Eine Einführung in Hegels theologisches Denken als Prolegomena zu einer künftigen Christologie* (1970). See also Christian Link, "Hegels Wort 'Gott selbst ist tot,' " *Theologische Studien*, vol. 114 (1974).
23. G. W. F. Hegel, *Lectures on the Philosophy of Religion*, trs. E. B. Speirs and
J. B. Sanderson (New York: Humanities Press, 1968), "The Absolute Religion," III, 98.
24. H. Küng, *op. cit.*, p. 208.
25. See the notes in Gabriel Wimmer's extensive explanation of the hymns, published in Altenburg in 1749 (I, 292f): "These words were defended by M. *Just. Wess.
Rumpaeus* in a special disputation under the presidency of D. *Jo. Nic. Quistorpii* in
Rostock in 1703, and he proved that it was incorrect when in the Dortmund hymnbook
in gratiam adversariorum the words were inserted, The Lord is dead. See *Olear. Hymnol.
Pass.* p. 101. Among others, this material was excellently disputed by D. *Dorscheus* in
Admirand. J. C. Septenar, p. 311 sqq. On the Sabellians and Theopaschites who taught
that God had suffered, but not in Christ but in a special person, see *Schamel. Vind. Cant.*
P. III, p. 25. Especially on this read *Serpilii Prüfung des Hohensteinischen Gesangbuchs*
['Examination of the Hohenstein Hymnbook'] p. 329. sq. and *Avenarii Evangel. Chris-
ten-Schmuck* ['Protestant Ornamentations of Christians'] *P. I.* p. 488, where not only
these words but the entire song is explained in great brevity. D. Steph. Klotz in a letter
to the author in 1650 vindicated and defended these words." The Protestant songbook in
use today does not contain the original version. Here we find, "God's Son lies dead"
("O Traurigkeit, O Herzeleid!"; *Evangelisches Kirchengesangbuch* [Hamburg: Friedrich
Wittig Verlag, 1959], nr. 73, verse 2).

eternally.[26] Yet the same Tertullian, fighting at another front against the thesis that God the Father suffered on the cross of Jesus, was crucified, dead, and was buried, rebutted that it was enough to say that the Son of God had died, and only because it was written in Scripture.[27] In debate with the Arians on the one hand and the Apollinarians on the other, Athanasius was concerned to confess the Crucified One as God,[28] whereby he thought it heresy to refuse to make that confession. And yet Athanasius dilutes his discussion of the crucified God by saying that Christ " '. . . suffered,' not in His Godhead, but 'for us in the flesh'. . . ."[29] Nonetheless, it is God who endures in the flesh, in the "outraged body" of Jesus Christ, the proof for which is seen in the eclipse of the sun on Good

26. See Tertullian, *Tertullianus Against Marcion* (*Ante-Nicene Christian Library*, vol. VII), tr. P. Holmes, eds. Rev. A. Roberts and J. Donaldson (Edinburgh: T. & T. Clark, 1868), bk. II, ch. 16, pp. 89f: "it is a part of the creed of Christians even to believe that God did die, and yet that He is alive for evermore." In the same treatise by Tertullian in which we find this discussion of the death of God, we also encounter the concept of the "crucified God," *deus crucifixus*; "God was found little, that man might become very great. You who disdain such a God, I hardly know whether you *ex fide* believe that God was crucified" (*ibid.*, bk. II, ch. 27, p. 113; see also pp. 111f). It is therefore incorrect when J. Moltmann says (*The Crucified God; The Cross of Christ as the Foundation and Criticism of Christian Theology*, trs. R. A. Wilson and J. Bowden [New York: Harper & Row, 1974], p. 47): "And it is here, in the theology of the mysticism of the cross in the late Middle Ages, that we first hear the monstrous phrase 'the crucified God,' which Luther then took up."

27. See Tertullian, "Against Praxeas," 29, in *The Writings of Tertullian*, vol. II (*Ante-Nicene Christian Library*, vol. XV), tr. P. Holmes, eds. Rev. A. Roberts and J. Donaldson (Edinburgh: T. & T. Clark, 1870), p. 401: "Christ died, the Son of the Father; and [let this suffice], because the Scriptures have told us so much." As evidence for God's inability to suffer, the words of Psalm 22 are used in "Against Praxeas," 30, *op. cit.*, pp. 404f, in particular the cry of God-forsakenness made by Jesus. This cry was uttered to show that God, who departed from the Son only as he gave Jesus the man up to die, was himself incapable of suffering: "You have Him exclaiming in the midst of His passion: 'My God, my God, why hast Thou forsaken me?' . . . this was the voice of flesh and soul, that is to say, of man—not of the Word and Spirit, that is to say, not of God; and it was uttered so as to prove the impassibility of God, who 'forsook' His Son, so far as He handed over His human substance to the suffering of death."

In this sense, Origen, in responding to the objection raised by Celsus that suffering and death were not fitting for a God, was led to say that it was the man Jesus but not God who was crucified (Origen, *Origen Contra Celsum*, in *The Writings of Origen* [*Ante-Nicene Christian Library*, vol. 23], tr. Rev. F. Crombie, eds. Rev. A. Roberts and J. Donaldson [Edinburgh: T. & T. Clark, vol. II (1872)], bk. VII, chs. 14 and 16, pp. 436f and 438f). Conversely, in an oracle of Apollo cited by Augustine from Porphyry, it is attested of a Christian woman, as an accusation, that she would not cease to "sing false laments to her dead God . . ." (Augustine, *The City of God*, tr. Marcus Dods, *NPNF*, 1st ser., II, bk. XIX, 23, p. 415; see also M. Hengel, "Mors turpissima crucis; Die Kreuzigung in der antiken Welt und die 'Torheit' des 'Wortes vom Kreuz,' " in *Rechtfertigung; Festschrift für Ernst Käsemann zum 70. Geburtstag* [Tübingen: J. C. B. Mohr, 1976], p. 127).

28. "Let them therefore confess, even they who previously denied that the Crucified was God, that they have erred; for the divine Scriptures bid them . . ." (Athanasius, "Ad Epictetum," "Letters of Athanasius," in *Select Writings and Letters of Athanasius, Bishop of Alexandria*, *NPNF*, IV, ch. 10, p. 574).

29. Athanasius, "Four Discourses Against the Arians," in *op. cit.*, III, 34, p. 412. Appealing to I Peter 4:1 ("Christ endured bodily suffering"), he demands that "these affections may be acknowledged as, not proper to the very Word by nature, but proper by nature to the very flesh" (*ibid*).

Friday: "For this reason it was that the sun, seeing its creator suffering in His outraged body, withdrew its rays and darkened the earth."[30] The early church's disputable talk about the death of God did not wait for the Reformation to find its continuation. The idea of the death of God was not alien to the mystical tradition: God died so that I might die to all the world and to all created things—that is how Meister Eckhart put it.[31] Luther, for other reasons, is then interested in the soteriological point of talk about the death of God. We shall return later to the relationship between the "Lutheran song" cited by Hegel and the theology of Luther.

In his treatise *Faith and Knowledge,* Hegel does not mention the origin of the statement "God himself is dead," but he certainly reveals its christological background by relating it to a discussion of Good Friday and the resurrection. In his use of this statement, Hegel's intention becomes plainer, which is to rework a cultural-historical content as a philosophical proposition: the phenomenon of modern atheism. The conclusion of the treatise *Faith and Knowledge,* which quotes from the "Lutheran song," is formulated in this way:

> But the pure concept or infinity as the abyss of nothingness in which all being is engulfed, must signify the infinite grief [of the finite] purely as a moment of the supreme Idea, and no more than a moment. Formerly, the infinite grief only existed historically in the formative process of culture. It existed as the feeling that "God Himself is dead," upon which the religion of more recent times rests; the same feeling that Pascal expressed in so to speak sheerly empirical form: 'la nature est telle qu'elle *marque* partout un Dieu *perdu* et dans l'homme et hors de l'homme.' [Nature is such that it *signifies* everywhere a *lost* God both within and outside man.] By marking this feeling as a moment of the supreme Idea, the pure concept must give philosophical existence to what used to be either the moral precept that we must sacrifice the empirical being (*Wesen*), or the concept of formal abstraction [e.g., the categorical imperative]. Thereby it must re-establish for philosophy the Idea of absolute freedom and along with it the absolute Passion, the speculative Good Friday in place of the historic Good Friday. Good Friday must be speculatively re-established in the whole truth and harshness of its God-forsakenness. Since the [more] serene, less well-grounded, and more individual style of the dogmatic philosophies and of the natural religions must vanish, the highest totality can and must achieve its resurrection solely from this harsh consciousness of loss, encompassing everything, and ascending in all its earnestness and out of its deepest ground to the most serene freedom of its shape.[32]

30. Athanasius, "Ad Epictetum," *loc. cit.*
31. See Meister Eckhart, *Meister Eckhart: A Modern Translation,* ed. R. B. Blakney (New York: Harper & Brothers, 1941) (Sermon—"The Will is Free"), p. 194: "And God died so that I, too, might die to the whole world and all created things."
32. G. W. F. Hegel, *Faith and Knowledge,* trs. W. Cerf and H. S. Harris (Albany: State University of New York Press, 1977), pp. 190f. Brackets as in the English edition.

(a) In this text by Hegel we can observe precisely how the concept of the death of God makes its transition from theological to philosophical significance. This transition corresponds exactly to the problem which Hegel was dealing with in the treatise *Faith and Knowledge*. It will aid in understanding this rather long concluding paragraph of the treatise if we return for the purposes of interpretation to its beginning and examine the problem Hegel is posing.

At the beginning of his work, Hegel states that the old contradiction between faith and knowledge has gained an entirely new meaning in the modern age. "Civilization has raised this latest era so far above the ancient antithesis of Reason and Faith, of philosophy and positive religion, that this opposition of faith and knowledge has acquired quite a different sense. . . ."[33] We note that, according to Hegel, this change in the meaning of the old opposition of faith and knowledge has arisen in *civilization*. But what happens within civilization is not yet fully grasped philosophically. Philosophy was involved in that change only to the degree that it ". . . has taken on the hue . . . of the latest cultural fashion."[34] In order to do justice to its task as philosophy, it must comprehend the reality given historically as civilization in its substantial truth and thus elevate it to the dignity of thought. In that sense, the "all-powerful culture of our time" fixes for philosophy its "standpoint."[35]

In "this latest era," as judged by Hegel, faith and knowledge were in fact related to each other in a new way. History had set philosophy and (positive) religion in a new relationship to each other in such a way that the old antithesis between knowledge and faith no longer appeared as the opposition of philosophy on the one side and religion on the other, but rather as a distinction *within* philosophy. According to Hegel, the completely new meaning of the opposition of faith and knowledge in the modern age consists of the fact that this opposition "has now been transferred into the field of philosophy itself."[36] It is in fact a transfer of the classic tension of faith and knowledge into philosophy in that the earlier opposition of faith and knowledge as religion and philosophy was carried out in such a way that reason was called on to serve faith as its maid. Philosophy had to battle that claim for the sake of its autonomy and finally conducted its own victorious battle "against the positive, against miracles and suchlike. . . ."[37] In "this latest era," the philosophical disputation with positive religion and its critical interpretation, as Kant had endeavored to do it, had become uninteresting, because "the positive form of religion," concretely Christianity, "no longer appeared to be worth the bother."[38] Reason does not even fight with faith anymore. The fighting relationship between faith and knowledge seems to be at an end.

An antithetical *struggle* between faith and knowledge was certainly not the beginning of the development drawn together by the civilization of "this latest era." There has been a struggle between knowledge and faith, philosophy and religion (theology), ever since late medieval Nominalism and the Refor-

33. *Ibid.*, p. 55.
34. *Ibid.*, p. 189.
35. *Ibid.*, p. 65.
36. *Ibid.*, p. 55.
37. *Ibid.*
38. *Ibid.*

mation. Older Scholasticism represented, by contrast, a completely different relationship between faith and knowledge, which can be defined as a totally *peaceful* tension. From the perspective of the modern concept of philosophy, it was a *peaceful* opposition—not really between philosophy and theology (religion) but rather one which can be defined as a peaceful opposition *within theology* (religion). Hegel apparently is referring to that when he recalls an expression from an earlier age which said that reason is "the handmaid of faith." Against that, of course, "philosophy has irresistibly affirmed its absolute autonomy," to the extent that from now on the antithesis of faith and reason is to be encountered in philosophy, even if it happens in a way which no longer takes faith seriously.[39] For our discussion of Hegel we must distinguish initially at least three "levels" of the development of the relationship of faith and knowledge:

(1) Faith and knowledge as a peaceful distinction within theology (religion).
(2) Faith and knowledge as a disputative distinction between theology (religion) and philosophy.
(3) Faith and knowledge as an unreconciled distinction within philosophy.

In this treatise Hegel is interested in the transition from the second to the third level and primarily then in the problematic relationship of faith and knowledge at the third level. He directs his attention to the victory of the Enlightenment and its problematic consequences. To be sure, the Enlightenment introduced the antithesis of faith and knowledge into philosophy, so that now philosophy is responsible for the resolution of the problems which result from that antithesis. However, philosophy has exercised its responsibility very poorly. Hegel regards the determination of the distinction between faith and knowledge, which now emerges in the philosophy of the Enlightenment, as unreconciled, an unresolved opposition, which renders critique necessary. Hegel's treatise *Faith and Knowledge* is his critical disputation with the victory of the Enlightenment and its consequences in philosophy.

If we examine the role which is ascribed to faith or to religion in Enlightenment philosophy, then we observe that the victory of the Enlightenment over religion is enormous. For that reason, this victory awakens skepticism. With concern, Hegel asks "whether victorious reason has not suffered the same fate that the barbarous nations in their victorious strength have usually suffered at the hands of civilized nations that weakly succumbed to them. As rulers the barbarians may have held the upper hand outwardly, but they surrendered to the defeated spiritually."[40] Accordingly he opines that the "victorious" Enlightenment has deprived reason of its victory because it vanquished a mere caricature of religion and fully missed genuine faith and reason in its very nature. *"En-*

---

39. *Ibid.* We will not deal with the question to what degree, in spite of the image of the philosophical handmaiden, there are issues already present within religion in which something like the autonomy of reason and the conscience is intended or even asserted, for example, in the context of the tractate "Treatise on Law" (Thomas Aquinas, *Summa Theologica,* in *The Basic Writings of Saint Thomas Aquinas,* 2 vols., ed. Anton C. Pegis [New York: Random House, 1945], First Part of the Second Part, qq. 90ff., vol. II, pp. 742ff).
    40. *Ibid.*

lightened Reason won a glorious victory over what it believed, in its limited conception of religion, to be faith as opposed to Reason. Yet seen in a clear light the victory comes to no more than this: the positive element with which Reason busied itself to do battle, is no longer *religion,* and victorious Reason is no longer *Reason.* The newborn peace that hovers triumphantly over the corpse of Reason and faith, uniting them as the child of both, has as little of Reason in it as it has of authentic faith."[41]

Thus Hegel regards the victory of the Enlightenment, to the extent that it was celebrated as the vanquishing of religion, as a negative process. (We are reminded that in November 1793 the cult of reason was introduced at Notre Dame in Paris. In broad sections of France an anti-Christian movement dominated which led to the closing of numerous churches and to the suspension of worship services.[42]) Hegel speaks expressly of the "negative procedure" of the Enlightenment, whose positive side "was a hubbub of vanity without a firm core,"[43] because it had not grasped its own negativity. But finally this negative procedure obtained a core "by grasping its own negativity."[44] This happened "in the philosophies of Kant, Jacobi, and Fichte."[45] What does that mean? What does it mean to say that the Enlightenment's "negative procedure" grasped "its own negativity"?

With this formula, Hegel expresses the fact that reason had become critical not only of religion, but more importantly of itself. The critique of pure reason took place as the self-critique of pure reason. Thus, reason came to its "self-awareness."[46] It is a part of the self-awareness of a reason which is criticizing itself and grasping its negativity that *reason* limits itself to *understanding* whenever knowledge and knowing are at stake. However, understanding is always and only focused on that which is finite and empirical. Thus, one can know only that which is finite and empirical. The (true) infinite, which Hegel also calls "the better part" of reason, cannot be known. It can only be believed, then. When knowledge declares itself to be incompetent, it simultaneously makes faith necessary. That which can only be *believed, must* be believed here. We are reminded of the famous sentence from Kant's "Preface to the Second Edition" of the *Critique of Pure Reason:* "I must, therefore, abolish *knowledge,* to make room for *belief.*"[47] The "old" antithesis of "faith and knowledge" is now encountered within philosophy in such a way that critical reason restricts knowledge to the finite and thus makes room for faith with reference to the infinite.

In this way reason deprived itself of the possibility of comprehending rationally its noblest subject. God cannot be known anymore. And thus "the better part of reason" has been translated into something "beyond reason." Hegel says that reason, "having in this way become mere intellect, acknowledges its

41. *Ibid.* (my italics).
42. K. Ploetz, *Epitome of History,* tr. W. H. Tillinghast (New York: Blue Ribbon Books, Inc., 1883), p. 455.
43. Hegel, *Faith and Knowledge,* p. 56.
44. *Ibid.*
45. *Ibid.* (italics in Hegel).
46. *Ibid.*
47. Immanuel Kant, *Critique of Pure Reason,* tr. J. N. D. Meiklejohn (*Everyman's Library,* 909) (London: J. M. Dent & Sons Ltd., 1950), p. 18.

own nothingness by placing that which is better than it in a *faith outside and above* itself, as a beyond. . . . This is what has happened in the philosophies of Kant, Jacobi, and Fichte. Philosophy has made itself into the handmaid of a faith once more."[48] However, in contrast with medieval Scholasticism, it happens here involuntarily. When the eternal or the infinite is understood as a Beyond put into faith, outside of and over reason, then that means that eternity is ". . . a beyond too vacuous for cognition so that this infinite void of knowledge could only be filled with the subjectivity of longing and divining."[49] In this sense Hegel speaks of the "nihilism of the transcendental philosophy."[50] As far as reason is concerned, eternity is "the incalculable, the inconceivable, the empty— an incognizable God beyond the boundary stakes of Reason."[51] As such, it is known and acknowledged by reason, which does so by making space for believing. Reason knows the eternal, knows God only as the unknowable. In the ultimate consequence of the Enlightenment we are dealing with a reason which is restricted to being the *antithesis of the absolute,* and yet it cannot absolutely posit that antithesis. The tragedy of the Enlightenment which Hegel perceived consists of a reason which "recognizes something higher above itself from which it is self-excluded"[52]—a formulation which one should remember.

For his part, Hegel then joins with these philosophies by acknowledging the negative meaning of the absolute as an infinite which is opposed to the finite, but he acknowledges it *only as a moment of the supreme Idea.* He criticizes his direct predecessors in philosophy in that he disputes the finality of the alternative between the God who exists outside of and above the "I think" (*cogito*), on the one hand, and the thinking ego, on the other hand. "Jacobi says, 'Either God exists and exists *outside* of me, a living being subsisting apart; *or else* I am God. *There is no third way.* Philosophy, on the contrary, says, *there is a third way.* . . .' For philosophy predicates of God not only being but also thought, that is, Ego, and recognizes him as the absolute identity of being and thought."[53]

To think of God as the absolute identity of thought (Ego) and being means, of course, to consider simultaneously that in pure thought all being is "destroyed," because thought only permits thought to *exist* as reasonable, and nothing else. Reason knows only itself to be reasonable, it knows only itself. It has been established since Kant "that reason only perceives that which it produces after its own design. . . ."[54] If God is supposed to be the absolute identity of thought and being, then he must also contain the negativity of thought. This negativity of thought would then, if it were *not* thought to belong to God himself, mean nothing other than that God is *nothing* for thought, that the eternity of reason is something *empty,* absolute emptiness. That was the precise situation of the relationship of faith and thought after the victory of the Enlightenment. Hegel absorbs as his own the philosophy he criticizes. It is fundamental to his thought that "the present world and the present form and self-consciousness of

48. Hegel, *Faith and Knowledge,* p. 56.
49. *Ibid.*
50. *Ibid.,* p. 170.
51. *Ibid.,* p. 60.
52. *Ibid.,* p. 61.
53. *Ibid.,* p. 169.
54. Immanuel Kant, *op. cit.,* p. 10.

the spirit contain with them all the stages which appear to have occurred earlier in history."[55] "Those moments which the spirit appears to have outgrown still belong to it in the depths of its present."[56] That is true here as well. That complex concluding paragraph of *Faith and Knowledge,* which draws together the philosophical past and reveals the depth of the "present" philosophy, makes this plain. Now we are in a better situation to understand that passage.

(b) According to Hegel, true philosophy conceptualizes what "only existed historically in the formative process of culture." That which was historically formed comes about in that a culture, with the help of certain philosophies (which by no means are identical with the *true* philosophy), *forms* its metaphysics by establishing "single dimensions of totality" as absolutes, and then works these absolutely established single dimensions of the whole into a system. Hegel conceives of "formation" thus as a transitive event. The culture of the modern age, characterized by "the hue of inwardness," has thus formed as its metaphysics, in the philosophies of Kant, Fichte, and Jacobi, the "metaphysics of subjectivity." In the systems of Kant, Fichte, and Jacobi "this metaphysic of subjectivity has run through the complete cycle of its forms, . . . [and thus] completely set forth . . . the formative process of culture . . . [and] brought this cultural process to its end."[57] If, then, "formation has ended," and the "complete cycle of its forms" is "run through,"[58] the external possibility is given "that the true philosophy should emerge out of this completed culture."[59] This happens in that philosophy sets aside the absolute establishment of certain dimensions of the whole ("the absoluteness of its finitudes") for the sake of the totality and thus "present[s] itself all at once as perfected appearance"[60] of philosophy, as it no longer reduces totality to these absolutely established single dimensions.

In the formation which is described as "the metaphysic of subjectivity," the feeling that God himself is dead belongs to the absolute establishment of certain dimensions of totality. As the "so to speak sheerly empirical form" of this feeling, Hegel quotes Pascal's sentence, "Nature is such that she testifies everywhere, both within man and without him, to a lost God and a corrupt nature."[61] This feeling has its origins in Protestantism. For "the religion of more recent times rests," according to Hegel, on this feeling, to the extent that the principle of subjectivity, dominant in the new metaphysics (the "principle of the

55. G. W. F. Hegel, *Lectures on the Philosophy of World History; Introduction: Reason in History,* tr. H. B. Nisbet (Cambridge: Cambridge University Press, 1975), p. 150.

56. *Ibid.,* p. 151.

57. Hegel, *Faith and Knowledge,* p. 190.

58. *Ibid.*

59. *Ibid.*

60. *Ibid.*

61. Pascal (*Pascal's Pensées,* nr. 441), in *Great Books of the Western World,* tr. W. F. Trotter, ed. R. M. Hutchins (Chicago: Encyclopaedia Britannica, Inc., 1952), XXXIII, 251. On the significance of the Pascal quotation, see the discussion in Ch. Link, *loc. cit.,* pp. 37ff. Link does not want to link this fragment, which is to be understood against the background of the doctrine of original sin, with the statement "Great Pan is dead" (*Pascal's Pensées,* nr. 695, p. 302), which Pascal "placed within the context of biblical prophecy . . . and interpreted as the condition of the epiphany of Christ ordained by God Himself" (p. 39). This interpretation is, however, traditional, as was shown above (p. 46, n. 3).

North"), is, "from the religious point of view," the principle "of Protestantism." Hegel's assertion that the religion of more recent times rests on the feeling that "God himself is dead" must be understood as the attempt to demonstrate the significance of the Reformation emphasis on "by faith alone" within the context of the subjectivity problematic. In faith, man, according to Hegel, is so oriented to the infinite God that his manifestation in some finite form, whether it be in an institution like the nation, the family, or the church, or a human work, is ruled out. Faith alone preserves the deity of God and prevents the dissolution of God by understanding and by intuition. The religion of Protestantism "builds its temples and altars in the heart of the individual. In sighs and prayers he seeks for the God whom he denies to himself in intuition, because of the risk that the intellect will cognize what is intuited as a mere thing, reducing the sacred grove to mere timber."[62] Protestantism thus avoids, for the sake of God's infinity, the finite perception of God in the institutions of finitude.[63] Thus Protestantism has raised to a principle an infinite and unbridgeable distinction between the subjectivity which longs for eternity and the eternal itself. That which is eternal does not mediate itself finitely, and subjectivity abhors the reconciliation of the infinite with the finite. Hegel calls this Protestant abhorrence of such reconciliation of God with finite (empirical) existence "the poetry of Protestant grief."[64] Later he will speak of the "unhappy awareness" in which subject and object, faith and knowledge, are divided and separate from each other. Without reconciliation with the finite, the infinite loses for subjectivity the character of objectivity and is supposed to do so. Subjectivity desires the grief of not being able to *have* God. For if it *had* God, then the infinite would be dissolved into objectivity. And that would not only be "a dangerous superfluity," but beyond that, it would be "an evil" if the infinite were objectified outside of the longing of subjectivity and "the intellect could turn it into a thing." If the feeling of grief at the imperceptibility of God "passed over into an intuition that was without grief, it would be superstition."[65] For in the context of the finite, God does not exist. To look on something finite as God and to worship it would be nothing more than superstition. In this sense the religion of more recent times rests on the "infinite grief," which was present as the feeling that God himself is dead.

The *formation* which followed Protestantism allowed this feeling to become historical in an antithetical, antitheological, or irreligious way, without overcoming the principle of subjectivity in the process. According to Hegel, the flight from the finite, as manifestation of the infinite, led ultimately to the sole recognition of the finite as reality, and thus the finite human ego was held to be infinite. Through this "flight from the finite, and [the] rigidity [of] subjectivity,"

62. Hegel, *Faith and Knowledge*, p. 57.

63. Hegel is concerned in this context to liberate the subject from the perception which claims the finite church to be infinite, as he saw it embodied in Catholicism. The proposition is to be understood not in the context of Christology but of Ecclesiology. The perception of God in the Crucified One as the condition for the possibility of "the freedom of the Christian man" is not addressed in this context.

64. *Ibid.*, p. 61.

65. *Ibid.*, p. 57. Accordingly, for Protestantism true faith cannot be had without the pain of testing. Faith without the painful experience of testing would already be superstition.

the "grove [turns into] timber."[66] The result was that "the reality with which it became reconciled, . . . was in fact merely empirical existence, the ordinary world and ordinary matters of fact (*Wirklichkeit*). Hence, this reconciliation did not itself lose the character of absolute opposition implicit in beautiful longing. Rather, it flung itself upon the other pole of the antithesis, the empirical world."[67] The formative process of the Enlightenment inherited to that degree the religion of Protestantism. In this formation, the cultural situation mirrored is one in which faith in God does not have an experienceable relationship to reality, and this causes its suffering. For if faith in God must be joined to a negative relation to experienceable finite reality, then the feeling must arise within the context of experience that God cannot be alive in the world.[68] In that sense the feeling on which the religion of "more recent times" rested, the feeling that "God himself is dead," "only existed historically in the formative process of culture." As a consequence, philosophy was no longer intended by its "fixed standpoint, which the all-powerful culture of our time has established," to "aim at the cognition of God, but only at what is called the cognition of man. This so-called man and his humanity conceived as a rigid, insuperable finite sort of Reason form philosophy's absolute standpoint. Man is . . . an absolute sensibility. He does, however, have the faculty of faith so that he can touch himself up here and there with a spot of alien supersensuousness."[69] But in truth, in this philosophy we have "finitude made absolute."[70] By contrast, the infinite is understood by Kant, Jacobi, and Fichte, who have "perfected . . . to the highest degree" the philosophy of the Enlightenment, as only the (empty) essence of the concept.[71] It is empty to the degree that the essence of the concept tends toward generality, and infinity is the purest form of generality or pure emptiness. In this sense the "pure concept or infinity [is] the abyss of nothingness in which all being is engulfed."[72] However, the pure concept itself cannot be satisfied with the mere ascertainment of what it is. Rather, it has to ponder itself, so to speak, and make the best of the "abyss of nothingness in which all being is engulfed." It is supposed to accomplish the negation implicit in it as the augmentation of infinity to the "Idea of absolute freedom." And that is possible only when "the feeling that God himself is dead" is not passed over or simply noted as an observation but is elevated to the dignity of a truth which belongs to God and is called forth by him. Only in doing that is the proposition "God is dead" saved from being made into an absolute.

(c) The true philosophy of the absolute, which Hegel announces in his

66. *Ibid.*, p. 58.
67. *Ibid.*
68. Ch. Link puts it well (*op. cit.*, pp. 43f): "Once separated from the reality of the 'second creation'—the realm of objective orders—the world of *faith* with all its contents is only the 'unreal' reflection of that which people in the world of enlightened knowledge do without. . . . Faith is no longer passed on in the reality of modern society. Its God has been forcibly ejected from the world of reality, and thus its truth, as far as knowledge is concerned, remains an uncommitted empty beyond. . . . Its 'death' marks the divorce of faith from the experience of the world."
69. Hegel, *Faith and Knowledge*, p. 65.
70. *Ibid.*, p. 66.
71. *Ibid.*, p. 61.
72. Compare *ibid.*, p. 191 with pp. 60f.

book *Faith and Knowledge,* has the task, in disputation with the philosophy which preceded it, of freeing finitude as an absolutely set single dimension of totality (and thus the feeling that "God himself is dead") from its absolute character, without destroying its truth. This can happen only by understanding infinity as a pure concept. As a pure concept, infinity is "the abyss of nothingness, in which all being is engulfed." To that degree, the pure concept comprehends the feeling that "God himself is dead." It represents that feeling in the form of comprehension. And because the supreme Idea for its part is comprehended in the pure concept and the concept thus becomes a moment of the supreme Idea, it must designate that feeling as a moment—"and no more than a moment"—"of the supreme Idea." Understood that way, the pure concept signifies ". . . the infinite grief [which] only existed historically in the formative process of culture . . . as the feeling that 'God himself is dead,' upon which the religion of more recent times rests"—as a moment of the supreme Idea. As a moment of the supreme Idea, the infinite grief receives from now on a "philosophical existence"—namely, in the philosophy of Hegel himself—whereas earlier it was in the formative process of culture (as "the moral precept that we must sacrifice the empirical being" in Fichte and as "the concept of formal abstraction" in Kant). That means that the unreconciled character of eternity as abstract infinity and finite world must be grasped as a moment of the Absolute itself, through which the eternal must pass in order to set aside the absolutization of the individual contradictory dimensions of totality for the sake of a reconciled totality, a true infinity.

By designating the feeling that "God himself is dead" as a moment of the supreme Idea, talk about the death of God gains a twofold meaning. First of all, in talk about the death of God, the situation of absolutized finitude expresses itself, which corresponds to abstract infinitude as empty negativity. Once that feeling is grasped as a moment of the supreme Idea, then the death of God is understood as an event of the *self-negation* of God, who does not desire to be "in and for himself" and does not desire to forsake the world in its finitude. Or must one perhaps say: who *can*not be in and for himself and *can*not leave the world to its finitude?

In the long-unknown aphorism (from his time in Jena), Hegel expresses this train of thought very simply: "God sacrifices himself, gives himself up to destruction. God himself is dead; the highest despair of complete forsakenness by God."[73] This is what is meant when we read at the end of *Faith and Knowledge* that the pure concept, in that it designates the infinite grief of the metaphysic of subjectivity as a moment of the supreme Idea itself, must grant to "philosophy the Idea of absolute freedom and along with it the absolute Passion, the speculative Good Friday." The idea of absolute freedom and absolute passion are linked together here because God gives himself up to destruction, and thus chooses suffering in absolute freedom. So the true philosophy of the absolute will restores "the speculative Good Friday in place of the historic Good Friday . . . in the whole truth and harshness of its God-forsakenness." That God himself were dead had in Protestant religion until then and in earlier philosophy only

---

73. F. Nicolin, *Unbekannte Aphorismen Hegels aus der Jenaer Periode (Hegel-Studien,* 4) (Bonn: Bouvier, 1967), p. 16.

the rank of subjective grief, but not the harsh dignity of a grief of God. That God himself is dead was a feeling of subjectivity, but not a moment of truth in God himself.[74]

To reproduce the basic atheistic feeling of the modern age in the whole truth and harshness of the God-forsakenness of Good Friday—that is the task of the true philosophy of the Absolute, which becomes Hegel's own philosophy. This philosophy may claim that it has taken the atheism of the modern age more seriously than it was able to take itself until then. At the same time it had to claim that it led beyond the atheism of the modern age. For the true philosophy which is announced in the concluding sentence of *Faith and Knowledge* not only claims to reproduce Good Friday speculatively in the whole truth and harshness of God-forsakenness, but to permit "the highest totality" to arise "in all its seriousness and out of its deepest ground to the most serene freedom of its shape."[75]

Therefore, whatever in the positive Christian religion faith in the Crucified is supposed to mean, is not to be left to faith alone, but is to be *thought* now through reason. And in the *concept of God* the divine being is to be understood as a sequence of events in which the eternity of divine life accepts and endures finitude up to and including the harshness of death as the end of the finite, in

74. It is worthy of note historically that Hegel, in his treatise "The Spirit of Christianity and Its Fate" (1798/99), found it to be an irritating offense for the "urge for religion" that "the form of a servant, the humiliation in itself," rather than "to be a mere veil and to pass away," is supposed to "remain fixed and permanent in God, belonging to his essence," according to the Christian faith ("The Spirit of Christianity and Its Fate," in Hegel, *Early Theological Writings*, tr. T. M. Knox [Chicago: University of Chicago Press, 1948], p. 293). Hegel counters this view with the thesis, "The nondivine object, for which worship is also demanded, never becomes divine whatever radiance may shine around it" (*ibid.*, p. 295). This is said with a view both to the "individuality" of Jesus and to the connected factor of the "humiliation" of the divine. Accordingly the death of Jesus is understood as the abolition of this humiliation, as an end to the concealment of the divine. The position which the church still takes, that "prayers are also offered to the man who taught, who walked on earth and hung on the cross," is criticized as a "tremendous combination" over which "for so many centuries millions of God-seeking souls have fought and tormented themselves" (*ibid.*, p. 293). There is similar irritation in Goethe in the "West-östlicher Divan," *Goethes Werke* [Weimarer Ausgabe] (Weimar: Hermann Böhlau, 1888), VI, 289: "Thou dost seek to make for me a God / such a lamentable figure upon a wooden cross!" Hegel parodies the faith of the church: "The veil stripped off in the grave, the real human form, has risen again out of the grave and attached itself to the one who is risen as God [!]" (*ibid.*). That death is to be understood as the definitive end of the "veil of reality" and as the revealing of deity is a point of view which Hegel firmly made, even later when he modified it. But later he also interpreted death as the last consequence of the servant form and the humiliation of God, and not just as its end. And what was a complaint in 1798/99, that humiliation should "belong to God's essence," becomes in 1802 a required concept to the degree that the feeling that "God himself is dead" is to be understood as a moment of the supreme Idea. Of course, it is to be understood as "not more than a moment." But this moment *is* now "the absolute suffering." In contradiction to W. D. Marsch (*Gegenwart Christi in der Gesellschaft; Eine Studie zu Hegels Dialektik* [München: C. Kaiser, 1965]), P. Cornehl properly emphasizes the difference between *Faith and Knowledge*, on the one hand, and the *Spirit of Christianity*, on the other, in his significant book *Die Zukunft der Versöhnung; Eschatologie und Emanzipation in der Aufklärung, bei Hegel und in der Hegelschen Schule* (Göttingen: Vandenhoeck & Ruprecht, 1971), pp. 125f.

75. Hegel, *Faith and Knowledge*, p. 191.

order finally to let God's being as the *history of the freedom of the spirit* become thinkable and real. The last sentence of *Faith and Knowledge* must then be a demand: "The pure concept . . . *must* signify the infinite grief . . . the feeling that 'God himself is dead' . . . as a moment of the supreme Idea" and thus "give [it] philosophical existence. . . ."[76] In the *Phenomenology of the Mind* Hegel then responded to this demand on philosophy. The concluding sentence of *Faith and Knowledge* was the self-heralding of "true philosophy."

2. In the lectures known as the "Jena Realist Philosophy,"[77] which Hegel gave in Jena in 1805/6, the concept of the death of God is taken up again. Here we encounter it in the context of a definition of the essence of "absolute religion." This enables us to understand more precisely the remarkable phrase "speculative Good Friday which otherwise was historical," which we found in the concluding sentence of *Faith and Knowledge*.

To put it in a phrase from his Berlin *Lectures on the Philosophy of History,* "It is in terms of religion that a nation defines what it considers to be true."[78] Therefore, every people has its own special religion, and that is true even if this religion might broadly duplicate the religion of another people. That special religion which is the *absolute* religion surpasses all the other special religions in that this "absolute religion" is no longer just a definition of what a people *regards* as true. The "absolute religion" rather, as defined in the *Jenaer Realphilosophie,* is the "knowledge that God is the depth of the Spirit which knows itself certainly."[79] This spirit must first arrive at its depth, however, just as it must first become certain of itself. This, significantly, does not happen through mere self-deepening, but rather through the spirit's going out of itself toward that which is alien to it, penetrating that which it is not. To become certain of itself in its depth, it must move toward that which is strange, without which the spirit would never come to know itself but would remain superficial. The strange is not merely traversed but is appropriated and processed. Thus Hegel speaks of the "course of life of God."[80] A life course is never just the sequence of all the periods of time passed through by a person, but rather the appropriation of those times as they are experienced and the processing of one's own lifetime into a history which at the end is identical with the person. God's course of life is also the identity of "person" and history. The decisive event of Good Friday belongs to this divine *curriculum vitae*.

The historical Good Friday is the day on which the historical person Jesus of Nazareth died. This day belongs to the past, and the further back in time the more so. As a past event, the crucifixion of Jesus is passed by time itself. In his Jena diary, Hegel wrote, "In Swabia they say of something which had long since happened: it's so long ago that soon it won't be true anymore. Thus Christ died for our sins so long ago that soon it won't be true anymore."[81] As an

76. *Ibid.,* p. 190.
77. G. W. F. Hegel, *Jenaer Realphilosophie,* ed. J. Hoffmeister (*Philosophische Bücherei,* 67) (Leipzig: F. Meiner Verlag, 1931, 1969).
78. G. W. F. Hegel, *Lectures on the Philosophy of World History,* p. 105.
79. Hegel, *Jenaer Realphilosophie,* p. 266.
80. See Küng, *op. cit.,* p. 230.
81. G. W. F. Hegel, *Dokumente zu Hegels Entwicklung,* ed. J. Hoffmeister (Stuttgart: Fr. Frommann, 1936), p. 358.

historical event taken for itself, Good Friday can affect the religion which lasted beyond the age of its founding just as little as its Founder, taken as an historical person, can be interesting over a long period of time or bind one to himself. In his Berlin *Lectures on the History of Philosophy*, Hegel says of the person of Jesus Christ that "this is indifferent to the absolute context and to itself, since the person is not the import of the doctrine. But the Christian Religion has this characteristic, that the Person of Christ in His character of the Son of God, Himself partakes in the nature of God."[82] These sentences, which anticipate the theological program which would later come, and whose influence on the theology of Martin Kähler, Karl Barth, and Rudolf Bultmann deserves study, are also valid for his earlier writings. If the death of Christ, understood as the sacrificial death for our sins, should not soon "no longer be true," then the "Good Friday which was otherwise historical,"[83] the death of Christ, may not be understood as though it "did not affect the nature of God."[84]

For Hegel, part of the absolute religion is the knowledge "that God, the absolute being beyond, became man."[85] The incarnation of God is then immediately related to the death of Jesus Christ. "It is not this man who dies, but the *divine*; that is how it becomes man."[86] In view of the dogmatic tradition of Christianity, with its docetic tendency which since the days of the early church had never been totally overcome, this was a monstrous statement. Where otherwise—we will come back to the exception of Luther—the death of Jesus Christ is interpreted as an event which affected only his human nature, in contrast with which the divine nature of the same person persisted to be,[87] Hegel wanted to understand the death of Jesus Christ expressly as the death of the divine. And it was on the basis of this event that he then interpreted the dogma of the incarnation. One may regret the underlying inadequate differentiation between the divine nature and the divine person. But that Hegel provided an interpretation of the dogma of the incarnation which is astonishingly in line with the New Testament's history of traditions when he sought to understand the incarnation on the basis of the death of Jesus Christ, deserves the highest regard. It cannot be theologically devalued when the christological truth is immediately diverted into the philosophical, in that the incarnation of God is discussed as the "divesting . . . of the abstract being,"[88] as "the sacrifice of divinity, i.e. of the abstract, beyond essence."[89] Understanding the divine essence as an "abstract essence from beyond" is certainly not biblical. Before this necessary theological critique is given more importance than our "readiness to learn," we should consider whether Hegel did not in his own way express the fact that a God

82. G. W. F. Hegel, *Lectures on the History of Philosophy*, trs. E. S. Haldane and F. H. Simson, 3 vols. (New York: Humanities Press, 1968), I, 71.
83. See above, p. 74.
84. *Ibid.*
85. Hegel, *Jenaer Realphilosophie*, p. 268.
86. *Ibid.*, n. 3.
87. ". . . The Word remaining quiescent, that He might be capable of being tempted, dishonoured, crucified, and of suffering death. . . ," asserts Irenaeus and with him the broad stream of dogmatic tradition. See *Against Heresies, ANF*, I, bk. III, ch. xix, 3, p. 449.
88. Hegel, *Jenaer Realphilosophie*, p. 268, n. 3.
89. *Ibid.*, p. 269.

understood in abstraction from the man Jesus will fail to be the God in his very divinity who is proclaimed by the Christian faith. Further, a 'fleshless word' (*logos asarkos*) is thus an abstract word of God, and to seek to understand and to proclaim God without the man Jesus is just as unchristian as the attempt to understand and proclaim this man without God.

Of course, part of the absolute religion is, as a consequence of God's incarnation, the total turning of God to the temporality of history, to the dimension of the "merely historical." Hegel expresses this with the statement "[that] this reality [*scil.* of the real man who was God] has annulled itself, has become something past."[90] God has submitted himself to death, to that which was most alien to him, and now he bears the mark of mortality in himself. In the reality of the God-man, God enters history and becomes a reality which is subject to perishing. As such it is not lost, but rather gives the spirit which is becoming certain of itself its depth which holds fast to death. Only in unity with the dead is the spirit alive and is its liveliness spiritual. This is the only way to arrive at the reconciliation of the infinite with the finite, so that the unending bears in itself the entire harshness of the fate of mortality. And this is the only way to arrive at that resurrection in which the spirit becomes certain of itself, so "that God is the depth of the spirit which is certain of itself." This *knowledge,* as Hegel defines the absolute religion, is itself another event of the divine being. Thus the chief part of the absolute religion is that "this God . . . [as] immediacy is the spirit of the common."[91] The incarnation of God interpreted as the death of God perfects itself as the reconciliation of the spirit "with its world,"[92] and in the church this reconciliation takes place when it is known.

In this knowledge, then, the "Good Friday which was otherwise historical" has become the speculative Good Friday. That special event of long ago has been elevated as a concrete event to the level of a general and enduring truth. Hegel's interpretation of the historical Good Friday as a speculative one is the attempt to exposit the death of the incarnate God as that event which is "not so long ago that it soon will no longer be true." The death of Jesus Christ is true as the direct presence of the spirit which comes to itself and to his church through this death.

3. The presentation of the way taken by this spirit who is coming to himself and knows himself as spirit in his purpose was given by Hegel in 1807 in his *The Phenomenology of Mind.* The impressive conclusion of this incomparable book expresses once more the relationship of the goal and pathway of the spirit coming to himself: "*The goal,* which is Absolute Knowledge or Spirit knowing itself as Spirit, finds its pathway in the recollection of spiritual forms (*Geister*) as they are in themselves and as they accomplish the organization of their spiritual kingdom. Their conservation, looked at from the side of their free existence appearing in the form of contingency, is *History*; looked at from the side of their intellectually comprehended organization, it is the *Science* of the ways in which knowledge appears. Both together, or History (intellectually) comprehended (*begriffen*), form at once the recollection and the Golgotha of Absolute Spirit, the reality, the truth, the certainty of its throne, without which it were lifeless, solitary, and alone. Only

90. *Ibid.*, p. 268.
91. *Ibid.*
92. *Ibid.*, p. 267.

> The chalice of this realm of spirits
> Foams forth to God His own Infinitude."[93]

(a) It should not be difficult to translate this conclusion—"dithyrambic and responsible, apotheosis and teaching proposition"[94]—back into the more mundane language of the system in *Faith and Knowledge*. Of course the distinction cannot be overlooked: the system now is, for the first time, fulfilled; the language is satiated.

Hegel's concern can be seen in scarcely surpassable clarity and urgency in the last secondary clause: that the absolute spirit is not "lifeless, solitary, and alone," not the abstract being from beyond, as we found it in the *Jenaer Realphilosophie*. In order not to be "lifeless, solitary, and alone," the absolute spirit takes his pathway in and through the realm of the spirits and takes these along as "comprehended history." The "spiritual forms (*Geister*) as they are in themselves" are the historical objectifications of the spirit. They emerge in existence as cultures, religions, philosophies. Appropriate to their historical existence is not simply the contingency of mere facticity but also the necessity of a systematically comprehensible context. As "mere" history their interrelationships are contingent. For Hegel, history is "conservation," in the sense of a context defined by contingency. It is not the absolute spirit, but only the sequence of individual spirits which are conserved in history, so that it can be called the "recollection of spiritual forms (*Geister*)." Yet to the extent that history is at the same time the pathway of the spirit to itself, the contingency of the series of spirits (or 'spiritual forms') must be understood as the essence of absolute necessity. The spirit's pathway as history through history is the comprehending of this history, the grasping of its necessity. For that reason the essence of the spirit is the comprehending of its own pathway, full of its renunciation, a pathway which it no longer forgets but carries with it as its "Golgotha." The phrase "Golgotha of Absolute Spirit" shows that Hegel is still oriented to talk about the death of God. The Golgotha of the Absolute Spirit is, as the throne of the spirit which knows itself, the same thing as what in *Faith and Knowledge* was the unending pain and the feeling that "God himself is dead" as a factor of the supreme Idea.

(b) The statement of the death of God is then explicitly encountered in *The Phenomenology of the Mind*. Before it is perfected in "Absolute Knowledge," it comprehends the "Spirit manifested in revealed religion," which has not yet itself grasped itself. That which is conceptualized in "Absolute Knowledge" is still "figurative thinking" or "representation" in the realm of religion. The distinction between the goal of "Absolute Knowledge" and this last section of the pathway consists of the difference between "comprehending" and "representing." It is, to be sure, true that without representing one cannot arrive at comprehending. For without representing, comprehending would have no object. If the "Spirit manifested in revealed religion" still remains in the dimension of

93. G. W. F. Hegel, *The Phenomenology of Mind*, tr. J. B. Baillie (*The Muirhead Library of Philosophy*) (London: George Allen & Unwin Ltd., 1964; 2nd rev. ed. 1949), p. 808. (The final quotation is an adaptation of Schiller's *Die Freundschaft*.)

94. This is the description of the concluding sentence of *Phenomenology* given by Ernst Bloch, *Subjekt-Objekt; Erläuterungen zu Hegel; Erweiterte Ausgabe, Gesamtausgabe* (Frankfurt am Main: Suhrkamp Verlag, 1962), VIII, 100.

representation, then that means that the "Spirit as a whole and the moments distinguished in it fall within the sphere of figurative thinking, and within the form of objectivity."[95] In revealed religion the spirit knows itself *only as the object* of consciousness and not yet as the unity of both, not yet as self-consciousness. Therefore religion must be overtaken by philosophy. But this final act in the history of the spirit is not simply an overtaking of religion by philosophy, and certainly not making faith superfluous through knowledge, as Hegel has constantly been accused. For, as far as the *content* of the representations is concerned, the truth of revealed religion is identical with absolute knowledge. "The content of religion, therefore, expresses earlier in time than (philosophical) science what spirit is. . . ."[96] This happens as *revealed* religion. Revelation is the spirit manifesting itself. In self-revelation the spirit manifests what it is. That which is manifested is then the content of revealed religion. In this content, the spirit presents itself as spirit. This is what distinguishes *revealed* religion from the forms of *natural* religion and *artificial* religion ("religion in the form of art"), which precede it.

    In natural religion, ". . . spirit knows itself as its object in a 'natural' or immediate shape."[97] Natural religion does not know of any contradiction between consciousness and nature. In it, the natural givens of the consciousness are directly divine. In artificial religion (or "religion in the form of art"), on the other hand, consciousness is produced as itself or as a self in such a way that in its object it does not really worship itself but rather beholds or perceives itself. The naturalness or immediacy of the spirit as a religious object is thereby set aside. In contrast to that, in revealed religion the spirit is so imagined that the immediacy of the spirit becomes a person, a self, and this self is immediate:[98] the spirit becomes self-consciousness in that the divine being becomes man.

    These distinctions between the three forms of religion are only apparently formal. They have their effect in the content of the religions. This can be shown in the statement about the death of God, which belongs to revealed religion, a statement which formulates a precise step of the relationship of being and consciousness, a relationship which is so decisive and full of tension for the history of the spirit. That being which is independent of any other, ". . . that which is in itself, and is conceived through itself," has been called "substance" ever since Aristotle.[99] It is characteristic of substance that it does not exist in something else. According to Hegel, this distinguishes it from the subject. Whereas substance rests in itself, for Hegel the subject is "the process of positing itself, or in mediating with its own self its transitions from one state or position to the opposite."[100] The subject *comes* to itself whereas substance has always *been* in itself. The essence of substance is autonomy, that of the subject is self-movement.

95. Hegel, *Phenomenology*, p. 789.
96. *Ibid.*, p. 801.
97. *Ibid.*, p. 694.
98. *Ibid.*
99. Compare the definition in Spinoza (*Ethics*, in *Chief Works*, 2 vols., tr. R. H. M. Elwes [New York: Dover, 1955], II, 39) with Aristotle, "The Categories of Interpretation," tr. H. P. Cooke, in *The Organon*, I (*Loeb Classical Library*) (Cambridge: Harvard University Press, 1938), 2a, 11ff, p. 19: "Substance . . . is that which is neither asserted of nor can be found in a subject."
100. Hegel, *Phenomenology*, p. 80.

Part of the self-movement of the subject is mediation by something else, which for its part is what it is through the subject. And the subject does not lose itself in that other thing, but rather together with that other thing, which exists because of it, it arrives at a freedom which surpasses the autonomy of substance, the freedom of self-consciousness. Therefore, in Hegel's view, ". . . everything depends on grasping and expressing the ultimate truth not as Substance but as Subject as well."[101] Only a substance which has become absolute subject and which is understood as absolute subject can be regarded as God.[102] From this point of view, the differentiation of the three forms of religion has taken place. They mark the pathway of the substance toward its being a subject.

In natural religion, the spirit knows itself to be substance and only substance; it is so immediately present to consciousness that it does not even experience itself as a *self*:

> *"Nothing is inside, nothing is outside;*
> *For what is inside is outside."* [103]

One could thus use Goethe's words to interpret the essence of natural religion in Hegel's sense. This identity of inside and outside could just as well be a contradiction without any relationship. That which is inward does not *express* itself. That *expression* or utterance which belongs to it remains *external* to it. It cannot express itself from inside toward the outside, because it is not yet able to make such self-distinctions. The self-distinction of that which is inward is the condition in which it is possible for it to express itself. And so natural religion's "ambiguous beings, a riddle to themselves—. . . the simple inner with the multiform outer, the darkness of thought mated with the clearness of expression—these break out into the language of a wisdom that is darkly deep and difficult to understand."[104]

"Through the Religion of Art spirit has passed from the form of substance in that of Subject. . . ."[105] If in natural religion the spirit had produced itself as an object, through "an instinctive kind of working, like bees building their cells,"[106] then the "artificer" in "religion in the form of art" "has become a spiritual workman."[107] Spiritual work is work which is conscious of itself. Part of it, therefore, is an inner knowledge of the individuality of spiritual work, which is gained only in that "this substantial objectivity and trust, in which the self does not know itself as free individual . . . in this inner subjectivity, in the

101. *Ibid*.

102. The outrage at Spinoza's definition of God as the only substance (see *Ethics . . .* , def. VI, with prop. XIV, pp. 39 and 49) is in Hegel's view justified since this definition seems to have given up the subject-character or personality (the self-consciousness) of God. See *Phenomenology*, p. 80: "If the generation which heard God spoken of as the One Substance was shocked and revolted by such a characterization of his nature, the reason lay partly in the instinctive feeling that in such a conception self-consciousness was simply submerged, and not preserved."

103. J. W. von Goethe, "Epirrhema," *Goethes Werke* [Weimarer Ausgabe] (Weimar: Hermann Böhlau, 1890), III, 88.

104. Hegel, *Phenomenology*, p. 707.

105. *Ibid.*, p. 750.

106. *Ibid.*, p. 704.

107. *Ibid.*, p. 709.

self becoming free, falls into ruins."[108] In that the spirit emerges ". . . as an extreme—that of self-consciousness grasping itself as essential and ultimate,"[109] the world of substance becomes for it mere material on which the inward reality can express itself as a self by forming that matter, giving it the form of the spirit. The "activity with which the spirit brings itself forth as object" is art. In art as mental *activity*, the "substance," which by definition is quiescent in itself, "has itself become this fluid and undifferentiated essence." As "pure form," that is, as pure act, art is "the night in which the substance was betrayed, and made itself subject."[110]

In order to understand Hegel's proposition that "the substance made itself subject," some terminological reminders are needed.[111] Originally "substance" was just another name for "subject." What was meant was that which was foundational (*hypokeimenon*), which was already present, which is present in and of itself. Everything which comes to be and was not already there arises out of something which was already there, which was its foundation or source. What is behind or beneath everything else is the foundation on which other things are able to exist. It is *subiectum*. Of course, there can be foundational things for which something else is the foundation. But what has nothing more beneath it or behind it bears its essence or nature (*ousia*) in itself. It is the foundation for other things but has itself no external foundation, and is identical with its own grounding. It is self-dependent. As something self-dependent it is its own foundation and the foundation for other things. The *identity* of essence or nature (*ousia*) and foundation (*hypokeimenon*), which as self-independence has always existed, is expressed in the word "*substantia*," which is differentiated from essence (*Wesen*), which is not its own foundation, as "*essentia*."

The formulation of the Christian doctrine of the Trinity took place within this terminology. But this dogmatic process paved the way for a terminological exchange which did not finally make its breakthrough until much later, and then with the barest memory of its earlier preparation. The doctrine of the Trinity asserted that God's essence (*Wesen*; that which God is: *ousia*) was self-dependent in relation to other nondivine things, but that this self-dependence existed in three differentiated ways of being, which were related to each other in the highest form conceivable. The divine essence had its own foundation, identical with itself, but this was threefold. Its self-dependence was grounded in a threefold manner: one essence in three foundational states (*mia ousia en trisin hypostasesin*), three *hypostases*. These three hypostases were conceived in terms of *persons* (the later term), based on the New Testament, that is, in the form of an existing one which can say "I" or can address another "I," as "Father," as "Son," and as "Spirit." Thus the terminological exchange was prepared which later was to

108. *Ibid.*, p. 711.
109. *Ibid.*
110. *Ibid.*, p. 712. One cannot deny totally the idea that Hegel is referring to the passion story in this citation. For "the Lord Jesus on the night when he was betrayed took bread . . . and said, 'This is my body. . . .' " For Hegel, the death of the Lord probably found its correspondent action in the process in which the substance of the bread and the wine was elevated to the dignity of the subject of the Lord arising from death.
111. See for the following brief explanation Martin Heidegger, *Nietzsche II* (Pfullingen: Günther Neske, 1961), pp. 296f, and "Aus der letzten Marburger Vorlesung," in *Zeit und Geschichte; Dankesgabe an Rudolf Bultmann zum 80. Geburtstag* (Tübingen: Mohr [Siebeck], 1964), pp. 491ff.

think of the subject as an "I," as "subject" in the modern sense of the word, so that the subject could be understood in its self-dependence (ego) as the foundation of the objectivity of all objects. This meant that it was conceived of in such a way that the old meaning of subject and substance (*subiectum, substantia*) was covered in a completely new fashion.

This terminological transformation had its effect not only within theological premises, but also in the sphere of epistemological and metaphysical premises. Since Descartes, the "I think" ('cogito') is regarded as the actual foundation of all that exists. The human ego is *subiectum* to the extent that it thinks, is mentally active. As mentally active ego the "*subiectum*" becomes "subject." Leibniz then ascribes to every substance a 'principle of action' (*principium actionis*), an 'active power' (*vis activa*) which is not dependent on anything else, an "original urge" which makes the substance a unit which unites itself, the monad. Based on this original urge, Leibniz regards the substance as the monad which is comparable to the ego: "I hold the substance itself, furnished with the original active and passive power, just like the ego or similar, to be the indivisible and perfect monad."[112] This definition of substance is oriented to the ego as the primary theme of substantiality, whereby the ego is still understood entirely in the sense of the self-dependence of the *subiectum* and yet already in the sense of the active subject. When this ego then "knows," what it knows becomes its "object." In knowing, the ego goes forth from itself as a seeker, finds something against which it "collides," and thus finds its "object." In knowing the subject is now dependent on the object. In that sense the subject as such is dependent on things outside of itself. It needs "mediation," is no longer what it once was when it was still called *subiectum*. That the knowing subject in the act of knowing draws the object into itself, overcomes its object as object and destroys it, reveals the degree to which the "subject" desires as ego to be the absolute *subiectum*. All objects should ultimately be dependent on the subject, which can endure its dependence on the world of objects only temporarily but not permanently. Therefore, the "I think" transforms itself into "I make."

According to Hegel the substance made itself subject in the activity of art. Here again the subject manipulates the world as its material and brings forth from it, without its help, as though out of nothing, the work of art in which it realizes itself. It sounds like a commentary on Schiller's famous poem[113] when

---

112. Letter to de Volder, June 20, 1703, as cited in Heidegger, "Aus der letzten Marburger Vorlesung," *op. cit.*, p. 496.

113. See F. Schiller, "The Ideal and the Actual Life," in *Poetical Works of Friedrich Schiller*, tr. P. E. Pinkerton (London: Robertson, Ashford, and Bentley, 1902), I, 85-89:

"When, through dead stone to breathe a soul of light,
With the dull matter to unite
The kindling genius, some great sculptor glows;
Behold him straining, every nerve intent—
Behold now, o'er the subject element,
The stately thought its march laborious goes!
For never, save to toil untiring, spoke
The unwilling truth from her mysterious well—
The statue only to the chisel's stroke
Wakes from its marble cell.
But onward to the sphere of beauty—go
Onward, O child of art! and, lo!

Hegel writes: "This pure activity, conscious of its inalienable force, wrestles with the unembodied essential being. Becoming its master, this negative activity has turned the element of pathos into its own material, and given itself its content; and this unity comes out as a work, universal spirit individualized and consciously presented."[114] Hegel understands the substance's "making itself into subject" as "the incarnation in human form of the Divine Being" beginning "with the statue."[115] In the religion of art, this incarnation of the Divine Being goes so far that consciousness is only completely certain of itself, while "all essential content is swallowed up and submerged."[116] To grasp this "light-hearted folly"[117] in its profound seriousness is the concern of revealed religion.

As revelation, revealed religion is the consummation of the religions and simultaneously the revelation of that knowledge which is known in philosophy as knowledge. For that reason, one cannot deal with the content of revealed religion without constantly addressing the relationship between religion and philosophy. The Hegelian use of the concept of the death of God, which does belong to the content of revealed religion, is correspondingly two-sided, if not ambiguous.

If the subject is distinguished from substance in that the subject is not itself without some other, then the self-certainty in which consciousness is only totally certain of itself is not yet the complete definition of the subject. As long as that "other" is only an object to be worked on by the subject, to be formed according to the image of the subject (the statue!), then the subject is its own object in that "other," it "possesses only the thought of itself," while the reality of that "other" is completely lost to it. "Consequently it is merely stoic independence, the independence of thought; and this finds, by passing through the process of scepticism, its ultimate truth in that form we called the 'unhappy self-consciousness' . . ."[118] The consciousness is unhappy because it is alone with itself, and outside of itself there is only death. "The statues set up are now corpses in stone whence the animating soul has flown."[119] Consciousness cannot become happy with itself in its self-certain isolation. In that it is a *self* for itself alone and denies self-existence to anything else, it not only loses that substance which is autonomous but basically also its own being, which was supposed to consist of coming to itself with some other. For that reason it is unhappy with itself. Jean Paul expressed religiously the unhappy loneliness of the self-consciousness which knows only death outside itself, in his "The Dead Christ proclaims that there is no God"[120]: "How every one is so alone in the vast crypt

---

Out of the matter which thy pains control
The statue springs!—not as with labour wrung
Airy and light—the offspring of the soul!
The pangs, the cares, the weary toils it cost
Leave not a trace when once the work is done—"
114. Hegel, *Phenomenology*, p. 712.
115. *Ibid.*, p. 750.
116. *Ibid.*
117. *Ibid.*
118. *Ibid.*, p. 752.
119. *Ibid.*, p. 753.
120. Jean Paul, *Flower, Fruit, and Thorn Pieces,* bk. II, ch. VIII, pp. 259-65. On the genesis of the treatise, see my essay "Vom Tod des lebendigen Gottes," in *Unterwegs zur Sache; Theologische Bemerkungen* (München: C. Kaiser, 1972), p. 109, n. 7.

of the universe! I am only next to myself. . . ."[121] Analogously, Hegel says, "It is consciousness of the loss . . . of substance as well as of self; it is the bitter pain which finds expression in the cruel words, 'God is dead'."[122]

In revealed religion this situation of consciousness becomes the *content* of consciousness. The concept of the death of God, which comprehends the unhappy consciousness, is revealed as a moment of the being of God and thus is seen as a necessity. For revealed religion distinguishes itself as absolute religion from the preceding forms of religion in that it perceives the necessity of becoming in which the substance becomes self-consciousness ". . . and, just on that account, is spirit."[123] The necessity of this becoming cannot be *produced*. Becoming *reveals* itself, rather, in the *immediate* perception, in which ". . . God is beheld sensuously and immediately as a self, as a real individual human being."[124] For Hegel, "this incarnation of the Divine Being . . . is the simple content of Absolute Religion,"[125] toward which the preceding forms of religion were pressing, without being able to produce it as their content. "The hopes and expectations of preceding ages pressed forward to, and were solely directed towards this revelation. . . ."[126] Their forms "compose the periphery of the circle of shapes and forms, which attend, an expectant and eager throng, around the birthplace of spirit as it becomes self-consciousness. Their center is the yearning agony of the unhappy, despairing self-consciousness, a pain which permeates all of them and is the common birth pang at its production. . . ."[127] This emergence can, however, take place only as revelation, although the *content* of revealed religion "has partly been met with already, as the idea of the '*unhappy*' and the '*believing*' consciousness,"[128] but not as revealed, as perceived necessity.

To be sure, revealed religion too, *as religion*, is limited to the *perceiving* of necessity. It has the notion of the spirit only as a figurative thought, but not yet as a notion which grasps itself, not yet as the notion of notions. To that degree, revealed religion is only the "first revelation"[129] of the spirit, and the perceived necessity of its content is not yet grasped as a necessity. Since revealed religion, instead of conceiving notionally, simply thinks pictorially, "it has the content without its necessity."[130] Thus, it works with "natural relations" like the relationship of father to son and transfers them "into the realm of pure consciousness,"[131] which is God. But as an "inner element," these pictorial thoughts possess the notion which knows itself to be notion, so that it would be irresponsible for Hegel to dispute the truth of the content of revealed religion and to degrade it "into a historical imaginative idea and an heirloom handed down by tradition."[132]

121. Jean Paul, *op. cit.*, p. 264.
122. Hegel, *Phenomenology*, pp. 752f.
123. *Ibid.*, p. 756.
124. *Ibid.*, p. 758.
125. *Ibid.*
126. *Ibid.*, p. 761.
127. *Ibid.*, p. 755.
128. *Ibid.*, p. 765.
129. *Ibid.*, p. 760.
130. *Ibid.*, p. 767.
131. *Ibid.*
132. *Ibid.*, p. 768.

In the form of pictorial thinking revealed religion makes known that the spirit comes to itself and is certain of itself only in a *movement* in which it divides into the most extreme *opposites* and yet recognizes the absolute opposites again as being *the same*. The religious ideas for this double movement are known as creation and reconciliation. Both pictorial thoughts are simultaneously the expression of negation, even though they appear to be positive. That the eternal, the "only eternal abstract spirit," becomes something else, that, to use Spinoza's terms, God thought of as *natura naturans* ('nature naturalized' or 'becoming') naturalizes himself into *natura naturata* ('nature perfected'), is expressed in the language of religion this way: "It creates a world. This 'Creation' is the word which pictorial thought uses to convey the notion itself in its absolute movement. . . ."[133] The created world is, however, not only that other which is set in contradiction to the "only eternal" spirit, but is as alienated spirit a "self-concentration" and thus also a separation of the inward and the outward, a division into opposites. The pictorial thought of religion calls this separation of the alienated spirit as world the fall of man (or the fall of the firstborn son of light concentrating on himself). The contradiction of good and evil emerges from the innocent spirit. The spirit itself, the selfhood of the spirit, is regarded now as the good, whereas the self-concentrating thought, who thinks the spirit, appears as the evil. In the opposition of good and evil the contrast is taken up between world and "only eternal" spirit. This contrast, too, is to be conceived of as movement, so that now the renunciation of abstract eternity or "the Divine Being 'humbling' Itself" is imagined as the good, to which evil is opposed "as an event extraneous and alien to the Divine Being. . . ."[134] The religious pictorial thought that evil belongs to the divine being in the form of divine wrath is, according to Hegel, only "the supreme effort, the severest strain, of which figurative thought, wrestling with its own limitations, is capable, an effort which, since it is devoid of the notion, remains a fruitless struggle."[135] The pictorial thought of divine wrath, viewed as fruitless, is, however, then connected to the religious idea that the self-humiliation of the divine being did not have to take place. Rather, "this is pictured as a spontaneous action"—an idea which Hegel immediately corrects, "but the necessity for its self-abandonment lies in the notion that what is inherently essential, and gets this specific character merely through opposition, has just on that account no real independent subsistence."[136] What religion imagines as the voluntary deed of God really happens with the necessity of the notion, namely, that the simple being of the substance "empties and abandons itself, vies itself unto death, and so reconciles Absolute Being with its own self."[137] This death sets aside the contradiction which religion had established with the idea of the creation of a world, so that the spirit alienated from itself through this "second process of becoming other" re-emerges as spirit: ". . . this death (of immediacy) is therefore its rising anew as spirit. . . ."[138]

The *death* of the divine being is therefore thought of in the *Phenomenology*

133. *Ibid.*, p. 769.
134. *Ibid.*, p. 773.
135. *Ibid.*
136. *Ibid.*, p. 774.
137. *Ibid.*
138. *Ibid.*, p. 775.

as integral to the divine self-humiliation. Here again the incarnation of God stands under the overarching sign of his death. Hegel interprets the succession of the contents of revealed religion, the dogmatic moments in the doctrine of the incarnation, from their end point. It is only after the necessity of this death has been conceived of that the ideas that "the Divine Being 'takes on' human nature" (*assumptio humanae naturae*) and that "the Divine Being empties Itself of Itself and is made flesh" (*incarnatio*) are understood.[139] The pictorial thought of the 'assumption of human nature' is intended, by calling on the doctrine "that the Divine Being from the beginning empties Itself of Itself," to mean "that implicitly and inherently the two"—God and man—"are not separate."[140] The pictorial thought of the incarnation of the Logos, further, expresses the *"reconciliation* of the Divine Being with its *other* as a whole," and especially "with the thought of this other—*evil*—", even if the expression is not spiritual but figurative.[141] It is essential to reconciliation with this other (evil) that this other (evil) as other (evil) must disappear. The Divine Being as it empties itself participates in this process of disappearance. It dies to that extent *in* its unity with the other. Its death is the death of the mediator. The "dead Divine Man, or Human God" is the perfect mediation between substance and subject, is "universal self-consciousness," if only *"implicitly."*[142] In the death of the mediator, not only the human nature but also the divine nature (in the sense of "the abstraction of Divine Being") died, and the contradiction between the two is set aside. Reconciliation appears as a double loss. The *"immediately* present God" dies with the individual person (Jesus) and "His being passes over into His *having been."*[143] This double loss is *felt* as the "bitterness of feeling of the 'unhappy consciousness', when it feels that God Himself is dead."[144] The "harsh utterance" which formulates the content of this feeling expresses the *movement of knowledge* which, through "the loss of the Substance and of its objective existence over against consciousness," allows "the return of consciousness into the depth of darkness where Ego is nothing but bare identity with Ego." That, however, allows "the pure subjectivity of Substance, the pure certainty of itself" to arise.[145]

Thus the death of God, in its consequences, is understood as an eminently positive event. As the negation of negation, the knowledge it makes possible has become "the spiritualization, whereby Substance becomes Subject, by which its abstraction and lifelessness have expired, and Substance therefore has become real, simple, and universal self-consciousness."[146] For the whole Hegelian undertaking, it is decisive that death has its natural meaning only on the level of religious pictorial thought. Revealed religion imagines the death of God as the death of a divine man, who experiences "death . . . *qua* death" as an human

139. *Ibid.*, pp. 775f.
140. *Ibid.*, p. 775.
141. *Ibid.*, p. 776.
142. *Ibid.*, p. 778.
143. *Ibid.*, p. 762.
144. *Ibid.*, p. 782.
145. *Ibid.*
146. *Ibid.*

individual.[147] It is only when religion *grasps* the imaginative idea "that through an event,—the event of God's emptying Himself of His Divine Being through His factual incarnation and His Death," "that the Divine Being is reconciled with its existence," only then for religion does death cease "to signify what it means directly—the non-existence of *this* individual—and becomes transfigured into the universality of the spirit, which lives in its own communion, dies there daily, and daily rises again."[148] To conceive of this daily dying and rising of the spirit as *one* context is a matter of the notion in which the spirit *knows* of its death and is thus already risen. In the consciousness of the necessity of death, it is itself overcome. Therefore, *knowledge* itself cannot really die "as the particular person is pictorially imagined to have really died"; rather "its particularity expires in its universality."[149] This knowledge, in its abstract negativity, sets aside death as such. It knows that it is a moment of life. On the basis of the death of God as imagined in revealed religion, it has always known the "spiritual resurrection."[150] As knowledge, its point of departure is the reconciliation of the absolute opposites which has already taken place, where religion's *imaginative thought* of reconciliation distinguishes itself from reconciliation itself as an event which took place "in the distance of the *past*," and sees it *own* reconciliation "as something remote, something far away in the *future*."[151] In contrast to the imaginative thought of religion with its eschatology, knowledge recognizes the reconciliation of opposites to be in the *present*. And "this knowledge breaks out into the 'yea, yea', with which one extreme meets another."[152] This does not happen outside of philosophy, but in philosophy the *Yes* of the spirit to itself takes place, the *Yes* which re-internalizes the *No* and preserves it inwardly.

(c) Philosophy, however, had to go to great labors in order to be able to produce such a Yes. It had to recognize its *historical* task and resolve it. This task, for Hegel, consisted of seeing through the Enlightenment's emptying of faith of its content as an unsatisfactory Enlightenment[153] and to aid the *truth* of enlightenment, that "heaven is transplanted to the earth below,"[154] to break

147. *Ibid.*, p. 780.
148. *Ibid.*
149. *Ibid.*, p. 781. On the significance of death as "the negation . . . of the individual as a factor existing within the universal," see *ibid.*, pp. 605ff. There this death is called "the sole and only word and deed accomplished by universal freedom," which negates the abstract existence of the freedom of the individual self-consciousness as the "unfulfilled punctual entity of the absolutely free self." Death as the negation of the particular individual is then for Hegel the "most . . . meaningless death of all, with no more significance than cleaving a head of cabbage. . . ."
150. *Ibid.*, p. 780.
151. *Ibid.*, p. 784.
152. *Ibid.*, p. 783.
153. *Ibid.*, pp. 588f.
154. *Ibid.*, p. 598. What Hegel called the truth of the Enlightenment in the *Phenomenology* was what he called the task "reserved . . . for our epoch" in his early treatise "The Positivity of the Christian Religion." There he made the characteristic differentiation between theory and praxis: "Apart from some earlier attempts, it has been reserved in the main for our epoch to vindicate at least in theory the human ownership of the treasures formerly squandered on heaven; but what age will have the strength to validate this right in practice and make itself its possessor?" ("The Positivity of the Christian Religion," in *Early Theological Writings*, tr. T. M. Knox [Chicago: The University of Chicago Press, 1948], p. 159). Even later, Hegel did not trust philosophy to exercise this power. "It is

through, against the apparently satisfied Enlightenment, by recapturing philo-sophically the content of faith. Philosophy had to grasp that in revealed religion heaven itself *has come* to earth. Philosophy had to reconcile Christianity with the Enlightenment. To do that, it needed and used the dark statement, the Death of God. Its usage reflected the historical reconciliation of Reformation and En-lightenment through Hegelian philosophy as the reconciliation of the spirit with itself, and thus it made a concept of God possible which will prove itself in historical reality because it comprehends this historical reality in the process.

The spirit which knows itself has, as was required in 1802, unending agony as an inherent moment of itself. The most painful negation, death, belongs to God's history and is constitutive for the speculative concept of God: *God is spirit.* For "the life of mind is not one that shuns death, and keeps clear of destruction; it endures death and in death maintains its being. It only wins to its truth when it finds itself utterly torn asunder. It is this mighty power . . . only by looking the negative in the face, and dwelling with it. This dwelling beside it is the magical power that converts the negative in being."[155]

That it is *revealed religion* which expresses what philosophical science brings to consciousness as true knowledge[156] makes clear how much for Hegel the "harsh utterance" that God himself is dead had retained its original *Sitz im Leben.* The indissoluble relationship of death and resurrection also indicates that the usage of the harsh utterance is more than just accidental. To be sure, the name Jesus Christ never appears in the entire *Phenomenology of Mind.* He even expressly considers "(avoiding) the name 'God', because this word is not in its primary use a conception as well, but the special name of an underlying subject, its fixed resting place. . . ."[157] But that the name "God" can become a notion only because God himself, God's Being, is *becoming* "over the under-lying subject, its fixed resting place," is a christological truth. Certainly, it is a christological truth translated into philosophy; but it is translated into a philos-ophy which places itself under the condition of truth which it claims to grasp. To affirm and to conceptualize one's own theological conditionedness—that is the translation task as which Hegel's philosophy is carried out.

4. Hegel's texts interest us as classical references for the emigration of talk about the death of God from theology to philosophy. At first it was a matter of the entry of talk about the death of God into philosophy, still full of chris-tological connections. But then that which "otherwise was historical" is thought

---

just as absurd to fancy that a philosophy can transcend its contemporary world as it is to fancy that an individual can overleap his own age. . . . If his theory really goes beyond the world as it is and builds an ideal one *as it ought to be,* that world exists indeed, but only in his opinions, an unsubstantial element where anything you please may, in fancy, be built" (*Hegel's Philosophy of Right,* tr. T. M. Knox [Oxford: Oxford University Press, 1949], p. 11). That sounds like a precautionary riposte to the Feuerbach thesis of Karl Marx, which caused such a furor: "The philosophers have only *interpreted* the world, in various ways; the point, however, is to *change* it" (from "Theses on Feuerbach," in K. Marx and F. Engels, *On Religion* [Moscow: Foreign Languages Publishing House, 1957], p. 72).
155. *Phenomenology,* p. 93.
156. *Ibid.,* p. 801.
157. *Ibid.,* p. 124.

anew as speculative philosophy. And that prepares the way for the emigration of talk about the death of God into an anti-theological philosophy.

The older Hegel did make the express claim once again that he had thought out anew the actual truth of theology, which had been forgotten by the theologians. With regard to the doctrine of the incarnation and of the death of God, his opinion was similar to what he remarked in a letter to the Halle theologian Tholuck (dated July 3, 1826), in response to reading an historical treatise by Tholuck on the development of the speculative trinitarian doctrine of the later oriental church:[158] "Does not the high Christian insight into God as the Triune merit a completely different awe than merely to ascribe it to an externally historical process? In your entire essay I could neither find nor feel a trace of your own sensibility for this doctrine. I am a Lutheran and through philosophy am all the more confirmed in Lutheranism. I will not permit myself to be satisfied with external historical explanation when it comes to such basic doctrines. There is a higher spirit there than merely that of human tradition. It is an outrage to me to see these things explained in a way comparable to the lineage and dissemination of silk manufacture, cherry growing, or the pox."[159]

Hegel also thought that he must perceive such a higher spirit than that of human tradition in the idea of the death of God. In his Berlin *Lectures on the Philosophy of Religion,* he interprets this concept expressly and pointedly as a true expression of Christian faith.[160] Talk of the death of God is then encountered explicitly in the context of the exposition of the story of Jesus Christ.

The Berlin lectures present the death of Jesus Christ as the turning point in the *understanding* of the story of Jesus. At the cross, according to Hegel, belief and unbelief separate in their capacity to understand. Up to the death of Jesus, his story is also accessible to unbelief: "This is the outward history of Christ, which is for unbelief just what the history of Socrates is for us. With the *death* of Christ, however, there begins the conversion of consciousness. The death of Christ is the central point around which all else turns, and in the conception formed of it lies the difference between the outward way of con-

---

158. A. Tholuck, *Die speculative Trinitätslehre des späteren Orients; Eine religions-philosophische Monographie aus handschriftlichen Quellen der Leydener, Oxforder und Berliner Bibliothek bearbeitet* (Berlin: Wiengandt & Grieben, 1826).

159. Hegel, *Briefe von und an Hegel*, ed. J. Hoffmeister, 4 vols., ed. R. Flechsig (*Philosophische Bücherei*, 238) (Hamburg: Felix Meiner Verlag, 1961), IV, 29. See also *Lectures on the Philosophy of Religion*, II, 345: "It is primarily philosophy which today represents orthodoxy *par excellence*; the propositions which have always been maintained, the basic truths of Christianity are maintained and preserved by it" [my translation—TR].

160. The Christian faith, according to the Berlin *Lectures on the Philosophy of History* (tr. J. Sibree [New York: Dover, 1956], pp. 347f), is grasped in the schematic of absolute revealed religion. This religion finds its counterpart in the world before it is elevated into the philosophy of absolute spirit. The world which corresponds to religion is the state. In place of the *contradiction* which has always been asserted between religion and the world, Hegel desires only to maintain that there is a difference between them. Religion is "a temple in which Truth and Freedom in God are presented to the conceptive faculty," "Reason in the soul and heart." This inner characteristic finds its counterpart in the worldliness of the state, which stands as "a temple of Human Freedom concerned with the perception and volition of a reality" (of God), next to the temple of "Truth and Freedom" which are merely "presented to the conceptive faculty" (*ibid.*, p. 347).

ceiving of it and Faith, i.e., regarding it with the spirit, taking our start from the spirit of truth, from the Holy Spirit."[161] How does this happen?

The "outward way of conceiving it," on which unbelief is fixed, understands the history of the man Jesus as a history without God. Faith, on the other hand, perceives, in contrast with unbelief, the historicity of the eternal God in the mortal history of Christ. It interprets the life of Jesus as the life-story of God. And just as faith "explains the life of Christ," so also "the teaching of Christ and His miracles are conceived of and understood in connection with this witness of the Spirit."[162] For only "faith is essentially the consciousness . . . of what God is in His true nature. . . . He is the life-process, the Trinity, in which the Universal puts itself into antithesis with itself, and is in this antithesis identical with itself. . . . Faith simply lays hold of the thought and has the consciousness that in Christ this absolute essential truth is perceived in the process of its development, and it is through Him that this truth has first been revealed."[163]

Faith can, however, understand his human existence as the appearance of the incarnate God only from the perspective of the end point of the human story of Jesus Christ. For the *life* of Jesus is, to say the least, ambiguous. Therefore, the understanding of the *death* of Christ is the decisive point at which one can recognize in his history more than, say, the story of Socrates or any other human history. For the passion and death of Jesus Christ do "away with the human side of Christ's nature, and it is just in connection with this death that the transition is made into the religious sphere; and here the question comes to be as to how this death is to be conceived of."[164]

Therefore, the death of Jesus Christ may not be understood as only a "natural death," caused by "injustice, hate, and violence."[165] Rather, faith must verify itself by this death, so that it begins to understand who Jesus Christ was on the basis of this death. "Christ's death is accordingly the touchstone, so to speak, by means of which Faith verifies its belief, since it is essentially here that its way of understanding the appearance of Christ makes itself manifest. Christ's death primarily means that Christ was the God-man, the God who had at the same time human nature, even unto death."[166]

161. *Lectures on the Philosophy of Religion*, III, 86.
162. *Ibid.*, p. 88. In the edition of the *Freunde des Verewigten*, XII, 249, it is put more clearly: "The doctrine, the words of this person are only perceived and understood truly by faith."
163. *Ibid.*, p. 87.
164. *Ibid.*
165. *Ibid.*
166. *Ibid.*, p. 89. Falk Wagner has analyzed the significance of the "death of God" for the unity of Christology and Ecclesiology in the Berlin lectures: *Der Gedanke der Persönlichkeit Gottes bei Fichte und Hegel* (Gütersloh: G. Mohn, 1971), pp. 273ff. Correctly, Wagner emphasizes (pp. 286ff) the theological progress in the understanding of God in the older Hegel over against the understanding of God in the *Phenomenology of Mind*: God does not first *become* self-consciousness in the knowledge of the church but *is* "as the personality who fulfills itself in the inner-trinitarian personal community" (*ibid.*, p. 288), which shows itself as eternal love in the death of Jesus Christ.

Michael Theunissen points in the same direction in his masterful commentary on the section of the *Enzyclopädie* which deals with the doctrine of the absolute spirit: *Hegels Lehre vom absoluten Geist als theologisch-politischer Traktat* (Berlin: de Gruyter, 1970).

It is fascinating to see in Hegel's exposition how Luther's dogmatic insights are made hermeneutically fruitful. The 'theology of the cross' (*theologia crucis*) asserts its material insights hermeneutically at this point. The crucifixion of Jesus Christ is regarded not only as *the decisive event of his life* but also as *the criterion for the proper understanding* of his being. It is therefore appropriate and useful to distinguish the various points of view under which the death of Jesus Christ is significant to Hegel.

First of all, this death is understood by Hegel as an experience which is constitutive of the human being of man. Dying is human. "It is the lot of finite humanity to die." To that extent, the death of Jesus Christ is, first of all, "the most complete proof of [the] humanity" of Christ. His death is the criterion for his "absolute finitude." And since, in addition, Jesus Christ died "the aggravated death of the evil-doer. . . , the death even of shame and dishonor on the cross," "in Him humanity was carried to its furthest point" at this ending of a human life.[167] In his dying, Jesus Christ is the ultimate realization of the human being. In his dishonor is demonstrated that he was completely a man.[168]

However, Hegel continues: ". . . a further determination comes into play— God has died, God is dead,—this is the most frightful of all thoughts, that all that is eternal, all that is true is not, that negation itself is found in God; the deepest sorrow, the feeling of something completely irretrievable, the renunciation of everything of a higher kind are connected with this."[169] The death of the man Jesus would not really have been understood theologically at all, in the strict sense, if it were taken to be only the end of a human life. As such it is only the negation of one individual existence, what Hegel called in the *Phenomenology of Mind* "that meaningless death . . . with no more significance than cleaving a head of cabbage."[170] It would be descent into the past, but nothing more. Only if God himself is present in the individual existence of this man can the death of Jesus Christ gain any religious significance. For that very reason faith confesses that God himself died. If God himself died, then what the *Phenomenology of the Mind* calls a "turning around" takes place: ". . . that meaningless death, the unfilled, vacuous negativity of self, in its inner constitutive principle, turns round into absolute positivity."[171] Accordingly, Hegel continues in the *Lectures on the Philosophy of Religion*: "The course of thought does not, however, stop short here; on the contrary, thought [now][172] begins to retrace its

167. *Lectures on the Philosophy of Religion*, p. 89.
168. After faith has recognized in a man killed in such a way that he was God himself, death by crucifixion must place the state which used such a means of execution radically in question. For "what the state characterises as degrading, is transformed into what is highest." But once the cross has "been elevated to the place of a banner, . . . inner feeling is in the very heart of its nature detached from civil and state life, and the substantial basis of this latter is taken away, so that the whole structure has no longer any reality, but is an empty appearance, which must soon come crashing down, and make manifest in actual existence that it is no longer anything having inherent existence" (*ibid.*, p. 90).
169. *Ibid.*, p. 91.
170. *Phenomenology of Mind*, p. 605.
171. *Ibid.*, p. 609.
172. Is this "now" one that denounces deduction, a "now" which construes and speculates treacherously? Or is it a "now" which tells about revelation and thus legitimately thinks through and speculates on what has happened? [N.B.: "now" is not in the English edition but is in the German original—TR.]

steps; God, that is to say, maintains Himself in this process, and the latter is only the death of death."[173]

In using the term "death of death" Hegel enters directly into the theological terminology of Luther. We find the expression "death of death" (*mors mortis*) a number of times in Luther, and its essence is also found in a genuine Luther hymn.[174] The issue here is a christological category which discusses the death of Jesus Christ from the perspective of his resurrection and of the salvation for the believer which is contained in that death. The death of the Crucified One reveals itself in the resurrection of Jesus Christ as the death of death for the benefit of humanity and thus as an event of God's love for godless men. Hegel's exposition is in the same general theological area, although we will have to deal critically with the unmistakable differences: "It is a proof of infinite love that God identified Himself with what was foreign to His nature in order to slay it. This is the signification of the death of Christ. Christ has borne the sins of the world, He has reconciled God to us, as it is said."[175]

For the crucifixion is understood, in the final analysis, as an event in which Hegel's most important category has, so to speak, its *Sitz im Leben*. In the death of Jesus Christ "this death of death . . . the negative of the negative" takes place.[176] The truth of divine life thus emerges from the depths of death: resurrection *from* the dead is conceived of as resurrection *out* of death, ultimately as the event of death's self-negation. Since God is in death, death negates itself. "God comes to life again, and thus things are reversed. The Resurrection is something which thus essentially belongs to faith."[177] Ultimately, ". . . it is faith . . . resting on the testimony of the Spirit . . . which explains the life of Christ. The teaching of Christ and His miracles are conceived of and understood in connection with this witness of the Spirit. The history of Christ is related, too [*scil.* only], by those upon whom the Spirit has already been poured out."[178]

Hegel summarizes once more: " 'God Himself is dead', as it is said in a Lutheran hymn; the consciousness of this fact expresses the truth that the human, the finite, frailty, weakness, the negative, is itself a divine moment, is in God Himself; that otherness or Other-Being, the finite, the negative, is not outside of God. . . . otherness, the negation, is consciously known to be a moment of the Divine nature. The highest knowledge of the nature of the Idea of Spirit is contained in this thought."[179] But for Hegel this highest knowledge implies that "man has attained to the certainty of being one with God, that mankind is the directly present Spirit."[180] According to Hegel, "it is this which creates the consciousness, the knowledge, that God is a Trinity."[181]

173. Hegel, *Philosophy of Religion*, p. 91.
174. "Die Schrift hat verkündet das, wie ein Tod den andern frass; Ein Spott aus dem Tod ist worden. Halleluja" (*Evangelisches Kirchengesangbuch*, nr. 76, verse 4) ("The Scriptures have proclaimed how one death devoured another; death has been scorned. Hallelujah"). See *WA*, 15, 218, 26f; Luther, *A Commentary on St. Paul's Epistle to the Galatians*, ed. P. S. Watson (Westwood, NJ: Fleming H. Revell, 1953), p. 273.
175. Hegel, *Lectures on the Philosophy of Religion*, III, 93.
176. *Ibid.*, p. 91 n.
177. *Ibid.*, pp. 91f.
178. *Ibid.*, p. 88.
179. *Ibid.*, p. 98.
180. *Ibid.*
181. *Ibid.*, p. 99.

This point of the whole undertaking, to translate theology into philosophy, is, of course, also the point at which theology and philosophy confront each other in strong opposition. We may certainly regard the fact that Hegel understood the trinitarian dogma as an explication of the meaning of the death of Jesus Christ as a demonstration of an admirable awareness of the problem, both from its historical and its dogmatic aspects. Hegel's *philosophy* of religion represents in any event a high-water mark of the first order in the *history of theology*, in that here the 'theology of the cross' and the doctrine of the Trinity mutually encourage and establish each other.

Regardless of any theological criticism which must be rendered, we are dealing here with a grand theological accomplishment, namely, a philosophically conceived theology of the Crucified One *as* the doctrine of the Triune God. Hegel unambiguously reminds the theologians of his day: "The reconciliation believed in as being in Christ has no meaning if God is not known as Trinity, if it is not recognised that He *is* but at the same time the Other, the self-differentiating, the Other in the sense that this Other is God Himself, and has potentially the divine nature in it, and that the abolishing of this difference, of this otherness, this return, this love, is Spirit. [Better: "this return of this love is Spirit"—TR.] . . . These are the moments with which we are here concerned, and which express the truth that Man has come to a consciousness of that eternal history, that eternal movement which God Himself is."[182]

Only after one has perceived how the philosopher has done theology as 'theology of the cross' (in contrast with the great Schleiermacher who in this regard has unfortunately nothing to offer) is it permissible to advance any *criticism* of Hegel's great theological achievement.[183] Once this has been perceived and properly honored, then the critical query is unavoidable as to whether Hegel's new attempt at developing a doctrine of God oriented to the crucifixion of Jesus Christ does not result in a restitution of the old doctrine that God became a man so that man might be deified. Although not as Alcides, who, as a perfected god, "cast down his garb of clay, / and rent in hallowing flame away / The mortal part from the divine. . . ,"[184] still man would become a spirit which develops his humanity into true divinity, becoming *utterly* spirit as a result. God became man in Jesus Christ in order to distinguish definitively between God and man forever, and this fundamental soteriological aspect is not dealt with by Hegel, but instead is turned into its opposite. Hegel's God needs man, who thereby becomes divine himself. It may be that the God who is in the process of coming to himself uses man and in that act of "development" elevates him to himself. It may be that man uses God while en route to the depths of the spirit, so that instead of crying out to God 'from the deeps' (*de profoundis*), he elevates himself

182. *Ibid.*, pp. 99f.

183. Wolfhart Pannenberg ("The Significance of Christianity in the Philosophy of Hegel," *The Idea of God and Human Freedom*, p. 159) has recently emphasized that Hegel, like no other "of the great thinkers of the modern age," has reasserted the "Christian religion . . . on the basis of the intrinsic rights of religion and the Christian revelation itself."

184. Friedrich Schiller, "The Ideal and the Actual Life," in *Poetical Works of Friedrich Schiller,* tr. P. E. Pinkerton (London: Robertson, Ashford, and Bentley, 1902), I, 89.

to his true height 'out of the deeps' (*e profundis*). Whichever option is chosen, the end result is that one has used, has exploited and destroyed the other.[185] It is irrelevant whether man is the being who uses God or God is the being who uses man—the latter is the more likely one—, the concrete distinction between God and man is jeopardized in either case. By contrast, it would be important here to recognize the human God in the Crucified One, who is both divine and human in that he prevents man from becoming God and liberates him to be man and nothing other than man.

5. We have noted that in 1802 and 1807, Hegel used the "harsh word" of the death of God with a surprising unconcern which leads us to suspect that talk about the death of God was already known to the reader of his day. In his lectures on the philosophy of religion, he names the source of this then common theme: "A Lutheran hymn." We may assume that Hegel was reaching back consciously beyond this Lutheran hymn to Lutheran tradition when he spoke of the death of God. There is further evidence for this available.

One of Hegel's co-students at Tübingen was the later professor of theology at Tübingen, Karl Christian Flatt (1772-1843), who like Hegel was a student of Gottlob Christian Storr (1746-1805). In 1797, Flatt published a book under the title *Philosophical-Exegetical Investigations of the Doctrine of the Reconciliation of Man with God*. At the beginning of this treatise, Flatt presented doctrinal opinions taken from the tradition. In so doing, he quotes, among other things, a statement made by the older Luther, from his essay *Von den Konziliis und Kirchen* ('Of Councils and Churches', 1539), which said in Flatt's version[186]: "If one were to put on the one side of the scales our sins and the wrath of God which they deserve, and on the other side the death and suffering of a mere man, then the first side would push us down into the lowest hell. But if one were to put on the other side God's suffering, God's death, God's blood, or God who suffered for us and died, then it would be much heavier and weightier than our sins and the entire wrath of God. . . ."

The christological function of speaking of the death of God was therefore

185. Hegel's sharpest critic was his earlier co-student in Tübingen, F. W. J. Schelling, whose own position was very close to that of Hegel. He objected, in his *Philosophie der Offenbarung,* to the identification of reality and reasonableness, saying that reason could only comprehend the real Something (*"Was"*), but not the reality of the "That" (*Sämmtliche Werke,* ed. K. F. A. Schelling [Stuttgart and Augsburg: J. G. Cotta, 1858], II/3, p. 65). According to him, Hegel, by thinking of God only in a concept, had like Kant been able to conceive of God only "at the end" (*ibid.,* pp. 45, 105, 172, for his terms), but could not conceive of God as the God "who can initiate something, who above all exists" (*ibid.,* p. 172). The "necessary consequence" was "that God was robbed of all transcendence" (*ibid.,* p. 173). On Schelling's own approach to a Kenotic Christology, see W. Kasper, *Das Absolute in der Geschichte; Philosophie und Theologie der Geschichte in der Spätphilosophie Schellings* (Mainz: Matthais-Grünewald Verlag, 1965); also Kasper, "Krise und Neuanfang der Christologie im Denken Schellings," *Evangelische Theologie,* 33 (1973), 366ff. As a consequence of Schelling's criticism of Hegel, it is not that inappropriate to break off at the correct time the reception of Hegel, although that break is neither "premature" nor certainly "suddenly and groundless" (see M. Welker, "Das theologische Prinzip des Verhaltens zu Zeiterscheinungen; Erörterung eines Problems im Blick auf die theologische Hegelrezeption und Gen 3,22a," *Evangelische Theologie,* 36 [1976], 225ff, especially 228 and 234).

186. C. Chr. Flatt, *Philosophisch-exegetische Untersuchungen über die Lehre von der Versöhnung der Menschen mit Gott* (Göttingen, 1797), I, 69.

not unknown in Hegel's direct setting. The Luther text[187] which Flatt paraphrased would have been known to Hegel, as a part of the Lutheran confessional documents. In the Solid Declaration of the Formula of Concord[188] it follows a few sentences from Luther's great treatise on communion from 1528, and states the following: " 'We Christians must know that unless God is in the balance and throws in weight as a counterbalance, we shall sink to the bottom with our scale. I mean that this way: If it is not true that God died for us, but only a man died, we are lost. But if God's death and God dead lie in the opposite scale, then his side goes down and we go upward like a light and empty pan. Of course, he can also go up again or jump out of his pan. But he could never have sat in the pan unless he had become a man like us, so that it could be said: God dead, God's passion, God's blood, God's death. According to his nature God cannot die, but since God and man are united in one person, it is correct to talk about God's death when that man dies who is one thing or one person with God.' So far Luther. From this it is evident that it is wrongly put to say or to write that the cited locutions, 'God suffered,' 'God died,' are merely empty words which do not correspond to reality." The Formula of Concord makes these statements in the context of its discussion of the doctrine of the *communicatio idiomatum* (the 'communion' or 'exchange' of the properties), which defines the relationship of the divine and human characteristics of Jesus Christ. The first implication of this doctrine of the 'exchange of the properties' is that "any property, though it belongs only to one of the natures, is ascribed not only to the respective nature as something separate but to the entire person who is simultaneously God and man. . . ."[189]

This version of the doctrine of the exchange of properties is a specifically Lutheran doctrine. The Formula of Concord, with its Luther quotation, is battling the Reformed, just as Luther himself was battling Zwingli in the statements of 1528 quoted earlier.[190] Hegel seems to have known about this antithesis when he appeals to a *Lutheran* hymn when speaking of the death of God. He agrees with Lutheranism in disputing a concept of the unity of the two natures in the person of Jesus Christ which remains abstract and rules out a real event happening between the divine and human nature. If God has become man, then the divine and human nature in the person of Jesus Christ must be thought of as in communication with each other so that their personal unity (*unio personalis*) is to be understood as the differentiated unity of one event. According to the Lutheran view, this unity must be conceived of strictly as limited to the person of Jesus Christ.[191] Hegel's view that through the incarnation and death of God

187. *WA*, 50, 590, 11-33.
188. Solid Declaration, Article VIII, Person of Christ, *The Book of Concord; The Confessions of the Evangelical Lutheran Church*, tr. T. G. Tappert (Philadelphia: Fortress Press, 1959), p. 599.
189. *Ibid.*, p. 598.
190. See *Vom Abendmahl Christi. Bekenntnis, WA*, 26, 261ff, 319ff.
191. See Martin Chemnitz, *The Two Natures of Christ*, tr. J. A. O. Preuss (St. Louis: Concordia, 1971), ch. XIII, p. 174: "But the property which belongs to the one nature [in Christ] is communicated or distributed to the person in the concrete." Along these lines, Wimmer explained the chorale "*O Traurigkeit, O Herzeleid*" in this way: "Because in the death of Christ only the natural bond between body and soul was broken, but the person between the divine and human nature remained firm (Acts 20:28; Heb.

there comes the resurrection of an absolute spirit which transforms the unity of divine and human nature into a universal must be disputed by theology as a threat to the concrete being of Jesus Christ and to the proper distinction between God and man. The *theological* criterion for the correct description of the christological unity of divine being and human being is respect for the uniqueness of Jesus Christ; the consequence of that uniqueness is the concrete distinction between God and man. To say that God does not desire to come to himself without man posits a permanent difference between the human God and the human man. To say that the death of Jesus Christ was the night in which the substance was betrayed and made itself into the subject can be acceptable only in the sense that *man* was *liberated* through this death to the freedom, always to be proven anew, of a subject. The dignity of that subject consists of the fact that he is nothing more than a man, to whom nothing human but everything divine is alien. By contrast, God, as the subject who in his love is always free, bears in his own being the fatal godlessness of man and is thus in his deity also human.

6. What should theology learn from Hegel's appropriation of the idea of the death of God?

Two things. Hegel's usage of the statement of the death of God should remind theology (1) of the *christological* origin of this concept and simultaneously (2) of *atheism,* which defines the modern period, as the situation which should not be permitted to have merely a superficial impact on the theological accountability for the Christian understanding of God. Theology must take atheism more seriously than it does itself by preventing it from becoming a substitute religion. Atheism as the negation of theism is a critical moment of Christian theology which should be brought to bear in the concept of God. Taken for itself, it is the other, free possibility of human existence, contested by faith; it can, however, be contested only when it is acknowledged. Both agreement with and criticism of Hegel's theological interpretation of atheism combine in this *ambivalence.* The systematic *connection* of the christological source of the idea of the death of God with the epistemological-metaphysical problematic of modern atheism could be Hegel's most significant achievement for theology. However, theology must deal with the objection which the Hegelian left wing raised against Hegel's concept of God. For the Hegelian understanding of the death of God was simultaneously the target of the attack leveled by the Hegelians who strove to "go beyond Hegel."[192]

7:3), the dead corpse of Christ was truly that of the Son of God and not a merely human body, so that we must necessarily sing and say: God Himself was dead, namely, the Son of God who had become man, not according to the divine nature but in and according to the human nature which he had indivisibly taken on in the unity of his person" (Gabriel Wimmer, *Liedererklärung* [Altenburg, 1749]).

192. Of course, Hegel knew that his lectures about the philosophy of religion could also be interpreted atheistically. With reference to a decree of the Prussian king, who commanded his official to insure that no doctrines would be propagated at Prussian universities "which lead to *Atheism,*" Hegel remarked in a letter to Niethammer, dated June 9, 1821: "I hope that any new danger will not touch me. . . . I am reading the philosophy of religion this summer and have a clear conscience in doing so" (*Briefe.* ed. J. Hoffmeister [*Philosophische Bücherei,* 236] [Hamburg: Felix Meiner Verlag, 1961], II, 271f). The politically clear conscience which needs to express itself that way knows of the possibility that these lectures might be the object of suspicion. Furthermore, this clear conscience happens to be in that period of time which was prejudiced by the argument with Schleiermacher about Hegel's altered political stance regarding the free-

7. It was chiefly Ludwig Feuerbach who made the connection between atheism and Christianity into grounds for accusation of Hegel. In doing so, Feuerbach shared Hegel's intent to think in a way which was appropriate for "the modern era." But he thought that he did so more appropriately than Hegel had been able to. In the letter with which he submitted his dissertation to his "respected teacher" in 1828, Feuerbach called for the "sole dominion of reason" and asserted that "reason has not yet been redeemed in Christianity,"[193] whereby he complained chiefly about the significance of death in Christianity. He was undoubtedly hoping that Hegel would be in agreement with him. However, Feuerbach later saw that his way of defining the relationship of philosophy and Christianity attacked Hegel's work at its core. "Whoever does not give up Hegelian philosophy does not give up theology,"[194] is how he put it in the "Preliminary Theses on the Reform of Philosophy" (1843).

In the "Principles of the Philosophy of the Future" (1843), Feuerbach expressly argues against Hegel's connection between Christology and modern atheism. This debate was a decisive step toward an atheism which had forgotten the theological origin of the idea of the death of God. Feuerbach accused Hegel of formulating a contradiction where Hegel saw it as reconciliatory: "The *contradiction* of the modern philosophy . . . consists of the fact it is the *negation of theology from the standpoint of theology* or *the* negation of theology which itself is *again theology*; this contradiction *especially characterizes the Hegelian philosophy.*"[195] For Hegel understood matter as the self-emptying of the spirit and thus posits that matter as God. And ". . . to posit matter as God is as much as saying, 'There is no God,' or as much as abolishing theology and recognizing the truth of materialism." To that extent, the anti-theologian could certainly learn from Hegel. Yet, in the Hegelian abrogation of theology, ". . . the fact remains that the truth of theology is at the same time taken for granted," much to Feuerbach's irritation.[196] Feuerbach's critical review of Hegel makes his own objections eminently clear: "Atheism, the negation of theology, is therefore negated again; this means that theology is restored through philosophy. God is *God* only through the fact that he overcomes and negates matter; that is, the negation of God. And according to Hegel, it is only the negation of the negation that constituted the true positing. And so in the end, we are back to whence we had started—in the lap of Christian theology. . . . The secret of Hegel's dialectic

---

dom of instruction, which came about as the result of the Karlsbad Edicts. Schleiermacher had called Hegel's statement that the state could remove teachers while continuing their salary contemptible. See on this Karl Heinz Ilting's Introduction (*Einleitung*) to his new edition of Hegel's *Vorlesungen über Rechtsphilosophie 1818-1831; Edition und Kommentar in 6 Bänden*, ed. Karl Heinz Ilting (Stuttgart: Fr. Frommann Verlag, 1973), I, 60-69.

193. Ludwig Feuerbach, *Werke in sechs Bänden*, ed. E. Thies (Frankfurt am Main: Suhrkamp, 1975), I, 353ff (357, 355, 357).

194. Literal translation; in *The Fiery Brook; Selected Writings of Ludwig Feuerbach*, tr. Z. Hanfi (Garden City, NY: Doubleday, 1972), p. 168, the translation reads: "He who clings to Hegelian philosophy also clings to theology" (*Gesammelte Werke*, ed. W. Schuffenhauer [Berlin: Akademie-Verlag, 1970], IX, 258).

195. "Principles of the Philosophy of the Future," *The Fiery Brook*, p. 204 (paragraph 21).

196. *Ibid.*, pp. 205f.

lies ultimately in this alone, that it negates theology through philosophy in order then to negate philosophy through theology."[197]

Therefore, for Feuerbach, Hegelian philosophy is the last "grand" but basically unfortunate "attempt to restore a lost and defunct Christianity through philosophy, and, of course, as is characteristic of the modern era, by *identifying* the *negation* of Christianity *with Christianity itself.*" Hegel had called for the development of a true philosophy, and then he set about doing it in order to overcome the metaphysics of false subjectivity which no longer permitted the thinking of God as concrete. But for Feuerbach, this was simply the *camouflaging* of the intolerable contradiction of the modern era. "The much-extolled speculative identity of spirit and matter, as of the infinite and the finite, of the divine and the human is nothing more than the wretched contradiction of the modern era having reached its zenith in metaphysics. It is the identity of belief and unbelief, theology and philosophy, religion and atheism, Christianity and paganism." In Feuerbach's judgment, Hegel thus concealed the contradiction, and it "escapes the eye and is obfuscated in Hegel only through the fact that the negation of God, or atheism, is turned by him into an objective determination of God; God is determined as a *process,* and atheism as a moment within this process."[198]

By contrast Feuerbach asserts that an identity of faith and unbelief, of God and the negation (death) of God, is not possible without the contradiction becoming the definitive negation of the one part of the contradiction by the other. For "a belief that has been reconstructed out of unbelief is as little true belief— because it is always afflicted with its antithesis—as the God who has been reconstructed out of his negation is a true God; he is rather a self-contradictory, an atheistic God."[199] Instead of believing atheistically in God, Feuerbach demands that faith be given up; in its place *man* should be acknowledged as the true and noncontradictory god, man as he is aware of his own contradictory nature. If "the secret of 'absolute' philosophy (was) therefore the secret of theology,"[200] then logically this philosophy—through the "negation without contradiction" of its theological character—[201] is to be developed in such a way that the secret of theology is disclosed as being anthropology. Only then will philosophy do justice to the modern era.

Hegel's restitution of theology through an atheistic concept of God, for that reason untenable, is adjudged by Feuerbach to be an undertaking which does not do justice to the "modern era." For "the task of the modern era was the realization and humanization of God," which is only fulfilled as "the transformation and dissolution of theology in anthropology."[202] If Hegelian philosophy, by restoring theology, has failed in carrying out the "task of the modern era," then this philosophy has also failed in terms of its own claim according

197. *Ibid.*
198. *Ibid.*
199. *Ibid.*, pp. 206f.
200. *Ibid.*, p. 209 (paragraph 23).
201. *Ibid.*, p. 204 (paragraph 20).
202. *Ibid.*, p. 177.

to which "philosophy too is its own time apprehended in thoughts."[203] To be
sure, it failed according to the logic of Feuerbach's arguments because it was
richer than its age. Feuerbach's critique of Hegel results in his impoverishment.
That critique wants to conceive of the death of God without resurrection.

To my knowledge, Feuerbach never *speaks* of the death of God. But with
his criticism of the Hegelian synthesis of "belief and unbelief, theology and
philosophy, religion and atheism, Christianity and paganism," he took the decisive step in separating talk of the death of God from its original significance
and ultimately using it in the sense of an atheism which disputes the Christian
faith. The criticism of Hegelian philosophy made by the theology of that day,
which also accused Hegel of atheism,[204] provided the appropriate orthodox counterpart to Feuerbach's argument, and so the death of God was no longer spoken
of in theology at all.

c. The Significance of Talk about the Death of God: The Problem of the Essence of God

Our observations on the usage of the statement that God is dead have
revealed a remarkable thematic. The christological origin of talk about the death
of God, the transfer of such talk into philosophy through Hegel, and the return
of talk about the death of God to theology as prepared by Bonhoeffer have all,
taken together, raised the question of the definition of the divine *essence* (*Wesen*)
to the level of a theme of discussion. The dark statement that God is dead does
not so much mean that the *existence* of God has been made a problem but rather
that the *essence* of God has become a problem. Of course, that must necessarily
mean that the divine existence is questioned. But we cannot underestimate the
significance of this insight that the questioning of the divine existence takes place
as a consequence of making the divine essence a problem. The process implies
that the traditional concept of the divine essence did not permit any contact by
God with the reality of the temporal and mortal. Through this process, theology
is reminded of one of its most important tasks.

1. It was already true of the early church and then of the Reformation
discussion of the significance of the death of Jesus Christ for his 'divine nature'
that it was a debate about the compatibility of the idea of God with the concept
of change, whereby the most extreme representative of change was considered
to be the event of death. How can the divine essence be thought of together with
the event of death without destroying the concept of God—that was the question
raised anew and radically by the Reformation, and theology should have dealt
with it. But it did not. It did not happen until the philosopher Hegel took up the
question in its radicality and sought to resolve it.

Hegel understands the harsh statement, "God himself is dead," as the
expression of the dreadful thought that "all that is eternal, all that is true, is
not," but continues immediately with the assertion that this "negation itself is

203. G. W. F. Hegel, *Hegel's Philosophy of Right,* tr. T. M. Knox (Oxford: Oxford University Press, 1949), p. 11.
204. I. Iljin, *Die Philosophie Hegels als kontemplative Gotteslehre* (n.p., 1946),
pp. 416ff.

found in God."[205] That means that Hegel is calling for a new and more radical definition of the essence of God by using the negation of the existence of God. The negation of existence should be thought of as a moment in the divine essence, namely, as that moment which enables and allows the divine essence to be thought of as a being of *history*. For without negation there is no history! For the sake of the historicity of God, for the sake of thinking the divine essence not only as a tautological subject but also as historical in itself, God's essence had to be thought of as a being defined by negation, which is divine solely as a being out of death, and is eternal only in the power of Easter.

As we shall discuss in greater detail, Nietzsche, proceeding from the impossibility of thinking of the essence of God, of God as God, negated the existence of God and let the divine essence "putrefy" like a corpse.[206] Here again, the concept of the essence of God is the actual theme under discussion. The "death of God" means for Nietzsche the necessary renunciation of even the *thought* of a divine essence: "Thou refusest to stand still and dismiss thy thoughts before an ultimate wisdom, an ultimate virtue, an ultimate power."[207] Thought cannot conceive of something ultimate, because it would then have to conceive of something beyond itself. But then it would have ceased to think. For thinking takes place "in full view of every danger." Any thought which thinks in full view of every danger must then conceive of that which is "beyond all beyonds."[208] If God is then asserted to be the essence which is absolute beyond everything, the ultimate beyond all beyonds, then the necessity arises to conceive of something which is beyond all other beyonds, which is the impossibility of even *thinking* of a definite, divine *essence*. This impossibility is an historical reality for Nietzsche. The unthinkability of the essence of God leads to the proclamation of the death of God as the greatest event of modern history.

For his part, Bonhoeffer, with regard to the historical reality of the world, speaks *hypothetically* of the nonbeing of God ('as though God did not exist'), but conceives of this hypothesis as the necessary expression of historical reality and of the divine essence which reveals itself on the cross. God's true deity is demonstrated for him in the very fact that he permits himself to be expelled from the world. The concept of weakness enters the concept of the divine essence—and as a consequence, the concept of death.

In his Christology in the *Church Dogmatics*, Karl Barth, taking a position close to Bonhoeffer's although based on exclusively New Testament and christological premises, interpreted the dogma of the true deity of Jesus Christ in such a way that the deity of this person was revealed in his lowliness and the true humanity of Jesus Christ was revealed in his majesty. Barth concludes that lowliness and inner-worldliness cannot be excluded from the concept of the essence of God. God, rather, is really thought of and understood in his divinity

205. Hegel, *Lectures on the Philosophy of Religion*, III, 91.
206. See Nietzsche, *The Joyful Wisdom* (in *The Complete Works of Friedrich Nietzsche*, vol. 10), nr. 125, pp. 167f.
207. *Ibid.*, nr. 285, pp. 220f.
208. E. Biser, *"Gott ist tot"; Nietzsches Destruktion des christlichen Bewusstseins* (München: Kösel Verlag, 1962), p. 187.

only when he can be believed to have suffered even death, without ceasing to be God.[209]

2. Where is God? We can no longer avoid the remarkable fact that this question, in its modern form, is not directed toward the existence of God, but toward his essence. *What* tradition has understood by "God" is what has become a problem. The "idea of God," which thought of God as the totally Other and thus as the Omnipotent One who controls everything, as the One Beyond and thus the supraterrestrial ruler over everything which is this-worldly, was questioned. Where is God, if that is what he is like? That is the question which must then be answered, "Nowhere." By questioning the divine essence, it becomes a question which casts doubt on the existence of God. But then it is really an answer in the form of a question. "Where is God?" really means, "God is nowhere, and thus he is not." The assertion that God is nowhere and thus is not is the practical consequence of an aporia in the concept of the divine *essence*. The statement of the death of God reveals that there is an aporia in the "natural" concept of God which makes the essence of God problematical, and it does so not only in its christological usage but also in its nontheological, expressly atheistic usage.

Both theism and atheism are afflicted by this aporia in the concept of the essence of God. Theism is afflicted because it plays the aporia down; atheism is afflicted because it lets itself be played down by the aporia. Only when this aporia has been recognized as such and we have learned from it, can the opposition of Christianity and atheism become genuine. Only when faith has worked through the 'particles of truth' (*particula veri*) of atheism, and only when atheism has acknowledged that faith in the crucified God is its twin, will the alternative be a firm one. Only then will the period of distorted polemics and even more distorted irenic-polemical dialectics ("only an atheist can be a good Christian, only a Christian can be a good atheist") be at an end, and the dispute between belief and unbelief will be rid of the dullness which has beclouded it till now.

A theology which is accountable for faith in God will, therefore, have to ask about the *aporia* in the concept of the divine essence, which led to the questioning of that essence in the first place. We must clearly understand that the contemporary theological discussion about the question of the relation of God's presence and absence, of his experienceability, more precisely, of the meaning of all talk about God, derives essentially from the aporia which makes the essence of God into the problem. We must also consider whether this question corresponds to an aporetic self-experience of the human ego which is rendered uncertain of itself by the overpowering weight of the world and is therefore concerned about its own security. The traditional concept of the divine essence has gradually but persistently become intolerable not only for theoretical thought but also for practical reason. The aporias of theoretical reason have probably anticipated those of practical reason. Thus it may be regarded as justifiable when, in what follows, primarily the intolerability of the traditional concept of the divine essence for our thinking is investigated. Hegel's usage of the idea of

209. See on this my various Barth interpretations: *The Doctrine of the Trinity: God's Being is in Becoming*, tr. H. Harris (Grand Rapids: Wm. B. Eerdmans, 1976); ". . . keine Menschenlosigkeit Gottes . . .; Zur Theologie Karl Barths zwischen Theismus und Atheismus," *Evangelische Theologie*, 31 (1971), 376ff.

the death of God has certainly made clear that the unhappy consciousness which thought of itself and only of itself had rendered the concept of the divine essence an empty one. If at one time the essence of God was the only essential thing, now the self-consciousness of the human ego thinking itself was the only essential thing, and God had become unessential. It was not possible to think of *what* or *who* he is. Human reason excluded the knowledge of his essence as an undertaking which exceeded the capacity of reason. But that happened under the presupposition of a very specific concept of the divine essence. Human reason rejected a thought which it knew well (perhaps too well), which made any real knowledge of its contents impossible. The reason for this must be sought in the relationship between the essence of God which ultimately is inconceivable and the human ego which conceives of it.

The systematic consideration of this aporia must deal with the *position* of this divine essence which is presupposed in the traditional concept of the divine essence. The position of the concept of God in regard to thinking was that of superiority. The "over us" aspect of this position is then expressed in the more detailed definitions of the divine being, for example, in the definitions of omnipotence and omnipresence. If, further, one thinks of omnipotence itself as omnipresent, which must follow, and of omnipresence as constantly active omnipotence, then absence is excluded as a matter of principle. The omnipotent and omniscient divine essence is then to be thought of as absolutely present, by virtue of his essence. Absolute presence is then a circumlocution for existence. The philosophical and theological tradition asserted therefore the identity of the essence and existence of God. The worldly necessity for a highest essence found its corresponding factor in the ontological necessity of the existence of this essence.

However, when the aporia which makes the divine essence a problem was discovered, then this identity of the essence and existence of God was put into question. Historical reflection about the position of the divine essence conceived of in the idea of God in relation to thought itself led to the self-limitation of thought to the human ego, because the position of superiority was accepted. This self-limitation took place as a rational grounding of the self in the "I think" of Descartes. Since this "I think" was supposed to secure the "I am" and also secure *existence in general* on that foundation, the human "I think" became the guarantor of the existence of the divine essence, which was still regarded as absolutely superior to thought. The identity of the essence and existence of God was destroyed by the intervention of something else. That something else, our thought, threatened not only the essence and existence of God, but logically, the very idea of God itself. Ultimately the result was, God is dead.

The development just outlined requires further historical examination. This is indispensable because the theological roots of the assertion of God's nonbeing in the presupposed concept of the essence of God must be laid bare. This must happen so that it becomes plain why an essence conceived of as absolutely present must, in fact, fail to do justice to the positive character of the divine being. To learn to think of the omnipotence of God as the *withdrawal* of his omnipresence and to think of the presence of God as the *withdrawal* of his omnipotence is the systematic goal toward which our historical examination is directed.

Our intention of arriving at that goal is guided hermeneutically by the common experience that part and parcel of the presence of a person is that person's withdrawn state. That is all the more true of the experience which we have with experience itself—namely, when God is experienced. Absolute presence is completely removed by one absence. But God's presence can only be experienced simultaneously with his absence. *Therefore,* his presence can be experienced only as *revelation.* This experience must then have its effect on the concept of the *divine essence.* That essence of God must therefore be thought of, on the basis of revelation, in such a way that revelation is thought of together with the concept of the divine essence, without revelation degenerating into coercion. To think of the divine essence means to think of it as an essence which *has* revealed itself and for which therefore a certain inner connection of presence and absence is essential.[210] Based on such a concept of God, the decision may then be made whether God must be declared as dead, or together with our thought of God our thinking in general requires renewing.

In one way or another, responsible theology must encounter the problem of the thinkableness of God. Without having thought of God, one can speak neither of the being nor of the nonbeing of God.

---

210. I am consciously avoiding the traditional language about the *concealment* of God as a way of being which is part of the concept of revelation. I am doing so in order to prevent burdening the considerations which follow with the misunderstandings and objections which the concept of *deus absconditus* must necessarily invoke. It is enough if the thoughts present here invoke their own misunderstandings and further provoke material objections, as I hope they will.

CHAPTER III

On the Possibility
of Thinking God

SECTION 8. The Position of Thought between God and God:
On the Problematic of the Modern Concept of God

1. The thinkability of something is not necessarily identical with its knowability. As Immanuel Kant said,[1] we can certainly think of something without knowing in the process that it exists or not. A part of knowledge is the judgment of existence, and for that either experience or at least perception of what there is or should be is necessary. Thus, a thing is made *less* thematic under the concept of its thinkability than it is under the concept of its knowability.

However, things can certainly be made the objects of knowledge without their having been thought of as what they really are, although they have been ascertained as things through experience or through the perception of their existence. If we ask in *this* sense about the thinkability of something, then we are not necessarily asking *more* than in the question about their knowability, but we are asking more *radically*. For, in order to be able to decide what is thinkable, thought must know itself. Furthermore, the discussion must include not only the essence of the thing to be thought of, but also the context of the world. The essence of *one* thing cannot be thought of without involving *other* things. With the introduction of the *context* of things, thought itself becomes thematic. For thinking means to grasp contexts and relationships and, further, to create a context in general.

What it means to think, and what thinking accomplishes, can be admirably demonstrated, in the European metaphysical tradition, in the concept of God. Since the beginnings of the European intellectual tradition, it has been the thought of God which has served as the concept which preserved the entire coherent context in general. In God, thought had a guarantor not only for the context of all things but also for the coherent context of thinking and being. But if it was thought itself which preserved the coherent context, then thought had to come to itself in the thought of God which generally represented all thought

---

1. I. Kant, *Critique of Pure Reason*, tr. J. M. D. Meiklejohn (*Everyman's Library*, 909) (London: J. M. Dent & Sons Ltd., 1950), p. 16 n.

itself, so that God had to be thought of not only as the thought object of thinking, but also as a thinking being.

Aristotle stated that the coherent context of thinking and being was thus that of thought: the "thinking of thought" preserved the entire structure. God was, accordingly, understood as *noēseōs noēsis*: as 'the thinking of thought,' God is the one who alone unites everything.

Christian theology followed this tradition in that it conceived of God as the absolute simplicity which holds together all creation in that it holds it all together with him, God. In the dimension of thought this context is called Truth. The 'divine intellect' (*intellectus divinus*) guaranteed the truth as the actual context of being. Truth was regarded as the 'equation of intellect and thing' (*adaequatio intellectus et rei*). But the human intellect arrived at such an equation only because the divine intellect as creative spirit had created both the things to be known and the human intellect which knows them, so that the 'created things' (*res creatae*) always had been in the relationship of equation to the divine intellect because as 'things to be created' (*res creandae*) they had been *in* the divine intellect earlier. This ontological-creative relationship of the divine intellect and the things to be created and already created (*res creandae/creatae*) guaranteed the 'equation' of the human intellect to the 'created things' (*res creatas*). The truth which forms the context of being, for its part, was dependent on the fact that the 'divine intellect' was absolutely at one with itself, both context and coherence *in nuce*, so to speak. Therefore, the absolute identity of the essence and existence of God was asserted: the existence of God follows with logical necessity from his essence. Accordingly, God was thought of as an 'essential being' (*ens per essentiam*), which as such was a 'necessary being' (*ens necessarium*).

Nevertheless, human thought had to distinguish linguistically between God's essence and God's existence when, for example, it wanted to prove that God exists. This distinction became all the more necessary when, for example, Thomas Aquinas sought to demonstrate the existence of God but at the same time had to say with regard to the *essence* of God: we can only know that of God which he is not.[2] Human reason had to *distinguish* something which it wanted to assert to be *identical*. How was that supposed to happen?

2. The tradition attempted to do justice to the difficult subject matter by making a further distinction. It taught that there was in fact no 'real distinction' (*distinctio realis*) between the 'essence of God' (*essentia dei*) and the 'existence of God' (*existentia dei*), so that if one had to make a distinction here, then we would always be dealing with an artificial differentiation of the human thought, a mere 'distinction of reason' (*distinctio rationis* or *ratiocinantis*). The serious assumption that there could be a *'real* distinction' (*distinctio realis*) between the essence and existence of God would have robbed the word "God" of any meaning. And that would be true whether the word "God" was to serve as the term applied by all thinkers to the essence which was assumed to exist at the end of the five "proofs of the existence of God" (a term to be used with great reservation) of Thomas, or this word "God" was to be used as the short form of the

2. We shall return to these problems from the point of view of the possibility of saying God (see below, pp. 232ff).

divine "self-introduction," "I am Who I am."[3] On the other hand, human thinking could not avoid the distinction between the essence and existence of God,
if it wanted to speak responsibly about God at all within the dimension of thought
and did not want to remain fully silent about him. It needed this differentiation
as a *methodical* distinction in order to be able to *initiate* responsible talk about
God within the dimension of thought. Mere insistence on the identity of the
essence and existence of God would have led, within the scope of classic metaphysics, to the closure of any exposition of the idea of God before anything had
been started at all. To that degree, it cannot be disputed that there was a necessity
present for a simple 'distinction of reason' (*distinctio rationis*) between the 'essence' and 'existence' of God. This necessity was an unavoidable given, part
and parcel of human thought[4]—regardless of whether it was explicitly asserted
or implicitly admitted by its factual indispensability in the systematic process of
thought. In order to think *God* really, the simultaneous originality and unity of
his essence and his existence had to be conceived of. But, in order to *think* God
really, one had to make a mental distinction between his essence and his existence. Thought, then, had to make a *rational differentiation* between something
which was in reality in identity, *because* of the *real identity* of the 'essence' and
'existence' of God.[5]

   3. Proceeding thus, the thinking which thought God was oriented as an
act of *human* reason to *worldly* distinctions, which it was required to make
anyway or at least was accustomed to make. The most fundamental distinction
in this regard was the difference between existence and essence. It was, after

---

3. See Thomas Aquinas, *Summa Theologica*, I, q. 2, art. 3, vol. I, p. 22.
   4. See C. H. Ratschow, *Gott existiert; Eine dogmatische Studie* (Berlin: Töpel-
mann, 1966), p. 24.
   5. There is controversy in the metaphysical tradition about the way in which essence and existence belong together or are to be distinguished. Even though it was
assumed in relation to God that a 'real distinction' (*distinctio realis*) was completely
inconceivable, the views diverged with regard to the created, finite being. Thomas Aquinas, and the school which followed him, looked on 'essence' and 'existence' as two
different 'things' (*essentia, existentia, res*), so that existence is added to essence only in
the case of God for reasons which reside in the essence of this God (*a principiis es-
sentiae*); with created things, this happened for reasons which resided outside of their
essence. No created thing is capable of being the cause of its existence out of its essence
(*Summa Theologica*, I, q. 3, art. 4, vol. I, pp. 30f). Therefore, there is a 'real distinction'
(*distinctio realis*) in force between the existence and essence of things whose being is
finite. Whatever is real in a finite way derives its reality from the 'composition' (*com-
positio*) of essence and existence. The opposite view was advanced by F. Suarez, who
provided orientation on the various opinions in the discussion in his "Disputationes metaphysicae" (*Opera omnia* [Venice, 1751], vols. XXII and XXIII), which had a strong
influence on modern philosophy both directly and indirectly. According to Suarez, the
distinction between the essence and existence of a real thing is possible only 'abstractly'
(*in abstracto*), with reference to that whose existence is created, and this is true for
general ontological reasons. The view he held—and not only he—was formulated: "existence and essence are not to be distinguished in the thing itself" (*existentiam et essentiam non distingui in re ipsa*) (disp. XXXI, sect. I, 13, *op. cit.*, vol. XXIII, p. 122).
The distinction is made 'for the sake of reason alone' (*tantum ratione*). Accordingly, as
Immanuel Kant would later object to what he called the ontological proof of the existence
of God, existence is not something which is added to essence (to the 'reality' of a 'thing'):
"*Being* is evidently not a real predicate, that is, a conception of something which is
added to the conception of some other thing" (*Critique of Pure Reason*, p. 350).

all, possible to think of the world as temporal and passing without making the essence itself a problem: ". . . For when the world is gone, then accidence is no more. The Essence, that remains."[6] In fact, the essence is that which really does persist to be. That which remains is essential. Does then, in that sense, existence belong to the world in such a way that if the world should possibly pass away then something like existence would also incidentally perish? Is existence an accident, whereas essence is a necessity?

If that were so, then *for God's sake* one could certainly never say that God exists. Fichte very perceptively came to this conclusion. For existence would mean to be in the world *de facto*,[7] and that would mean that the existing thing would have to be thought of under the conditions of space and time. In view of the axiom that world, space, and time were first created by the God who exists, such a conclusion of thought would sound absurd with regard to the existence of the divine essence. Metaphysics was protected from such conclusions as long as it was held that the assertion of a mere 'rational distinction,' as a distinction of *human* thought, between the essence and existence of God was not applicable at the level of the higher peace of divine reason, where the 'divine intellect' (*intellectus divinus*) held sway. For the 'divine intellect' was as an act of the divine essence understood as 'Infinite Spiritual Essence' (*essentia spiritualis infinita*),[8] thus an act of real existence and thus the event of the identity of divine essence and divine existence. To conceive of this 'divine intellect' meant then for all thinking, including human thinking, to be grounded on it and to derive the standard of truth from it. The 'divine intellect' in its agreement with itself (and subsequently the agreement which results between it and all 'created things' [*res creandae*], which come into being only out of that 'divine intellect'), was the guarantor of truth, which then the 'human intellect' could realize as 'the equation of intellect to created things' (*adaequatio intellectus ad res creatas*).[9] Thus the mere 'rational distinction' between the essence and existence of God was already caught up in the dependence of human thought, which makes that distinction, on the divine thought which from its very origin is in agreement with itself.

4. Now all of that had to change fundamentally when human thought came on the idea of grounding itself on itself. That is what happened. That event has been, not inappropriately, called the beginning of the modern age. For our problem of how to think God it means a reorientation rich in consequences. For whatever human reason held to be a necessary distinction could no longer be held as valid for a higher reason, either a priori or ex posteriori. Of course, the thinking of the modern age needed, and still needs, time to recognize all of the fateful significance of the consequences which suddenly emerged. And it certainly needs time to work through what it has seen and perhaps to transform it into something new. But before that we must consider what happened as the

6. See p. 24, n. 14.
7. See Ratschow, *op. cit.*, p. 23.
8. See H. Schmid, *The Doctrinal Theology of the Evangelical Lutheran Church, verified from the original sources*, trs. C. A. Hay and H. E. Jacobs (Philadelphia: United Lutheran Publication House, 1889), p. 112.
9. See Martin Heidegger, "On the Essence of Truth," in *Existence and Being*, trs. R. F. C. Hull and A. Crick (Chicago: Henry Regnery Company, 1949), p. 324.

'mere rational distinction' between the essence and existence of God stabilized
as a distinction which apparently could no longer be resolved, so that reason
now set about making a real differentiation between God and God. Human
thought now found its natural place between God's essence and God's existence.
The old 'rational distinction,' which expressly disputed that there was a 'real
distinction' between God's existence and essence, provided as a mere 'distinction
of ratiocinating reason' (*distinctio rationis ratiocinantis*), that is, an act of thought,
an opportunity to modern thinking to establish itself between God so differentiated, that is, between God and God.[10] In the act of 'ratiocination' (*ratiocinari*),
the mere 'distinction established by reason' (*distinctio rationis ratiocinantis*) becomes something like a 'distinction of ratiocinated reason' (*distinctio rationis
ratiocinatae*), which as such *from now on* (in contrast with the delimited meaning
of the expression in Scholasticism[11]) did not merely discover the 'foundation of
the thing' (*fundamentum in re*) for this 'distinction' but actually created it to
begin with. This is what one could call the "subjective" side of the crisis of the
idea of God in the modern area. The *thought* or idea of God became a threat to
the unity of the divine being, as an event of thinking. Of course, this was
possible only because, in thinking the divine essence, the "objective" side of
the crisis of the idea of God was already latently present. The "subjective" side
of this crisis reveals the way it was made possible by its "objective" side.

The possibility of a crisis of the idea of God as a thinking event, a possibility already anticipated in the metaphysical tradition of the concept of God,
became an acute problem at the point when thinking began to ground itself in
the event of the human "I think." This happened in the philosophy of Rene
Descartes, who became the decisive figure for modern thought. In what follows,
we shall examine the problem just described in Descartes himself. We are not
so much interested in repeating the already well-known thinking of Descartes
but rather in grasping as precisely as possible the theological problematic in that
thinking. This will happen by demonstrating that the modern grounding of thought
in the Cartesian *cogito* is the initiation of the destruction of the metaphysically
based certainty of God (sect. 9).

10. It is not important that the assertion of a 'real distinction' between the essence
and existence of God was expressly maintained, as in the example of Descartes. It is not
seldom in intellectual history that two things happen simultaneously: something is explicitly asserted and the opposite of the assertion is implicitly carried out.
11. Scholasticism made a distinction between a 'real distinction' (*distinctio realis*;
the expression indicated a difference given in the being of a subject under discussion),
a 'distinction of ratiocinated reason' (*distinctio rationis ratiocinatae*; this expression
indicated a differentiation to be made for rational reason but which as such had its basis
in the being of the subject: 'it has its foundation in the thing'—*habet fundamentum in
re*), and a 'distinction established by reason' (*distinctio rationis ratiocinantis*; this expression indicates a differentiation exclusively grounded in the operation of reason but which
has no basis in the being of the subject under discussion). This whole differentiation of
the varying ways of drawing distinctions carried out a significant hermeneutical function
in the treatment of theologically complex problems, and played an important role, for
example, in the question of how the discussion of the variety of divine characteristics
was to be understood. Further information about these and other differentiations in the
concept of 'distinction' can be found in F. Suarez, *On the Various Kinds of Distinctions*
(disp. VII of *Disputationes Metaphysicae*), tr. C. Vollert, S. J. (Milwaukee: Marquette
University Press, 1947), sect. I, pp. 16ff.

5. The question which results for Christian theology from the analysis of Descartes is whether or not the destruction of the metaphysically based certainty of God must mean the impossibility of any certainty about God at all. Therefore we shall attempt to deal with this question in what follows. It will not be our intent to obtain surreptitiously shallow theological certainty via the modern crisis of the thought of God, but rather to work through the crisis in order to arrive at a theological answer in the very act of thinking through the crisis. A theology of revelation—and Christian theology according to the position taken in these studies can be only and exclusively revelational theology—should not and will not seek to discredit revelation and faith by making them substitute solutions and simply recommending that one should *believe* rather than *think* when it comes to the concept of God—or even worse, neither to believe nor to think, but instead to *act* finally. Everything at its time and in its place! Everything in the proper context! What we want to do is to *think* what we *believe*. And to that extent, the resolution of the question of how to think God remains our task—or else we are threatened by superstition.

In order to think through the crisis of modern thought about God and thus to arrive at a possible theological answer to the question of certainty about God, the theological consequences of the Cartesian basing of thought in the "I think" are to be considered by using as examples three statements, one by Johann Gottlieb Fichte, another by Ludwig Feuerbach, and finally one by Friedrich Nietzsche. It will be shown that the metaphysical thought of God had to become the presupposition for the modern disputation of the possibility of thinking of God (sect. 10).

If it is the purpose of theology to understand and thus to think what we believe, then the steps of argumentation just described require of us that we not simply oppose the metaphysically based certainty of God and its destruction with such a certainty of faith which excludes thinking. Rather we should incorporate modern criticism of the metaphysical concept of God into the questioning process of faith as it understands itself, so that, through the modern crisis of the meta-physical idea of God, God will be *thinkable in a new way*, on the basis of the certainty of faith. The mere antithesis of the God of the philosophers to the God of Abraham, Isaac, and Jacob has become just as irresponsible as the mere antithesis between the unbelief of the philosophers and the faith of Abraham, Isaac, and Jacob would be. Even to set up a contrast between the doubt of the philosophers and the faith of Christians is ultimately not a responsible theological act. For a faith which is abstractly antithetical to doubt makes faith itself doubt-ful, and doubt which abstractly opposes faith makes doubt unworthy of credi-bility. Faith does, of course, exclude doubt—there is no doubt of that. But faith can really exclude doubt concretely only when it contests that doubt as the other possibility which is set in opposition to faith. Therefore, faith can *exclude* doubt only by *confronting* it. In order to overcome doubt, faith would virtually have to summon up doubt, unless faith does not want to stop being faith. Therefore, all *mere antitheses* of this kind are irresponsible because they set up *false alter-natives*. The criterion of a false alternative is the sterility of thought which results from it. Basically, all the ways in which the God (or the unbelief or the doubt) of the philosophers is set in opposition to the God of Abraham, Isaac, and Jacob (or of the faith of Christians with all that challenges it) are theologically irresponsible. That is because they have become, quite simply, sterile.[12]

For this reason it is a theological task of the first order to explicate that the certainty of faith in God, that God's being is *thinkable again*, precisely by our reception of the problems of modern thought (sect. 11). To be thinkable does not mean that something must be thought necessarily. At most the thinkability of God is a necessary thought. But it is not our intent here to develop the necessity of thinking God totally apart from the certainty of faith. *That* kind of natural theology is precisely what is supposed to be overcome. But, in contrast with that, what we are intending to do is to retain or regain the biblical position *without* neglecting the questions of our age and thus leaving it on its own. The "knot of history" may not be untied in such a way that modern thinking against God marches on into the future and the Christian faith mindlessly proceeds down its pathway. On both sides that leads to superstition which must be resolutely battled both in its antiquated and in its modern forms. The strictest form of resolute battle against superstition will be in following the command to define the relationship of faith and thought as thoroughly and understandably as possible. This is what we shall attempt to do with regard to the thinkability of God.

SECTION 9. The Self-Establishment of Modern Thought in the Cartesian "I Think" as the Premise for the Destruction of the Metaphysically Established Certainty of God

Descartes' thought brought about an historical decision which is acknowledged to have provided the foundation for man's modern understanding of himself and the world. The fact that *I* think when I *think* led in Descartes to the self-establishment of thought in the "I think." *Cogito* thus becomes a *foundational* term in Cartesian thought.

The intellectual decision made in the thought of Descartes did not just organize anew man's understanding of himself and the world but also man's understanding of God. This is what we shall address in what follows. Our point of departure must be the self-establishment of thought in the "I think," the Cartesian organization of man's modern understanding of himself. The new organization of man's understanding of God has depended on it since Descartes. We must consider again the well-known Cartesian rationalization of human self-certainty through the power of methodological doubt (sect. 9a). For methodological doubt in Descartes is capable not only of establishing the self-certainty of the human ego. In this context it has also the function of demonstrating the necessity of God. In the theological analysis of Cartesian thought, however, it will be shown that Descartes secured the existence of God in such a way that it necessarily had to lead to the destruction of the concept of God and of the metaphysically grounded certainty of God (sect. 9b).

---

12. The correctness of the famous differentiation, well known from Pascal's *Memorial*, is not thereby contested, as I have shown in the *Epilegomena 1975* of my Barth paraphrase; see *Gottes Sein ist im Werden; Verantwortliche Rede vom Sein Gottes bei Karl Barth; Eine Paraphrase* (Tübingen: J. C. B. Mohr [Paul Siebeck], 1965[1], 1967[2], 1976[3]), pp. 126f. An English translation is available, but the Epilogue is not included in this edition. See also *The Doctrine of the Trinity: God's Being is in Becoming*, tr. H. Harris (Grand Rapids: Wm. B. Eerdmans, 1976).

a. The Power of Doubt: Methodological Doubt as the Premise for the Establishment of the Necessity of God

That Descartes organized human understanding of God in a new way is seen not so much in the proofs for the existence of God which he thought through and partially redeveloped anew, although there are some remarkable aspects to consider here as well.[1] More than with regard to the structure of the proofs of God, the *function* which these proofs have in Descartes' philosophizing makes plain the extent to which the relation of human thought to God was defined in a *new* way. Because of the way it was done, the question which had to result was, Where is God? Our attention, in what follows, is directed not so much to the line of argumentation in proving God's existence as to the movement of the thought itself, in which talk about God and the necessity of proving his existence have their very definite meaning.

1. Descartes molded the character of the so-called modern era in that he attempted to provide it an 'unshakable foundation of truth' (*inconcussum fundamentum veritatis*). To lay an unshakable foundation for that which merits being called true means, however, that the question of truth is being guided by the question of certainty. That which is, should be authenticated as existing beyond all doubt. One can only build, can only construct knowledge on the foundation of that which is undoubtedly existing. For that reason, Descartes, who doubted everything, was the thoroughgoing enemy of the doubtful. It was the declared purpose of his thinking to arrive at certainty of knowledge.[2] The strength of his

---

1. Descartes' ontological proof of God has two peculiarities in contrast with Anselm's ontological argument. A *first* difference is the concept of God taken as the point of departure of the argument, a concept of God in which his existence is to be proven on the basis of his essence as understood (see on this the analysis in D. Henrich, *Der ontologische Gottesbeweis; sein Problem und seine Geschichte in der Neuzeit* [Tübingen: J. C. B. Mohr, 1960], pp. 3f and 10ff; also G. Runze, *Der ontologische Gottesbeweis* [1882], p. 33). For Anselm, it is the concept of the *perfect* essence, and for Descartes it is the concept of the *necessary* essence. Of course, the concept of the perfect essence also plays a role in the Cartesian argument in that God certainly must be the more perfect essence in contrast with man, or man must be the less perfect essence in contrast with God. Often it appears that Descartes is only following Anselm's patterns for the ontological proof: for example, in the Fifth Meditation and in the *Principia philosophiae*, I, 14. But Descartes drew a clear line of separation with regard to the Anselmian approach to the ontological proof of God; see the reply to the objections to the Fifth Meditation.

A *second* difference is found in the *occasion* which preceded the concept of God. Of course, it is not only in Descartes that the occasion for a proof of the existence of God stands in a close relationship to the selection of the *ontological* argument. In the case of *Anselm* one must remember that he does know other proofs of God, but nonetheless the fact that he developed the ontological proof first of all gives this ontological proof a special significance for the theological understanding we find in Anselm's theology. There is, however, in *Descartes* a *necessary* connection between the proofs of God and the approach of his thought, as it sets about to establish metaphysics anew. This necessary connection is such that an analysis of this thinking must show why this thought system, which establishes certainty through doubt, sees itself under necessity to prove the existence of God, doing so through two arguments derived each from *ideas of deity* which are already present in the consciousness of the 'knowing thing' (*res cogitans*).

2. See G. Ebeling, "Gewissheit und Zweifel; Die Situation des Glaubens im Zeitalter nach Luther und Descartes," in *Wort und Glaube II; Beiträge zur Fundamentaltheologie und zur Lehre von Gott* (Tübingen: Mohr [Siebeck], 1969), pp. 138-83.

thought was that he based this certainty on its very opposite, on thoroughgoing doubt. In order not to have to doubt anymore, he used the ability to doubt. The total grounding of human certainty through doubt could succeed in the long run only because Descartes made God into the comrade in arms of doubt. At the beginning of modern metaphysics, God and doubt are a united front against— doubt. This mutuality would have far-reaching and grave consequences.

For Descartes, doubt bears the function of an hermeneutical principle. Initially doubt is exercised "to distinguish the true from the false."[3] This is, of course, possible only when in the course of an undoubtedly true insight it is made simultaneously quite plain what it is that makes the insight true knowledge. And that is what I can comprehend clearly and distinctly: ". . . everything which we conceive very clearly and very distinctly is wholly true."[4] In order, however, to arrive at such a knowledge event, doubt must come first. That is the only way in which one can initiate the process of learning to distinguish the true from the false. The demand for truth ascribes hermeneutical priority to the suspicion of error, a priority which is initially methodologically necessary. Whoever wants to learn to distinguish true from false must encounter all that has been known until now with mistrust, in order to find that point from which the true can be ascertained as true. Therefore, everything must be doubted, which means "think everything false."[5] That clearly means taking leave of the accumulated past and thus of the authority of the history of knowledge and thought until now—re- gardless of whether it might later prove to be a temporary leave-taking or a permanent one. The Cartesian demand for truth remands the thinker entirely to his own intellectual present: ". . . and I was thus constrained to embark on the investigation for myself."[6]

That person who risks directing himself, and who refuses to be led by anyone else at all, that person is totally dependent on himself as a being which is totally present to itself, and is absolutely contemporary. The ego can bring itself only in total restriction to itself, which means in total subjection to itself. That means that the ego is also subjected to its own weaknesses and deficiencies, and it is one of the chief tasks of the self-directing ego not to succumb to those weaknesses. The best way to evade the danger of succumbing to one's own weakness is to assert that weakness as a weakness. For Descartes, this self- direction takes place in one's submission to oneself as a being which is defined by a specific weakness: the necessity of doubt. I must doubt because I *can* doubt. It is part of both the dignity and imperfection of the human being that it can

3. Rene Descartes, *Discourse on Method*, tr. L. J. Lafleur (*Little Library of Lib- eral Arts*, 19) (New York: Liberal Arts Press, 1960), p. 2: "Besides, I was always eager to learn to distinguish truth from falsehood" (p. 11).

4. Rene Descartes, *Meditations*, tr. L. J. Lafleur (*Little Library of Liberal Arts*, 29) (New York: Liberal Arts Press, 1951), III, 34. See below, p. 117, n. 21.

5. Descartes, *Discourse on Method*, p. 21; that does not mean: to prove that every- thing is false; see *Meditations*, I, 17.

6. *Discourse on Method*, p. 11. Time as the present is thus the unnamed presup- position which stands behind the entire undertaking. To be certain of oneself as intellec- tually present means that one is both the person *deciding for* doubt and the one who *in* doubt *gains* himself *through* doubt, that is, the one who *rejects everything* and the one who *asserts existence for himself*.

doubt.[7] The unity of man's excellence and imperfection is expressed by Descartes in the statement that it is part of man's definition to be "not wholly perfect."[8] Man's ability to doubt is identical with his not being able not to doubt, in that he is subjected to the doubtful and yet is not supposed to give in to it. Of course that does not mean that he *must* doubt *everything*, but rather that he can doubt everything but must doubt in principle.

To doubt *everything* was Descartes' historical decision, which then brought doubt to its essence. Doubt is brought to its essence when it is driven to its extreme. Descartes drives man's lack of perfection, which is essential to man, and which is his ability to doubt, to its extreme, and in so doing, he allows man to arrive at the essence of his human existence. Thus Descartes *carries through* this humanly essential *lack* of total perfection in order to make the *best* of it. And he makes the best of it by turning this lack of total perfection against his own fallibility. Doubt gives birth to its own death. For doubt of everything cannot doubt the doubting of the doubter. But at that point there emerges in the sea of doubt, discovered by doubt itself, an island of indubitable *being*.

We said that doubting means "to think everything false." This leads necessarily, for Descartes, to the conclusion ". . . that I who thought so was something. . . . I think, therefore I am. . . ."[9] "*Ego cogito, ergo sum.*"[10] This is certainly not a syllogistic deduction but the consequence of different moments of an event, the event of a methodically made discovery.[11] "I think, therefore I am"—that is knowledge as event. It implies that I must think *myself* as a thinking person: *cogito me cogitare*, "I think myself thinking." But if I must

7. *Ibid.*, pp. 20-22.
8. *Ibid.*, p. 22.
9. *Ibid.*, p. 21.
10. Rene Descartes, *The Meditations and Selections from the Principles*, tr. J. Veitch (Chicago: Open Court Publishing, 1927), I, vii, p. 132: "Accordingly, the knowledge, *I think, therefore I am*, is the first and most certain that occurs to one who philosophizes orderly."
11. In the Second Meditation, Descartes did not give this 'first knowledge' the form of a proposition which can be interpreted as a syllogism. In spite of the *ergo*, there is no syllogism here, as has frequently been emphasized. For "this conclusion would have to have as its major premise, 'that which thinks, is,' and the minor premise, 'I think,' with the conclusion, 'Therefore I am.' However, the major premise would only be a formal generalization of what lies in the proposition, 'I think—I am.' Descartes himself emphasizes that no inference is present" (Martin Heidegger, *What is a Thing?*, trs. W. B. Barton, Jr. and Vera Deutsch [Chicago: Regnery, 1967], p. 104; see Heidegger, *Nietzsche II* [Pfullingen: Günther Neske, 1961], pp. 158ff). Descartes emphasizes that before the 'first and most certain proposition' one must know ". . . that there is nothing really existing apart from our thought . . ." (. . . *Selections from the Principles*, I, x, p. 133). *Ergo* points out that *movement* inheres in *cogitare*, movement which understands and expresses itself as *being* and without which *nothing* can be understood and addressed as being. This movement is called: I, the ego. Descartes' "analytical unity" of being and thinking in the ego stands before Kant's synthetic unity of transcendental apperception (". . . the presentation *I think* . . . must necessarily be capable of accompanying all our representations"). The ego must be able to accompany all thinking (imagining); and that is where the certainty of "I am" rests, and thus the certainty of being in general (see Heidegger, *What is a Thing?*, p. 104).

think myself thinking, then I have myself as being. Through doubting it becomes clear to doubt that the *being* of an existing thing is indubitably evident, namely, the being of man, who is characterized by the nature of doubt, if one can put it that way.

It is very significant that Descartes, in calling this insight the Archimedean point of certainty,[12] established the existence and the essence of the human person as being, in fact, one and the same. "I think, therefore I am" means then "I am a thinking essence." *Cogito sum* means *sum res cogitans*. Descartes does realize his knowledge of the existence of man and his knowledge of man's essence *one after the other* in both the *Discourse* and the *Meditations*.[13] That accords with his requirement that every problem should be divided "into as many parts as possible."[14] Objectively, the response to the question mark about what or who I am is only the reformulation of the proposition which secures my existence: "I think, therefore I am." I am (exist) because I am *what* I am. A part of my essence as a 'thinking thing' (*res cogitans*) is thus the knowledge *that* I am because I am *this essence*.

2. However, this 'first principle' of philosophy, which insures the unity of human existence and human essence with the "that" of human existence, is not capable of securing the unity of existing itself. For the certainty of this *cogito me cogitare* ('I think myself thinking') is the certainty of reflective doubt which can assure me only of my *present* existence. If I exist as a 'thinking thing' (*res cogitans*), and if doubt is part of its essence, then this doubt can, and methodically must, direct itself *anew* against every knowledge ever arrived at, unless it is a knowledge which has just been arrived at for the first time; the reason for this is that *memory* is not removed from the suspicion of deception. Descartes says expressly ". . . that this proposition: *I am, I exist*, is necessarily true [only] every time that I pronounce it or conceive it in my mind."[15] I must *constantly* and *initially* ascribe my being to myself, conceive of my being for myself. The certainty of thought as the affirmation of being is limited to the time of that affirmation or to the time in which the thought is conceived.[16]

But that means that man is constantly thrown back to the zero point of *cogito me cogitare*, that he must constantly establish his being anew. For, "the present time is not dependent on that which immediately preceded it; for this

---

12. As an example in Descartes, *Meditations*, p. 12.

13. See *Discourse*, p. 21: "I then examined closely what I was . . ."; *Meditations*, p. 24: "But I do not yet know sufficiently clearly what I am, I who am sure that I exist."

14. *Discourse*, p. 12—the second of the four basic rules which Descartes sought never to violate in his thinking: "The second was to divide each of the difficulties which I encountered into as many parts as possible, and as might be required for an easier solution" (p. 12).

15. *Meditations*, II, iii, p. 24. This "every time" obviously is true of every other knowledge, which would be all the less certain in comparison with self-knowledge (see *Meditations*, III, v, p. 34), since the knowledge "I think—I am" is the basic criterion for all true knowledge (see the *Discourse*, pp. 20-22).

16. *Meditations*, II, vi, p. 25: "I am, I exist—that is certain; but for how long do I exist? For as long as I think; for it might perhaps happen, if I totally ceased thinking, that I would at the same time completely cease to be."

reason, there is no need of a less cause for conserving a thing than for at first producing it."[17] The certainty of one's own existence does not yet imply the continuity of this certainty and thus the certainty of the continuity of one's own existence.[18] But it is precisely this certainty of continuity which is required in order to project a *world* from the Archimedean point of the *cogito me cogitare*. Without its own continuity the ego would remain without a world to which a *unity* belongs which surpasses and comprehends the moment.

The certainty of "I think—I am" (*cogito sum*), therefore, by no means excludes doubting the continuity of "I am," and thus doubting the existence of the world. However, according to Descartes, doubt is that particular weakness of the human essence which can be turned against man's fallibility. One doubts in order to arrive at certainty. "The fact that all 'thinking' (*cogitare*) is essentially 'doubting' (*dubitare*) means nothing else than this: to re-present (*vor-stellen*) is to assure (*sicher-stellen*)."[19] Accordingly, the purpose of doubting the continuity of "I am—I exist" (*ego sum, ego existo*) is to arrive at assurance of this continuity. To provide such assurance, it is necessary to press this doubt to its extreme. That happens by doubting not only the continuity of certainty and thus of human existence, but even doubting the existence of God.[20]

3. Thinking claims that God is necessary in order to be able to secure the continuity of the ego with his help. How does that happen? We remember that the unique characteristic of man, according of Descartes, consists of the fact that the human essence is not a completely perfect essence. Therefore, a man can delude himself. Therefore, he must doubt. But doubt can be pressed methodically to its extreme in such a way that the best is made of this weakness, namely, a proof of the existence of the doubter. This proof of the existence of the doubter as a not completely perfect essence, in contrast with which something more perfect can and must be conceived of, provides the criterion for all true knowledge. The existence of the doubter was *very clearly and very distinctly comprehended* in doubting itself. "To conceive very clearly and very distinctly" (*clare et distincte percipere*) may be taken as the criterion of certainty or of truth

17. Rene Descartes, "Appendix from the Reply to the Second Objections," Axiom II, in *The Meditations and Selections from the Principles*, p. 218.

18. See *Meditations*, III, xxxi, p. 47: "For the whole duration of my life can be divided into an infinite number of parts, no one of which is in any way dependent upon the others; and so it does not follow from the fact that I have existed a short while before that I should exist now, unless at this very moment some cause produces and creates me, as it were, anew or, more properly, conserves me." For Descartes, creation and maintenance are distinguished from each other 'by reason alone' (*sola ratione*), but not intrinsically (*ibid.*).

19. Martin Heidegger, *Nietzsche II*, p. 152; see also W. Schulz, *Der Gott der neuzeitlichen Metaphysik* (Pfullingen: G. Neske Verlag, 1957), p. 38.

20. H. Blumenberg referred to the Nominalistic tradition in which the concept of the 'absolute power of God' (*potentia dei absoluta*) made "time the dimension of absolute uncertainty," an uncertainty "both of the identity of the subject, for whom the present moment provides no guarantee of the future, and of the duration of the world, whose radical contingency can from one moment to the next alter being into appearance, reality into nothingness." Blumenberg sees in this traditional Nominalistic problem the "central motivation for the doubting approach made by Descartes" (H. Blumenberg, *Die Legitimität der Neuzeit* [Frankfurt am Main: Suhrkamp, 1966], p. 121).

with regard to *all* things[21]—*as long as it never occurs* that something conceived of in this way as clear and distinct should prove to be false.[22]

This reservation must, however, be shown to be unjustified if any certain knowledge beyond the "first knowledge that I am a thinking thing" (*prima cognitio, me esse rem cogitantem*) is to be possible at all. Such an occurrence, where something conceived of clearly and distinctly is proven to be false, must not take place. There must be a *guarantee* that that which is clearly and distinctly conceived of cannot be proven to be false. This guarantee is provided through *doubting*. Therefore we must doubt that something clearly and distinctly conceived of cannot be proven to be false. This is where *God* is called into play.

In the *Discourse*, following the presentation of the criterion of truth, various arguments for the existence of God are cited without any initial reference to that criterion being clearly made. Only after Descartes has shown that there is adequate reason to doubt the existence of things (like bodies, constellations, earth) represented in our thinking as well as to doubt the false representations of our dreams, does he return to the criterion of truth with the assertion that this criterion can be accepted as true only ". . . because God exists, and because he is a perfect Being, and because everything in us comes from him."[23]

By contrast, in the *Meditations* Descartes arrives at the same destination by what appears to be a detour. There he does not cite the various arguments for the existence of God but rather advances the possibility that this God could be a deceiver.[24] This possibility had already been used at the end of the First Meditation in order to have a just reason to *doubt everything*.[25] In the Third

21. *Meditations*, III, 34: "And therefore it seems to me that I can already establish as a general principle that everything which we conceive very clearly and very distinctly is wholly true." On the definition of "clearly and distinctly" see the *Principles*, I, xlv: "I call that clear which is present and manifest to the mind giving attention to it, . . . but the distinct is that which is so precise and different from all other objects as to comprehend in itself only what is clear" (*Meditations and Selections from the Principles*, pp. 152f). The criterion for truth is thus limited *by the present* or, better, *to the present*.

22. *Meditations*, III, 34: ". . . the clear and distinct perception. . ., but this would really not be sufficient to assure me that what I affirm is true if it could ever happen that something which I conceived just as clearly and distinctly should prove false."

23. *Discourse*, p. 25. Original: ". . . à cause que Dieu est ou existe, et qu'il est un être parfait, et que tout ce qui est en nous vient de lui."

24. *Meditations*, III, 35: ". . . I must examine whether there is a God as soon as an opportunity occurs, and if I find that there is one I must also investigate whether he can be a deceiver; for as long as this is unknown, I do not see that I can ever be certain of anything."

25. *Meditations*, I, 22. There the 'evil spirit' (*genius malignus*) is introduced as the *opponent* of 'God who is very good' (*optimus deus*), whereby the latter is methodically inhibited in his being, so to speak. The 'evil spirit' is termed 'this great deceiver' and thus is introduced as that quality which according to Meditation III could possibly be ascribed to God. The 'evil spirit' is *previously* 'god.' That extreme nominalistic tradition which conceived of God as a possible deceiver was probably known to Descartes. On the historical problem, see K. A. Sprengard, *Systematisch-historische Untersuchungen zur Philosophie des 14. Jahrhunderts* (Bonn: Bouvier, 1967), I, 99ff. According to Blumenberg (*op. cit.*, p. 163), we find in Descartes the "radicalization of the nominalistic hypothesis of the 'absolute power' to that of the 'evil spirit'." On the function of the concept of a 'false god' (*deus fallax*) within the scholastic problem of evidence, see Blumenberg, *op. cit.*, pp. 153-73.

Meditation, Descartes picks up this methodical fiction, but no longer as the motivation for the totality of doubt, but rather to guarantee the criterion of truth as valid for *all* knowledge, without God!

This recourse, already encountered in late medieval Nominalism, to the possibility of a deceiving God is monstrous in the context of both metaphysical and theological judgment. It must be seen for what it really is. It is nothing less than the doubting of the essence of God, the questioning of the deity of God. For a 'deceiver god' (*deus deceptor*) is not god at all but rather the opposite of the 'God who is good' (*deus optimus*),[26] who merits the appellation God only because he is the superlative, the highest form of the good. The 'deceiver god' is the 'evil spirit' in the language of knowledge, and in the language of faith it is the devil.

Descartes then opposes this imagined devil with the "God who is good," so that by destroying the methodically necessary 'deceiver god' he can guarantee the totality of the truth criterion. Only by making the 'god who is good' certain can he exclude the possibility of deception, even in relation to 'conceiving clearly and distinctly.' On the one hand, he had to image an 'evil spirit' and place God in doubt in order to come to certainty about God through doubt; on the other hand, he needs God just as much in order to free himself from the spirit which he had conjured up. One could say that God has to be made into his opposite first, in order to be guaranteed as the opposite of the opposite and thus as the power who provides certainty. If we bear in mind that Descartes' philosophy and Luther's theology[27] cannot really be compared with each other, then we could interpret this by quoting Luther: "God cannot be God unless He first becomes a devil. We cannot go to heaven [*scil.* of certainty] unless we first go to hell [*scil.* of doubt]."[28] But only God himself can destroy the character of the devil ascribed to him, so that ultimately we may say: "For great is his steadfast love toward us; and the faithfulness of the Lord endures for ever" (Ps. 117:2).[29] That Descartes must *prove* the existence of this God only underlines how *necessary* this 'God who is God,' God himself, is in order to set aside the 'deceiver god.'

26. See also *Discourse*, p. 25: "It is evident that it is no less repugnant to good sense to assume that falsity or imperfection as such is derived from God. . . ."

27. See on this Ebeling, *op. cit.*, pp. 138ff.

28. Luther, "The Exposition of the 117th Psalm (1530)," in *Selected Psalms III* (*Luther's Works*, vol. 14), ed. Jaroslav Pelikan (St. Louis: Concordia Publishing House, 1958), p. 31. In the preceding sentence, Luther described this devil's character ascribed to God (on the term "devilhood" see *ibid.*, p. 32): "I know well that God's Word must first become a great lie, even in myself, before it can become truth." While remembering the qualitative differences between Luther and Descartes, we may still be reminded of the common nominalistic legacy they shared.

29. Martin Luther, *op. cit.*, p. 32. The "overcoming" of the devil and the destruction of the "evil spirit" (or, better, his disclosure as the spirit of the double man) represents for both Luther and Descartes the overcoming of an extreme Nominalism (see Schulz, *op. cit.*, p. 38, for Descartes). Blumenberg (*op. cit.*, p. 163 and often) misses the point of the Cartesian thought process, I think, when he sees the significance of that process chiefly in the fact that Descartes "developed the implications of theological absolutism a further decisive step and brought them to such an acutely threatening level that the reaction could only be found in absolute immanence."

Nemo contra deum nisi deus ipse ('No one is against God unless it is God himself').[30]

4. Part and parcel of the stringency of the Cartesian approach is the idea that God is *necessary* for the human 'thinking thing' (*res cogitans*). Therefore we can understand that Descartes understands God as a necessary essence, as a 'necessary being' (*ens necessarium*).[31] Based on his necessary existence, God's perfect existence becomes a developed theme. God is *necessary* for Descartes initially not as the most perfect essence (*ens perfectissimum*), but only as the essence which is *more perfect* than man. The idea of God which man finds in himself and is not made by him and cannot be shown to have come to him through his own perception of the external world, that is, the 'innate idea' of God,[32] is the very idea which requires of me that I think of "a nature that was really more perfect than I was."[33] Such a nature more perfect than man is necessary because man can perceive his doubt as a lack only in relationship to such a nature. The God who is supposed to overcome doubt must first of all verify doubt as a lack.[34]

Therefore, God must be one who is superior to me. At the same time, he must also be superior to the 'evil spirit.' But that is an invention of imperfect man. In fact, is the 'evil spirit' anything other than man doubting everything, or, more precisely, man forcing himself to total doubt, who then abjures this compulsion to total methodical doubt as an epistemological devil? We will have done justice to Cartesian radicality only when we answer this question positively. The 'deceiver god' is the "divine" wraith (*Doppelgänger*) of man who is made by man himself. For the will to deception represented by the 'deceiver god' is the precondition of the possibility, or the rightful basis for total doubt. Man himself establishes this precondition. It is his invention. In it, he divorces himself from himself and assumes the role of the epistemological devil. If it is insane, there is still method to this madness. For the sake of the method, the mad figure of the 'deceiver god' results. God, who is doubted as the 'evil spirit,' is basically man as he repudiates his will to doubt as the will to methodical self-deception, which is itself destructible. For doubting man hardly lacks perfection more than 'the deceiving god.'[35] Thus, 'God who is against the evil spirit' (*deus contra*

30. See J. W. von Goethe, *The Autobiography of Goethe, Truth and Poetry; From My Life*, ed. P. Godwin (New York: Wiley & Putnam, 1846), pt. IV, bk. XX, p. 107.

31. See above, p. 112, n. 1.

32. Descartes distinguishes these three kinds of ideas: "Among these ideas, some seem to be born with me, others to be alien to me and to come from without, and the rest to be made and invented by myself" (*Meditations*, III, 36). On the Cartesian concept of the "idea," see Heidegger, *Nietzsche II*, pp. 151ff.

33. *Discourse*, p. 22; see also *Meditations*, III, 45f.

34. See *Meditations*, III, 44: "For how would it be possible for me to know that I doubt and that I desire—that is, that I lack something and am not at all perfect—if I did not have in myself any idea of a being more perfect than my own, by comparison with which I might recognize the defects of my own nature?"

35. *Meditations*, III, 50: "And from this it is quite evident that he cannot be a deceiver, since the light of nature teaches us that deception must always be the result of some deficiency." This insight of natural human reason leads to the destruction of the concept of a 'most powerful deceiver' (*deceptor potentissimus*) as we find it in the fiction of an 'evil spirit of great power' (*genius malignus summe potens*) (*ibid.*, p. 22).

genium malignum) is nothing other than 'God against doubting man' (*deus contra hominem dubitantem*). To that extent, then, all that is really needed is something *more perfect* than *man* is, in order to be capable of definition as the power which is *superior to everything*.[36] When the existence of that power has been assured, when God's existence has been proven, then the devilish double role of man is abrogated and his identity, as it was threatened *by that role*, is secured. Man has played his role as an epistemological devil to its end.

But he *had* to play out the role so that God would become necessary. If the 'evil spirit' had not been invented, man would have *had* to doubt first in order to be able to prove God's existence. For Descartes' proofs of God all are connected to an idea of God which I discover in my consciousness as a form of it.[37] One could also say: they are a way with which I discover myself. The fact *that* I am, *that* I am a 'thinking thing' (*res cogitans*), *that* I discover myself as existent with the idea of God, all had to be secured through my doubt. Without 'doubting' (*dubitare*) there is no 'I think—I am' (*cogito sum*), without 'I think—I am' (*cogito sum*) there is no certainty of a 'thinking thing' (*res cogitans*), without a 'thinking thing' there are no 'modes of cogitation' (*modi cogitationis*) and thus no 'ideas,' including no idea of God! Without an idea of God there is no proof of God, and without a proof of God there is no certainty of God! Without the certainty of God there is still the self-certainty which was arrived at through doubt, but there is no assurance of this self-certainty beyond the present moment. The self-certainty which I owe to my doubt must therefore be guaranteed through the assurance of the existence of God. God is necessary as the back-up insurance against my own doubt. The successful proof of the existence of God might be called the title of nobility for doubt, which has been steered into a more fitting path by the destruction of the 'evil spirit': noblesse oblige. The doubter can no longer oppose himself playing the role of the epistemological devil.

5. The proof[38] of the existence of the "God who is good" has now insured the continuity of human existence. This has been accomplished in a twofold fashion:

(a) For one, the context of the ego has been insured in that "clear and distinct perception" must no longer be subject to questioning and can therefore

---

36. Since man knows himself as one who is "not a completely perfect essence" ("I am not at all perfect"; *Meditations*, III, 44), that which is more perfect is already the most perfect, and his perfection is already a "perfection of all perfections." Descartes then defines God, along the lines of tradition, as the essence to whom "all perfections" are ascribed (*ibid.*, V, 64; see also pp. 48, 50). The intensification from the *defective* perfection of man to the idea of the *more perfect*, or even *most perfect*, is presented in the *Meditations*, IV, 54f: "And it appears to me to be very remarkable that, of all the other qualities which I possess, there is none so perfect or so great that I do not clearly recognize that it could be even greater or more perfect. Thus for example, if I consider my faculty of conceiving, I immediately recognize that it is of very small extent and greatly limited; and at the same time there occurs to me the idea of another faculty, much more ample, indeed immensely greater and even infinite, and from the very fact that I can imagine this I recognize without difficulty that it belongs to the nature of God."

37. *Meditations*, III, 35f.

38. The form of the proofs is not of interest in this context. But see above, p. 112, n. 1.

serve as a general criterion of truth. The 'evil spirit' can no longer deceive me. The criterion of truth is guaranteed. This has also secured the transition from the present tense of my 'thinking myself thinking' (*cogito me cogitare*) to other "clear and distinct perceptions" as well as to every other present tense of the 'thinking thing.'[39]

(b) Second, the continuity of human existence has been secured in that I know myself to be finite in the knowledge of God himself.[40] For the idea of something more perfect,[41] which assures me that my doubt is a lack (out of which the best is to be made), can only have been placed in me by that which is more perfect itself. Since I, as a doubting being with deficiencies, am dependent on that which is more perfect,[42] I can encounter him only *passively*. Because I cannot be considered the *originator* of the idea of infinity or that which is more perfect, I am *established* in my finitude. The ability to doubt is thus a proof of my finitude just as it is the proof for the existence of something more perfect. Together with my finitude, the identity or continuity of my existence is also assured. I cannot disintegrate. "For the whole duration of my life can be divided into an infinite number of parts, no one of which is in any way dependent upon the others; and so it does not follow from the fact that I have existed a short while before that I should exist now, unless at this very moment some cause produces and creates me, as it were, anew or, more properly, conserves me."[43] Since, however, such a power does not inhere in the human 'thinking thing,' it recognizes itself as being absolutely dependent—Schleiermacher's formulation is entirely appropriate here.[44] This dependence as "proof of one's own finitude is the internal meaning of the argumentation."[45] It makes man in his dependence so secure that man can understand himself as secured.

It is possible only by virtue of the existence of God to assure the continual existence of man, who as a deficient essence makes the best of his deficiency,[46] "because this God in His absolute power confers myself upon me."[47] And with that, I have really been given to myself. I am no longer just certain of my existence at this very moment, but rather I am certain now of my identity. Just as doubt as defect made me certain that I did exist, now dependence as a defect makes me certain of myself as one who is identical with himself. The defective character of man is proven to be a major form of power. The defectiveness of

39. *Meditations*, V, 61-67.

40. On what follows, see Schulz, *op. cit.*, pp. 38ff. Schulz sees in the following thoughts the point of Descartes' metaphysics.

41. See *Meditations*, III, 44.

42. *Discourse*, p. 23.

43. *Meditations*, III, 47; see also above, p. 116, n. 18.

44. Schleiermacher's definition of piety as the feeling of absolute dependence probably stands in an historical relationship to Descartes' definition of the existence of the 'thinking thing' as a knowledge of absolute dependence. The mediator may well have been Spinoza to whose name the reader of *On Religion* is summoned to "offer a reverent tribute" (F. Schleiermacher, *On Religion; Addresses in Response to its Cultured Critics*, tr. T. N. Tice [Richmond: John Knox Press, 1969], p. 84).

45. Schulz, *op. cit.*, p. 38.

46. See *Meditations*, III, 49f.

47. Schulz, *op. cit.*, p. 39.

man is ontologically justified. The weakness of the Cartesian ego is shown to be, in fact, its actual strength.[48]

There are two things about the human ego which are implied by Descartes' securing of the continuity (unity) of human existence by doubting God.

(a) First, Descartes expresses here the fact that doubt of the human ego as such is not strong enough to produce the securing of the continuity of human existence which he wants. He needs God as a comrade in arms. God is a methodological necessity for the continuity of the 'thinking thing' which is securing its existence.

(b) God will not do as the comrade in arms of doubt if he would be established as an entity removed a priori from all doubt and superior to all doubt, which would put doubt in doubt. The securing would then be by no means final, because the course of the assurance would not have gone through doubt and thus not secured by the doubter. If God is really to be able to provide this assurance, which doubt itself cannot provide, then God must be put in doubt and in the process be secured. To that extent, a "methodological will to atheism"[49] does belong to this second meaning of the proposition that God must be doubted in order to assure the continuity of human existence.

b. The Securing of God as the Disintegration of the Certainty of God

The new Cartesian approach to metaphysics contains an explosive theological power whose outworking is known to us but whose cause has not been understood at all adequately. We must therefore particularly emphasize the extent to which the Cartesian securing of God for the purpose of providing assurance for the human ego had to lead to the disintegration of certainty about God.

In order to demonstrate that the actual strength of man is his weakness, a proof of the existence of God was needed which showed God to be a 'necessary essence' (*ens necessarium*) which was free of that very human defect. For man could be defined as man only by referring to something which is "more perfect than man." God could then be God only in that he is not less perfect than he is. But if the perfection of God is an important theme only because man is not quite perfect and needs something more perfect above himself, then paradoxically the idea of a perfect God is dependent on the postulate of a less perfect reality— that is, on the self-understanding of man. God ends up in the position of a predicate of perfection, which is conceived of in terms of the defectiveness of a not quite perfect human essence. Thus, by identifying God with that which is highest, God is totally relativized by man. The understanding of God makes itself its own problem.

1. The entire problem of this understanding of God, which Descartes inherited from the tradition, can be seen if we formulate the decisive proposition a little differently. The decisive proposition was this: ". . . the God who possesses all these high perfections of which my mind can have some slight idea, without however being able fully to comprehend them; who is subject to no

---

48. The *Discourse on Method* came to the same conclusion without having to make use of the 'evil spirit.' It could be demonstrated, however, that the path taken by the *Meditations* only clarified what the *Discourse* intended and accomplished.
49. Schulz, *op. cit.*, p. 34.

defect and who has no part of all those qualities which involve imperfection."[50] God possesses all perfection, which man cannot comprehend (Kant would say: cognize) but can somehow attain to through thought, and is in no way at all subject to any defects. This idea could also be put in this way: God cannot do without any perfection and must do without any deficiency. *God must lack defects*. The defect which God must lack is anything which can be considered as a hindrance of *power*. That means that God must be free of every *weakness*, from anything remotely like a limitation of his power which could be interpreted as a tendency toward weakness. If his existence is to be provable and thus my existence is to be secured as identical, then his name must be understood to denote an infinite, independent, most intelligent, and most potent substance: "By the word 'God' I mean an infinite substance . . . independent, omniscient, omnipotent. . . ."[51]

Obviously it is not a problem for theology that God should be not only an intelligent, but the most intelligent essence. But intelligence is thought of here primarily according to the model of power. And theologically that is problematic. Highest intelligence here excludes all weakness, vulnerability, powerlessness. That calls forth theological mistrust. From an anthropological perspective the rule would be: the more intelligent, the more vulnerable. It would thus appear appropriate to ascribe to the "highest intelligence" highest vulnerability and *thus* not to exclude weakness from it in principle. Certainly faith in the crucified God forces us to contest the view that God is an absolutely invulnerable essence.

However, mistrust is also called for in precisely the opposite direction, when we consider the Cartesian thought process. In it, the actual strength of man was found to be his weakness. It was the defect of the ability to doubt which made Cartesian man powerful. Would one not then suspicion that, conversely, the God understood as the *highest* power would be the one who was *totally* defective? The highest power could ultimately be found to be the actual weakness.[52] The unconditional independence of God could ultimately be disclosed to be the absolute dependence of God on man. God, who is moved above all doubt through the process of doubt, would become the most doubtful thing of all. That which exists necessarily (*ens necessarium*) would become superfluous. This theological suspicion, expressed in such questions, is proven to be justified when we examine it more closely. Descartes' approach, which determines the metaphysics of the modern period, is, judged objectively, the beginning of the disintegration of the presupposed understanding of God and thus of the certainty of God which had developed until now.

2. We are dealing with a disintegration in a very precise sense of the word. For the new metaphysical approach of Descartes requires, in spite of the historical disclaimers he made, that God's being be so radically divided into his

---

50. *Meditations*, III, 50. The opposition of "without . . . being able fully to comprehend them" and "of which my mind can have some slight idea" (see also *Meditations*, III, 44), with respect to God, is a typically scholastic reservation; compare Thomas Aquinas, *Summa Theologica*, I, q. 12, art. 7, vol. I, pp. 101f with I. q. 13, art. 2, reply to obj. 3, vol. I, p. 116. Also on this, see above, p. 7.

51. *Meditations*, III, 43.

52. The Cartesian God on the cross—and the cross would collapse! The 'infinite substance, independent, omniscient, and omnipotent' is too heavy. And that is its weakness.

essence and his existence, that the understanding of God must disintegrate. It is being disintegrated. And the certainty of God until now is also disintegrated by the decomposing understanding of God. Seen objectively, what Descartes conjured up is almost precisely the opposite of the thrust which inheres in the ontological proof of God. As Descartes understood its thrust, the argument proceeded from the *essence* of God as an *ens necessarium* to the existence which necessarily belongs together with this essence. But conversely, the Cartesian metaphysical approach, which makes something like a proof of God necessary as the grounding of the self-securing given in "I think, therefore I am," requires that a fundamental distinction be made between the certainty of the essence of God (I am certain that God is such and such) and the certainty of the existence of God (I am certain that God is).[53] How so?

Descartes regards that knowledge as *true* which demonstrates that something exists undoubtedly. In that sense, that which is true for Descartes is that which is comprehended clearly and distinctly. That which is clearly and distinctly comprehended is that which is present and unconcealed to the attentive mind (*quae menti attendenti praesens et aperta est*). That which is unconcealed and present to the attentive mind is therefore regarded as existent beyond doubt.

In a most original sense, only the clearly and distinctly comprehending spirit itself is present and existing beyond all doubt: 'I think, therefore I am.' *Thus the clearly and distinctly comprehending ego becomes the place of presence in general.* Only the ego can be present in a total way. For the ego, as the experience of being with oneself, is the event of present existence in an absolute sense. Whatever otherwise lays claim to being present and to being beyond all doubt must therefore be present *in me*, must participate in the being-with-itself of the ego. As that which is most originally present, the Cartesian ego is also that *where*, that *place*, where something present is capable of being present at all: the place of presence in general. Absolute absence must, by contrast, mean nonbeing.

Therefore, God is proven to exist beyond doubt only in that he is *present with me*. But God has been defined as "infinite substance, independent, omni-

---

53. Remaining at the level of rational knowledge of God, for Luther too there is a fundamental cognitive difference between the "that-being" and "what-being" of God, between the 'existence' and the 'essence' of God: There is "a vast difference between knowing that there is a God and knowing who or what God is." See Luther, *Lectures on the Minor Prophets II: Jonah, Habakkuk* (in *Luther's Works*, vol. 19), ed. Hilton C. Oswald (St. Louis: Concordia Publishing House, 1974), p. 55. Whereas Descartes begins with the 'essence of God' which is comprehended in the 'idea of God' and moves to the ascertainment of the 'existence of God' through the ego (see above, pp. 119f), Luther takes another route: "Reason . . . knows that there is a God, but it does not know who or which is the true God" (*ibid.*, pp. 54f). And it is the misfortune of reason overstepping its boundaries that it wants to move from the knowledge that there is a God somehow to the knowledge of who God is, as Luther says: "Thus reason also plays blindman's buff with God; it consistently gropes in the dark and misses the mark. It calls that God which is not God and fails to call Him God who really is God. Reason would do neither the one nor the other if it were not conscious of the existence of God or if it really knew who and what God is. Therefore it rushes in clumsily and assigns the name God and ascribes divine honor to its own idea of God. Thus reason never finds the true God, but it finds the devil or its own concept of God ruled by the devil" (*ibid.*, p. 55). For "Nature knows the former [*scil.* that God exists]—it is inscribed in everybody's heart; the latter is taught only by the Holy Spirit" (*ibid.*, p. 55). This difference does not obtain for faith. For faith knows that God is in that it experiences who or what God is.

scient, omnipotent," as that which is absolutely *superior* to me. As such, he confers my self on me.[54] In that I am always the place of presence in general, God, in conferring my self on me, gives himself to me at the same time. More precisely, in that God confers my self on me, I also appropriate God himself. Modern man is man appropriating God, and only in doing so does he have a relation to God; man is responsible for God.

But at that, the being of God must necessarily disintegrate. On the one hand, God cannot, in terms of his essence as the one who is absolutely superior to me, be thought of as restricted to the presence of the ego. It is part of the essence of God (also according to Descartes) that he is not only present with me. On the other hand, the existence of God can be asserted only to the degree that he is present within the dimension of my presence. For "according to Descartes beingness is representedness through and for the subject," which "I" am.[55] The following aporia results:

(a) In that the essence of God is represented (imagined) by me, the existence of God is secured through me.

(b) With regard to his *essence* God is the almighty Creator, who is necessary in and through himself and through whom I am (both in general and in terms of what I actually am).

(c) In terms of his *existence*, however, God is through me, in that *his* existence can be understood only as representedness through and for the subject, which "I" am.

3. Descartes himself did not make the contradiction which arises here into a separate theme. Instead, he remained true to the tradition in asserting the indissoluble unity of the 'essence of God' and the 'existence of God' and then constructed his ontological proof of God on it. Descartes could avoid the *problem* by appealing to the tradition because he agreed with its assertion that the infinite God cannot be really comprehended and grasped by the finite ego (as 'thinking thing') but can only be arrived at, in a certain sense, in one's thoughts.[56] The concept of being (of the substance) could not be expressed, therefore, of both the finite and of God univocally.[57] With that, Descartes had in effect concealed the problem he raised, by resorting to traditional theological means.

The concealed problem consists of the fact that God only enters into the presence which allows him to *be*, when he is *represented* (imagined) *as God*.[58] The ego as 'thinking thing' has become the 'subject' (*subiectum, hypokeimenon*) of all existence. That means that God, when he is conceived of by me *as* God, must in terms of his *essence* be *above me* and with himself, *only with himself*. But in terms of his *existence*, as this essence, God must be *with me* and *only*

54. According to Schulz, *op. cit.*, p. 39.

55. Heidegger, *Nietzsche II*, p. 172.

56. See *Meditations*, III, 11 ("Preface"); III, 45; III, 49f and 54ff; see also the edition of the *Meditations* edited by A. Buchenau, p. 103, the Answer to the First Objections.

57. *Principles*, I, li (*Meditations and Selections from the Principles*, p. 156): "And accordingly, the term substance does not apply to God and the creatures *univocally*, to adopt a term familiar in schools; that is, no signification of this word can be distinctly understood which is common to God and them."

58. See *Principles*, I, lii (*ibid.*, p. 156): "But yet substance cannot be first discovered merely from its being a thing which exists independently, for existence by itself is not observed by us."

with me, because only *through me* can he be present. Therefore, when God is *conceived of* as the Creator who is necessary in and through himself, he is made by the representing subject into the object, even if he can never be totally comprehended as such.

4. This is, to be sure, a contradiction which disintegrates the being of God: namely, into a *highest essence over me* and into its *existence through me and with me*. This contradiction which disintegrates the being of God results in the factual *establishment* of God as being at once over me and with me. To conceive in a new way the bringing together of God's essence and existence in this antithesis became the task in which modern metaphysics failed and had to fail. Once God has been established in such a contradictory fashion, then he can be removed *as God*. This contradictory definition of God would have to be followed sooner or later by the removal of God, thus doing away with the contradiction. In fact, to the extent that God, as the absolutely superior highest essence, cannot be limited to presence within the dimension of my present existence, he is already disappearing. But this is happening not in spite of, but because his existence has been secured through my ego. This securing of God must necessarily lead to Nietzsche's question, "Where has God gone?" The man who is proving God's existence precisely misses that essence whose existence he is proving.

However, it would be a short-circuited conclusion if one sought to conclude from this aporetic situation, into which the concept of God has come through the self-grounding of thought in "I think," that theology is supposed to battle directly against this self-grounding of thought. That might be the conclusion one drew, intending to protect the thought of God in this fashion from its disintegration through the "I think" proposition which imposes itself between essence and existence, or perhaps to rescue the thought of God from that process of disintegration. Certainly the metaphysics of subjectivity cannot have the last word, and theology must indeed do its part for the "self-renewal" of thought. But it is theologically more important at this point to grasp the insight that the idea of God taken over by Descartes from tradition, the metaphysical concept of the divine itself, was a precondition for the process of disintegration. The problem of this concept of God—which has always been sensed in metaphysics but has been corrected in dubious ways—must be perceived by theology as the actual theological aporia. Perhaps the greatest service which the modern metaphysics of subjectivity, as decried by theology as it has been, has done for Christian theology has been to focus sharply the entire problem of the presupposed concept of the divine essence within the dimension of the proposition, "I think." Within the dimensions of this "I think," the metaphysical concept of God which has also defined theology, although not exclusively, has become progressively less conceivable and finally unthinkable. We shall now turn to this process by seeking to clarify it with the use of three texts.

SECTION 10. The Metaphysical Concept of God in the Modern Disputation of the Possibility of Thinking God

In Johann Gottlieb Fichte's *Gerichtlicher Verantwortungsschrift gegen die Anklage des Atheismus* ('Judicial Defence against the Accusation of Atheism'), he demands, "He [*scil.* God] should not be thought at all because this is impossible."[1]

In Ludwig Feuerbach's book *The Essence of Christianity,* we find the assertion, "Only when thy thought is God dost thou truly think, rigorously speaking."[2]

In Friedrich Nietzsche's *Book for All and None, Thus Spake Zarathustra,* the question is asked: "Could ye *conceive* a God."[3]

If we take each of these three statements out of its context, they then relate to each other in a remarkably tense fashion. Feuerbach seems to contest what Fichte demands. And what Feuerbach asserts, Nietzsche appears to question. This double antithesis appears to move Nietzsche's question very close to Fichte's demand, so that these two statements create the impression of being both in extreme contradiction to Feuerbach's proposition.

This contradictory character, which appears to be present in the relationship of the three thinkers' statements to each other, becomes, however, problematic when we remember that Nietzsche's statement, although it appears to question what Feuerbach asserted and thus to be close to Fichte's proposition, which was opposed by Feuerbach's thesis, functions in total opposition to Fichte's position in the whole context of Nietzsche's philosophy. This is because Nietzsche felt that he, as the *prosecutor* of Christianity and of theology, had to assume the role of the *Antichrist,* whereas Fichte with his call not to think God at all was defending himself against an *attack on atheism* initiated by the church authorities of Saxony and thus was defending the very essence of Christianity against its "literal" alienation. Feuerbach, on the other hand, whose assertion appears to be the crassest contradiction of both Fichte's demand and Nietzsche's question, felt that he had to view *anthropology as the mystery of theology*, so that he does appear to be fighting alongside Nietzsche after all, just as Nietzsche did, in fact, appropriate quite a few of Feuerbach's arguments.

To be sure, Nietzsche's question implies an answer which, if one considers the nature of thinking itself in order to think of God as unthinkable, might be formulated using Feuerbach's approach: "Only when thou dost think of God as unthinkable, dost thou truly think, rigorously speaking." Although this formulation of the answer which is contained by implication in Nietzsche's question appears to be in total contradiction to Feuerbach's assertion, the exact opposite is, in fact, true. Both propositions correspond to each other precisely if they are understood in the context of the thought from which they are derived. And again, although our formulation of Nietzsche's implied answer to his question appears to be a rather exact duplicate of Fichte's demand, both propositions do contradict each other utterly when we consider the thrust of both Nietzsche's and Fichte's thought. What appears to be total contradiction in the relationship of

1. J. G. Fichte, *Der Herausgeber des philosophischen Journals gerichtliche Verantwortungsschriften gegen die Anklage des Atheismus,* in *Sämmtliche Werke,* ed. I. H. Fichte (Berlin: Veit & Company, 1845, 1971), V, 266.
2. Ludwig Feuerbach, *The Essence of Christianity,* tr. G. Eliot (New York: Harper & Brothers, 1957), pp. 36f.
3. Friedrich Nietzsche, *Thus Spake Zarathustra; A Book for All and None,* in *The Complete Works of Friedrich Nietzsche,* ed. O. Levy, tr. T. Common (New York: Macmillan, and London: George Allen & Unwin Ltd., 1930), "In the Happy Isles," XXIV, 99.

Nietzsche's question to Feuerbach's thesis is in fact merely an external antithesis. And although Nietzsche's questioning of a contradiction appears to affirm that which is negated in Feuerbach's contradiction (namely, Fichte's demand to protect the deity of God by respecting his unthinkability), in truth he is really contradicting what appeared to be affirmed—he is radically denying God.

Precisely because of these false appearances and because of the possibility of destroying them, the three thinkers' propositions are admirably suited for use in interpreting the basic positions which post-Cartesian thought can take on the question of the thinkability of God. This can be done when such thought insists on a metaphysical concept of God as its presupposition, be it the presupposition for the possibility of thinking God, or the presupposition for contesting this possibility. That is precisely the case in Fichte's demand quoted above, as well as in Feuerbach's assertion and Nietzsche's question. The disputation of the thinkability of God also requires a concept of God as its presupposition. It is not disputing nothing. All three thinkers are presupposing, in one way or another, the metaphysical concept of God.

Fichte contests the thinkability of God, for the sake of the glory of God. But it is the glory of a highest being metaphysically understood. Feuerbach asserts the conceptual necessity of God for the sake of the dignity of human thought. But it is the dignity of man identifying himself with the highest being, metaphysically understood. Nietzsche questions the thinkability of God, for the sake of the praise and justification of all mortality. But it is the praise and justification of a mortality from which God, metaphysically conceived as the highest being, must be and remain removed, because all mortality is by definition excluded from the metaphysically conceived highest being. Until that common factor in the statements of all three thinkers is overcome, it will scarcely be possible to discover a new basic position of thought in relation to the question of the thinkability of God.

In what follows I shall provide a brief explication of what has been anticipated here in summary.

a. Fichte's Demand: "God should . . . not be thought at all"

1. Fichte's demand that God should not be thought at all is supported rather concisely with the statement, "because this is impossible."[4] The reason for the demand that one not think God is itself a disputation of the thinkability of God. Although Fichte with his demand merely seeks to answer "in passing" a question which someone may have raised "in passing," his answer confronts the central issue. What is purportedly said "in passing" hits the center of the target. The reasoning for the demand not to think God at all makes this plain.

4. Fichte's demand interests us here only systematically in the context of the guiding perspective of our treatise as a possible position in relation to the problem of the thinkability of God in the modern period. Therefore, the development of Fichte's thought and also the difference between the late Fichte's position and that view espoused during the period of the atheistic controversy can be left totally aside here. In order to understand the development of Fichte's concept of God, see the newer monographs by Falk Wagner, *Der Gedanke der Persönlichkeit Gottes bei Fichte und Hegel* (Gütersloh: G. Mohn, 1971), and Günter Bader, *Mitteilung göttlichen Geistes als Aporie der Religionslehre Johann Gottlieb Fichtes* (Tübingen: J. C. B. Mohr, 1975).

To assert the *impossibility* of something requires more than an occasional thought as a presupposition. The impossibility of something can be asserted only on the basis of the highest degree of certainty. To predicate an "impossible" in all seriousness can never be the result of a mere presumption nor of a simple ascertainment. Rather, there must be the certainty here that the thing which is declared to be impossible stands in total contradiction to something which is unquestionably certain. Certainty about the existence of an extreme contradiction to something which is already unquestionably sure is a very high level of certainty. Thus, one can say "impossible" only when one is obliged to do so by a very high degree of certainty. Of what is Fichte so extremely certain that he dares to assert the impossibility of thinking God?

The only possible answer to that question is this: of God himself. Fichte is so certain of *God* that he sees himself obliged to contest the *thinkability* of God. Put in the theological language of Protestant tradition, the certainty of God is salvific. The certainty of God is the blessedness of man. In a Berlin lecture, Fichte said, "The Metaphysical only, and not the Historical, can give us blessedness. . . ."[5] This statement, made after the period of the atheistic controversy in Jena (we are neglecting entirely the problem of the development of Fichte's thought here), provides a clear reference for the understanding of the impossibility of thinking God, as it was asserted in the atheism controversy. It is the Metaphysical understood in contradiction to the Historical; it is this metaphysical certainty of God which makes us blessed. That makes perfectly clear that for Fichte the impossibility of *thinking* God was based on the certainty of a metaphysically conceived God. The disputation of the thinkability of God is carried out for the sake of God, so understood. Apparently, thought cannot, under any circumstances, do justice to the deity of God.

What was Fichte thinking, then, when he understood *thought* as inadequate for the deity of God?

In order to answer this question precisely, it will be helpful to reflect back on Kant's question with regard to the thinkability of God, which was presupposed by Fichte. In the self-criticism of reason, which Kant recognized and executed as the prime task of the philosophy of his age, a further turning-point was reached in the self-grounding of thought, judged from the perspective of Descartes. Kant for his part presupposes the Cartesian self-grounding of thought in the proposition "I think," and this is expressed in his fundamental proposition of the synthetic unity of transcendental apperception: ". . . the representation *I think* . . . must necessarily be capable of accompanying all our representations."[6] We shall discuss the significance of this proposition for the problem of the thinkability of God, but only to the degree necessary to understand better Fichte's demand that God should not be thought at all.[7]

2. In the foreword to the second edition of the *Critique of Pure Reason*, Kant defended the indisputably *negative* results of his work, "that it only serves

5. J. G. Fichte, *The Way Towards the Blessed Life; or, The Doctrine of Religion*, tr. W. Smith, in *The Popular Works of Johann Gottlieb Fichte* (London: Trübner & Company, 1889), p. 392.

6. Immanuel Kant, *Critique of Pure Reason*, tr. J. M. D. Meiklejohn (*Everyman's Library*, 909) (London: J. M. Dent & Sons, 1950), p. 94.

7. See G. Bader, *op. cit.*, pp. 29-48.

to warn us against venturing, with speculative reason, beyond the limits of experience," as nevertheless *positive* in its usefulness. The positive usefulness becomes plain when we observe that crossing over the boundaries of experience by means of speculative reason results, in reality, in a limitation of the use of reason, rather than the intended expansion of its use. For "the principles with which speculative reason endeavors to transcend its limits" really belong to the sphere of the senses, so that these principles in such transcending of the boundaries "threaten to extend the limits of sensibility . . . over the entire realm of thought, and thus to supplant the pure (practical) use of reason."[8] If in the use of practical reason any expansion of pure reason should be possible at all, then the theoretical use of reason must have its boundaries assigned in advance. "I must, therefore, abolish *knowledge*, to make room for *belief*."[9] This statement requires explanation.

(a) The knowledge Kant feels he must abolish is understood by him as a *cognizing* of objects. For Kant, cognizing is not identical with thinking. The difference between cognizing and thinking is seen in that "I can *think* what I please, provided only I do not contradict myself; that is, provided my conception is a possible thought, though I may be unable to answer for the existence of a corresponding object in the sum of possibilities. But something more is required before I can attribute to such a conception objective validity, that is, real possibility—the other possibility being merely logical. We are not, however, confined to theoretical sources of cognition for the means of satisfying this additional requirement, but may derive them from practical sources."[10] The additional requirement which allows me not only to think an object but also to *cognize* it in a theoretical sense, consists for Kant in this: "In order to *cognize* an object, I must be able to prove its possibility, either from its reality as attested by experience, or *a priori*, by means of reason."[11] Even when, in the case of God, the objective validity is derived from practical sources of cognition, there must also be at least a concept of God as a given, so that the thinkability of God is assured and realized.

In the sense of this distinction between thought and cognition, Kant disputes the theoretical cognizability of God, of freedom, and of immortality, but he does not contest their thinkability, to which then the demand for cognition on the part of practical reason can appeal.[12] Cognition in the context of the

8. Kant, *op. cit.*, p. 15. Conversely, "in respect of all our ideas of the supersensible, reason is restricted to the conditions of its practical employment, [which] is of obvious use in connection with the idea of God. It prevents *theology* from losing itself in the clouds of *theosophy*, i.e., in transcendent conceptions that confuse reason, or from sinking into the depths of *demonology*, i.e., an anthropomorphic mode of representing the Supreme Being. Also it keeps *religion* from falling into *theurgy*, which is a fanatical delusion that a feeling can be communicated to us from other supersensible beings and that we in turn can exert an influence on them, or into *idolatry*, which is a superstitious delusion that one can make oneself acceptable to the Supreme Being by other means than that of having the moral law at heart" (Kant, *Critique of Judgement*, in *Great Books of the Western World*, vol. 42, tr. J. C. Meredith, ed. R. M. Hutchins [Chicago: Encyclopaedia Britannica, Inc., 1952], 599f).
9. Kant, *Critique of Pure Reason*, p. 18.
10. *Ibid.*, p. 16.
11. *Ibid.*
12. To develop a concept of God, Kant makes use of the principle of analogy. See below, pp. 263ff.

theoretical use of reason would subject God, freedom, and immortality to the conditions of space and time, because "we have no conceptions of the understanding, and consequently, no elements for the cognition of things, except in so far as a corresponding intuition can be given to these conceptions. . . ,"[13] whereby space and time have been defined by Kant as forms of sensible intuition. To subject God, freedom, and immortality to the conditions of space and time means to formulate a thought which is contradictory in and of itself. That becomes immediately evident with the concept of immortality: immortality within time—that is an intrinsic contradiction.

Whoever asserts the *cognizability* of God, freedom, and immortality attains the opposite in that he thus makes the *thinkability* of God, freedom, and immortality impossible. For, as we saw, one of the elements of the thinkability of an object is the noncontradictory nature of the thought. But if, "on behalf of the necessary practical use of my reason,"[14] things like God, freedom, and the immortality of the soul are going to be acceptable at all, then the thinkability of God must be secured, and thereby the contradiction avoided which would arise with the assertion of the cognizability of God by means of theoretical resources of reason.

If we follow Kant thus far, then based on his premises, the exact opposite from what Fichte wanted to accomplish for the sake of God, namely, the disputation of the thinkability of God, must result, and that must be prevented at all costs. According to Kant, a concept of God must then be developed in a struggle with theoretically indispensable doubt, a theistic concept of God must be designed anew, in order to be certain of God in a practical sense.[15] However, Kant himself connected *thinking* with the cognizing *ego* in such a way that it is difficult to distinguish thinking from intuition, and from space and time as its forms as well. This is where Fichte links up. For that reason, the rather complicated argumentation in Kant should be presented in greater detail.

(b) It is well known that Kant regarded it as a "scandal to philosophy" "to be obliged to assume, as an article of mere belief, the existence of things external to ourselves. . . ."[16] For that reason, he sought to replace this mere belief with the proof of the existence of things outside ourselves. To do this, Kant resorts to the *"empirical consciousness of my existence,"* because man, the ego, cannot relate "a determination of my existence by *intellectual intuition"* to the *"intellectual consciousness* of my existence, in the representation: *I am."*[17] Kant derives the fact that "I am conscious . . . of my *existence in time"* from "internal experience" through the "internal sense" rather than from *intellectual* intuition, so that the empirical consciousness of my existence in time must correspond to the intellectual consciousness of my existence in the representation "I am," if my being is to be regarded as definite in any sense at all.[18] Thus, a *determination* of my existence is already given through the internal experience of the internal intuition through which I am conscious of my existence in time.

13. *Critique of Pure Reason,* p. 16.
14. *Ibid.,* p. 18; however, my translation—TR.
15. See G. Bader, *op. cit.,* p. 47.
16. Kant, *Critique of Pure Reason,* p. 22 n.
17. *Ibid.,* p. 22 n.
18. *Ibid.*

Determination is only present, however, where something *permanent* is present which can be determinative. Since internal experience does not discover such a permanence in me, it must then depend on something permanent "which is not in me, which can be, therefore, only in something external to me, to which I must look upon myself as being related."[19] To that extent, it is also true that "I am just as certainly conscious that there are things external to me related to my sense, as I am that I myself exist, as determined in time."[20] Things outside of me are, therefore, just as certain as I am certain of myself.

What has been gained to this point is only the certainty that *some* things exist outside of me *at all*. By means of my internal sense I am not certain of *definite* things at all. That very certainty of things external to me, which is given in the very same certainty which I have of myself, thus forces me to comprehend the things outside of me *clearly and distinctly*. I must move from the general certainty that things may exist outside of me to the cognition of specific things, if the certainty gained through internal intuition, about the existence of things outside of me, should not ultimately be ascribed merely to my imagination.

Kant's approach to cognition appears now to be in direct opposition to that of Descartes. Whereas Descartes had demanded and grounded knowledge, based on *uncertainty* and *doubt*, through 'clear and distinct perception' (*clara et distincta perceptio*), for Kant the necessity of a clear and distinguishing comprehension of the cognizable results from the *certainty* given through internal intuition, the certainty of my self and of the world of things outside of myself in a general sense. If there is "something external to me, to which I must look upon myself as being related," then I must attempt to draw this "something external" before myself in such a way that I can imagine it to be something definite. To do that, thinking is needed. For without "I think," the relation in which I find myself to other things outside of myself remains dark. Nothing *appears* to me even though I am as certain of the existence of something outside of myself as I am of my own existence in time. The relation to other things, in which I find myself, can only be illuminated through representations which then receive their clarity and distinctiveness through an "I think." The light which illuminates being in such a way that that which exists can encounter me, is derived from the ego. It is the light of reason. "The representation *I think* . . . must necessarily be capable of accompanying all our representations."

This statement implies that the ego which realizes its own identity in the act of thinking unites the intellectual consciousness of its existence (I am) with the empirical consciousness of its existence and thus links together the variety of things outside of itself into a clear and distinct unity of representations. This proposition is therefore the formulation of the objective condition of cognition in a general sense. In order to be able to use reason for cognition at all, this reason must, through the mere analysis of its self, gain the fundamental knowledge that the self-consciousness is *an ego which is active in thinking*. The ego is active in thinking in such a way that it links together the varieties of things out there into clear and distinct unities in that it processes *itself* as the original unity. "The first pure cognition of understanding, then, upon which is founded

19. *Ibid.*
20. *Ibid.*

all its other exercise . . . is the principle of the original synthetical unity of apperception."[21]

(c) Although "perfectly independent of all conditions of mere sensuous intuition,"[22] this first pure cognition of understanding is in fact conceived of with reference to the objects of sensuous intuition. There is an involuntary example of this in Kant, where, in order to illustrate the priority of the first pure cognition of understanding, he argues as follows: "But, in order to cognize something in space (for example, a line), I must draw it, and thus produce synthetically a determined conjunction of the given manifold, so that the unity of this act is at the same time the unity of consciousness (in the conception of a line), and by this means alone is an object (a determined space) cognized."[23] Without the "I think," there would be no concepts at all, without which in turn the manifold could not be comprehended as a unity and thus could not be thought of at all.

This means in effect that without the "I think" nothing can become a cognizable object for me, not to speak of its being recognized as an object. "The synthetical unity of consciousness is, therefore, an objective condition of all cognition, which I do not merely require in order to cognize an object, but to which every intuition must necessarily be subject, in order to become a subject for me; because in any other way, and without this synthesis, the manifold in intuition could not be united in one consciousness."[24]

Kant himself expressly states that this proposition, "although it constitutes the synthetical unity (as) the condition of all thought,"[25] is *analytical*. An analytical (affirmative) propositional judgment is present, according to Kant's well-known dictum, when "the connection of the predicate with the subject is cogitated through identity."[26] Now the fundamental proposition of the synthetic unity of apperception is for Kant an analytical proposition because "it states nothing more than that all my representations in any given intuition must be subject to the condition which alone enables me to connect them, as my representatives with the identical self, and so to unite them synthetically in one apperception, by means of the general expression, *I* think."[27] Therefore, if the synthetic unity can be established only through an "I think," which analytically identifies my representations as *mine*, then that identity is given in the thought of the ego which makes both analytical and synthetic judgments possible. Based on the self-identification of the ego in "I think," the connection of nonidentical things can only begin to happen. The self-identification of the ego in "I think" is indispensable if the cognizing ego is supposed to be able to represent the variety outside itself at all. In this "I think" the self-identification of the ego takes place as that of a subject relating itself to objects through its representations.

To "represent" means, to present something to oneself in such a way that the representing ego brings itself into a clear position of oppositeness to that

21. *Ibid.*, p. 97.
22. *Ibid.*
23. *Ibid.*
24. *Ibid.*
25. *Ibid.*
26. *Ibid.*, p. 30.
27. *Ibid.*, p. 97.

which is represented. If this "I think" must accompany all my representations, then with the self-identification of the ego in "I think" the "illumination" of that which is opposite to me takes place, within which existing things first can become objects for me and thus appear and be recognized as objects. The subjective nature of the "I think" is, accordingly, the condition for the possibility of cognizing objects. As such, it is always directed toward the objectification of being, factually speaking. The cognition of being results only when the manifold variety is already *given* to an ego. But what is given must be fixed by an "I think" and brought into representation in such a way that for this ego it becomes an object, appears as such, and then can be cognized as an object. In this "I think" there is, thus, a tendency toward the factual *subordination* of thought to the given manifold variety on which it is dependent in order to become active in cognition at all. To that extent, there is in Kant's "I think" a remarkable ambivalence between the *independence of thought* from sensuous intuition and the "I think" *which conceives of itself in relation to the given manifold variety,* that "I think" which must be able to accompany all my representations.

(d) Of course, Kant then sets a decisive limitation. He does not want to have the fundamental proposition of the synthetic unity of apperception "regarded as a principle for every possible understanding," "but only for that understanding by means of whose pure apperception in the thought *I* am, no manifold content is given."[28] That is human understanding. The self-consciousness of the human ego does not comprise any more than this, that I am given to myself. From "I am," the way leads to another being only via "I think," if it is intended to be a *way of cognition.* Without "I think" there is no cognitive route which leads from "I am" to an "S is P." Therefore, it is true of human reason that it can have experiences with other existing things only because "the conditions of the possibility of experience in general are at the same time conditions of the possibility of the objects of experience. . . ."[29]

On the other hand, for a possible different understanding "which contained the manifold in intuition, in and through the act itself of its own self-consciousness, in other words, an understanding by and in the representation of which the objects of the representation should at the same time exist,"[30] the special act which connects the manifold content into the unity of consciousness would not be necessary. An "I think" would not have to accompany its representations. In contrast to such a *divine* understanding, which could traditionally be called an *intuitus originarius* ('original intuition'), the *human* understanding is defined by the differentness between its self-consciousness and everything else in such an original way that without an "I think" it is totally incapable of comprehending the other for what it is. For that reason human understanding is so very limited to its "I think," "that we cannot form the least conception of any other possible understanding. . . ."[31]

To say that the human understanding cannot conceive at all of such a divine understanding does not mean for Kant that one cannot think God at all. For the purposes of the *practical* use of reason, Kant can certainly think God; he must

28. *Ibid.,* pp. 97f.
29. *Ibid.,* p. 128.
30. *Ibid.,* p. 98.
31. *Ibid.*

do so.[32] The practical cognition of reason which implies both the thinkability and the conceptual necessity of God is possible because God does not fall under the condition of sensuousness in it.

The basic concept of the synthetic unity of transcendental apperception produced a certain *ambivalence* with regard to the significance of the "I think," an ambivalence which forces us to ask whether Kant's concept of thought is not in fact bound to his concept of intuition in such a way that it is impossible for the "I think" to think anything independent of whatever *is given by intuition.* The practical necessity of thinking God cannot be carried through without at least thinking God *in analogy* to the representations accompanied by the "I think"—even though God as the moral law-giver does not fall within the conditions of sensuousness.[33]

3. In the atheism controversy, Fichte clearly related the "I think" terminologically to the objects of intuition. To think means therefore to make mortal, to bring under the conditions of space and time. At the same time and together

32. In this context, Kant speaks terminologically of faith. "Belief or assent from a reason which is objectively inadequate, but subjectively adequate, relates to objects with respect to which we not only can know nothing, but also can have no opinion—nay, cannot even allege probability, but only can be certain that it is not contradictory to conceive such objects in the way in which we do conceive them. The rest is a *free* assent, which is necessary only in a practical *a priori* point of view; an assent, therefore, to that which I assume from *moral* ground, and so that I am certain that *opposite* can never be proved" (*Kant's Introduction to Logic*, tr. T. K. Abbot [New York: Philosophical Library, 1963], p. 58). Belief, therefore, is not a special source of knowledge, but is rather regarding something to be true which as knowledge has a special relationship to *actions*. "This is an assent which is sufficient for action, that is, a Belief" (*ibid.*, p. 58 n.). In that sense, even the merchant needs faith: "Thus, for instance, a merchant, in order to enter upon a business transaction requires not merely the opinion that something is to be gained by it, but the belief, that is, his opinion must be firm enough to run the risk" (*ibid.*, p. 58 n.). The *religious* understanding of belief also accords with this. "The acceptance of the fundamental principles of a religion is faith *par excellence (fides sacra)*" (*Religion Within the Limits of Reason Alone,* trs. T. M. Greene and H. H. Hudson [New York: Harper, 1960], p. 151). I make only passing reference here to Kant's various distinctions within this religious concept of faith: between pure rational faith and revealed faith, faith freely assented to (*fides elicita*), commanded (*fides imperata*), freely accepted and commanded (*fides historice elicita*—'faith historically elicited'), and blindly accepted and commanded (faith which obeys the command blindly—*fides servilis*) (*ibid.,* pp. 151ff). This difference, implied in these distinctions, between a moral and rational faith and an historical faith constitutes for Kant the Christian religion in its ambivalence as a natural and a revealed religion, or as a natural and a taught religion. The criterion for its possible agreement must be, according to the presupposed general understanding of faith, the relationship to action, obviously, which is the question whether a proposition of faith which is regarded as revealed and thus must be taught (in order to be persuaded of its truth) produces something "practical" (see *Der Streit der Fakultäten,* in *Werke in sechs Bänden,* ed. W. Weischedel [Wiesbaden: Insel-Verlag, 1966²], VI, 303). However, in spite of such considerations, Kant certainly never suppressed the original meaning of faith. He remembers, "*Fides* is properly faithfulness *in pacto,* or subjective trust in one another, that one will keep his promise to the other—*Faith and Credit.* The former when the *pactum* has been made; the latter when it is about to be made. Speaking by way of analogy, the practical reason is, as it were, the *promiser,* man is the *promisee,* and the good expected from the act is the *promissum*" (*Kant's Introduction to Logic,* p. 60).

33. We shall deal in greater detail with the phenomenon of analogy, and the way Kant used it and allowed it to be used in discourse about God, when we come to our section on the possibility of speaking of God.

with Kant and the entire metaphysical tradition, he understood God as that being which under no circumstances may be placed under the conditions of time and space. For that reason, God may not be thought at all. Thinking and God do not get along with each other because God and the sensuous world exclude each other so much that they cannot even be conceived of as mutually exclusive.

(a) Fichte understood thought in this sense as an act of mortalization always related to space and time. This is made plain in the context of Fichte's demand that God not be thought at all. "One might ask in passing and I will answer in passing: Should God then be thought of as united with the world? My answer: neither as united with it nor as different from it; he should not be thought of at all in relationship to it (the world of the senses), nor should he be thought at all, because this is impossible."[34] This thesis, "this is impossible," puts Fichte in plain contradiction to Kant. What leads him to do that?

This question asked in passing, whether God should be thought as united with the world, was produced by Fichte's double thesis that on the one hand God cannot be thought as a substance because substances are matter extended in space, and on the other hand that one cannot think God outside the world because then the world is excluded from God, and God is then conceived of as an imperfect being defined by negation. The reader is confronted with an aporia which Fichte expects him to endure. This aporia consists of the fact that an either-or becomes a neither-nor.

Either I think of God as a definite substance and predicate being for him. But then, according to Fichte, I have constructed God from extended matter and imposed on him a predicate which contradicts his infinity. For, according to Fichte, "those conditions in our thought which we signify in our language with the predicate of *being* (persistence and endurance)" apply only to that which is located within the region of *external* experience.[35] To aver the being or substantiality of God would mean in consequence to make God a thing. A thing-God would be, however, the mortalization of the infinite God. He would have to perish when the world perishes. But "what kind of God would this be who went to his end with the world?"[36] Whoever "conceives of God in this fashion is thinking irrationally."[37] Therefore, God may not be thought. God does not occur within the world. There is no pathway out of the world to God. Thus, there appears to be only an "or" left to thought:

Or I think God as outside the world. But here again I have set an end to the infinity of God, this time by cheating infinity of the finite world. "That *otherworldly* God which I should perhaps have taught as the consequence of hostile understanding is certainly *not* the world because he is beyond the world. His concept is thus defined by negation and he is not infinite, and thus not God."[38] The negation of the world is not a pathway which leads to God.

34. Fichte, *Gerichtliche Verantwortungsschriften*, V, 265f.
35. *Ibid.*, p. 260. Fichte accuses his opponents of not being able to distinguish between this ontological understanding of the predicate "is" and the logical copula "is."
36. Fichte, *Appellation an das Publicum gegen die Anklage des Atheismus*, in *Sämmtliche Werke*, ed. I. H. Fichte (Berlin: Veit & Company, 1845 [=1971]), V, 223.
37. Fichte, *Gerichtliche Verantwortungsschriften*, V, 261.
38. *Ibid.*, p. 265.

The either-or has proved to be a neither-nor. Nothing leads to God.[39] When asked whether God, if he cannot be thought of as otherworldly, must not then be thought of as "united with the world" (then one would have convicted Fichte of pantheism), the defendant against the accusation of atheism answered, "neither united with it nor separate from it." But then God "cannot be thought at all."

(b) The aporia into which Fichte leads his reader is the result of Fichte's one-sided development of the Kantian understanding of thought. Fichte says expressly, "All our thinking is *schematizing,* that is, a constructing, a limiting, and a formation of a foundation (*schema*) to be presupposed for our minds when thinking."[40] "There are two kinds of such *schemata: Action* (pure, autonomous, absolutely initiatory action, grounded solely in itself), and *extended matter.*"[41] Action as absolutely initiatory event is not defined by space as is extended matter which is encountered in space; but as absolutely initiatory, it is also not yet in time, although as a beginning it enters into a relationship with time. Fichte then states that time stands between the two *schemata* as the mediator between them.[42] That corresponds to Kant's teaching of the internal meaning through which I am conscious of my existence in time but whereby I must always understand myself as existing in relation to what exists outside of myself. Time was also for Kant the mediation of the autonomous ego and the being of things external to me in space. However, for Fichte, time mediates between extended matter and the ego as a *moral actor.* To that degree, it is a later connection between theoretical and practical reason.

However, this action as such can be deduced neither from space nor time. It is given to us "through the command of duty," that is, "through the absolute thought, founded in no other thought or being, that we should simply *do* something. This thought, and the *schema* of activity engendered by it, is the basis of our natures; it is that through which we solely exist, and in which our true being alone consists."[43]

The true man is, thus, the acting, and only the acting man. But as actor, man is no longer member of a sensuous but of a "supersensuous world-order." In that region, and only there, man encounters God. For "purely philosophically, one would have to say of God that He is not a being but rather is pure activity (Life and principle of a supersensuous world-order), just as I, a finite intelligence, am not a being but am pure activity."[44] The indisputable *difference* be-

39. See (in what is clearly another context) Bader, *op. cit.,* p. 46: "Nothing *leads* to religion; religion is immediate."

40. Fichte, *Gerichtliche Verantwortungsschriften,* p. 259.

41. *Ibid.*

42. "Time is located between the two and mediates them to each other" (*ibid.*).

43. *Ibid.,* pp. 259f.

44. *Ibid.,* p. 261. To the extent that *time mediates* between the *schema* of extended matter and the *schema* of pure activity, one could "apply the concept" of a God understood as pure activity to something "which is not in *space* but which is extended in *time,*" so that "certain predicates could be ascribed" to God as the logical subject. This is the way that a proposition like "God is spirit" could arise. For an activity which is extended solely through time "is called *a spirit.*" But Fichte warns against such a procedure, which "can introduce much too easily theoretic errors and superstition" (*ibid.,* p. 264). If we remember this warning, then we could understand Fichte's critique of the

tween God and man consists of the fact that God is the "principle" whereas I am simple a *"member* of that supersensuous world order" defined by this principle: I am "activity out of duty."[45]

(c) If we examine Fichte's usage of language, we note that he calls the "schematizing" which forms the *schema* of pure activity, thought. One could then ask if Fichte does not, in point of fact, *think* God after all, in that he thinks him as *pure activity*. Fichte does then say that "God is to be thought [!] as an *order of occurrences*."[46] And he speaks of the possibility of perceiving the supersensuous "through pure thought alone."[47] But for Fichte that is not yet the comprehension of God himself, but rather just a *schema* of God.

As we saw, "schematizing" is "a limiting." "All our thinking is a limiting, . . . and in that regard it is called *grasping;* to grasp together from a mass of definable things, so that always something remains outside the limits drawn, something not grasped or comprehended, and thus does not belong to that which is grasped."[48] A God who is *thought* as "pure activity" or as "the order of occurrences" and is *grasped* within such a concept has thereby been limited and thus not really thought *as God*. As schematizing, thinking always falls short of the pure activity comprehended in its first, supersensuous schema. "Thus it is clear that as soon as one makes God the object of a concept, he then ceases to be God, that is, to be infinite."[49] Therefore, God should "not be thought at all."

This paradox that the supersensuous schema always falls short of the truth which it grasps is related to the fact that we basically apprehend everything comprehended *in* the first supersensuous schema only *through* our sensory capacity to represent things (our power of imagination). "What we perceive is always the first [schema]; the instrument, the tinted glass, so to speak, through which alone under certain conditions we can perceive it, is the power of imagination; and in this tinted glass, it alters its form and becomes a second" schema.[50] The first schema, more clearly than with Kant and his "I think," is always

---

concept of God in the sense of a special substance—a concept which is supposed to emerge independent of all relationship of God to us (see *Appellation. . .* , in *op. cit.,* V, 214 with 216)—as the preparation for Hegel's famous statement that the substance, in the night in which it was betrayed, became subject. However, this subject may not be imagined as a being independent of its activity, or as a being which can be known apart from its relationship to us—even if it is a being understood *morally!* On the contrary, God may not be *imagined* at all because every imagination (or representation) would have to intervene between the divine activity and us, in order then to distort the event of the divine relationship to us. Schleiermacher regarded Fichte's position (which reminds us of the first edition of Melanchthon's *Loci*) as religiously apt and recalls Fichte's polemics against the distortion of God into an idol when he contradicted those "who rejoice in the possession of an original idea of the Supreme Being derived from some other quarter, but who have no experience of piety" (*The Christian Faith*, trs. Mackintosh and Stewart [New York: Harper & Row, 1963], p. 25; in the German edition edited by M. Redeker [1960[7]], I, 40, there is a Fichte quotation provided by the editor as a footnote which fully misses the problem being discussed by Schleiermacher, but the appropriate quotation from Fichte could be found in the vicinity of the statement used).

45. Fichte, *Gerichtliche Verantwortungsschriften*, V, 261.
46. *Ibid.*
47. *Ibid.*
48. *Ibid.*, p. 265.
49. *Ibid.*
50. *Ibid.*, p. 260.

designed in the direction of the second and can only be articulated through it. All statements about God would move in the second schema and fall short of God, and would violate his majesty. Thus Fichte cannot ascribe *personality* and *consciousness* to God, because deity, although it is "according to matter, . . . total consciousness, . . . intelligence, pure intelligence, intellectual life and activity," is "absolutely incapable of being comprehended in a concept" *as* this pure intelligence.[51]

To assert impossibility, we said, presupposes a high degree of certainty. The question remains as to how Fichte can be so utterly certain of God that he contests God's thinkability, if he cannot ever be certain of God *through thinking*. The answer has already been implied when we noted that God and man are pure activity. God and man encounter each other only in activity. However, the activity must be distinguished from the schema in which we think the activity. It is not in schematized activity but in the event of activity that man is certain of God. If activity is the basis of our own nature, then we implement the truth of our beings *in that we act*. If God, for his part, is pure activity, then we come to terms with God in activity. As an *actor* the human ego is certain of itself as pure activity and then also certain of God as pure activity: of itself as the one who is obliged to act through freedom, of God as the one who through activity obligates to freedom. In the freedom of the act, man, who is obliged to pure activity for the sake of this freedom, encounters God, who is himself pure activity, *actus purissimus* ('purest act') free of all passivity and limitation: utterly and totally free.

(d) Fichte, as an advocate of the metaphysically conceived deity of God, is anything but an atheist, as has become clear. To say that God is not thinkable is not a statement *against* but *for* God. Of course, Fichte is "thinking" something in the process when he prohibits the thinking of God. And what he is "thinking" here is that highest of all beings which traditionally is understood as "pure intelligence, intellectual life, and activity,"[52] as 'pure act' (*actus purus*), but who is given to man only immediately, only in the pure act which God himself is, only as the *execution* of the "relations" of an order of moral activity, which "relations are revealed directly in man's inwardness."[53]

Man, who lifts himself up to pure activity, is compensated for the unthinkability of God with the immediacy of God. I can be certain of God as pure activity only in pure activity, and in acting God *reveals* himself to me as the one who acts. The direct affirmation of such revelation is what the Christian tradition calls *faith*. Thus, faith steps, for Fichte, into the place of thought. For him, faith is the certainty with which human activity is certain of divine activity and thus endures. "Thus faith remains with that which is immediately given and stands unshakably firm. . . ."[54] It is then a misunderstanding to say that it is doubtful that there is a God or not. It is not at all doubtful but rather the most

51. *Ibid.*, p. 266.
52. *Ibid.*
53. Fichte, *Appellation. . .*, in *op. cit.*, V, 208.
54. See Kant, *Critique of Pure Reason*, p. 469: ". . . I must not ever say: *It is* morally certain that there is a God, etc., but: *I am* morally certain, that is, my belief in God and in another world is so interwoven with my moral nature, that I am under as little apprehension of having the former torn from me as of losing the latter."

certain thing there is, the very basis of all other certainty."[55] And because God is the *most certain thing* for faith, it is prohibited of thought that it limit God and thus make him *uncertain*. If Kant had abolished *knowledge* in order to make room for faith, but expressly asserted the thinkability of the God of faith and even postulated it in a moral sense, then Fichte had to abolish *thought* in order to leave room for faith as immediate certainty.

> *"Only study and never rest,*
> *Thou dost not come far with thy conclusions;*
> *Of philosophy it is the last and best*
> *To know that, after all, we must believe,"*

was the scornful comment of Emanuel Geibel.[56] We must of course note that the faith understood here as the opposite of thought and knowledge is something completely different from the faith defined in the Old and New Testaments.

4. Fichte's argumentation is convincing only if two presuppositions are accepted. On the one hand, thought must be defined as always having been and always being defined by the human ego as a mortal (perishing) subject. On the other hand, God, within the basic structure of the metaphysical understanding of God, is asserted to be the perfect and infinite being, which can tolerate absolutely no limitation of any kind. Fichte shares the metaphysical concept of God with the entire European tradition. God, established as pure activity, is the 'purest act' (*actus purissimus*), the pure activity of thinking thought (*noēseōs noēsis*) directed toward the moral. Fichte shares his understanding of thought with Descartes and Kant, whereby he one-sidedly expounds a certain ambivalence in Kant's terminology through the clear definition of thought as "setting boundaries and ends." That results, obviously, in Fichte's express rejection of the possibility of stating the existence of God, in contrast with Descartes. "The concept of God cannot under any circumstances be defined through existential statements."[57] For Fichte, existence is a concept which is explicitly and completely determined by "I think"—and in that he is more consequently Cartesian than Descartes himself. It is the old metaphysical principle, "the finite is not capable of comprehending the infinite" (*finitum non capax infiniti*), which is emphasized to the utmost degree in the name of the metaphysics of finite subjectivity: "You are finite; and how could the finite comprehend and grasp the infinite?"[58]

In the atheism controversy, Fichte remains faithful to the metaphysical

---

55. Fichte, *Über den Grund unseres Glaubens an eine göttliche Weltregierung,* in *Sämmtliche Werke,* ed. I. H. Fichte (Berlin: Veit & Company, 1845 [= 1971]), V, 187f. This statement is opposed to Kant's limitation of theoretical reason to the thinkability of God and thus to the rejection of the knowability of God from theoretical sources. See on this Bader, *op. cit.,* p. 47.

56. E. Geibel, *Juniusleider,* in *Gesammelte Werke,* 8 vols. (Stuttgart: F. G. Cotta, 1883), vols. 1-2, Spruch Nr. 4, p. 118.

57. Fichte, *Rückerinnerungen, Antworten, Fragen,* in *Sämmtliche Werke,* ed. I. H. Fichte (Berlin: Veit & Company, 1845 [= 1971]), V, 371. See Kant, *Opus postumum (Akademie-Ausgabe)* (Berlin: Georg Reimer [subsequently W. de Gruyter], 1938 [= 1971]), XXII, 116.

58. Fichte, *Über den Grund unseres Glaubens an eine göttliche Weltregierung,* V, 187.

understanding of God as a being which is infinitely superior to the world (this was also emphasized by Descartes). But in order to avoid the contradiction in the existence of God summoned up by Descartes, Fichte renounces the *imagining* or *representation* of God and the *securing of God's existence*, and he believes that in doing so he is protecting the deity of God: "In summation: in that something is grasped, it ceases to be God; and every alleged concept of God is necessarily that of an idol. Whoever says, Thou shalt not make a concept of God, is saying in other words: Thou shalt not make any graven images, and his commandment means intellectually the same thing as the sense of the old Mosaic commandment: 'You shall not make for yourself a graven image, or any likeness. . . .' "[59] Augustine's statement, "for if you comprehend, it is not God" (*si enim comprehendis, non est deus*), is translated by Fichte's philosophy into the setting of the problem in the modern age. Fichte drew the conclusion which one must draw if, after Descartes' division of the divine being into an independent essence above me and its existence with me which is totally dependent on me, one wants to maintain the understanding of God as this essence which is independent in every respect.

By contrast, Nietzsche, proceeding on the basis of the unthinkability of this essence, proclaimed the death of God, God's death as our act. That means that Nietzsche understood that the consequence of the Cartesian concept of existence can be emphasized against Descartes only in such a way that the "ego" which decides about existence also decides about the divine being. To be able to decide about God means, however, to have made the decision already that there can be only *one* "ego" which decides about existence and being, and thus God must be done away with. "I believe in the primitive Germanic statement: All gods must die."[60]

Can one think dying gods? Before we turn to the question of Zarathustra, we must analyze Feuerbach's apparent antithesis to Fichte's demand that God is not to be thought at all.

b. Feuerbach's Assertion: "Only when thy thought is God dost thou truly think, rigorously speaking"

Whereas Fichte declared that his demand not to think God at all was an answer given in passing to a question raised in passing, Feuerbach's assertion is to be understood as something "rigorously spoken." What Fichte answered in passing was in effect the central proposition of his philosophical theology. Feuerbach's rigorous statement is only one example of a language understood throughout as basically rigorous, but which cannot be called strict. The rigorousness of this language is to be found neither in the strictness of its formulations nor in the strictness of the thought expressed through it, but exclusively in the rigorousness of the intention which is expressed in it.

The rigorously formulated assertion of Feuerbach, "Only when thy thought is God dost thou truly think," reveals very clearly the intent of the endeavor

---

59. Fichte, *Gerichtliche Verantwortungsschriften*, V, 267.

60. F. Nietzsche, "Aus den Aufzeichungen zur Geburt der Tragödie" (1870), *Die Unschuld des Werdens*, I, *Der Nachlass*, ed. A. Baeumler (*Kröners Taschenausgabe*, Bd. 82) (Stuttgart: Alfred Kroener Verlag, 1956), p. 3.

which Feuerbach carries out with his interpretation of the essence of Christianity: The mystery contained in the word "God" should profit man in such a way that everything implied by the word "God" should be asserted of man. The proposition belongs in the context of a critical exposition of the traditional metaphysical concept of God. With constant reference to the essence of the Christian faith, this exposition is to be completed with the rigorous intention to demonstrate that what theology asserts to be the contrasting relationship between God and man is really the mere division of man within himself. The result is to be that *man*, now coming to himself out of that dichotomization, can be asserted to be that being which rightfully and solely merits being called *divine*. The rigorousness of the undertaking is unmistakable.

1. If we ask first of all about the possibility of such a daring endeavor, then we must confirm that Feuerbach was right that theology itself made it possible for him to contest its truth. This should not be taken as an accusation to be levelled at theology—as Karl Barth did[61]—but rather as a statement of a fact which makes clear the degree to which Feuerbach was dependent on the Christian faith and its theology in order to be able to carry out his endeavor at all.

In the context of this question, it is instructive to see the outline of his thoughts which Feuerbach adopted in his *The Essence of Christianity*. In pursuing his goal of returning religion (not destroying it) to its alleged truth by demonstrating its anthropological essence, the ordering of Feuerbach's thought is not without significance. I shall limit myself to a comment which applies to the first three chapters of the first part (chs. 3 to 5).

In accordance with the definition of the human essence through the triad reason–will–heart, he treats first "God as the essence of understanding," then "God as moral essence or law," and finally "God as the essence of the heart." This order could be regarded as irrelevant if one were to follow Feuerbach's explanation that "we think for the sake of thinking; love for the sake of loving; will for the sake of willing,"[62] that each of the three "powers" which are constitutive of the human essence exists for its own sake, and that "that alone is . . . divine, which exists for its own sake."[63] According to this explanation, it would be possible to delineate the divinity of human understanding, the divinity of the human will, and the divinity of human love, and then to assert that the genus man constituted by the unity of this triad was a divine being.

In spite of his assertion that each of these three human capacities exists for itself and is thus divine, Feuerbach points out expressly through the connection of the chapters at the beginning of the first part of his book that the God who is interpreted *only* as the essence of understanding is precisely not seen as the God who is in truth *human*, hence *human* understanding too cannot actually be presented as *divine*. At the level of thought, God is thought as a God who remains abstractly *opposite* to man ". . . as a being *not* human."[64] "The under-

61. See, for example, Karl Barth, *From Rousseau to Ritschl*, tr. B. Cozens (London: S.C.M. Press Ltd., 1959), p. 357; J. Glasse, "Barth zu Feuerbach," *Evangelische Theologie*, 28 (1968), 459ff.
62. L. Feuerbach, *The Essence of Christianity*, p. 3.
63. *Ibid.*
64. *Ibid.*, p. 34.

standing knows nothing of the sufferings of the heart"[65]—that is the anthropo-logical reason for this, and it certainly is subject to dispute.[66] In order for the abstract perfection of the divine rational essence to become the concrete perfec-tion of the human essence, the *abstract oppositeness* of God and man, established by God as a rational essence, must be shown to be a painful lack in man, a self-alienation of the human essence.

This happens in that the perfection, in which God is God, is expressed as man's own *possibility* of being perfect, through the *demand* for human perfec-tion. Thus, the chapter on God as the essence of understanding is followed by a chapter about God *as law*—a chapter which enables the transition to the "incarnation of God" and hence to the demonstration of the divinity of man. It is only within the dimension of the law that movement in the oppositeness of God and man is introduced. For in order to fulfill the law, *love* is required. In love, however, the antithesis of God and man is abrogated—an antithesis which is abstract in the oppositeness of man to God as the essence of understanding, but which comes fluid and concrete in the oppositeness to God's demanding perfection. In Feuerbach's understanding of religion, it is the law which first enables the gospel of the incarnation of God. Judged anthropologically, the law makes understanding historical and thus mediates the anthropological unity of reason, will, and love.[67]

The result for our explanation of the Feuerbachian proposition of the ne-cessity of thinking God is that the concept of God placed at the level of under-standing, or of thought, has only a kind of contextual function for the *Christian* concept of God, which Feuerbach wants to interpret. This leads to the interesting presumption that Feuerbach could not have become a relatively convincing critic of religion, or better, of theology, *without* an interpretation of the essence of *Christianity*.[68] This presumption is strengthened historically by the fact that Feuerbach's so-called critique of religion is consistently nourished by Hegel's

---

65. *Ibid.*

66. I mention as one of several counterarguments the insight already underlined, which may be briefly summarized: the more intelligent, the more vulnerable.

67. One of the unique features of Feuerbach's thought is the assertion that the demand for perfection directed to man does not initiate with God but is attributable to man. According to Feuerbach, the contradiction between perfection and imperfection resides in man himself. Since man cannot endure this difference, he has hypostatized the perfection and set it apart from himself. The *sensitiveness* of man which cannot tolerate the pain of this difference between human perfection and imperfection functions in Feuer-bach's view as the actual reason for the existence of religion (*ratio essendi*). *Sensitiveness*, as a kind of existential factor, suppresses the human contradiction between human per-fection and imperfection in such a way that man, now only imperfect, sees his possible perfection as something outside of himself, as God. This sensitiveness then requires that this contrast between the imperfection of man and the deified perfection be made tolerable in the perception of God as the heart-essence which takes mercy on imperfect man in the act of becoming a man (incarnation), so that man can endure the perfection, originally separated from himself, next to his own imperfection. It would appear to me that for Feuerbach's philosophizing, this sensitiveness can be regarded as a kind of heuristic principle, even in a biographical sense.

68. This circumstance becomes fully clear from the perspective of the identity of God and love, which is asserted by the Christian faith. We shall deal with Feuerbach's interpretation of the New Testament statement "God is love" (I John 4:8) in our discussion of the humanity of God (see below, pp. 314ff).

interpretation of "revealed religion." What Hegel understood as a stage of religion, however decisive, the "unhappy consciousness," is taken by Feuerbach as
the absolute starting point of religion, which he then tries to overcome through
a critique of a theology which allegedly holds on to this starting point as an
absolute, whereby Hegel's interpretation of Christianity as a religion of reconciliation is the guiding idea.

The *general* reason for the thesis ". . . that the true sense of theology is
anthropology, that there is no distinction between the predicates of the divine
and human nature, and, consequently, no distinction between the divine and
human subject,"[69] is logically inadequately established.[70]

Feuerbach's critique of religion sustains itself as a critique *de facto* on the
material statements of the Christian faith and its theology, which certainly does
not always answer as well as it should for this faith. This can now be seen in
his remarks about "God as a Being of Understanding."

2. The statement, "Only when thy thought is God dost thou truly think,
rigorously speaking," assumes that God in his deity is to be thought as the one
than whom nothing greater can be thought. It connects up, therefore, with An-

69. Feuerbach, *The Essence of Christianity*, p. xxxvii.
70. To reach this conclusion, Feuerbach appeals to the alleged Aristotelian rule
that "wherever, as is especially the case in theology, the predicates are not accidents, but
express the essence of the subject, there is no distinction between subject and predicate,
and the one can be put in the place of the other; on that point I refer the reader to the
Analytics of Aristotle, or even merely to the Introduction of Porphyry" (*ibid.*, p. xxxvii).
But neither Aristotle nor Porphyry ever asserted anything like that. "A *property* is
something which does not show the essence of a thing but belongs to it alone and is
predicated convertibly of it" (Aristotle, *Topica*, tr. E. S. Forster [*Loeb Classical Library*]
[Cambridge: Harvard University Press, 1960], I.v, 102a, pp. 18f); for Porphyry, see
Isagoge, chs. 4 and 17). Although, accordingly, a property (*proprium*) in the strict sense
signifies a characteristic *solely* ascribed to the essence of a definite thing, the *essence* of
that thing is by no means exhausted in this one property. Neighing, for example, is a
characteristic of a horse and only of a horse, although it does not reveal the essence of
the horse; but "when a thing is a horse, then it can neigh, and if something can neigh,
then it is a horse" (Porphyry, *op. cit.*, ch. 4). The reason the reversibility rule is valid is
that the property can function in the logical universe of judgment as the predicate of
one and only one logical subject. If then, according to Feuerbach, "there is *no* distinction
between the predicates of the divine and human nature," then the result is precisely the
opposite, that "the predicate" can *not* "be put in the place of the subject." Feuerbach's
conclusion that "consequently [!] [there is] no distinction between the divine and human
subject, and they are *identical*," is scarcely grounded according to the rules of logic to
which he appeals. Only if it were certain from the outset that two subjects, God and
man, are identical, would the logical rule of reversibility be applicable, for only then
would the identical predicates refer to only one subject. However, the logical operation
then serves to prove what had been presupposed. Feuerbach, by contrast, sets up God
and man as distinct in the religious consciousness, so that according to him there are at
first two different subjects present in the religious consciousness.

Apart from the unfortunate reference to Aristotle and Porphyry, one might also
ask if not in fact, if the predicate does express the full essence of the subject, the predicate
and subject are exchangeable, and God and man become identical. The theological tradition never ascribes the same predicates *univocally* to God and man, for that very reason.
For Feuerbach too, therefore, a more earnest grappling with the doctrine of analogy
would be needed, which doctrine makes the equation of the predicates expressing the
divine essence with those expressing the human essence problematic. Feuerbach could
well have known of this problematic with the theological doctrine of analogy through
Kant's *Prolegomena,* section 58.

selm of Canterbury's[71] famous description of God as "a being than which nothing greater can be conceived" (*id quo maius cogitari nequit*). Together with traditional dogmatics, Feuerbach assumes that God is thinkable in his *essence,* his deity, with initially no reference to the identity of this essence with the concrete trinitarian subsistence and certainly by ignoring the identity of God with the concrete existence of the man Jesus of Nazareth. According to Feuerbach, it is not until the concept of the incarnation enters, which understands God as the essence of the heart and thus deprives him of his deity, that the essence of God is understood as that of a *human* deity which then, obviously, is seen to be a divine humanity. Thus Feuerbach sets up God's deity as an only apparent counterconcept to that of the human essence. God is rather thought of "as the antithesis [*Extrem*] of man, as a being not human, i.e., not personally human."[72]

Since Thomas Aquinas, the dogmatic tradition of Christianity has sought to define the essence of God in a similar abstraction of the three divine persons and of the divine-human person.[73] The most radical form for this was the development of the knowledge of God as natural theology. This kind of theology thinks God to the extent that the human capacity of thought finds it possible to think God. Feuerbach completes this tradition when he derives the abstract concept of the essence of God, which concept is maintained by the human thought of God, from the concept which human thought must have of itself. For to the extent that God is thought "as a purely thinkable being, an object of the intellect," he "is thus nothing else than the reason in its utmost intensification become objective to itself."[74] The presupposition here is that reason itself must become objective.

This presupposition is based on the hermeneutical theory that everything human ". . . must express itself, reveal itself, make itself objective, affirm itself." Human reason expresses what it is in that it thinks of God. "It is asked what is the understanding or the reason? The answer is found in the idea of God." For, ". . . what reason is, what it can do, is first made objective in God." In this sense, "God is a need of the intelligence, a necessary thought. . . ."[75] In all this, Feuerbach is always presupposing that God is that "than which nothing greater can be conceived." Only on the basis of that presupposition is it sensible to assert that "God is the reason expressing, affirming itself as the highest existence."[76]

Hence the critical derivation of theology from anthropology moves in a circle, in that the concept of the highest being, the highest *object* of thought, is understood precisely as "the *highest degree* of the thinking power"[77]—a post-Hegelian variation of *noēseōs noēsis* ('thinking thought'). The concept of the highest being is used not only for God but also for reason, because reason attains

71. Anselm of Canterbury, *Proslogium,* in *St. Anselm; Basic Writings,* tr. S. N. Deane (LaSalle, IL: Open Court Publishing Company, 1962), pp. 7-9.
72. Feuerbach, *op. cit.,* p. 34.
73. See on this, Karl Rahner, "Remarks on the Dogmatic Treatise 'De Trinitate,' " in *Theological Investigations,* tr. K. Smyth (Baltimore: Helicon Press, 1966), IV, 77ff.
74. Feuerbach, *op. cit.,* p. 36.
75. *Ibid.*
76. *Ibid.*
77. *Ibid.*

its very essence only in the thought of a highest being, and it comes to itself and satisfies itself there. "Because with the conception of this being [reason] first completes itself, because only in the idea of the highest nature is the highest nature of reason existent, the highest step of the thinking [and abstraction] power attained: and it is a general truth, that we feel a blank, a void, a want in ourselves, and are consequently unhappy and unsatisfied, so long as we have not come to the last degree of a power, to that *quo nihil majus cogitari potest* . . ." ('than which nothing greater can be conceived')[78]—for that reason it is true that "only when thy thought is God dost thou truly think, rigorously speaking."

3. There are two remarkable things about Feuerbach's statement: (1) God is established as that beyond which nothing greater can be conceived; (2) as that beyond which nothing greater can be conceived, God is the intrinsic nature of reason. But if God, as 'that than which nothing greater can be conceived,' is the intrinsic nature of reason, then the magnification of self is given as the essence of thought. Thought magnifies itself, but it cannot surpass itself. In thinking, the empirical ego is surpassed, but not the ego as a genus of existence. As a genus of existence, the ego represents the boundary of thought. For Feuerbach, that boundary is God. For at that point where the ego can magnify itself no further, it thinks God. God is, therefore, the boundary concept, produced by thought itself, and immanent to thought, of thought magnifying but not able to surpass itself. As this boundary concept, God is a *thought*. And as a thought God is one, or better, the most authentic accomplishment of thought. Thinking is then, so to speak, a creator and God is its noblest creation (*ratio creatrix divinitatis* = reason the creator of divinity!); with this creation, the creative ability of this creator is exhausted: ". . . for only God is the realised, consummate, exhausted thinking power."[79] Thought cannot think more than God.

In the thinking of God, then, the self-fulfillment of thought takes place, as that which exhausts the creative self. Thought fulfills itself only at the point where it exhausts itself. What Feuerbach fails to consider in this context is that the stringency of the Anselmian concept of God is that of an argument which constrains thought to ascribe *being* to this conception, in distinction from mere thinking. This must remain unconsidered if the mystery of theology is supposed to be anthropology.

c. Nietzsche's Question: "Could you conceive a God?"

Zarathustra's question, "Could you *conceive* a God?", is closely related to the parallel inquiry, "Could you *create* a God?" Both of these questions are preceded by the assertion, "God is a conjecture."[80] In both instances, no objection is made to conjecture. But conjecture should be restricted. Man must conjecture. His life is lived out in conjectures. But the conjectures must be meaningful. And they can be so only when they find their measure in that of which man is capable. For that reason, conjecture should be restricted. However, the restriction

78. *Ibid.*, pp. 36f.
79. *Ibid.*, p. 37.
80. Friedrich Nietzsche, *Thus Spake Zarathustra; A Book for All and None*, in *The Complete Works of Friedrich Nietzsche*, p. 99 (ch. XXIV, "In the Happy Isles").

of conjecture is blocked by the unrestricted conjecture, God: ". . . but I do not wish your conjecturing to reach beyond your creating will . . . but I should like your conjecturing restricted to the conceivable."[81] In what way does God block the restriction of conjecture?

1. For Nietzsche, or for the tradition against which he is contending, God is the conjecture of infinity. "Once did people say God, when they looked out upon distant seas."[82] "Seas" are for Nietzsche, as well as for the earlier language of the metaphysical tradition, a metaphor for infinity.[83] Tradition made an identification between the infinity surrounding finite man and God. By making such an identification, infinity became a *firm antithesis* to finitude, particularly when the incarnation of the infinite God was disregarded in this context, which is what usually happened. An infinity *not* identified with God, on the other hand, could be looked on as the open aspect of finitude, its horizon, and it then would be the essence of man to go toward that horizon and to prohibit the emergence of any opposition between the finite and infinity. In that sense, Nietzsche, overcoming both metaphysics and Christianity, speaks of the death of God as that great event which finally opens up the horizon again: "The sea, *our* sea, again lies open before us; perhaps never before did such an 'open sea' exist."[84] In this understanding, the death of God is the setting aside of a fixed oppositeness between finitude and infinity. The dominion of that oppositeness, now finally overthrown, signifies the devaluation of human finitude in favor of the infinitely greater value of the opposing infinity of God: "What? Time would be gone, and all the perishable would be but a lie?"[85] The conjecture of infinity destroys the finitude of the one who conjectures. It imposes finitude on him, instead of comprehending finitude in and of itself. For that reason Zarathustra wants to restrict human conjecturing. For that reason it should not "reach beyond your creating will." For that reason it should be restricted to "the conceivable."

The will to restrict conjecture to the creative will might well be the horizon for the will to restrict conjecture to the conceivable. The infinite God opposed to finite man is fundamentally outside the creative will of man; in that, Nietzsche agrees with the tradition he is criticizing. The infinite God is so opposed to the creative will of finite man that he always casts the creative will back to its finitude, understood as the repulsive opposite of infinity. Since more is conjectured in the thought of God than can be presumed of the creative will, this will is thrown back behind its own real possibilities as a result of that "more." The

---

81. *Ibid.*

82. *Ibid.*, p. 98.

83. In his book *"Gott ist Tod"; Nietzsches Destruktion des christlichen Bewusstseins* (München: Kösel Verlag, 1962), pp. 44f, Eugen Biser cites Gregory of Nazianzus, John of Damascus, and Augustine, as well as Meister Eckhart, Angelus Silesius, and Hölderlin.

84. Friedrich Nietzsche, *The Joyful Wisdom* (in *The Complete Works of Friedrich Nietzsche*, vol. 10), tr. Thomas Common, ed. O. Levy (Edinburgh, London: The Darien Press, 1910), nr. 343, pp. 275f. In section nr. 124 ("In the Horizon of the Infinite"), it is expressly said of the "ocean" that it is "infinite" (p. 167). The "Preface to the Second Edition" notes that the entire book is nothing other than "the frolicking of returning energy, of newly awakened belief in a tomorrow and after-tomorrow; of sudden sentience and prescience of a future, of near adventures, of seas open once more" (*ibid.*, p. 2).

85. *Thus Spake Zarathustra*, p. 100.

problem of the "thinkability" of God "defined" by identification with infinity becomes a very different problem if one differs from the tradition which saw in a God understood as outside the creative will of man the positive beginning point of theology. Instead of seeing it that way, Nietzsche regarded such a view as a fixing of man in a position of finitude understood as the mere opposite to infinity, and in that he finds the grounds for the impossibility of responsible talk about God. "Could you *create* a God—then, I pray you, be silent about all Gods!"[86] That which man cannot create is not worth discussing. But how can one *think* something which must remain silent because it is not worth discussing? Nietzsche's antipathy is directed toward the thinkability of a God set apart from the creative human will.

2. This antipathy applies to the definition of God as 'that than which nothing greater can be conceived,' the ontological argument of Anselm, as well as against the Cartesian approach of a metaphysics which makes being dependent on the 'thinking thing' (*res cogitans*). Nietzsche's position in opposition to both the Anselmian argument and the Cartesian approach to metaphysics is contending against the same thing in both, which is the illusion of a self-mediation of thought into being.[87] The metaphysical approach of Descartes, which dominates the modern period, is opposed by the principle of "the immediacy of life to itself" which restricts the *conceivability* of being, set as the restriction of conjecture, by means of human discernment: "Your own discernment shall ye follow out to the end!"[88] If one's own discernment (senses) is thought out to the end, then finitude is constituted out of itself and ceases to be the mere opposite factor of infinity. For Nietzsche, the power for the finite's "being beyond itself"[89] rests in the discernment of the senses: creative power. The will to restrict conjecture to the conceivable is thus determined by the will to direct the conceivable toward that which is capable of being done.

There is, then, a precise correspondence to this in the attack made on the conceivability of a God understood as that 'than which nothing greater can be conceived.' When the Cartesian approach to metaphysics is bound to the stringency of the ontological argument, without which the self-certainty of the 'thinking thing' in Descartes cannot arrive at any certainty of its own continuity, then God understood this way is not only *necessary* (because 'that than which nothing greater can be conceived' would not be necessary if it were given only 'in the mind' [*in intellectu*] and did not have to be thought of as existing 'in reality' [*in re*]); God, so understood, is then the *only* necessarily existing thing, because this existing thing is the only thing 'than which nothing great can be conceived' and as such cannot possibly have *come* into being and certainly cannot have been *created*. If one wanted to think God, then one would have to think him as one who could not be created because he has always been. Only in that way is he something than which nothing greater can be conceived.

However, as that "than which nothing greater can be conceived," God becomes automatically inconceivable outside the boundaries of that conceivabil-

---

86. *Ibid.*, p. 99.
87. See on this, Biser, *op. cit.*, pp. 100ff.
88. Nietzsche, *Zarathustra*, p. 99.
89. See Martin Heidegger, *Nietzsche, Volume 1: The Will to Power as Art*, tr. D. F. Krell (San Francisco: Harper & Row, 1979), pp. 211ff.

ity restricted by the creative will. That thought which is supposed to think something than which nothing greater is conceivable would in conceiving such a thought restrict itself by an act which always and immediately surpasses this self-restriction. It must think God as the highest object of *thought* and yet see his highest value for thought in the fact that he may not be thought of as something which is *only thought.* Thought must, in a sense, "take off its own harness." In thinking *this* thought, thinking must reel, which is tantamount to giving up thought altogether: "God is a thought—it maketh all the straight crooked, and all that standeth reel. . . . To think this is giddiness and vertigo to human limbs, and even vomiting to the stomach: verily, the reeling sickness do I call it, to conjecture such a thing."[90] The thought of God, always presupposed in a metaphysic which understands God as that 'than which nothing greater can be conceived,' causes giddiness because it forces thought to compare itself to a height to which it is forbidden to climb. Thought cannot think such a height without setting itself fully aside. The thought of God is totally enervating.

With his argument against the thinkability of God, Nietzsche is linking himself to the aporia which Hegel had already formulated when he drew his conclusion from the philosophy of subjectivity: reason ". . . recognizes something higher above itself from which it is self-excluded."[91] To think something "higher above itself" demands too much of the humanity of thought and thus of the existence of thinking man who cannot tolerate being expected to think higher and further beyond himself than he is able to go in the power of the creative will. "But that I may reveal my heart entirely unto you, my friends: *if* there were Gods, how could I endure it to be no God! *Therefore* there are no Gods."[92]

3. This unique syllogism directs our thinking back to the boundaries of conceivability restricted by the creative will. Thought which returns to these boundaries has, according to Nietzsche, a power *capable of transforming everything.* In the context of the question (which bears its answer within itself): "Could you *conceive* a God?", we thus read, "But let this mean Will to Truth among you, that everything be transformed into the humanly conceivable, the humanly visible, the humanly sensible! Your own discernment shall you follow out to the end."[93]

Of everything which must be transformed into that which is humanly conceivable, God must above all be transformed. But God is transformed into the humanly conceivable only when he ceases to be that infinity which as superego is opposed to finite man. According to the logic of the presupposed concept of God, he then ceases to be God in any sense at all. By opposing infinity with the finite, the creative will does away with God and in his place creates itself as the will to the human superego (*Über-Ich*) which surpasses the finite ego. The infinite divine superego is displaced by the will of the finite ego to be the human superego, the superman: "Once did people say God, when they looked out upon the distant seas; now, however, have I taught you to say, Super-

90. Nietzsche, *Zarathustra,* p. 100.
91. G. W. F. Hegel, *Faith and Knowledge,* trs. W. Cerf and H. S. Harris (Albany: State University of New York Press, 1977), p. 61.
92. Nietzsche, *Zarathustra,* p. 99.
93. *Ibid.*

man."[94] The *infinite* is now transformed into the dimension of the *becoming* or *emergence* of the Superman, that is, into the dimension of a finitude which is restricted from outside: "The finitude comes out of the world itself."[95] To *think* the Superman does, indeed, raise thought to a new height. But this height of thinking is no longer the height of some other thing which is over against thought but rather the height of thought itself which is both dominated by and restricted by the will.

4. In terms of the matter itself, Nietzsche was thus asserting the same thing Feuerbach stated with his thesis of the perfection of human thought attained only in the thought of God. In both instances an alien height, superior to human thought, is reduced to the level of human thought. This reduction takes place in both cases in such a way that the human essence is intensified or magnified, a self-magnification which in both Feuerbach and Nietzsche cannot be achieved by thought alone.

Therefore, Nietzsche excludes God from the realm of the conceivable for the same reason which led Feuerbach to make the assertion that "only when thy thought is God dost thou truly think, rigorously speaking." In both cases, God is presupposed as 'that than which nothing greater can be conceived,' but with the decisive difference that Nietzsche takes seriously the stringency of the Anselmian argument bound up in this understanding of God, whereas Feuerbach does not reflect on the ontological argument at all in this context and thus really misses the actual point of this way of speaking of God. That provides the explanation for the differing, even antithetical formulations of what is actually the same thought in Feuerbach and Nietzsche. What is the epitome of thought for Feuerbach cannot be, for Nietzsche, an object of thought which is to be distinguished from thought. That difference may explain why Nietzsche can say with one simple question what Feuerbach must express with such effort in a rigorous assertion.

d. The Actual Inconceivability of the Metaphysical Concept of God for
   Thought Which Establishes Itself on "I Think"

Fichte, Feuerbach, and Nietzsche share the understanding of God derived from the metaphysical tradition. All three thinkers are, however, also thinking in terms of the modern self-grounding of thought in "I think," even though Fichte surpasses "I think" with "I act," Feuerbach accepts the essence of understanding only as the context for the concept of God which is rightly grasped as the essence of the heart, and Nietzsche opposes the self-grounding of thought with the restriction of thought through the will. The results of this self-grounding of thought for the metaphysical concept of God were already seen in their approach in Descartes. This "I think" (*cogito*), which decides about something like existence, interposed itself between the 'essence of God' (*essentia Dei*) and the 'existence of God' (*existentia Dei*) and destroyed the concept of God understood as the unity of essence and existence. This "I think" now stood between God and God. And thus it destroyed its own certainty of God.

In Fichte, Feuerbach, and Nietzsche, the destruction of the metaphysically

94. *Ibid.*, p. 98.
95. Heidegger, *Nietzsche I* (Pfullingen: Günther Neske, 1961), p. 345.

based certainty of God is demonstrated in varying ways. But the same thing is always seen: God's essence and God's existence are separated. The differences between the basic positions of Fichte, Feuerbach, and Nietzsche are thus eminently suited, in their very differentness, to point out the same basic problem of modern thought with regard to the thinking of God as that aporia without whose resolution theology will, in fact, not be able to think God.

Fichte's demand that God not be thought at all was intended to protect the deity of God. According to the Cartesian view of thought as ascertainment and the resulting understanding of existence as that which is ascertained through representation, this could take place only by denying the proposition, God exists. But since a being conceived without existence cannot be God, it became necessary for the sake of the divinity of God to demand that God not be thought at all.

Feuerbach, like Fichte, was interested in the preservation of the metaphysically defined divine. But it was not the divinity of God but the divinity of man which was to be secured. Thus Feuerbach criticized the metaphysical tradition because it reduced the concept of an existing God to the concept of the divine, thus making the divine a predicate, positively predicated of man as a genus of being. The existence of God had to fall so that the divine essence as the essence of humanity could be claimed. If for Fichte thinking was a "mortalizing" and the existence secured through "I think" a mortalizing predicate which could never be attributed to God, then Feuerbach had to deny the existence of God in order to be able to think God's essence as infinite and thus attribute to man infinity as a predicate. Like Fichte, Feuerbach had to declare that God's essence and God's existence were mutually irreconcilable, so that the concept of God as the highest and infinite being which combines all perfections and lacks all imperfections could be preserved. Only in this way could Feuerbach realize his rigorous intention of elevating the mortality of human existence to the heights of the divine essence. For that very reason, the conceivability of the divine must be expressly asserted, in contrast to Fichte. That a God which may not exist is not thought as God at all, and that Feuerbach's thought thus does not even measure up to Kant's sole criterion for all thought, that of noncontradiction, makes all the clearer how much the metaphysical concept of God has become inconceivable under the premise of thought which grounds itself in the "I think." This thought of God contradicts itself.

Nietzsche drew the only possible consequence from all this. He no longer says *God* when he wants to elevate man to the heights reserved for God in metaphysics; instead he says, *Superman*. "God hath died; now do we desire— the Superman to live."[96] Thus Nietzsche destroyed once more the concept of the essence of God already deprived of its existence, in that he denounced the

96. F. Nietzsche, *Zarathustra*, p. 351. The expression "Superman" is used by Nietzsche as a "simile" in order to claim the place no longer occupied by God as man's possession. Like the way in which Nietzsche speaks of the death of God, this expression is a dense metaphor which effectively articulates processes which are described in greater detail elsewhere. However, the expression should not be regarded as a "central category" in Nietzsche's thought. This is underlined in an impressive essay by B. Taureck, "Nihilismus und Christentum; Ein Beitrag zur philosophischen Klärung von Nietzsches Verhältnis zum Christentum," *Wissenschaft und Weltbild*, 26 (1973), 116, n. 7.

concept of this essence, conversely, as an impossible thought which destroys all thought. In doing so, he equated partially Platonic and Christian traditions without distinction.[97] Accordingly, the Christian concept of God is for him a bad conjecture. In distinction from Fichte and Feuerbach, Nietzsche logically negated the *essence* of God and to that degree God's *existence*. Not to be able to *think* God means, in precise contrast to Fichte, that thinking would be discredited by a divine essence and *thus* this divine essence as well as its existence, a God, would have to be declared unthinkable. The destruction of the thought of God is now clearly perceived to be an act of the "ego." To do this, it requires a *new* thinking. Only that kind of thought which had to think something *new* and thus renew itself, could note how far the thought of an immortal highest being had fallen. The real degeneration and hostility toward humanity of the metaphysical thought of God, which was already destroyed by the "I think," could first be fully perceived when thought finally set about praising and justifying mortality: "Evil do I call it and misanthropic: all that teaching about the one, and the plenum, and the unmoved, and the sufficient, and the imperishable! All the imperishable—that's but a simile, and the poets lie too much.—But of time and of becoming shall the best similes speak: a praise shall they be, and a justification of all perishableness!"[98]

One of the remarkable and marvelous contradictions in Nietzsche's thought is that at another place he was able to perceive the "God on the cross" as the God who "solidarizes" himself with mortality, if only then, conversely, to assert the impossibility of *such* a God. We shall return to this. Our intention here was to clarify the consequences of the Cartesian intellectual approach for the metaphysically based certainty of God in all its various possibilities. Nietzsche's consequence was the most consequent because it began to take leave of the results. In this leave-taking it becomes completely certain that the last certainty of modern metaphysics is that of the factual inconceivability of God. Atheism could now become a foregone conclusion.[99]

SECTION 11. The Word as the Place of the Conceivability of God

Augustine, and the tradition which followed after him, resisted the temptation to want to *comprehend (comprehendere)* God. To comprehend God meant to miss God entirely. Since Descartes, the Augustinian concern appears to be

97. See Nietzsche, *Twilight of the Idols,* "Things I Owe to the Ancients," nr. 2: "In reality my distrust of Plato is fundamental. I find him . . . so pre-existently Christian" (in *The Complete Works of Friedrich Nietzsche,* vol. 16, tr. A. M. Ludovici, ed. O. Levy [New York: The Macmillan Company, 1911], p. 114). B. Taureck (*op. cit.,* p. 129) has raised well-substantiated objections to the assertion of an undifferentiated identification of Christianity and Plato in Nietzsche, and he has shown that the "thought expressed" in the term Platonism (as a devaluation of the 'sensible world') "is only an *unimportant* part of Nietzsche's judgment of Christianity."

98. Nietzsche, *Zarathustra,* p. 100. See below, pp. 203-25.

99. The genesis of atheism as an obvious truism is treated here only from the perspective of so-called *theoretical* reason. Within the context of the conceivability of God, atheism as an obvious truism is dealt with only as a possibility. The reality of a fully obvious and self-evident atheism would include further conditions, primarily the condition that God has become dispensable if not actually an obstacle for *morality.*

relatively harmless. The thought which comprehends God is not threatening to miss God but rather to encounter God in such a way that human thought *penetrates* God. The thought of God, in its reference back to the "I think," calls forth the very danger of its own destruction: Can God be thought at all in such a paradoxical situation?

1. The paradoxical situation of the self-abrogation of the traditional thought of God contains an opportunity: it is possible that the thinking which decides about the existence of God could be replaced by a thinking which accords with the existence of God, and such thinking could lead to a new constitution of the thought of God. To do that, a transformation of the relationship of thought to the God to be thought is absolutely necessary. If God is supposed to be able to be thought at all, then the tendency of the "I think" which seeks to penetrate the existence of God, coupled with the destruction of the God thought in that way which has been called forth by this penetration in the modern age, must be overcome as even a mere possibility. This presupposes that the assumed metaphysical thought of God, which virtually produced the destructive effect of modern thought as it penetrated the identity of essence and existence and then destroyed this identity, must be radically overcome.[1] It will be necessary to arrive at a new definition of the relation between God and thought in order to do this.

Thus, we are faced with two tasks. On the one hand, *God* must be thought as the one who he is. And this must be done in such a way that no distinction emerges between the essence and existence of God, the distinction which made it possible for the "I think" to intervene between God and God. That obviously means that we must learn to think God in a new way. Who and what is God? On the other hand, *thought* itself must be so conceived of that it can no longer even *intend* to intervene between the essence and the existence of God. This can happen successfully only if thought, when it turns to questions of existence, learns to reject any interloping between essence and existence. Instead of doing that, the crucial thing would be to perceive existence as that which is essential, and thus to show that act of perception which preserves the original unity of existence (*Dasein*) and nature of being (*Sosein*); that act of perception is what

---

1. If one does not want to leave metaphysics to itself, then "mastery" can only be "overcoming" in matters of metaphysics, which means to take a "step backward," allowing us to enter into that which is to be mastered and to overcome it. The thinker who has made this plain to us, who has attempted to learn how to think and to teach how to think in the struggle with metaphysics, is Martin Heidegger. Theology will obviously have to go its own direction, and it cannot simply be identical with the intellectual path of the philosopher. But this can also be learned from Heidegger if one has not already learned it in one's own work. There is one thing, however, which theology may do without apology: to pay its respects to a thinker whom the most modern philosophy thinks it can evade. Philosophy? However that may be, if philosophy thinks it has to practice the art of forgetting, then for better or worse it will have to learn from theology that Heidegger's thought is an *event* of philosophy which the history of thought can deal with only through thought, and not through thoughtlessness. The respect which theology also owes this thinker can be paid only when theology gives undivided attention to its own concern, which means that *as theology* it must be prepared to learn what may be learned from a philosophy. Theology cannot desire to become philosophy in the process. Then it would just degenerate into a "mixophilosophicotheologia" (on this expression borrowed from Calovius see Karl Barth, *Evangelical Theology: An Introduction,* tr. G. Foley (New York: Holt, Rinehart & Winston, 1963), p. 3.

was progressively distorted by the 'thinking' (*cogitare*) which sought to make everything sure. That obviously means that one must learn to think thought in a new way. What does it mean, to think?

These two tasks, to learn to think both God and thought anew, cannot be separated from one another theologically. It is therefore all the more important from which of the two tasks one approaches the other one. This question, which requires initial clarification, is in actual fact the issue of the self-understanding of theology itself. The first decision to be made will have to do with the difference between philosophical and evangelical theology. A theology which is responsive to the gospel, meaning a theology which is responsive to the crucified man Jesus as the true God, knows that it is fundamentally different from something like philosophical theology in this one thing: single-mindedly and unswervingly, based on its specific task, it attempts to think God from the encounter with God, and *thus* to think thought anew. For Christian theology, the decision about what *thought* means is to be made in relation to the possibility of thinking the *God* who is an event. The possibility of thinking God is, for evangelical theology, not an arbitrary possibility, but rather a possibility already determined by the existence of the biblical texts and claimed already by faith in God. Theology must think God in the concrete context of a history which, beyond the momentary aspect of the "I think," implies experiences of God which have happened and are promised.

Evangelical theology is distinguished from philosophy in that it does not desire to be *lacking in presuppositions,* but rather implies certain decisions in its approach to being evangelical theology. A dialogue with philosophical theology, which is really conceivable only as an argument, or a disputation with atheism, must begin accordingly with the exposition of these hermeneutical decisions of evangelical theology. Only in this way does it proceed in a precise and scientific fashion. And above all, this is the only way for it to be honest.

Evangelical theology *explicates* its basic decisions immediately as decisions of thought, and not solely as decisions of faith. There is a difference whether faith believes or whether thought also understands this. When thinking becomes involved with faith, it will also understand that God cannot be thought without faith. That is the initial point from which evangelical theology proceeds.

More precisely, there are three basic hermeneutical decisions which are implied in the approach of an evangelical theology.[2] First of all, the decision has already been made in this approach that one cannot arrive at a concept of God by beginning with a new definition of thought and proceeding to such a concept as it emerges from the analytics of thought. Only in resolving the material task of thinking God as God can a theological renewal of thought emerge—which of course does not exclude the possibility that a "renewal" of thought should be striven after and achieved in other ways than theological ones. Second, the decision has already been made in the evangelical approach to theology that the task of thinking God as God is guided by a very definite possibility which is given with a very special experience of God (formulated anthropologically), with a special relationship of God to human thought which

2. By *evangelical* theology we mean talk about God which expresses the identity of God with the crucified Jesus as the gospel. As evangelical theology, it is catholic.

claims to have general validity. Third, the decision has already been made in
the approach of evangelical theology that this possibility which guides thought
in the task of thinking God as God is steered by the reality of the biblical texts.
All three decisions revolve around the same basic content which states that the
place of the conceivability of God is a Word which precedes thought. We shall
attempt to come closer to this basic content as we proceed through a discussion
of the basic decisions just mentioned, all of them contained in the approach of
evangelical theology.

2. Christian theology arose as the explication and self-criticism of faith
in Jesus of Nazareth. To believe in Jesus means to understand him as that person
through whom and in whom God has become definitively accessible. Our access
to God is thus really understood as God bringing us to himself. Therefore, that
event in which one comes to the thinking of God is also to be understood as an
event in which God brings us to himself, "retrieves us." The *thought* of God
results from this event, and is not therefore its presupposition. We must oppose
the contrary view. Since it is always being asserted, we shall turn first of all to
its rebuttal.

The supporting argument of the view we are contesting is the objection
that even in the original emerging situation of the Christian faith and of its valid
theology, the thought of God was the general anthropological presupposition of
the Christian faith, which is not present today in that form and which must then
be regained. This objection contains an assertion which, under certain and carefully defined conditions, is correct. But in its qualified correctness it cannot
authorize one to draw the conclusion that one must first of all work out the
general anthropological presupposition for the thought of God in order then and
thereafter to be able to think God as the God who became accessible in and
through the man Jesus. If that conclusion were correct, then the presupposition
already asserted that God had become definitively accessible in and through
Jesus would have to be disputed. Since, however, it is the intention of this
conclusion that through a general anthropological exposition of the thought of
God no other God should become thinkable than the God who reveals himself
as God in Jesus and through him, our presupposition is at least shared finally in
this conclusion, even though not *as* a presupposition. But if, conversely, our
presupposition is correct, then the 'portion of truth' (*particula veri*) of that
conclusion (which as such would be a wrong conclusion) could only be that a
God who definitively discloses himself in *one* man and through this *one* man to
all men ontologically defines with such an act of definitive self-disclosure the
human existence of all people so that based on such a revelatory act anthropological phenomena in man would have to become understandable which are
indebted to that divine act but which by no means have their reality only in
relation to that act.

To clarify this, we refer to the basic character of the singular self-disclosure
of God as *address*. The fact that man is *addressed by God* makes him a fundamentally *addressable being*. Addressed by God, man is by no means only
addressable by and for God. He is free to allow himself to be addressed by
everything and everyone. In this freedom of addressability he is man. This also
explains why the *obedience* with which man properly responds to the God who
addresses him, in that he allows himself to be addressed and defined by him, is

a *realization of freedom*. It is part of the worldly nonnecessity of God that man is constituted by his relationship to God as a being to whom the special freedom of an existence in response to God and in harmony with God is entrusted, together with the freedom of addressability. The obedience which man owes God would be perverted into disobedience if it did not grow out of freedom. Because he is determined for freedom when God addresses him, he can only respond in freedom to this claim laid on him when addressed by God. Part of this freedom ascribed to man, which implies an ontological definition of his human existence, is necessarily the general openness of addressability. To put it pointedly: because man is the being addressed by God, he is also addressable by the devil. This freedom is not to be adjudged as a necessary evil which gives man the possibility of responding to other claims than that of God and thereby to end up in opposition to the divine claim. Rather, it is to be understood as the wealth of human existence made possible by God's relationship to man.[3]

The erroneous conclusion which deduced the possibility of the thought of God from general anthropological premises, if not even his necessity, and whose 'portion of truth' we attempted to summarize, does in fact have a very problematic premise. Only under very qualified circumstances is it possible for one to admit that the Christian faith at the period of its emergence presupposed the "thought of God" as a general anthropological 'human condition' (*conditio humana*). Faith in Jesus as the Son of God was judged by many of those proponents of religions and philosophies, who based their claims on this 'human condition,' to be either blasphemous, or as putting the thought of God in question, or even as atheistic. That was logical in that the faith pointedly rejected the divine existence of those powers who functioned as gods within the context of the thought of God. That Paul (I Cor. 1:18ff) described the word of the cross as foolishness and a scandal for the "natural man" of both races (Jew and Greek) is understandable only if the word of the cross implies a radical break with the thought of God which appears to be presupposed as generally valid. Even the doubtless different situation of our age cannot be allowed to move Christian theology to even a transitory hermeneutical abstraction of its original situation, if the accusation of atheism leveled at emerging Christianity is to have nothing to do with the modern atheism which has been asserting itself against Christianity. For any abstraction of its original situation (the opposite would obviously not be the attempt to re-create that original situation; that would be just as abstract) would necessarily lead to an abstraction of the definitiveness of God's

---

3. It is only in this wealth that we can be "beggars" at all before God. But man is not a beggar in the sense that, through analysis of the wealth of his being, he could demonstrate his greater neediness and the corresponding infinite dependence on a being which then should be called God (see Martin Luther's last statement, which relates to the inexhaustible wealth of the Bible, February 16, 1546 [*WA*, 48, 241]; on that, H. A. Oberman, "Wir sein pettler. Hoc est verum," *Zeitschrift für Kirchengeschichte*, 78 [1967], 232ff). This confession, "We are beggars, that is true," is not an act of self-recognition which then leads to the beginning of the knowledge of God, but rather a self-recognition which comes about because of the encounter with God. For that reason, neither the recognition of man's capacities nor the recognition of his needs leads to a concept of God which thinks God as God, but the knowledge of God certainly does lead to a *new* encounter of man with his own capacities and with the deficiency of his being which is grounded in his wealth.

self-disclosure in the crucified Jesus, and that means to a *theological* inhibition of the claim which the Johannine Christ expressed in the very unambiguous formulation: "No one comes to the Father, but by me" (John 14:6). This statement, however, must stand as a fundamental proposition of evangelical theology, also with regard to the *knowledge* of God.

3. To assert that the unique relationship between God and Jesus is the presupposition of evangelical theology, which thought is then to illuminate, means this: special significance is to be acknowledged of those biblical texts which speak of this relationship. They talk about God because, in that they articulate the history of his humanity, they participate in this history in authentic and original objectivity.

There is, however, one limitation of this original objectivity which must be registered here. It is this, that God, even in these texts, does not disclose himself *directly*. The New Testament texts themselves are already the results of God's self-disclosure. And one might say that the Old Testament texts are pathways leading to those results. The biblical texts are, as fixed processes of tradition which express the event of God's self-disclosure in original objectivity, an irreplaceable reality. But they themselves are to be strictly distinguished from the event by the very fact that they talk about it. They do not speak the language of God, but rather our human language.[4] Yet, although they do not depart from the boundaries of our language, they speak of the fact that God himself has spoken. They reveal *God as the one who speaks*. In doing that, they prohibit the misunderstanding that the Bible itself is a talking God. 'Sacred scripture is not the person of God speaking!' (*Scriptura sacra non est dei loquentis persona*).

Thus we have designated the reality of the biblical texts as a possibility which leads theology in its task of thinking God as God, but we have called it only a *possibility*. The reality of the Bible *makes it possible* to think God as God. The process of thought itself, however, must be carried out in each period of time, led by *this* possibility. It is not replaced by the reality of the biblical texts, just as, conversely, the success of the attempt to think God as God cannot replace the biblical texts, and cannot even desire to replace them. After all, a part of their reality is the function of narration and proclamation, which no concept of God can take over as such, although it must include them in itself. This function is included in the thinking of God only when God is thought as the one who speaks. If God himself is not thought as the one who speaks, then the thought of God has really nothing to say with regard to God. To think God means to think God solely as the one who has something to say 'about God' (*de deo*): "God rightly speaks of God."[5]

Consequently, evangelical theology, based on the decisions implied in its

4. What one could describe as "the language of God" would have to be an event which involves the difference between God and the world as well as the advent of God in the world, the latter not being allowed to abrogate the former. It would have to formulate authentically the difference between God and world and God's arrival in this world—a difference which cannot be thought out too stringently. And only God himself can do that. To that extent it is true that 'the word of God *is* the person of God speaking' (*verbum dei est dei loquentis persona*).

5. B. Pascal, *Pascal's Pensées*, nr. 799 (*Great Books of the Western World*, vol. 33), tr. W. F. Trotter, ed. R. M. Hutchins (Chicago: Encyclopaedia Britannica, Inc., 1952), p. 328.

whole approach, proceeds from a material definition of God which has fundamental significance for the task of thinking God as God and for the whole
business of thought itself. When thinking endeavors to think God, then the God
who is to be thought has already laid claim on it. What constitutes it as *thinking*
is that it cannot reduce itself to a zero point with regard to God, in order then
'apart from God' (*remoto deo*) to construct a thought of God. It can arrive at
something like a thought of God only because thought is already addressed by
God. If thought does not then have the primary role in first bringing up the
subject of God, but is in fact always and already addressed by God, then it can
explicate its condition of being addressed only in a thought of God which thinks
God 'materially' (*materialiter*) as the *one who speaks out of himself*.

4. The thought of a God who speaks out of himself does exclude the idea
that the thought which thinks God can be grounded independently of the God
who is to be thought. To think God cannot mean that human reason could, so
to speak, prescribe for God how he is to reveal himself to it. Of course, reason
is dependent on its own designs in order to gain insight into anything. But the
fact that the designs of reason are called forth themselves by the perceptions of
reason is by no means excluded by Kant's famous thesis that ". . . reason only
perceives that which it produces after its own design. . . ."[6] Even the thought
of God must be "constructed," so to speak, as a thought by human reason. But
the "construction" as such is guided by that which reason *perceives* when it
allows itself to be addressed by the God who speaks *out of himself.* Reason is
rational when it comprehends that it cannot construct a God out of itself. Reason
is rational when it comprehends that a God is *thought* as God at all only when
he is thought as a God who *reveals himself.*

However, even in evangelical theology, revelation is a term which is little
esteemed. That may be related to the excessive use of this expression as well as
to its categorical misuse in the last two centuries. Too often the weakness of the
theological argument and of one's own decision was offset by an appeal to
revelation. With regard to one's own decisions, even if they are churchly ones
and as such necessary, one ought not appeal to revelation in the sense that it is
claimed to be the authority which not only makes one's own decisions legitimate
but beyond that is even infallible.[7] Revelation is by no means an authority which
renders something infallible.[8] It is as little that as it is an instance which im-
munizes against the labor of thought. In the current context of our discussion,
revelation means only that God is the unconditional subject of himself and as
such is accessible only because and to the extent that he makes himself accessible. Apart from the access to himself which he himself *affords,* no thinking
will ever find its way to him. Without revelation, thinking will at best construct
a thought of God which it can then disintegrate and at some point must disintegrate.

6. Immanuel Kant, *Critique of Pure Reason,* tr. J. M. D. Meiklejohn (*Everyman's Library,* 909) (London: J. M. Dent & Sons, 1950), p. 10.
7. Neither "orthodoxy" nor "orthopraxis" is *correct* when it can claim revelation
as an authority which renders this doctrine or that action infallible.
8. In this we would give unqualified support to Hans Küng. See his book *Infallible? An Inquiry,* tr. E. Quinn (Garden City, NY: Doubleday, 1971), as well as the
collection of essays edited by him, *Fehlbar? Eine Bilanz* (Zürich/Einsiedeln/Köln: Benziger, 1973).

5. The fact that God makes himself accessible to man presupposes that God has something to do with man. This, in turn, implies that God himself proceeds along a pathway. That God concerns us, unconditionally concerns us, must be demonstrated anthropologically. But the anthropological verification of this content lives from the implication that the God who unconditionally concerns us makes his own pathways on which he desires to go. In his ways, he is God. The ways which God goes cannot be distinguished from the one going, like a pathway from the path-walker. They are rather more like the way of a man's life which in a certain sense is identical with the living man. Ways of life are the ways of the living person to himself. And they are still that even if he should become alienated from himself.

God's ways are also his ways to himself. They are different from our ways of life in that his "to himself" is not removed from the divine subject— "God's way is his work"[9]—like the man who must seek himself and find his way to himself. But they are like the human ways of life in that the way is inextricably united with the subject. On the human way of life, a man becomes what he is. On the divine way of life, God makes himself into that which he is. The formulation of this content is this: God's being is in coming. That will have to be explained more precisely later. In our present context it will suffice to say that God makes himself accessible in that he goes on ways to himself.

God goes on ways to himself even when they lead to other places, even to that which is not God. God's ways to himself include something like distance from himself too. God becomes *accessible* to something else only when he does not exclude it from his ways but rather takes it along with him on his ways. That other which God takes along with himself on his way is what the Bible calls his *creation*, and that which is excluded from his ways is called *chaos*.

One very definite, although certainly not the only, way of being taken along is thought. To think God means to be taken along by God. Theological thought is in a profound sense a process of being taken along. For its part it comes to itself only in that it permits God to take it along, and does not shy away from any rigors of the way. Only in this way can it become independent and critical. The passivity of being taken along liberates the independence of one's own movement of thought, which is most appropriately called "thinking after" something. It is in grasping that one is being taken along by someone else that we acknowledge that the one taking us along precedes us as those being taken along. As "thinking after" (reflection), this thought is free; it is a movement of thought which is genuinely human. In this movement of thought, there then comes a "construction" of a thought of God which thinks God as the subject of himself.

Theological thinking cannot, therefore, set aside God initially, in order then to develop a self-definition of thought separate from that which is really supposed to be thought in theology, and then to arrive at something like a thought of God which is intended to function as the context for the definitions of God gained through revelation. It was no accident that the result of this approach was the fateful distinction between the doctrine of a divine *essence* on the one hand

9. Martin Luther, *Deutsche Auslegung des 67. (68.) Psalmes (1521) (WA,* 8, 25, 8).

and the doctrine of a *triune* God on the other. Instead of this, theological thinking must proceed from the fact that God gives himself to be thought. In theology, then, thinking means to attempt to conform to God with the capacity of human reason. God goes *his* ways. Thought will not touch (*attingere*) God if it goes other ways.

These considerations will stimulate objections with which they must deal. We shall seek to deal with some of the most important of these. This provides us an opportunity to focus that which we have said more precisely.

6. Can God be met at all? Is not God, as the one who goes his way, infinitely ahead of our thought (Isa. 55:8f)? In a theology of revelation, is not thought forced into the role of the eternal laggard who must always arrive too late, come what may? In order to meet God in our thoughts, should not one think his ways in advance of him rather than after him? Is not thinking the power which opens up the future? Must not thinking be eschatological rather than archeological? Can we then merely think *the world* without *in our thought* projecting our decision about whether and how we ought to *change* and *form* it? Is not a world comprehended by thought a projected, a thoroughly formable world? And would not a God comprehended by thought also be a projected and formable God?

This objection becomes more pointed when we ask the further question whether man, who constructs the world and in his productivity constantly expands it, is not dependent on the gods he creates in his projections. In order to think *the world* and to make it formable in the process, is it not virtually indispensable that one transcend the present world and construct a divine *"more than the world"* (in the sense of a step beyond the world)? Is the world not dependent on such a *"more than the world"* in order to attain *"more of the world"* through thought and formation? Is not the modern world fundamentally threatened in its very existence if it is not constantly focused on a *"more of the world"*? But can one attain *"more of the world"* if one has not previously conceived of something *"more than the world"*? Therefore, is not the modern world much more dependent, much more urgently dependent, on projecting and constructing gods which are *more* than the world as it currently exists, as were the god-producers scorned by Deutero-Isaiah (Isa. 44:9ff)? And are not the gods so projected and constructed not much more "useful" if not necessary than the idols made in the blacksmith's shop? Must not a world thought of as formable constantly project and fabricate new gods, one after the other, in order to anticipate steadily the new horizons of a continually changing world with the projected construction of a new *"more than the world,"* so that a really new *"more of the world"* can really result, and so on? Must not the useful gods get used up by virtue of their usefulness, become spent and worthless (Isa. 44:9)? Do we not have, do we not need, an unending atrophy of gods? Must not eschatological thought be atrophic thought to the same degree that it is projecting and constructing thought? Do we not live on the basis of eschatological atrophy? Is not the modern world an eschatological process of atrophy without end? And is not "God" the code word for this unending process of atrophy?

All of these questions would have to be answered with an unqualified Yes *if God were speechless.* Basically, the hypothesis of the world implied in all of the above questions is one great abstraction of the concept of God as one who speaks, a concept which is indispensable for any thinking which seeks to proceed along God's ways. It is an abstraction derived from the basic fact that *Christian* theology exists only because there is such a thing as faith in a God who speaks. Christian theology cannot claim responsibility for the world hypothesis which is abstracted from God as one who speaks. It cannot do this for the sake of God. But it also cannot do it for the sake of the world. For, to the extent that this world hypothesis is abstracted from the word of God, it is simultaneously the concept of a world which is in and of itself speechless. For what can be regarded as speech in any exclusively projective-constructive and thus atrophic thinking is a "speaking" which is exclusively constructed and informed by construction. What it lacks is one, if not the essential dimension of the language, that which is the truly characteristic thing about language, namely, the *event of addressing and being addressed.* Apart from the address character of language, all that is left of language for us is the variety of the possible systems of symbols. That is, of course, something. As such, it certainly is not to be underestimated, but rather affirmed in its necessity. The best can and should be made of this because it is something which is certainly good. But it is always an abstraction of that which is essential in language when words become mere symbols. A world which worked exclusively with symbols and systems of symbols would be, in any case, an abstraction of the humanity of man, who is not a truly human person apart from being addressed and allowing himself to be addressed. A world without addressability and addressedness would be a speechless world. Man would exist in it, but he would not be truly *human.*

Our insight into the true speech character of the human being as a lingual being who is addressed and can be addressed has still not conclusively settled the issue as to what extent a hypothesis which constructs man and his world as speechless is also an abstraction of God as one who speaks, an abstraction of the word of God. There is not even a pathway from the addressability of the human person, a pathway which could substantiate itself with evidence, leading to God. All of the alleged ways of this kind imply presumptions which as such are bereft of evidence. Careful thinkers have called these presumptions by name and expressly presumed them of those who think along with them. Where that does not happen and evidence is offered, there demonstrably erroneous conclusions result, through which the alleged evidence came about. To what extent then can we still assert that the hypothesis of the world, advanced above, is one large abstraction from the word of God, that is, that it thinks God as speechless? For if no pathway which is supposed to claim evidence for itself leads from the speech character of man to God, then how much less to the word of God! Logically speaking, the term "God" has less content to it than the term "word of God." Must not then a theology of revelation make a presumption of the person who thinks along with it—that is, the presumption of the word of God?

7. An unqualified Yes must be given to that question. Christian theology does, indeed, work with a presumption, which is a presumable presumption. The difference from the contested concept is only this, that this theology, which confesses its presumptions, *begins* with them. Logically, that is far more presumable. For the concept of the word of God implies as such the presumption that God be taken seriously as one who speaks. Theology must begin with this presumption if it wants to be and to remain exclusively theology, from the outset

onward. Theology is responsible talk about God. But it would not be talk about God if it wanted to avoid, at first, the God who speaks. The presumption of God must begin with the definition of God as one who speaks, essential for the understanding of God, and not with the presumption of the existence of an X which one then calls "God." The presumption of the *existence* of a God cannot be carried out by putting the *essence* of God aside—as the presumption of an existing unknown, so to speak.[10] Talk about God, if it is supposed to be talk about a God who for his part speaks, must begin as such. That is just as true of theology. If it wants to speak about God anyway and must then speak of God as one who speaks out of himself and about himself, then theology cannot first express itself incognito and then at some appropriate or inappropriate point in the dialogue with other sciences reveal its true colors just because at this point in the dialogue it regards its existence to be justified or thinks that it must now instruct its partner in dialogue about the necessity of theology. "Such scenes of recognition . . . bear an inexcusable error in that they shame one, and the manipulator wanted to fabricate a little praise for himself; this shame and this vanity set aside the effect, for they cast away the instruction which was bought at this price." Theology should certainly not be so naive as to think that it could "like the minister in the comedy go through the entire play in a costume and in the last scene then unbutton it and let the light of wisdom shine forth."[11] Theology must always begin with the admission, which only honors it, that it is nothing other than theology, and that it expresses God as the one who speaks of himself. Talk about the God who speaks should not be a surprising thing in theology—as surprising as God himself is for any person. Rather, theology is essentially the doctrine of the word of God. As such, it is doctrine of the addressability of the human person. If man is the being who is addressed by God, and thus can be addressed about God and therefore ontologically constituted by language, then the presumption that one should become involved with the word of God is a presumption which accords with the very nature of man. It is certainly not something beyond presuming. Man can engage himself in it.

8. Our understanding of this content can be deepened by discussing a further characteristic of the act which thinks God. It is a characteristic of the act which thinks God, if not of all thought in general, that the thinking "subject" experiences himself in the process of this thought as an "object" known by God. The ego which recognizes God discovers itself in the act of thinking to be an ego which is known by the God who is to be thought. This interweaving of activity and passivity of knowledge in the thought of God can be represented temporally, in that the passivity of being known in the act of thinking calls forth the experience of already being in relationship to God. That is also true of the active process of knowing. In that one knows God, one knows that one is already known. In this "reduplication of knowledge" (if these words be permitted) the

10. One cannot treat a (good) acquaintance like someone who is unknown simply because one wants to introduce him to others whom he does not know. A known person must be introduced as the person whom one knows. And that implies, of course, that he is an acquaintance already.

11. G. W. F. Hegel, *Wer denkt abstrakt?*, *Sämtliche Werke*, ed. H. Glockner (Stuttgart: Fr. Frommann Verlag, 1958), XX, 446.

encounter and event character of the concept of God is demonstrated. That thought experiences itself in the moment of knowledge as already having been known is the expression of a prevenient ontic bond between thought and its object which only in the act of thought becomes experienceable as a relationship which takes place in the act of thought. The process may be compared with the structure of joy which defines the rejoicing ego in such a way that it cannot decide to have joy, cannot really begin with joy, but rather, when it has joy, encounters itself as a rejoicing ego.[12] The fact that the ego which thinks God experiences itself as an ego in the act of thinking, an ego which has always begun with the knowledge of God, is another expression of the ontic bond of the concept of God to faith and through faith to the God who is to be thought. Thought experiences itself when it begins to think God, and is already being taken along by God. It is taken along because when it thinks God it is following faith, which is the most original way in which God takes one along with himself. Only through the fact that faith exists does thought, with regard to God, become reflective and reflecting. It follows faith and pursues its unique characteristics, and in this way allows itself to be taken along.

Reason can, therefore, only think God in that it follows after faith. It does not itself believe. It thinks. Thought does not believe anything. It thinks about things (reflects). But part of the sincerity of thought is that it thinks this: with the thought of God the thought of the necessary interrelationship of faith and God has been thought. Thinking cannot think God without thinking God and faith together. It is therefore honest to ascribe to faith its constitutive function for the thought of God. In the thought of God, this is expressed when God is thought as the one who speaks and thus as the one who is the absolutely addressing being.

9. The presumption directed to thought that it involve itself in God's word in order to learn to think God as God is, therefore, not immediate. It implies the presupposition that there is such a thing as faith. Faith is understood here as the relation of man who responds to the God who addresses him, a relation which is made possible by the event of the God who speaks and which is existentially called into being. Thus another understanding of faith is rejected which subordinates faith to thought as a lower form of knowing. Faith is anything but a lower form of knowing.[13] Faith can, therefore, not replace thought.[14] Rather, it is that behavior in which man, in the most original way possible, accords with God as well as with himself. To that degree, faith is not only a being defined by God's word but also and simultaneously a self-definition of

12. The tragicomedy of a figure like the apparently royal thinker on the throne in Georg Büchner's comedy consists of the fact that he ("What a state of affairs! Everything's going to pot.") can say of himself, "And I had resolved to have such rejoicings!" (Georg Büchner, "Leonce and Lena," Act III, Scene 3 in The Plays of Georg Büchner, tr. Victor Price [London/Oxford/New York: Oxford University Press, 1971], pp. 98 and 100).

13. See my essay " 'Theologische Wissenschaft und Glaube' im Blick auf die Armut Jesu," in Unterwegs zur Sache; Theologische Bemerkungen (München: C. Kaiser, 1972), pp. 11ff, especially 20ff.

14. See M. Heidegger, Phänomenologie und Theologie (Frankfurt: Klostermann, 1970), pp. 13-33.

man.[15] But this self-definition excludes self-grounding. In faith, rather, I allow myself to be defined by God for self-definition. Yes, faith as the most original being taken along by God is the experience of the definition of man for self-definition and as such is his liberation from the compulsion to ground himself. Put anthropologically, faith is the emergence of freedom.

That which truly merits being called freedom is determined in this act in which an ego becomes so involved with another ego that it permits that other ego to remain precisely what it is,[16] in order to define its own ego. Freedom, therefore, always benefits more than one being, more than one human ego. It takes place between I and Thou, but also between I and It. In that sense the freedom of faith does not benefit just the believing person. It also benefits God— we should not shrink back from this statement—for example, in that man gives God the glory, in that man *thanks* him (II Cor. 4:15). However, with these considerations we are moving beyond the problem to be dealt with in these paragraphs, in which it has been our intent to show that faith, in any event, implies for man that freedom in which he becomes free for a *self-definition* which does not have to revert to the *self-grounding* of the human ego. In faith, rather, the ego defines itself for a well-founded renunciation of self-grounding. For faith is the immediate being taken along of the ego by God and thus is already beyond any self-grounding. The attempt to think God takes its departure from this relation between God and the ego.

10. Now we can take up again the question raised above which formed an obstacle to our definition of thought as "being taken along" and "thinking after": Can God ever be met by a thinking which is merely reflective ("thinking after")? Is he, as the one who goes his ways, not infinitely beyond thought so that thought, if it is to catch up with him, must take fully other paths? Does not a merely reflective theology shrivel up into theological anthropology?

When God permits himself to be known as the one who speaks and who is to be thought as such, then the answer to these questions depends on our understanding of what *word* is.[17] If word were only an informative symbol which the speaker can leave behind himself, without continuing to be in relationship with it, then reflection would indeed be a curatorial undertaking. But that particular understanding of the word breaks down because of the very essence of the word of God. If faith is the position of man to God which is made possible by this word, a position in which man accords not only with himself but also, and just as originally, with God, then this accordance has the character of an *encounter* between God and man. God's word is then not a relict which goes its own way, distant from and without relationship to God; rather, this word is full of relationship, in every regard it is a relational word. In it, God relates himself

---

15. Karl Barth developed the structure of self-determination in the experience of faith in the first volume of his *Church Dogmatics*. The relevant passages (*CD*, I/1, pp. 217-26) have, significantly enough, been almost fully neglected in the discussion of Barth—with no small damage to the discussion.

16. On the structure of freedom as allowing to be, see Martin Heidegger, "On the Essence of Truth," in *Existence and Being*, p. 330.

17. On what follows, see G. Ebeling, *Introduction to the Theological Theory of Language*, tr. R. A. Wilson (Philadelphia: Fortress Press, 1973), pp. 43ff and 166-211.

to us in such a way that we must discover ourselves to be already in relationship to him. Faith then carries out in a human way this already-being-in-relationship of man to God.

If thought now follows the movement of faith (without itself therefore becoming faith[18]), then it thinks the *word* of God as an *event* which prohibits the separation of the one who spoke the word from that word, like the shoemaker from the shoe which he has made. By contrast, the function of the word in which God shows himself to be the one who speaks out of himself is to be understood as an *addressing interruption* through which the one who addresses comes near to the one who is addressed in an incomparable way. The essence of the addressing word is *approach through interruption.*[19]

This approach through interruption which takes place in the power of an addressing word does not exclude distance but includes it. God is not present in his word like the wine in the barrel or the foot in the shoe. The word is not a vessel containing God. As its content, he would be in principle separable from this "vessel," capable of being distanced from it. But instead, the word preserves the *apartness* of God which, for its part, need not be thought of as a deficit for man.[20] What is generally true of word and language is also characteristic of the word of God, which is that ". . . language does not directly unite the speaker and person or persons to whom he is speaking. The encounter always takes place within the context of a particular matter."[21]

The word of God preserves thus a relationship to which faith corresponds: a relationship in which God comes near to us without setting aside his apartness

18. It must be contested whether faith is the subjective condition for the thinking of God. One can certainly follow along the movement of faith without believing—just as one can understand joy while being sad. We must warn against an *existential* narrowness here. It suffices that one believes at all in order to pursue the movement of faith and thus to learn to think God. This must be strictly regarded later on when we discuss the certainty of God as the condition for the thinkability of God. It is a completely different question whether it is *beneficial* to proceed in that fashion, that is, to seek to follow along the movement of faith without personally believing. To reflect on joy without personally rejoicing could increase one's sadness to an unbearable level.

19. What is true of the function of the word of God may be presumed to be true by analogy for the function of the word in general. That the metaphysical tradition liked to define man as *zōon logon echon* ('living being having the word') may be interpreted as an indication of that. The oldest metaphysics had understood man as the living being in which the context of existence is so interrupted that the result can be the coming near of the one who exists. Heraclitus seems to have conceived of this "going into the nearness" (*angchibasiē*) as the rhythm of being permeated by the logos (the word) (B 122, *Heraclitean Fragments; A Companion Volume to the Heidegger/Fink Seminar on Heraclitus,* eds. John Sallis and Kenneth Maly (Tuscaloosa: The University of Alabama Press, 1980), p. 15. And according to Plotinus, it is the unique characteristic of that which exists as such to be both present and yet absent in the same fundamental sense (*Enneads* VI/4), thus being everywhere and nowhere (as property of that which exists specially) in order freely to come as near as it can to that to whom it wishes to come near without becoming its property (Plotinus, *The Enneads,* tr. S. MacKenna [London: Faber & Faber, 1956], Sixth Ennead, Fourth Tractate, part 3, pp. 520f).

20. The distinction between *theologia viatorum* ('the theology of the pilgrims') and the *visio beatifica* ('the beatific vision, the theology of the saints') may not hastily be called on here in the sense of a differentness of values.

21. Ebeling, *op. cit.,* p. 172.

in this nearness.[22] The presence and absence of God are no longer to be thought of as alternative in the word of God. Rather, God is *present as the one absent* in the word.

If thought in this sense must reflect on one who is absent and as such is present in the word, then such reflection cannot possibly be an archaeological endeavor, but rather an event which considers the one who is absent together with the one who is present, the future together with the present. If God in the word is so present as the one absent that he brings himself near to us through the word, then it is certainly not impossible to meet God. To permit oneself to be met by God is then by no means impossible but the most likely thing that could happen. This event of letting oneself be met by God is not, however, thought, but faith. Thought is affected by God only to the extent that it does not interpose itself between God and the faith. It can do that only by not believing itself. On the other hand, it shares with faith the fact that it lets God be and be considered as the one who speaks out of himself. That is, in any event, a *logical* necessity of the thought of God, which makes clear that thought can be affected by God only in the form of thought. Thought so affected by God affirms the word as the place where God is thinkable.

11. Going beyond the special theological thematic, thought would then be understood as a way of "being taken along" in which the ego which is taken along proceeds in its perceptions out of itself in order to correspond critically to that which has been perceived. In thought, the ego desires to become true together with that which has been perceived. To do that, it must fix the perceived as a something (an object) in such a way that the other thing can be followed in its own order, structure, and movement and be recognized as itself in this act of following after it. Cognition would then be that particular act of thought in which following after that other object leads to its representation and the ego comes back to itself with the representation of the other thing in order to grasp the representation. In this, the ego remains related to the way on which it has gone out of itself to the extent that it processes this way to the other thing *linguistically* as a way of its self into itself. Judged ontologically, thought is a way gone by the subject out of itself and to the same degree a way of the subject into itself. In thought, the ego intensifies itself in that it departs from itself, its inwardness. In that sense, thought is a *psychēs . . . logos heauton auxōn.* ("Soul has its own principle of growth.")[23]

With the twofold direction of the thinking ego, going out of itself and returning to itself, thought is a reflexive form of the process of "being taken along" in which the ego is not only taken along but also relates itself critically to this process of "being taken along." It *distinguishes (krinei)* between itself and that which is to be thought. Thought can only begin when it begins with *something* which is already there, independent of all thought. For that reason the ego must in thinking proceed out of itself, must "think after" (reflect). At the same time, thought must demonstrate its independence over against that which is to be thought, must relate back to itself and formulate concepts with which it

22. The way to define the relationship between the nearness and the apartness of God more precisely and concretely will be the chief problem of our discussion of the speakability of God (ch. IV).

23. Heraclitus, *op. cit.* (Wheelwright, B 115 [W 45]), p. 58.

comprehends not only its objects but also itself. The formation of concepts done by thought is its creative act, initiated by the object but yet derived solely from the power of reason. That thought *can* form concepts at all is made possible by an even more original fact, the fact of addressing language. In language, the ego is already and always outside of itself and at the same time deeply oriented to itself. It listens outwardly and thus inwardly in order, in the interplay of the two movements, to gain its representations and concepts. Even the logical formation of concepts is an act of thought made possible by language, which counters the object with that resistance without which cognition would end up being the poor conformity of the "subject" to "objects." Thought can think something as existing only when it does not leap over the contrast between thinking and being. It must *carry out* that contrast. Only in carrying out the contrast between thought and being does this contrast then become transformed into the correspondence of thinking and being.

12. In the attempt to think *God,* thought is "taken along" in that it thinks *faith* and what faith believes in. Faith, however, is the immediate form of being taken along by God. Faith is the ego's going out of itself unceasingly. There is no way back. For faith is always located with that which is believed; it does not have to get there first. Therefore, in faith the difference between the act of faith and the object of faith is always surpassed in favor of the concrete difference between faith and that which is believed, between faith and God. The concrete distinction consists of the fact that faith does not desire anything for itself. It does not return to itself but rather remains with that which is believed. In contrast, thought, when it arrives at its content, always returns to itself: in essence, it is reflection, a reflexive form of "being taken along." In the act of reflection, the ego remains independent of the fact that it is being taken along.

But then, just as faith is an original act of self-definition, 'thinking after' is the precise opposite of a "thinking" which does not have to make the effort to do its own thinking but simply "thinks" what someone has already thought out for it. Thought is never imitation. That kind of 'thinking after' which sees itself obligated to 'think after' God is always the thinker's own pursuing of his own way. For that reason, thought does not believe in that which is thought. It must as thought always begin itself and desires to see its own thoughts judged only by the authentic thoughts of others. To 'think after' means then not to believe in something which has been thought through by someone else. That which is 'thought after' never becomes something pre-thought for someone else, never becomes a thought. That which is 'thought after' becomes a *being,* which as such is something to be thought, that which most authentically is to be thought and remains that: the being of God. To the extent that this being of God is *coming* to itself on all its ways, the thought which 'thinks after' is a thought which is setting out on the way into the future, a thought which lays claim on the future in the act of thinking. To think means to set reason into movement, through a return to an origin not caused by reason, toward the future, so that reason departs from a movement of circling constantly around itself. Reason will be set into motion toward the future only when it is preceded by something which then should be 'thought after.'

As such 'thinking after', theology is in a very strict sense *'theologia in via'* (theology underway), as it was called by the early Protestant fathers. It is *'theo-*

logia in via' not only because people are "still" *viatores* ('wanderers, pilgrims'), but because thought as such is in motion, underway, when it 'thinks after' something. It is indispensable that any thinking which sets about learning to think God, although it can proceed along no *other* way than God's way, that is, the way of revelation, must go along this way as its own process: the way of being as the way of thinking. This too belongs to the true nature of the word: to allow the act of following after to become possible only as a process which each follower must go through himself. A true word teaches and will always enable us to proceed along a foreign way as our own pathway.

13. While going along this way, each will have his *own experiences*. If God is the issue, then experience can never be ruled out. But it cannot be regarded as programmed. Faith does not reject any experience which has been had. But it is not oriented to experience because, as it were, it had to fill itself up with experience, but rather because, as faith, it is already full of experience. Certainly faith is not simply an identifiable experience among others, but rather it is the realized readiness to have new experiences with experience itself, so that one must define it as *an experience with experience*.

To conceptualize this experience with experience is the task of the movement of thought. The direction of movement of faith will have to be measured, of course, by the word of God. Experiences tend to make themselves absolutes. Then they threaten the purity of faith. Faith has been most seriously threatened by some of its best experiences. For that reason, an indispensable *critical* instance emerges for faith and for its experiential power in theological thought. While faith can always answer to the word of God alone, that is, can only carry out man's *relatedness* to God, thought going its own way must distinguish itself from the existential realization of this relatedness to the extent that it also has to comprehend the origin of this relatedness, God's placing himself in relationship to us and thus the movement of the word of God itself. Because thought consciously presses the claim of the existential,[24] it can do what it must do without presumption when it is supposed to 'think after' God in his word through the mediation of faith.

What is now to be said about the problem of the thinkability of God cannot be the event of thought which 'thinks after' God—that should have become sufficiently clear in what we have said until now. At best it is the beginning of that event, namely, a sketch of the aporias and tasks which the analysis of the crisis of the metaphysical concept of God in the modern age has revealed. It should also have become plain that what was said before about the word of God as the location for the thinkability of God should now be integrated in such a way that is definitive for the formulation of the requirements which are set for theology in dealing with the problem of the thinkability of God.

As a countermove to the securing of God through the "I think," which ultimately destroys all certainty of God, we shall expound the certainty of faith as the deprivation of security (sect. 12). "I think" is to be opposed by "I believe" in such a way that the *ego* does not decide what *faith* means. It should be fully clear by now that the mere replacement of an ego which is the grounds for thought with an ego which is the grounds for faith will not assist toward the

24. See above, p. 165, n. 19.

thinkability of God. It would therefore be a good thing not to oppose "I think" with "I believe," although the issue certainly is that of the certainty of faith and also of the statement "I believe." In this context, that the New Testament speaks of "I believe" only when it is accompanied by "we believe" is of a significance which cannot be underestimated. This already implies that the ego cannot be regarded as a suitable place for the self-grounding of faith. Of course, "we believe" is just as incapable of serving for the self-grounding of faith. Faith, rather, excludes self-grounding as its very antithesis. For that reason, and only for that reason, the certainty of faith (in rebuttal of "I think" as the self-grounding of thought) can only validate the word as the place for the thinkability of God, and does so in such a way that it again becomes possible to think God.

The way that God is to be thought can be more precisely defined on the basis of the insight that God is present in the word as the one who is absent. If God comes to the world in the word, then in contrast to metaphysical concepts of God and their own aporias of the absolute nature of God, the necessity and possibility of thinking God in union with mortality will have to be discussed (sect. 13). God's union with mortality will be shown to be the most profound grounding for the thinkability of God. What Nietzsche felt had to be denounced as the frightful deceptiveness of a symbol is the true basis for the only possible way to think God: God on the cross.

SECTION 12. The Certainty of Faith as the Deprivation of Security

1. Christian faith and the theology related to it have a special historical function in a situation which, theologically, is largely defined by those aporias which found their coerced solution in the thesis of the inconceivability of God. If all talk about God is not to be irresponsible, then it is theologically indispensable that that dimension of faith be worked out and historically asserted which makes God thinkable (again). To do this, constant rethinking of the history in which God threatened to become unthinkable is needed.

The actual obstacle to the thinkability of God was found to be both the traditional concept of God and the modern self-understanding of thought as a process of making secure. God became necessary in this thought as the back-up insurance for one's own process of self-security (Descartes), but in the process of thought which progressively came to see itself as self-securing, God became an impossible thought (Nietzsche). The concept of God needed as back-up insurance for thought was shown to be unthinkable as a consequence of self-securing thought (Fichte). The position taken by the self-securing ego with regard to itself as well as everything else had to lead, as far as God is concerned, either to the collapse of thought or to the destruction of the presupposed concept of God, if not to both.

In this situation, theology receives the assignment to help both the presupposed concept of God and thought itself to engage in a process of criticism which permits God to become thinkable in a new way. This criticism can only be executed, however, when it is carried out as the explication of a *positive set of contents*. The content which is to be asserted critically against the thesis of the unthinkability of God is the indisputable fact that there is a very definite kind of certainty which is appropriate for faith. The critique of the tradition which leads to the unthinkability of God would, positively, assert the *certainty* of faith (*certitudo fidei*) as the expression of a concept of God which must still be formulated. This obviously is not to be done so that the the the aporias of thought may be done away with by means of the certainty of faith. The certainty which is given with faith by definition excludes neither existential testing nor intellectual doubt, but is rather bound up with both in a complex fashion.

In our context, the certainty of faith is of significance chiefly because it shifts the ego into another position from that of securing itself. Whoever is certain of something does not need to secure it. And whoever is certain about a person certainly has no need of security. The process of making something secure is the methodological consequence of doubt and the existential result of mistrust. Certainty, on the other hand, is the implication of a trust which, with regard to persons, is borne by the trust of the one in whom trust is placed. Where trust is borne by trust, there is no need for security.

In the relationship of mutual trust, an elementary *deprivation of security* takes place almost automatically. Certainty, as the implication of trust, has a "desecuring" function. In a historical setting defined by the thinking which seeks to establish security, theology has the task of challenging the thinking ego in the midst of his self-securing with the deprivation of security, a deprivation which thought finds responsible and which permits one to think God as the one who he is.

In order to make this dimension of faith historically fruitful for thought and the concept of God, we need to concentrate more precisely on the desecuring certainty of faith. Our discussion must deal with the structure of faith which we already addressed when we described faith as that human position in which man perceives God as the one who speaks out of himself. It is the very essence of faith that it correspond to the God who speaks out of himself. An analysis of the structure of faith must, therefore, explicate this correspondence character of faith. To that end, we must clarify the significance which God, as the one who speaks out of himself, has for the ego which is to correspond to him in faith.

Therefore, we must query the insight gained in the previous section, that God's word is to be looked on as the location for the thinkability of God, in order to find its further implications. In doing so, the significance of the word for both the thinkability of the God who addresses us and for the being of the man who is addressed must be illumined. What does it mean for the thinkability of God that God comes to man in the word and, in a specific sense, as the word? If the word is the location of the thinkability of God, then we should not only ask about what the word *as God's word* has to say to the person addressed in a material sense—that is chiefly the task of material dogmatics—but we must also clarify hermeneutically what function the word of God *as addressing word* has for the addressed ego. In order to be able to define this function, we shall have to pursue further a few essential elements of the word as an event which addresses the ego. It is useful to proceed on the basis of the distinction between the relation of existing things to the present ego, on the one hand, and the relation of the addressing word to the presence of the ego which is being addressed, on the other hand.

2. Words of address qualify the situation of the presence of an ego in a fundamentally different way from things which are present. If one does not take the things present here and now as signs (*signa*) of things actually elsewhere

(res), then it is true that their presence is disclosed to a present ego as a "here and now point." What is there right now is somewhere, has its place at a specific location, has its "here." This place can change, so that the thing may be here and then there. But this present thing is always either here or not here. If one says of a thing that it is present, then one must be able to say that it is now here and only here. The present of a thing is, therefore, always for a "now" and restricted to a "here." The present thing exists in the identity of Here and Now.

The Here and Now of a present thing can be expressed meaningfully only when there is an ego present in relation to which the thing is now here. If there were no ego there, it would not be meaningful to say "now" and "here." The present thing is *now here as this thing* to the extent that I am there. But the ego, on the other hand, is *here now in and of itself,* if it is *there at all.* Martin Heidegger, therefore, called the existence of the human ego *Dasein* ('being there'), whereas he always called the here-and-now-being of things which were related to such *Dasein* their *Vorhandensein* ('being present'). However, the ego, although it is here now in and of itself, is profoundly determined by what encounters it from outside itself, that which lays external claim on it. If this ego were challenged by only one present thing, then the situation of the presence of the ego would be reduced to the identity of here and now through such a present thing. Personal presence would then appear to be a mere series of ego–here–now points. The state of 'being there' would be, in this mere claim made by an externally present thing, fixed on the unopened, closed identity of the ego–here–now point and would resemble the bud of a rose which never blossoms. That would be the case if, beyond the present things, the ego were not also challenged by an event which defines the situation of presence in a way which opens up the ego–here–now point, which in an elementary fashion differentiates the identity of here and now.

This elementary differentiation which defines the situation of presence originates in the fact that the ego is always defined by a word which lays claim to it, so that its ego character is constituted by language. In that sense, the ego is the *zōon logon echon* ('living being having the word'). The ego has the command of the word because language has power over the ego. This is also negatively valid in that language can bewitch the ego (not only its mind but also its heart). Language also dominates man at that point where man is supposed to dominate language. But this negative use of language is possible only because language is a power which fundamentally defines man, while disclosing his 'being there,' his existence. This assertion is to be discussed in terms of the structure of the word.

Words have the structure of speaking of something to someone so that one is addressed in terms of the subject under discussion. The *logos* has as the *logos tinos* ('the word of something') the structure of *pros ti* ('toward something'). It relates the addressed ego to something. This can happen in such a way that the word appears to make itself superfluous, as in an informative communication. But it can also take place in such a way that the relatedness of the addressed ego to that which is under discussion exists only in the linguistic relationship of the addressing word. In any event, the ego is put into a relationship with its own being here and now through the word which addresses it. Every addressing word approaches the addressed ego in such a way that it lets this ego come to itself. In listening I relate myself to myself and approach myself with the word which

addresses me: I am here now, and yet in that I listen I come to myself at the
same time. One might say that the point of now expands itself. It has a future
and becomes thus the present. The structure of the word thus differentiates the
dull identity of here and now. The addressing word, like the present thing, is
here now. But it is here now in such a way that it relates the Here and Now to
each other in a specific way. It is now here, and at the same time it is beyond
the identity of Here and Now. It gives the Now, so to speak, space beyond the
point of Here and it gives the Here time beyond the point of Now. The word is
what first discloses the present. It does this as a word which *addresses*. It
discloses to the addressed ego the ego–here–now points in that it sets aside their
punctual character, as the present. In that sense, addressing words are distinguished from present things in that they, as Rilke[1] aptly put it, transcend being
here. Being here can be transcended only if the identity of here and now is
differentiated.

A present thing, judged from the perspective of the ego, is now here and
only here, or in another place and thus not here at all. Whoever wants to remain
with a present thing must be where its Here is, either following that thing as it
moves away or taking the thing with himself. But the thing is also characterized
there, where it is, in its present by the identity of here and now. And it holds
on to the ego which wants to remain with it firmly, so that it fixates the ego to
its being Here and Now. By contrast, an addressing word is also now here when
it addresses one. But in that it addresses the ego about something which does
not necessarily belong to the identity of ego–now–here, it refers the person
addressed beyond the "here and now." This experience of the ego's being referred
beyond the Here and Now is the existential *distancing* of the ego into a state of
absence, through which process existence begins to come near to him. The entire
process corresponds to the experience of *coming near*, discussed above, which
takes place through a word which *interrupts* reality. In that the ego is addressed,
something like a distancing from the immediate identity of Here and Now always
takes place. In that the ego is addressed about something, the situation of the
presence of the ego is qualified in such a way that the ego shifts into a distance
from its immediate being here and now and thus can be related to something
else. If then the other thing to which the ego is related through an addressing
word is something *absent*, then the ego is related, spatially put, to something
which is Not–Here, or, temporally put, to something which is Not–Here–Now.
But since this Not–Here–Now is not nothing, the addressed ego is addressed
with regard to another being. Thus the dimension of an existential distance is
asserted through which the ego is set in relationship to its own "Here and Now"
in such a way that together with the spatial difference of Here and Now, the
Now is encountered by the past and the future. What is not here requires the
addressed ego, when addressed about it, to relate the past and the future to its
now. That is the only way in which it experiences time, in that it gains time.[2]

1. See Rainer Maria Rilke, *Sonnets to Orpheus*, tr. M. D. Herter Norton (New
York: W. W. Norton & Company, Inc., 1942), Part I, Fifth Sonnet, p. 25.
2. See, on the entire section, M. Heidegger's analyses in *Being and Time*, and the
statement there "that temporality, as an ecstatical unity, has something like a horizon"
(*Being and Time*, trs. J. Macquarrie and E. Robinson [New York: Harper, 1962], p. 416).
The analyses presented in *Being and Time* do not proceed on the basis of the significance

The ego is removed here and now into either the past or the future. In that it is addressed about something absent, it is addressed about the past or the future.

But such an existential distancing into the past or the future is not a distancing *away* from the "Here and Now." Rather, the ego *in* its "Here and Now" is brought sufficiently near to them that the ego–here points can then be qualified as an integrated *present.* Through distancing from the identity of "Here *and* Now" they are differentiated into a time which discloses the being here and now as the *present.* The Here gains temporal function itself. Out of the merely punctual identity of "Here and Now" the difference of a "Here *in* the Now" emerges, through the power of the addressing word, and thus the present is disclosed to the ego as temporal space. It is only through the distancing of the ego, which differentiates that identity, a distancing in the direction of a past and a future ascribed to the ego, that the ego's own status of being there is disclosed to it as the present. The lingual character of the human being, which has always served to interrupt the dull identity of the ego–here–now point, is the source of that distance from oneself without which no ego ever comes near to itself. It is out of that distance from oneself that the person approaches himself. Thus he *has* time. Thus he *is* man. It is only within the self-revealing present that the Now as moment attains the character of a temporal event.[3]

The word of address, therefore, provides the experience of a temporal distancing, which makes the experience of the present possible. One can go so

of the addressing word for the disclosure of time as the horizon of temporality. Accordingly the interpretation of language found there is oriented differently. It is guided by the existential of understanding, so that he can state, "Being-There hears, because it understands" (*ibid.,* p. 206). By contrast, theology understands listening on the basis of the event of being addressed, out of which understanding then emerges. The state of 'being-there' understands because it hears. And it hears because it 'is there' (exists) as one who is addressed.

3. The moment as the *time for decision* is first disclosed through a relationship which differentiates the identity of "Here and Now," through a word which surpasses the being-here-and-now. Only the one who transcends the moment can actually perceive it as such. It is only within a present which integrates the moments that a decision, a *"hic Rhodos, hic salta"* ('Here is the rose, dance thou here'), becomes meaningful or requirable at all. Hegel then translates the demand, "Here is the rose, dance thou *now*" (*Hegel's Philosophy of Right,* tr. T. M. Knox [Oxford: Oxford University Press, 1949], p. 11). To understand the blossoming rose as a summons to dance presupposes the disclosed present and the word which discloses it. It must be *said* to someone, Here is the rose, dance thou here! For that reason every decision presupposes an addressing word which so surpasses one's being-here that the present is disclosed as the present. Moreover, on the basis of an understanding of man as a lingual being, oriented to this function of the word, one must theologically question whether man is a *deficient being*. To be sure, the animal, who is fully at the mercy of the *plethora* of the "Here and Now" which surrounds it, may well perceive *more* of that "Here and Now" than does man. But it does not perceive this "Here and Now" *as* "Here and Now," so that it does not arrive at a "Here *in the* Now." In being forced toward the fullness of existence, that fullness is in effect closed to it. The animal lacks the hermeneutical "as." Man, who lacks much that animals "still" have, is characterized by this hermeneutical "as," because, and to the extent that, man is a word-being. Man belongs to the word, which surpasses his being-here and which translates man, as a mere animal, from being *forced* to fullness into the *event* of fullness. In this event, the force to *be-now* and to *be-here* is certainly experienced as a deficiency, but *the freedom for the disclosure of the present* is experienced as a particular distinction.

far as to say that the better we understand that which is past and the more intensively we hope for that which is future, or seek to bring it about, the more present we are. It is the *ego as spirit* which becomes present to itself in that it works through this experiential distancing. Spiritual presence is the most original capacity of the ego, to be fully present through the surpassing of the state of being-here which is identical with the state of being-now. This capacity is the unique characteristic of the ego as a *zōon logon echon* ('living being having the word, or speech'). Spiritual presence would be falsely understood if one sought to understand it as the opposite concept to the sensual presence of the ego. In contrast to such a spiritualizing or intellectualizing view, spiritual presence is rather to be understood as the ego's state of being present in its entire sensuality. In its sensuality as a body, the ego is here now, whereas as spirit it draws this its sensual state of being here through distancing into the past and the future and qualifies it thus as the present. This present which is always coming to itself out of the past and the future could be called the continuity of the human ego. The continuity of the human ego would then not be grounded in the ego itself but rather in the *word* which qualifies the ego's state of present existence.

In order to avoid misunderstandings, it should be expressly noted here that the ego within the horizon of language is always understood as a subject which is defined by sociality. Whoever calls man a being distinguished by its language, has also understood him as the ego within a lingual and living community. We shall return to this later.

3. The general anthropological content we have presented is of the greatest theological significance because, as we saw, theology sees God as the one who speaks out of himself and thus sees man as the being who is addressed by the God who speaks. Theologically, man is relevant as the being which is defined by the "word of God." The "word of God" is to be understood as the abbreviated formulation of the entire fact that God addresses us about himself and thus about ourselves. In that process, what happens is that a "word" which addresses us "surpasses our being-here," and this happens in a much more radical way. In that man is addressed by God about God, a *total distancing* of the ego takes place over against its being-here and being-now, and accordingly a *completely new qualification of man's state of being present* results, which one could call *eschatological spiritual presence*. Every word of God which addresses us surpasses our being-here in that it places us *before God*. The "here and now" are surpassed not only in the sense in which the addressing word otherwise differentiates the identity of being-here and being-now through the distancing of the ego into the past and the future for the sake of the disclosure of the present. In that the word of God, distancing us from ourselves, allows us to be 'in the presence of God' (*coram Deo*), it brings us into a relationship of *total distancing* not only to the "here and now" which is to be disclosed as the present but also to the being-here and being-now which human words have already disclosed as the present. Even the "here in the now" is surpassed. Thus the distancing of the ego into the past and the future is surpassed—not in the sense of a quantitative increase, but rather in the sense of what I would like to call *eschatological outdistancing*. The word which addresses man about God surpasses the entirety of the ego's worldly context. But in that way, it directly encounters the ego. And thus it discloses to the ego a new way of being present, it discloses to it worldly

presence as presence defined by God, as eschatological presence.[4] The eschatological outdistancing of the worldly context of man through the God who addresses us provides the experience of a newness which makes the entire world old. It is no accident that Paul expresses this thought in a word of *address:* "The old has passed away, behold, the new has come" (II Cor. 5:17).

The eschatological character of man's distancing from himself has an eminently critical dimension. For, to the extent that this distancing surpasses everything which is, everything which is *for itself* is made nothing. Every word which addresses man about God is, in that sense, a *negating or destroying* word. It brings about an annihilation in that it surpasses not only our being-here, but also our past and our future. But distanced from himself in such a way, the man addressed about God is brought into a new, ultimate nearness to himself. That is, to be sure, a nearness of the ego to itself which includes its being before God. The New Testament understands this as the presence which is eschatologically oriented through the guarantee of the Holy Spirit.

The word of God which addresses man about God has, then, an annihilating effect, for the sake of something new. Evangelical theology may not remain silent about the fact that it is destructive.[5] But, and this is what evangelical theology must chiefly speak of, it is destructive only on the basis of the *positive* fact that God addresses us about himself in such a way that he *promises* himself to us. One should not understand it in such a way that God would permit what exists to be made nothing in order then to be able to begin all over again from the beginning, so to speak. The reverse is true: because God, in addressing us about himself in such a way that he promises himself to us, always creates something new, that which is old becomes nothing.[6]

4. It should be carefully noted that evangelical theology understands the being of Jesus, his life, death, and resurrection, as that history within which the God who speaks out of himself has expressed himself. Accordingly the eschatological distancing of man, which could be called the destruction of all his worldly contexts, is still not a distancing into infinity but rather a distancing into the concrete past represented by his death on the cross and into the concrete future of Jesus Christ represented by his resurrection and parousia. This eschatological reference to the God who has come and is coming in Jesus Christ is then the reason for the fact that the now surpassed worldly contexts have gained finally their true, theological, and concrete significance. By virtue of their radical eschatological relativization, they become unavoidable as a task of human life, from which not even religion can give dispensation.

5. See on this my essay "Die Welt als Möglichkeit und Wirklichkeit; Zum ontologischen Ansatz der Rechtfertigungslehre," in *Unterwegs zur Sache; Theologische Bemerkungen* (München: C. Kaiser, 1972), pp. 206ff, especially pp. 217ff.

6. Thus sin passes away only when it is forgiven; but the forgiveness of sins is always *more* than the passing away of sin. And in exactly the same way the godless person passes away *because* he is justified, not *in order* that he can be justified; the justification of the godless is always *more* than the passing away of the godless. The actual contrast between the theology of Karl Barth and Friedrich Gogarten appears to me to consist of this contrasting definition of the theological relationship between passing away and becoming, of death and life, of judgment and grace. See on this the analysis of Gogarten's writings with special attention to the Luther statements which he cites in W. Hüffmeier, *Gott gegen Gott; Hermeneutische Untersuchungen zum Gottes- und Todesverständnis Friedrich Gogartens unter besonderer Berücksichtigung seiner Lutherinterpretation* (Tübingen dissertation, 1972). On the relationship between Barth and Gogarten I refer to the insightful investigation presented by P. Lange in *Konkrete Theologie? Karl Barth und Friedrich Gogarten "Zwischen den Zeiten" (1922-1933); Eine*

It would, therefore, be advisable not to say that the word of God leads into a crisis. At best, it *leaves* a "crisis" behind it in that through outdistancing our reality *within* being, it forces us to consider also that *nothingness* so that *critical distinctions* become possible and indispensable. The positivity of the eschatological distancing of the man who is addressed about *God* is that it is now possible to make theological and political distinctions between that which has been *done away with* and that which has become *possible,* and with the help of such distinctions one can assume responsibility for the *world.* The word of God provides therefore an understanding of ourselves and thus an understanding of the world. It requires that we *think* ourselves in that it lets us *work through* the provided understandings of self and the world.

And yet, theologically, it is still an abstract concept of God which has been introduced here. The decisive thing is thus the question whether the person who is addressed about God is given an understanding of God which goes beyond the experience of merely being addressed about "something like God." When God is experienced as the one who speaks, does he permit himself to be thought as the one who he is? Or do we have to stay with the fatal proposition, "We can only say about God what he does to us but not what he is"?[7] Is theology condemned to be able to think about *our relatedness* to God and yet to have to answer the question about the thinkability of God with the tautological response, "God is . . . God"? Is the restriction of thought to the tautology "God is God" the only possibility for avoiding placing thought *between* God and God and disintegrating the concept of God by opposing essence and existence?

4. The restriction of the thinkability of God to the tautology "God is God" contradicts the very essence of that faith which is derived from the addressing word of God. For the certainty of faith is the certainty that it is dealing with God himself. Faith is participation in God himself.[8] Certainly faith does not force itself into a position *between* God and God. It is the essence of faith to let God be who he is. But if faith does participate in God himself, without penetrating God in such a way that it forces itself between God and God, then God's being must be thought as a being which allows that it be participated in, that is, a being which turns *outward* what it is *inwardly.* This happens in the word and only in the word of God. For it is part and parcel of the essence of the word to allow participation in the being of the one who speaks by bringing that being to turn itself to someone else. In the word, the being of the speaker expresses itself. From an anthropological viewpoint it is often true that in the word often

---

theologiegeschichtlich-systematische Untersuchung im Blick auf die Praxis theologischen Verhaltens (Zürich: Theologischer Verlag, 1972). Karl Barth's dogmatic approach, to define the judgment of God on the basis of grace, that is hermeneutically to say that on the basis of the new the old has become old and passed away (II Cor. 5:17), has been taken up chiefly by Ernst Fuchs and independently developed further hermeneutically.

7. See W. Herrmann, *Die Wirklichkeit Gottes* (1914), p. 42 (in *Schriften zur Grundlegung der Theologie,* ed. P. Fischer-Appelt [München: Chr. Kaiser, 1967], II, 314). The first half of this sentence was cited approvingly by R. Bultmann in *Faith and Understanding,* I, tr. L. P. Smith (New York: Harper & Row, 1969), 63: "Faith can only be the affirmation of God's action upon us. . . ."

8. See G. Ebeling, "Jesus and Faith," in *Word and Faith,* tr. J. W. Leitsch (Philadelphia: Fortress Press, 1963), pp. 201ff, especially pp. 209ff.

more of the being of the speaker is expressed than this person knows or wants—
an ontological fact from which psychoanalysis, for example, derives its whole
existence. In a theological regard, the word is not to be looked on as involuntary
or even traitorous expression. The Johannine identification of the logos with God
himself (John 1:1) says instead that God in the word expresses his most inward
being without reservation. He turns himself outward, without holding back any
part of himself. He gives himself entirely in the word which he speaks. In this
sense it is true "that God alone comes in the word alone."[9] If God makes
participation in himself possible through his word, then this gift of participation
is an event of the divine being itself. The explicit cognition of this gift of
participation, the thinking of what faith is, implies then the possibility of thinking
God as he really is, in and of himself. It is a part of the truth of faith that God
is to be thought as he is, based on his self-disclosure. Any restrictive reservation
which one might want to register here would move faith very close to superstition. Hegel hit the nail on the head: "Whoever says that God cannot be known,
says He is jealous, and so makes no earnest effort to believe in Him, however
much he may speak of God."[10] One proviso may be mentioned: there may well
be something like the 'hidden work of God' (opus dei absconditum). But if God
is the one who speaks of himself, then there is no deus absconditus ('hidden
God') in the sense of the principle of the unrecognizability of God.

If then the self-disclosure in which God makes participation in himself
possible is the expression of the divine essence, what appeared to be a tautological statement, "God is God," now becomes expoundable for thought. To carry
out this exposition, thought must come to terms with its self-grounding in the
proposition "I think." Theology is the site of thought's debate with thought to
the extent that the perspective of God leads thought to question its self-grounding
in the "I think." For this purpose we resume our debate with the Cartesian
approach to metaphysics in the modern age, with its consequences.

5. The Cartesian approach to modern metaphysics understands thought to
be ascertaining through representing. The subject of ascertainment is as the
'thinking thing' (res cogitans) the human ego. The ego first of all ascertains
itself, as being present to itself, in order then to ascertain God and the world
and thus its own continuity.

A theological debate with this approach to modern metaphysics cannot
ignore the achievement of this approach within the history of thought. The
establishment of thought on ascertainment led to worldly results in the form of
the mastery of the world through production of the world. "Safety first" (or
better, "Certainty first"—TR) is a motto which in many ways should not be
despised. One might conjecture that in the modern age, which is so concerned
about the ascertaining, or securing, of everything which exists by the human
subject, the security risk would have to grow to monstrous dimensions because
only the ascertaining "ego" of man functions as the decisive agent over all
existence and non-existence. But even if one does make that conjecture, it can

9. G. Ebeling, "Die Evidenz des Ethischen und die Theologie," in Wort und
Glaube II; Beiträge zur Fundamentaltheologie und zur Lehre von Gott (Tübingen: Mohr
[Siebeck], 1969), p. 41.
10. Hegel, Lectures on the Philosophy of Religion, trs. E. B. Speirs and J. B.
Sanderson (New York: Humanities Press, 1962), III, 148.

and may not lead to the irrational attempt to seek to retreat back behind the approach of the metaphysics of subjectivity in such a way that the Middle Ages return—even though that age has been unjustly degraded into a negative metaphor. Every context of our world has already been too thoroughly permeated by the ascertaining function of the human subject for that to be possible.

The "I think" was understood as the 'thinking thing' (*res cogitans*) which secured or ascertained the existence of the one who exists through the process called *representation*. The problem which remained unresolved was this: how can one move from the being of representation to the being of that which is represented if God is not conceivable anymore as the guarantor of the unity of the 'thinking thing' (*res cogitans*) and the 'extended thing' (*res extensa*)? In view of that problem, the "I think" had to be transformed into "I act," which initially found itself to be moral action, but soon became producing, making activity, carried out beyond any consideration of good and evil. Now, all of my representations are supposed to be accompanied by the principle, "I should act." The necessary consequence of the Cartesian understanding of man as the 'thinking thing' who secures the existence of what is through representation is the mastering of the world, guided by man's thinking and planning. The world now is only the pure object of the human subject. As the object of the human subject the *represented* world becomes fundamentally *producible*. It is only one step from representation (as 'clearly and distinctly conceiving,' *clare et distincte percipere*) to production (as 'clearly and distinctly constructing,' *clare et distincte construere*). The represented object is as such also makeable. The thinker has become the producer, the maker. And this has happened, not although but because he thinks.

The Cartesian process of securing through representation has long since become, in strict consequence, a securing through production, whereby the decision-making function of the human subject over being and nonbeing has been increased in its potency qualitatively and in accordance with the safety risk has become *de facto* (and not just *in intellectu*) a worldwide risk. Our world differs from that of the Middle Ages and the Ancient World precisely at this point, that in almost all of its factors it is a produced world and in that fact it finds and proclaims its only security. However, the more exclusively the security depends on the producer, the more exclusively is then the producer the point of the security *risk*.

Obviously this cannot be dealt with by simply ending the production process. A world which is secured by production depends for its existence on the continuity and increasing of production. The process of world mastery through world production is irreversible. Productive man has long since passed the Archimedean point of the *beginning of world-production*[11] and thus is now so much defined in his very being by *that which is produced* that he can only continue the process of production. The power of the subject who secures the existence of what is through representation and production returns from that produced world back to the subject as the inability to do without the exercise of that power. The *will* to power has become *de facto* the *compulsion* to exercise power.

---

11. This point is completely different from the production *within* the world, which has always been characteristic of man as *homo faber*.

And with that, the man who was to secure the world has become not only the actual but also the irrevocable security risk of the world. He must endure this by working through it.

The theological debate with the Cartesian approach to modern metaphysics cannot be so irresponsible as to want to reverse or even set aside the securing of the world through man. And even if it wanted to, it could not do that. Modern man *must* secure his world according to the law under which he has begun, and he must do so through constantly continuing production. And in this context he *must* secure himself as the subject of this securing process. If the world is to continue to be there for him, then man *must* be there as its maker, the function which he has made for himself. There is no theological alteration to be made here. Genesis 1:28 cannot be diluted at that moment when the danger which is given with the command to domination becomes evident. The only way not to become the victim of that danger is to refuse to flee from the command to assume responsibility for the world.

6. The theological debate with the Cartesian approach to modern metaphysics and with its consequences must, however, raise the question whether the human essence has really been fully grasped when man is known only as the subject of production and securing. We must ask whether man can secure himself *totally*, and in every regard. That the man who secures the world must secure himself as the *one who is responsible for the process of securing* certainly does not mean that he has secured himself *as man*. Can man secure himself as man?

According to Descartes, he can do so only when he is certain of God as his back-up insurance, that is, when he also secures God as the one who secures him totally and completely. However, this additional provision cannot be thought through to a conclusion without having the concept of God disintegrate into contradictory concepts and making the presupposed concept of God as the absolute and independent essence inconceivable. That alone speaks against the approach of the whole undertaking. Theological argumentation cannot ignore this matter. Yet, it will not let itself be led by this negative aspect if it really wants to raise any objections to the fundamental approach here. For theological argumentation *against* a position can be done only on the basis of an argument *for* another position. Otherwise it would not really be *theological* argumentation. The failure of a respectable undertaking cannot itself function as a theological argument. Theology must then have some other objection if it believes that it must negate the question whether man can totally secure himself *as man*.

The *positive* argument which can be raised theologically against the possibility of a total self-securing of man by man consists first of all in a reference to the fact that a totally secured man would cease to be man. Human existence is something more and something other than "being secured." A totally secured human would be merely a piece of the world, a robot-like *Doppelgänger* ('double') of man, a horrifying caricature of man. Our theological argument, now put positively, is this: man is truly human in that he is able to place himself in dependence on someone other than himself. That entails his ability to be dependent. To be human means to be able to depend, to trust.

Of course, this argument has not been understood theologically when this proposition is understood heroically or even tragically. Theologically man is understood as an ego which can depend or trust only because this ego can depend on or entrust itself *to someone else*. That is not a word game, although it may sound like one.* What may appear to be a mere word game to superficial reading may be exegetically verified in the Old Testament significance of the terms "truth" and "faith."[12] But it can also be explained systematically.

The understanding of man and his world based on the Cartesian "I think" states that man secures *everything* through himself, and that this constitutes his humanity: the human ego exists for itself and to that extent for everything else which is secured through its being represented by the human ego. The basic principle of this understanding of man and his world may be formulated in this way: *I am human because and to the extent that I*, as the one who secures, *exist for something*. In more recent morality and the theology permeated by it, this is then varied into the (equally respectable) definition of man as engaged being for others: *I am human, because and to the extent I am there for other people*.

This definition of human existence, however, must be contested to the degree that it intends to be the primary definition of man. On the basis of man's relatedness to God constituted by the event of the word of God, that God who allows man to participate in his being, this definition is to be countered with the assertion that the humanity of the human ego consists of my allowing someone else to be there for me. Only on the basis of that can I be there for someone else. The main theological point is that *I am human in that I let someone else be there for me*.[13] That can also be called trust, and with regard to the 'someone else' who as God has promised himself to us, we must call this *trust in God*. This is precisely what is meant when we speak of *faith*.

Trust in God is no more heroic than is the trust which evolves between persons who love each other. It implies, of course, the expectation that one will rely or depend *totally* on God. And one can rely totally on God only when one 'forsakes oneself.' Really to forsake oneself and depend on another means to

---

*The author refers to a "word-play" because of his use of *"sich verlassen."* This reflexive verb means "to depend, to rely, to trust." But it carries also the connotation "to forsake oneself, to depart from oneself." When joined with a preposition (*auf*) it becomes "to depend on someone." The implication is that man can forsake himself and rely or depend on someone else—TR.

12. See D. Michel, "'ÄMÄT. Untersuchung über 'Wahrheit' im Hebräischen," *Archiv für Begriffsgeschichte*, 12 (1968), 30ff; R. Smend, "Zur Geschichte von האמין," in *Hebräische Wortforschung; Festschrift W. Baumgartner, Vetus Testmentum*, S 16 (1967), pp. 284ff; H. Wildberger, " 'Glauben'; Erwägungen zu האמין," *ibid.*, pp. 372ff; H. Wildberger, " 'Glauben' im Alten Testament," *Zeitschrift für Theologie und Kirche*, 65 (1968), 129ff.

13. The definition of human existence which states that I permit another to be there for me obviously does not add anything to that other ego, which I permit to be there for me as my Thou. The human ego can permit another ego to be there for me only if he opens himself up for me. What is at stake here is the fundamental anthropological factor that man is dependent on *the freedom of the other* man. This general definition of human existence as letting another one be there for me corresponds precisely to the definition of thought as permitting existence (see above, pp. 162ff). In relationship to the world, that is, in the relationship of the ego to the it (I-It), permitting the existence of the world as a context for that which is to be used implies its *being used*—precisely to that boundary which is set for usage if the entire context of that which is to be used is supposed to be maintained. It is part of the mystery of the world that the man who makes use of it is also able simultaneously to supply the world the possibility of its regeneration for new usage—or, at least, *until now* man has been able to do this.

renounce all self-grounding. Faith is, in fact, that self-definition of man in which man, on the basis of his being defined by God, renounces all self-grounding. But faith *can* renounce all self-grounding because self-grounding has already been surpassed by trust in God. This is how Jesus' statement is to be understood when he says that the one who wants to gain his life will lose it, but he who loses it will gain it. The logion in Mark 8:35 is a statement about certainty in God. And like all forms of certainty in God, this statement (which is to be exegeted from its end to its beginning) expects of man that he will remove his own securities. If I am human in that I permit another to be there for me, then I am only certain of myself in that other one. Therefore, it is not a law but a promise when we formulate the anthropological principle: *Only he who forsakes himself will come to himself.* This promise, more than any law, constitutes the being of man as man.

Now we see that faith, what one might call the concave, has the same structure as the word of God, which is its convex. Faith, too, does not allow one's being-here and being-now to continue in its directness. Just as the word surpasses our being-here and being-now, faith too *permits* the surpassing of our being-here and being-now. And since the word of God not only surpasses our "here and now," but also that being-here and being-now which has been surpassed by human words, the "here *in* the now," *with* its past and all of its producible future, therefore faith permits our *entire existence here* to be outdistanced through a radical distancing of ourselves from ourselves. This is a distancing which brings us to a *new* nearness to ourselves, so that we become present to ourselves in a new way.

7. This new nearness of man to himself is, as a nearness caused by the word of God, a presentness which man cannot promise to himself. It takes place when God promises himself to us. This nearness of man is *new* in a unique sense in that before God it allows all that to be *destroyed* which man has done on his own in order to come near to himself. For all human attempts at self-approach which man does to himself realize, to be sure, a distance-less nearness of man to himself. But this nearness is accomplished without coming near to the other, to God. And therefore they must be destroyed before God. For the *self-realization* of man results in the *forfeiting* of man's nearness to himself, increased from out of the distance, a nearness which includes the presence of God. The self-realization of man forfeits the beneficial nearness of man to himself, that nearness which is qualified by the Holy Spirit of God. Man's eschatological nearness to himself is also forfeited because all human attempts at self-nearing have the penetrating tendency to want to come near to oneself in such a way, to want to come to oneself in such a way that man is neighbor to himself, and the sole neighbor. The ego wants to become identical with itself. "Each man is his own neighbor"—that is an ancient utopia, one which betrays resignation, however, a utopia of man seeking his identity.

In the Cartesian "I think" this utopia appeared to be palpably close to its full realization. At least in the moment of 'thought' (*cogitare*) the ego appeared to have come so close to itself that man as the 'thinking thing' (*res cogitans*) became his own neighbor in the process of carrying out the "I think"—again, his only neighbor. 'I think myself thinking' means 'I think myself being' (*cogito me cogitare; cogito me esse*). "I think" meant "I am." The ego was, as the place of the identity of thought and being, the identity event in an absolute sense. In the egocentric identity of thought and being, the ego had become its own neighbor.

However, within the perspective of metaphysics it became clear that no one can *remain* his own neighbor. God had to be called on in order to preserve the continuity of identity with itself. That is a reference to the fact that in truth no person can be identical with himself without being with someone other than himself. No person *is* really his own neighbor. For that reason, the penetrating self-nearing attempts, with which man seeks to come so close to himself that he ultimately is his own neighbor, must be destroyed when the word of God brings us into a new nearness to ourselves. That kind of new nearness of man to himself, new because it is a nearness which destroys that which has been forfeited, is what we call *eschatological* nearness.

The word of God creates this eschatological nearness of man to himself in that it relates man to the God who addresses him in such a way that God comes *nearer* to man than man could ever come to himself.[14] God is my neighbor. He comes nearer to me than I am to myself. Faith opens itself up to this nearness of God. That in faith I come near to myself in an eschatologically new way is based on God's own coming near. In that God comes near to man he brings man to himself. That we, for our part, cannot come to ourselves without being brought to that point is the expression of an identity of the ego with itself which can be found only in another. Man can become identical only to the extent that someone other than he is, is with him. The ultimate nearness of man to himself takes place only at that point where God's word surpasses the being-here of man.

8. Important consequences for the concept of God result from what has just been discussed. We recognized the aporia of the metaphysical concept of God in the fact that God had to be thought as the one who is absolutely present. Absence then had to signify something like the non-existence of God so conceived. If the word of God surpasses our being-here, then God for his part cannot be there in the sense of a surpassed being-here. He would then be surpassed himself. Faith also preserves in this regard the structure of the addressing word. In the word, God *is* present as the absent one. Faith *allows* God as the absent one to be present. It lets God be so near that man in the midst of his being-here and being-now moves into that *radical* distancing *from* this "here and now" without which our presentness is not disclosed to be God's presentness. God does not come near to us without moving us out of our self-realized nearness to ourselves: 'he puts us outside of ourselves' (*ponit nos extra nos*). God is only present to the ego which has been moved outside of itself. On the other hand, God with me is removed from me for the very reason that he comes nearer to me and is nearer to me than I am able to come near to myself. That very thing which *is closest* to me is that which is radically removed from me. It can be experienced only in the ecstatic structure of this 'we being outside ourselves' (*nos extra nos esse*). As a result, the 'putting us outside ourselves' (*nos poni extra nos*) is the structure of that experience with experience which we had understood as the experience of God.

Faith thus preserves the withdrawal of that one who as God is my neighbor. Without a fundamental *extra nos* ('outside ourselves') faith knows of no *deus*

14. See below, pp. 295-98.

pro nobis ('God for us') and certainly no *deus in nobis* ('God in us'). God is only *near* to us in that he distances us from ourselves. As the one who distances us from ourselves, God is certainly the one who is farthest away from the man who seeks to exist in and of himself, who seeks to will in and of himself, and who thus insists on himself. The converse is simultaneously true: this fundamental 'us being outside ourselves' (*nos extra nos esse*) is as such identical with the nearness of God. God's being-for-us is not added to this *nos extra nos esse*. It is not an undefined and abstract *extra nos* which then would become defined and concrete in God's *pro nobis* ('for us'). When we, in listening to his word, are outside of ourselves, then God is already there for us. Therefore the distance into which the believing ego moves in the midst of his presentness is not a distancing into something *undefined*. In this regard as well, every notion of heroic risk and the possibility of the tragic implied in it is to be dismissed. Man is removed—through the word of God addressing him—in faith into that very defined *extra nos* which has in the series of human being-here and being-now a concrete historical place in a very definite 'here and now' (*hic et nunc*), namely, in the 'there and then' (*illic et tunc*) of the cross of Jesus Christ. *God came* in this concretely definable past. In the 'then and there' of the death of Jesus God came to man. That is what the word proclaims and states, the word to which faith corresponds: the word of the cross. In it, that which the word addressing us says about the God who speaks out of himself (God on the cross as our neighbor) and the *structure* of the relationship between word and faith are congruent.

We still have to discuss in detail what this 'then and there' means for the being of God which is to be thought. In the present context it is sufficient to make clear to what degree our existence is so surpassed by the word of God that the faith which responds to it relates us to the Crucified One as to the *extra nos* of God which brings us to a precise and concretely defined distance from our own existence here, in the very midst of that existence. Faith is the reference back to the Crucified One. The word of the cross surpasses our being-here and our being-now, yes, our entire existence here, in such a way that the present now is disclosed as the presentness of God and as our own presentness simultaneously.

This presentness is not to be set up as absolute over against history. The reference back to the Crucified One is as such a reference to the past which forbids us to think of all the history which has happened as merely an accumulation of events, as the refuse of failed actions. It forbids this because, since Jesus' crucifixion, the word of the cross has been *proclaimed* and at all times has been able to surpass human being-here and being-now in such a way that the presentness of God was an event. And the believer, on the basis of his faith, opens himself up to the hope that the word of the cross will continue to be proclaimed in the future and will always be able to surpass again human being-here and being-now, until the Crucified One comes (I Cor. 11:26). God comes out of this future, that is, the God who has already come to man in the death of Jesus. He comes as the one who has come in that way.[15] The backward reference of faith finds its corresponding expression in the no less relevant dis-

---

15. See W. Kreck, *Die Zukunft des Gekommenen; Grundprobleme der Eschatologie* (München: C. Kaiser, 1966).

tancing to our being-here and being-now, which we call the future reference of hope. The present is disclosed to us from that believed-in past and, similarly and based on it, from this hoped-for future. There is no presentness which is disclosed as present which is not disclosed from the future of God in the same way and thus is open for all earthly future. The distance which the nearness of God brings with itself is to be understood with regard both to the past in which God came and to the future out of which God is coming. But this doubly-oriented distance is always a definite and concrete distance. It does not remove us, in the midst of our existence here, further from ourselves than to God. And it removes us to God in that it permits us to *endure* that removal. Being removed to God means to have a share in the withdrawal of God as withdrawal, but not as the abrogation of that withdrawal. God is near to us as the one who has withdrawn himself. That is the certainty of faith which as such is certainty of God and thus the de-securing of self-certainty.

Even self-certainty! For with God's presentness our own presentness is disclosed to us through the word from the cross. But self-certainty is precisely the opposite of self-founding through ascertainment. As the certainty of faith it is rather the absolute deprivation of man's security. That becomes completely clear when we add the final point to the problem of the thinkability of God, which we do by turning to the consideration of the unity of God with perisha-bility. The word of God speaks of God's unity with perishability when it defines the Crucified One as the Son of God.

SECTION 13. God's Unity with Perishability as the Basis for Thinking God

The necessity of thinking God together with perishability brings us to the final turn in our debate with the Cartesian approach to modern metaphysics and its results which continue to the present; this final turn will open up for us the basic lines of the concept of God. We now move completely into a critical position over against the traditional metaphysical conception, which also was presupposed and passed on by Descartes. It is the concept of God which permits him to be thought only as a highest, absolute, and independent being and for that reason ultimately prevents his being thought at all, in order to be able to assert that he is that kind of being.

We shall also have to attend to the protest of weighty theological voices when we take seriously the necessity of thinking God and Jesus together in such a way that the *Crucified One* must be the criterion for any possible concept of God, and take it seriously as a theological and intellectual necessity which corresponds to the being of God. We hear those weighty voices from the Ancient Church, from Scholasticism, from the Reformation (chiefly represented by Zwingli), and from Orthodoxy as well, especially Reformed Orthodoxy. We are especially conscious of the voice of the great Schleiermacher. We are certainly conscious of their protest, which is directed against the attempt at submitting God's absoluteness and independence, his being over us as absolute causality, his infinity and his omnipotence, his immutability and his immortality—sub-mitting all of that to *perishability* and to the negating reality of *death*. When we make the attempt here to think God together with perishability, then we certainly are not doing it as though these weighty voices did not exist or were not all that weighty. One cannot ignore or take lightly the protest of such a cloud of witnesses. One can only proceed along the pathway which one feels constrained to go in following the word of the cross *in full view* of such protest and challenged by the weightiness of the protesting voices, and one must receive the undebatable 'elements of truth' (*particula veri*) which are found in this protest. "Plato is a friend to me, all these teachers are friends to me, but the greater friend is truth."

We shall discuss first of all the necessity (13a) and then the possibility (13b) of thinking God's unity with perishability. In both cases we shall be led by the believed-in unity of God with perishability which is real as christological unity. Since, at the same time, we are considering the problem of modern thought raised by the "I think," we shall be dealing with a double necessity and a double possibility of thinking God together with perishability.

a. The Double Necessity of Thinking God's Unity with Perishability

The examination of a few basic elements of modern metaphysics led to a clear view of the problem of how God and perishability can be related to each other appropriately. This entire problem has gradually and progressively become the actual basic problem of any philosophy which asks about God. And as this basic problem appeared to be irresolvable, the philosophy derived from this tradition gradually stopped asking about God. There is some evidence for the supposition that the atheism born out of modern philosophy is a child of resignation. Must then theology also be resigned?

The answer will depend on the possibility of thinking God and perishability together. Such a possibility will disclose itself only through an appropriate understanding of the necessity of thinking God's unity with perishability. This necessity is a given for Christian theology in two ways: on the one hand as an objective necessity through the christological exposition of the biblical tradition, and on the other hand as a consequence of the historical consciousness which has grown out of modern metaphysics. Both aspects shall be presented in greater detail. At the same time we should expose the approaches to the possibility of thinking God and perishability together.

1. That *man* is perishable is experienced by modern man in an especially notable radicality compared to earlier ages. Medieval man experienced his perishability over against the imperishability of his God. The eternity of God led man to become aware of his own futility. The imperishability of the eternal God made finite man see his own perishability with horror, but also let him ultimately set his hope on this imperishable God. "In the midst of life we are surrounded by death"—that was a truth experienced by man in his position over against God. In the modern age, by contrast, man experiences perishability's threat to himself only over against himself. The experience of perishability is an automatic one, independent of any contrast to the imperishability of an infinite being.

That was made extremely distinct as early as Descartes. The Cartesian "ego" was, as we saw, forced to secure its existence, because the "ego" is capable of doubt. The ego must doubt because it can deceive itself. Through turning this ability and necessity to doubt into methodological doubt of all existence—*de omnibus dubitandum*—the "ego" attained the indubitability of its own doubt and the certainty of itself as a 'thinking thing' (*res cogitans*). The certainty obtained, however, only for the moment of the "I think." The "ego" could not secure the continuity of its existence through itself alone. Thus we are dealing with the experience of perishability in a twofold fashion from the outset.

First of all, the securing of the "ego" in the "I think" is already the consequence of an ontological *deficiency,* which is represented gnoseologically as the deficiency that man is able to deceive himself and thus as the necessity of doubt. Ontologically, this gnoseological deficiency is represented as the finitude of the "ego" which can deceive itself and thus must doubt. However, the limitation of finitude (which is certainly conceivable as imperishable) does not necessarily imply an affinity to deceivableness. That arises only with finitude experienced *as perishability* which, lacking all defenses and support, cannot even secure itself out of itself: 'the thinking thing desires to be deceived' (*res cogitans vult decipi*) could be the pointed way of putting it. In the process, though, this desire liberates the power to defend oneself against such perishability and thus to secure one's imperishability as proof of the immortality of the soul. The ego experiences its perishability as a general threat to its security. But it has this experience in that it becomes aware of itself as an ego which can doubt and must doubt, which creates its imperishability through the destruction of its perishability, so to speak. Perishability is experienced in the encounter of the ego with itself.

Furthermore, the experience that the certainty of "I think" is *limited* to the actual moment in which one thinks is an even more profoundly gripping experience of the way in which perishability threatens the ego. For now, the ego, which had secured itself for the moment in which it thinks as the 'thinking thing' (*res cogitans*), is threatened with regard to the certainty of its own continuity beyond the precise moment in which it is thinking. Perishability is now experienced within the experience of the "ego" as something already secured. The experience of perishability is a part of the self-experience of the ego which secures itself and everything else. In order to overcome the experience of perishability with something lasting, God is drawn into the picture.

We can call the Cartesian metaphysical approach, in spite of the thesis of the immortality of the soul, the factual basis of a metaphysics of perishability. The threat of perishing forces one to the self-grounding of thought in the "I think" as a self-securing "ego," which for its part then *vastly increases* the ego's experience of threatening perishability. Man's knowledge of his perishability is concealed in Descartes' approach. For that reason, the human ego secures itself. If man were imperishable, he would not need to secure himself.

If, however, perishable man, as the subject of the process of securing through the method of representation, is the one who decides about all that may be predicated *to exist,* then all that has been secured by this subject can only be regarded as perishable and secured in a finite way alone. Within the structure of modern metaphysics, therefore, to *exist* ultimately and necessarily means *to be perishable.*[1]

---

1. This is certainly true also of the assertion of the alleged imperishability of the 'thinking thing,' which requires, in order to be certain that it can endure, a detour via the securing of a God which is carried out by the self-same 'thinking thing.'

If, under these presuppositions, one then says that "God exists," one has basically subjected God to perishability because one has secured him as perishable. Following the metaphysical tradition, one then completely stopped talking *about God* at all. Even the assertion that "God exists *necessarily,*" intended to secure existence from its own perishability, cannot resolve the aporia which has emerged. The aporia has rather been intensified, as Kant demonstrated with his proof of the impossibility of a concept of unconditional necessity. For that reason, Fichte refused to use the predicate of *existence* about God, for the sake of the deity of God, and demanded that God not be thought at all, whereas conversely Nietzsche declared God to be an inconceivable being for the sake of perishability and thus to be dead: "All the imperishable—that's but a simile, and the poets lie too much."[2]

2. Christian theology today must make a decision. It must decide whether it will follow Fichte and his theological heirs and renounce the thinkability of God. Or it must (as the only possible alternative, in actuality) be prepared to destroy the presupposed understanding of the divine being 'superior to us' (*supra nos*) in order to think God in the way that he has revealed himself in his identity with the man Jesus. Such a destruction would be given in and of itself if one were to align oneself with the *consequences* of the Cartesian concept of existence in such a way that God would consciously be thought of as a being subject to perishability—in contrast with Descartes' own view and rather more along the lines of Nietzsche's thought. But in contradistinction from Descartes, this could not be done in such a way that God would be secured in the process. If man cannot secure himself *totally as man,* then he certainly cannot function as the subject which would secure God. Rather, the element of finitude and perishability, once combined with God, would have to contend against the element of security. That would be precisely what happens if Descartes' presupposed metaphysical concept of God, as that highest being which lacks and must lack every deficiency, were given up. With the metaphysical idea of God, God drops out as the final guarantor for self-securing man. This would mean further that God would be removed entirely from the context of the securing of the human subject.

The converse would then also be true of man, which is that he can function as God's securer as little as God can function as his guarantor. The *securing* function of man would remain limited to the *production of the world,* in such a way that producing man is responsible for his world without any other guarantor. The security risk is by no means reduced in this regard. Rather, it is increased even more.

Theology, therefore, if it sees itself obligated to think of the relationship of God's being and existence as being without contradiction, in such a way that God and man can be together, is required to make the following decision:

(a) One conceives of the noncontradictory nature of God's being and existence in such a way that one reverts to the metaphysical concept of the being of God and does away with the existence. Then one can think of God only as the unthinkable. For a non-existing God is unthinkable. Man, who is supposed to be *with God* based on this premise, must then elevate himself *over his own existence* in order to be with God beyond the dimension of finitude and perish-

2. See above, p. 152, n. 98.

ability. Then he is only with himself abstractly. The result is the distinction between the empirical "ego" on the one hand, and the ideal, relationless, transcendental, and even moral "ego" on the other hand. And this must lead to the conclusion: "The Metaphysical only, and not the Historical, can give us blessedness. . . ."[3]

(b) One thinks of the noncontradictory nature of God's being and existence in such a way that man comprehends the existence of God as the epitome of the divine being. Then, however, the traditional concept of the being of God must be given up because existence demonstrably includes one's being perishable within temporality. The noncontradictory unity of being and existence can also be thought of as projected on perishable man. But it cannot be thought of as something that man has projected. The noncontradictory unity of being and existence cannot be secured through representation and does not exist at all in the form of something which is secured. That very possibility which led to the disintegration of the unity of being and existence would be excluded.

If one sees the decision for the second form of this alternative as the theologically proper approach, then immediately the acute question is where this noncontradictory unity of God's being and existence is revealed in such a way that it must be thought of as a unity which projects itself on man.[4] Where is the indisputable site of the unity of God's being and existence, which would be as such the place where God and man are together and where God is thinkable?

3. The answer to this question which forces its way into the foreground is this: the historical fact. Thus, not seldom is the theological thesis advanced that God comes in the dimension of *historical factuality,* if not to himself then as he himself to man. In that history and also time are asserted to be the place for the thinkability of God, this answer is to be accepted. Since however, if God is to be thought as an event within human history, differentiations between different kinds of factuality within history are easily made, or historical facts are regarded as divine (even as proofs for divine actions), the dimension of historical factuality appears to be an extremely ambivalent thing which promises a kind of unambiguity which it really lacks. Then one speaks of salvific facts and not only argues about what a salvific fact is but also about whether such salvific facts are perceivable as having that quality by everyone or only with the help of a divine spirit.

We will not become involved in this kind of argument because we regard the category of salvific fact as erroneous. The misformation of this category is closely related to the presupposed thesis that God appears as God within the dimension of historical factuality. It is all the same whether one imagines this in such a way that God *intervenes* in history in order to make himself noticeable through such interventions, or that God *anticipates* the end of all history in certain givens which are in fact unique but in principle always possible, bearing in mind that God is present as God at the end of history anyway. Whichever way is taken, God is thought as an independent being over against the event of

3. See above, p. 129, n. 5.
4. See S. Kierkegaard, *Philosophical Fragments,* tr. D. Swenson, rev. H. V. Hong (Princeton: Princeton University Press, 1936, 1962[2]), pp. 107ff.

perishing existence.[5] The salvific fact is then supposed to participate in the independence of God.

Within the dimension of history a *fact* is an event which as such has already taken place and can only be regarded as something happened. A *salvific fact*, however, is supposed to be an event which persists in its factuality and thus represents a *nunc stans* ('persisting or lasting now') *within* history. Such salvific facts are exempt from perishability from the outset. In and of themselves, they do not know nothingness. For that very reason, we must object, they do not know God. The construction of the category of the salvific fact is a theological self-misunderstanding. With the best of intentions, it seeks to protect God from all perishability and preserve him from all devastation, and thus overleaps the requirement (which is anything but automatic or obvious) of thinking God and the death of the man Jesus of Nazareth together in such a way that God and man are thought together and God's being and existence are thought of as the same. Under the rubric of the category of "history," ancient Christology's dislike of thinking the eternal God in a radically temporal way is repeated: "Since they can admit no change in the deity, they also admit no actual *incarnation* of the logos."[6] And this happens because the relationship of eternity to time is defined at the cost of time, and God's eternity remains a thought which thinking believes it must think because it is afraid of time. "From the very beginning, time was the evil conscience of all empty metaphysics, the point which they liked to avoid."[7]

4. The dimension of historical factuality can be regarded as the place of the thinkability of God only when the character of the temporality of historical reality is taken seriously. Time includes the experience of perishing, which for its part is experienced as perishing only on the basis of the experience of being present. Presentness, in turn, discloses itself over and beyond the dull identity of the ego–here–now point as presentness through a word which addresses the present ego. The word is to be seen as the actual core of historical reality because it interrupts the natural context of existence in such a way that something like historical reality becomes possible. Further, within the dimension of historical reality the word interrupts the life context of the ego or of a community which

5. The thesis that certain historical events were anticipations of the end of history which at some time will reveal all of history as an *entirety* has the advantage of being a reflected kind of naiveté which must then deal with an even more naive and more reflected counterquestion: What is then supposed to happen with the entire course of history brought to a conclusion in such a way? What comes after the end? A new entirety? But what kind of entirety would that be that permitted one to think of another entirety next to it or beyond it? And how is God related to an entirety which he is *not* but which is supposed to be an *entirety without* him? Or is God ultimately the entirety himself? How then is God kept from being ultimately without a "future"? It appears to me to be more appropriate to drop the category of the "entirety" or the "whole" as a theological category and to assert the element of truth in it through the use of the category of the *context*. Contexts presuppose only relative unities, and can thus be thought of without the postulate of an entirety which comprehends everything. "The entirety" thus remains open. And this principle of the openness of "the entirety" is able to give *everything* both movement and direction, in that the "entirety" is now open for "more than the entirety."

6. F. W. J. Schelling, *Philosophie der Offenbarung*, in *Sämmtliche Werke*, ed. K. F. A. Schelling (Stuttgart and Augsburg: J. G. Cotta, 1858), II/4, p. 162.

7. *Ibid.*, p. 108.

says "we" in such a way that presentness is ascribed as present (and thus as the arriving future) but also is experienced as constantly perishing. In the word, that which is separated in history is *ontologically* together: present, future, and past. That every word is spoken *ontically* only within the historical sequence and thus has "its time," that it is therefore ontically thoroughly defined by history, may not be allowed to mislead one about the ontological priority of language over against history. Language is the inner ground of history, whereas the latter is the outer ground of language. Only through the addressing word does the community of subjects come to be, and within it that kind of ego-intensity which makes history.

To make the emergent answer to our question about the place in which the being of God may be identified as his existence more precise, we have advocated in this study up to now the Reformation thesis, developed in our own way, that the place where God is thinkable is the *word* which enables *faith*. One of the major reasons that the word is to be considered as the place for the thinkability of God is that it unites within itself a high degree of perishability with the most intensive power of becoming. What else is simultaneously as perishable and as creative as the word? Where else do perishing and becoming, past and future, reality and possibility, being and nonbeing reside so closely together as in the word? In the word, man interacts with man as man, which is the reason that language reveals human inhumanity in the most sensitive fashion. In the word, we are together and yet we distinguish ourselves in such a way that each person is he himself.

If the word is the place for the thinkability of God, then before that it must be the place where God and man are together, a being together which renders it impossible to disintegrate the unity of God's being and existence into a being which is over us and an existence which we have secured. God and man must be with each other in the word in such a way that they are definitively distinguished in this being together: God a God who is human in his deity, and man, instead of penetrating God and thus deifying himself, who is a human person, always becoming more human.

Thus we state a condition which in reality is by no means simply an intellectually produced postulate. Rather, Christian proclamation understands itself as that kind of word. The condition we have defined is thus in reality a claim which Christian proclamation makes about itself. How does Christian proclamation come to this claim?

This can be answered only with reference to the event about which this word speaks. Christian proclamation speaks of the event of the unity of God with the executed Jesus of Nazareth. God himself spoke through the Crucified One. And as the Crucified One, he desires to continue to speak. The ancient church's dogma of the incarnation of the word of God sought to formulate this event of the identification of God with a man who submitted not only to the perishability of earthly existence but also to the deadening power of the law. With that intention, it is still a criterion for proper Christian proclamation today.

Together with John's Gospel, Christian theology understands the *logos*, who was "in the beginning" (John 1:1) and thus deserves to be called the *word of God*, as the addressing word in an absolute sense. The decisive thing is that in this word the self-communication of the one who speaks takes place: God speaks out of himself, and as such he addresses us. And here again, the decisive thing is that such addressing self-communication of God takes place under the ontic conditions of historical reality, in indissoluble identity with the particular history of the man Jesus. The word became flesh (John 1:14a) in such a way that the self-communicating glory of God continues to address us and to share itself within the context of historical reality (John 1:14b, c and John 1:16), to the extent that its focus is faith. Faith, however, is essentially one's self-involvement with the God who expresses himself. The reality of the man Jesus for faith within the context of historical reality is characterized therefore chiefly in the fact that it is nothing other than the history of the God who speaks out of himself, communicates himself, and thus addresses us: 'not apart from the word did the human nature of the man Jesus exist' (*numquam seorsum a verbo extitit humana natura hominis Jesu*). To that extent, faith confesses the man Jesus as the word of God who in this particularity completely expresses himself and to that degree empties himself, to use the formulation of the Philippian hymn. And in that self-emptying in which God's glory subjects itself to perishability for the sake of perishing man, faith recognizes the means and the foundation of the particular historical reality of the man Jesus, so that, 'other things not being equal' (*ceteris imparibus*), we can assert with Schelling, "This *kenosis* . . . was the *unique* cause of the existence of the man Jesus."[8]

Part and parcel of Christian proclamation therefore is that it discovers God and man already to be together in Jesus Christ. It is addressed and impressed by that. And in that it attempts to say this to all people, it expects of all those so addressed that they will *involve* themselves in this co-existence of God and man. That means that the word which speaks of God expects *faith* of the person addressed. Without involving oneself in this co-existence of God and man, one cannot be a part of that co-existence.

This is equally true of the possibility of thinking God. The anthropological requirability of trust in God corresponds to the christologically experienceable humanity of God, as the access to the possibility (which existentially increases its capacity) of understanding God. Whoever does not understand God cannot think God. Trust in God, if not as an existential act then in any event as an explicable phenomenon, is thus the condition for the possibility of the true thought of God. Without faith, and if not in its full emergence, then at least thinking through the process of faith, God cannot be thought at all. Trust and faith are nothing other than those human acts with which man affirms God for God's sake (and not for the sake of some other necessity) in such a way that he allows him to be there where he is, which is with man. In this *existence* of God with the man Jesus, the divine *being* is realized. Faith preserves the identity of God's being and existence in that it perceives God's being as a being with the man Jesus and thus as a being for all people. For that reason, and only for that reason, faith is the precondition for the thinkability of God (and not because personal piety or holiness is the *conditio sine qua non* of the thought of God). Faith as the precondition of the possibility of the proper thought of God is that

---

8. *Ibid.*, p. 159. With this sentence, Schelling formulates precisely the traditional christological thesis of the anhypostasis of the human nature of Jesus Christ: "Not apart from the word did the human nature of the man Jesus exist." See also *ibid.*, p. 158.

instance which prevents thought from making a distinction between the being and existence of God. *Faith takes God's existence as his being.* Basically everything is said for faith when it experiences that God is. Schelling's objection to Hegel, which was that reason could only grasp the being of a thing, its 'what it is' (*quid sit*), but not its unanticipatable existence, its 'because it is' (*quod sit*), because the quiddity withdraws from reason which considers necessity,[9] is to be taken seriously theologically because the existence of God can under no circumstances be secured by reason but rather is a given as an unanticipatable facticity. But Schelling's distinction between *Quid* and *Quod* (what, and because, or why)—which is directed against a false identification of existence and thought— must be developed further by the attempt to understand the existence of God as the being of God, so that the thinking of a difference between God's being and existence becomes impossible. The highest achievement of that thought which distinguishes between the being and existence of God is only the proof of the identity of what had been differentiated, a proof which is expressed in the statement, God is necessary. In opposition to such high achievements of thought, faith must assert that the divine essence which derives from the unpreconceivable existence of God, and is thought of as such, teaches one to think of God as one who cannot possibly be understood as necessary in identity with the *particular* historical reality of the man Jesus, for logical reasons. Rather faith must emphasize that in this very uniqueness of an historical person, God is interesting for his own sake and is in this more than necessary.

　　5. This content can also be elucidated anthropologically. If thought is to think God as the one who finds his counterpart solely in faith, then thought is directed toward a particular human *attitude* in relation to God. Faith is that human attitude toward God which is called forth by God himself, in which man, completely without *coercion* and gladly, relates himself to God. The most original attitude of one ego toward another person, an attitude called forth by that other one, completely uncoerced and realized gladly, is *joy.* For that reason, one can say "joy in God" instead of "faith." For faith permits God to be that one who in and of himself *is for us* and *takes us unto himself* so that we do not *want to be* what we are without him. The self-definition for which man is determined in faith can thus be only the immediacy of a defined joy. Joy in God would then be the origin, the source, of the true thought of God, to the extent that joy is that "existential" in which God is thinkable *for the sake of his own self.* For joy is always joy in something for its own sake. Thus, it is indeed the real origin of thought—over against the disquieting *thaumazein* ('to wonder') at the madness of existence. But regardless of that, whoever does not think God *for his own sake* has not yet begun to think *God* at all. To think God without joy in God is a self-contradiction which must lead even the most logical proof of God to absurdity. All attempts to prove the necessity of God are therefore so distressing as well as paradoxical, because they can arrive at God only at the end of the process and thus can know him only as the "God at the end." They cannot *begin* with God,[10] because they do not begin with God for his own sake. But if God

　　9. See F. W. J. Schelling, *Philosophie der Offenbarung,* II/3, pp. 57ff; *Philosophie der Mythologie,* II/1, pp. 562ff.
　　10. On this critical objection of Schelling, see above, p. 95, n. 185.

is thought for his own sake, on the basis of a joy summoned forth by God himself, then the very act of thinking God is the demonstration of the fact that God is *more than necessary.*

If one thinks God's being on the basis of this "more than necessary," that is, his relationship to the world out of the superabundance of his being, his deity out of his self-determination to become human, and his eternity out of his identity with the crucified Jesus of Nazareth, then one has begun to think God and perishability together and thus to think God for his own sake.

The necessity of thinking God in unity with perishability is a necessity given by the word of God itself. This material necessity, however, coincides with the necessity of thinking God and perishability together which emerges from the consequences of modern metaphysics. Both necessities can be combined only in *disagreement* with each other. Yet if the necessity of this disagreement is recognized, then the possibility of its being transformed into *fruitful tension* is not ruled out. There are disputes in which the desire to win is prohibited from the outset, but out of which the freedom of understood closeness to each other can emerge as something new.

6. It would be helpful to reformulate what has just been said more precisely in the form of a discussion with the modern approach to securing God, with its consequences. If thinking is to advance, then it should not resist repetition.

"Where is God?" That is the question which emerges at the conclusion of the metaphysics newly established by Descartes. According to Descartes, the answer to this question has to be that God is over us. In that, Descartes was totally faithful to traditional metaphysics. For him, God is exclusively that superior power beyond which nothing superior can be thought. The specific Cartesian factor was that he secured this "over us" *as* "over us" through reflecting on the human "ego" (in such a way that first of all I secure my own self). But by securing God over us in this way, God threatened to become fixed in a realm beyond in such a way that, as the highest essence (or nature), he was required to procure his existence from within the worldly sphere. That made him a highest essence which existed at the grace and favor of those subject to him. In the modern concept of God, the fate of European monarchies is anticipated.

The Christian faith, in countering this dilemma in the thought of God, had to return to a reconsideration of its own approaches to the understanding of God. Long before Descartes, the Christian faith had cited the Socratic dictum against a God who is localized only over us: 'Things that are above us are no concern of ours' (*quae supra nos, nihil ad nos*).[11] That was a theological warning.

---

11. Martin Luther, *Luther and Erasmus: Free Will and Salvation,* trs. E. G. Rupp, P. Watson, and B. Drewery (*Library of Christian Classics,* vol. 17) (Philadelphia: Westminster, 1969), pp. 109, 200f. (*WA,* 18, 605, 20f and 685, 5ff); in the earlier passage, Luther summarizes Erasmus's position which he is rejecting; in the following quotation he expresses himself positively against the use of the concept of '*deus absconditus*' ('concealed God'): "To the extent, therefore, that God hides himself and wills to be unknown to us, it is no business of ours. For the saying truly applies, 'Things above us are no business of ours' " (pp. 200f). On the interpretation of the Socratic dictum, its origin, and Luther's theological use of it, see my essay "Quae supra nos, nihil ad nos;

Modern metaphysics had to disregard it totally. It could not permit itself to be irritated by theology, particularly when the issue was thinking God. Descartes himself may serve as the example for this.

In his dedication to the Sorbonne which prefaces his *Meditations* Descartes sought to draw a sharp distinction between theology and philosophy by saying that he understands theology to be for the believer, whereas philosophy has to do with the unbeliever, and he means here, preferentially has to do with the unbeliever. For this reason, he has "always thought that the two questions, of God and of the soul, were the principal questions among those that should be demonstrated by [rational] philosophy rather than theology. For although it may suffice us faithful ones to believe by faith that there is a God and that the human soul does not perish with the body, certainly it does not seem possible ever to persuade those without faith to accept any religion, nor even perhaps any moral virtue, unless they can first be shown these two things by means of natural reason. . . . It is absolutely true, both that we must believe that there is a God because it is so taught in the Holy Scriptures,[12] and, on the other hand, that we must believe the Holy Scriptures because they come from God. The reason for this is that faith is a gift of God, and the very God that gives us the faith to believe other things can also give us the faith to believe that he exists. Nevertheless, we could hardly offer this argument to those without faith, for they might suppose that we were committing the fallacy that logicians call circular reasoning."[13] This was an attack on theological talk about God, which is not lessened by the immediate appeal to the tradition of natural theology and the biblical texts which substantiate it.[14] *Theological* talk about God, according to this view, is of no import for unbelief, because it discusses God as one *to be*

Eine Kurzformel der Lehre vom verborgenen Gott—im Anschluss an Luther interpretiert," *Evangelische Theologie,* 32 (1972), 197ff.

A question which has frequently been discussed is how Luther's critique of metaphysics relates to the new approach of Cartesian thought, with particular regard to the modern age which is fundamentally conditioned by both the Reformation and Descartes' thought. I would remark in this regard that *one* decisive difference between the theology of the Reformer and the philosophy of the thinker who based thought on "I think" would be this: Descartes *took over* the metaphysical thought of God and thus brought it into a crisis which was certainly not intended. In contrast, Luther *battled* the metaphysical concept of God on the basis of a certainty of God which implied a *new* understanding of God. Luther destroyed the older approach because and in that he built something new. Descartes, on the other hand, initiated a destructive process precisely by holding onto that which was older. This is, at any rate, the situation from the perspective of the concept of God, which, after all, did not belong to the obvious components of thought in either that philosophy or this theology. G. Ebeling has provided a penetrating analysis of the problem of the relationship between Luther and Descartes: "Gewissheit und Zweifel; Die Situation des Glaubens im Zeitalter nach Luther und Descartes," in *Wort und Glaube II; Beiträge zur Fundamentaltheologie und zur Lehre von Gott* (Tübingen: Mohr [Siebeck], 1969), pp. 138ff.

12. Descartes was Catholic —.

13. "Letter of Dedication" (to the Faculty of Theology of Sorbonne), *Meditations on First Philosophy,* tr. L. J. Lafleur (*Library of Liberal Arts,* 29) (New York: Liberal Arts Press, 1951), p. 3.

14. See W. Schulz, *Der Gott der neuzeitlichen Metaphysik* (Pfullingen: G. Neske Verlag, 1957), p. 39: ". . . but at the same time this dedication signified an attack."

believed in. Apparently Descartes presupposes here that unbelievers could be and had been brought to faith through evidences and proofs.

Immanuel Kant, later, put the same accusation in a more ironic form: "That there is a God is proven by biblical theology by the fact that he has spoken in the Bible."[15] And Kant says of an "historical faith, grounded solely on fact,"[16] a faith related to *history*: "Historical faith 'is dead, being alone'; that is, of itself, regarded as a creed, it contains nothing, and leads to nothing, which could have any moral value for us."[17] Thus Immanuel Kant. One might, however, ask if, for the Cartesian 'thinking thing,' the *faith* which spoke of God in its own way over against securing thought was not "dead, being alone," because the God which the Christian faith expresses could not be considered as the highest power over us, providing the necessary assurance for human self-certainty, and thus had to be irrelevant for the self-criticism of human reason carried out as a soliloquy.

We certainly must ask whether, conversely, a God postulated as the necessary assurance for the self-securing 'thinking thing' or as the guarantor for the unity of sensuality and morality would not be a stillborn God, if that expression be allowed. This "infinite substance, independent, omniscient, omnipotent," was absolutely incapable of tolerating any deficiency. Can something like that be alive? Such a being could, should not be human by definition. Then the opposite question is raised: Does such a God, which may not be human, deserve to be called divine? The "I think" of modern metaphysics could distinguish man from God only by distinguishing God from man, by holding God far away from man and from man's history. But did not that in fact rob God of his divinity? Is not the actual 'crime of the offense of majesty' (*crimen laesae maiestatis*) against God's deity the disputation of his humanity? And is not the ultimate intention, either conscious or unconscious, of this disputation of the humanity of God the drive to be able to incorporate divinity into the human will in such a way that the better part of man can be spoken of no longer as human but rather as exclusively divine, whereas the remaining part of man is left as "an earthly remnant, painful to bear," until finally "God separates himself from man in flames, and the ponderous vision of earthly life sinks and sinks and sinks . . ."?

The faith which interposes such questions is a disturbance. But should not faith be seen as a disturber of the metaphysical thought of God, as even its greatest menace? Was it not necessary that a study of religion within the boundaries of pure reason would have to come to the aid of the metaphysical concept of God in order to reduce the all too human discourse about a God who reveals himself in history to a rational level? Did not faith have to be subordinated to that morality which was established without faith, if it were not to become irrational in and of itself and thus be dead?

15. I. Kant, *Der Streit der Fakultäten,* in *Werke in sechs Bänden,* ed. W. Weischedel (Wiesbaden: Insel-Verlag, 1966²), VI, 285 (for partial translation, see H. Reiss, "The Contest of Faculties," in *Kant's Political Writings,* tr. H. B. Nisbet [Cambridge: Cambridge University Press, 1970]).
16. I. Kant, *Religion Within the Limits of Reason Alone,* trs. T. M. Greene and H. H. Hudson (New York: Harper, 1960), Book Three, Division One, V, 94.
17. *Ibid.,* VI, 102.

But then faith will reply with the question whether it really is such a rational capacity that a theoretical or practical use of reason, separate from the event of faith, can prescribe reason's function. What becomes of God when an abstract "I think" or an abstract "thou shalt" sets the context from the outset within which one then may and must decide what merits being called God? Although the intention to maintain the strictest possible distinction between God and man cannot be supported too strongly by theology, does not this approach lead to a result which is totally opposed to that intention? And finally, if God has been established as the *securing factor* for man, has not then the decision been already made that from now on the securing must become the *god of man*? Is not ultimately the categorical imperative the grand attempt to establish the morally understood security of the human race as its highest good? If "nothing can possibly be conceived in the world, or even out of it, which can be called good without qualification, except a *good will,*"[18] then does not the good will which secures the welfare of the human race become the god of man?

Theology must point out the *possibility* of such a reversible equation as the actual danger of the metaphysical thought of God within the context of modern thought. If the *consequent realization* of this possibility is to be hindered, then that thought which secures not only everything, but also God and man (theologically, that is "more than everything"), must be opposed theologically by an instance which liberates the relationship of God and man from the framework of security without having to abrogate all thought entirely. Such an instance is the trust which takes away security on the basis of the certainty of God. Trust can be defined accurately as *certainty which removes security*. It is true in many respects that "trust is good but control is better." Mastering the world through production of the world is unthinkable without control, not to speak of actually doing it. Control provides security, and is thus indispensable within the structure of that which is securable. But every interpersonal relationship, every contact from person to person, would be destroyed by the performance of that securing process which provides for control. Man lives on trust. Trust is an existential factor which constitutes the humanity of man. For in trust man can rely on an instance outside of himself, he can go out of himself without having to be concerned about himself. In this sense, unlimited trust (not as a requirement, for trust cannot be required, but rather as an event which takes place, not without good reason) is the basic process between man and God. Man's relationship to God stands and falls therefore with trust in God, that is, with an event of certainty which removes security.

Within the structure of theological thought, then, the *removal of security* is the task at hand. The time has come for the removal of security. It should be noted that we are speaking of the removal of *man's* security, not of his works' security nor of the world's security which is itself progressively more defined by his works. On the contrary, to remove man's security, as a person, can be done today only in combination with the increased securing of his works and his world. In this regard, one will have to learn to understand in a new way the old Reformation distinction between person and work. It is precisely because man

18. See I. Kant, *Fundamental Principles of the Metaphysic of Morals,* tr. T. K. Abbott (Indianapolis: Bobbs-Merrill Company, 1949), p. 11.

must secure his world in his drive to produce his world that he is in danger of insisting on the securing of his own self as person. Man mistrusts himself. In contrast with that, faith insists that man is a being which, by the merits of divine justification, merits trust and which can itself exercise trust. For that reason, man needs to distinguish his person from his works. The de-securing of man is necessary both theologically and anthropologically for the sake of man's trust-worthiness. It should be sufficiently clear from all that has been said that the process of removing security is the exact opposite of making one insecure. The trust which removes security does not make one insecure, but rather free.

This is then a freedom from the drive of the ego toward itself. It arises from the freedom of a relationship in which God as he himself can *encounter* man. In order to be able to *think* this encounter of the free God with man who is to be freed, the thought of God must be liberated from the framework of security which is both theoretical and practical in its derivation. The destruction of this thought structure cannot happen, however, without the accompanying destruction of the metaphysical concept of God which is its presupposition. That thought which "thinks after" faith must emphasize that God and man *encounter each other in freedom* and must then be capable of being *thought* as encountering each other in freedom. That means for the capacity of thought itself that theology requires of reason that it realize itself not only as a soliloquy but that it remain open, or reopen itself, so that it can be addressed.

7. Theology can do its assigned task only when, in answering the question "Where is God?", it does not refer solely to "above us." God is also below us. And that is the very way in which he is God. God is ". . . not in a mere divinity which is obviously presented to man in the mere humanity intended for man. . . . When man tries to make this mad exchange [between God and man], his first and supreme error is in relation to God. It is not only that he cannot succeed in worshipping the true Deity in himself, but that in positing himself as absolute what he thinks to see and honour and worship in himself is already the image of a false deity, the original of all false gods. Ignoring the grace of God. . . , man chooses himself, and in so doing even in this . . . respect he chooses that which is not. . . . he makes God the devil. For if . . . there 'is' a devil, he is identical with a supreme being which posits and wills itself, which exists in a solitary glory and is therefore 'absolute.' The devil is that being which we can define only as independent *non-being*."[19]

---

19. K. Barth, *CD*, IV/1, p. 422. The Barthian statement does not appear to be correct (in German), and so I have corrected it by adding brackets. In terms of the history of theology, Descartes did overcome the nominalistic dichotomy in the concept of the *essence* of God (*potentia dei ordinata* ['ordained power of God']—*potentia dei absoluta* ['absolute power of God']) by first of all describing the one side of this inner-divine distinction as the 'evil genius' (*genius malignus; deus deceptor*) and then proving the impossibility of such a devilish god. But what was the price to be paid for that! In fact, the twofold and divided essence of God was replaced by the separation of the essence and existence of God. What then was imagined to be the essence of God corresponds to what Luther called 'God in his majesty and in his nature' (*deus in maiestate et natura sua*). The existence of this God was secured by Descartes through the idea of the essence of God. Thus the nominalistic concept of God was brought in fact to absurdity. In contrast, Luther appeared to remain committed to the nominalistic tradition in that he left 'God in his majesty and in his nature' within the realm of unlimited freedom as 'the

If then God is not essentially (*essentialiter*) over us but under us, then obviously we must ask once more: Where is God? The theological answer to that is, God is in God's word. This answer implies a polemic which we could formulate with Luther's words: "God must therefore be left to himself in his own majesty, for in this regard we have nothing to do with him, nor has he willed that we should have anything to do with him. But we have something to do with him insofar as he is clothed and set forth in his Word, through which he offers himself to us. . . ."[20] That could have been written against Descartes. It was written against Erasmus. But basically, it is written *for* the unbelief with which theology must deal because it has to deal with belief. In responding to unbelief's question, "Where is God?", there is no double answer, but rather only *one*[21] answer: God is in God's word. As such, he is there for us, he works life and salvation in that he shares in the lostness and death of man. And with regard to the "infinite substance, independent, omniscient, omnipotent. . . ," which is supposed to be the concept of God, that is, with regard to the God who causes everything which is *without distinction,* it is certainly true that 'things that are above are no concern of ours' (*quae supra nos, nihil ad nos*). For the abstract imperishability of God above us is the expression of a God who in his abstractness (or, as Luther could say, in his nudity) is a terrible and in his terribleness ultimately a boring God. Terror without end ultimately kills all attentiveness. Even fascination at the abstract majesty of God over us results in a sense of horror which kills *concrete* attentiveness toward God, results in a thoroughly terrifying boredom. And for that very reason, the wordless, dumb, and perfectly abstract divine majesty does not concern us. In trying to think it through to the end, we could really only "unharness" thinking, to use Nietzsche's idea. In such a case, thought ceases to be interesting.

In contrast with that, it would be faith's task to interest thought in God, if it properly understands itself. But faith can do that only by stating the place where God is accessible to thought. This place is that particular word in which God is present temporally. It is the presupposition for thinking God and perishability together. In this, it is the presupposition for the thinkability of God.

8. The resulting task with regard to the formation of a concept of God is to work out a way of thinking God which in the very formulation of divine being does justice to the insight which Luther stated so neatly and cleanly, "For these

---

concealed God' (*deus absconditus*). It appears that Luther could not think of a securing of God comparable to the Cartesian approach, because that would bring theology to the point of absurdity. But the contrast emerges at another point, namely, where Luther leaves nominalism in the concept of God and then, on the basis of the revelation of God in the word, asserts the 'proclaimed God' (*deus praedicatus*) as that counterpart on which man can depend. For this reason, in Luther the category of the *word of God* occupies that position in which according to Descartes the securing *representation of God* should stand. The subject which secures through representing is the ego as the 'thinking thing,' that is, man, who knows that God is above him. The subject of the word of God, on the other hand, is God himself who in his word is below us.

20. Martin Luther, *Luther and Erasmus: Free Will and Salvation*, p. 201.

21. This should be worked through critically also against Luther's nominalism within his discussion of the "concealed God."

two belong together, faith and God."[22] The *conditio sine qua non* for this is the destruction of the "God of the philosophers" as the 'most perfect being' (*ens perfectissimum*) above us.[23] But the result may not be that we do not think God at all anymore. In theology, God must be *thought*. He must be thought because nothing can be done against the "God of the philosophers" by renouncing the thinkability of God. Christian theology, rather, in working through the concept of God, must carry on the business of thinking far more rigorously than philosophy has done with its concept of God. Taking leave of the "God of the philosophers" is anything but taking leave of the obligation to think God. Taking leave of the "God of the philosophers" would rather be a departure from Pascal's distinction between the "God of the philosophers" and the "God of Abraham, Isaac, and Jacob,"[24] a distinction which was necessary then but which has become sterile today. The time has come for giving up this alternative. To do that, one must make the effort to think God in such a way that the thought of God corresponds to the being of God. God's being must then provide the possibility of thinking God and perishability together, as a unity. That which the word of God makes necessary must be made possible in God himself.

How then, if God and faith formally "belong together" just as God and man materially belong together in perishability, must God be thought in such a way that they can be definitively distinguished from each other? How can God and perishability so be thought of together that a Christian concept of God results? We shall endeavor to answer this question in that we now attempt to interpret ontologically and positively the word of the death of God within the horizon of the word of the cross.

b. The Double Possibility of Thinking God's Unity with Perishability: The Ontological Significance of Christological Talk about the Death of God

1. The necessity of thinking God in unity with perishability emerges as the result for that thinking which is prepared to perceive the event of faith as the precondition for, and the possible word of a God as the place of, his thinkability. This necessity results all the more when thought follows the movement of Christian faith and affirms the word which announces God in the man Jesus as the place of the thinkability of God. To that extent, the indispensability of a thought which conceives of God not without perishability is a *theological* necessity. The word of the cross requires it.

Intellectual necessities, however, may not ignore the historical place of

22. Martin Luther, "Great Catechism," in *The Book of Concord; The Confessions of the Evangelical Lutheran Church*, tr. T. G. Tappert (Philadelphia: Fortress Press, 1959), p. 365.

23. Of course, in doing so, one will have to take account of the *intended* distinction between God and man as 'elements of truth' in this philosophical concept of God; although intended, it is still incorrect, realized in a disastrous fashion, and thus transformed ultimately into the very opposite of what was intended.

24. See also the *Epilegomena 1975* in my book *Gottes Sein ist im Werden; Verantwortliche Rede vom Sein Gottes bei Karl Barth; Eine Paraphrase* (Tübingen: J. C. B. Mohr [Paul Siebeck], 1965[1], 1967[2], 1976[3]), pp. 126f. An English translation is available, but the Epilogue is not included in this edition; see *The Doctrine of the Trinity: God's Being is in Becoming*, tr. H. Harris (Grand Rapids: Wm. B. Eerdmans, 1976).

thought itself, especially if they are to do justice historically to what is to be thought. Whatever must be necessarily thought can only possibly be thought in the historical context of thought. That does not mean that the position of our thinking within the history of thought is ultimately decisive with regard to what can still be thought today. Thinking must, rather, defend itself constantly against such a tyranny of the spirit of the age, as a critique of itself. But it cannot do that by ignoring with seeming sovereignty the spirit of the age, the place of our thinking within intellectual history. There is progress in thought only when thought pursues its own concern reflectively *and* in doing so attends to the historical context of thought and of the spirit of the age in such a way that the intellectual necessities which arise out of the business of thought lead into debate with the current spirit of the age and the aporias of thought which derive from it. Whoever wants to change the spirit of the age must first of all have understood it. But whoever really understands the spirit of his age cannot evade grasping this spirit in its temporality. The life of the spirit is as such temporal. If then the spirit is in and of itself temporal, then it is always pushing beyond the spirit of the age at any given time. And where is it going?—the self-critique of thought should at least participate in the making of that decision.[25] Just as that is true of any thought, it is also valid for theology, that is, for the thought which reflects on the word of God based on the certainty of faith.

Theological reflection, consequently, will not be able to dissociate itself from the intellectual history defined by the dominance of "I think" as though it simply could move beyond the historical situation of thought with its plenitude of problems. It was probably a decisive weakness of so-called dialectical theology that it did not protect itself adequately and clearly enough against possible misunderstandings, and at times favored or even encouraged such misunderstandings.[26] Whichever proponent of the so-called theology of the word desires to think further in that school's direction responsibly will have to see and struggle against the results of this weakness, facing expressly the fact that it is the great

25. Basically, of course, every thought which really led history further was more or less aware of this historicity of thought, even though it was not until the modern age that it was experienced in a particularly marked way. Plato reveals the extent to which he saw himself called on to work through intellectual traditions which conflicted with each other and transform them into something new. And Aristotle reflected expressly about the "place in the history of thought" in which his philosophy belonged. Even those philosophers who allegedly thought unhistorically, such as Immanuel Kant, did in fact deal responsibly with the historical position of their thought, either implicitly or explicitly. With regard to Kant, it must be asserted that it was the keen analysis of the historical situation in which philosophy at that time found itself which led to the critical intellectual achievement which so radically altered the situation of thought. See, for example, the Foreword to his *Prolegomena to any Future Metaphysics*, ed. L. W. Beck (Indianapolis and New York: Bobbs-Merrill Company, Inc., 1950), pp. 13ff.

26. That this is a grave *misunderstanding* of the "Theology of the Word" will be undoubtedly clear not only to the reader of the writings of Friedrich Gogarten and Rudolf Bultmann, but with careful thought also to the unprejudiced reader of the *Church Dogmatics* and the other writings of Karl Barth which accompany it. It would be extraordinarily interesting and rewarding to research historically and systematically the theology of these theologians from the point of view of their own presentation of the historical context within which, and in confrontation with which, they went their various theological ways. Such research is a prerequisite without which no truly instructive history of the theology of the twentieth century can be written.

threat to all truly scientific advance in theology. It is scarcely less of a hindrance to objective progress in theology than disregard or even scorn for the content comprehended in the category of the word of God, an attitude which dishonors theology.

It is incontestable, then, that that thinking which follows the movement of faith can no longer seek to ground itself in "I think," nor even attempt to ground itself at all. Rather, as the thought of faith, it is grounded in the selfsame word which makes faith possible. As incontestable as that is, it is equally indubitable that it is the *human person* who is thinking when theology is being done (we are speaking here of 'the theology of the pilgrims or wayfarers'—*theologia viatorum*). In reflecting on the ways of God, the "I think" situation does not become alien to the thinker, although it is integrated immediately into "*we* think," which is the characteristic situation for the Christian faith. The reason that this is so is that in faith nothing *human* is alien to the believer, but rather can only become all the more familiar. It is thus entirely out of the question to say that theology passes by man because it devotes its *undivided* attention to God.[27] Where, then, is the God who is being "thought after" here *because* he revealed himself? Where else could he be than with mankind? And who thinks after God if he follows the movement of faith in his thinking? Who else but man? There is a Christian understanding, an understanding of the theological necessity of the old pagan statement, "I am a man, and nothing that concerns a man do I deem a matter of indifference to me."[28] That "deeming" belongs to the confession of faith, the credo.

For our problem of the thinkability of God, that means that the theological necessity of thinking God together with perishability cannot be realized while ignoring the problem which has emerged for modern thought from the relationship of thought and mortality, thought and God, as well as God and perishability. The threefold relationship of God, thought, and perishability, which we find as an unresolved problem in the historical context of modern thought, must be brought into movement if thought is to deal adequately with the theological necessity of thinking God and perishability together. Otherwise one cannot "think after" the word of the cross, if such "thinking after" is really supposed to be thought. The *possibility* of thinking God's unity with perishability is to be sought today in the debate with the historical situation of modern thought and thus is

27. It is impossible to say, then, that a theology of revelation would be justified in or forced to disregard the so-called humane sciences, or any other sciences at all, merely because it claims, as theology, to be its own science. To "think after" something (to reflect on it) never means to hasten away from the situation of the thinker in order to leave it behind in isolation. To "think after" something, rather, means to draw thought into motion together *with* the situation of the thinker. That would be, at least, the theological way in which theology should carry on its dialogue with other sciences, from which it must be strictly distinguished but yet can never be separated. Such a dialogue will not allow these other sciences to be preempted as theological disciplines, nor will the theological disciplines be allowed to lose themselves in the other sciences, however undebatably they may have affinities to the various other disciplines. Both *sides* in a fruitful relationship will emphasize that they must proceed "without admixture and untransformed."

28. Terence, *Heauton Timoroumenos*, Act I, Sc. i (see "The Self-Tormentor," in *The Complete Comedies of Terence*, tr. and ed. P. Bovie [New Brunswick: Rutgers University Press, 1974], p. 84).

to be sought as a debate of thought with thought. If the historical situation of modern thought must be described theologically as *atheistic*, then the question of the *possibility* of thinking God and perishability together is at the same time an intellectual debate with thought's atheistic fate. Is atheism the fate of thought?

2. With this question we return to the level of talk about the death of God. The aporia should have been worked through in our discussion until now to the point that agreement about the meaning of talk about the death of God can be reached between faith and reason. Such an agreement does not need to be a unified view. It can consist of the recognition of a clear alternative. With regard to talk about the death of God, that is in fact the case.

Over against the confrontation of thought grounded in "I think" with that reflection which sees in the word from the cross the place for the thinkability of God, the dark word of the death of God reaches the clarity of an alternative which in any event forces theology toward the unambiguity of a decision: *either* to think God's unity with perishability in such a way that God and faith belong only to the past and atheism is the fate of the spirit, *or* to think God's unity with perishability in such a way that we recognize that both God and perishability have been thought inadequately until now, and the pathway of the spirit can be prepared through the (poor) alternative between theism and atheism into a situation in which the spirit is present so that God can finally be thought again.

Theology oriented to the word of the cross will opt for this second possibility, since to choose the other possibility unavoidably forces theology into a role (which many theologians accept with special pleasure) in which it exists only in order to be the executrix of its own legacy. The one who thinks that he can evade this clear decision in order to do theology while ignoring it will have to accept the charge that he is theologizing right past the problem of modern thought as well as thinking right past the word of the cross. Of course, we would have to ask, in the first case, how much thinking and, in the second case, how much theology is really being done. The justified accusation of deficient awareness of the problem, which must be leveled against such decisionless theology, bursts every claim of scientific integrity as well as theological objectivity. What remains is at best a kind of liturgy, and that is certainly a miserable liturgy, because genuine liturgy has another *Sitz im Leben* than the academic podium.

The theology formed by the Reformation, in any event, did think God and perishability together in that it thought God and the man Jesus together on the one hand, and human faith and God together on the other hand. The intimate connection of God and Jesus, which must verify itself in the death of Jesus, is the actual ground for the intimate connection of God and faith. God and faith belong together—Luther's statement is properly understood only when every possibility is ruled out that the believer will be removed from the perishable world through the connection of faith with God, in the process of which removal from the world the believer is even "deified." Rather, God belongs to faith in the sense that God and faith are subjected in the same way to the perishability of the world in which the believer believes. If God is to be thought because the word of the cross must be thought after, then God and faith do not belong together in another "world" but rather *in perishability*. But then God himself must be thought as belonging together with perishability.

Talk about the death of God is the most stringent form of reminder of this task. Even the atheistic use of this kind of talk knew that it was obligated to this task in its own way, so long as it was not merely thoughtless. The dark word of the death of God can alternatively be interpreted then so that two ways become visible in which God can be thought together with perishability. Both ways have their own origins and beginnings and certainly differing destinations, but yet they have much in common. They often overlap, and for long stretches they appear to be identical with each other. This makes it all the more necessary that we distinguish them.

3. Based on the premises of modern metaphysics, talk about the death of God is a meaningful but inauthentic expression of the impossibility of continuing to think God, postulated metaphysically as independent absoluteness, in the unity of divine essence and divine existence. In that sense, the expression "God is dead" is the paradoxical code word for the beginning of the end of metaphysics, which could think of reality without God and could not maintain the unity of thought and being without God—that is, a metaphysics which understood itself as "theo-onto-logic." But as one of the last thoughts of metaphysics, the thought of the death of God, understood that way, totally belongs to this "theo-onto-logic." It remains under the sway of that which originally was affirmed and now is denied. The metaphysical thought of God shows itself, even in the way it is abrogated, still as the royal thought of that thinking which dethrones it.[29]

The thought of God's death understood thus remains metaphysical because that thinking which conceives it is unable, or unwilling, to understand the metaphysically postulated essence of God as a contradiction to the true deity of God. The broad concept of the divine essence, namely "that than which nothing greater can be thought," remains uncontested wherever that essence so defined is asserted to be unthinkable, whether for positive reasons (Fichte) or for negative reasons (Nietzsche). The result is that that beyond than which nothing *greater* can be thought is itself not capable of being *thought*. "That than which nothing greater can be thought" is subjected one way or another to the principle, "it cannot be thought" (*cogitari non potest*).

Based on the premises of modern metaphysics, talk about the death of God makes pointedly clear that the concept of God which modern metaphysics took over from the older metaphysics cannot tolerate the finitude of thought. The paradoxical aspect of the statement "God is dead" is intended to express the absurdity of the concept of God. The attempt to think God and perishability together (and that is what "thinking" ultimately means on the presupposition of the Cartesian "I think": it means to think of what is thought in combination with perishability) makes the metaphysically conceived God himself perishable and allows him to perish; "God is dead." One cannot think God and perishability together without setting aside the metaphysically conceived thought of God. Perishability disintegrates him.

4. What is revealed to be the actual premise of the ultimate thought of that metaphysics which understands itself as theo-onto-logic is the *negative* metaphysical evaluation of perishability. Its basic ontological structure is fixed as that of annihilation. That which perishes is destroyed. The word of the cross speaks

---

29. See my essay "Vom Tod des lebendigen Gottes," in *Unterwegs zur Sache; Theologische Bemerkungen* (München: C. Kaiser, 1972), p. 122.

in opposition to that. Its objection does not imply that perishing is a harmless affair. Rather, in the word of the cross, the seriousness of death is expressed in an unsurpassable way. The objection is directed toward the ontological discrediting of that which is perishable.

The consequences of such a negative metaphysical evaluation of perishability conceal the unique worth of that kind of perishing which corresponds to the process of becoming and which is not violently realized. One only perceives the curse of perishing. It is not possible then to enjoy the blooming rose without lamenting its fading: ". . . fair flower, Being once display'd, doth fall that very hour."[30] One discredits "the glories of the earth" because they must "become smoke and ashes."[31] What is never considered is that the ability to perish can also be positive. The negation in perishing is multiplied into annihilation and the shadow of nothingness falls on all that is perishable. Because, as something which is coming into existence, it must perish, it is *worthwhile* that it be destroyed—that is the mephistophelian logic of this metaphysics: ". . . for all, that doth begin/Should rightly to destruction run;/'Twere better then that nothing were begun."[32]

The significance of the motto "God is dead," as the expression of the ultimate theo-ontological thought of metaphysics, consists accordingly of the conclusion that God has become unthinkable, because he cannot be thought in the context of this world and its perishability. Significantly, talk of the death of God is then taken to be paradoxical. The expression itself may not be thought, as a result. Talk of the death of God is speaking of death only as an image.[33]

30. William Shakespeare, "Twelfth Night; Or, What You Will," Act ii, Scene iv, *The Complete Works of William Shakespeare* (New York: Books, Inc., 1948), p. 81.

31. Thus the chorale by A. Gryphius (No. 328 in *Evangelisches Kirchengesang-buch*), who uses the rose as the model for the nothingness of the perishable, because nothing makes plain more quickly than this image how little worth there is to something which appears to be so glorious:

Wie eine Rose blühet,	As a rose blooms
wenn man die Sonne siehet	When one sees the sun
begrüssen diese Welt,	Greeting this world,
die, eh' der Tag sich neiget,	Which, ere the day has ended,
eh' sich der Abend zeiget,	Ere evening has arrived,
verwelkt und unversehens fällt	Withers and falls unseen,
so wachsen wir auf Erden. . . .	Thus do we grow on earth. . . .

Accordingly, the moral of the chorale is put:

Verlache Welt und Ehre,	Scorn the world and honor,
Furcht, Hoffen, Gunst und Lehre	Fear, hope, favor, and doctrine,
und geh den Herren an,	And go toward the Lord,
der immer König bleibet,	Who always remains the king,
den keine Zeit vertreibet,	Whom time cannot drive away,
der einzig ewig machen kann.	Who alone can make eternal.

32. J. W. von Goethe, *Faust*, I, 1339ff, in *Goethe* (*Great Books of the Western World*, vol. 47), tr. G. M. Priest (Chicago: Encyclopaedia Britannica, 1941), p. 33.

33. The question which then surfaces is whether the talk about God presupposed in the pointed image of the death of God was not inauthentic. Did not Nietzsche express what the significance of talk about God which precedes talk about the death of God really was when he interpreted the imperishable as merely a simile for perishability? Was not that also the presupposition under which Feuerbach could even dare to state that the true mystery of theology was anthropology? In order to debate Nietzsche's confrontation with Goethe's verse, "All the perishable—that's but a simile," it would be necessary to think

It is the coded expression of the idea that we can, should, and may no longer think of a God. But it does not conceive of the idea that God *comes together* with death. For, if God may not be brought together with and thought together with perishability, then the point of speaking of the death of God in this intellectual context is that a real *death* of God cannot be thought at all. The metaphysically established God is supposed, rather, to be destroyed by his own perfection. That *essence,* established as perfect, highest, and perfectly independent, is forced into destruction by the *existence* defined by human subjectivity, because this God cannot exist humanly and may not exist humanly. Existence, which must go through the needle's eye of "I think," becomes a threat to the divine essence in the same way that one human breath can be a threat to a balloon which is blown up too far: it bursts. However, if at some point the highest essence of all is destroyed in this way, its reputation is irrevocably ruined.

The thesis of the incompatibility of perishability with the metaphysical concept of God is, however, only a shift from the theo-ontological structure of metaphysics into atheism. But there is *another* route from metaphysics to atheism which presents itself in a more penetrating fashion as an antithesis to the specifically Christian, or better, christological understanding of the unity of God with perishability. Next to the thesis already discussed, that the metaphysically conceived God cannot tolerate perishability, there is the opposing assertion that perishability, allegedly understood as free of metaphysics, cannot tolerate "God on the cross." Nietzsche said that "God was dead" in this sense. His thoughts come very close to the Christian truth which he was opposing. They merit special attention.

5. When speaking of the death of God, Nietzsche was contesting the *thinkability* of the metaphysically conceived God, but that was not all. At the same time, he vehemently opposed the possibility of thinking God and perishability together in the way in which the Pauline discourse about the crucified Son of God expected thought to do. Nietzsche's statement "God is dead" attacks with the sharpest polemic the presumption that God and death are seriously to be thought of together on the basis of the word of the cross.

In his "Antichrist" there is a statement which cannot be surpassed in both its precision and its polemics: "A God of the kind created by Paul is the negation of God" (*deus, qualem Paulus creavit, dei negatio*).[34] This statement deserves special attention. First of all, it implies that Paul had made a special understanding of God possible, in contrast with the tradition of thought. For Nietzsche, the special characteristic of Paul's thinking goes so far that he feels compelled to say that Paul has, in fact, *created* a God, a new God: "*deus, qualem Paulus creavit. . . .*"

---

about the nature of similes in general. What does "*but* a simile" really mean? Would not Nietzsche's antithesis to Goethe's verse have become impossible if one had understood the essence of the simile to be the distinction accorded to one who exists when it is enabled to express something other than its own self with its own self? All that is perishable is *even* a simile—would not such a statement more appropriately serve to sing the praise of perishability as perishability? See on this below, pp. 210f, n. 47.

34. F. Nietzsche, "The Antichrist," in *The Complete Works of Friedrich Nietzsche,* tr. A. M. Ludovici, ed. Dr. O. Levy (New York: Macmillan, 1911), vol. 16 (*The Twilight of the Idols*), nr. 47, p. 196 (Latin not translated—TR).

Nietzsche puts the word "God" in this context in quotation marks in order to show that the "God which Paul created" least of all deserves to be called a god. For the "God" allegedly created by Paul is a God who ". . . confounds the wisdom of this world."[35] The reference is to Paul's statements in I Corinthians 1:18ff, where Paul speaks of the word of the cross, which do in fact seek to think together God and perishability in the person of the Son of God who has become man. Nietzsche takes Paul at his word and insists that the apostolic discourse about God does not want to be anything else than talk about the crucified Christ (I Cor. 2:2).

For Paul, the Crucified One is weak, subject to death. But Paul does not celebrate this thought with melancholy, but rather thinks of it as the gospel, as a source of joy. What is joyful about the weakness of the Crucified One? The weakness of the Crucified One is for Paul the way in which God's power of life is perfected (II Cor. 13:4). Weakness is then not understood as a contradiction of God's power. There is, however, only one phenomenon in which power and weakness do not contradict each other, in which rather power can perfect itself as weakness. This phenomenon is the event of *love*. Love does not see power and weakness as alternatives. It is the unity of power and weakness, and such is certainly the most radical opposite of the will to power which cannot affirm weakness. Pauline 'theology of the cross' (*theologia crucis*) is, accordingly, the most stringent rejection of all deification of self-willing power. Nietzsche did then acutely and clearly see that a *new* understanding of God has been initiated here. He really saw it much more clearly than a broad theological tradition did which followed Paul. "*God on the cross*—does no one yet understand the terrible ulterior motive of this symbol? Everything that suffers, everything that hangs on the cross is divine. . . ."[36]

What angers Nietzsche is the distinction granted to that which is perishing in its *negative* quality in that God is to be thought in the midst of perishing not only as God, but especially as the *suffering God*. For Nietzsche, God is at best a simile, as is everything imperishable. Here too the metaphysical concept of God remains the presupposition, in that the God asserted to be imperishable is still seen as the simile for the *strength and power* of the perishable. But then the *deus crucifixus* ('crucified God') must be asserted to be the *dei negatio* ('negation of God'). The Antichrist understands itself as Antichrist in this, "that we can discover no God, either in history, or in nature, or behind nature,—but that we regard what has been revered as 'God,' not as 'divine,' but as wretched, absurd, pernicious; not as an error, but as a *crime against life*. . . . We deny God as God. . . . If the existence of this Christian God were *proved* to us, we should feel even less able to believe in him.—In a formula: *deus qualem Paulus creavit, dei negatio*."[37]

The text reveals how precisely Nietzsche grasped the incompatibility of the Christian understanding of God with the metaphysical concept of God. That Nietzsche felt "even less able to believe" in the God of the Christians, even if this God should be proven to him, provides Nietzsche's talk about the death of

---

35. *Ibid.*
36. *Ibid.*, nr. 51, pp. 204f.
37. *Ibid.*, nr. 47, p. 196. The reference to Pascal's idea of *dieu perdu* ('lost God'), also quoted by Hegel, is clear.

God a double orientation. On the one hand, it points to the unthinkability of the metaphysically conceived highest essence. On the other hand, it is also intended to point to the *incredibility* of the Christian understanding of God, which is the former's precise opposite. The metaphysical concept of God enervates thinking and must then be rejected as unthinkable. The worship of the Christians' God is the self-abrogation of a God, namely, of a metaphysically thought God, but now not only in the medium of thought but also in the medium of perishability. "Modern men, with their obtuseness as regards all Christian nomenclature, have no longer the sense for the terribly superlative conception which was implied to an antique taste by the paradox of the formula, 'God on the Cross.' Hitherto there had never and nowhere been such boldness in inversion, nor anything at once so dreadful, questioning, and questionable as this formula: it promised a transvaluation of all ancient values."[38]

In view of his insight, one wonders then that Nietzsche did not see the 'negation of God,' which he ascribed to the Pauline understanding of God with regard to the metaphysical concept of God, as the beginning of another, a *new* understanding of God which would certainly have been appropriate to "praise and justify all that is perishable." The reason for this anti-theological narrow-mindedness is probably to be sought in the fact that Nietzsche was prepared to praise and justify the perishing of the perishable only as a perishing which was natural and free of all weakness and suffering.[39] And *in that*, Nietzsche remained deeply obligated to metaphyics even as its opponent: in that he wanted to conceive of the perishable without pain, of perishing without suffering and without the mourning of leave-taking, and in that he then had to condemn the worship of a suffering God as a "crime against life." From the perspective of the theology of the Crucified One the hard judgment cannot be evaded that Nietzsche, to the extent that he polemicized against the crucified God, conceived of the *perishability* of life *abstractly*. This is not affected in any way by a certain self-glorification of suffering which results for Nietzsche from the loneliness of one's own superiority. The abstraction of which this thought is guilty, and which was unavoidable in view of what he willed to do, consists of his wanting to justify perishable life only at the *heights* of his own vitality. To bring man to the height of *superman* was the declared purpose of the will to power. Nietzsche understood himself and declared himself to be a thinker of the heights.[40] Zarathustra comes from the heights and returns to them—possibly even higher.

38. F. Nietzsche, "Beyond Good and Evil," in *The Complete Works of Friedrich Nietzsche,* tr. H. Zimmern, ed. Dr. O. Levy (London and Edinburgh: The Darien Press, 1914), vol. 12, ch. III, nr. 46, p. 65.

39. See B. Taureck, "Nihilismus und Christentum; Ein Beitrag zur philosophischen Klärung von Nietzsches Verhältnis zum Christentum," *Wissenschaft und Welt-bild,* 26 (1973), 126: "Nietzsche's gravest accusation against Christianity is that it wants to weaken the strong men."

40. Nietzsche's mad man announces that "all who are born after us belong to a higher history than any history hitherto" (*The Joyful Wisdom,* in *The Complete Works of Friedrich Nietzsche,* vol. 10, tr. T. Common, ed. Dr. O. Levy [Edinburgh and London: The Darien Press, 1910], nr. 125, p. 168). And according to Nietzsche's opinion, as found in his writings whose sphere is "the air of the heights," humanity is entitled to its "great right to a future" ("Preface," *Ecce Homo,* in *The Complete Works of Friedrich Nietzsche,* vol. 17, tr. A. M. Ludovici, ed. Dr. O. Levy [Edinburgh: Morrison & Gibbs

However, "thought does not overcome metaphysics by surpassing and cancelling it in some direction or other and ascending even higher: it descends into the nearness of the nearest. The descent, especially where man has ascended too far into subjectivity, is more difficult and more dangerous than the ascent. The descent leads to the poverty of the existence of the *homo humanus*."[41]

6. Nietzsche's statement "The god of the kind created by Paul is the negation of God" can, however, be understood in a completely different way. Nietzsche did, in fact, distantly perceive the possibility of a God understood in unity with perishability. As an objection to himself, he did consider the possibility that God could be thought in a different way than as an ensemble of metaphysically understood highest essence and bourgeois morality. "Actually, the opposite would be possible, and there are indications of it. God, thought of as one liberated from morality, the entirety of life's contradictions forcing themselves into him, and in divine agony *redeeming* and *justifying* them."[42] Then the death of the metaphysically understood God, announced by Nietzsche, would only be the overcoming of the "moral God," as Nietzsche himself notes: "Basically only the moral God is overcome."[43] And God would be thinkable anew "as the transmundane, that which is above and beyond the miserable street-corner morality of 'good and evil'."[44] We come closest to Nietzsche's envisioned possibility when we seek to understand "the god of the kind created by Paul" in terms of what Paul himself said and thought when he spoke of God, so that on that basis such a statement could arise to describe the Pauline understanding of God. But thought would then have to descend to the poverty of "the existence" of that particular *"homo humanus"* about which Christian proclamation says that this man was the Son of God (Mark 15:39). Thought would have to learn to think God in the poverty of the existence of this man.[45]

Ltd., 1911], nrs. 2 and 3, p. 2). For him, Zarathustra "is not only the loftiest book on earth, literally the book of mountain air,—the whole phenomenon, mankind, lies at an incalculable distance beneath it" (*ibid.*, nr. 4, p. 4). Speaking of his books, he says, "they sometimes attain to the highest pinnacle of earthy endeavor" ("Why I Write Such Excellent Books," *ibid.*, nr. 3, p. 61). And Nietzsche would like to have himself understood as ". . . the harbinger of joy, the like of which has never existed before; I have discovered tasks of such lofty greatness that, until my time, no one had any idea of such things. Mankind can begin to have fresh hopes, only now that I have lived" ("Why I Am a Fatality," *ibid.*, nr. 1, p. 132). One cannot escape the parody here of the Christmas angel who comes "from heaven above" as the joyful ambassador of God.

41. Martin Heidegger, "Letter on Humanism," tr. E. Lohner, in W. Barrett and H. D. Aiken, *Philosophy in the 20th Century* (New York: Random House, 1962), pp. 294ff.

42. F. Nietzsche, *Nachgelassene Fragmente*, in *Werke; Kritische Gesamtausgabe*, eds. G. Colli and M. Montinari (Berlin and New York: Walter de Gruyter, 1974), VIII/2 (Autumn 1887), p. 247.

43. *Ibid.*, VIII/1 (Summer 1886–Autumn 1887), p. 217.

44. *Ibid.*, VIII/2 (Autumn 1887), p. 247. H. Gollwitzer (*Von der Stellvertretung Gottes; Christlicher Glaube in der Erfahrung der Verborgenheit Gottes; Zum Gespräch mit Dorothee Sölle* [München: Ch. Kaiser, 1968²], pp. 160f, n. 93) comments aptly on Nietzsche's self-objection: "Nietzsche senses here that in the Christian message of the cross something could be at work which was completely different from the 'nihilism' of Christian morality which he disliked so much." And this something other is what he "suspects in the 'divine agony'."

45. For this reason, theology cannot expound the poverty of existence of the *"homo humanus"* (which Heidegger regards as that which must first be considered philosophically) apart from the identity of God with the man Jesus. Conversely, only on the

The important thing, however, will be to do away with the unhappy distinction between the essence and existence of God, which "I think" had added to the metaphysically conceived God—it must be seen as sheer intellectual nonsense. In the unity of the divine essence with the existence of Jesus the man, God's existence must be thought in such a way that God's essence is understood *as* his existence. And this must be done in such a way that no 'distinction of reason' can be made between the 'essence of God' and the 'existence of God' (*distinctio rationis; essentia dei; existentia dei*). Accordingly, talk about God's existence and God's essence is to be replaced by a kind of talk which leaves that distinction behind itself: talk about the *being* of God.

The being of God so understood is then already comprehended out of its unity with perishability. In fact, it is understood as the negation of the divine essence, which Nietzsche parodied, although not inappropriately, as ". . . the one, and the plenum, and the unmoved, and the sufficient, and the imperishable."[46] If one understands the divinity of God out of its unity with the poverty of the existence of the Crucified One, then God's being can no longer be thought as infinite in contrast with every finitude, and certainly not as independence in contrast with every dependence, and obviously not as an eternity which excludes time, nor as a highest essence which does not know nothingness. The God who is in heaven *because* he cannot be on earth is replaced by the Father who is in heaven in such a way that his heavenly kingdom can come *into the world*, that is, a God who is in heaven in *such a way* that he can *identify himself* with the poverty of the man Jesus, with the existence of a man brought from life to death on the cross.

7. If God's identity with the Crucified One is believed, then an *ontological* task is put to our thinking, which is to grasp God's being in perishability in such a way that talk of the death of God gains a more profound meaning than that of

---

basis of the event of this identity of God and man can theology say and think what the word "God" really is supposed to mean. Thus it cannot agree with the philosopher when he permits the essence of deity to be thought only out of the essence of the holy, or the essence of the holy only out of the truth of being, and only then in light of the essence of deity conceived out of the truth of being and out of the essence of the holy permits the thinking and expressing of "what the word 'God' is to signify" (Heidegger, *op. cit.*, p. 294). Heidegger (*op. cit.*, p. 294) asserts: "Only from the truth of Being can the essence of the holy be thought. Only from the essence of the holy can the essence of divinity be thought. Only in the light of the essence of divinity can it be thought and said what the word 'God' is to signify." Depending on the position taken with regard to these thoroughly philosophical sentences, the decision will be made as to whether a theology, which wants to learn from Heidegger at all, will remain *theology* in its dialogue with philosophy. A theology will also reveal in its stance toward these statements of the thinker, considering the nature of being, whether or not it is *Reformation* theology. The position with regard to these statements of Heidegger is thus particularly appropriate when examining whether the new question of *natural theology* (which must necessarily be asked in a new way) is really going new directions or merely returning to the old ways with a new vocabulary—new patches on old clothes. Heidegger knows very well that for the Christian faith "that existence which is primarily revealed and which as revelation effects faith . . . is Christ, the crucified God" (*Phänomenologie und Theologie* [Frankfurt: Klostermann, 1970], p. 18). Therefore, the theology of the Crucified One must comprehend the essence of deity out of the unity of God with the proverty of existence of the true man who is called Jesus.

46. F. Nietzsche, *Thus Spake Zarathustra; A Book for All and None*, in *The Complete Works of Friedrich Nietzsche*, tr. T. Common, ed. O. Levy (New York: Macmillan; London: George Allen & Unwin Ltd., 1930), p. 100.

a pointed metaphor for the self-destruction of the metaphysical concept of God. Theology must regain the most original meaning of this statement. That is possible only when it understands that "God on the cross" is not only the negation of all arbitrary concepts of God but positively is a God who with his own being confronts the nothingness which is present in all perishability. Nietzsche's statement "a god of the kind which Paul creates is the negation of God" is understood in a Pauline fashion only when that which Nietzsche calls "the negation of God" is understood as a negation through which the being of God is first adequately defined. That is the case when God is thought as one who excludes from himself any abstract opposition of imperishability and perishability, and thus is imperishable only to the extent that he subjects himself to perishability. Only when God's being is thought in that way does the thought of God comprehend God himself. In order to do this, of course, the essence of *perishability* must be adequately determined, that perishability to which *God's being* is supposed to be subjected. What is then "perishable?"

Theology oriented to the word of the cross necessitates our questioning an exclusively negative metaphysical qualification of perishable and perishing. It must also ask about the positivity of that which is perishable. Only then will thought find it possible to disclose the *actual negativity* of perishability. Only when what is perishable is as such not valued as negative ontologically, can what is truly negative in it be seen and defined. And with that, the positive aspect of perishability has become thinkable. The destruction of the exclusively negative ontological qualification of perishability reveals that which is actually affirmative in perishability. We must then ask, What is negative about perishability, and what is positive about it? What is that which is actually negative in perishability? And what can be distinguished from it as that which is actually affirmative in perishability?

8. According to the metaphysical tradition, the negative aspect of the perishable is its temporality—in contrast to the eternal characteristic of the imperishable. But the negativeness of perishability has not yet been grasped if we were merely to see it in the contrast between the temporality of perishable being and eternity. Then one would have still qualified perishability as exclusively and totally negative, without gaining a perception of its positiveness. Doubtlessly even the farthest future will at some time be past. But conversely every present will also have a future. And that the past has no future is not all that settled, as it might appear to "healthy common sense." The temporality of the perishable is, just like perishability itself, dependent on its being freed from an exclusively negative ontological qualification. In this regard as well, Goethe's saying is not the last word on the matter, "All the perishable—that's but a simile!"[47] Temporality, as much as the perishable, conceals the difference in

47. Nietzsche, *Zarathustra*, p. 100. The reference to Goethe is unmistakable. It is confirmed in a poem entitled "To Goethe," which may be found in the appendix to *The Joyful Wisdom*, among "The Songs of Prince Free-As-A-Bird" (*The Joyful Wisdom*, in *The Complete Works of Friedrich Nietzsche*, p. 357):

        "The Undecaying"
        Is but thy label,
        O God the Betraying
        Is poets' fable.

itself between that which is truly negative and truly positive in perishable being. What is it?

A *tendency toward nothingness* certainly appears to be an aspect of that which is actually negative in perishability. For the tendency not to be is a threat to everything perishable! We can assert that only on the basis of certain appearances *in that which exists,* such as anxiety at nothingness or the drive to endure. For we do not know nothingness. It does not disclose itself to us on its own. Nothingness does not show itself. It can appear "only" in a simile, in the simile of something which is not nonbeing. In the form of simile one can experience something which cannot be recognized as such. But such a simile is never nothingness itself. But if we do not know nothingness in itself, but rather only in the simile of something else, which is not nothing, but is rather something, then the *tendency toward nothingness* can be expressed only in similes. For in order to know the tendency toward nothingness as such, we would have to know the nothingness toward which it is tending.[48] Similes for ontological contents cannot be arbitrarily chosen, however. They cannot be invented, they must be found. They are similes which being brings along with itself, they are similes of being. That is also true of those similes which express the tendency toward nothingness. The similes in which we experience nothingness and the tendency toward nothingness are not developed after we have had certain experiences with what is; rather, they are similes which are themselves experienced. They are within being itself. Thus they are unsurpassably pregnant and as similes they are irrevocably evidential. Everyone knows them and experiences them in their sinister power as analogies of nothingness and the tendency toward it. I will name two similes of this kind. Everyone knows *death* as the simile of nothingness which encounters us in the context of life. And everyone knows *perishing* as the simile for the tendency toward nothingness which encounters us in perishability.

Because death and perishing are ontological similes for nothingness and the tendency toward nothingness, it is very easy for perishability to be judged exclusively as a negative phenomenon. This is seen most clearly in the defensive fashion in which man seeks to escape from the perishability which is qualified as exclusively negative. Man's defense against that perishability which has been alleged to be exclusively negative, a defense which is metaphysically decisive, is the construction of a Now which stands in the midst of perishing time. In the

---

Our aims all are thwarted
By the world-wheel's blind roll:
"Doom," says the downhearted,
"Sport," says the fool.

The world-sport, all ruling,
Mingles false with true:
The eternally fooling
Makes us play, too!

48. W. Weischedel (*Der Gott der Philosophen; Grundlegung einer philosophischen Theologie im Zeitalter des Nihilismus,* vol. II: *Abgrenzung und Grundlegung* [Darmstadt: Wissenschaftliche Buchgesellschaft, 1972], p. 202) remarks aptly: "The experience of questionableness is not the experience of nonbeing, but rather merely the experience of the possibility of nonbeing." The possibility of nonbeing can be experienced only within the sphere of being.

midst of the process of *perishing,* there is supposed to be something which *remains*: the Now. The moment, that being of shortest duration, is declared to be something permanent,[49] is made into a *nunc stans* (a 'standing now').

In defending himself against the sinister character of an exclusively negatively defined perishability, man feels driven to say to the moment: do stay, thou art so beautiful. That means that one wants to make the moment a 'permanent now' (*nunc stans*). 'Permanent now' is an old expression for eternity. As such, it is a denunciation of time as a mere phenomenon of flight, from which one must seek to escape. Perishing man wants to elevate himself in an instant and for an instant, moving out of perishing time. He wants to elevate himself beyond time into imperishability, which is the way he imagines eternity: eternity appears accordingly as the Now which is timeless, imperishable, and thus permanent. In the name of this permanent, this enduring instant, objection is raised against the temporality of perishability or, what appears to be the same, against the perishing character of time. Therefore, man seeks something in time which will allow him to move *beyond* time. One event which elevates man beyond time is thought to be desire:[50]

> *"Woe saith: Hence! Go!*
> *But joys all want eternity—*
> *Want deep, profound eternity."*

Pain longs to perish, and woe finds its comfort in the fact that it has an *end*. But desire ("joys") wants to remain, wants to be endless. Desire is thus a twin to religion. Religion too summons up the permanent now against the

---

49. It is undoubtedly the ontological character of the moment, which allows it to be defined as the being of shortest duration, out of which the possibility is derived to assert that the Now is what is most enduring. For the character of perishing appears at the very least in the Now as a "mere instant." Something which is there "for an instant" appears to leap over nothingness, becoming, and perishing. The man who is seeking to flee from perishability asks whether this instant is not, in fact, forever. Must he not be eternal, between the times, suddenly? Everything lasts only for its own time. But what does not last—is that not the only lasting thing, which is the 'standing now'? We shall not discuss here the extent to which the metaphysical understanding of the moment as a 'standing now' (*nunc stans*) can be traced back to Parmenides (see the discussion of the permanent now in Leonardo Taran, *Parmenides* [Princeton, NJ: Princeton University Press, 1965], Fragment 8,5, p. 85) and to Plato (see the discussion of the 'moment' in "Parmenides," *The Dialogues of Plato,* tr. B. Jowett, 2 vols. [New York: Random House, 1937], II, 156, p. 126). We shall restrict ourselves to the unfortunately still necessary remark that Parmenides and Plato are not the frightful phantoms which they are often said to be in recent theology. To be sure, "truth is the greater friend," but may one say that before having submitted to the threat implied by saying "Plato is my friend?" Whoever did not learn to love those thinkers while studying them has no reason to fear what they thought. But he has even less right to denigrate their thought into the smallness of his irritable antitheses. It is a lamentable thing that one must make Parmenides or Plato, not to speak of Aristotle, into a black backdrop against which one thinks one can let one's own flickering light shine a little. Shouldn't one put his light *on* the bushel from the outset? The indispensable debate with the metaphysical tradition inaugurated by "the Greeks" cannot take place in such a way that one does not even endeavor to think through the thoughts of this tradition, in order then instead to quote as a contrast to biblical truth something which one has never even read in its own context.

50. Nietzsche, *Zarathustra,* pp. 279f.

perishing character of time: "In the midst of finitude to become one with the infinite, and to be eternal in every instant—this is the immortality of religion."[51] What is should not be nonexistent. In the midst of perishability, there should be an 'eternal being' (*aei on*), countering all perishing. For that reason, thought invents for itself the permanent now, a '*nunc stans*' as the expression for eternity.[52]

Yet the idea of the 'permanent now' misses the true dignity of time, and along with it the positive character of perishability. Perishing also has its honor and its value. To be sure, it is a simile for the tendency toward nothingness. But as such a simile it is then also more than *only* a tendency toward nothingness. Perishability has by no means been adequately defined through that tendency not to become anymore and thus to be annihilated, which is so threatening to reality. In the process of perishing, there is rather a positive intention of time which holds sway, an intention which one can for the time being simply call the *limitation of the real*. In the process of perishing, that which is real arrives at its boundary, beyond which it no longer is real. But that certainly does not mean that it is nothing. The boundaries of reality are not the end of being. Thus we must continue to ask, What is that which is ontologically positive about perishability? What is actually affirming in that which is perishable and thus is still perishing? What is the true dignity which is ascribed to the process of perishing?

9. We answer this question with the thesis which is fundamental for everything which will follow: *That which is ontologically positive about perishability is the possibility.* The possible is what is actually affirming in perishable being. We say that initially to point out that there are affirmations which surpass the real without removing us from the context of the real. We have already learned to understand the event of the word as such a basic event of affirmation, that word which surpasses our being-here and being-now in such a way that only through it our "here and now" are disclosed to us *as* the present. The present, the disclosed present, contains beyond the reality of the "here and now" a further factor, which is that it lives *with the possible*. The word discloses the present in that it gives reality possibilities which elevate the real beyond the mere tautology of the purely factual and makes it an historical existence rich in relationships. Disclosed presentness insists not only on that which is real, but also exists out of the possible, and toward the possible. Thus, nearness and farness are mediated within the dimension of the possible. Therefore the possible is what inheres in the event of the word and in unity with it is the actual affirmative component in perishable being.

We can clarify what we have just said by looking at the opposite concept. We saw that the usual antithesis to perishability is eternity in the sense of timeless imperishability. What is timelessly imperishable, the 'permanent now,' is traditionally defined as *the real and only real*, as pure realization in the form of having been realized, as pure *energeia* ('actuality') without *dynamis* ('po-

---

51. F. Schleiermacher, *On Religion; Addresses in Response to Its Cultured Critics*, tr. T. N. Tice (Richmond: John Knox, 1969), p. 157.

52. A comparison could also be made to the metaphysical concept of the theory, according to which mortals resemble the immortals in the moment of 'reasoning' (*theōrein*): 'reasoning' as 'immortal' (*athanatizein*) (see Aristotle, *Ethica Nicomachea*, tr. W. D. Ross, *The Works of Aristotle*, ed. W. D. Ross [Oxford: Oxford University Press, 1954], IX, 1177a 12–1178a 8, pp. 29f).

tency'), as the 'purest act' (*actus purissimus*) without 'potentiality' and 'possibility' (*potentia et possibilitas*), as the realized without possibility: self-realization in the sense of being self-realized. That *possibility* which arises over against perishability was accordingly understood as a *deficiency in reality*. This happened as a result of the basic Aristotelian decision regarding the fundamental understanding of being in general: ". . . that actuality is prior to potency [or potentiality]."[53] Based on this metaphysical decision, whose consequences appear to have become our fate, tradition has consequently thought God as pure reality, as the purest act of self-realization in the sense of one who has always and already realized himself. In that sense, God is so and not anything else; he has, so to speak, always made himself necessary. It is the intellectual task assigned to the Christian faith to take leave of this concept of God, first of all because of the word of God itself, and then because of the aporias of this concept of God in an age which is surrendering itself to atheism, on the basis of that very concept of God(!). For that reason we think God in unity with perishability. And in doing so, we oppose the fundamental Aristotelian approach of European metaphysics, which ascribed to pure reality an ontological primacy over possibility and thus assigned necessarily an exclusively negative ontological quality to perishability. If the ontological primacy of being was assigned to the real, then the possible had to appear as what actually is impotent and thus perishability would be deprived of any aspect of positiveness.

We oppose the fundamental Aristotelian decision in favor of the ontological primacy of reality in that we assert in antithesis to it that possibility is the ontological plus of being.[54] The possible is then also the plus of perishability. Possibility is the positive thing about perishability. And that means further that perishing itself, even what is past, is not without possibility.[55]

It was Søren Kierkegaard's great service to have clearly expounded this content, stimulated probably by Schelling. He wrote, "The possibility from

---

53. Aristotle, *Metaphysica*, in *The Works of Aristotle*, tr. W. D. Ross (Oxford: Clarendon Press, 1954), VIII, theta, 1049b, p. 5. On the problem of the ontological primacy of reality before possibility and the theological critique of it based on the justification of man through God, I refer to my essay "Die Welt als Möglichkeit und Wirklichkeit; Zum ontologischen Ansatz der Rechtfertigungslehre," in *Unterwegs zur Sache*, pp. 206ff. My discussion there deals with details about the relationship of word, possibility, reality, and nothingness, as it might be conceived on the basis of the doctrine of justification.

54. The entire work of Martin Heidegger is to be compared with the philosophical debate with the fundamental Aristotelian decision in favor of the primacy of reality.

55. Whoever denies that the past is not only real but also has no capacity for becoming is ascribing to the perishable the quality of immutability. That does not lack a certain air of paradox since the perishable allegedly must perish because of its mutability. It would then be the mutability of the perishable which aids it in attaining the immutability (of its being in the past). Hegel sought to elevate this paradox to the rationality of an ontological content, as he looked on the *past being* as the mode of being of the *essence* and emphasized the mediation of *memory* as the way of knowing from immediate being to essence. See Hegel, *Science of Logic*, trs. W. H. Johnston and L. G. Struthers (*The Muirhead Library of Philosophy*) (New York: The Macmillan Company, 1961), II, 15: "Only when knowledge, coming out from the sphere of immediate Being, *internalizes* itself, does it through this mediation discover Essence.—Language has in the verb *Sein* ('to be') preserved *Wesen* ('Essence') in the past participle *gewesen* ('been'); for Essence is Being which has passed away, but passed away nontemporally."

which that which became actual once emerged still clings to it and remains with it as past, even after the lapse of centuries. Whenever a successor reasserts its having come into existence, which he does by believing it, he evokes this potentiality anew, irrespective of whether there can be any question of his having a more specific conception of it or not."[56] Thought in this way, the possible is not cancelled by its realization. It remains.

Thus, there remains within the context of the perishable the capability of becoming. For possibility is the capability of becoming. Kierkegaard then rightly ascribed to what is past the capability of becoming[57]—on the basis of the word of God which preserves the past, and the present, and the future as being originally together, his theological right to do so can certainly not be doubted. But in doing so, he then contradicts the view that the past is only a chain of events and things which follow each other, and which, when they have had their time, make room for what is to follow by disappearing into nothingness. Such a temporal chain would basically be only the *unhistorical* sequence of isolated moments. The unhistoricity of this sequence would consist of its being unable to determine itself the context of time. But if, on the other hand, the possibility of the past may be repeated, then what is past remains related to the future as something past.

In that sense, the essence of perishability is disclosed as *history*, which does not permit what has been to remain nothing. The past does not have to disappear into nothingness. It does not have to be nothing, does not have to be destroyed.[58] The loss of its reality is not also the loss of its possibility. Even the

56. S. Kierkegaard, *Philosophical Fragments*, p. 107.
57. Thomas Aquinas formulated the exact opposite position (compare B. Lakebrink, *Klassische Metaphysik; Eine Auseinandersetzung mit der existentialen Anthropozentrik* [Freiburg: Rombach, 1967], p. 66: "it must be observed that the power and potentiality of a thing extend not to what has been, but to what is or will be: wherefore possibility has no place in the past" (*The Summa Contra Gentiles*, tr. English Dominican Fathers [London: Burns, Oates and Washbourne, 1923], vol. II–II, ch. 84, p. 249).
58. It may be noted that the anthropological dimension of the category of possibility certainly must not necessarily be *futuristic*, and that it must not be exclusively dealt with as a *principle of hope*. Possibility is not *identical* with a "principle of hope," neither for philosophy nor for theology. Theologically, rather, man's primary relationship to the possible is *faith*, and then following that, hope. The anthropological component in this theological relation to possibility is, initially, a relationship back to history which has happened for the sake of the present event of history. In history, the past is also accompanied by the power of becoming, if it can find words to express itself, or better, when words find it.
A Christian eschatology would thus think of *eternal life* as the revelation of life as it is lived with all of the possibilities which surround it, that is, not merely as the eternalizing of the possibility *out* of which our life became possible, but rather as the revelation and implementation of all those possibilities *into* which our life constantly moves without ever having realized them. Then all of the possibilities, the missed ones and the concealed ones, all of which define us, will as such reveal the truth of our life, to each individual as the *subject* of the life he is living. This may be taken as an expansion on the corresponding discussion in my little book, *Death, the Riddle and the Mystery*, trs. Iain and Ute Nicol (Edinburgh: St. Andrew Press, 1975), pp. 115ff; apparently my remarks there were not adequately insured against misunderstandings along the line that the eternalizing of a lived life meant the setting aside of my person as the subject of my life.

elementary fact of historical memory contradicts that. 'Memory' (*memoria*) preserves the possibility of past reality.

10. Based on its historical essence, perishability can then be ontologically defined in terms of what is actually negative as well as what is actually positive. For the nothingness which menaces the perishable can now be more precisely described on the basis of the similes in which it is illuminated. It is not to be understood as a possibility of what is perishable, but rather as that rendering of being impossible which destroys every possibility. Nothingness is the absolutely impossible, the incapacity to become. From nothingness, nothing is derived.

But that is not all! Beyond that we must say that *because* nothing is derived from nothingness, nothingness is, in relation to being and its possibilities, a negatively virulent emptiness without a place in being, a destructive undertow, a negative ontological whirlpool, a 'nihilating nothing' (*nihil nihilans*). The existing as such, and the perishable as such, does not tend in and of itself toward nothingness. Perishing is something other than to be annihilated. What appears as a tendency toward nothingness in what is perishable is itself still ambivalent. The perishable tends, as what is perishing, back toward the possibility out of which it came. It is then at an end, but has not therefore become nothing. In the form of having been, it continues to participate in being. What then appears to be a tendency toward nothingness in the existent is really only a tendency toward the state of having been. It is then nothingness itself which usurps this tendency in that it draws the process of perishing into the undertow of annihilation, which no longer permits what was to be possible anymore. Then what has been becomes as such impossible.

That nothingness which cannot become something out of itself is then in its own incapacity something like the power which renders impossible, the despotism of the nothing. This is the tyranny of a power which builds on nothing and only on nothing, and which empowers the negativeness of perishing until it becomes annihilation.

With these remarks we are in a sense ascribing to perishability what was asserted of possibility, following Aristotle: namely, that it is related equally both to being and to nonbeing, that as 'pure potency' (*pura potentia*) it permits being and its opposite nonbeing at the same time. E. Przywara cites Aristotle for the view that in the realm of "possibility in general" (in contrast to reality as "the possibility which has been implemented"), "the proposition of contradiction is not valid, either noetically or ontically"[59]: "Every potency is at one and the same time a potency of its opposite. . . . That, then, which is capable of being may . . . not be."[60] It should be pointed out that in *this* ontological conception, the possible is interesting only as the origin of the real, that it is understood as the 'weakest being' (*ens debilissimum*) that marks everything derived from it with the "blemish of its origin out of the 'nothingness' of the possible."[61] By contrast, in *our* understanding, possibility is the particular distinctive of the perishable,

59. E. Przywara, *Analogia Entis; Schriften* (München: J. Kösel and F. Pustet, 1932; Einsiedeln: Johannes Verlag, 1952, 1962), III, 113.

60. Aristotle, *Metaphysica*, in *The Works of Aristotle*, VIII, theta, 8, 1050f, pp. 11f.

61. B. Lakebrink, *op. cit.*, p. 76.

so that "the possible" is understood not only as a designation of origin but also and chiefly as a designation of the future, so that it is not understood as a category of deficiency and defect but rather of capacity and promise. "I say that is possible which has the potency to be nothing."[62]

The being of what is perishable is thus basically a *struggle*. Perishability is the *struggle between possibility and nothingness,* the struggle between the capacity of the possible and the undertow toward nothingness. And to the extent that we have understood possibility as being ontologically primary over against reality, we can also say, Perishability is the *struggle* between being and nonbeing.[63] But then, how is *God* to be thought when it is our task to comprehend God in unity with perishability? How is God to be thought in the struggle between possibility and nothingness, the struggle between being and nothingness?

11. The answer is provided by the positive significance of talk about the death of God, which is by no means to be taken only metaphorically. The positive meaning of talk about the death of God would then imply that God *is* in the midst of the struggle between nothingness and possibility. It corresponds to God's deity, and certainly does not contradict it, *to be* in the struggle between nothingness and possibility. Of course, the *essence* of God can no longer be put outside of this struggle, and one can no longer define God as an essence 'above us' (*supra nos*). Rather, the *essence* of God is to be thought as being absolutely identical with his *existence*.

Obviously we must then state as what God's being is to be thought, if his *essence* is identical with his *existence* between nothingness and possibility, that is, if he shares in the struggle between the ontological undertow toward nothingness and in the capacity of the possible. *Who* is God, if he is in such a way that he *exists* in this struggle?

First of all, we would answer that God is the one without whom this

---

62. The definition is taken from the *Compendium* of Nicholas of Cusa. He understood the "potency than which nothing is able to be more potent or prior" as the "omnipotent principle," even more original than being or nonbeing, "For it is before being and nonbeing." See Nicholas of Cusa, *Compendium*, X/29, 5f, in *Opera omnia,* vol. XI/3, eds. B. Decker and K. Bormann (Hamburg: Meiner, 1964), p. 23.

63. I prefer the category of struggle as describing the position of perishable existence in a more ontologically relevant way than the category of suspension, which Weischedel prefers. Weischedel's analyses of questionableness can be used for the understanding of the perishable. I agree with his definition of the mystery of the questionableness of the world: "that the world holds itself in a situation of unsupportedness and in holding itself has no hold; that it is and yet verges on nonbeing; that it is nothing and yet verges on being; that it is not swallowed up by nothingness and yet is menaced by it; that it is constantly threatened by nonbeing and yet holds itself [!] above the abyss of nonbeing; in short, that it is not absolute and yet does not fall into nonbeing" (*op. cit.*, p. 203). With a few modifications, that could be understood as an analysis of perishability. But Weischedel's statements themselves suggest that one should understand the content described more as a struggle than a state of suspension between being and nonbeing. The assertion that "the truth of that which exists experienced in the experience of questionableness" is "the state of suspension of its reality" (*ibid.*) threatens to render the opposition of being and nonbeing harmless, since nothingness is not seen with all its nihilistic aggressiveness. Apparently his aversion to mythological speech led the philosopher to a dangerous neutralizing of nothingness, which then makes it possible to say that the world *holds itself* over the abyss of nonbeing. The objection of Christian theology would be that the world *is held* there.

218 comma ON THE POSSIBILITY OF THINKING GOD

struggle would not be there at all. God is, after all, the Creator, without whom nothing is, no struggle between the capacity of possibility and the undertow toward nothingness! Without God there would not be any perishability. But, as the Creator and the ground of all that is perishable, is he not then the one who is only transmundane, who must be totally distinguished from all that is perishable? It cannot be contested that not only metaphysics speaks this way. So does the faith, and so does the Holy Scripture, the Word of God, speak of God: God shows that he is God by summoning that which exists from nothingness into being (Rom. 4:17). Thus God's being is understood as creative, as the being which creates 'out of nothing' (*ex nihilo*). Is not God as Creator removed from and infinitely superior to the *struggle* between being and nonbeing? Is God not the one who elevates himself above this struggle?

Based on the word of the cross, which emphatically proclaims that the one *who was raised from the dead is the Crucified One,* we answer that the being of God is first revealed as creative being in the struggle with the annihilating nothingness of nothing. This means hermeneutically that we are not to expound the word of the cross on the basis of the biblical statements about the imperishability of God, which are directed toward God the Creator. Rather, conversely, we learn how to understand who God the Creator is on the basis of the biblical statements directed toward the Crucified One, which statements force us to think God in unity with perishability. A theology of the Crucified One does not abstract itself from creation—precisely the opposite, it establishes *proper* theological talk about God the Creator. But such a theology is not to be designed on the basis of a theology of creation. To be sure, Israel's confession of God the Creator grew out of its faith in the God who had redeemed his people from slavery in Egypt and went with his people through the desert. But as much as that is true, it is all the more true that God himself in his being which creates from nothing is to be thought on the basis of the history in which he went to death with the man Jesus, in order to be himself in the struggle between being and nonbeing.[64] Then we must say that there is really only a struggle between nothingness and being because God exists.

Talk about the death of God implies then, in its true theological meaning, that God is the one who involves himself in nothingness. This is not contradicted by belief in the resurrection from the dead. On the contrary, the proclamation of the resurrection of Jesus reveals the sense in which God involves himself in

64. Christian theology, in its talk about God, distinguishes itself from a philosophy inquiring about God in that the theological concept of the Creator cannot simply be derived from the creation. "Philosophical theology," on the other hand, can recognize as its only presupposition for a possible concept of God the context of being in its questionableness, and it cannot see this as something creaturely (see Weischedel, *op. cit.,* pp. 184ff). But there is an analogy between the theological and the philosophical question about God to the extent that the philosophical question of God, if still placed today at all, begins with a questioning of being, that is, from a *particular* event within the context of being. As *radical* questionableness, the inquiry may soon envelop the whole and comprehend the *general character* of the context of being, but it still arises from a *particular* process which must then move from the particular to the general. To that extent, philosophy ought to be able to understand, at least formally, the way in which theological talk of God is oriented to the *particular* event of the *revelation* of God in Jesus of Nazareth.

nothingness. He does not do so in order to destroy nothingness but rather so that nothingness will be drawn into God's history. God battles nothingness by not leaving it to itself. A nothingness left to itself would be what is absolutely undefined and as such chaotic. But by involving himself in nothingness, God does define and determine it. And in that God defines it, he contradicts and resists the annihilating power of nothingness. For according to our understanding, this was the annihilating power of nothingness which, in its absolutely undefined and empty state as a negatively virulent vacuum without a nameable position, in this its ontological placelessness, creates for itself a phantomlike attraction, an annihilating undertow into itself, into nothingness. Nothingness does not let itself be precisely located. It is undetermined. And for that very reason, that nothingness has no place and is undetermined, it leads to chaotic consequences. It absorbs being until it is full, so to speak, by annihilating what exists. But because it takes being into itself only in the attraction of annihilation, it never *has* being. And because it never has being, it must constantly seize hold of being in the act of annihilation. Because it has nothing, its "egoism" is total, and it wants everything.

Talk about the death of God means, accordingly, in its interpretation through the proclamation of the resurrection of Jesus: (a) that God has involved himself with nothingness; (b) that God has involved himself with nothingness in the form of a struggle; (c) that God struggles against nothingness by showing it where its place is; (d) that God gives nothingness a place within being by taking it on himself. In that God identified himself with the dead Jesus, he located nothingness *within* the divine life. But by making for nothingness a place within divine being, God took away from it the chaotic effect of its phantomlike attraction. In bearing annihilation in himself, God proves himself to be the victor over nothingness, and he ends the negative attraction of "hell, death, and the devil." By proving himself to be this victor, God reveals what he truly and ultimately is. God is that one who can bear and does bear, can suffer and does suffer, in his being the annihilating power of nothingness, even the negation of death, without being annihilated by it. In God nothingness loses its negative attraction and thus its annihilating effect. Once it is taken up into God's being, it creatively sets for itself a new function. It receives its own *determination* and thus loses its abstract emptiness and its phantomly attraction.

The determination of nothingness is nothing other than *concrete negation*. Nothingness becomes concrete negation which gives to concrete affirmation its critical edge. In its determination as concrete negation, nothingness receives the new function of raising the possibilities of being to a new level of power. It becomes the differentiating power in the identity of being.

12. If it is then true that God has defined his deity in that event which we have understood as God's identification with the dead Jesus, then we must say that God is not only the one who is identical with himself for his sake alone. As the one who suffers endlessly, God is rather the *one who exists for others*. Being for others he is identical with himself. The localizing of nothingness within divine being is, as an act of God, an act of divine being, an act of divine self-determination. Whoever really is *for others* and seeks to *be* himself in that, always subjects himself immediately to nothingness. In this self-determination

for the sake of others, this peculiar dialectic of being and nonbeing, of life and death, takes place, which as pacified dialectic is called *love*.

Thus, the actual meaning of theological talk about the death of God is revealed as the most original self-determination of God for *love*, whereby this self-determination of God itself already belongs to love. God defined himself as love on the cross of Jesus. God *is* love (I John 4:8).[65]

Although this statement is formulated on the basis of the death of Jesus, it obviously may not be understood to mean that God did not become love until the event of the death of Jesus. Understood that way, love would then be a kind of self-distortion of God. What happened on the cross of Jesus is an event which in its uniqueness discloses the depths of deity. The special eschatological event of the identification of God with the man Jesus is at the same time the innermost mystery of divine being. In the special event of God's identification with the Crucified One, God expresses himself as the one who he has always been, in himself.

Then, however, God is the one who expresses himself in himself. His "inner being" *is* itself a turning toward what is "outside." God communicates

65. In dealing with the problem of death and the death of God, I have frequently alluded to this New Testament interpretation of the death of Jesus as an event which concerns God himself. For example, in radio lectures on "The Dark Word of 'The Death of God' " (which were printed in a shortened form in the *Evangelische Kommentare* [1969]), I stated, following Karl Barth, that God "in his Son surrenders deity to the grasp of death in order to be God *for* man, by enduring death. To be there for someone means to relate to that person. And when God does not cease relating to us, even in death, then that means that he contradicts the relationlessness of death with his own being. In this selfless self-involvement of God, he betrays who he is. Love is the motive not only of divine action but also of divine being. Where everything is lacking in relationships, only love can create *new* relationships" (*Evangelische Kommentare*, 2 [1969], 199f). "God vanquished death . . . in that he took death with himself into that life which he, God, is himself" (*ibid.*, p. 200). "We can really learn who God actually is only on the basis of this fact. God's life does not exclude death but includes it" (*ibid.*, p. 201). The trinitarian conception of the paschal history, which was already present in *The Doctrine of the Trinity; God's Being Is in Becoming*, is intended to be made more precise in this as well as in other discussions. (The lectures are reprinted in *Von Zeit zu Zeit; Betrachtungen zu den Festzeiten im Kirchenjahr* [München: C. Kaiser, 1976], pp. 15ff; see chiefly the theses for establishing Christology in *Unterwegs zur Sache; Theologische Bemerkungen* [München: C. Kaiser, 1972], pp. 274ff, and especially the programmatic statement, "God's being is no longer to be thought as the 'altogether simple being' [*omnino simplex esse*]. God's eternal being is more differentiated and also more temporal than we are capable of thinking" ["Vom Tod des lebendigen Gottes," in *Unterwegs zur Sache*, p. 120].)

It is all the more surprising that Jürgen Moltmann in his book *The Crucified God (The Cross of Christ as the Foundation and Criticism of Christian Theology*, trs. R. A. Wilson and J. Bowden [New York: Harper & Row, 1974]), which surprisingly often says materially the same thing even to the same formulations but which apparently is thinking in an entirely different direction formally, feels that he must make the following objections to my position:

1. that Jesus' death is to be thought of as "death *in* God" (p. 207);
2. that in Jesus' death not death but rather *love* becomes a "phenomenon of God" (p. 234);
3. that God may not be thought of "*in genere*," independently of Jesus' death on the cross, but rather God is to be thought on the basis of Jesus' death on the cross, and thus in a trinitarian fashion (p. 204 and often).

What should we say to this?

with himself without withholding himself from others. As love, he makes it possible to share in his life, in the life of love. His identification with the man Jesus is, consequently, the *revelation* of the *eternal* being of God, as a special and unique event. (Otherwise the event between God and Jesus would be a private affair, so to speak.) From all eternity, God *is in and of himself* in such a way that he is *for* man. As the Eternal he is for perishable man, whose perishability has its ground in this Pro-Being of God, a ground which prevents the process of perishing from ending in nothingness.

This content finds its simple but great formulation in the Pauline question which summarizes the entire Bible in one argument: "If God is for us, who can be against us?" (Rom. 8:31). Note that Paul expressly includes death as representative of nothingness in the list of the powers which "cannot separate us from the love of God which is in Christ Jesus" (Rom. 8:38f). Note further that Paul in this context unmistakably identifies the being of God concretely with love: God's love in Jesus Christ. And note finally that Paul, for this reason, *differentiates* God's being in that he distinguishes between "God" and "his only Son." The thought which follows faith is not to distinguish between the essence and existence of God, but rather between God the Father and God the Son. In unity with the man Jesus, God differentiates himself from himself, without ceasing to be the one God in this self-differentiation. We shall have to dwell in greater detail on the trinitarian implications of this content later. For the matter at hand it will suffice for us to make plain that the special eschatological event of God's identification with the Crucified One and God's struggle with nothingness which takes place in this event *moves* the eternal being of God not to a self-distortion but rather to a self-definition. It has been quite properly stated that the incarnation of God may not be deduced from his being as triune God. How should that even be possible if one can experience who or what God actually is only on the basis of this event?! We shall have to understand the *freedom* of God's self-identification with the man Jesus as a *substantive* moment of his self-definition. Uncoerced, without *inner* necessity, but with the innermost involvement, God shares himself with others. And in that this happens in *freedom*, it is just as divine as it is in the fact that it *happens*. God *is* the freedom to self-determination which for its part is as such defined, concrete freedom: the freedom of love.

If it is shown theologically that God happens as love in the death of Jesus but did not first become love there, then on the basis of the word of the cross, God's being as God can be thought as a being which submits itself to perishability because it involves itself in nothingness. The statement "God is love" implies two determinations which are related to each other nondialectically, in spite of all the tension present: (1) God is (to be sure) the one who involves himself in nothingness and as such is love. (2) God is (however) love in and of himself and not only through the nothingness with which he involves himself. Both determinations say the same thing from opposite sides; however, both are necessity in order to be able to express the inward movement of the divine being. They are necessary in order to think God's love as freedom, but also to think his freedom in no other way than as love. Just as love can never be coerced, but rather in a very exact sense engages itself *in and of itself,* so God is what he is, love, *in and of himself.* In that sense, freedom is a constitutive moment in love. For that reason it is not only superfluous but also completely inappropriate to

append dialectically to the determination of divine being as love the *further* determination of the divine being as freedom. Freedom is not a counterpoint to
love, as little as freedom is lost in love. Love as such takes place in freedom,
and freedom longs for love in which alone it can maintain and expand itself.

Therefore, God's being does not first become love because love is necessary
to counter nothingness. Rather, because God is love as he is himself, he counters
nothingness and its power. Because God is love, this is then God's *being*: to be
related to nothingness.[66]

In that God is, there is a difference between God and nothingness. In that
God is, he is as the one who is different from nothingness. But this difference
is under no circumstances to be thought of as being relationless and to be taken
as abstract. As the one who is different from nothingness, God is also the one
who is related to it. The difference between God and nothingness is not the
logically neutral difference between being and nothingness, but rather an event
of differentiation in which God in and of himself relates himself to nothingness.
We would not have thought God, and we would not have begun to speak of the
being of God, without having considered at the same time nothingness and its
representative, death. The being of love unites love and death in that in the event
of love life goes beyond itself. Therefore it may be asserted that, in that God is,
he is already beyond himself. And in precisely that, he is God. Thus, "in the
beginning" the "word" is with God, belongs to God as the word of love in that
he expresses himself in order to address others.

13. We may grasp this content with an old but apt concept, by calling
God *overflowing being*. To begin with God alone means to begin with the *infinitely abundant* God whose abundance, significantly, can be understood a priori
not as *possession* but only as *overflowing,* as a going with himself beyond
himself. Before all "self-having," all "self-possession," God is self-communication in the most original form.[67] In *this* fashion, God is related to nothingness.

---

66. Whoever thinks God must have all being begin with God *alone*. And that
thought which lets God alone be the beginning knows of nothing outside of God's being
in the 'reason for knowing' (*ratio cognoscendi*). If there were some other thing outside
of God, something which does not exist *through him*, then God would be a being limited
by that which exists, and there is no reason why that other existing thing should not be
just as divine; there would be a competing God established with God. Against such
dualistic conceptions, Christian theology must think God and otherwise nothing. That
theology, in this way, arrives at thinking *everything* on certain terms (but not on any
terms) is what might be called the reward for this restrictive approach of thinking God
and nothing else: "For if he had grasped one thing, he would have grasped all—in God,
I mean, since whoever does not 'grasp' God never 'grasps' any part of his creation"
(Martin Luther, *Luther and Erasmus: Free Will and Salvation,* p. 108). Talk about the
beginning of being is anything but necessary with regard to what exists. It is the concept
of God which necessitates that all being have its beginning with God alone. And the only
reason that is true is because faith experiences God as the one who directly concerns
what already exists, the people who are already alive. The *gracious* God, whose grace
takes place unconditionally, evokes the confession of the Creator God who as such is first
grasped when he and only he begins to be thought as the *beginning* of all being.

67. This thesis is a rebuttal of the view that all things that are "strive to return to
themselves, want to come to themselves, to take possession of themselves," that the
"meaning of being" is "*self-possession.*" We are contradicting then the axiom expressed
by Karl Rahner, following Thomas Aquinas: "All activities, from the sheerly material to
the innermost life of the Blessed Trinity, are but modulations of this one metaphysical

In order not to have himself solely for himself, God *creates* for himself, in the act of original self-communication, a living counterpart out of nothingness, to whom he can communicate himself as love and has in fact communicated himself in the act of creation in an irrevocable fashion. God is already related to nothingness in his being and then, beyond that, as the 'Creator out of nothingness' (*creator ex nihilo*). God is Creator out of love and thus Creator out of nothingness. This creative *act* of God is, however, nothing else than God's *being*, which as such is *creative* being.[68] In that God relates himself *creatively* to nothingness, he is the one who distinguishes himself from nothingness, he is the opponent of nothingness. God's being, as overflowing and creative being, is, so to speak, the eternal reduction of nothingness, which for its part only "is" in that God distinguishes himself from it and relates himself to it. 'Creation from nothingness' (*creatio ex nihilo*) is a struggle against nothingness which carries out this reduction positively. As such, it is the realization of divine being. In the work of creation, God's being not only *acts* as love but *confirms* itself to be love. Therefore, that God is love is the reason that anything exists at all, rather than nothingness. Borrowing from a famous statement of St. Augustine, one could say, Because God is love, we are.[69]

We draw these theological considerations together into their ontological *concept* when we grasp the being of God as a Going-Out-Of-Himself into nothingness. God involves himself with nothingness in that, in his existence out of himself he goes beyond himself, he goes out of the depths of his self into nothingness. This going out is his essence.[70]

With this ontological concept of the divine being we have comprehended the essence of God *as* existence. Existence which is identical with the essence of deity means: *a se in nihilum ek-sistere* ('to ex-ist, stand, out of himself into nothingness'). The tradition had already understood God's being as '*esse a se*' ('being out of himself'), but had understood 'existence' (*existentia*) as '*extra (causas et) nihilum sistere*' ('to stand outside of nothingness [and of cause]'). The ontological gain made by a theology which thinks the crucified God as the

---

theme, of the one meaning of being: self-possession, subjectivity" (Karl Rahner, *Hearers of the Word*, tr. M. Richards [New York: Herder & Herder, 1969], p. 49). To be sure, according to Rahner, part of "self-possession" is "a flowing outwards, an exposition of its own essence from its own cause." But this is only a phase to which that other phase corresponds which Rahner calls "a withdrawing into itself of this essence, which has expressed itself in terms of its specific cause—which has, as it were, revealed itself" (*ibid.*). It would be interesting to make a comparison of Rahner's interpretation of Thomas with Heidegger's exposition of Schelling in his *Schellings Abhandlung Über das Wesen der menschlichen Freiheit (1809)*, ed. H. Feick (Tübingen: M. Niemeyer, 1971).

68. On the problem of the identity of the 'external and internal works' (*opera ad extra et ad intra*), see below, pp. 371f.

69. See St. Augustine, *On Christian Doctrine*, NPNF, 1st ser., II, 531, and Aquinas, *Summa Theologica*, I, q. 13, art. 2, vol. I, pp. 114f: "Because He is good, we are."

70. Building on this concept of divine being, the concept of eternity as infinity would become theologically and ontologically relevant: God's most authentic Going-beyond-himself is, as 'going out toward *nothingness*' (*in nihilum ek-sistere*), a being which constantly renders impossible (and destroys) its own possible end, and is thus the projection of eternity as infinity. Mere endlessness does not merit being called infinity, but rather that being which constantly overcomes its own end and its own boundaries should, with good reason, be called eternally unending being.

true God is that the being of God now becomes understandable as a 'going' (*ek-sistere*) eternally and inexhaustibly 'out of itself into nothingness' (*a se in nihilum*), which does greater justice to both the divinity and the humanity of God than does the concept of existence understood as 'standing outside of nothingness' (*extra nihilum sistere*). The fundamental aspect of the *victory* over death is not the 'standing outside of nothingness' (*extra nihilum sistere*) which flees from nothingness, but rather the creative 'standing into nothingness' (*in nihilum sistere*). In that God is, he is this victor. To that degree, God does not start to be when he creates his creature, but rather he is "in" himself eternally creative being.

However, in order to think God as God, which means as the only God, we shall have to refine our concept of God even further. If God alone is to be God, then nothingness, into which God goes out, should not be equally original with God. Otherwise it would attain to the dignity of a counter-God. Thus, part of the concept of God is to think of the difference between God and nothingness as constituted by God. It is part of the being of God which is in itself creative to establish the difference between God and nothingness. God is not coerced by nothingness to 'go out into nothingness' (*in nihilum ek-sistere*). Rather, because God is eternally creative being in that he *goes out of himself*, and only for that reason, there is a *difference* between being and nothingness so that God *goes out 'into nothingness.'* This difference between being and nothingness is carried out not as a difference in nothingness, but rather in being. Since God is creative being, going out of himself into nothingness, the issue of the difference between being and nonbeing is a struggle within being which for its part cannot be *decided* without God involving himself in this struggle in such a way that he is present in unity with perishability.

If we think God in this fashion, then we have ceased to think him as the one elevated infinitely above all nothingness and perishability, or as intrinsic being untouched by nothingness and perishing, or as absolute essence which must avoid finitude as well as death, and death again as well as its own eternal end. God does not stand then "before the fascinated gaze" of thought, "slender and light, as though sprung out of nothingness." If, ultimately, "all doubts, all struggles are silenced in the victory of higher certainty," still, based on the God who is thought in unity with the Crucified One and based on the thinking which corresponds to this being of God, it will never be possible to continue, "all witnesses of human need have been rejected." Rather, not only in his going out into nothingness, but also in his victory over death, God has become a person with the man Jesus, without thereby ending his being as God. Thus, God's being remains in a process of becoming: *going into nothingness* and yet always, at the same time, *coming from himself.* As certainly as God comes *from God,* he does not come to himself without subjecting himself *to nothingness.* His way *out of it* is nothing other than the innermost work of his being.

The Christian doctrine of the Trinity speaks of this concretely when, *on the basis* of the 'outward works of the Trinity' (*opera trinitatis ad extra*), it understands the process of becoming, in which God's being is, as the 'internal works' of deity (*opera ad intra*). The concept of the trinitarian God emphasizes that God's abundance is to be thought as something other than that hostile "teaching about the one, and the plenum, and the unmoved, and the sufficient, and the imperishable."[71] In the challenge placed by the word of the cross to thought, which expresses itself positively in talk of the death of God, we are ultimately dealing with the issue whether "one will give assent to God's having come into existence, by which God's eternal essence is inflected in the dialectical determinations of coming into existence."[72] If our thinking assents to this, then it has opted for the capacity of the possible which it must do if God is to occur as himself in the struggle between nothingness and being. If God is to be thought as present in this struggle, then we are to set our hopes in good faith on the outcome of the struggle in favor of that which is truly affirmative in perishability.[73]

However, if we have reason to affirm the *ontological primacy* of possibility in this sense as an *ontic plus* as well, then God is thinkable in even an atheistic reality. The thinkability of God is indebted to the primacy of the possible.

71. See above, p. 152, n. 98.

72. S. Kierkegaard, *Philosophical Fragments,* p. 109. [With all due respect to the translators, it might correspond more readily to Prof. Jüngel's argumentation to translate *Werden* as "becoming" rather than "coming into existence" in this passage—TR.]

73. At the end of our consideration of the thinkability of God, it should be expressly noted that it has been no accident that there has scarcely been any mention of man's *sin* until now. There has been theological reason for this. Certainly God's identification with the Crucified One took place, according to the witness of the New Testament, in order to remove *our sins*. Certainly Christ died *for us*. And it is just as certain that the definition of sin is to be made on the basis of the justification of the sinner; sin is the *intensified empowerment of nothingness,* that nothingness into which God goes out and out of which he calls his creation into being, an empowerment *to the level of a power summoning back to destruction.* Sin makes nothingness into something; it builds up nothingness into an anti-deity. And it does this by keeping God out of the struggle between being and nonbeing.

Sin, then, is nothing other than the presumptuousness of man to be able to deal with nothingness himself, to justify himself as *coming* from nothingness (instead of being created from it), and thus to understand his own being as a going 'out of nothingness' (*ex nihilo*). Man, then, insists on nothingness as his origin and source, which he has now vanquished. In this, he gives nothingness the opportunity to convict him of the very opposite. He *falls prey* to nothingness. In death, the apparent vanquisher of nothingness is vanquished by it. When man avers that nothingness is the origin which he has overcome, he surrenders himself to nothingness as the unvanquishable purpose of his being; for God is kept back from the struggle with nothingness to the extent that man claims that he *comes* out of nothingness, rather than to be called forth from it. Again, this is the way in which nothingness becomes *powerful.* Thus, sin becomes the 'creatoress of divinity' (*creatrix divinitatis*), of an anti-God whose destructive power consists of its keeping the true God away from itself. It is for the sake of this sin that Christ died, that God went to death 'once and for all' (*ephapax*).

The relationship between God and death has, then, its particular focus in the fact that death is the wages of sin. But *this ontic,* and theologically decisive, confrontation of God with the *annihilating* power of nothingness does not exclude but rather includes the fact that God's own being is subject to nothingness in such a way that the confrontation is made possible, *without* God contradicting himself in the process. The 'once' and 'once and for all' (*hapax, ephapax*) of that christological event are to be thought as made possible in the being of God himself. Christ does offer himself only once, but does so with his *own* blood; for that reason, he did not have "to suffer repeatedly since the foundation of the world" (Heb. 9:26). The once-and-for-all character of Christ's death is an eschatological uniqueness both with regard to our sins and with regard to God's being.

CHAPTER IV

On the Speakability of God

SECTION 14. The Statement of the Problem

1. Theology is talk about God. But one can talk about God in a variety of ways. Even the Bible, which is as a collection of texts an authoritative and certainly instructive book on the usage of the word "God," speaks of God in many different ways. Not only the predicates change, but also the subject terminology. And the predications can even be opposed to each other. Christian dogmatics, therefore, has attempted to set up a structure for the meaningful and legitimate use of the word "God," or better, for a meaningful and legitimate paraphrase of this word, by enumerating God's essential characteristics, borrowing from the metaphysical discussions of God. Although the attempt to set up such a framework for talk about God is certainly problematic, especially in the form of a list of characteristics,[1] we must certainly honor the intention which is behind it, namely, to prevent the misuse of the name of God. The manifold nature of talk about God raises the question whether then all talk about God can be meaningful and legitimate. The Bible agrees with other traditions that the name of God may not be abused. Even the atheist is sure that there is an abuse, which he shows by pointing out the corrupting results of religious talk. And certainly there is no more corrupting abuse than that of the word "God." It is indispensable for talk about God that a basic distinction be made between the right kinds of usage and the equally manifold abuses of the word "God." One can abuse this word crudely and with refinement, and even "utter unworthily" the name of God. What does such abuse consist of?

The answer to this question draws together all that has been discussed until

---

1. Virtually every better Christian dogmatic has been more or less aware of the problematic of its doctrine of the characteristics of the divine essence. This is seen in, among other things, the subtle discussions of the distinguishability of such characteristics from the divine essence on the one hand and from each other on the other. In more recent times, F. Schleiermacher reminded us of the many problems which are raised for dogmatics in this regard, and renewed the awareness of the problem which has been present since Scholasticism (*The Christian Faith*, trs. Mackintosh and Stewart [New York: Harper & Row, 1963], vol. I, pars. 50ff, pp. 194ff). For a comparison, it is instructive to study the corresponding discussion in G. W. F. Hegel, for example, in his "Lectures on the Proofs of the Existence of God," in *Lectures on the Philosophy of Religion*, vol. III, trs. Rev. E. B. Speirs and J. B. Sanderson (New York: Humanities Press, 1962), pp. 203ff. Special significance in the debate with the dogmatic treatment of the divine characteristics as pursued by Schleiermacher should be attached to the study by H. Cremer, *Die christliche Lehre von den Eigenschaften Gottes* (*Beiträge zur Förderung christlicher Theologie*, 1, 4) (Gütersloh: Bertelsmann, 1897, 1917²). This book merits more attention than has been given it in the theological discussion.

now. The abuse of the word "God" is certainly present when the opposite of what we have seen to be responsible talk about God is achieved. Human talk about God merits being called responsible when its only intention is that God should be permitted to speak. We call that kind of human talk about God which wants to let him speak himself, "corresponding to God." Therefore, talk about God is responsible when it is its intention to correspond to God. And it *corresponds* to God in that it *lets him come*. That human speech corresponds to God which allows God to speak in such a way that it permits him to be the *subject* of the speaking, the one who speaks. The criterion for the proper usage of the word "God" is whether human speech allows and achieves this or prevents it, for whatever reasons it may be. Whether human speech is so used that God can *come* and is able to be *present in the power of the word*—that is the question which must constantly be dealt with in theology as responsible talk about God.

Theology, in distinction from all possible other usages of the word "God," is talk about God which in its positive usage is obligated to prevent the misuse of this word. As such, it constantly must attend to the kind of speech which corresponds to God, in that it allows him to speak himself. In this, the Christian faith proceeds from the prejudgment that God has definitively spoken in the word of the cross as the gospel for all mankind. Theology, therefore, orients itself to that speech which corresponds to the crucified Jesus Christ. Only in that fashion does it do justice to its claim that it is talk about God, that is, that talk about God which regulates all talk about God.

This orientation implies the task of thinking God. Whoever wants to speak responsibly about God must think God. He may not shrink from the work done in thinking God. Part of that labor is to be involved oneself in the traditional thinking about God because that which always has been thought does not dispense with one's own thinking. It is also part of this labor to reject the traditional thinking about God to the extent that what has always been thought makes it impossible to think the thought of God in every age anew, or to think God in a new concept of God. Part of the task of theology is constantly to begin the labor of thinking God anew, even if the results should prove that the traditional way of thinking God is completely identical with the newly arrived at thought of God. Even in such a case, the labor would certainly not have been superfluous. There is a very special way in which the process of thinking itself belongs to the thought of God.

2. The way in which the thought of God and the event of thought belong together is further based on the fact, elementary for every responsible thought about God, that God is thinkable only as the unconditional subject of himself, and that it inheres in this unconditional being as subject that God reveals himself as God if man is to be able to think the unconditional subject of himself as such. The way in which the thought of God is dependent on the revelation event corresponds to the way in which the thought of God is dependent on the event of thought. Revelation can be comprehended in thoughts only to the degree that these thoughts themselves constantly refer back to something which must be thought anew. God can be thought only as something constantly to be thought anew.

In general, God can be thought as the one who he is only on the basis of revelation which *has taken place*. The possibility of the thought of God which thinks God as God is conditioned by the fact that God *has* revealed himself.

Faith is the anthropological realization of the fact that God *has* revealed himself. For revelation is, in its facticity, not primarily an occasion for knowledge, but rather an event of self-sharing in the being of the one revealing himself, an event which implies knowledge. Accordingly, faith is not primarily a human mode of knowing, as Plato and his tradition taught, but rather an event of human participation in the being of that one who allows such participating in his being— and again, an event which implies knowledge. Of course, God is always known somehow in the event of faith. But this way in which God is somehow known is totally obvious to faith. It is an implicit knowledge. Beyond that, faith seeks to explain what is obvious to it, for many reasons, of which we may mention the one, which is that we should always be ready to give an answer for the hope which is founded on our faith (I Pet. 3:15). Faith then is concerned about thinking God.

3. Thought, when it really wants to think God, can proceed only by "thinking after" faith (reflecting on faith). It will do this with the critical reservation that faith as a human attitude toward God is affected by every possible kind of human attitude about one's self and the world. There is, to be sure, the act "of pure faith," but the person of the believer is never a person defined solely by his faith and nothing else. In the *person* of the believer, belief itself is affected essentially by the world. Thought must constantly give attention to the problem which results from this worldly influence on faith; as such it is opportunity, and only then is it a danger. The danger that man's attitude toward God is determined by his attitudes to himself and his world, instead of determining the former, is therefore to be borne in mind when God is to be thought as the one in whom we believe and always have to believe anew. The knowledge of God implied in faith can be dissembled or even distorted. But thought cannot escape this problem by dispensing with faith and, in its place, seeking to think God 'apart from faith' (*remota fide*), and to construct this or that concept of God. Such an endeavor would be related only to man's attitudes toward himself and his world and would have to postulate a relationship of man and his world to God on the basis of those attitudes. Thus, in a greatly increased way, it would be subject to those dangers, and would fall prey to them, from which it was seeking to escape. Instead of driving out the devil with Beelzebub in that fashion, self-critical thought should establish faith as the condition for the possibility of thinking God, in order then, based on this possibility, to resist the dangers it brings. This can, however, happen only when thought constantly refers faith back to its source, to that event in which God, expressing himself, permits participation in himself.

We defined that event as the event of the word in which God speaks in such a way that he communicates himself. It is precisely because thought can perceive God only as the one who is believed and to be believed that the word which enables faith is the place where God is thinkable. The theological responsibility of thought consists of bearing responsibility for a word which is not added later to God as one who is to be thought, but in which God is present as God. For this reason, this word is called the word of God. The question of the thinkability of God is then resolved by whether God is *speakable* on the basis of such a word of God. However, since thought, in order to work through a concept of God, is dependent on God's *having* revealed himself, the word of

God must *already have happened*, regardless of whether there might possibly be a further event of this word. The attempt to think God is meaningful only under the presupposition that God *has* spoken. Everything else remains a postulate, even if the opposite should be asserted. Logic makes this plain. When it wants to argue philosophically, theology must refer to traditions which claim to speak of God because he himself has spoken. Every theology is dependent on "positive religion," even if it is only in order to negate them. Thus, theology is always related to history. These traditions must be taken seriously in their claims and critically evaluated in terms of their claims. It could then be the task of philosophical theology to engage all the theologies, bound up in and obligated to their historical religious traditions as they are, in a critical discussion with each other. A *criterion* for the truth of each "positionally" raised theological claim can be developed only in conversation with the historical traditions and their respective theologies. Such a criterion can be found only in the struggle for truth. In fact, it is probable that the criterion for the truth will be more contested than truth itself.

4. *Christian* theology will come to terms appropriately with this content by seeking to show, as best it can, how unambiguously Christian faith is indebted to certain language events in which God has spoken. The problem of the speakability of God, and of the thought of God developed on its basis, cannot be tackled abstractly, with no regard for certain speech traditions. The discussion about whether and how God is speakable must take place with regard to very specific speech events which claim that God has spoken. For Christian theology, those are the *particular* speech events which make Christian faith possible. With reference to them, the problem of the speakability of God must be discussed in as *principled and general* a fashion as possible, and work on the thought of God must be governed by an interest in a concept of God which is *generally binding*.[2]

A universal theological problem is to be worked through in terms of the particular character, the "proprium," of the Christian faith. The particular character of the Christian faith, however, is the word of the cross, to put it as succinctly as possible. Everything which is intended to be Christian must be measured by that one thing. The word of the cross is talk about God's unity with the man Jesus who was killed on the cross, and about the distinction between God and man, grounded in that unity, as an event which justifies man in his being as human and thus benefits all mankind. In that sense, the word of the cross is a proclamation which allows God to speak definitively, a proclamation which takes place in the name of God. We can also say that the word of the cross is the self-definition of God in human language, which implies a definition of man.

2. It should be noted in this context that of course the principial consideration of the relationship between the thinkability and speakability of God was already guided by the self-understanding of the Christian faith. This was equally true of the critique of the destruction of the concept of God inaugurated by Descartes and made possible by the metaphysical concept of God which he and all of modern metaphysics presuppose. The hermeneutical circle is not only unavoidable in such discussions, but is demanded. To "admit" is part and parcel of the integrity of thought. To polemicize against it betrays either something like a religious naiveté (which presents itself as rationalism), which should be respected, or a fatal tendency to theological charades.

The principal and general problem which is raised for Christian theology in the context of the speakability of God has to do with the relationship of God to human language, or better, the relationship of human language to a God who can be thought only as one who speaks out of himself. We had to understand the word in which God is supposed to have expressed himself, as that word which belongs to God's own being. But as such, it does not necessarily belong to human language. As God's word, it is not necessarily also human language. On the other hand, the expression "word of God" is not very meaningful if it is supposed to mean a word which does not belong to human language. Human language knows only human words. Yet the fundamental distinction between God and man threatens to be lost if God's word is not basically differentiated from all the words of human language. It appears that the problem of the relationship of the presence and absence of God repeats itself here with reference to the word of God, whereas we had sought to resolve this problem by turning to the hermeneutical distinctiveness of the word which addresses us. As a result, we shall have to consider the significance of the hermeneutical distinctiveness of the word in relation to the mediation of presence and absence when we now turn to the relationship of God's word and human language. In what way can we say of human language that it allows God to speak? The problem of theology, which ultimately decides the issue of the thinkability of God, is the question as to how one can talk about God humanly and not miss his divinity in so doing. We call this the problem of the speakability of God.

The problem arises both *because* we are talking about God and also *so that* we can talk about God. If there was not already talk about God, thinking would scarcely ever come up with the thought of God. The construction of a thought of God and the need to do so emerge out of the preceding talk about God, or at least out of a preceding sense of being addressed which we call "God," even when man responds to this address with silence. Even such silence would be a way of talking about God, resulting from its own process. That is all the more true for every outspoken or silent negation of God. However thought decides about God, it presupposes talk about God. Whether we are considering the presupposed talk about God, or that talk about God which may yet take place, the question remains, whether and how God is humanly speakable.[3] How can one correspond to God humanly?

3. Since the days of so-called dialectical theology, the thesis has often been advanced that theological thought is responsibility for the word of God. There is debate about whether the being of God itself is something for which one can be responsible, or only the word "God" or its human usage. Further debated is whether one can be responsible for something like the word of God if one illuminates the meaning of the word "God" without this word and thus makes responsible usage of the word "God" possible, for example, through the existential interpretation of human existence as lingual being. Since here God has been thought within the context of language, but he himself has been thought without language, apart from the event of the word of God, such an approach could ill defend itself against the accusation that the word character of the divine being was introduced after the fact. If God is thought within the human context as a lingual being, but initially apart from the word in which he is, the danger of a transcendental concept of God looms anew, that concept which led into the aporia of the unthinkability of God. For this reason, the opposite approach is taken in this study. On the basis of the event of the word of God, *God and man* are to be thought of as lingual beings, each in his own special way.

5. In actuality, one cannot—that is the answer to this question given by a mighty tradition in not only philosophy but also Christian theology. Although theology is talk about God, the assertion crops up very early in theology that one cannot really say who God is. Talk about God can actually state only what God is *not*: 'God is incapable of definition' (*deus definiri nequit*).

In what follows, this old and often still maintained position will be rebutted. The reason for rebuttal is faith in the justification of man through God, which took place in the death of the man Jesus. The Christian belief in justification excludes the opinion that God only permits one to say what he is not, saying that such an opinion is self-contradictory. If God is one who justifies mankind, then that is already a statement about who or what God is. For justification implies recognition. Recognition, however, requires that the one who is recognized *permit* himself to be recognized. Therefore, justification takes place solely on the basis of faith. To permit oneself to be recognized implies, in turn, that the one who is recognized knows the one who is recognizing. In the event of recognition, such knowledge is realized in that the recognizer must reveal himself if his recognition is to mean anything at all. No one can be recognized by a totally unknown person, nor even by someone who is more or less known. Faith that justifies asserts, therefore, that God reveals who he really is in that he justifies men. And since the justification of the godless by God took place in the event of God's identification with the crucified man Jesus, theological thought must hear from this christological event what both God and man ought to mean. This event also provides information about how talk that corresponds to God is possible.

In our discussion up to now, we have dealt with the certainty of faith, but not with that which makes faith possible, and so now we will turn to answering the question of the speakability of God. But before doing so, we shall discuss briefly the thesis of the unspeakability of God, in its own way a classic stance, which will then make it possible for us to develop all the more clearly our opposing thesis in this study. To accomplish this, we shall interpret a statement of St. Thomas Aquinas, who developed the classical thesis of the unspeakability of God in a classical way (sect. 15). Then, since a theology which asserts the unspeakability of God still claims to be talk about God, the hermeneutical disputation which is occasioned by the theme of the speakability of God focuses itself sharply in the question whether talk about God is more relevant if we are made more aware of the inadequacy of such talk or if our talk about God is accompanied by the certainty of ultimate adequacy and such certainty is affirmed as relevant. We shall endeavor to respond to this controversial question by discussing the theological concept of mystery. There, thesis and antithesis agree that God is to be thought as mystery (sect. 16). But how one thinks about God as mystery will decide whether God can be expressed in human words in such a way that these words really correspond to his being. The problem of the speakability of God is ultimately seen to be the problem of the possibility of analogous talk about God. Under the title of analogy, the whole dispute returns again, in that this is also debated: what does it mean to correspond to God? The discussion of the theological concept of analogy brings the dispute about the speakability of God to its conclusion (sect. 17). At the end, it will be seen whether faith that justifies is hermeneutically justified. Only then will we see

how God's being is to be thought in unity with perishability on the basis of the
word of the cross (sect. 18).

SECTION 15. The Classical Thesis: "The Deity, therefore, is ineffable and incomprehensible"

1. Thomas Aquinas elevated the Socratic thesis, "I know that I know
nothing," to the rank of a fundamental theological proposition, whose validity
is, however, restricted to the knowledge of God. The ultimate form of the human
knowledge of God (*"ultimum cognitionis humanae de deo"*) is the statement
"man reaches the highest point of his knowledge about God when he knows that
he knows him not."[1]

The uncontested beginning point for all theological endeavors to arrive at
responsible talk about God is the insight, ". . . we cannot know what God is,
but rather what He is not, we have no means for considering how God is, but
rather how He is not."[2]

Thomas shares this insight with the theological tradition which he quotes
in this context. So, for example, in discussing the question whether God (himself) is the subject-matter of 'sacred doctrine' which claims to be a science, he
quotes John of Damascus in order to support the view (later proven to be irrelevant) that God himself cannot be considered as the 'subject-matter of this science': ". . . for Damascene says: *It is impossible to express the essence of God.*"[3]
The cited thesis of the ancient theologian is not doubted by Thomas as he sets
about destroying the consequences derived from it. Rather, it is expressly taken
up, although in the variant form that we cannot *know* of God what he is.[4] The
Damascene had said in the quotation that we cannot *express* ('say') what God
is. Does knowledge fail because language fails? Or is the unspeakability of God
a result of lacking knowledge? Before we pursue the problem further in Thomas,
the tradition which he cites should be reviewed briefly.

2. The ancient tradition that asserts that God's essence is unspeakable
(ineffable) has its beginning in the pre-Socratic insight into the more than qualitative distinctiveness of the divine over against everything' else. Heraclitus had
already spoken of the one who is "apart from all else," one above all that is, set
apart and thus totally special, the one who rules all things.[5] This insight was
coupled with harsh criticism of any humanization of the divine, especially criticism of the pedagogical authority of Homer. Heraclitus and Xenophanes are
known as relentless critics of anthropomorphic talk about God. At the same
time, such criticism did not rule out the possibility of talking about God at all.

1. Thomas Aquinas, *On the Power of God* (Three Books in One), tr. English
Dominican Fathers (Westminster, Md.: Newman Press, 1952), bk. III, q. 7, art. 5, reply
to obj. 14, p. 33.

2. *Summa Theologica* (hereafter *STh*), I, q. 3, introd., vol. I, p. 25.

3. *STh*, I, q. 1, art. 7, obj. 1, vol. I, p. 12.

4. *STh*, I, q. 1, art. 7, reply to obj. 1, vol. I, p. 12.

5. Heraclitus, B 108 and B 41, in Philip Wheelwright, *Heraclitus* (Princeton, NJ:
Princeton University Press, 1959), 7, p. 19, and 120, p. 102. On the whole issue here,
I refer to my monograph, *Zum Ursprung der Analogie bei Parmenides und Heraklit*
(Berlin: De Gruyter, 1964).

The proper knowledge of the divine, and the proper word which corresponded to it, were rather the presupposition of such criticism. In Plato, the pre-Socratic tradition was developed further, even though the various drafts of the Platonic philosophy do not immediately reveal to what extent they were reworkings of the questions of earlier thinkers. The oldest documentation for the usage of the word "theology" is found in this context, which takes into account the pre-Socratic critique of overly generous talk about the divine.[6] Its counterpart is found in Plato's definitions of the relationship between myth and logos with regard to the possibility of doing justice in speech to that First, Highest, and Ultimate which "far exceeds essence in dignity."[7] Plato's remarks about the impossibility of expressing in speech this "beyond" by means of the logic of the logos have become decisive in the history of thought. The seventh letter is undoubtedly the most penetrating witness for the Platonic decision to withhold the stringency of the concept from the still greater stringency of that being "beyond all being," which actually can be grasped only as the incomprehensible. In the dialogue *Phaedo,* the great disciple states through the mouth of the dying teacher that the logos has delegated to the divine irony of the myth what its own logic is prevented from expressing.

One must be reminded of this basic philosophical decision if one wants to understand why, in Christian theology, the assertion could have arisen that we could not say who God is, in spite of the fact of the Bible. Of course, the thesis of the ineffability and incomprehensibility of the divine is given its biblical grounds—for example, in John of Damascus with reference to John 1:18 and Matthew 11:27. But this reasoning came after the fact. It is the spirit of Plato[8] which is expressed in this fundamental statement, "The Deity, therefore, is ineffable and incomprehensible."[9] Mediated by Neo-Platonism, the basic Platonic decision about the speakability of God made its way into Christian theology. It was especially the theologian known under the pseudonym Dionysius the Areopagite (see Acts 17:34) who brought this philosophical decision to its position of influence within Christian theology.[10] The Platonic experience of "that which far exceeds the essence" goes beyond the *surpassing* of being and presents itself as *transcendence* over everything which exists and every being,

6. Plato, "Republic," in *The Dialogues of Plato,* tr. B. Jowett, 2 vols. (New York: Random House, 1937), II, bk. II, 379, p. 643.

7. As early as Middle- and Neo-Platonism, there had been talk of a regular "theology of Plato" in the sense of a systematic onto-theological design. "Proclus was the one who finally arrived at the designation, 'Platonic theology' " (J. Hochstaffl, *Negative Theologie; Ein Versuch zur Vermittlung des patristischen Begriffs* [München: Kösel, 1976], p. 65, with reference to Proclus, *Platonic Theology,* ed. Aemilius Portus [Hamburg, 1618; repr. 1960], and Proclus, *The Elements of Theology,* ed. E. R. Dodds [Oxford: Clarendon Press, 1933]).

8. See the "Republic," bk. VI, 509, in *op. cit.,* p. 770, where the idea of the good as "far exceed(ing) essence in dignity" is given.

9. John of Damascus, *Exposition of the Orthodox Faith,* tr. S. D. F. Salmond, *NPNF,* 2nd ser., vol. IX, 1899, bk. I, ch. I, p. 1.

10. The writings of Dionysius the Areopagite, dating from the late fifth century, were translated into Latin around 850 by John Scotus Erigena. "This and a few later medieval translations made possible the great influence which the writings gained upon European, medieval thought" (J. Hochstaffl, *op. cit.,* p. 121).

into a transmundane realm, "far exceeding everything,"[11] so that even the superlative of being has to be surpassed if one wants to arrive at the divine. Such a transcendence would be a step into the unfathomable depths which necessarily would wipe out the entire capacity to think and conceptualize as it strides forward on the foundation of what exists. In view of the impossibility of such transcendence, the affirmative language shifts over into negation, which withholds that being which cannot be transcended away from God, who is to be sought beyond being and existence in a beyond which is always further beyond and thus cannot be found. One can do justice to the God who is *over* being only by the *negation* of what he is not. "With regard to the divine, negations are true, whereas affirmations are inadequate."[12] In that God is the one who is above all thought, he is called and he is the Incomprehensible. And in that God is that goodness which surpasses all speech, he is called and he is the Ineffable. Because he is a God who can be expressed through no word, whose deity surpasses every word, this Trans-Word is described most adequately as Non-Word, and accordingly, Non-Name and Non-Knowledge.[13] To prefer negative statements (*apophaseis*) about God over affirmative statements (*kataphaseis*) may not be

11. Compare in Dionysius the Areopagite, *On the Divine Names and the Mystical Theology* (*Translations of Christian Literature*, Series I), tr. C. E. Rolt (New York: Macmillan, 1920), ch. I of "The Mystical Theology," pp. 191f, with ch. I/1 of "On the Divine Names," pp. 51f. This concept of "exceeding or beyond all things" which developed in continuation of Plato's "exceeding the essence" appears to have become the key theological term of the patristic doctrine of God. An impressive documentation of the theological function of this formula is found in the well-known hymn of Gregory of Nazianzus (see p. 258, n. 30), which is translated here from the German translation by U. H. Theill-Wunder (cited in Hochstaffl, *op. cit.*, p. 108):
"Beyond all things! How else might I praise Thee?
How should one word extol Thee? For Thou art unspeakable by every word.
How should one thought perceive Thee? For Thou art incomprehensible by every thought.
Thou alone art unnamed: for Thou didst make every name.
Thou alone art unknown: for Thou didst make every knowledge.
Everything which can speak and cannot speak praises Thee.
Everything which can understand and cannot understand honors Thee.
For the common desire, the common woes of all
Are directed to Thee. All things plead to Thee!
Understanding Thy sign, all things sing Thee a silent hymn!
In Thee the One remains everything; to Thee presses everything at once.
Thou art the goal of all, art One, and All, and No one,
Not being of one, not everything. Name of everything,
How shalt Thou be called, Only Unknown One?
Which celestial understanding penetrates the
Veil lying above the clouds? Be gracious to me!
Beyond all things! How else might I praise Thee?"
12. *De coelestia hierarchia*, II/3, SC 58, 79:2ff (Migne, *Patrologia Graeca*, III, 141). Accordingly Dionysius the Areopagite terms his theology "apophatic theology," perhaps in derivation from Proclus. He uses the expression both in the plural (parallel to "positive theologies"; "The Mystical Theology," in Dionysius the Areopagite, *On the Divine Names and the Mystical Theology*, I/1, pp. 192f) and in the singular (*ibid.*).
13. "The Divine Names," in Dionysius the Areopagite, *op. cit.*, I/1, pp. 52f: ". . . the Super-Intellectual Unity surpasses Intelligences, the One which is beyond thought surpasses the apprehension of thought, and the Good which is beyond utterance surpasses the reach of words. Yea, it is an Unity which is the unifying Source of all unity and a Super-Essential Essence, a Mind beyond the reach of mind and a Word beyond utterance, eluding Discourse, Intuition, Name, and every kind of Being."

misunderstood as a decision which lessens the divinity of God. The affirmative statements are understood here rather as predications which burden God with lesser values which reduce the divinity of God, whereas the negative statements are looked on as the affirmative predications of the absolute superiority of God because they remove everything nondivine from God. The ontological transcending beyond the superlative of being can find its counterpart only in a language which sets it apart to a point beyond which nothing can be thought further: the negation. We correspond to God only from the most extreme distance.[14]

In this sense, John of Damascus also asserts the ineffability of God. But a fundamental part of his ineffability is talk about this ineffability. The unspeakable may not be kept silent, but must instead be expressed. "In the case of God, however, it is impossible to explain what He is in His essence, and it befits us the rather to hold discourse about His absolute separation from all things. For He does not belong to the class of existing things: not that He has no existence, but that He is above all existing things, nay even above existence itself."[15] The thesis of the ineffability of God must then still state two things about God if it does not want to negate God entirely while asserting his ineffability. The assertion of the ineffability of God must state God's existence, in some category or other, in order to assert itself theologically. And it must also state the absolute superiority of God as the actual reason for his ineffability.

John of Damascus did then delimit the proposition "The Deity . . . is ineffable and incomprehensible" in two ways. To put it more precisely, one should say that God himself delimited the fundamental assertions of ineffability and incomprehensibility made about him. For God did not leave us in a state of total theological ignorance. That is, however, an assertion which presupposes a particular event, which breaks through this fundamental ineffability and incomprehensibility of God with divine sovereignty. Such a revelatory event is then expressly mentioned: "Moreover, by the Law and the Prophets in former times, and afterwards by His only-begotten Son, our Lord and God and Saviour Jesus Christ, He disclosed to us the knowledge of Himself as that was possible for us. . . . He revealed that which it was our profit to know; but what we were unable to bear He kept secret."[16] Such an event, which a Christian theology will scarcely be able to deny, could certainly have made the fundamental proposition of the ineffability of God a theological problem. But the Damascene's interest is oriented in precisely the opposite direction. It is revelation itself which leads directly into the ineffability of the divine essence. Obviously, then, it is all the more important that there be certainty about the *existence* of such an Ineffable. Therefore, the proposition "The Deity . . . is ineffable and incomprehensible" is delimited in another way. That limitation of this thesis consists of the assertion that the knowledge of the *existence* of God is implanted in *all* humans by their very nature.[17] The mere quiddity of an ineffable is a certainty for man, without the ineffable divine having broken through its ineffability by means of special language events.

14. We shall return to Dionysius the Areopagite below, pp. 255ff.
15. John of Damascus, *op. cit.*, bk. I, ch. IV, p. 4.
16. *Ibid.*, bk. I, ch. 1, p. 1.
17. "For the knowledge of God's existence has been implanted by Him in all by nature" (*ibid.*, bk. I, ch. 1, p. 1).

We are now dealing with the actual premise of the thesis of the ineffability of God. It consists of the self-evident assumption that there is a God. The self-evident aspect of this assumption must then elevate itself above everything else which is self-evident when one is to reflect on the deity of this God whose existence is self-evident. The self-evident aspect of the assertion that a God is may not express anything at all about what a God is. Otherwise this self-evidently existing God would occur within the context of the self-evident, and then he would not be God at all. He would resemble the spirit which comprehends him and thus would be deprived of his absolute superiority and independence. Therefore, the self-evidentness of the fact that a God exists is, in a reflected theology, accompanied by the insight that we cannot know what a God is. "It is plain, then, that there is a God. But what He is in His essence and nature is absolutely incomprehensible and unknowable."[18]

And yet, how can one express in language and give a name to an existence about which one cannot describe *what* it is? Neither the assertion "there is something," nor the assertion "there is something which is completely other," can justify calling this unknown something *God*. The gnoseological distinction between the self-evident existence of God and the totally non-self-evident, totally unknown essence of God confronts us with the fundamental hermeneutical question, What does God mean? More precisely put, What does God properly mean? The thesis of the ineffability of God cannot be maintained if it does not resolve the aporia which arises with the distinction between the self-evident existence and the ineffable essence of God.

3. Thomas Aquinas worked through this tradition and its problems. In the process, the axiom of the ineffability of God is restated in the narrower proposition, ". . . we cannot *know* in what the essence of God consists" (*"quod de deo non possumus scire quid est"*).[19] Thomas reveals that he believes it to be possible to *speak* of God in his assertion that God himself is the subject of that science which as sacred doctrine takes its place next to the 'philosophical disciplines' (*philosophicae disciplinae*).[20] 'Sacred doctrine' (*sacra doctrina*) talks about God. But how can it do that if we do not know what God is?[21]

(a) The answer which Thomas gives to this question sounds very much like the Reformation to us. Thomas refers to the *effects* of God. Although we do not know *what* God is, we do know certain effects of God. Such effects, which we experience both as nature and as grace, can take the place of a definition of essence. In terms of the logic of concepts, it is possible to let the known 'effect' (*effectus*) of an unknown 'cause' (*causa*) replace the definition of the essence of the 'cause,' in order to arrive at valid statements about this 'cause.' Thus theology proceeds along the lines of a generally accepted scientific rule: ". . . even as in some philosophical sciences we demonstrate something about

18. *Ibid.*, bk. I, ch. IV, p. 3.
19. *STh*, I, q. 13, art. 2, vol. I, pp. 114f.
20. See *STh*, I, q. 1, art. 1, vol. I, pp. 5f.
21. The treatment of this theme is also the subject of the commendable study by B. Welte, "Bemerkungen zum Gottesbegriff des Thomas von Aquin," in *Zeit und Geheimnis; Philosophische Abhandlungen zur Sache Gottes in der Zeit der Welt* (Freiburg: Herder, 1975), pp. 219ff.

a cause from its effect, by taking the effect in the place of a definition of the cause."[22]

Therefore, theology is certainly *talk* about God. The only way in which it is that is that it takes the essence of God as the 'cause' of an 'effect.' Only when talking about the effect of this cause can it express God. This does not only apply to the so-called natural knowledge of God as expressed in the "preamble to the articles."[23] It is also to be related to the revealed knowledge of God expressed in the "articles of faith" so that talk about God's effects enables one also to speak of God himself: ". . . in this doctrine we make use of His effects, either of nature or of grace, in the place of a definition, in regard to whatever is treated in this doctrine concerning God. . . ."[24]

The problem resulting from the thesis of the impossibility of knowing God's *essence* emerges immediately when Thomas turns to the discussion of the doctrine of God in the narrower sense. This takes place first of all in the form of a discussion of the question 'whether God exists' (*an deus sit*). The question of the *existence* of God is inextricably connected to our problem in that the existence of a total unknown can hardly be made the object of a study. There must at least be names (designations) for that unknown essence whose existence is supposed to be demonstrated. Significantly, Thomas presents the question of the *existence* of God as *part* of the study of the *essence* of God, namely, as the first part: "Concerning the divine essence, we must consider: —1) Whether God exists? 2) The manner of His existence, or, rather, what is *not* the manner of His existence. 3) Whatever concerns His operations—namely, His knowledge, will, power."[25] The general rule, ". . . the question of its essence follows on the question of its existence. . . ,"[26] functions here to legitimize the nominal definition in place of the essence definition as the place at which the proofs of God may begin.[27] The fact that the question of the existence of God is treated

22. *STh*, I, q. 1, art. 7, reply to obj. 1, vol. I, pp. 12f.

23. *STh*, I, q. 2, art. 2, reply to obj. 1, vol. I, p. 21, *"praeambula ad articulos fidei."*

24. *STh*, I, q. 1, art. 7, reply to obj. 1, vol. I, pp. 12f.

25. *STh*, I, q. 2, introd., vol. I, p. 18. See I, q. 3, introd., vol. I, p. 25: "When the existence of a thing has been ascertained, there remains the further question of the manner of its existence, in order that we may know its essence."

26. *STh*, I, q. 2, art. 2, reply to obj. 2, vol. I, p. 21.

27. Therefore, one cannot strictly speaking take the question "where God is" as the "preliminary question . . . to the main question, 'how God is' " (G. Ebeling, "Existenz zwischen Gott und Gott," in *Wort und Glaube II; Beiträge zur Fundamentaltheologie und zur Lehre von Gott* [Tübingen: J. C. B. Mohr (Siebeck), 1969], p. 268). It is a partial question which helps to answer the question, 'how is God?' The knowledge of the existence of God necessarily implies at least a partial knowledge of the essence of God. "Therefore, the Scholastics rightly say, 'Now the knowledge of the *existence* of God involves some knowledge of his *essence*, in so far that it is known as the prime immovable mover, the first cause, the necessary being, the ultimate being, and the governor of all things" (B. Lakebrink, *Klassische Metaphysik; Eine Auseinandersetzung mit der existentialen Anthropozentrik* [Freiburg: Rombach, 1967], p. 169; on the quotation, see J. Gredt, *Elementa philosophiae Aristotelico-Thomisticae*, 2 vols. [Freiburg: Herder, 1929], II, p. 257, nr. 818, 4). There is a strict methodological distinction to be made between this problematic of the relationship of the knowledge of the essence and knowledge of the existence of God, and the priority of the 'who is' (*qui est*) as the name of God over all other 'divine names' (*nomina divina*). The 'absolute being' (*esse absolutum*)

as a part of the question of the essence of God also merits attention even if one considers that God's 'essence' (*essentia*) is immediately identical with God's 'being' or 'existence' (*esse, existentia*),[28] that is, that the distinction between the essence and existence of God is only a 'rational distinction' (*distinctio rationis*) and not a 'real distinction' (*distinctio realis*). This points out that Thomas deals with the study of the existence of God as a preliminary decision relating to the answering of the question of the essence of God. That means that we now encounter emphatically the significance of *talk* about God for the knowledge of God.

(b) First of all, Thomas rebuts the difficulties which could possibly stand in the way of the positive answering of the question of the existence of God (in the sense of a "proof" of the existence). Two difficulties could emerge. On the one hand, the a priori *evidence* for the existence of God could make a "proof" of this existence appear irrational. On the other hand, the existence of God belongs to the *articles of faith* which remove themselves from access through the rationality of proof so that a "proof" of the existence of God would have to appear as unbelief. The two possible obstacles are thus exactly contrary to each other: if the existence of God were evident to reason a priori, then one would not have to *believe* it, and if the existence of God were the content of an 'article of faith' (*articulus fidei*), then it could not be *demonstrated with reason*.

If God's existence were *self-evident* to man (*per se notum*), then it could not be debatable and also would not need to be "proven." The special question of the existence of God would not be necessary but rather superfluous. Thomas must abrogate this possibility in order to demonstrate the *necessity* of researching the existence of God. To accomplish this, Thomas distinguishes between two kinds of self-evident things, of which only the second corresponds to the currently held meaning of self-evidence. First, something can be self-evident in and of itself without its self-evidence being acknowledged by knowing man. Second, something can be self-evident in and of itself *and simultaneously* self-evident for us. The self-evidence of the thing is then also a self-evidence of our understanding.[29] Now, God's existence is *not* one of those kinds of knowledge which is

---

expressed by the 'name "who is"' (*nomen "qui est"*) may not be understood as the opposite concept to God's essence (in the sense that "*without essence* it stands upon itself as 'subsistent being' [*esse subsistens*]"), which is demonstrated by Lakebrink's citation from the *Commentary on the Sentences* (I. sent., dist. 8. 1. 1. 4; Lakebrink, *op. cit.*, pp. 89f), apparently meant as evidence for this distinction: "They say that each name accords with its own determined nature, just as the wise man says something. But this noun, 'who is,' names absolute being and not being which is determined by anything else. And so John Damascene says that God does not signify something but signifies a kind of infinite sea of substance as though non-determined" (the 'triple way' follows). The distinction at issue here is not that between 'essence' and 'being' (*essentia, esse*), but rather that between 'being someone' (*esse aliquid*) in the sense of 'determined being' (*esse determinata*) and 'absolute being' (*esse absolutum*) in the sense of the infinity of an undefined essence. The early Protestant fathers defined God in this sense as 'infinite spiritual essence' (*essentia spiritualis infinita*).

28. *STh*, I, q. 3, art. 4, vol. I, pp. 30f.

29. "I answer that, A thing can be self-evident in either of two ways: on the one hand, self-evident in itself, though not to us; on the other, self-evident in itself, and to us" (*STh*, I, q. 2, art. 1, vol. I, p. 19).

self-evident in a double sense. It is, to be sure, self-evident in and of itself. But its self-evidence must then be made understandable for human understanding.

This thought sequence interests us from the perspective of the speakability of God. The question of the existence of God in this context is a problem for *talk* about God to the extent that the self-evidence of a content which may be formulated as a logical judgment consists in the judgment's predicate being contained in its subject.[30] If this logical self-evidence is not only to be valid for the thing in and of itself but also valid 'to us' (*quoad nos*), then all people must know *what* the thing designated by expressions which function as logical subject and logical predicate *is* (in its essence).[31] If, on the contrary, the meaning of the subject and predicate is not known to everyone in this sense, then the content formulated in such a logical judgment may be intrinisically self-evident, but for cognitive man it is not self-evident.[32]

Since God's existence and God's essence are one (as Thomas promises to demonstrate later), the statement "God exists" is self-evident in and of itself.[33] But since we do not know what God is, so that the "being-as-what" of this essence designated by the term which functions as the logical subject of the sentence is not adequately known, the statement "God exists" cannot be regarded as self-evident for us. Rather, it must be "proven."[34] But the proof *can* be developed only when that thing whose existence is supposed to be proven is not absolutely unknown to us. The proof still requires some means of proof. Since, however, God's essence is unknown to us, yet he is introduced as the cause of certain effects and those effects are known to us, the proof of the existence of God can be developed out of these causes.[35]

30. "A proposition is self-evident because the predicate is included in the essence of the subject" (*ibid.*).
31. "If, therefore, the essence of the predicate and subject be known to all, the proposition will be self-evident to all" (*ibid.*).
32. "If, however, there are some to whom the essence of the predicate and subject is unknown, the proposition will be self-evident in itself, but not to those who do not know the meaning of the predicate and subject of the proposition" (*STh*, I, q. 2, art. 1, reply to obj. 2, vol. I, p. 19). For this reason, Thomas rejects the premise of the so-called ontological argument; for it is by no means true that everyone agrees that God is to be understood as that "than which nothing greater can be thought" (*STh*, I, q. 2, art. 1, reply to obj. 2, vol. I, p. 20).
33. By asserting the identity of the essence and existence of God, Thomas is not 'begging the question' but rather referring back to Christian revelation; this is emphasized by O. H. Pesch, contesting G. Ebeling, in Pesch's essay "Der hermeneutische Ort der Theologie bei Thomas von Aquin und Martin Luther und die Frage nach dem Verhältnis von Philosophie und Theologie," *Tübinger theologische Quartalschrift*, 146 (1966), 177.
34. "Now because we do not know the essence of God, the proposition is not self-evident to us, but needs to be demonstrated . . ." (*STh*, I, q. 2, art. 1, vol. I, p. 19).
35. ". . . but needs to be demonstrated by things that are more known to us, though less known in their nature—namely, by His effects" (*ibid.*). G. Ebeling answers the question, whether the existence of something absolutely unknown can be queried, rather imprecisely when he says only that "the traditional talk about God" is "the presupposition of the question whether God exists" (*op. cit.*, p. 269). For that reason, his immanent criticism of Thomas's approach, which uses Thomas to make the objection that we "can never know what God is in the strict sense" (*ibid.*), is somewhat off the mark. It is *because* we do not know in a strict sense what God is that the "proof" via the effects is developed, and "traditional talk about God" is itself oriented to that proof from the effects. The traditional talk about God includes, namely, the "names" of God which are

We now turn to the other possible obstacle to a "proof" of the existence of God. If the statement "God exists" is an 'article of faith' (*articulus fidei*), it cannot be proven. For "what is of faith cannot be demonstrated."[36] Thomas bases this thesis in our context biblically on Hebrews 11:1: faith is related to that which is invisible. However, proof leads to knowledge: ". . . demonstration produces scientific knowledge. . . ."[37] For Thomas, knowing means seeing. That which is known (*scitum*) is something seen (*visum*). Through the inflowing light of faith, the articles of faith are *discernible* (understandable) in their truth by the person who has faith (but only by that person!), but the only reason for this is that the believer sees God himself in this light as the one "who reveals himself in the articles of faith illuminated by the light of faith," and who thus "lets one see" these articles of faith as "truths of salvation addressed by him to the believer."[38] The light of reason which makes knowledge possible is, by contrast, not dependent on the perception of God as that one who permits one to see what is knowable. At another place, Thomas argues the thesis that a thing cannot be both known and believed by a person—which obviously does not rule out that something which *is still* believed could be known in the eschaton, or that something which one person knows or sees could certainly "still" be believed by another person who has not yet come to know it.[39] With regard to the same object, faith and knowledge cannot be simultaneous, at least not in the same person. The contrast between faith and knowledge here asserted is exclusively to be found in the knowing person. In terms of the object itself, it is entirely possible that it can be taken in terms of both knowledge (*scibile*) and faith (*credibile*).[40]

Thomas rebuts this other possible obstacle for a proof of the existence of God by asserting that the existence of God influences the realm of the visible and thus can be proven by its visible effects; he then decides about this knowledge that it does not belong to the 'articles of faith' but rather to the 'preambles to the articles of faith' (*praeambula ad articulos fidei*).[41]

If, however, the existence of God is 'demonstrable and knowable' (*de-*

---

oriented to the effects of God, those names which permit one to use the meaning of the name "God" as a nominal definition: "Now the names given to God are derived from His effects. . . . Consequently, in demonstrating the existence of God from His effects, we may take for the middle term the meaning of the name *God*" (*STh*, I, q. 2, art. 2, reply to obj. 2, vol. I, p. 21).

36. *STh*, I, q. 2, art. 2, obj. 1, vol. I, p. 20.

37. *Ibid.*

38. L. Oeing-Hanhoff, "Gotteserkenntnis im Licht der Vernunft und des Glaubens nach Thomas von Aquin," in *Thomas von Aquin 1274/1974*, ed. L. Oeing-Hanhoff (München: Kösel, 1974), p. 117.

39. ". . . it is impossible that one and the same thing should be believed and seen by the same person. Hence it is equally impossible for one and the same thing to be an object of science and of belief for the same person" (*STh*, Second Part of the Second Part, q. 1, art. 5, vol. II, p. 1061).

40. "Nevertheless, there is nothing to prevent a man, who cannot grasp a proof, from accepting, as a matter of faith, something which in itself is capable of being scientifically known and demonstrated" (*STh*, I, q. 2, art. 2, reply to obj. 1, vol. I, p. 21).

41. "The existence of God and other like truths about God, which can be known by natural reason [reference to Romans 1:19 is made in the Latin original but not in the ET—TR], are not articles of faith, but are preambles to the articles . . ." (*ibid.*).

monstrabile et scibile) and not 'credible' (*credibile*) in the strict sense, then the problem of *talk* about God truly becomes a problem.

(c) Something is *provable* only when one can *talk* about it somehow. However, the proof for the existence of a God who is not immediately accessible in his essence cannot then connect to the definition of that essence. We already noted that "the question of its essence follows on the question of its existence."[42] On the other hand, if one wants to prove that something exists, then somehow or other one must be able to state what that thing is whose existence is supposed to be proven. Consequently, the concept which defines the essence of a thing (whose existence is to be proven) must be replaced by another *form of speech*. However, since in terms of both revelation and reason God is thematically a 'cause' which is knowable on the basis of its *effects* (if we cannot know what he is, we can still recognize what he is not), then the knowledge of his existence falls under the general rule of the knowledge of a cause based on its effects. The effect of a 'cause' permits a certain kind of talk about the 'cause.' Based on the effect, it is possible to state material characteristics of the 'cause' which give meaning to the 'name' (*nomen*) used to designate the 'cause,' without defining the essence of the thing which is being regarded as the 'cause.'[43] We are dealing here with a kind of speech which, based on its effects, gives meaning to the 'name' which designates the thing whose existence is to be proven.[44]

Thus, the approach taken by Thomas to develop "proofs" for the existence of God becomes transparent. An elementary worldly content, without which the world would not be what it is, can be taken as that effect of God from which the 'name' "God" derives its meaning as the designation of the cause of this effect. If the existence of this cause is proven, then the existence of the God who is designated in the 'name' "God" based on his effects is also proven. The special characteristic of this "proof" is that the "elementary world content,"[45] together with the logic attached to that experienced world content, requires that this content be thought of as a *context* of contents which would not have constructed itself independently but rather requires that it be conceived of as a construct. Thus, for example, the elementary world content of movement, in line with the principle that "everything which is moved is moved by something else," requires that a context of movement be thought which can be initiated only by a *unmoved mover* who is not part of the context of movement. "The world should[46] not hold me *in infinitum* so that it would replace God."[47] Or, to phrase it more like the Thomas citation: The world cannot maintain itself infinitely, so that God's existence must be brought in. God's existence enters in to the degree that the instance which constitutes the world context from outside of

42. See *STh*, I, q. 2, art. 2, reply to obj. 2, vol. I, p. 21. As a general rule, the statement is especially important since according to Thomas existence and essence coincide only in God.
43. ". . . in order to prove the existence of anything, it is necessary to accept as a middle term *the meaning of the name*, and not *its essence*" (*ibid.*).
44. "Now the names given to God are derived from His effects. . . . Consequently, in demonstrating the existence of God from His effects, we may take for the middle term the meaning of the name *God*" (*ibid.*).
45. Ebeling, *op. cit.*, p. 270.
46. Thomas would probably say "can."
47. Ebeling, *op. cit.*, p. 271.

itself is exactly what everyone means with the name "God," when they designate that 'first cause' in terms of its effects.[48] If the natural knowledge of God is to have any meaning at all, then it is self-evident for Thomas that God himself, as the Revealer, lets it be known through his effects that he *is* himself this 'cause.'[49]

(d) For Thomas, then, talk about God presupposes accomplished knowledge. God is brought *to speech* in that he is *named* on the basis of the world contexts which are *recognized* as his effects. Talk about God is a human *naming* which derives its right from the preceding knowledge of that which is to be named. The general hermeneutical principle that a thing can be named only to the extent that it is known also applies to God.[50] We can *know* God only in that we know him as the 'cause' of certain 'effects,' based on his effects.

The *natural* knowledge of God arrives, first of all, at the knowledge of the *existence* of God as the 'first cause,' so that then the knowledge of everything else may necessarily be ascribed to God *as* the cause of all things, far surpassing everything which is caused.[51] 'Natural knowledge' (*cognitio naturalis*) recognizes, accordingly, three things. It recognizes (1) that God, as the 'cause of everything' (*causa omnium*), is related to all creatures *in the relationship* of causing. It recognizes (2) that God, as the *absolute* causer, is infinitely *distinct* from all things which are made. And it recognizes (3), by considering points one and two together, that the *predicate of creaturely being* must be *kept from* God, not because of some deficiency in him, but rather because of his perfection far surpassing all things made.[52] The naturally gained knowledge of God presents him to us as one who is profoundly unknown. It acquaints not so much with God as with his Unknownness.

48. According to Thomas, the name "God" is generally used as a designation for a "universal providence," for which reason this name, as a word in our language, is fitting "to signify something existing above all things, the principle of all things, and removed from all things" (*STh*, I, q. 13, art. 8, text and reply to obj. 2, vol. I, pp. 126f).
49. Older Protestant Orthodoxy appealed expressly to the 'innate ideas' (*ideae innatae*) in this context. See, for example, the *Prooemium de natura theologiae* in Johann Gerhard's *Loci theologici* (ed. E. Preuss [Berlin, 1863], I, 4, Prooemium 17): "Natural theology is . . . *natural in itself,* which is made up of those common ideas which are innate to us, because God exists. . . ." When Thomas, at the end of the five ways, makes the assertion that "all call it God," or "we call it God," he is not expressing an anthropological consensus but rather "the judgment of the Christian faith about the results of the philosophical endeavor" (O. H. Pesch, *op. cit.,* p. 177). If that is true, it would deprive the entire undertaking of its character as *natural knowledge of God,* which leads us to be doubtful about this interpretation.
50. "For everything is named by us according to our knowledge of it" (*STh*, I, q. 13, introd., vol. I, p. 112).
51. ". . . we can be led from them [*scil.* the effects] so far as to know of God *whether He exists,* and to know of Him what must necessarily belong to Him, as the first cause of all things, exceeding all things caused by Him" (*STh*, I, q. 12, art. 12, vol. I, p. 109).
52. "Hence, we know His relationship with creatures, that is, that He is the cause of all things; also that creatures differ from Him, inasmuch as He is not in any way part of what is caused by Him; and that His effects are removed from Him, not by reason of any defect on His part, but because He superexceeds them all" (*ibid.*). This inner order of the natural knowledge of God is reflected in the sequence of the questions in that, after the discussion of the existence of God, the next point of discussion is how God is not, and then only is there a treatment of how God can be known and named by us.

Over against the natural knowledge of God, the knowledge of God which arises through revelation goes beyond this acquaintance with the unknownness of God in a very limited way. *In this life,*[53] the supernatural knowledge of God only brings the knower into a relationship with the God who is all the more unknown. To be sure, we are related to God through grace during our earthly life, but it is to a God who is, so to speak, concealed in his own light. Knowledge based on revelation is dependent on the *effects* of God, and it does indeed *improve* natural knowledge of God in that it allows us to know more and nobler 'effects' of this 'cause.' Beyond that, revelation with its *gracious effects* makes statements about God possible which natural reason could never arrive at, such as, that God is triune.[54]

If then the *knowledge* of God in earthly human life is always related to the earthly context in its natural and gracious effectedness, then, according to the established hermeneutical rule, the *names* of God are directed by his effects. Thus, the names of God do not express in language the divine *essence.*[55] Even the names which we give to God name him only in that they state what God is not. In that God's essence is *above* everything which we may know of God and name with words, God remains exalted above every designation given to him.[56]

(e) This seems to be contradicted by Thomas when he regards it as possible to make statements of God not only in terms of the 'negative way' and the 'eminent way' (*via negationis, via eminentiae*)[57] but beyond that, knows "names

---

53. In eternal life, by contrast, man can know God's essence with God's gracious help, and in fact he *must* fundamentally *be able* to know it. For it would contradict not only the faith which prepares one for the 'beatific vision' but also the nature of human reason if the latter could not recognize God's essence. For does not the human nature in its rationality strive toward the knowledge not only of the *existence* of causes, which explain that which is known to be as effects, but also toward the knowledge of *why*, that is, the cause in its essence which determines what is caused? On this, compare *STh*, I, q. 12, art. 1, vol. I, p. 92, with the beginning of Aristotle's *Metaphysica:* "All men by nature desire to know" (*The Works of Aristotle,* tr. W. D. Ross [Oxford: Clarendon Press, 1954], VIII, A. I, p. 980).

54. "Although by the revelation of grace in this life we do not know of God *what He is,* and thus are united to Him as to one unknown, still we know Him more fully according as many and more excellent of His effects are demonstrated to us, and according as we attribute to Him some things known by divine revelation, to which natural reason cannot reach, as, for instance, that God is Three and One" (*STh*, I, q. 12, art. 13, reply to obj. 1, vol. I, p. 111). Through revelation, God is known as the "highest cause" beyond his effects, which as such are known in the creatures naturally. Revealing himself, God shares himself with others as he is known only to himself (see *STh*, I, q. 1, art. 6, vol. I, p. 11).

55. "It follows, therefore, that we can give a name to anything insofar as we can understand it. Now it was shown above that in this life we cannot see the essence of God; but we know God from creatures as their cause. . . . In this way therefore He can be named by us from creatures, yet not so that the name which signifies Him expresses the divine essence in itself . . ." (*STh*, I, q. 13, art. I, vol. I, p. 113).

56. "The reason why God has no name, or is said to be above being named, is because His essence is above all that we understand about God and signify in words" (*STh*, I, q. 13, art. I, reply to obj. 1, vol. I, p. 113).

57. See *STh*, I, q. 12, art. 12, vol. I, p. 109; I, q. 13, art. 1, reply to obj. 1, vol. I, p. 113.

of God said absolutely and affirmatively, as *good, wise,* and the like. . . ."[58] The fact of such absolutely affirmative names of God is something the Bible reader can ignore as little as the believer who celebrates the liturgy. Revelation accomplishes its own validity. Thomas had to do justice to this fact hermeneutically.

The way he does this is in reversing his approach until now so that he now posits the perfect divine essence as the ground of divine causation. God is not called the perfect one because there are perfections within creaturely being, which is incontestable. Rather, because God is absolutely perfect, he gives to his creatures creaturely perfections. In that sense, he is to be called "The Good." It is not because he is the cause of the good that God is called "The Good," but because he is good, he goes beyond himself and grants being and goodness so that one can say with Augustine, *"Because he is good, we are."* [59] The absolutely affirmative statements about God, in that they name God, name him no longer merely as the cause, but rather they speak of God in such a way that the why of his causation is also stated. Since this Why rests within God himself, God is not expressed here on the basis of his effects, although not without reference to them.

Apparently, then, more is expressed about God than only what he is not. Thomas then expressly affirms that the names of God expressed 'absolutely and affirmatively' designate the 'substance' (*substantia*) of God, that is, speak of God essentially.[60] In making this assertion, Thomas is interested in then placing it under the already mentioned rule that our names of God are not able to express his *essence*. So Thomas immediately restricts this assertion, saying that the names which speak substantively of God are intrinsically just as imperfect as the creatures which, in their perfection, can only be regarded as imperfect images of the divine perfection when they are set over against the most originally perfect God. Even the names which speak 'absolutely and affirmatively' of God remain captive to creatureliness and thus state the divine perfection only imperfectly. *This* is the sense in which Thomas seeks to understand the Damascene's thesis: "The Deity, therefore, is ineffable and incomprehensible." Versus total skepticism, he interprets the thesis in this fashion: "Damascene says that these names do not signify what God is because by none of these names is what He is perfectly expressed; but each one signifies Him in an imperfect manner, even as creatures represent Him imperfectly."[61]

Thomas, therefore, has subjected the names of God which speak of him absolutely and affirmatively to his hermeneutic of the greater dissimilarity between God and the word which speaks of him. Even the names which express the perfection of God only imperfectly name God's perfection and imply that God is always the more perfect. 'God is always greater' (*deus semper maior*).

58. *STh*, I, q. 13, art. 2, vol. I, pp. 114f. When, in what follows, the "name" is frequently mentioned, then this is done in order to preserve the continuity with the Aristotelian-Scholastic usage. The term "name" in this chapter is not to be understood in the sense of modern logic.

59. *Ibid.*

60. "Therefore, we must hold a different doctrine—namely, that these names signify the divine substance, and are predicated substantially of God" (*ibid.*). It is certainly not a coincidence that Thomas now shifts from the term *"essentia"* to the term *"substantia."*

61. *STh*, I, q. 13, art. 2, reply to obj. 1, vol. I, p. 115.

The hermeneutical difference between God and the word which speaks of him is based by Thomas in this instance in a differentiation in the language process itself. In that *which* those 'names' signify, as they speak of God 'absolutely and affirmatively' ('what is signified' = *id quod significant*), they do capture the divine perfection and are thus validly *authentic* talk about God; the perfection of God of which they speak applies, of course, to God in the most authentic sense and in its most original meaning. But *in the way in which* these words exercise their naming function ('mode of signification' = *modus significandi*), they remain the captives of the lesser perfection of creatures and thus must be regarded as *inauthentic* talk about God.[62]

Thomas responds to the hermeneutical problem of the speakability of God, which arises here anew, with the doctrine of analogy, which we shall deal with shortly. As far as our understanding of the hermeneutical significance of the thesis, "Ineffable is the divine," and the theological implications it has, our discussion of Thomas's exposition of this thesis may suffice. What we have just treated should have made plain that talk about God is fundamentally understood 'according to the receiving person' (*secundum hominem recipientem*). Talk about God is defined itself by man's conditions of knowledge. Since language must follow knowledge, and knowledge is defined through the mode of being of the knower, the language which speaks of God always remains behind God to the extent that it is the language of speaking man, the language of the world. Every approach toward God, as close as it may come, always implies a still greater distance. The hermeneutic of the unspeakability of God appears to preserve the essence of God as a *mystery*. When theology speaks of God, it keeps him silent all the more.

But over against this impressive conception, the question must be raised whether it is not defining the concept of the mystery of God solely(!) through the limits of human knowledge. But is God a mystery because we are not able to know him adequately? Or is he full of mystery in his being? Does not a mystery constitute itself only through itself?

In answering this question, the relationship of nearness and farness, presence and absence of God will be decided in our talk about God. That the greatest linguistic approach toward God implies a still greater distancing cannot be looked on as settled as long as it has not been decided how God as mystery relates to the word which speaks of God.

62. "Therefore, as to the names applied to God, there are two things to be considered—viz., the perfections themselves which they signify, such as goodness, life, and the like, and their mode of signification. As regards what is signified by these names, they belong properly to God, and more properly than they belong to creatures, and are applied primarily to Him. But as regards their mode of signification, they do not properly and strictly apply to God; for their mode of signification befits creatures" (*STh*, I, q. 13, art. 3, vol. I, pp. 116f; compare *The Summa Contra Gentiles*, tr. English Dominican Fathers [London: Burns, Oates & Washbourne, 1924], vol. I, I, ch. 30, pp. 72f: "Wherefore as Dionysius teaches, such terms can be either affirmed or denied of God: affirmed, on account of the signification of the term; denied, on account of the mode of signification"). The words which speak of God's perfection imperfectly are spoken, as a result, in another sense of God than of creaturely existence: "the diverse perfections of creatures" (*STh*, I, q. 13, art. 4, vol. I, p. 118).

SECTION 16. The Disputed Mystery

a. The Question about God

Faith knows God as the ultimate and authentic mystery of the world. Yet at the same time, faith understands God as that which is most self-evident. Whoever has ears to hear and eyes to see would have to understand God. Would God then become bereft of mystery?

Mysteries awaken questions. That is an incontestable fact. But the more exact relationship between question and mystery is disputed. How does God as mystery relate to our questioning? Does he call it forth? Or does our questioning ultimately call forth God as mystery? How does man's question about God come about?

It is beyond question that one *can ask* about God. Thus we shall have to probe the possibility of the question about God to find out its origin. Where does this possibility for man come from? What permits us to ask about God?

The nearest answer to this question, the one preferentially given today, says that it comes from the questioning itself. In a certain analogy to the procedure with the "proofs" for the existence of God in the theological *Summa* of Thomas Aquinas, man in this case is understood as an essence which is led to questions through the world processes and his own life process. It is essential in man that he can and must ask questions. To question is human. But questions demand answers. However, as a rule, answers can themselves be questioned further. They awaken new, further questions. The more profound and thorough the answers are, the more probing the questions become which they provoke. Real questioning is not only radical questioning, but a questioning which radicalizes itself all the more with the assistance of the answers which are given. The one who truly questions, it is said, ultimately places everything in question— until, after so many questions about himself and his world, and on the basis of these questions, he raises the ultimate question about the meaning of his questioning and thus about meaning in general. "It is precisely He, Man, who drives me to the ultimate despairing question: why is there anything at all? Why is there not nothing?"[1] The last question, which seeks to do justice to questioning itself, places being itself in question as it raises the question of meaning. And thus it is asking about the ground which separates being from nothingness— God. In that the questioner experiences himself and everything else in ultimate questionableness, the distress of questioning turns itself to talk about God.[2]

The question about God is raised here entirely without God. It is raised automatically. The question about God arises out of questioning as questioning. Thus it is basically identical with the question about the meaning of questioning and thus about the meaning of the being of the one who must question because he can question. It lies within the flow of such an approach that the questioning

1. F. W. J. Schelling, *Philosophie der Offenbarung, Sämmtliche Werke,* ed. K. F. A. Schelling (Stuttgart and Augsburg: J. G. Cotta, 1858), II/3, p. 7.
2. As representative of the vast literature on this problem, I refer to the careful analysis of the structure of questioning which leads to talk about God which Peter Eicher has presented in his debate with Karl Rahner's corresponding concept: *Die anthropologische Wende; Karl Rahners philosophischer Weg vom Wesen des Menschen zur personalen Existenz* (Freiburg/Schweiz: Universitätsverlag, 1970).

form then directs all further talk about God. The question about God, if it really is to be the last of questions, gives its own answer. As a question which is automatically placed, it possesses nothing which it could query in order to get an answer other than itself alone. And all the more irrevocably it will then regard its own answer as valid. Questions which answer themselves because they were automatically raised signalize the end of questioning. In that sense, too, the question about God which arises as a forced question directs all further talk about God. It has at least a latent tendency toward infallibility.[3] The material aspect of the question is seen in the fact that the God who is articulated as a result of automatically raised questions is a God who appears to be a power absolutely removed from and superior to all questions. As such a power, it must obviously also be superior to all talk about him. Talk about God which is born out of questioning and thus tends toward infallibility can scarcely give enough attention to the hermeneutical distinction between God and talk about God in the sense of the absolute superiority of God over the word. It must appeal to God as mystery. And it presupposes a very definite understanding of mystery: Mystery is that which is inaccessible.

The explanation of the origin of the human question about God in man's ability to question, and thus his necessity to question, is countered by the phenomenological fact that questions do not customarily put themselves automatically. That explanation, too, must begin at specific processes in the world or in life before it makes the questions initiated in such processes into principles. To trace the question about God back to man as the essence which can and must raise questions, an essence which not only has questions but is ultimately himself a question, appears to phenomenological criticism as merely a variation of the Cartesian self-grounding of thought in "I think." The parallelism is unmistakable, up to and including the demonstration of the necessity of God.

If, by contrast, we proceed from the position that questions must be *summoned forth*, then the definition of man as a questioning essence is anthropolog-

---

3. It is indeed worth considering that a philosophical theology like that of W. Weischedel, dwelling so much in radical questions as it does, in spite of the necessarily postulated "hovering attitude," in spite of the understanding of God as "the source" "of radical questionableness" and as "the call to the question," in spite of the definition of "philosophical-theological existence" as "openness," still finally proclaims that "leavetaking" is the basic philosophical-theological attitude, and expressly explains: "Leavetaking" means "to gain distance from the questionable world." What else does that mean but no longer to be placed in question by the questionable world, while in the attitude of radical questionableness? To take leave in order not to return implies so much as to have made a definite judgment about that from which one has taken leave. This definitiveness is, to be sure, nihilistic. For what is the difference between an "openness" which realizes itself as unending "leave-taking" and an openness for nothing? If "leave-taking" is always departure "into the uncertain," then leave-taking has been made absolute as the suspense between destroyed certainty and principial uncertainty. In consequent fashion, the promise is made to the person who thus "conducts himself philosophically-theologically" that he "will understand himself as the language of God" (*Der Gott der Philosophen; Grundlegung einer philosophischen Theologie im Zeitalter des Nihilismus* [Darmstadt: Wissenschaftliche Buchgesellschaft, 1972], II, 255; all other quotations are taken from pp. 253-56). The author would probably then insist that, not in spite of, but because of his beginning with the radical questionableness of man, the infallibility of "the language of God" as the most actual possibility arises. It is after all the infallibility of absolute suspense, which is *always* true because it *never* says the truth.

ically suspicious. Before man begins to ask questions, he is already addressed as man—wherever that may be from. It is out of his being addressed that man starts to question. Questions which arise automatically merit full mistrust. They awaken the mistrust that wonders if they will not produce answers which cannot be grounded in anything else than the questions which preceded them. There are such "answers" which as such have their basis in themselves, and apart from themselves have no grounds at all. Why should a ground be given to them in that one makes the question as question into their basis?

The theological objection to this grounding of the question about God in human questioning is that it does not permit one to think of God as the one who speaks out of himself. Rather, God can be brought to expression only through the person who is asking about him. God is summoned up as the mystery which is contained in the questionableness of all being. In opposition to that, the anthropological point must be made that the man who asks about God is a being who has already been addressed by God, a being who in his questioning has already been justified.[4] The question about God would then be the result of a being already addressed by God. God is asked about, because God has already spoken. In this sense, we counter the obvious thesis, so frequently advanced today, of the origin of the question about God in the radical questionableness of human existence with the phenomenologically more obvious assertion: God can be asked about only because there has already been talk about him.

That there has already been talk about God is not to be interpreted in such a way that this already present talk about God is a datum already given with human existence. God is the one who speaks *out of himself.* To be addressed by God can therefore only and always be an *event.* The ontological relevance of the understanding of man as a being addressed by God presupposes, rather, the externality and event character of addressing word over against the addressed person. Otherwise talk about God and the question about God could not really be distinguished. A *datum* of talk about God, given with the existence of man, would, because of such an inability to make the distinction, necessarily lead talk about God back to the question about how, for example, talk about God as the Highest presupposes as a condition of its possibility the question about that which is higher and its capacity to be heightened.

The assertion "God can be asked about because there has already been talk about him" understands talk about God as an event which encounters the existence of man. This does not exclude, but rather includes, the fact that man enters existence as a word of God relevant to him happens to him and makes man a hearing counterpart. Man would then be ontologically constituted by that counterpart who addresses him. He enters existence as one who is called on, and thus as one who is acknowledged.

In this case, the word which encounters human existence, in which God is spoken of, is the event which controls the question about God. The question is raised because a word happened which makes God accessible for his own sake. All questioning happens because something is there and makes itself no-

4. See on this E. Jüngel, "Der Gott entsprechende Mensch; Bemerkungen zur Gottebenbildlichkeit des Menschen als Grundfigur theologischer Anthropologie," in H.-G. Gadamer and P. Vogler, eds., *Neue Anthropologie* (1975), VI, 342ff.

ticeable as existent. Thereupon the question is asked, What is it that is there—
qu'est-ce que c'est que ça? Such questioning is called Thinking. Questions are
asked because what exists discloses itself in its existence. Only to the extent that
it discloses itself can it also withdraw or close off itself. The sense of unrest
which then leads to questions always presupposes that what has withdrawn had
earlier disclosed itself. In that sense, talk about God raises questions because it
has something to give. More precisely, talk about God arouses the question about
God because and to the extent that God has disclosed himself as word. Talk
about God is then talk out of God.[5] It opens itself up to questioning which is
free from the compulsion to fix itself on itself and even to ground itself in the
structure of radical questionableness which is then itself an infallible answer. If
questioning is initiated by a preceding "answer" in such a way that it turns all
the more intensely to the event which started the questioning the more it understands and experiences of it, then the event which initiated the questioning merits
being called *mystery*.[6]

We have presented two possible answers to the question as to where man's
question about God comes from. Traditional theology has only seldom opted for
one of these two possibilities, both of which exclude each other. Rather, as a
rule it has claimed both possibilities 'without distinction' (*promiscue*) and then
sought to deal with the resulting aporia, with God having to be thought on the
one hand as the answer to preceding questions and on the other hand as the one
who speaks out of himself, by resorting to the distinction between the natural
and the revealed knowledge of God. With regard to the concept of God, this
aporia became manifest in the rationally drawn distinction between the existence
and essence of God, a distinction which for its part virtually had to provoke
reason to assert itself between the essence and existence of God, in spite of all
assertions that there was no real difference. It could do this either to mediate
the two parts correctly to each other, and it could be to dispute the existence of
a divine essence. Faced with such developments which derail theology, it helps
little to call on God as mystery. Theology, instead, should have seen its responsibility in preventing such philosophical developments from ever happening. To
appeal to God as a mystery is always too late. Man can only be called into the

---

5. See R. Bultmann, "What Does it Mean to Speak of God?", in *Faith and
Understanding*, I, tr. L. P. Smith (New York: Harper & Row, 1969), 55.
6. In his last lecture, "Die Frage nach Gott im skeptischen Denken" (ed. W. Müller-
Lauter [1976], pp. 28f), W. Weischedel provided a definition of the relationship between
radical questioning and mystery, which not only corrects his earlier thoughts, but also is
quite close to the position taken in this study. Weischedel writes: "It is not actually the
case that *we* touch upon the mystery, but rather it touches us. . . . The mystery is not
called for by skeptical questioning; rather, this latter encounters the mystery as the most
extreme reality which it can reach, which encounters it out of itself. . . . Radical questioning would never start if the mystery, into which it is asking, had not previously
announced itself as the impulse to questioning. Thus the mystery as that which precedes
all thought is what cannot be preconceived, what is in advance of all thought. . . . The
mystery as the unpreconceivable precedes radical questioning and makes it possible. There
would be no radical questioning if there were no mystery which attracts it." For me it is
all the more difficult to understand why Weischedel, with reference to the Christian faith,
thinks that he must restrict *this* concept of mystery to the 'secrets' (*secreta*) of the 'hidden
God' (*deus absconditus*) (*ibid.*, p. 30) and asserts that talk about the 'revealed God' (*deus
revelatus*) is contradictory to the concept of mystery (*ibid.*, p. 31).

mystery which God is. The Christian faith asserts that this is what has happened, and in doing so, this faith disputes the closedness of this mystery.

b. God as Mystery

1. There is a statement by the early Wittgenstein, nr. 7 in his *Tractatus logico-philosophicus,* which is widely referred to by theologians: "Whereof one cannot speak, thereof one must be silent." The sentence does not dispute that there is something about which one must remain silent. In proposition 6.522 it is expressly stated, "There are unspeakable things. This is *shown,* it is the mystical." Traditionally that about which one must remain silent because it is inexpressible has been called a mystery. This is regarded as a characteristic of all religion. "Investigation into the inner nature of all kinds of faith which concern religion invariably encounters a *mystery,* that is, something *holy* which may indeed be *known* by each single individual but cannot be *made known* publicly, that is, shared universally."[7]

This understanding of mystery is oriented negatively. Although the *negative* concept of mystery is also widespread in theology, we shall seek to show in what follows that a theology oriented to New Testament usage will counter it with a *positive* concept of mystery.

In contrast with the negative concept of mystery, the New Testament designates that to be a mystery which must be *said* at all costs and which may under no circumstances be kept silent.[8] Goethe's "So grasp without fail / the holy open mystery"[9] approaches quite close to the New Testament understanding of mystery. The phrase "holy open mystery" might well be taken from the New Testament (I Tim. 3:16). The public realm belongs, according to that, to the essence of the mystery. And another positive peculiarity of the mystery is that it wants to be grasped, and, as Goethe aptly notes, without fail, that is, *now*—although, of course, Goethe is referring to the mystery which presents itself "in the observation of nature."

Part of the structure of the positive concept of mystery is then, on the one hand, that it does not cease being mystery when it has been grasped. This distinguishes the mystery from the riddle which ceases being a riddle when one has comprehended it. Mysteries, on the contrary, cannot be resolved, uncovered,

7. Immanuel Kant, *Religion Within the Limits of Reason Alone,* trs. T. M. Greene and H. H. Hudson (New York: Harper, 1960), Book Three, Division Two, p. 129. Kant distinguishes (p. 129 n.) mysteries which are "hidden things in nature (*arcana*)" and "mysteries (secrecies, *secreta*) in politics which *ought* not to be known publicly" from the holy mystery (*mysterium*) of religion. Whereas *arcana* and *secreta* fundamentally are capable of being known to us, the *mysterium* is the "genuine" mystery, "and it may well be expedient for us merely to know and understand that there is such a mystery, not to comprehend it."
8. Speaking of the mystery, which man does not volitionally produce but which "encounters him and concerns him," G. Ebeling says aptly, "Such a mystery should not be concealed and kept silent by man, but rather should be perceived, preserved, and thus under certain circumstances be expressed in an appropriate way" ("Profanität und Geheimnis," *Wort und Glaube II; Beiträge zur Fundamentaltheologie und zur Lehre von Gott* [Tübingen: J. C. B. Mohr (Siebeck), 1969], pp. 197ff).
9. J. W. von Goethe, "Epirrhema," *Goethes Werke* [Weimarer Ausgabe] (Weimar: Hermann Böhlau, 1890), III, 88.

or exposed.[10] On the other hand, a part of the structure of the positive concept of mystery is that it is essential to the mystery that it permits itself to be grasped. Although it cannot be "resolved," it desires to be grasped. A true mystery draws us to itself and into its confidence. It allows itself to be known in confidence *as* a mystery. The mystery is therefore the subject of the process of letting itself be grasped: it *reveals* itself *as* mystery.[11]

One of the dark puzzles of the history of theology is the way in which this positive New Testament understanding of mystery has constantly been suppressed hermeneutically in theology. Talk about God is often understood in the tradition as mysterious talk. But it was thought to be mysterious because its object, God, cannot actually be known by our thinking. *Talk* about God is accordingly regarded as *inauthentic* talk.[12] This hermeneutical skepticism with regard to the speakability of God can be so intensified that the demand is made not to speak of God at all because our thought cannot genuinely know him. It is virtually a kind of theological self-commendation to introduce "God" as an unspeakable term. As doubly enlightened theologians, we have been taught that what cannot be *known* is something we cannot *talk* about. And "whereof one cannot speak, thereof one must be silent."

The negative understanding of mystery has far-reaching implications. If mystery is defined as that about which one must remain silent and really only can remain silent, then it is entirely logical to dispute the thinkability of God with Fichte. The strictest reference to God as mystery would then probably have to be a finger placed to the lips. The gesture is well known as an expression of Buddhist piety, but could well serve as the last gesticulation of European metaphysics. Any and every word would be too much for God because every thought would be too little for him. And objections to this result must necessarily place the mysterious character of God in question, if they do not seek to rethink the basic concept of mystery anew; in order to be able to speak of God rationally, an unmysterious God must be postulated. "Christianity not mysterious"[13] is then

---

10. ". . . A mystery is not something still undisclosed, which is a second element along with what is grasped and understood. This would be to confuse mystery with the still undiscovered unknown" (Karl Rahner, *Theological Investigations*, tr. K. Smyth [Baltimore: Helicon Press, 1966], IV, 108). See also G. Ebeling, *op. cit.*, p. 200.

11. Against Rahner (*ibid.*): "Mystery on the contrary is the impenetrable which is already present and does not need to be fetched. . . . It is the indomitable dominant horizon of all understanding, that which makes it possible to understand other things by the fact that it is silently there as the incomprehensible." That Rahner must define mystery as the "horizon of all understanding . . . that . . . is silently there as the incomprehensible" results with iron necessity from his basic transcendental-theological approach, which grounds talk about God in the questionableness of the question.

12. Thus, for example, Dionysius the Pseudo-Areopagite asserts that Jesus remained "concealed, even after he had revealed himself. . . . For the mystery of Jesus remains concealed and is not accessible to any concept or spirit; rather, even when it is spoken, it remains unspeakable, and when it is thought, it remains unknown" (Epistle 3, in Migne, *Patrologia Graeca*, III, 1069).

13. This is the title of a once well-known book by the Irish Deist, John Tolland. It appeared in 1696 and "made the name of its author well-known throughout England and on the Continent." Of course, the result was that it "cost him not only the prospects for a fitting place in life but also closed all good society in England to him" (E. Hirsch, *Geschichte der neuern evangelischen Theologie im Zusammenhang mit den allgemeinen Bewegungen des europäischen Denkens*, 5 vols. [Gütersloh: C. Bertelsmann, 1949], I, 296).

the motto under which talk about God is to be carried on. Now, whether God as mystery is to be disputed in the name of an all too eloquent enlightenment, or is to be honored by an idealism which crests in silence, with either option mystery is regarded as what cannot be thought and thus must remain silent. And whether God is affirmed or negated depending on one's definition of mystery, the decision is guided by an hermeneutical approach which understands the psychologically welcome recommendation, "First think and then speak!", as an ontological order. Before God can speak, reason must first of all have arrived at the thought of God.[14] The negative concept of mystery arises from a hermeneutical approach whose fundamental principle is the ontological priority of thought before speech. Here, thought is not only the principle of order, but rather the constitutive principle of language and as such ontologically precedent to it. Thought tells speech what it really has to say. That thought itself has something *to say* and is therefore always linguistic remains unconsidered. Rather, this hermeneutical approach maintains that thought leads to the speaking of what is to be said. What was not first brought to speech by thought and nevertheless was said anyway is regarded as inauthentically spoken.

Various consequences can be drawn from the theological implications of this negative understanding of mystery. These consequences of the negative concept of mystery, which have generally taken place or are at least possible, may be summarized in the following models with regard to their effect on talk about God:

(a) It is possible *to remain silent* about God and in that silence to *affirm* him, since he is totally unthinkable and therefore unspeakable.

(b) It is possible to *speak* of God as the one who is totally unthinkable and therefore unspeakable, and so speaking to *negate* him. This is primarily the way in which atheism answers the question of God.

(c) It is possible *to remain silent* about God as one who is totally unthinkable and thus unspeakable, and remaining silent to *negate* him. To deal with the question of God in this way would be that form going beyond mysticism, theism, and atheism which as the only real alternative to Christian faith could be considered, to the extent that this faith would no longer come under consideration, as *a scandal* in any way. As Christian faith, it would have been surpassed. For a faith which is in no way a scandal anymore would not be Christian faith, under the circumstances of the world. But as long as some find Christianity a scandal, they are taking a position which is located not *beyond* atheism.

(d) It is possible to speak of God as one who is not unthinkable in every regard and thus is somehow speakable, and speaking thus to affirm him: 'not in order that it be spoken, but that it not be entirely kept silent' (*non ut illud diceretur, sed non taceretur omnino*). This is the way in which theism, deism, and, in combination with the first model, the metaphysical tradition in Christian theology have dealt with the question of God.

The Christian faith, if it understands itself properly, can only protest against

14. Perhaps when Kant asserted that one cannot say, "*It is* morally certain that there is a God, etc.," but only, "*I am* morally certain," he was thinking of the necessary coincidence of these two elements, and then of a third: that I must come to myself if God is to speak and reason is to arrive at the thought of God (Immanuel Kant, *Critique of Pure Reason,* tr. J. M. D. Meiklejohn [*Everyman's Library,* 909] [London: J. M. Dent & Sons, 1950], p. 469).

each of these possibilities as well as against any combination of them. Neither the second nor the third negative possibilities, nor the first and the last positive possibilities are possibilities for the Christian faith. Whenever the theological tradition has associated with either of the two positive possibilities, then it must be thoroughly criticized. Theological criticism is relevant with regard to the two negative possibilities only to the extent that they have arisen out of the debate with the positive possibilities.[15]

2. The theological objection against the above-mentioned negative and positive possibilities for resolving the problem of God's speakability as a part of the question about God is to be formulated on the basis of the New Testament understanding of mystery. The hermeneutical approach which undergirds this understanding of mystery does see thought as the principle of order for language, but does not understand it as the principle which constitutes speech. This approach does not then imply that it is thought which first articulates what is to be said. Rather, it proceeds from the assumption that what is to be thought is preceded by what is spoken.[16] Speech calls to thought and thought follows after speech, thoroughly critical, and that means, critical of what is spoken. Obviously, not a temporal sequence is meant, but rather a material one. In terms of time, it is always a case of the coincidence of thought and speech, in line with Schleiermacher's insight: "Speaking is the existence of thinking."[17] Criticism of thought cannot consist of deciding about what should be expressed in speech.[18] Speech has its own sovereignty. This is demonstrated in the elementary

15. It is not a concern of Christian talk about God to present an apology (defense) over against atheism. The attitude of the Christian faith toward atheism which is preferable to any apology would be what results in occasional harassing fire and constant attentiveness to what could be of Christian concern within atheism.

16. See Ernst Fuchs, *Jesus; Wort und Tat* (Tübingen: J. C. B. Mohr [Siebeck], 1971), p. 78: "It has to be turned around: Speech is not merely thought's means of expression, but rather thought is abbreviated speech. Speech has the prior place, the priority over all thought." In the best work yet to appear on Fuchs, J. B. Brantschen has dealt with the function of this and similar propositions within Fuchs's theology; see Brantschen, *Zeit zu verstehen; Wege und Umwege heutiger Theologie; Zu einer Ortsbestimmung der Theologie von Ernst Fuchs* (Freiburg/Schweiz: Universitätsverlag, 1974), especially pp. 214ff.

17. F. Schleiermacher, *Dialektik*, ed. I. Halpern (Berlin: Mayer & Müller, 1903), p. 114. See also p. 73: ". . . the independence of pure thought is bound to the possession of speech"; p. 87: ". . . inwardly as well, every thought is already word"; J. Stalin, "Marxism and Linguistics," in *The Essential Stalin: Major Theoretical Writings, 1905-52*, ed. B. Franklin (Garden City, NY: Doubleday, 1972), p. 433: "Bare thoughts. . . , free of the 'natural matter' of language—do not exist."

18. M. Heidegger was one who "recognized language as the realm within which the thought of philosophy and every kind of thinking and speaking reside and move" (*Phänomenologie und Theologie* [Frankfurt: Klostermann, 1970], p. 39). But at the same time, he emphasized the critical function of thought over against speech: "Language speaks. Man speaks only in that he accords with language. . . . Language is an original phenomenon whose peculiar nature cannot be demonstrated through facts, but which can be perceived only in an unprejudiced experience of language. Man can artificially invent sounds and signs but can do that only in relationship to an already spoken language, and in derivation from it. However, thought remains critical, even over against original phenomena. To think critically means to differentiate constantly . . . between what requires proof for its justification and what requires mere perception and reception in order to be proven. It is always easier to give a proof in a given situation than to involve oneself in receptive perception in the other situation."

speech act of address. It is sovereign, even though it can be manipulated in spite of its sovereignty. It is not reason which leads to speech, but rather speaking leads to reason and to thought,[19] which then for its part has to preserve speech's own order, for example, with the help of the critique of speech.[20]

In this sense it is certainly true of the relationship between the thinkability and the speakability of God that God must first of all speak, if he is to let himself be thought. But every language which we know is human language. God, too, if he wants to speak, can speak only in a human fashion. But how can he still be thought of as God? The theological tradition answered this question by appealing to God as mystery, in its negative concept, and by pointing out the *inappropriateness* of our language for talk about God. It was taught that every human designation of God was inappropriate for him, so that every human word could only speak of God inauthentically. We shall debate this doctrine from the position of the positive understanding of mystery in what follows.

'Whatever is received is received according to the condition of the recipient' (*quidquid recipitur, secundum modum recipientis recipitur*)—so goes a scholastic principle.[21] It is indisputable. But how can one talk about God without missing him entirely in such talk? The humanity, or better, the worldliness of our language appears to make it a priori impossible to talk about God himself. If God permits himself to be known only when he has been brought to speech, if God can be asked about only because there already has been talk about him, then the impossibility of articulating God in speech appropriately is compounded by the fundamental questioning of the knowability of God. And there would be no other option left for theology than to ask about God within the schematic of the negative understanding of mystery, in spite of the New Testament's positive understanding of mystery as what must unconditionally be articulated in language.

The problem of the speakability of God has, in fact, been handled this way in the theological tradition. Based on the New Testament understanding of 'mystery,' there was no other option than to *talk* about God (I Cor. 9:16). The necessity of the "that" was indisputable. But if God can be spoken of only

19. To put it in F. W. J. Schelling's words (Introduction to *Philosophie der Mythologie, Sämmtliche Werke*, ed. K. F. A. Schelling [Stuttgart and Augsburg: J. G. Cotta, 1858], II/1, p. 52): "Since neither a philosophical nor any other kind of human consciousness is conceivable without language, the ground of language could not be laid with consciousness. Nevertheless, the deeper we penetrate into it, the more certainly we discover that its depth surpasses by far that of the conscious product."

20. Linguistic-analytical philosophy, which operates as language criticism, functions within the realm of spoken language. To that extent, "contemporary 'philosophy', coming from its extreme opposite positions (Carnap → Heidegger)," namely, from the so-called "technical-scientistic view of language" and the so-called "speculative-hermeneutical experience of language," moves toward a "still concealed middle point" (M. Heidegger, *op. cit.*, p. 39). See also the report by J. Habermas, "Zur Logik der Sozialwissenschaften," *Philosophische Rundschau*, Beiheft 5 (1967), and K. O. Apel, "Heideggers philosophische Radikalisierung der 'Hermeneutik' und die Frage nach dem 'Sinnkriterium' der Sprache," in O. Loretz and W. Strolz, eds., *Die hermeneutische Frage in der Theologie* (Freiburg: Herder, 1968), pp. 86ff.

21. See, for example, Thomas Aquinas, *STh*, I, q. 75, art. 5, vol. I, pp. 689f; I, q. 76, art. 2, obj. 3, vol. I, p. 700; I, q. 79, art. 6, vol. I, p. 755. As early as Dionysius the Pseudo-Areopagite we read: ". . . Divine things are revealed unto each created spirit in proportion [*kata tēn analogian*] to its powers . . ." (Dionysius the Areopagite, "The Divine Names," in *On the Divine Names and the Mystical Theology*, I/1, p. 52).

"according to the condition of the recipient," then ultimately it is only possible to speak of him inauthentically; silence is the only authentic way to deal with God. What nevertheless can be said about him is basically a silence which is made more precise through speaking. The ultimately unspeakable God cannot be reached by way of language. The only sense which talk about him can have is to cause, with the help of language, something like a self-removal of the inauthenticity of human talk about God and thereby to reach God himself at least in silence. The tradition defined by Dionysius the Pseudo-Areopagite accordingly attempted to encounter the linguistically unattainable God through a hermeneutical self-exclusion of language.

c. Silencing God through the Exaggeration of Language

How can human language be excluded in order to arrive at the unspeakable God? The nearest answer, "through remaining silent," is inadequate in that silence is itself ambiguous. If one wants to attain something definite, one cannot exclude language through unmediated silence, unless the situation in which this unmediated silence is to happen is unambiguous. But then this situation itself mediated the silence. Appropriate silence, which as silence is supposed to mean something definitive, must be introduced, must be mediated. Only such a silence is eloquent. Such a mediation of silence is indispensable if there is really to be silence about *God*, if *God* is truly to be silenced. For silence as such either conveys nothing or conveys more than one meaning.

The indispensable mediation of silence about God is not necessary just once but constantly if the danger should not arise that God should be *forgotten* and thus involuntarily *silenced to death* through a penetrating silencing which is mediated once and for all and thus constantly asserts itself in the future. Appropriate silence about God would thus depend on constant, renewed, necessary mediation. Who or what provides such constant mediation of silence?

That mediation which aids human language to be excluded constantly for the sake of a relevant silence about God can be provided only by human language itself. It is only with the help of language that a silencing can be introduced which is neither meaningless nor ambiguous, but rather allows silence about something specific in such a way that one can experience what is being kept silent and why. Human language must, therefore, exclude itself. It must talk about God in such a way that thereby appropriate silence about God becomes possible.

In some forms of monasticism Christianity has produced structures of the Christian life in which spoken expression has no other function than to practice appropriate silence. Theology has also designed a theoretical model which ought to fulfill the set task of moving through speech to correct, namely, to concrete silence. The classical path for such self-exclusion of human language for the sake of appropriate silence about God is that of negation through exaggeration or exaggeration through negation. This path is identified with the name of Dionysius the Pseudo-Areopagite.

Dionysius the Pseudo-Areopagite may be looked on as the father of so-called negative theology in that this theology has cited a few of his propositions in attempting to resolve the problem of the speakability of God by use of linguistic negation. Language's own possibility for negation was viewed as the hermeneutical method which permits one to move beyond the inappropriateness of human language for the purpose of responsible talk about God, precisely with the help of language. As we have already noted, according to Dionysius the Pseudo-Areopagite it is not so much the affirming but rather the negating statements which are hermeneutically appropriate for expressing the divine, so that such talk does not completely miss God.[22] The systematic implications of this approach are significant, among other things, because they dominate theology to the present day, and especially strongly in those places where no one notices that apparently revolutionary theological endeavors are really taking place under the law of a very old tradition.

The thesis which undergirds this theological interest in the negating power of language is that every spoken designation of God says too little about God. This is true even when the spoken designation increases a positive statement until it is a superlative. True similarity with deity is not attainable through positive designation, because deity exists "above all being and life."[23] But if superlative statements about God still say too little about God, then the attempt must be made to overcome the hermeneutical discrepancy between such superlative affirmative predicates on the one hand and God himself on the other by articulating in language the chasm which separates the worldly superlatives from God himself. One way to attempt this is to express the inability of even the most superlative predicates to comprehend God. This is not only a matter of negating what these predicates express as content, but of negating the adequacy of the power of expression (capacity of comprehension) of these predicates.[24] This negation of the adequacy of such expressions takes place through the express spoken negation of the articulative adequacy (capacity of comprehension) of all statements directed toward God. This negation expresses the chasm which separates these statements from God himself. Such express spoken negations of the linguistic sufficiency of all statements about God must always be made as the condition of human talk about God, if human words are really supposed to be

22. Dionysius the Pseudo-Areopagite, *De coelesti hierarchia*, II/3, SC 58, 79 (Migne, *Patrologia Graeca*, III, 141); see above, p. 234.

23. *Ibid.*, II/3, SC 58, 78, 38f (Migne, *Patrologia Graeca*, III, 140).

24. Although we intend to draw attention here only to a few systematic implications of the approach of so-called negative theology, so that we are not setting out to present an interpretation of the Areopagite, still we surmise that the hermeneutical preference for negative statements for talk about God in *The Celestial Hierarchies* is based not only on the negation of certain contents, but rather on the negation of the sufficiency of the power of expression of all predicates related to God in a general sense. For the point of the negative predications is the justification of the *dissimilarity* between human talk about God and God himself. The presupposition here is that there are, in the order of creatures, certain similes and similarities of the creative powers in God (see Dionysius the Areopagite, "The Divine Names," in *On the Divine Names and the Mystical Theology*, VII/3, pp. 151f). But if in all the similarity between God and the world, the dissimilarity becomes thematic, then God can most readily be "celebrated supramundanely" (*hyperkosmiōs hymneitai = supermundialiter celebratur*) by means of the formulation of dissimilarity, a formulation arrived at methodically, using the negation of the worldly being similar to him. Talk about God is then appropriate only when it withdraws itself in the very act of being done. In that sense, the only predicates which are proper for talk about God are those which state not what God is, but what God is not—*ta ex hōn ou ti estin, alla ti ouk estin sēmainetai* (*De coelesti hierarchia*, II/3, SC 58, 78, 42f, and 44f [Migne, *Patrologia Graeca*, III, 140]).

aimed at God in such a way that they lead talk about God over into that silence which is appropriate to him.

What are the spoken expressions of negation which might serve as express spoken negations of the adequate power of expression of all statements which focus on God? All those expressions might serve which point out "not what God is but what he is not." These include, above all, the negations of those acts which normally *grasp* the existent, that is, the negation of thinking, of knowing, and of speaking, or of naming. If thought endeavors to grasp God, then when stating the resulting predicates, one must state at the same time that such predicates do not have the adequate power to express what they are about: God is thought of, but he is thought as the one who cannot be completely thought; over against knowing, he is the Non-Knowable. If speech seeks to grasp God, then when stating the resulting predicates one must also state that such predicates do not have the adequate power to express what they are about: God is unspeakable; over against all speaking and naming, he is rather the Non-Word, the Non-Name.[25]

In this way, God is expressed, in fact, as the one who is infinitely superior to every predicate. And then one can affirm the three ways, outlined by Dionysius the Areopagite, by which using language one can move toward God, although not totally reach him. These are the classical ways, known as the 'way of negation' (*via negationis*), the 'way of eminence' (*via eminentiae*), and the 'way of causality' (*via causalitatis*).[26] For the three classes of "definitions" of God which emerge along these three ways do remain with their predicates in the realm of worldly existence. But by virtue of the spoken negation of the adequacy of their power of expression, which is always to be stated, that is, by using the 'negative way' once more on all three 'ways,' they are elevated infinitely above all earthly existence so that this negation achieves an unending intensification of the predicates, which actually are meaningful only within the realm of earthly existence.[27] Only when they no longer say what they really say, are they predicates of the subject God, and do they speak about him. The "definitions" of God

25. Dionysius the Areopagite, "On the Divine Names," in *On the Divine Names and the Mystical Theology*, I/1, pp. 52f; see above, p. 234, n. 13.

26. *Ibid.*, VII/3, p. 152: ". . . we mount upwards (so far as our feet can tread that ordered path), advancing through the Negation and Transcendence of all things and through a conception of an Universal Cause, towards That Which is beyond all things. . . . He is All Things in all things and Nothing in any, and is known from all things unto men, and is not known from any unto any man. 'Tis meet that we employ such terms concerning God, and we get from all things (in proportion to their quality) notions of Him Who is their Creator." The text discloses the transition to the Scholastic doctrine of analogy ("proportion"), which is expressed in the paraphrase of Pachymeres on the passage (Migne, *Patrologia Graeca*, III, 885-88).

27. The three ways to define God are not equivalent to each other in that they all require the application of the 'negative way.' If one does not apply the 'negative way' to all three ways, then the thought of God remains within the structure of that thinking which conceives of the world, in that God is definable only as the flawless ('negative way') summit ('eminent way') and ground ('causative way') of existence. God has thus been thought when one pursues the world, freed of all its flaws, to its basic ground by intensifying the world to its highest form. On the problem of the equality of all three ways, see F. Schleiermacher, *The Christian Faith*, trs. Mackintosh and Stewart (New York: Harper & Row, 1963), I, par. 50, p. 197.

prove themselves to be potentializations of his indefinability. "Apophatic theology asks, so to speak, just that much more than kataphatic theology can answer.
. . . In that the mysterious God *in and of himself* emerges and is known in faith, theology may not stop at the methodological moment but must inquire about this moment with a view to the emergent mystery."[28] Through *a rejection of language which takes place within language,* God becomes assertable as a "super-being" which is infinitely superior to all earthly being, and as the "Super-word" which is infinitely superior to all language he becomes, so to speak, silenceable. The actual function of this talk about God is to make possible a silence which becomes *concrete* through such talk. To that extent, the negative predications possess mystagogical rank. In them, deity is "celebrated transmundanely."[29] That silence about God which becomes *concrete* through them is basically the celebration of his absolutely superior divinity.[30] And that is a celebration which also elevates the celebrators above themselves and thus above everything.[31]

This approach, which conceives of talk about God as the process of making silence about God precise, is significant because of the possibility it opens up to interpret the *biblical* statements about God critically. The biblical texts ascribe, as it would appear, predicates to God in an almost naive unconcern, predicates which poorly fit into the context of an essence which is infinitely superior to all that exists. Especially those predicates which present God in a human fashion, as, for example, with reference to anger or jealousy, have constantly been felt to be completely inappropriate ways to talk about God.[32] The biblical texts present the problem of *anthropomorphism,* and do so drastically.

The same problem presents itself more subtly with those predicates which do not describe God in quite such a human way, in that basically the hermeneutical rule applies, 'Whatever is received is received according to the condition of the recipient.' So-called anthropomorphism in religious discourse has not been adequately grasped hermeneutically if it is understood only as a peculiarity of talk about God. Talk about God is anthropomorphic for the simple reason that language as such is that event in which man relates himself to his world in such a way that he exists as man. Thus every spoken utterance of man is anthropomorphic in the sense that man, whatever he says, is expressing himself either explicitly or implicitly. In that through language not only man turns to himself

28. J. Hochstaffl, *Negative Theologie; Ein Versuch zur Vermittlung des patristischen Begriffs* (München: Kösel, 1976), pp. 133f.

29. *De coelesti hierarchia,* II/3 (Migne, *Patrologia Graeca,* III, 140); see above, p. 256, n. 24. The celebrative component of negative theology finds its counterpart in the exuberant language which leads to concrete silence: "Often the pomposity of the Areopagite style has been lamented, or his almost superhuman language has been praised. Even Thomas Aquinas noted, '. . . because the blessed Dionysius used an obscure style in all his books' " (Hochstaffl, *op. cit.,* p. 143, n. 413; for Thomas, see the preamble of his commentary on *De divinis nominibus*).

30. Gregory of Nazianzus (Song 29 [Migne, *Patrologia Graeca,* XXXVII, 507f) speaks accordingly of the God who exists "beyond everything," to whom "everything sings a silent hymn."

31. See, for example, Dionysius the Areopagite, "On the Divine Names," VII/3, in *On the Divine Names and the Mystical Theology,* pp. 151-53.

32. F. Schleiermacher called it "the business of Christian dogmatics" to regulate these ideas of God enslaved in the finite "so that the anthropomorphic element, to be found more or less in all of them, and the sensuous which is mixed with many, may be rendered as harmless as possible" (*The Christian Faith,* I, par. 50, p. 195).

but his world is turned to him and he *experiences* that encounter, he also expresses the fact that he as man must first find himself and then, when he does so, he always brings more into that process than he himself is. In the very fact of man's relating everything to himself in speech he goes beyond himself so that he no longer can be taken in isolation, but rather must become the "measure of all things," if not through ignoring himself then certainly in looking beyond himself. Only because man can look beyond himself in this sense can he be the measure so that everything must appear to be related to him. In the sense of this human peculiarity of looking beyond oneself, not only human thought and knowledge[33] but also the entire area of language is anthropomorphic.[34] And this is an enrichment shared with the entire context of existence.

Normally, however, the anthropomorphism of human speech has been felt

33. See M. Heidegger, *Hinweise zum Problem des Anthropomorphismus in den Vorlesungen, Schellings Abhandlung Ueber das Wesen der menschlichen Freiheit (1809),* ed. H. Feick (Tübingen: M. Niemeyer, 1971), pp. 196f. In raising objections to Schelling's treatise, Heidegger remarks: "The most important thing in all positions regarding the 'anthropomorphistic' objection is that one admits at the outset what is generally cited anyway, which is that everything is measured according to the figure of man.

"But the questions really begin following and as a result of this admission. The 'anthropomorphic' objection subjects itself to the most incisive counter-objections in that it is satisfied with having asserted itself. What is behind it is the conviction, seldom discussed further, that whatever man is is generally known by everyone.

"But the dangerous thing about anthropomorphism is not that it measures according to the figure of man, but that it regards this criterion as self-evident and its closer definition and grounding as superfluous. The objection to anthropomorphism does the very same, but with the one difference that it rejects this criterion. The decisive question is raised by neither the users of customary anthropomorphism nor its rejectors, namely, Is not this criterion necessary, and why is that so? If one's thinking proceeds this far, then one sees that behind the dispute for and against anthropomorphism there are essential questions which belong on a completely different level. We name a few of these:

1. Can human thinking and knowing proceed in any other way than in constant reference to human existence?

2. Is the result of this fact that man remains the 'criterion' a humanization of everything which is recognizable and knowable?

3. Is not a preceding and necessary question, which must be placed, this one: Who is man?

4. Does not every definition of man's essence, as the question about who he is shows, go beyond man just as certainly as every insight into the absolute falls well below it?

5. Is it not a necessary conclusion of this that the position upon which man's essence is defined is neither man alone as everyone knows him, nor is it the non-human, nor is it the absolute which one so readily believes to be comprehended?

6. Does not man exist in such a way that, the more originally he is himself, he is not only and not primarily himself?

7. If man, as that which exists which it is not only itself, becomes the criterion, what does humanization mean? Does it not mean the very opposite of that which the objection sees in it?"

34. See Bruno Snell, *The Discovery of the Mind: The Greek Origins of European Thought,* tr. T. G. Rosenmeyer (New York: Harper & Row, 1960), pp. 191ff. Also helpful in illuminating the theological problem of anthropomorphism are Helmut Gollwitzer, *The Existence of God as Confessed by Faith,* tr. J. W. Leitch (Philadelphia: The Westminster Press, 1965), pp. 141-201; H. M. Kuitert, *Gott in Menschengestalt; Eine dogmatisch-hermeneutische Studie über die Anthropomorphismen der Bibel,* tr. E.-W. Pollman (München: C. Kaiser, 1967). See also E. Jüngel, "Metaphorische Wahrheit; Erwägungen zur theologischen Relevanz der Metapher als Beitrag zur Hermeneutik einer narrativen Theologie," *Beihefte zu Evangelische Theologie* (1974), pp. 71ff, especially 76f.

to be a deficiency which needed to be removed. But if language as such is anthropomorphic, then the only possible solution was to get rid of the deficiency of anthropomorphism by having language remove itself. Thus the hermeneutical direction given to theology by the Areopagite approach was to speak of God within anthropomorphically structured speech in such a way that the result was an appropriate silencing of speech. One felt all the more obliged to follow this direction as one found the more or less explicitly anthropomorphic language about God in the biblical texts, which was God's Word, to be a theological problem, which had to be resolved in favor of a theology which preserved the divinity of God.[35]

In order to arrive at this solution, the Areopagite approach required hermeneutical expansion. This took place through the theological reception of the doctrine of *analogy*. Among other things, its purpose was to abrogate the scandal of anthropomorphism; it did so through the negation, or better, the premise of the negation of the adequacy of expression in all human talk about God, by intensifying those statements directed toward God within human language. To the extent that an absolute superiority of God is supposed to be asserted, a superiority over the meaning intended in the human utterances, God can be asserted to be an entity which transcends once more all meaning of being: he "is" beyond the meaning of being. Since this "being" beyond is expressed *with the help* of meanings which are transcended in the act of utterance, this "beyond the meaning of being" can be asserted as meaningful, or at least as not simply meaningless. This is the imposing achievement of the old theological doctrine of analogy, which saw itself obliged to support the thesis of the inexpressibility of God. We shall contradict it, and in its place seek to develop another view of the analogy between God and man, but our reason for doing so is that biblical talk about God forces us to define in a new direction that classical doctrine of analogy. What needs to be done is to arrive at an understanding of talk about God which does not merely tolerate anthropomorphism, or which finds its inappropriateness appropriate because of the way it expresses the complete differentness of God, but which applies positively and from the outset the anthropomorphic structure of human speech. In doing so, the concern of so-called negative theology, which was to avoid understanding God as in any way conditioned by the world, no matter how sublime that may be, is to be preserved. Whereas the tradition we've described understood the revelation of God solely as the enabling of proper talk about the still greater hiddenness and mysterious superiority of God over the world, now God is to be grasped as a mystery which is communicable in and of itself in language.

In doing so, the dominant concepts of traditional thinking about God, the concepts of divine dominion, omnipotence, and supremacy over the world, are radically subordinated to the definition of God as love, a definition which expresses the divine essence more stringently. To grasp God as love, that certainly means to grasp God as self-communication. That, however, explodes the thesis of the unspeakability of God. For this definition, which both allows and requires

35. Negative theology, as practiced by the Areopagite, had also the function of justifying the imagery of Holy Scripture as talk about God which was appropriate in its very inappropriateness (see *De coelesti hierarchia*, II/3, SC 58, 78f [Migne, *Patrologia Graeca*, III, 141]).

that God's communicability be asserted on the basis of his self-communication taking place as love, prohibits the thinking of God as a silent mystery. And "that ineffability of the Divine Being" must not necessarily be replaced by "an explanation in due theoretic form," as Schleiermacher feared.[36] God is no more degraded or reduced in his being through his communicability than is a lover deprived of his power through his self-communicating love. All theological concern of this kind leads astray. It fails to see that God is not envious. Hegel was correct: "*Plato* and *Aristotle* were opposed to the idea of divine jealousy, and the Christian religion is still more opposed to it since it teaches that God humbled Himself even to taking on the form of a servant amongst men. . . ." Therefore, "it is absurd to say of the Christian religion that by it God has been revealed to man, and to maintain at the same time that what has been revealed is that He is not now revealed and has not been revealed."[37]

But with this concept of mystery, we have already plunged into the discussion before us of the material definition of God as love. We shall return to it in greater detail in the last part of this study. Before that, we must discuss further the more formal hermeneutical problematic. This will be done in an attempt to understand the *gospel* as the human word which *corresponds* to the divine mystery. We are seeking therefore a doctrine of analogy which is appropriate to the gospel.

In what follows, we must investigate the contrarily oriented classical figures of the doctrine of analogy, at least to the extent that we establish the possibility of carrying out the dispute about *God as mystery*. On the basis of the New Testament's positive understanding of mystery, we shall endeavor to arrive at a new theological usage of analogy, one appropriate to the gospel, in contrast with the traditional usage of analogy in theology. It is in the evangelical understanding of analogy that, in our opinion, the adequate grounds of the speakability of God are opened up. Using Karl Barth's terminology and receiving a New Testament phrase,[38] we call this 'theological use of analogy' (*usus theologicus analogiae*) the *analogy of faith*. But we understand this term, to use Erich Przywara's language, as a 'reduction' (*reductio*), or better, as an 'introduction to mystery' (*introductio in mysterium*).

SECTION 17. The Problem of Analogous Talk about God

1. The doctrine of analogy, which is of special interest within the context of the problem of the appropriateness or inappropriateness of human talk about God, which it would appear is always humanizing talk about God, is known

36. Schleiermacher, *op. cit.*, I, par. 50, p. 196.
37. G. W. F. Hegel, "Lectures on the Proofs of the Existence of God," in *Lectures on the Philosophy of Religion*, III, trs. E. B. Speirs and J. B. Sanderson (New York: Humanities Press, 1962), pp. 193f.
38. The usage, in what follows, of the term "analogy of faith" (*analogia fidei*) goes beyond the meaning of the Pauline phrase in Romans 12:6: "in proportion [*analogian*] to our faith." The Greek term 'analogy of faith' (*analogia tēs pisteōs*) has its own history in which the hermeneutical aspect of its meaning is dominant. A first examination of the history of the term is provided by B. Gertz, *Glaubenswelt als Analogie; Die theologische Analogie-Lehre Erich Przywaras und ihr Ort in der Auseinandersetzung um die analogia fidei* (Düsseldorf: Patmos-Verlag, 1969), pp. 49-86.

under the title *analogia nominum* ('analogy of the name'). This doctrine of the analogy of the name, or better, of the *naming*, must, of course, always consider as well which *existing thing* is to be named. For there is a similarity or an analogy of naming only where various existing things are expressed with the same word or are designated by the use of synonyms, and can thus hermeneutically be legitimately called by the same word. Thus the analogy of naming cannot be absolutely separated from the question of the being of what is existing. It implies, in some sense or another, an analogy of being. The doctrine of the analogy of being is known under the title *analogia entis*.[1] Plato is thinking of the so-called analogy of being when he calls 'proportion' (*analogia*) "the fairest bond" of all bonds (between what exists in constantly different ways).[2]

Although one must differentiate hermeneutically between the 'analogy of the name' and the 'analogy of being,' it must be noted that the two kinds of analogy are related to each other and in fact interpermeate each other.[3] For our purposes, only partial aspects of the many-leveled classical doctrine of analogy are interesting. We shall orient ourselves initially with several statements by Kant on this theme. In order to understand Kant's statements more precisely, we shall then turn to a few texts which reveal the Aristotelian origins of the doctrine

1. The term *analogia entis* has become an often cited although very seldom understood controversial theme of theology in this century through the major work by Erich Przywara on the theme, a work which cannot be admired enough. Although it has often been so asserted, the term itself does not derive from Przywara himself but from the Scholastic tradition. It has been known since the end of the fifteenth century, at the very least. See on that J. Teran-Dutari, "Die Geschichte des Terminus 'Analogia entis' und das Werk Erich Przywaras," in *Philosophisches Jahrbuch der Görres-Gesellschaft*, 77 (1970), 163ff. In his late book *In und Gegen; Stellungnahmen zur Zeit* (Nürnberg: Glock & Lutz, 1955), pp. 278f, the aged Przywara took ironic note of the controversial theological usage of the term and also of Karl Barth's pithy remark that he "regards the *analogia entis* to be *the* discovery of the Antichrist and thinks that one cannot become catholic *on its account*" (*CD*, I/1, p. VIII). According to Przywara, it was chiefly Karl Rahner who, in the German-speaking world, offered an impressive religio-philosophical interpretation of the Thomistic doctrine of the "analogy of having being." This doctrine is of special importance in our context because it educes from the *question* of being the answer that man as man is necessarily a hearer of the word, namely, of the possible word of God. On the basis of the analogy of having being, the anthropology which works through the question of being understands itself as "the metaphysics of a *potentia oboedientialis* for the revelation of the supernatural God" (Karl Rahner, *Hearers of the Word*, tr. M. Richards [New York: Herder & Herder, 1969], p. 162). The debate with the work of Przywara and Rahner would require another book. The thought process of our study, therefore, will restrict itself to an implicit dialogue which certainly is aware of what the religious philosophy of Rahner ultimately promises: that the person who must attend to the possible word of God as an anthropological necessity will, once he has grasped this necessity, not find it difficult "to recognize the holy Roman Catholic Church as the seat of the genuine revelation of the living God" (*ibid.*, p. 177). Such an expectation will lead the Protestant reader to respond to this understanding of analogy, which undergirds such an expectation, as a typically Catholic understanding, and to counter it with an evangelical understanding of analogy, knowing full well that the doctrine itself is indispensable; the ecclesiological consequences of such a doctrine could be perhaps more ecumenical.

2. Plato, "Timaeus," in *The Dialogues of Plato*, tr. B. Jowett, 2 vols. (New York: Random House, 1937), II, 31, p. 15.

3. On what follows, see G. Söhngen, "Die Weisheit der Theologie durch den Weg der Wissenschaft," in J. Feiner and J. Löhrer, eds., *Mysterium Salutis; Grundriss heilsgeschichtlicher Dogmatik* (Einsiedeln: Benziger, 1965), I, 930ff.

of analogy and then the theological elaboration of this doctrine provided by Thomas Aquinas.[4]

2. Immanuel Kant sought to answer the theological and philosophical question about how to speak appropriately of God by appealing expressly to the logical figure of analogy. In that, Kant stood within a classical theological tradition, even though he very likely was unaware of it. In the context of the question of responsible talk about God, Kant's appeal to analogy has special meaning because here that particular philosopher who thought it to be necessary to abrogate metaphysical knowledge believed that he could give a positive answer to the question whether God can be expressed in language in a rationally responsible way. After all, according to Kant, the "idea of God can under no circumstances be represented in experience. . . . God cannot be imagined perceptually." On the other hand, God must be "known after the style of appearance because all knowledge is bound to experience." Kant resolves the aporia with the help of the possibility "of representing the idea of God . . . after the analogy of appearances."[5] What does this mean?

The critique of pure (theoretical) reason had led to the conclusion for Kant that we on the one hand may not go beyond the boundaries of understanding with our judgments if we do not want to make irresponsible judgments, but that on the other hand we cannot dispense with the idea of God, which surpasses the empirical (immanent) uses of our understanding, if, for example, we are not to be coerced into thinking of the world as infinite, which would mean that the world were God. Then, the critique of practical reason had shown that for the sake of the proportionality of virtue and happiness, the existence of a God must be postulated who ensures us of that *unity* of virtue and happiness which the world does not provide. This presents us all the more bluntly with the difficulty of defining more precisely what the essence of God is supposed to be, and how it is supposed to be possible to define it. Thus we need the idea of a God who is distinct from the world without being able to say on the basis of our experience as what the essence of this God is to be defined. God can, of course, be thought of as "a mere product of the mind alone," as "an intelligible object,"[6] but that does not make it possible to define him more nearly *as God* with various predicates. The concept of God remains meaningless. "If we represent to ourselves a being of the understanding by nothing but pure concepts of the understanding, we then indeed represent nothing definite to ourselves, and consequently our

4. On what follows, I refer with highly selective reference to the plethora of literature and beyond the relevant works by E. Przywara to, above all, G. Söhngen, *op. cit.*, pp. 905ff, and L. B. Puntel, *Analogie und Geschichtlichkeit* (Freiburg/Basel/Wien: Herder, 1969), vol. I. In addition, see the essay by M. Reding, "Analogia entis und analogia nominum," in *Evangelische Theologie*, 23 (1963), 225ff, for the understanding of which the later corrigenda are indispensable (*ibid.*, p. 336). Instructive for me was the essay by G. Scheltens, "Die thomistische Analogielehre und die Univozitätslehre des J. Duns Scotus," *Franziskanische Studien*, 47 (1965), 315ff. E. Przywara especially commended the book by H. Wagner, *Existenz, Analogie und Dialektik; Religio pura seu transcendentalis* (1953).

5. E. K. Specht, *Der Analogiebegriff bei Kant und Hegel* (Kant-Studien, E 66) (Köln: Kölner Universitätsverlag, 1952), p. 12.

6. Immanuel Kant, *Critique of Pure Reason*, tr. J. M. D. Meiklejohn (*Everyman's Library*, 909) (London: J. M. Dent & Sons, 1950), p. 333.

concept has no significance; but if we think of it by properties borrowed from
the sensuous world, it is no longer a being of understanding, but is conceived
phenomenally and belongs to the sensible world."[7] To resolve this aporia, Kant
makes use of the schematic of analogy: ". . . no other course remains for us
than to follow analogy, and employ the same mode in forming some conception
of intelligible things, of which we have not the least knowledge, which nature
taught us to use in the formation of empirical conceptions."[8] For if we keep
ourselves "only at the boundary of all permitted use of reason," then, in Kant's
opinion, we can say something about God which is responsible and meaningful.[9]
However, this talk about God which keeps to the boundary of all permitted use
of reason follows the rule of knowledge "by means of this analogy."[10]

What is meant is that the concept of a God "lies beyond all the knowledge
which we can attain within this world."[11] Yet we keep to the boundary of knowledge of which we are capable within the world when in our talk about God "we
limit our judgment merely to the relation which the world may have to a Being
whose very concept lies beyond all the knowledge which we can attain within
the world. For we then do not attribute to the Supreme Being any of the properties in themselves by which we represent objects of experience, . . . but we
attribute them to the relation of this Being [*scil.* the highest essence] to the
world. . . ." Kant asserts that in such an approach we would avoid "*dogmatic*
anthropomorphism," but would permit ourselves a legitimate "*symbolical* anthropomorphism," which is legitimate because it "in fact concerns language
only and not the object itself."[12] We speak of a highest essence "*as if*" the world
"were the work of a Supreme Understanding and Will."[13]

Kant ascribes to language a hermeneutically decisive function for the definition of the relation of God and the world, and thus for the problem of the
thinkability of God. On the one hand, less objective knowledge is required of
language, so that language can permit the thinker more than can the knowing
which is directed to the object. Language is differentiated from the object. On
the other hand, language with its apparently small claim with regard to knowledge makes God first thinkable as God, so that we can then formulate a *concept*
of God. The "symbolical anthropomorphism" is the corresponding achievement
of language. Through such "symbolical anthropomorphisms," which are limited
to mere statements about relations, God is not actually known, but nevertheless
has been expressed in language to such an extent that "there remains a concept
of the Supreme Being sufficiently determined *for us,* though we have left out

7. Immanuel Kant, *Prolegomena to any Future Metaphysics*, ed. L. W. Beck
(Indianapolis and New York: The Bobbs-Merrill Company, 1950), pp. 103f.

8. Kant, *Critique of Pure Reason*, p. 333; here is a literal translation of the citation
used by Prof. Jüngel: ". . . there remains no other course to us than the analogy, according to which we use the concepts of experience in order to formulate some concept
of intelligible things about which we actually do not have the least knowledge"—TR.

9. Kant, *Prolegomena to any Future Metaphysics*, p. 105.

10. *Ibid.*, p. 106.

11. *Ibid.*, p. 105.

12. *Ibid.*, pp. 105f. In this way, thought keeps "exactly to the boundary between
deism and theism," so that it both stands up to Hume's critique of theism and avoids the
skeptical results of Hume's approach. See E. K. Specht, *op. cit.*, pp. 37f. "Properly
understood theism in the form of analogous knowledge of God is according to Kant that
natural theology which keeps exactly to the boundary of reason" (Specht, *op. cit.*, p. 38).

13. Kant, *Prolegomena. . . ,* p. 106.

everything that could determine it absolutely or *in itself;* for we determine it as regards the world and hence regards ourselves, and more do we not require."[14]

"Whatever is received is received according to the condition of the recipient"—the rule also applies here. But through this talk about God "according to the condition of the recipient" the infinite difference between God himself and the person who talks about God, the infinite difference between God himself and human (anthropomorphic) talk about God, is not silenced, concealed, or circumvented, but rather is directly expressed.[15] This happens through the analogical power of language. For, according to Kant, analogy "does not signify (as is commonly understood) an imperfect similarity of two things, but a perfect similarity of relations between two quite dissimilar things."[16]

Kant cites a few such analogies: "If I say that we are compelled to consider the world *as if* it were the work of a Supreme Understanding and Will, I really

14. *Ibid.*, p. 106.

15. Epistemologically the expression in language of this infinite difference between God and man means that analogy permits the remaining within the boundaries of mere reason. Through the analogy which preserves the infinite difference between God and man, man is referred from purely *theoretical* reason to *practical* reason. In *The Critique of Practical Reason* (tr. T. K. Abbott, *Great Books of the Western World,* vol. 42 [Chicago: Encyclopaedia Britannica, 1952], pt. I, bk. I, ch. I, sect. II, p. 314), Kant emphasizes that "even in the case where we [conceive] supersensible beings (e.g., God) according to analogy, that is, a purely rational relation, of which we make a practical use with reference to what is sensible," "the application to the supersensible solely in a practical point of view does not give pure theoretic reason the least encouragement to run riot into the transcendent." In *The Critique of Judgement* (tr. J. C. Meredith, *Great Books of the Western World,* vol. 42 [Chicago: Encyclopaedia Britannica, 1952], p. 602), Kant accordingly explains that "in the case of two dissimilar things, we may admittedly form some *conception* of one of them by an *analogy* which one bears to the other, and do so even on the point on which they are dissimilar; but from that in which they are dissimilar we cannot draw any *inference* from one to the other on the strength of the analogy—that is, we cannot transfer the mark of the specific difference to the second." The analogical *inference* is permissible only when we have "exactly the same reason" ("par ratio") "for putting" dissimilar things (in regard to the relevant definition) "in the same genus with one another" (*ibid.*, p. 602). The distinction between the thinkability and the knowability of a thing (see above, p. 105) returns again here within the phenomenon of analogy. In correspondence with his contesting the *knowability* of God, Kant also negated the possibility of *inferring* God 'by analogy' (*per analogiam*). God and man are never to be regarded within the same genus; God is, after all, not *in genere* at all. But this does not mean for Kant, as Lakebrink appears to assume (*Klassische Metaphysik; Eine Auseinandersetzung mit der existentialen Anthropozentrik* [Freiburg: Rombach, 1967], p. 139), that "no analogy of any kind is possible between the two" because of the missing identity of genus for God and man. In expounding this text, Lakebrink failed to note the difference between *infer* and *think* which Kant pointedly emphasizes. Kant then states, "In the same way the causality of the supreme world-cause may be conceived on the analogy of understanding, if we compare its final products in the world with the formative works of man, but we cannot, on the strength of the analogy, infer such human attributes in the world-cause. For the principle that would make such a mode of reasoning possible is absent in this case, namely the *paritas rationis* for including the supreme being and man, in relation to their respective causalities, in one and the same genus. The causality of the beings in the world which. like causality by means of understanding, is always sensuously conditioned, cannot be transferred to a being which has no generic conception in common with man beyond that of a thing in the abstract" (*Critique of Judgement,* p. 602 n.). We find the same argumentation in Kant's *Religion Within the Limits of Reason Alone,* trs. T. M. Greene and H. H. Hudson (New York: Harper, 1960), Book Two, Section One, Part B, p. 59 n.

16. Kant, *Prolegomena. . . ,* p. 106.

say nothing more than that a watch, a ship, a regiment, bears the same relation to the watchmaker, the shipbuilder, the commanding officer as the world of sense (or whatever constitutes the substratum of this complex of appearances) does to the unknown,"[17] which is called God. Involuntarily one is reminded of the corresponding expositions of Thomas Aquinas, even though the examples speak the language of another age. God is articulated as the "builder" of the world, as the "artistic constructor," or as the "commander" of the world. The name used for God in each instance is ascribed to the "highest essence" in another sense than to worldly builders, artistic constructors, or commanders—that is, in an analogous sense.

If one examines the examples chosen by Kant, then one notices that he always uses as analogies for the relation between God and the world relationships between dissimilar things which express *dependence*. God is called *God* through a comparison with dependent relationships. Apparently, when described by analogy, God must be expressed as that essence which itself is not dependent but rather totally independent in that God is that entity on which everything else depends: as the *highest* essence, or the *first cause*. The mere similarity of two relations between very different things is thus always presented as the similarity of dependent relationships, so that in the *analogy of relationships* a certain *relative order* is also at work. The concept of relationship which is presupposed in this analogy is expressly called "the concept of cause" by Kant.[18] In his *Critique of Judgement*, Kant then defines analogy ("in a qualitative sense") as "the identity of the relation subsisting between *grounds and consequences—causes and effects*—so far as such identity subsists despite the specific difference of the things, or of those properties, considered in themselves (i.e. apart from this relation), which are the source of similar consequences."[19] Two different kinds of analogy thus are intermixed in Kant, which the tradition was more or less accustomed to distinguish from each other. To make that clear, we shall turn to a few older texts on the problem of analogy, which are intended to acquaint us with the two basic hermeneutical models of the analogy of naming.

3. The two basic models which are known as analogies within the context of the doctrine of the 'analogy of the name' (*analogia nominum*) were given more precise analysis by Aristotle,[20] although he called only one of the two models an analogy. It has been shown that Aristotle was influenced by the older philosophical tradition, especially that of Plato and Speusippus, both in his use of the term 'analogy' (*analogia*) and in his development of the two models.[21]

17. *Ibid.*
18. *Ibid.*, n.
19. *Critique of Judgement. . . ,* p. 602 n.; my italics.
20. See F. Brentano, *Von der mannigfachen Bedeutung des Seienden nach Aristoteles* (Freiburg im Breslau: Herder, 1960), pp. 85ff and 108ff.
21. See Erich Frank, *Plato und die sogenannten Pythagoreer; Ein Kapitel aus der Geschichte des griechischen Geistes* (Halle: Niemeyer, 1923[1], 1962[2]); E. Jüngel, *Zum Ursprung der Analogie bei Parmenides und Heraklit* (Berlin: De Gruyter, 1964); L. B. Puntel, *op. cit.*, pp. 14ff; H. J. Krämer, *Zur geschichtlichen Stellung der aristotelischen Metaphysik (Kant-Studien,* 58) (Köln: Kölner Universitätsverlag, 1967), pp. 313ff, and especially pp. 341f; E. Heitsch, "Die Entdeckung der Homonymie," *Abhandlungen der Akademie der Wissenschaften und der Literatur in Mainz, Geistes- und sozialwissenschaftliche Klasse (AAWLM.G)* (1972), nr. 11, pp. 37ff and 49ff.

(a) Aristotle deals with analogy in several contexts, and among them in the framework of his analysis of metaphor. Analogy is a special case of 'metaphor' (*metaphora*).[22] Metaphor is the result of a transference in language (*epiphora*). The thought here is of the transference of a name to a bearer for whom this name is actually alien. According to Aristotle, such a transference of name can take place in four different ways, namely, either from the genus to the kind, or from the kind to the genus, or from one kind to another, or 'according to analogy' (*kata to analogon*). "Accordingly," such a transference is oriented to the parity of relations between two completely dissimilar entities, or, to put it in Kantian terms, to the perfect similarity of two relationships between quite dissimilar things. Aristotle says: "That from analogy is possible whenever there are four terms so related that the second (B) is to the first (A) as the fourth (D) to the third (C); for one may then metaphorically put D in lieu of B, and B in lieu of D. Now and then, too, they qualify the metaphor by adding on to it that to which the word it supplants is relative."[23] The presupposed concept of analogy is that of proportion in the mathematical sense of that expression (a:b=c:d). With the aid of such proportions, one can compare things with each other and name them 'according to analogy' (*kata to analogon*) even though they have nothing to do with each other as far as their *essence* is concerned. What makes them comparable is rather exclusively a *relation* here and there. Aristotle explains this: "Thus a cup (B) is in relation to Dionysus (A) what a shield (D) is to Ares (C). The cup accordingly will be metaphorically described as the 'shield of *Dionysus*' (D + A), and the shield as the 'cup of *Ares*' (B + C). Or to take another instance: As old age (D) is to life (C), so is evening (B) to day (A). One will accordingly describe evening (B) as the 'old age *of the day*' (D + A)— or by the Empedoclean equivalent; and old age (D) as the 'evening' or 'sunset *of life*' (B + C)."

To name something 'according to analogy,' it is presupposed that the transference (*epiphora*) is *understandable*. One needs to *know* that the shield belongs to Ares and the cup to Dionysus. Naming after analogy presupposes that the situation of those existing things to be named is well known. This situation must be one which is *commonly expressible in language*. If one wants to say something in this sense about God 'by analogy' (*per analogiam*), then God's *relation* to himself and to other existing beings (or to everything existent which is to be distinguished from him) must be correspondingly known. In this sense, Kant presupposes that the situation of the world's dependence on God is commonly known, so that talking about God "according to analogy" is possible.

(b) The other hermeneutical model of the analogy of naming which has been significant for talk about God is also oriented to relationships, but not to similar relations between dissimilar things. In this model, we are no longer dealing with the phenomenon of metaphor, which really belongs to rhetoric, but

22. Aristotle, *De Poetica*, tr. I. Bywater, *The Works of Aristotle*, ed. W. D. Ross (Oxford: Clarendon Press, 1952), XI, 1457b, 1ff. See on this E. Jüngel, "Metaphorische Wahrheit; Erwägungen zur theologischen Relevanz der Metapher als Beitrag zur Hermeneutik einer narrativen Theologie," *Beihefte zu Evangelische Theologie* (1974), pp. 88f.
23. *De Poetica*, ch. 21, 1457b, 16ff; see *Metaphysica, op. cit.*, VIII, Δ. 6, 1016b, 31-35; *Ethica Nicomachea, op. cit.*, IX, V. 3, 1131a, 30-1131b, 10.

rather with the logical problem[24] raised by the question, in which sense the same word can be used for different things without becoming a meaningless word usage. The point at which this question initiates is that process, which can be observed daily in our common speech, according to which words are used with many meanings. For example, the German word *Bank* can be used to name that framework on which one likes to seat oneself (*bench*) as well as for those agencies which today are violently misused frightfully often for illegitimate gain by robbers (*bank*). Aristotle also analyzed this phenomenon of the ambiguity or multiple meanings found in our language usage, and in doing so he made a distinction between three different forms of naming, of which one was later called analogy—although Aristotle did not give it that name.

The multiple meanings which adhere to our words in daily usage force a science concerned with unambiguity to clarify the various possibilities which language has to call different things by the same name. Aristotle[25] distinguished three different possibilities which become known in later terminology as the *univocal, equivocal,* and *analogous* predications.[26] Aristotle is starting with things. They are of interest, as far as their naming is concerned, in that different things are named with the same word. But this can take place in varying ways.

First of all, Aristotle distinguishes that kind of statement in which the same word (*onoma*) is used of different things with the same or identical meaning, so that the differing things not only share the same 'name' but also the 'word of the essence' (*logos tēs ousias*). That is contrasted with the precisely opposite kind of statement in which the same word is used of different things in a totally different meaning, that is, expresses a totally different sense in each usage, so that the differing things share the same 'name' but not the same 'word of the essence.' In the first instance, the word is expressed unambiguously for every existent thing which it names. So, for example, the term "living being" expresses exactly the same thing about humans as it does of oxen. And the word "human" says the same thing about all people. Every human can not only be called "human" but also fundamentally be addressed *as* human: the essential concept is the same in each instance. The word "human" in this case is correctly regarded

---

24. The distinction made here between rhetoric and logic is intended only to clarify matters. It was not first made until Aristotle.

25. Aristotle, *The Categories of Interpretation,* tr. H. P. Cooke, in *The Organon I (Loeb Classical Library)* (Cambridge: Harvard University Press, 1938), 1a, 1ff, pp. 13ff; see *Metaphysica, The Works of Aristotle,* VIII, Γ. 2, 1003a, 33ff; K. 2, 1060b, 31ff.

26. St. Thomas interprets Aristotle (Thomas Aquinas, *Commentary on the Metaphysics of Aristotle,* tr. J. P. Rowan [Chicago: H. Regnery Company, 1961], bk. IV, lesson 1, nr. 535, pp. 217f): "But it must be noted that a term is predicated of different things in various senses. Sometimes it is predicated of them according to a meaning which is entirely the same, and then it is said to be predicated of them univocally, as animal is predicated of a horse and of an ox. Sometimes it is predicated of them according to meanings which are entirely different, and then it is said to be predicated of them equivocally, as dog is predicated of a star and of an animal. And sometimes it is predicated of them according to meanings which are partly different and partly not (different inasmuch as they imply different relationships, and the same inasmuch as these different relationship are referred to one and the same thing), and then it is said 'to be predicated analogously,' i.e., proportionally, according as each one by its own relationship is referred to that one same thing." On the interpretation of St. Thomas' text, see G. Scheltens, *op. cit.,* pp. 317f.

as 'univocal' (*synōnymōs, univoce*). It is a word used in a simple, identical sense, a *monachōs legomenon*. In the second instance, the word is used in a completely different meaning of each existent thing which it names. Thus, for example, the word "living being" expresses something else when used for a painted figure of a person than for a living person, just as the German word *Bank* is used for two completely different things, depending on its application. Every *Bank* (bench) in the park can be called that, just as every *Bank* (bank) with its cashiers' windows can be called that. But neither of them can ever be called *Bank* with the same meaning of the word. The one usage cannot keep the promises made by the other: the essential concept is different in each instance. The word *Bank* in this case is used 'equivocally' (*homōnymōs, aequivoce*).[27] It is one of those words which is used with many meanings, one of the *pollachōs legomena*.[28]

But, according to Aristotle, there is something in the middle between equivocity and univocity, which is so-called *analogous* speech, in which the same word can be used for different things without the meaning of the word having to be completely identical or completely different. There is analogy present, in this sense, when the same word is used of differing things without being totally identical in meaning (univocal) nor totally and extremely different in meaning (equivocally), but rather expressing some things as the same, and others as different. Those different things named by the same word are addressed not in the same sense but in a *similar* sense. This similarity is based on the fact that the same word addresses the various things which it names on the basis of *something mutual to which they are all related,* each in a different way.

Therefore, in the model of analogy, the same word has relatively different meanings[29] in its various usages but still these meanings are all related to *one identical thing,* on the basis of which the varying usage of the word is justified as similar usage. This *one thing* to which the various things called by the same word are related is then the hermeneutical *first thing,* on the basis of which and in relation to which other things can also be named. Aristotle calls these namings 'paronyms' (*parōnyma,* i.e., a derived word), in distinction from 'synōnyma' and 'homōnyma.' A word which functions paronymously belongs to the 'hom-

---

27. The terminological distinction between 'homonym' and 'synonym,' which is obviously somewhat differently oriented, derives "from Speusippus and is arbitrarily established by usage in daily language: both words were previously used in the same sense, as far as '*synōnymos*' was in usage at all." Aristotle distinguishes in a way different from Speusippus, but does reveal at times "some dependence upon Speusippus' terminology" (E. Heitsch, *op. cit.,* p. 57, n. 2; see pp. 71f).

28. Aristotle analyzes *language usage*: In the many usages of the same word he does not see an arbitrariness of language but rather a substantial content which is forcing itself into language. Thus, for example, the analysis of the various meanings of the word *on* ('to be') leads to the exposition of ontological contents (*Metaphysica, op. cit.,* Z. 1, 1028a, 10: "There are several senses in which a thing may be said to 'be' . . ."). See F. Brentano, *op. cit.*

29. G. Scheltens (*op. cit.,* pp. 317f) emphasizes that for Thomas, in contrast to Cajetan, for example, the analogously predicated name is not the expression of a concept which permits a certain variation of meaning within its inherent unity, so that Thomas' doctrine of analogy is not phased by Duns Scotus' critique, which disputes that such concepts even exist. For Thomas, rather, analogous predications are "the predication of a common word which in its various applications also covers a different concept."

onyms,' and also to the words of many meanings (*pollachōs legomena*), but is often used in another way than the word which names different things homonymously.[30] For example, the human body is called "healthy"; medicine, urine, the color of one's face, and the clothing which protects health can, however, also be called "healthy," although they are totally different things. In spite of their difference, it is entirely correct to call them "healthy" in an analogous sense, because they all are related to one identical thing, each in its own way. Urine is related to health in that it *demonstrates* that the corresponding organism is healthy. Medicine is related to health in that it *effects* the health of the body. The body relates to health, in that it *is* (or has been made) healthy. Health itself is the *prōton hygieinon* ('first health') as the principle and ground for healthy being. The reason for the analogous namings then consists of the fact that *different* things have *different relations* to a *common thing,* on which as the ontological first thing "the other things depend, and in virtue of which they get their names."[31]

4. Now if we return to the first model of analogy, the one expressly called 'analogia' by Aristotle, then we see that there is an agreement between the two models insofar as in each instance there is a naming based on relations. Whereas in the first model two similar (identical) relations between totally dissimilar things allow the naming by analogy, in the second model the different relations of differing things to one common thing legitimize the assertion of an analogous meaning of the same word which is used for these different things. The first model of analogy understands analogy to be a proportion which, on the basis of similar (identical) relations between dissimilar things, allows comparison with each other within the relations of relations. Thus one speaks of an *analogy of proportionality,* an *analogia (proportio) proportionalitatis*. The second model of analogy understands analogy, on the basis of the noncomparable relations of different things to the one thing they have in common, as *simple analogy of relation (analogia proportionis)* or also the *analogy of attribution,*[32] that is, as the dependence of different things on one common thing in varying relations. If, in the analogy of proportionality, A relates to B as C to D, then in the analogy of attribution, B, C, and D all relate in varying ways to A, on the basis of which they are commonly named. If "the same proportion of two things to a third" is the rule in the first instance, then we could borrow from Thomas and say of the

30. Aristotle, *Metaphysica, op. cit.,* Γ, 1003a, 33ff. He is discussing the non-homonymous ways of speaking of "related to one central point," which are not in every way identical with the 'paronyma.' On this problem, see J. Hirschberger, "Paronymie und Analogie bei Aristoteles," *Philosophisches Jahrbuch der Görres-Gesellschaft,* 68 (1959), 191ff; H. J. Krämer, *op. cit.,* pp. 338ff.
31. Aristotle, *Metaphysica, op. cit.,* Γ. 2, 1003b, 16f.
32. On the development of the term 'analogy of attribution' (*analogia attributionis*), see L. B. Puntel, *op. cit.,* p. 39, n. 18. The expression probably goes back to the Latin translation of the Greek *pros hen* with *attribuere:* "That is said to be predicated analogically which is predicated of many things whose reasons and definitions vary but which are *attributed* to the same thing" (compare Aristotle, *Metaphysica, op. cit.,* Γ. 2, 1003a, 33, with Thomas Aquinas, *De principiis naturae,* in *Opuscula Philosophica,* ed. R. M. Spiazzi (Torino-Rome, 1954), cap. 6, nr. 366).

second instance, "which related in different ways to the same thing,"[33] or to quote Thomas, "but the name which is thus used in a multiple [*scil.* analogical] sense signifies various proportions to some one thing."[34]

Now, however, we must point out a special peculiarity of the analogy of attribution by virtue of which it is significantly different from the pure analogy of relation (*analogia proportionalitatis*). Whereas the analogy of proportionality requires nothing of the proportions except their correspondence, the analogy of attribution or the analogy of relation presupposes that the 'many things' (*multa*), which each have different relations to the one thing they have in common (the *unum*), are all related to that one common thing in a relationship of *dependence*. The differing proportions of the different things are definitely ordered relationships because of the dependence with which they are related to the one thing. The one common thing is hermeneutically the first thing to which the differing things which are called by the same word are ordered in this naming. Thus the 'analogy of attribution' is also called the *analogy of order*,[35] whereby the hermeneutical order is primarily meant that this analogy is constituted by an *analogans* ('one who makes the analogy') on which the thing named after it depends as the *analogatum* ('that which is analogized').

We find as early as Aristotle the analysis of the dependence relationship as the reason for naming different things by the same word. To describe the

33. In his commentary on Aristotle's *Metaphysica* (*op. cit.*, Δ.6, 1016b, 31ff), Thomas says, "any two things are related in different ways to one third thing" (*Commentary on the Metaphysics of Aristotle*, bk. V, lesson 8, nr. 879, p. 341). To distinguish the two models of analogy, one follows Thomas in contrasting the analogy 'according to differing proportions to the same subject' (*secundum proportiones diversas ad idem subiectum*) (*analogia attributionis*) and the analogy 'according to one proportion of two things to different subjects' (*secundum unam proportionem duorum ad diversa subiecta*) (*analogia proportionalitatis*); compare Thomas Aquinas, *Commentary on the Nicomachean Ethics*, tr. C. I. Litzinger (Chicago: H. Regnery Company, 1964), bk. I, lecture 7, nr. 96, p. 41, and Aristotle, *Ethica Nicomachea, op. cit.*, I. 6, 1096b, 25ff. Accordingly, G. Patzig makes this distinction: "Paronymy . . . is a relationship between objects which exists when the objects (a) are designated with the same term and (b) are defined through their varying relationship to an *identical thing*, the 'first in every category.' By contrast, there is, according to Aristotle, an analogy between objects when (a) they are designated by the same term and (b) can be defined by their *identical* relationships to *something different*" (G. Patzig, "Theologie und Ontologie in der 'Metaphysik' des Aristoteles" [*Kant-Studien*, 52] [Köln: Kölner Universitätsverlag, 1960/61], pp. 204f).

On the development of the term "analogy" from its original function as the designation of the 'proportion of proportionality' to its later function as the designation as well for the so-called 'analogy of attribution,' see L. B. Puntel, *op. cit.*, pp. 22-27 and 38-40. According to G. Scheltens, Thomas did teach the 'analogy of proportionality' in *De Veritate*, but those passages should not be heavily weighted with regard to his understanding of analogous predication. Whereas Cajetan based his entire interpretation of the Thomistic doctrine of analogy on those passages, *De Veritate* reveals only a point of view which Thomas gave up as soon as he expressed it. "It really only appears clearly in *De Veritate*, but also begins to disappear there" (*op. cit.*, p. 320). If the interpretation which I now present is correct, then the material here will have to be evaluated in a more differentiated fashion.

34. Thomas, *STh*, I, q. 13, art. 5, vol. I, p. 120.

35. Later Thomas says "usually '*respectus ad unum*,' '*ordo ad unum*,' etc.," instead of *attributio* (L. B. Puntel, *op. cit.*, n. 18).

lingual-logical relationship of different things which are "referred to something single and common,"[36] on which everything else depends and after which it is named,[37] he uses the term 'anagoge' (*anagōgē*). Under the influence of Neo-Platonic commentaries on Aristotle, the aspect of dependence was translated from the logical and hermeneutical context to the ontological during the period of Scholasticism, so that the hermeneutical dependence of any *analogatum* on the *analogans* flowed over into the ontological dimension of dependency of being. The hermeneutical first thing appears as the ontological origin which under certain circumstances can also be thought of as the ontic causer. The so-called analogy of attribution now functions in such a way that the *analogans* possesses what is meant with the same word more originally than the other things named by the same word and thus appears as the cause in a causal nexus. In this sense, Dionysius the Areopagite stated that it was "meet that we employ such terms concerning God, and we get from all things (in proportion to their quality) notions of Him Who is their Creator."[38]

Analogy thus understood gained special significance in Thomas Aquinas for human talk about God and still determines Kant's usage of analogy in the context of the formation of concepts which are appropriate for God.

5. Thomas Aquinas used analogy, understood as the middle point between univocity and equivocity, in order to answer the question in which sense we can use common affirmative predicates, taken from the world's language for the naming of creaturely being, to speak of God.[39] One must reject the 'names' (*nomina*) which *univocally* may be ascribed both to God and the creatures, because then God would not be adequately distinguished, as the highest cause, from everything which he had caused.[40] But since, on the other hand, we do know God *from his creatures,* it cannot be said that such 'names' of God and creatures can only be expressed *equivocally.*[41] The only way out remaining is

36. Aristotle, *Metaphysica, op. cit.,* K. 3, 1061a, 11.

37. *Ibid.,* Γ. 2, 1003b, 16f.

38. Dionysius the Areopagite, *On the Divine Names and the Mystical Theology* (*Translations of Christian Literature,* Series 1), tr. C. E. Rolt (New York: Macmillan, 1920), VII/3, p. 152. We already made reference to the paraphrase of Pachymeres (Migne, *Patrologia Graeca,* III, 885ff), so important for the doctrine of analogy (see above, p. 257, n. 26).

39. Out of the vast literature on the Thomistic understanding of analogy, I will mention only the book by H. Lyttkens, *The Analogy Between God and the World; An Investigation of Its Background and Interpretation of Its Use by Thomas of Aquino* (Uppsala: Almqvist & Wiksells, 1952).

40. "Univocal predication is impossible between God and creatures. The reason for this is that every effect which is not a proportioned result of the power of the efficient cause receives the similitude of the agent not in its full degree, but in a measure that falls short" (*STh,* I, q. 13, art. 5, vol. I, pp. 119f). See the further reasoning in *The Summa Contra Gentiles,* vol. I, I, ch. 32, pp. 76f.

41. "Neither, on the other hand, are names applied to God and creatures in a purely equivocal sense. . . . Because if that were so, it follows that from creatures nothing at all could be known or demonstrated about God; for the reasoning would always be exposed to the fallacy of equivocation" (*STh, loc. cit.*). See here also the further reasoning in *The Summa Contra Gentiles,* vol. I, I, ch. 33, pp. 78f. Luther was similar to Thomas in his adherence to the rule that equivocation calls forth false assertions. See, for example, "All equivocation is the mother of errors" (*Disputatio de sententia: Verbo caro factum est [1539] [WA,* 39/II, 28, 28]).

that such 'names' for God and the creatures are to be expressed "in an *analogous* sense, that is, according to proportion."[42]

Completely independent of the question of talk about God, Thomas makes a general hermeneutical distinction with regard to the common naming 'according to analogy (proportion),' a division into two different kinds of analogy based on the *number* of different things related to the one identical thing. There is either a dominant relation of the *many* to the *one* or there is one sole and dominant relation of the *one* to *others*.[43] Since it is always presupposed that at least two different things have two different relations to the one common thing, in the second instance the one thing (*unum*) might relate to itself as that one common thing to which the other one relates itself in another fashion.

The examples which Thomas uses clarify the difference. Thomas chooses the examples, already found in Aristotle, of the human body, medicine, and urine, all of which can be called "healthy." The one thing to which all three things are related is, for Thomas, health per se, but it is thought of as subsisting in a definite existing thing. The 'one thing' (*unum*) is in a concretely existing being.

In the first instance of analogy, therefore, the health of the body is the *unum* to which healing medication and the urine which indicates health are ordered.[44] The 'one thing,' which may be regarded here as the hermeneutical first thing and provides a reason for naming other existing things the way this 'one thing' is named, is exclusively thematic as a first thing in the *order of knowing*. That accords with Thomas' hermeneutical rule that the order of language is to follow the order of knowing.[45] If in the *order of knowing* the health

42. *Ibid.*; compare *The Summa Contra Gentiles*, vol. I, I, ch. 34, p. 79: ". . . they are relinquished because . . . those things which are said of God and other things are predicated neither univocally nor equivocally, but analogically; that is, according to an order or relation to some one thing."

43. "Therefore it must be said that these names are said of God and creatures in an *analogous* sense, that is, according to proportion. This can happen in two ways: either according as many things are proportioned to one . . . or according as one thing is proportioned to another" (*STh, loc. cit.*). Compare the more extensive differentiation in *The Summa Contra Gentiles*, vol. I, I, ch. 34, p. 79: ". . . analogically, that is according to an order of relation to some one thing. This happens in two ways. *First,* according as many things have a relation to some one thing: thus in relation to the one health, an animal is said to be *healthy* as its subject, medicine as effective thereof, food as preserving it, and urine as its sign. *Secondly,* according as order or relation of two things may be observed, not to some other thing, but to one of them: thus being is said of substance and accident, in so far as accident bears a relation to substance, and not as though substance and accident were referred to a third thing." Just as in the theological *Summa*, Thomas declares here that the first form of the 'analogy attribution' cannot be considered for talk about God: "Accordingly such names are not said of God and other things analogically in the first way, for it would be necessary to suppose something previous to God, but in the second way" (*ibid.*). We shall return to this shortly.

44. ". . . as many things are proportioned to one (thus, for example, *healthy* is predicated of medicine and urine in relation and in proportion to health of body, of which the latter is the sign and the former the cause" (*STh*, I, q. 13, art. 5, vol. I, p. 120).

45. "For the relationship of the name is consequent upon the relationship of knowledge, since the name is the sign of intellectual conception" (*The Summa Contra Gentiles*, vol. I, I, ch. 34, p. 80. See *STh*, I, q. 13, art. 4, reply to obj. 1, vol. I, p. 118: "because a name signifies a thing only through the medium of intellectual conception." The mediatory function of knowing for the naming of things is based on the similarity between the things and the structures of knowledge, which for their part are designated by spoken

of the body is to be regarded as the first thing and thus as the reason for calling
other things like medicine and urine "healthy," then that does not necessarily
imply[46] that in the *order of being* the healthy body is also the first thing, with
its health then being the ontic reason for the health ascribed to medicine and
urine. Ontically, the health of the medicine is the hermeneutical first thing, so
that it is to be regarded as the 'cause' of the health of the body.[47] The ontic
priority of the 'one thing' after which the analogous naming of the 'other things'
follows does not play a constitutive role for the 'mode of signification' (*modus
significandi*). The analogy of being, which is the basis of the spoken analogy,
is presupposed, with its order defined by participation and causality, but it is not
independently emphasized.

With regard to talk about God, the first type of the second model of the
analogy of naming ("where many things are related in different ways to one
third thing") does not come into question because God in this case is not upheld
as the origin of being, but, conversely, would be joined with the 'many things'
in relationship to a 'one thing' (*unum*) which necessarily was higher than all of
them. With the second type of those forms of naming 'according to analogy'
given in the *Summa*, the ontic order between two things named with the same
word is expressly mentioned. Since it has to do with a proportion between One
Thing and only one Other Thing, that which is the hermeneutical first in the
order of knowledge must subsist in one of the two. One of the two must also
be ontically earlier. Thomas uses as an example for such an analogous naming,
"according as one thing is proportioned to another," the word "healthy" again,
but this time only with reference to medicine and the body: ". . . thus *healthy*
is said of medicine and an animal, since medicine is the cause of health in the
animal body."[48] If the analogous naming is oriented to the order of knowing,
then medicine cannot really be given as the reason for the fact that both it and
the body may be called "healthy," unless one should consider the ontic characteristics of the 'proportion' together with the definition of the proportion be-

---

structures—this is asserted by Thomas following Aristotle (Thomas Aquinas, *Aristotle:
On Interpretation*, tr. Jean T. Oesterle [Milwaukee: Marquette University Press, 1962],
lesson III, 16a13, pp. 31f): "Since according to the Philosopher, words are signs of ideas,
and ideas the similitudes of things, it is evident that words function in the signification
of things through the conception of the intellect" (*STh*, I, q. 13, art. 1, vol. I, p. 133).

46. Of course, it can also be true that the order of being and the order of naming
or knowing correspond to each other: "Now in this analogical predication the relationship
is sometimes found to be the same both as to the name and as to the thing, and sometimes
it is not the same. For the relationship of the name is consequent upon the relationship
of knowledge. . . . Accordingly when that which comes first in reality is found to be
first also in knowledge, the same thing is found to be first both as to the meaning of the
name and as to the nature of the thing" (*The Summa Contra Gentiles*, vol. I, I, ch. 34,
p. 80).

47. "On the other hand, when that which comes first according to nature, comes
afterwards according to knowledge, then in analogical terms, there is not the same order
according to the reality and according to the meaning of the name: thus the healing power
in health-giving (medicines) is naturally prior to health in the animal, as cause is prior
to effect; yet as we know this power through its effect, we name it from that effect.
Hence it is that *health-giving* is first in the order of reality, and yet *healthy* is predicated
of animal first according to the meaning of the term" (*The Summa Contra Gentiles*,
vol. I, I, ch. 34, p. 80).

48. *STh*, I, q. 13, art. 5, vol. I, p. 120.

tween the 'one thing' and the 'other thing.' But then we must immediately clarify whether the order of being and the order of knowing accord with each other.

According to Thomas, this is not true with reference to God since we know God only from his effects, as the cause of these effects. Thus the problem of the analogy of naming is raised to a new level of difficulty theologically. For if God is known only as the cause of his effects, then the most which could be said of God is that he is *the cause* of the perfections which are expressed absolutely and affirmatively *about him.* God would then be called "good" because he is the cause of good, and only for that reason. But Thomas would have rejected that as irrelevant.[49] Therefore, the analogy of naming must be understood in another way as only in the pattern of causality, even if it is necessarily presupposed *that* God is the 'cause of all things' (*causa omnium*).

The actual theological analogy of naming is given for Thomas only when the 'one thing,' which as the common element in different things is the hermeneutical reason for the analogy of naming, first subsists in God himself and *therefore* in the creatures caused by God. The content of what is expressed analogously with the same word is thus ascribed to God, in the most original form. Only in that God himself, for example, *has* the perfection of goodness in its most original form, does he as the 'cause' of his creatures distribute this perfection to them; they then have it in their particular way of being as those who have been caused, and thus based on that we can know and name what has its original *being* in God himself.[50]

The analogous naming "according as one thing is proportioned to another" is thus connected for Thomas, in point of fact, with the first model of analogy of naming (which derived from rhetoric), the 'analogy of proportionality.' For within the proportion of the 'one to the other,' which is seen in the second instance of the second model of the analogy of naming as a causal nexus, the

49. "And in this way some things are said of God and creatures analogically, and not in a purely equivocal nor in a purely univocal sense. For we can name God only from creatures. Hence whatever is said of God and creatures is said according as there is some relation of the creature to God as to its principle and cause, wherein all the perfections of things pre-exist excellently" (*STh*, I, q. 13, art. 5, vol. I, p. 120). Compare that passage with *STh*, I, q. 13, art. 6, vol. I, pp. 121f: "For the words *God is good,* or *wise,* signify not only that He is the cause of wisdom or goodness, but that these exist in Him in a more excellent way. Hence as regards what the name signifies, these names are applied primarily to God rather than to creatures, because these perfections flow from God to creatures." The 'mode of signification' remains in this case a peculiarity of the language of this world, so that, as explained above (pp. 245f), the divine perfections can only be expressed by us imperfectly: "But as regards the imposition of names, they are primarily applied by us to creatures which we know first. Hence they have a mode of signification which belongs to creatures, as was said above" (*ibid.*).

50. "Accordingly, since we arrive at the knowledge of God from other things, the reality of the names predicated of God and other things is first in God according to His mode, but the meaning of the name is in Him afterwards. Wherefore He is said to be named from His effects" (*The Summa Contra Gentiles,* vol. I, I, ch. 34, p. 80). If in the first instance of the second model of analogy two different things are related to the first thing as a third thing in differing ways, then in the second instance the one thing is related to itself and then only to the other thing (or rather, that other is related to it). Therefore, only the second instance can be the *theologically* relevant one within the second model of the analogy. For God, for the sake of his deity, cannot be related to a third thing which would put him hermeneutically in one line with other things.

'one thing' spoken of as the cause *relates itself* to the common element which is the hermeneutical basis for analogical naming in that it *has* this common element in the most original way, that is, on the basis of this originality it possesses this element in such a way that it is identical with it. "Having" necessarily means here "being," because the *unum* has this common element in the same way in which it has itself. The 'other thing' (*alterum*), as that 'which is caused' (*causatum*) and as the 'creature' (*creatura*), *relates itself* to the common element (which is in fact identical with the 'cause' of the 'other thing which has been caused') by *having* this common element, even if only in a derived and thus less perfect fashion. The so-called 'analogy of attribution' has drawn into itself the so-called 'analogy of proportionality' when the issue is analogous talk about God.[51]

We are dealing here with a connection similar to that found in Kant. But whereas in Thomas the use of the so-called analogy of attribution for talk about God does *in fact* comprehend the so-called analogy of proportionality, Kant emphasizes as the indispensable presupposition of his theological use of the analogy of proportionality the causal nexus of the so-called analogy of attribution ("the one has proportion to the other in that the one is the cause of the other"). This factual intermingling of the two analogies is declared in Catholic textbooks to be indispensable for the knowledge of God and for the corresponding talk about God: "Only by the formula of the analogy of proportionality (just as God holds to his being, so the creature holds to its being) is God made knowable, for if some similarity in the very rationale of being is admitted, which is not known to us, except inasmuch as the being of the creature supposes some other being, thus according to dependence and attribution (internal in any case)."[52] Whereas in the 'mode of signification' the language of the world functions as the hermeneutical *analogans,* and talk about God as the hermeneutical *analogatum,* the content expressed by this analogous talk about God is structured in precisely the opposite fashion: God is expressed in the hermeneutical *analogatum* as ontic *analogans* (*causa*), the world on the other hand as ontic *analogatum* (*causatum*).

6. The incorporation of several basic aspects of the traditional doctrine of analogy into our discussion was intended to aid us toward a more precise formulation of the problem which is given with the dispute about God as mystery.

51. This is not to say that Thomas, conversely, connected the so-called analogy of proportionality with regard to talk about God with the so-called analogy of attribution. Thomas wants to distinguish the pure analogy of relations, the naming "according to the similitude of proportion," as *merely metaphorical* expression from the so-called analogy of attribution (or of proportion), that is, from the common naming "from the fact that one has a proportion to the other," as by contrast a more authentic way of speaking when naming God. If one calls God a lion, then that means only that God in his actions is similar in strength to a lion in his actions: the naming is completely determined by the mode of existence of the creature and can be shared by God only after the fact and in an inauthentic fashion: "So it is that all names applied metaphorically to God are applied to creatures primarily rather than to God, because when said of God they mean only similitudes to such creatures . . . by proportionate likeness; so the name of *lion* applied to God means only that God manifests strength in His works, as a lion in his" (*STh,* I, q. 13, art. 6, vol. I, p. 122).

52. W. Brugger, *Theologia naturalis; Institutiones Philosophiae Scholasticae* (Pullach bei München: Berchmanskolleg Verlag, 1959, 1964²), pars. VI, nrs. 272, 257.

The question to be decided is whether God is speakable only as the one who actually is unspeakable, and can be made known only as the one who is actually unknown. Within the framework of analogy, the problem has confronted us up to now as the question of how human talk about God could be possible without a "humanization" of the divine essence which is inappropriate to God, since language in all its forms of expression is bound to the form of being of speaking man. To put it somewhat less anthropocentrically: How can one speak of God in the language of this world without "humanizing" the divine essence in a way inappropriate to God when language in its lingual character is oriented to the world and thus is told by the world how it is to speak? By using the pure analogy of relation (analogy of proportionality), which preserves the absolute different-ness of the things being related to each other, it appeared that a possibility which maintained the difference between God and man (world) was given for appro-priate talk about God. According to the analogy of proportionality, one thing (A) of several totally different things is named after another thing (C) only to the degree that the relation in which one of these two things stands to another thing (a:b) can be named on the basis of a similar relation of the other of these two things to again another thing (c:d). For this reason, Kant stipulated that the pure analogy of relation was the philosophical enablement of responsible talk about God.

However, a more precise analysis of this model of analogy revealed that it at least presupposes a lingual *acquaintance* with the *situation* of the thing to be expressed; the *relations* of the two things to the further thing must be known to us if the naming is not to be meaningless. The relation of an unknown thing to another unknown thing cannot be compared with a known relation. The re-lation of this unknown which is supposed to be called God to something known must be known if that unknown is supposed to be expressed in speech, at least in its unknownness. If God were *fully unknown within* the world and its human language, then responsible talk about God on the basis of the pure analogy of relation would be impossible. Therefore, this model of analogy had to be com-bined with another model, which permits God to be expressed on the basis of a *nameable* relation to the world (or to something in it) *as* the unknown, who in his unknown state relates to the world in a way which we know of. The so-called analogy of attribution accomplished this in that through it God is addressed as the origin and the condition (in Thomas he is even the original proprietor) of what is conditioned or caused in the world. Thus God is presupposed as the unconditioned condition of the world. His absolute unknownness has been more precisely defined as the unknownness of the origin or of the condition of the world and thus of us ourselves (and of our language). But God himself is preserved in this way as the unknown who is absolutely distinct from the world.

Now the actual accomplishment of this theological and philosophical tra-dition is this: God's unknownness has become obtrusive in an unavoidable way. For we know it as *the unknownness of our origin,* so that we refer ourselves to an Unknown without which we would not exist.

Thus the theological critique to be directed against the great accomplish-ment of this metaphysical tradition focuses on the fact that in its obtrusiveness the unknownness of God has become an unbearably sinister riddle. For it is intolerable to live in the awareness of a condition which comes into view only in order to disappear again into unknownness. It is difficult enough for a person, within his earthly conditionedness, to have an unknown father, as a procreator but not as a father. Theologically, such an understanding of God as mystery results methodologically in the establishment of the event for whose sake the New Testament, yes, the Bible came to be: the event of God's turning to mankind in such a way that *trust* in God was made possible. By contrast, the analogy of attribution defines so precisely the unknownness of God that it vastly increases that unknownness into God's total inaccessibility. That fact is not softened, but rather hardened by the formulation of concepts 'on the analogy of proportionality,' based on the presupposition of the so-called 'analogy of attribution.' For when God, along the lines of the analogy of the human intellect and will which plans and executes within the world, is thought and then named as "intellect" and "will," he by no means becomes better known to us in his unknownness. Such names are always accompanied by the insight that they are inappropriate as anthropomorphic terms, and thus they increase the distance between such talk and God, and thereby emphasize the uncanny strangeness of God so understood.

Kant, then, maintains that we express the unknownness of God only when we use the analogy of relation. What is made known in such language really applies only to language, and not to the "object." God and man do agree in terms of language that they can be named "intellect" and "will"—but the difference is that God and man each have a very different relation to what "intellect" and "will" are. God as Intellect and Will is *creative*. Thus the mutual name excludes any similarity with human will and intellect, which have their *effect* on the world, but only within the *presuppositions* of the world.[53] In any event, God

---

53. It should be pointed out here that Spinoza, in his energetic polemic against every anthropomorphic expression which goes beyond the concept of "the *immanent* cause of all things" or of the *sole substance,* was focusing expressly on the designation of God as intellect and will. "Further (to say a word here concerning the intellect and the will which we attribute to God), if intellect and will appertain to the eternal essence of God, we must take these words in some significations quite different from those they usually bear. For intellect and will, which should constitute the essence of God, would perforce be as far apart as the poles from the human intellect and will, in fact, would have nothing in common with them but the name. . . ." For God, expressed as intellect, would have to be understood as the cause of all things (of the essence and the existence of all things). "Now the intellect of God is the cause of both the essence and the existence of our intellect; therefore the intellect of God . . . differs from our intellect both in respect to essence and in respect to existence, nor can it in anywise agree therewith save in name, as we said before." Anthropomorphic talk about God as intellect and and will is, according to Spinoza, pure equivocation: "there would be about as much correspondence between the two as there is between the Dog, the heavenly constellation, and a dog, an animal that barks" (Spinoza, *Ethics,* in *Chief Works,* 2 vols., tr. R. H. M. Elwes [New York: Dover Publications, 1955], II, pt. I, prop. 27, note, pp. 56f). In this regard, Kant does not dispute the total difference between various entities called by the same name, but thinks instead that he can express God in his differentness from the world through the analogous use of the name, as the cause of the world. To that extent he shares Spinoza's polemic against "dogmatic" anthropomorphism. However, the "symbolic" anthropomorphism of analogy works in the interest of the strong differentiation between God and the world (man). This difference is, for its part, made absolute as the difference between cause and effect, based on the critique of reason of the kind found in Spinoza. Schleiermacher will then put this difference, so absolutized, into the category of absolute dependence. Of course, the consequences for doctrine are found in Christology, where no other course remains but to take Zwingli's side against Luther.

is always thought of as the absolutely causative essence. Schleiermacher will construct his doctrine of faith on this concept of God.

That Kant in all the analogies mentioned thinks of the relation of God to the world as a *causative* relation characterizes, as a consequence, the unique features of this talk about God. The category of the creator, supreme over the world, dominates the very approach of this way of conceptualizing according to analogy. The *symbolic* anthropomorphism, which Kant asserts as his position in his analogous talk about God, has the very function of keeping God out of the world with the help of language. This is expressed most clearly in that Kant uses even the phenomenon of *love* in his approach to analogous talk about God to "obtain a notion of the relation of things which absolutely are unknown to me." Following the law which has been adopted (Schleiermacher will pursue the same line), divine love is now placed under the category of *cause:* ". . . as the promotion of the welfare of children ($=a$) is to the love of parents ($=b$), so the welfare of the human species ($=c$) is to that unknown character in God ($=x$) which we call love; not as if it had the least similarity to any human inclination, but because we can suppose its relation to the world to be similar to what things of the world bear to one another. But the concept of relation in this case is a mere category, namely, the concept of cause, which has nothing to do with sensibility."[54]

That Kant places the relation of God to man, which merits being called love, within the category of cause, which is free of all "human inclination"(!), is theological reason enough to mistrust the usage of the analogy of attribution. The procedure indicates that what love really is cannot be conceived of in this model. The love of God articulated in this way will never be able to overcome the chasm between God and man (the world), which is characterized by infinite superiority. That God spoken of as love in this way remains 'above us' (*supra nos*) in the dimension of causer. And that is, all the way through, the actual *theological* weakness of the classical form of the doctrine of analogy. Analogy understood this way puts God, as the unknown initiator of this world, firmly above the world and exclusively beyond it, in order then to use analogy to articulate the unknownness of this initiator to the limited point that his unknownness is all that is expressed. Kant's *formula* is altogether apt: $a:b=c:x$. But the function of this formula is to name "that unknown character in God . . . which we call love." This makes very plain that analogy so understood does not reach beyond the realm of what we have always called "love" in this way. Talk about God does not transcend the human experience which is presupposed to be generally known. On the other hand, it does not express anything about the being of God. Because it does not transcend human experience as it is generally presupposed to be known, it manages to articulate the unknown essence, "God," only in his activity as the initiator of everything, together with his infinite superiority over and differentness from the world. What not only remains unknown, but is *de facto* excluded, is that together *with* human experience as such a further experience is possible which does not derive *from* human experience.

The traditional theological usage of *analogy* as we observe it in Kant is predominantly agnostic—for the sake of God's perfection. Here, too, Spinoza

54. Kant, *Prolegomena to any Future Metaphysics,* p. 106 n.

stated more clearly that something cannot be which may not be. He objects to the doctrine that God is pursuing *purposes* in his causative being by saying that this doctrine removes the perfection of God. For, if God acts because of a purpose, then he must necessarily desire something which he lacks: "Further, this doctrine does away with the perfection of God: for, if God acts for an object, he necessarily desires something which he lacks."[55] Spinoza insists: ". . . but in philosophy, when we clearly perceive that the attributes which make men perfect can as ill be ascribed and assigned to God, as the attributes which go to make perfect the elephant and the ass can be ascribed to man; here I say these and similar phrases have no place, nor can we employ them without causing extreme confusion in our conceptions."[56]

In his reception of the classical doctrine of analogy, especially his application of the 'analogy of proportionality,' Kant refuted Spinoza's logical fears, but the effect was to enhance all the more the premise which he shares with Spinoza and the metaphysically conceived doctrine of God, which is that God and man not only remain infinitely *distinct* from each other but also *toto coelo different* ('by all of heaven'). The divinity of God excludes humanity. God is not permitted to be human. Spinoza expressed this with extreme clarity in a letter to Oldenburg: "The doctrines added by certain churches, such as that God took on himself human nature, I have expressly said that I do not understand; in fact, to speak the truth, they seem to me no less absurd than would a statement that a circle had taken on itself the nature of a square."[57]

The Christian faith has no other course than intellectually to oppose this suspicion of absurdity which is directed toward the most important assertion of the faith. And in this case, attack is not only the best defense, it is better than all defense. Faith in the God who is identical with the man Jesus forces theology to dispute the very premises of the metaphysical tradition, which are the source of that suspicion of absurdity. Over against that tradition, and for both christological and hermeneutical reasons, the question is raised which is decisive for the problem of the speakability of God: Can the indispensable articulation of the *distinction* between God and man be done only through the assertion of the *total differentness* of God and man? There is christological reason to ask whether there is not a God-enabled, a God-required, even a God-demanded anthropomorphism which moves far beyond the naiveté of "dogmatic" anthropomorphism as well as the skepticism of "symbolic" anthropomorphism. Briefly: is there a theological use of analogy which corresponds to faith in the incarnation of God?

Although this question may appear to be a matter of formulation, it does in fact go to the very heartbeat of the Christian faith, a fact which may be indicated through reference to the monk Sarapion, who according to Cassian had become a theological problem for his church because of his adherence to

55. Spinoza, *op. cit.*, pt. I, Appendix, p. 73.

56. Spinoza, "Letters," in *Chief Works*, 2 vols., tr. R. H. M. Elwes (New York: Dover Publications, 1955), II. letter 36, p. 353. See also K. Löwith, *Gott, Mensch und Welt in der Metaphysik von Descartes bis zu Nietzsche* (Göttingen: Vandenhoeck & Ruprecht, 1967), pp. 209f.

57. *Ibid.*, letter 21, p. 303.

the heresy of the Anthropomorphites.[58] He was formally accused and opposed by theologians and the bishop. ". . . at length the old man was shaken by the numerous and very weighty assertions . . . and was drawn to the faith of the Catholic traditions. The prelates' satisfaction was of short duration, however, Cassian continues, for the next morning Sarapion spoke up and said, 'Alas! wretched man that I am! they have taken away my God from me, and I have now none to lay hold of; and whom to worship and address I know not.' His faith had not survived the zealously conducted enlightenment"[59]—and it should be noted that it was an enlightenment 'to the greater glory of God' (*ad maiorem dei gloriam*). Apparently the monk Sarapion took John 1:14-18 too seriously, according to which the glory of God is supposed to have become experienceable in a man. However, theology should no longer have to be ashamed on account of the monk Sarapion.

SECTION 18. The Gospel as Analogous Talk about God

1. If human talk about God is supposed to correspond to him, then it must be analogous to him. Therefore, theology must devote concentrated attention to analogy. The opinion that one could evade the problem defined by the term analogy and theologically ground appropriate talk about God on the basis of an exposition of the conditions of its possibility is thoughtless. There can be no responsible talk about God without analogy. Every spoken announcement which corresponds to God is made within the context of what analogy makes possible. Even that silence which corresponds to God could only be made possible, as we saw, by an analogy which reaches its purpose in the end of speech.

However, the indispensability of analogy for every thoroughgoing theology, and the unavoidability of theological preoccupation with analogy, can and may not lead us to overlook the fact that this always involves a decision about what may be considered as analogy within the realm of theology. We reminded ourselves of the fact that there are different models of analogy. What must be decided now is what makes analogy the analogy *of faith* (*analogia fidei*). And that will also decide how we are to use analogy *theologically* so that it will be entirely accurate to say of human words that they correspond to God. It is no accident that analogy is the theme of theological debate.

To be sure, the debate about analogy has usually been carried on within recent Evangelical theology with an astonishing lack of understanding and horrifying carelessness. In the dispute about analogy, the deficiency in the area of the consciousness of the problem is scarcely less acute than the lack of any awareness of the necessity of analogy and of the struggle for its proper usage. The confusing thing about this struggle is that, on the side of Protestant theology, the criticism of the genuinely Catholic doctrine of so-called 'analogy of being' (*analogia entis*) is directed against the very thing against which this doctrine

58. John Cassian, *The Confessions of John Cassian,* "The Second Conference of Abbot Isaac," X, ch. III, "Of Abbot Sarapion and the heresy of the Anthropomorphites . . . ," *NPNF,* 2nd ser., XI, 402.

59. H. M. Kuitert, *Gott in Menschengestalt; Eine dogmatisch-hermeneutische Studie über die Anthropomorphismen der Bibel,* tr. E.-W. Pollman (München: C. Kaiser, 1967), p. 5.

itself is directed. With unshakable imperturbability, the objection is made to the theological concept of analogy known as *analogia entis* that, on the basis of this presupposition, God, world, and man, or creator, creation, and creature, are drawn together into a structure of being which then makes it possible to understand God on the basis of the ordering of the created world under him. The creature which understands itself as the simile of God will also understand God, conversely, as the image of the creature and thus fall into that very godlessness which Paul attacked in Romans 1:23. The *analogia entis* as grasping after God—that was the horrible phantom which was making the rounds in Protestant theology and against which one felt one had to confront man in the name of God, calling out: You resemble the spirit which you grasp, not me! Protestant polemics are strengthened in their imperturbability by Karl Barth's blunt statement, "I regard the *analogia entis* as the invention of Antichrist, and think that *because of it* one cannot become Catholic."[1] The remark has often been cited but little understood. Its understanding is, of course, obstructed by other statements by Barth,[2] so that even within the Barthian school the change of his views remained concealed, that change which was caused precisely by his discovery of the analogy of faith as the precondition for the possibility of proper talk about God. "We need it, we need it through the whole affair"—that was a remark he later made with regard to analogy. But he still adhered to his rejection of the so-called *analogia entis*. However, his objection was no longer defined by the concern that with the help of the so-called *analogia entis* one would try to overcome in Promethean fashion the qualitatively infinite chasm between God and man, described with the term "the totally Other"—or that one would have to want to do this. That was the concern of the "dialectical" Barth, which, however, went through a process of transformation during his labor on the *Church Dogmatics*. To be sure, Barth continued to be concerned about the difference between God and man in a way seldom found in theology since Luther. But in contrast with the rest of Protestant polemics, the "late" Barth feared that the so-called *analogia entis* would not do justice to the difference between God and man by overlooking the *nearness* of God.[3] And that does, in fact, lead us to the real aporia of the use of analogy to which we have alluded.

The theological aporia into which the classical form of the doctrine of analogy leads became visible in Kant's philosophy as the actual accomplishment

1. *CD*, I/1, p. x. In distinction from the common opinion held in Protestant literature, E. Mechels recently worked through the intention of *analogia entis* in E. Przywara's sense (*Analogie bei Erich Przywara und Karl Barth; Das Verhältnis von Offenbarungstheologie und Metaphysik* [Neukirchen-Vluyn: Neukirchener Verlag, 1974]). There one finds debates with the pertinent Protestant literature—unfortunately, it is somewhat too schematic. The remarks directed against my work on the problem impressed me so little that I prefer to neglect them here.

2. On the criticism of Barth's misunderstanding of *analogia entis*, see Hans Urs von Balthasar, *The Theology of Karl Barth*, tr. J. Drury (New York: Holt, Rinehart & Winston, 1971), pp. 135ff, and B. Gertz, *Glaubenswelt als Analogie; Die theologische Analogie-Lehre Erich Przywaras und ihr Ort in der Auseinandersetzung um die analogia fidei* (Düsseldorf: Patmos-Verlag, 1969), pp. 251ff. Gertz (p. 259) summarizes his criticism with von Balthasar's judgment (p. 269): "There is no trace of the phantom of the analogia entis, which Karl Barth makes it out to be, to be found in him (Przywara)."

3. See E. Jüngel, "Die Möglichkeit theologischer Anthropologie auf dem Grunde der Analogie," *Evangelische Theologie*, 22 (1962), 535ff.

of this doctrine of analogy. The "knowledge after analogy" used by Kant for talk about God establishes analogy as the means for the more precise determination of an idea of God which otherwise remains empty. The X which is to be known is regarded, however, as something unknown. Only with the help of conceptualization through analogy can it be articulated. The way it is done, however, means that the talk about God which results is justified only as inauthentic talk. The God, who initially is regarded as unreachable, for whom the word "God" is then used only as the circumlocution of an X, is expressed in language with the aid of analogy only to the point that his relationship to the world becomes speakable, but this relationship cannot be taken as a statement about God's being. *What remains unthinkable is that God himself relates in this relationship, relates to himself and at the same time to the world.* And thus that talk about God made possible by "knowledge after analogy" is basically only a linguistic ingredient which is indispensable only to the point that the objects must let themselves be *defined* by thoughts. What can be formulated here is the knowledge of the unknowability of God. In order to know God's unknowability, something must in fact be said about God. If this were not possible, then not even the unknowability of God could be known. No knowledge at all would result. Analogy serves, therefore, to make expressible in speech the unknowable God in his unknowability. It does this by positing God as X, as the sum of everything which is the case, in a relation which equals a relation within the sum of everything which is the case: $x:a=b:c$. God is inaccessible, and remains beyond the boundaries of all grasping and any concept that could define him. All talk about him has ultimately no other meaning than to preserve his mystery. And that mystery, so understood, permits nothing more to be known about it than the fact that it is a mystery.

Those theological objections normally raised against this doctrine of analogy generally miss the point of the so-called *analogia entis* entirely. For this usage of analogy applies primarily to the inaccessibility of God, applies to it only too much. Following the Fourth Lateran Council (1215), Erich Przywara cited as the basic law of analogy, with unsurpassable parturience, the rhythm of "greater dissimilarity in so great a likeness" between God and the creature.[4] And then, appealing to St. Augustine,[5] the consequent assertion is made that "in the analogy as 'the analogy of the greater dissimilarity' the God is powerful and makes himself known who 'is not God if you do not grasp him.' "[6]

The structure of analogy which Przywara asserts as "the greater dissimilarity within so great a likeness" is, as far as its content is concerned, also presupposed by Kant. This is so to the extent that with "a perfect similarity of relations between two quite dissimilar things"[7] the (perfectly similar) relations

4. Denzinger, *The Sources of Catholic Dogma,* tr. R. J. Deferrari (St. Louis and London: Herder, 1957), par. 432, p. 171: ". . . between the Creator and the creature so great a likeness cannot be noted without the necessity of noting a greater dissimilarity between them."

5. St. Augustine, *Sermo* 117, iii, 5, in Migne, *Patrologia Latina,* XXXVIII, 663; see above, p. 8, n. 9.

6. E. Przywara, "Metaphysik, Religion, Analogie," in *Analogia entis; Schriften* (Einsiedeln: Johannes Verlag, 1962), III, 334.

7. I. Kant, *Prolegomena to any Future Metaphysics,* ed. L. W. Beck (Indianapolis and New York: Bobbs-Merrill, 1950), p. 106.

are nothing in and of themselves so that the relation is to be understood as an *ens minimum* ('minimal being') over against which the (perfectly dissimilar) things are something in and of themselves and thus have their own, higher value as being than does the *ens minimum*. Thus the stated perfect similarity of relations is surpassed by a still greater dissimilarity of the *relata* ('related things'). And whereas three of these *relata* may be presupposed as known, the fourth will be known only as something unknown. The analogy established as the means of knowledge permits each of the *relata* to be in and of itself, so that the relations remain completely external to them. The dependent relationship of the 'analogy of attribution' is not asserted within the 'analogy of proportionality' in a way that the analogy appears as something new over against the *relata* in relationship to each other, as something which could define the *relata* anew. The structure of relations outside the *relata* determines the analogy, but the analogy as this structure of relations does not determine the *relata* so that through the analogy a *new being* could emerge. Therefore this analogy (as far as language is concerned) is exclusively an 'analogy of naming' (*analogia nominum*): the *relata* come into consideration as far as language is concerned only in terms of their naming. The language which is subordinated to knowledge is essentially naming language, relating *signa* ('signs') to *res* ('things'), and in such language meaning exhausts itself in designation. The only thing in this analogy, established as a means of knowing, which is linguistic in nature is the *relata*, but not the relations. What dominates in the proportional ordering of $x:a=b:c$ is itself presupposed as *nonlingual*.

Analogy thus understood has doubtless the advantage of being the most thoroughgoing *hindrance* to a closed system which forces together God, man, and the world. As the "pendulating middle point" between Creator and created being, it destroys at the roots any and every deductive and inductive derivation of the One from the Other. The mediation of Creator and creature to a reconciling Third Entity is also totally excluded through the so-called *analogia entis* and the 'analogy of naming' which inheres in it.[8] As the "penetrating structure of something purely and freely factual,"[9] it protects the holy grail of the mystery, and as such is really the opposite of what Protestant polemics have made it out to be.

Very often the Protestant polemic against the so-called *analogia entis* also completely misses the genuinely Evangelical approach to theological thought. This does not happen because an understanding of analogy which has not been understood is being disputed, but rather because these critics are thinking much too much in the same direction as the opponent which they believe they are combating. If all that were at stake were to respect God as the Totally Other, nothing would be more appropriate than to think up the much-scorned *analogia entis*. But that cannot ultimately be the concern of a theology which accords with the gospel. The great Przywara did then insist, in a certain tension with the tendency of his argumentation, that the constantly new experience of still greater similarities between God and creature may not fail to take place. "There is only

8. E. Przywara expressly refers to this again in his essay "Stellungnahmen zur Zeit," in *In und Gegen; Stellungnahmen zur Zeit* (Nürnberg: Glock & Lutz, 1955), pp. 279f.
9. E. Przywara, *loc. cit.*

the constantly new rhythm in which the 'still greater similarity' is radically broken open into the radically surpassing (experience) of a 'still greater dissimilarity' of the 'God who is above everything which can be thought'—but this happens in such a way that even this 'still greater dissimilarity' cannot be transferred into an alogical logical principle of an absolute 'Totally Other,' but rather brings the experiencing and thinking person down anew from the 'giddy heights' to a new experience of 'still greater similarities' in the (even religious and theological) 'fertile bathos of experience.' "[10] That man is brought down into a constantly new experience of God's similarity with us, without being betrayed of something higher in the process, is the function, to be sure, of an 'analogy' which does its work 'according to the gospel' (*analogia, kata to euangelion*). What Przywara adds on would be both the reason and approach of a theological doctrine of analogy. For Przywara, the "constantly new experience 'of still greater similarities' " is significantly only a moment in the rhythm of that "pendulating middle-point" which is crossed, immediately and essentially, by the "still greater distance." As a pendulum, analogy so understood never arrives at a conclusion. Its stigma is that Augustinian "unrest for God" which arrives at *no* end, and its symbol is the *night* which bears within itself the origin and all new becoming.[11]

   In contrast with that, our task is to develop an understanding of analogy in the light of the gospel whose metaphor would be the rising sun of the new day ("Every morning is fresh and new. . . !"): that light in which the owl of Minerva gives in to the dove of the Holy Spirit. One must understand analogy as an event which allows the One (x) *to come* to the Other (a) with the help of the relationship of a further Other (b) to even one more Other (c). The issue is an *analogy of advent*, which expresses God's arrival among men as a definitive event. But when the analogy contains *God* as one of its members (x:a=b:c), then, on the basis of the relation of God (x) to the world (a), the world-relationship (b:c) which corresponds to that relation appears in a completely new light, in a light which *makes* this world-relationship *new*, an eschatological light. The world-relationship (b:c), which of itself can give no reference to God, now begins to speak for God: not as 'natural elements' (*natura*) which God has brought to their highest form and made perfect, but rather as a worldly obviousness speaking in the service of something even more obvious, and thus as a completely new case because of the new light which illuminates it. The God who comes to the world (x→a) makes use of the obvious in this world in such a way that he proves himself to be that which is even more obvious over against it. It is all too obvious that one will give everything for the value of the treasure buried in the field in order to have that greater value. This obviousness appears then in a totally new light when it is expressed as a parable for the kingdom of God which lets itself be found. Then the treasure in the field moves into the

---

10. *Ibid.*, p. 280.
11. Thus, according to Przywara, "the mystery of God in Christ flows into the One Word which penetrates through revelation either expressed or unexpressed: night" (*Evangelium; Christentum gemäss der Offenbarung,* vol. I: *Christentum gemäss Johannes* [Nürnberg: Glock & Lutz, 1954], p. 286). B. Gertz (*op. cit.,* p. 108) refers to the influence exercised by J. Görres (also) on Przywara's theological reception of the metaphor "night."

series of those things over against which God is the value to be found, or the value already found. But that can be experienced only when God conquers, so to speak, the worldly obviousness (b:c) and establishes himself in it and with its help as the one who is more obvious, that is, when b:c is *talked about* in such a way that it *corresponds* to the relation between God and the world (x→a), and God then ceases to be the unknown (x). In the event of the analogy x→a=b:c God ceases to be x. He introduces himself in that he arrives. And this his arrival belongs to his very being which he reveals as arriving.[12] But this is possible only when this arrival itself takes place as an arrival-in-language so that in such an analogy not only the *relata* but also their relations to each other and their correspondence are lingual. Briefly put: the gospel is to be understood as the event of correspondence.

The criterion for what may be considered correspondence or analogy if the gospel is to be understood as correspondence can, then, be only that event about which the gospel speaks. The formal structure of the analogy which as hermeneutical enabling and as ontological release may be considered as talk about God corresponding to God cannot be derived from general principles, such as the principle of contradiction, but can be exposed only on the basis of an analysis of talk about God which has already taken place. The claim of such talk that it corresponds to God is to be presupposed as an hypothesis. The verification of the claim itself cannot be the task of theology anyway. But it certainly is the task of theology to name the conditions under which such a claim can be meaningful at all. However, these conditions are to be taken from the context to which that claim relates itself. Methodologically, then, the formal law of structure is to be exposed out of the material peculiarity of Christian talk about God, that law which all talk which corresponds to God must satisfy according to the claim of such talk.[13]

12. What M. Heidegger says about the analogy of being (*Schellings Abhandlung Über das Wesen der menschlichen Freiheit* [1809], ed. H. Feick [Tübingen: M. Niemeyer, 1971], p. 233) does not then apply to the 'analogy of faith' understood as the analogy of advent: "The existent 'corresponds,' it complies in what it is and how it is, it subordinates itself under the dominating cause as that which is caused. . . . *Analogy belongs to metaphysics* in a double sense:
    1. that the existent 'corresponds' to the highest existent,
    2. that thought and explanation are oriented to correspondences, similarities, generalities.
Where, on the other hand, one thinks directly from being itself, analogy has no place anymore." Where one thinks from God, a totally new understanding of analogy arises, which does away with the concept of the "highest existent."
    13. A precautionary note is needed to point out that, with this method, not all questions can be dealt with which arise in the context of the claim of human talk to correspond to God. What Schleiermacher set about to discuss in the lemmata which head his doctrine of faith, but also much of what is discussed today in the way of "scientific and theoretical" problems with regard to the word "God" (not seldom in a rather tumultuous way), will gain indisputable relevance if one is prepared to engage in the method described above. In the current debates about theological method, the issue cannot be to set aside methodically whole areas of the problem of talk about God, perhaps even out of arrogance. But the hermeneutical decision must be made about the direction from which a problem area can be opened up for discussion. The method used in this study simply seeks to prevent that distraction which tries to take Christian talk about God seriously by not taking its content seriously until after the fact.

2. To understand the gospel as correspondence means first of all to ask about the event which is the subject of the gospel. A short form for what *euangelion* is would be the Pauline phrase *logos tou staurou* ('word of the cross').[14] According to Paul, talk about the death of Jesus Christ on the cross is the point at which not only the spirits but also the fates of those who hear them are judged: "For the word of the cross is folly to those who are perishing, but to us who are being saved it is the power of God" (I Cor. 1:18). Talk about God which speaks of the death of Jesus Christ on the cross is drawn here into the event of which it speaks, in its being as discourse. The event character of this event, its *dynamis* ('power'), is shared with the speech which speaks of it. In communicating this content, not just information about it is being passed along. The content shares itself in such a way that a distinction between it and talk about it can be made only through an abstraction. What is expressed in the "word of the cross" is thus itself the full relation of language.

Paul expresses this both theologically and hermeneutically significant content in II Corinthians 1:18-21 in such a way that he asserts that the human speech of the apostle in its relationship to speaker and hearer ("our word to you") and the event of which it speaks are one entire event context. It is no accident then that what is spoken of is described as a language event. Paul bases his assertion that his apostolic discourse was not "Yes or No" (vv. 18f) on the subject of the apostolic 'word': The Son of God, Jesus Christ, proclaimed by the apostolic speaker to the Corinthian hearers, was not "Yes and No"; rather an unambiguous "Yes" has become an event in him (v. 19). He speaks a "Yes." God is to be regarded as the speaker of this "Yes," so that in the apostolic talk about Jesus Christ God's own word, his "Yes," is expressed and directed to the apostle's hearers. The difference between the apostolic and the divine word consists of the fact that the 'word' of the apostle is not "Yes and No" but *is* clearly "Yes," whereas God's word *became* an event not as "Yes and No" but clearly as "Yes" (v. 19). In its character as the present, the human word lives from the definitiveness of the divine word. The name of Jesus Christ as the Crucified One is responsible for this definitiveness. For in him all God's promises are "Yes," so that, in prayer, through him human speech must become "Amen." Then, in the human confirmation of the definitiveness of the divine word, God is honored (v. 20).

These observations on the Pauline text II Corinthians 1:18-21 prohibit one's taking the divine "Yes" about which we are speaking as an inauthentic mode of expression. To be sure, there is "translation" in this mode of expression. "Yes" is a human word which one person says to another person. The translation of this word to an event in which it is to be said of a *divine* speaker to a *human* hearer allows one to see in this case both the enabling and the structure of such translation. The apostle translates the model of human speech to God because he can understand his own apostolic speech only as the explication of a divine

14. On the parallelism of gospel (Rom. 1:16f) and the word of the cross (I Cor. 1:18) see H. Braun, "Exegetische Randglossen zum 1. Korintherbrief," in *Gesammelte Studien zum Neuen Testament und seiner Umwelt* (Tübingen: J. C. B. Mohr, 1962), pp. 178-81; E. Jüngel, *Paulus und Jesus; Eine Untersuchung zur Präzisierung der Frage nach dem Ursprung der Christologie* (Tübingen: Mohr [Siebeck], 1972⁴), pp. 30-32.

judgment reaching its conclusion in it.[15] The translation of the model of human speech to God is based on the certainty that God has shown himself to be human in the execution of his divinity. To think of him as one who speaks, to speak of him as one who speaks, is not a "dogmatic anthropomorphism," which comes too close to God, but rather the result of that *event* in which God becomes accessible as God in language, which the Bible calls *revelation*. In and as this event, the analogy of faith takes place, in which human words do not come too close to God but rather God as the word comes close to man in human words.

3. In that in Evangelical speech God comes close to men, he carries out his divinity's own humanity, in order to make concrete the difference between his divinity's own humanity and the humanity of man. The difference between God and man, which is constitutive of the essence of the Christian faith, is thus not the difference of a still greater dissimilarity, but rather, conversely, the difference of a still greater similarity between God and man in the midst of a great dissimilarity.

This hermeneutical thesis does presuppose the *event* in which the analogy of faith, so understood, was carried out. The Christian faith confesses that God's becoming man, the incarnation of the word of God in Jesus Christ, is the unique, unsurpassable instance of a still greater similarity between God and man taking place within a great dissimilarity. This event makes clear, however, that the difference of such still greater similarity is not a matter of relationless identification. That the still greater similarity between God and man remains an *event* and only as such is true and real is the actual mystery of God which is revealed in the identification of God with the man Jesus, an identification which preserves this difference. Through this christological event of identification, a nearness between God and man is expressed which from the outset surpasses anything like the "result" of an identity of God and man which sets aside every difference. Identity in the sense of the removal of every difference knows nothing of nearness. It would be, obviously, the end of the original distance between two entities which had become identical. But it would be the end of distance without the entrance of nearness. Identity as the ending of distance without nearness is the establishment of *absolute* distance. Two entities which had become identical in this sense would be apart from each other in an *absolute* sense. By contrast, the mystery of the God who identifies with the man Jesus is the increase of similarity and nearness between God and man which is *more than mere identity* and which reveals the *concrete difference* between God and man in its surpassing mere identical being. It is only in this sense that the Easter confession may be risked, that confession that Jesus Christ is true God and true man. And in the sense of the still greater similarity between God and man in the midst of such great dissimilarity, one can and must say that the man Jesus is *the parable of God (Gleichnis)*, understanding the being of the man Jesus on the basis of the Easter kerygma. This christological statement is to be regarded as the fundamental

15. It would be worth researching the extent to which the conclusive character of the divine judgment of justification corresponds to a peculiarity of the logic of language. On the problem of the logic of language, see Josef Simon, "Satz, Text und Diskurs in transcendentalphilosophischer und sprachlogischer Reflexion," in *Sprache und Begriff: Festschrift für Bruno Liebrucks* (Meisenheim [am Glan]: Hain, 1974), pp. 212ff.

proposition of a hermeneutic of the speakability of God. As such, it is the approach to a doctrine of analogy which expresses the gospel as correspondence.

4. The understanding of the man Jesus as the parable of God begins systematically with the insight which led us to this christological proposition. This insight said that the translation of the model of human talk to God is based on the certainty of a God who is human in his divinity. God is thinkable as one who speaks because and to the extent that he is human in and of himself. God relates to his word not only in a way similar to that in which man relates to his word, but God relates to his word in such a way that he thereby relates to man, and in a very particular way relates to man's relationship to his own word. The analogy is also here in its relations a matter of language. It is not only a case of an analogy of naming based on an analogy of being. What is truly interesting here are the relations between the beings who are to be named or are named. If these relations are themselves lingual, then the names appear only as a moment of the language context which still is defined in a *primarily verbal* way. The relations *happen* to the degree that in them—and not only in one of them—God relates to himself. The relations are therefore not external relationships over against the *relata*, but rather the *executions* of language behavior which bring the *relata*, who are entering into relationship to each other, to a new relation which profoundly determines their very being. The analogy itself is in an eminent sense a *language event*. Because what happens in it is that God relates himself to the world and to man and thus is expressed in language, the event of the correspondence of human talk to God is not a capacity of language itself; it is not its own possibility, but rather an alien possibility which is opened up to language and required of it. It is not possible for language as such to correspond to God. To correspond to God is a possibility which comes to language from God, and certainly not as a matter of chance.

It will be helpful to portray this content more concretely by turning to the parables of Jesus. A consideration of the parables of Jesus would be necessary in any event if the christological proposition that the man Jesus is the parable of God is not to remain abstract. For the emergence of the confession of the early Christian churches that the crucified Jesus is God's Son, which Paul is presupposing as known in the quoted text II Corinthians 1:18ff, is not conceivable apart from the proclamation of the earthly Jesus and its consequences for the person of Jesus himself. The *son* is the *personal parable of the father;* he represents the father, so that Bultmann's famous question as to how the proclaimer became the proclaimed can be put this way: How did the move from the parables of Jesus, so representative of the proclamation of Jesus, to faith in Jesus as the parable of God come about? The understanding of parable as analogy leads to the answer to this question. In order to discuss the analogy-structure of the parable more precisely, we shall turn from the christological context again to the general hermeneutical problem.[16]

5. The parable is regarded as an extended metaphor, or the metaphor can be called an abbreviated parable. The difference consists of the fact that a parable narrates while a metaphor coalesces the narrative in a single word. But the

---

16. See Gottlieb Söhngen, *Analogie und Metapher; Kleine Philosophie und Theologie der Sprache* (Freiburg/München: K. Alber, 1962).

narrative structure is also immanent in the metaphor, at least of the metaphor understood as the 'epiphora according to analogy' (*epiphora kata to analogon*). But whereas metaphor *implies* narrative in the form of *naming* and thus is directed toward a *certain word*, the parable always presupposes language's process of naming and is rather directed to portraying a process, an event through the movement of language.[17]

In any event, both metaphor and parable have in common that they are *addressing* speech. What is *expressed* in the form of metaphor and parable, *addresses one*. This happens because metaphors and parables depart from customary language usage and represent a lingual renewal—just as language in general is an absolutely new usage of existence over against the nonlanguage activity with what exists. This new usage makes what exists communicable in a qualitatively new way: to be able to *say* what a "hammer" is or what is "just" signifies a new way of dealing with the world and each other. Thus language is the absolutely new way of dealing with what exists, and in it parable and metaphor are a self-renewal of language. What is new, however, addresses one.

That is true, first of all, for the one who forms fortunate metaphors and successful parables. But it is also true, and even more so, for the relationship of emerging and emerged metaphors and parables to hearers, who are implicitly always present at the creative language act of the formation of parables and metaphors. The attention of the listener is awakened and directed to what is the concern of the speaker when he uses a new figure of speech which departs from the dominant usage—assuming that the metaphor or the parable is successful. Aristotle, therefore, praised metaphorical speech because it made easy learning possible.[18] What is new is what has been absent up to now in relation to what is already known, and this is true even if it is very obvious yet undiscovered. But, Aristotle says, men are "struck by what is out of the way,"[19] so that they open themselves more easily to what appears to have been brought to them from far away. It is obviously presupposed that the new thing moves in the direction of what is already known, so that the spoken innovation can be combined with what is known. That is the case when an analogy is at work between the new and the accustomed. Something *absolutely alien* would not grip one. What grips us is that correspondence which mediates between the unknown and the already known, the foreign and the customary, the far away and the near, the new and the old. Analogy grips us. It causes the character of address found in metaphor and parable.

17. Metaphor and parable are anything but inauthentic ways of speaking. The opposing assumption that language was originally completely metaphorical and parabolic is probably closer to the mark. There is even reason to ask whether *truth* is really anything else than the "translation" of what exists into language, which for its part is first constituted by such "translation" and thus contains and preserves the process of translation as a basic process of language. The "translations" within language would then be remembrances of the "translation" of what exists into language, through which it first became what it is. See on this my study "Metaphorische Wahrheit; Erwägungen zur theologischen Relevanz der Metapher als Beitrag zur Hermeneutik einer narrativen Theologie," *Beihefte zu Evangelische Theologie* (1974), pp. 76ff.

18. See *ibid.*, pp. 94f.

19. Aristotle, *Rhetorica*, tr. W. R. Roberts, *The Works of Aristotle*, ed. W. D. Ross (Oxford: Clarendon Press, 1952), XI, iii.2, 1404b, 10-12.

This is true not only of the relation of such language processes to their hearers. The one who develops the metaphor and "discovers" the parable must be gripped by the same proportion which later will grip the hearers of his speech. What distinguishes him from them is that he *first of all discovers* the engaging correspondence and then expresses it. But the metaphorical discovery is not only a discovery for the one who first made it. The stating of a discovered correspondence in the form of a metaphor or a parable preserves the character of discovery so that the hearers are drawn into the process of discovery. Analogy as a process of speech is an eminently socializing phenomenon in that it binds together in a fellowship not only the addressed hearers but also the speaker engaged by the analogy with his hearers. This is a fellowship in which the process of discovery on the part of the one who formulates can be recapitulated through his metaphorical language. The discovery shares itself as an event of discovery. As discovering language, metaphors and parables are social.[20] As analogous talk about God, they (with the help of the "speaker who is communicatively competent"[21]) create situations in which the subject of the talk becomes generally understandable, because those addressed become discoverers to all of whom the same thing discloses itself.

This sociality has, however, a *special* character, in a certain sense a *playful* character. The sociality of metaphors and parables distinguishes itself from other kinds of addressing speech, such as the command, in that the discovering language of metaphor and parable is, in a very special way, really not necessary, but is forceful in its nonnecessity. It is not necessary to call Achilles a lion. It was also not necessary to call Jesus God's Son. It was equally unnecessary to tell about the kingdom of God and to say that it is like a treasure buried in a field or like a very precious pearl or like an unjust steward. In such talk, a certain reality is expressed through *possibilities* in such a way that this possibility leads forcefully to the discovery of a new dimension of reality and to greater precision in talk about what is real. Metaphors and parables thus express more in language than was real until now. They do this by involving the person who is addressed in the being of what is being talked about, or they mediate the topic of talk to the being of man. But they do this in such a way that they delve into the reality and do not pass by it or go beyond it. The individual metaphors and parables are, certainly, never necessary as these particular ones. They are *free* formations of language, one might say representatives of the freedom of lan-

---

20. Thus the discovering speech of metaphor and parable is comparable to the social function of the true wise man of classic antiquity, who spoke in parables, and not by chance. See the references to Ben Sira (37:19-26) in Martin Hengel, *Judaism and Hellenism; Studies in their Encounter in Palestine during the Early Hellenistic Period,* tr. J. Bowden (Philadelphia: Fortress Press, 1974), I, 132: "Thus Ben Sira put his wisdom to the service of his people." He was not merely wise for himself. That distinguishes him from Kohelet.

21. See J. Habermas, "Vorbereitende Bemerkungen zu einer Theorie der kommunikativen Kompetenz," in J. Habermas and N. Luhmann, *Theorie der Gesellschaft oder Sozialtechnologie; Was leistet die Systemforschung?* (Frankfurt: Suhrkamp, 1971), pp. 102f. A hermeneutic of analogous talk about God has accordingly as its task "the post-construction of regulatory systems according to which we" not only "produce or generate" "situations of possible speech in general" but the specific situation of addressing talk about God (*ibid.,* p. 102).

guage. That distinguishes them from the necessity of the concept. It is another question whether metaphors and parables, once they have been successfully articulated, can then become dispensable. This question can be answered only in a differentiated way and with regard to the *Sitz im Leben* of any such formulation. For our purposes, it is sufficient to know that the discovering language of metaphors and parables implies a language event of creative freedom. The speaker who formulates a successful metaphor or parable is creative in freedom, and the hearers of successful metaphors and relevant parables involve themselves in that same creative freedom when they permit themselves to be addressed and "gripped" by what is said. It is this very creative freedom of language which is so forceful. The original lingual unity of freedom and forcefulness is nothing more than the essence of analogy. That the relation of a to b through that of c to d is expressed in language is anything but necessary—it could perhaps also be expressed by the relation of y to z. But once it has happened, it is forceful. Analogy is the addressing event of gripping freedom. As such, it is both an enhancement of language and its precise focusing.

Therefore, it is an hermeneutical error of grave consequences when parables and metaphors are understood as a kind of veiling which is supposed to make something "more mysterious" than it already is. One cannot even say that metaphors and parables are indirect discourse. They are distinct from the "normality" of direct discourse as it manifests itself in the indicative statement: for example, Socrates is a dialectical person. But they are distinct from the "normality" of direct discourse not through indirectness but through a higher degree of directness. This higher level of directness, which surpasses the "normality" of direct discourse, this level which belongs chiefly to the essence of the parable, is called concreteness. This talk is obviously not concrete in that it makes perceivable things more objective, so to speak, so that it portrays the green tree as greener and more treelike than normal language does. The concreteness of the parable really does not have primarily to do with the representative or naming function of language, although this function clearly cannot be excluded. The higher level of directness which surpasses the "normality" of direct discourse, which is what we are calling concreteness, is rather the turning of what is being talked about into the speech which then reaches the hearer in such a way that he is drawn into the relationship of word and thing. An event results in which the subject of the discourse, the discourse itself, and the ones addressed are represented in a differentiated unity. In a parable, language is so focused that the *subject* of the discourse *becomes concrete in* language itself and thus defines anew the people addressed in their own existence.[22] Something happens *in* the

---

22. In his book *The Parables; Their Literary and Existential Dimension* (Philadelphia: Fortress Press, 1967), Dan Otto Via has relevantly pointed out that "parables as aesthetic objects are able to engage non-referentially the focal attention of the *whole* man upon configuration of happening existence" (p. 92). Although Via thinks that he is thereby presenting certain corrections of my hermeneutic of parables as I presented them in *Paulus und Jesus* (*op. cit.,* pp. 135ff), I believe that this rather exactly corresponds to what I intended with the thesis that in the parable the kingdom of God is expressed *as* parable. What Via (*op. cit.,* p. 92) calls "the non-referential engagement of the attention" (that is, the linguistic assertion that "this engagement of the attention" was "non-referential") is precisely what I had called the *collective* power of the parable, that is, the power which collects or assembles the narrative elements or the perceptive elements of the parable and at the same time collects human existence. Thus I see myself in agreement

parable, and it happens in such a way that then something also happens *through* the parable. The metaphor already has a tendency toward event, because the metaphor surpasses the directness of indicative speech with its greater concreteness. "Socrates is a horsefly" says more than "Socrates is a dialectical person"— under the presupposition that one understands the *situation* of the naming process (Socrates torments the citizens of Athens the way a horsefly torments a horse— a:b=c:d).

6. Biblical talk about God knows the parable as one of many possible language forms in which faith expresses God. But basically all language forms of faith participate in the structure of parabolic language. In that sense parables serve as the language of faith generally. Of all parables as representatives of the language of faith generally, Jesus' parables of the kingdom of God are especially instructive because, although they are not the adequate ground, they are the hermeneutical preparation for kerygmatic talk about Jesus as the Son of God. The nearness of the kingdom of God which Jesus proclaimed finds in the parable that hermeneutical model which prepares in language form for the still greater nearness which will be expressed in the confession that the word of God has become flesh and has dwelt among us. The Easter kerygma, in point of fact, makes use of the possibilities which the parables of Jesus had initiated. Jesus' parabolic discourse about God had the function of catachesis for the event of the God who is coming near. The parables of Jesus do not speak of God as a man. But they speak of God in such a way that they tell about the world of men. They don't do this by putting the world in God's place so that some kind of general wisdom would emerge as the point of the parables. The points of Jesus' parables disclose that their concern is the kingdom of God, and that means that they are dealing with the intertwined network of God's relationship to Jesus' hearers and their relationship to God. The points of these parables virtually prevent equating God and the world in some way or other.

The equation of God and the world would to all intents leave the world to itself. The world would remain in its old state, and God would remain as he was: nothing would happen. Jesus' parables about the kingdom of God are *events* whose points are supposed to "ignite" in the hearer himself. At the end, that about which the parable spoke is concrete in the hearer. For that to happen, *during* the discourse the listener must be drawn into the talk in such a way that he is *taken along* by the word event of the parable on the way toward its point. But that cannot be achieved by any equation of God and the world.[23] Rather, it leaves the hearer where he is and God and the world in that place where they always were. Equation means basically that an announcement is made "in spoken form" about what had always been. If the parable were an equation, then it

with Via and can only regret his objection that I had understood the parable as an event which "combines the individual ideas or elements of a narrative to one theme" (*sic*!: taken from *Die Gleichnisse Jesu; ihre literarische und existentiale Dimension* [München: C. Kaiser, 1970], p. 92; the English original does not have quite this wording—TR), perhaps a misunderstanding of me. I hope that I have done away with this misunderstanding, caused perhaps by my formulations, when I explicitly assert that that *about which* the parable speaks becomes concrete *in* the parable itself (thus, is "non-referential").

23. Karl Barth therefore sought to emphasize the parable (the analogy) against the equation. See his Reformed reservations about the Lutheran doctrine of communion: "Approach and Intention in Luther's Communion Doctrine," in *Theology and Church; Shorter Writings, 1920-28,* tr. L. P. Smith (New York: Harper, 1962).

would be a thesis, and then its "content" would in fact be a theme which could be abstracted from the "form" of the parable. But a parable is not a thesis and has no theme at all. Rather, it is an event which then makes something else happen. It is probably most comparable in this regard to the joke which must happen if it is to be successful, and which then encounters a person in such a way that something happens within him: he laughs. For that reason, the parables of Jesus never say, The kingdom of God *is*, for example, an especially valuable pearl or a treasure in a field. Rather they say, The kingdom of God *is like* a treasure in a field. And then a story is told: a story about a man who discovers a treasure, and in his joy he goes and sells everything he has and buys the field (Matt. 13:44f). And *while* this story is being told, the listener is being focused on its point. He is being collected in that the parable collects itself, so to speak. And with the point, the kingdom of God itself in the parable *arrives* in the hearer if he engages himself in the parable and lets himself be gathered by the parable into it.

For this reason it is hermeneutically important to comprehend that the parables of Jesus are developed out of their point. For that reason I argued against Adolf Jülicher and the rhetorical tradition that the point of the parable was a *tertium comparationis* ('third point of comparison') between the image half and the content half.[24] Rather it is a *primum comparationis* ('first point of comparison') which at the end of the parable emerges as *the point*. Whoever looks for the *tertium comparationis* here destroys *the event* of the parable. Basically he understands the parable as a comparison of firmly established things (a:b = c:d). This presupposes that the content half is already known, that is, as a relation (c:d) which *remains* completely different from the narrated relation (a:b), just as different as thing and image, as *res significata* and *res significans* ('signified thing' and 'signifying thing'). But that is not at all the way it is. If we want to express what happens here by using the difference between *signum* and *res significata* ('sign' and 'signified thing'), a difference which hermeneutically is totally inappropriate for Jesus' parables, then we would have to work with the *sacramental* relation of *signum* and *res significata*, so that the *signum* would be understood as *signum efficax* ('efficacious sign'). The sign would be *used up* in what it signifies, just as the wine and bread are consumed in the communion in that they announce the presence of Jesus Christ. In being used up, in the destruction of the sign, the *res significata* happens. But the hermeneutical distinction between *res significans* (*signum*; 'signifying thing' or 'sign') and *res significata* ('signified thing'), between the image half and the content half, is too encumbered to be applied here appropriately. Ultimately it cannot free itself from the structure of analogy as the "still greater *dissimilarity* in so great similarity." The issue at stake here is the overcoming of this understanding of analogy if one wants to understand Jesus' parables of the kingdom of God.

These parables do presuppose the dissimilarity of the kingdom of God and the world in the sense of a fundamental difference, but they only emphasize this difference so that the great dissimilarity in a still *greater similarity* is emphasized. That means that the kingdom of God expresses itself in the language form of the parable, which certainly is to be understood as analogy, so that its strangeness,

24. See Jüngel, *Paulus und Jesus*, p. 138.

its abstract differentness from the world, is ultimately surpassed by a greater familiarity in the sense of a *concrete differentness* from the world which benefits the world. That is possible only when the relations which have been placed in relationship to each other are defined by the activity of the kingdom of God. Strictly speaking, one cannot even say that *it* is like this *with* the kingdom of God. . . ; rather, one must say, The kingdom of God itself is like this so that the following relationship corresponds to it. To put it another way, the kingdom of God (x), unknown in the world and not even knowable within the world's terms, relates itself to the world (a) in a relationship which in the world corresponds to the way things happened in the story of the treasure in the field: $x \rightarrow a = b:c$. At an earlier point I put it this way: the kingdom of God comes into language in the parable as a parable, and thus comes to the hearer. I would emphasize now more strongly than in *Paulus und Jesus* that it *comes* to language in that people *bring* it into language. It is certainly true of b:c that 'it is received according to the mode of the receiver' (*secundum modum recipientis recipitur*). But the kingdom of God cannot as such be *brought* into language without *coming* into language, without $x \rightarrow a$. Its "reception according to the mode of the receiver" presupposes 'according to the speaking God' (*secundum dicentem deum*). God *comes* into language. He is discussed, *enters* into words. And only to that extent can he also be *brought* to language. Bringing God to expression in language thus follows after the relation of the kingdom of God to the world and consequently has as its criterion the fact that the *very great distance away* of the eschatological kingdom of God is surpassed by a *still greater nearness*. Thus the parable, although it speaks the language of the world, speaks at the same time in truth and speaks genuinely of God.[25]

The still greater nearness of the far distant kingdom of God evidences itself in the point of any parable. In the point of the parable, the kingdom of God

---

25. Jesus' parables of the kingdom of God achieve hermeneutically exactly what Luther ascribed to synecdoche. But whereas the synecdochical form of speech *presupposes* that there is a highly intimate nearness of two different things already present, in order *then* to express the one with the help of the other, the parables of the kingdom of God, or the analogical power of the gospel, first brings about this special nearness of elements which are distinct from each other in principle. One might say that analogy brings God and man together as it is spoken. Thus it is the structure of the event in which God addresses himself to man in such a way that man is determined now outwardly and inwardly to speak of God. Inwardly too! The indispensable emphasis on the externality of the God who speaks of himself may not lead to a denial of the fact that man in the process is addressed in his inmost being and in this fashion is drawn out of himself. In every human discourse about God, man is also expressing himself—although this certainly need not take place in the form of direct communication about himself. Man says more about himself in that he must talk about God, that he wants to talk about God, and that he likes to talk about God. In the human will to and human joy at talk about God the fact that 'God is more intimate to me than my inmost being' proves itself to be the kind of liberating power that means that the inner necessity of having to speak about God is experienced as the self-expressive freedom to want to talk about God. And this is on the basis of the analogical power of the parable in which the God who is coming to speech enables man to speak about God. Johann Gerhard was thus well-advised when he insisted, while retaining the traditional theologoumenon of the 'incomprehensibility of God,' that the 'knowledge of God is sought from the word,' because it is 'sufficient for salvation' and must be called a 'perfect knowledge' (*Loci theologici,* ed. E. Preuss [Berlin, 1863], vol. I, p. 286, loc. II, cap. 5, nr. 90).

comes near to the hearer in an unsurpassable way. Ultimately it is nearer to me than I am to myself—similar to a successful joke which forces laughter even if one should be so close to himself that he does not want to laugh at all. Where the point of the parable of the kingdom of God arrives, the hearer is no longer his own closest neighbor. God is closer to him: 'God is more intimate to me than my most intimate part' (deus interior intimo meo).[26]

7. Proceeding from the parables of Jesus, an opportunity now presents itself to overcome the alternative between a so-called dogmatic (i.e., naive) anthropomorphism and a so-called symbolic anthropomorphism. The parable as talk about God prevents the naiveté of "dogmatic" anthropomorphism which destroys the distinction between God and man by speaking of God as of a man, raised to his highest form. The fatal thing about this naiveté of "dogmatic" anthropomorphism is first seen in its consequences. For a God conceived of as man to the highest degree cannot really be concretely distinguished from man. For the sake of the deity of God, then, "dogmatic" anthropomorphism must necessarily call forth that criticism which objects that the anthropomorphism which thinks of God like a man cannot think God as God. It was in this sense that Heraclitus and Xenophanes criticized the humanization of deity in myth. Obviously, the consequence then is that, in countering the inappropriate human-ization of God in "dogmatic" anthropomorphism, an even more inappropriate dehumanization of God is called for in a critique of "dogmatic" anthropomor-phism, a critique which is no less dogmatic. The threat then is that God can no longer be distinguished from man. He disappears into the distant realm of the unspeakable and thereby loses his concrete distinctiveness from man.

The fatal thing then about naive "dogmatic" anthropomorphism is ulti-

26. I refer to Augustine's famous statement: "Thou wert more inward to me than my most inward part; and higher than my highest" (Confessions, bk. III, ch. VII/11, NPNF, 1st ser., I, 63). To understand the Augustinian esse ('to be') as venire ('to come') is, however, essential for the understanding of gospel as analogy. This is not in the sense of a being-present of the creative ground in what exists, which was always there, as Paul Tillich thought ("God . . . is nearer to them than they are to themselves"; Systematic Theology, 2 vols. [Chicago: University of Chicago Press, 1957], II, 7). It is also not meant in the sense of the identity of God with the "mystery of the obvious that is closer to me than my own I," as Martin Buber put it (I and Thou, tr. W. Kaufman [New York: Scribner's, 1970], p. 127). Rather, in the sense of a self-communication which takes place as an arrival, God "is" closer to me than I am able to be close to myself.

It was probably in this sense that John Calvin, arguing against Osiander (De unico mediatore Jesu Christo et iustificatione fidei; Confessio [Königsberg, 1551]), understood every dwelling of Christ in our hearts, every union of the highest degree which becomes ours in relation to Christ and which lets us share in his blessings, as the event of fellowship with Christ which is constituted by his coming. Thus he is not only outside us but also in us in such a way that we are outside ourselves. See Calvin, Institutes of the Christian Religion, ed. J. T. McNeill, tr. F. L. Battles (Library of Christian Classics, vol. 20) (Philadelphia: Westminster, 1960), I, bk. III, ch. 10, p. 737: "Therefore, that joining together of Head and members, that indwelling of Christ in our hearts—in short, that mystical union—are accorded by us the highest degree of importance, so that Christ, having been made ours, makes us sharers with him in the gifts with which he has been endowed. We do not, therefore, contemplate him outside ourselves from afar in order that his righteousness may be imputed to us but because we put on Christ and are engrafted into his body—in short, because he deigns to make us one with him. For this reason, we glory that we have fellowship of righteousness with him."

mately that it cannot withstand theological enlightenment but rather, when once theologically enlightened, asserts that God is in the final effect not speakable at all. Since one is no longer allowed to think God as a divine ego according to the analogy of a human ego, a divine ego which is addressable as Thou, he becomes unspeakable as his own subject, that is, as God. What is called for today *as a substitute,* the talk about God's co-humanity (as an appropriate definition of what is meant by the word "God"!), is in truth the hermeneutical dehumanization of God. It would be correct to say of a God so understood that all things human were alien to him.[27] But since all things human are alien to him, he must be rejected as a counterpart who encounters man. The dehumanized God cannot be concretely distinguished from man. That excessive distance into which God is hermeneutically shifted in this way leads to man's seeing such a divinity as an ideal which he must strive to attain. Man alienates himself from his own humanity in order to seek after the place of the distant God, man himself now being an essence of the distant.

In opposition to "dogmatic" anthropomorphism *and* the fatal consequences which may be ascribed to it, it may be said of the *parable* as analogous talk about God that it preserves the *concrete distinctiveness* of God and man (world). It preserves this distinctiveness, however, in that it combines God ("the kingdom of God") and man in one and same event, in the parable itself.

The parable, as concrete spoken implementation of the analogy between God and man, does not recede into a merely "symbolic" anthropomorphism, which would articulate in spite of such a great similarity between God and man a still greater dissimilarity. Parable as analogous talk about God prevents both "dogmatic" anthropomorphism and "symbolic" anthropomorphism which renders the difference between God and man as a *total differentness.* If "dogmatic" anthropomorphism speaks of God *like* a man, the no less fatal "symbolic" anthropomorphism forbids speaking of God *as* a man. Thus it contradicts what the Christian faith asserts to be true: that God was among men as the man Jesus. This unique identity of God and man, confessed in faith, excludes in its uniqueness one's speaking of God arbitrarily *like* a man, but also opposes the prohibition of speaking of God *as* this particular man. Christian theology must therefore be inflexible with regard to both "dogmatic" and "symbolic" anthropomorphism. For Christian talk about God stands and falls with its being able to speak of God *as* a man without falling prey to some kind of "dogmatic" anthropomorphism. God and perishability are thought together in the Christian faith when the faith speaks of God as a man and *in the process* says "God," and does not require that one always speak of a man *instead* of God. Rather, what must be done is to speak of God as a man in such a way that *this man* whose name *is Jesus* can

27. It would be worth conducting exhaustive research to see to what degree the major currents within the so-called God-is-dead theology represent the ultimate consequence of "dogmatic" anthropomorphism. It could probably be demonstrated that in fact this is a last form of naive anthropomorphism, working itself out on the basis of the intellectual and historical premise of the critique of anthropomorphism. Even if God is understood as co-humanity, the critique of anthropomorphism (as it was worked through in its most pointed form in Feuerbach's suspicion of illusion) has only appeared to be radicalized, whereas *de facto* a radicalization of naive "dogmatic" anthropomorphism has been achieved.

be named, confessed, and called on *as God*. If it is true of the parables of Jesus that God comes closer to their human hearers in them than they are to themselves, then it is true of Jesus as the parable of God that God has come closer in him to *humanity* than humanity is able to come close to itself. Through that process he brings humanity into a new relationship to itself whose form is the ecumenical community of Jesus Christ.

If God comes closer to humanity and in it to me than the human ego, individually and generically, is able to come close to itself, if God in this sense is "more inward to me than my most inward part," *then* he is not "higher than my highest" in such a way that my perishability would not touch him and his highness would not touch me. What is evidenced *hermeneutically* with regard to talk about God as the still greater similarity in such a great dissimilarity must also be expressible and be formulated *ontologically* with regard to the being of God. What should one call that being which in such great dissimilarity is concerned for the greater similarity, in such great distance is concerned for the still greater nearness, in such great majesty is concerned for the greater condescension, in such great differentness is concerned for the still more intensive relationship? To ask it in a Pauline way (in all of this we are dealing with God's relationship to 'sinful man'): How is that being to be named who counters growing sin with still greater grace (Rom. 5:20)?

The answer does not have to be sought. It is both anthropologically and theologically evident and is called *Love*. The basic hermeneutical structure of Evangelical talk about God, namely, the analogy as the still greater similarity within such a great dissimilarity between God and man, is the linguistic-logical expression for the being of God, which being realizes itself *in the midst of such great self-relatedness as still greater selflessness,* and is as such *love.* But love is compelled to express itself in speech. Part of love is the declaration of love and the confirmation of love. Since God is not only one who loves, but is love itself, one *must* not only speak about him, but one *can* speak about him. Love possesses the power of speech: *caritas capax verbi* ('love is capable of the word').

CHAPTER V

On the Humanity of God

SECTION 19. The Humanity of God as a Story to be Told; Hermeneutical Preface

1. Where is God? One reference to the answer to this question was provided for us in the dark statement of the death of God. The illumination of its atheistic meaning out of its christological origin led to the insight that God's place is his unity with perishable man. In distinction from the meaning which atheistic usage assigned to the dark statement of God's death, its christological origin demands that the unity of God with perishable man be understood as the identification of the living God with the crucified Jesus of Nazareth and the event of that identification as the revelation of the life of the crucified God. The original and indispensable meaning of talk about the death of God is not the identification of man with God, which necessarily must lead to the replacement of God with man (understood generically), but the identification of God with the *one* man Jesus *for the sake of all men*. Its original sense, now to be regained, is not to express man's striving for divinity, but rather the *humanity of God*. It reminds us that that "which is primarily revealed for faith and only for it, that existing one which as revelation chiefly brings about faith . . . [is] Christ, the crucified God."[1] Understood this way, this discourse directs us toward the task of thinking God himself as the union of death and life for the sake of life. Since the "union of death and life for the sake of life" is a way of defining the essence of love, we shall have to think *God as love* together with the christologically understood humanity of God.

The task of thinking God's humanity confronted us with the problem of the thinkability of God in an historical situation characterized by the self-grounding of thought in "I think." In this historical situation, the metaphysical concept of God was undermined by the *cogito* ('I think') which established itself between the essence and the existence of God. The *material* insight into the humanity of God taught us to think of God as the subject of himself who is *free* in the very event of love, and that led to the *formal* insight that God can be known and thought only on the basis of his own being. God is thinkable as God solely on the basis of his self-sharing of his being, which has taken place. This

1. M. Heidegger, *Phänomenologie und Theologie* (Frankfurt: Klostermann, 1970), p. 18.

299

self-sharing of God is to be understood, as we saw, as the self-communication and self-emptying of a subject who speaks and addresses out of himself, to whom anthropologically only faith corresponds. For God, as the one who comes from himself and who comes to this world in this unconditional sovereignty, can be understood only when he is thought of as the one who addresses us about himself out of himself and that means as the one who comes in the word. The God who comes only in the word finds his only correspondence in faith, because only faith lets God's being be a being that is coming, that is, lets God be present as the one who is absent. This necessary linkage of God and faith came to be seen as the condition for the possibility of thinking God. And the *thought of God*, as that which thought thinks, must follow the *word* which makes *faith* possible—just as in a general sense language is seen to be that more original phenomenon over against thought or consciousness.[2]

But we also saw that it was absolutely essential to resist the flight away from thought, which understandably can follow the disintegration of the metaphysical concept of God. What belongs "together with God" is not a 'faith fleeing from understanding' (*fides fugiens intellectum*) but a 'faith seeking understanding' (*fides quaerens intellectum*). The God who is human in his divinity is the precise opposite of an essence which in ill-willed fashion closes itself to all human thought and knowledge. God is not envious[3]—just as little as love is envious. As love, rather, God is thinkable, without a distinction capable of being made between essence and existence. Love is essentially existing lovingly. As love, God is thinkable in the concept of an overflowing being which subjects itself to nothingness, a concept which understands God's essence and existence as a unity which cannot be differentiated: God's being is *a se in nihilum eksistere* ('to perdure out of itself into nothingness'). As we shall now present in greater detail, he *is* the event of the unity of life and death for the sake of life. Thus he *is* the event of a still greater selflessness in the midst of such great self-relatedness. That is how he *is* God.

To think God's being as love means then to think God's thinkability on the basis of his speakability, and his speakability on the basis of the *correspondence* he has established between God and man. The analogy of faith brings God into speech in such a way that he comes nearer to humanity and thus nearer to the individual person than they and he are capable of coming near to themselves.

The word which corresponds to God, which God lets come to earth as that word which comes solely from God and which proves him to be the one who, coming still closer from and in spite of the great distance, can thus only be a word *event*, can only be a *movement* of speech which corresponds to the self-movement of God. Human speech corresponds to the being of God, which is coming, in that it moves every statement, each of which is as such unrenounceable, on into movement again, that is, it is not ashamed of its *temporality*, preferring instead some kind of timeless concept, but rather carries out purposefully that temporality.

The language which corresponds to God is, in an eminent sense, temporal word (or, verb). The characteristics of language and time, understood as an original unity, work together to make the word which corresponds to God the

2. See above, p. 253.
3. See above, p. 261, n. 37.

location of the humanity of God. This is true in a *material* sense in that God as the one who speaks out of himself (*ho logos*) has expressed himself, through the event of the identification with the history of Jesus of Nazareth, in the period of time of one man's life, and has ascribed in the event of the resurrection of Jesus from the dead an eternal future to this period of time, so that one must say: God has entered as man into the temporality of human history ('the word has become flesh'), and in so doing has changed that history in a way in which it could not change itself. This is also true in a *formal* sense in that the human word which speaks of this event has to announce, both as 'proclamation' (*kēryssein*) and as 'confession' (*homologein*), the history of Jesus Christ as the time of God's humanity which has come once and for all. The word which corresponds to God, the human language which corresponds to God, is something like an eschatological declaration of time,[4] which *interrupts* world history as it proceeds "through the course of time" with the announcement of its end based on the turning point which has taken place in the history of Jesus Christ; in doing so, it promises humanity "a new attitude of man to the world in which he lives."[5] But since both the end which is to be announced to the world[6] and the turning point which has already happened are possibilities which *have come* to the world together with the God who has come to the world, and thus can neither be derived nor explained from the history of the world, the announcement of a new age in the history of the world can assert itself only indirectly in that it demonstrates itself in terms of the being of the world until now. This happens in that the announce-

4. See E. Fuchs, "Die Zukunft des Glaubens nach 1. Thess. 5,1-11," in *Glaube und Erfahrung; Zum christologischen Problem im Neuen Testament, Gesammelte Aufsätze* (Tübingen: J. C. B. Mohr, 1965), III, 362: "The time of Jesus Christ as the time of the children of God *is* already the language event on which everything depends. It is not words, but the word of this time announcement itself which is the event which alone gives entry into the eschatological age. And thus is it precisely this word which not only 'preserves' in faith, in love, and in hope, but which is to be actively used as what it is: as the medium of the revelation of God. For God does what he *says*."

5. Friedrich Gogarten, *Christ the Crisis*, tr. R. A. Wilson (Richmond: John Knox Press, 1970), p. 117 (a literal translation of the original German title may be useful: 'Jesus Christ; Turning Point of the World; Basic Questions of Christology'—TR). Gogarten defines "this new relationship through which the world is constituted anew in the sense that the salvation which comes with the kingdom of God is present in it" (literal translation from German original, p. 91) as the relationship of responsibility *for* the world, not *to* the world (ET, p. 118). Since man's relationship to God is, from now on, decided solely by God, man is free "to forsake the domination of the present world and its ordinance" (*ibid.*, p. 118) and to take over responsibility so that the world through its cultic piety can no longer make man responsible *to* the world and thus be the world "which dominates him and separates him from God" (translation from original edition; see ET, p. 118—TR). Gogarten was politically rather conservative, but one can see in terms of his Christology how he could become one of the theological predecessors of a "theology of revolution."

6. For the genesis of the New Testament announcement of the end of history out of the historical understanding of prophetic thought, see H. Gese, "Geschichtliches Denken im Alten Orient und im Alten Testament," in *Vom Sinai zum Zion; alttestamentliche Beiträge zur biblische Theologie* (München: C. Kaiser, 1974), p. 98: "For prophetic thought, history is pushing toward its goal. And the more this goal is identified with the salvific acts of Yahweh, which once established the covenant, the stronger the eschatological molding of historical thought had to become: History finds its end. . . . The end of history broke in when the kingdom of God appeared in history, a kingdom which is not of this world."

ment of the new age makes the world's being up to now appear as a being *which has been made old* by the *new age* and which is predetermined now to pass away—just as Adam first *becomes* the old Adam through Jesus Christ as the new man.[7]

The announcement of a new age, which declares the humanity of God, is thus an announcement which does not understand itself based on the world's self-understanding, but it transforms this self-understanding as the announcement of a *change of the ages* and a *turning point in history.* It is no accident that thinkers like Kant and Schleiermacher, who weighed their words carefully, spoke of the Christian faith as a revolution which has given both the human ego and the history of the world an incomparable turning point. But such a change of the ages can introduce itself only *temporally,* and such an historical turning point can make itself known only *historically.* The form of that talk which expresses God in language, that talk about the humanity of God, must accordingly be a language which structurally expresses time and history. Only in that way can it render the eschatological change of the ages understandable as a world turning point which has happened historically and which also addresses every future present age in the world. The language which corresponds to the humanity of God must be oriented in a highly *temporal* way in its *language* structure. This is the case in the language mode of *narration, telling a story,* which, if one wants to look for something like an original mode of speaking, can most probably be understood as the "original language" because of its inner order which genuinely unites the characteristics of language and time, along with the qualities of interjection and evocation.[8] God's humanity introduces itself into the world as a story to be told. Jesus told about God in parables before he himself was proclaimed as the parable of God. There is an hermeneutically persuasive reason that the eschatological event of the identification of God with the Crucified One became an integral[9] part of the life of Jesus as it was lived[9] and thus became a rich story which demanded explication. In that sense, no theology of the Crucified One can or may do without the narration of the life and suffering of Jesus, as a life in the *act of the word* which tells of God's humanity. Yes, it will not even be able to grasp the life, death, and resurrection of Jesus as a story which is unified in itself without going further back into the narrative context of the

7. See on this E. Fuchs, *Zum hermeneutischen Problem in der Theologie; Die existentiale Interpretation, Gesammelte Aufsätze* (Tübingen: J. C. B. Mohr [Siebeck], 1965²), p. 284 [compare E. Fuchs, "The New Testament and the Hermeneutical Problem," in *The New Hermeneutic,* eds. J. M. Robinson and J. B. Cobb, Jr. (New York: Harper & Row, 1964), vol. II].

8. Myth is earlier than logos, the metaphor is earlier than the concept, and the stories of the gods (*theologiai*) are earlier than the philosophical theology which regulates them (*typoi peri theologias*). Schelling (Einleitung, *Philosophie der Mythologie, Sämmtliche Werke,* ed. K. F. A. Schelling [Stuttgart and Augsburg: J. G. Cotta, 1858], II/1, p. 52) even supposes that "language itself is only faded mythology," that is, faded narration—which agrees with Jean Paul's famous statement that "every language is a dictionary of faded metaphors looking back on mental relationships" (*Vorschule der Ästhetik,* in *Werke,* ed. N. Miller [Munich: Carl Hanser Verlag, 1973³], vol. V, par. 50, p. 184).

9. See on this my essays "Jesu Wort und Jesus als Wort Gottes" and "Thesen zur Grundlegung der Christologie," in *Unterwegs zur Sache; Theologische Bemerkungen* (München: C. Kaiser, 1972), pp. 126ff and 274ff.

history of Israel, in which "what is new and has never yet been" identifies itself as one reaches out to what has long since happened because "what is new and has never yet been can only be introduced in narrative."[10] Based on the context of this history of Israel, which tells of God's coming, but which through God's coming is always brought to the possibility of its ending,[11] even the creation can become a story to be told as the *history* of creation. Apart from this telling of the creation story, it would scarcely be possible to understand the God who identifies himself with the crucified Jesus as the one who not only calls forth being out of nonbeing but also calls forth new life out of the death which *annihilates* all being. He could not be understood, further, as the one who introduces himself as the God who is eschatologically active and who in his reliability is never old but always coming into language in a new way. That thinking which wants to understand God will always be led back to narrative. The thought of God can be thought only as the telling of a story, whereby the concepts are to be carefully controlled. If thinking wants to think God, then it must endeavor to tell stories.

In this way, it comes to know itself in a new way *as thinking,* in that consciousness now appears to be constituted not only by the egocentricity of "I think" but rather by history, and thus discovers itself to be a consciousness which is "entangled in history."[12] Consciousness is structured in a thoroughly temporal way both by the stories which it always has in its past, which ontically mold it, and by the history which essentially lies before it, which ontologically molds it. "Tell me your story, and I will tell you who you are"—the conclusion could be expanded to read, "I will tell you how you think." This is true, in any event, of the we-consciousness[13] of fellowships and to a certain degree of human

10. J. B. Metz, "A Short Apology for Narrative," in *The Crisis of Religious Language* (*Concilium: Religion in the Seventies,* vol. 5, nr. 9), eds. J. B. Metz and J.-P. Jossua, tr. D. Smith (New York: Herder & Herder, 1973), p. 86.

11. See my essay "Die Welt als Möglichkeit und Wirklichkeit; Zum ontologischen Ansatz der Rechtfertigungslehre," in *Unterwegs zur Sache,* p. 223. The eschatologically new has no other tie with the old than that it is what makes the old into the old. To do that, it must explicate itself in relation to the old in such a way that it can be identified as the new over against it. It cannot make itself understandable by *basing* itself on what has been. Its evidence must rather be made understandable on its own terms. But this happens in that it introduces itself *as narrative* into the context of what has been, which context cannot say anything eschatologically new in its own power. In narrative, the new explicates itself in relation to the old so that it really becomes understandable as the new.

12. "Entangled in Stories" (*In Geschichten verstrickt;* it could also be 'histories'— TR) is the title of a book by the Husserl student W. Schapp, who asserts the entanglement of consciousness in stories over against the intentional character of consciousness; Schapp, *In Geschichten verstrickt; Zum Sein von Mensch und Ding* (Hamburg: R. Meiner, 1953). See by the same author, *Philosophie der Geschichten* (Leer: G. Rautenberg, 1959), above all pp. 177ff and 271: "Wherever one speaks, it is people who are entangled in stories who are speaking."

13. This is also true of the ego-consciousness. "*Individuum est ineffabile*" would be a true statement only if the individual were a being without history. The statement becomes incorrect if the individual is identical with a story. Then it becomes relatable. For in narrative the unique and individual are mediated through language into generality without losing their uniqueness and individuality. See F. Mildenberger, *Theologie für die Zeit; Wider die religiöse Interpretation der Wirklichkeit in der modernen Theologie* (Stuttgart: Calwer Verlag, 1969), p. 161, n. 13; W. Pannenberg, *Theology and the Philosophy of Science,* tr. F. McDonagh (Philadelphia: Westminster, 1976), p. 61, n. 111.

reason as generic consciousness. Hegel's *Phenomenology of the Spirit* is built on this. And if Dilthey's call for a "critique of historical reason" should ever be carried out, then not only the narrative depth structure of reason will have to be dealt with, but also all the traditions which have been perceived through narrative and been received into the general consciousness. Many traditions may well be diverted into the unconscious part of general consciousness. But as long as the tradition of the humanity of God remains both scandal and foolish as the announcement of the world's turning point, which does not arise out of worldly possibilities, then it will only very partially be integratable into general consciousness. Man can correspond in his language to the humanity of God only by *constantly telling the story anew.* He thus acknowledges that God's humanity as a story *which has happened* does not cease being history *which is happening now,* because God remains the subject of his own story. To put it another way: it is the power of the Holy Spirit in which God's humanity constantly encounters human reason as a story to be told anew, although it cannot be captured once and for all in that act of perception. God's being remains a being *which is coming.*

2. The task which remains for us in the last part of this study, the task of defining the humanity of God more precisely, proceeds from the presupposition that God requires that he be *told about.* A few remarks about this presupposition should expose our approach to the task we still have to do. We have said that man is able to correspond to the humanity of God only by narrating it. We have based this on the knowledge of the humanity of God as an event which turns human history around and which became reality not out of this history and its possibilities but solely out of the 'alien power' (*potentia aliena*) of the God who comes to the world. The language which corresponds to history is narration. The language which corresponds to the turning point of history is even more so narration. *"History* tells stories."[14] The special significance which this general

14. This is the principle of linguistic-analytical philosophy so often cited in more recent hermeneutics of history (A. C. Danto, *Analytical Philosophy of History* [Cambridge: Cambridge University Press, 1965], p. 111); see the critique of this in F. Fellmann, "Das Ende des Laplaceschen Dämons," in R. Koselleck and W.-D. Stempel, eds., *Geschichte—Ereignis und Erzählung (Poetik und Hermeneutik; Arbeitsergebnisse einer Forschungsgruppe,* vol. V) (München: Wilhelm Fink Verlag, 1973), pp. 115ff; on the entire problem, see W. Pannenberg, *op. cit.,* pp. 58-224, above all pp. 58ff, 71, 145ff.

The narrative structure of biblical language and of theologically responsible talk about God has been dealt with in a variety of ways in more recent theology. Next to the diverse statements by Karl Barth, see above all G. von Rad, *Old Testament Theology,* 2 vols., tr. D. M. G. Stalker (New York: Harper & Row, 1962), I, 115-21, esp. p. 121 ("Thus, re-telling remains the most legitimate form of theological discourse on the Old Testament"); K. H. Miskotte, *When the Gods are Silent,* tr. J. W. Doberstein (New York: Harper & Row, 1967), pp. 199-214; F. Mildenberger, *op. cit.,* pp. 157ff; F. Mildenberger, *Gotteslehre; Eine dogmatische Untersuchung* (Tübingen: J. C. B. Mohr, 1975), pp. 80-86 and *passim*; J. B. Metz, "The Future in the Memory of Suffering," in *New Questions on God (Concilium: Religion in the Seventies,* vol. 76), ed. J. B. Metz, tr. J. Griffiths (New York: Herder & Herder, 1972), pp. 9ff; J. B. Metz, "Erinnerung," article in H. Krings *et al.,* eds., *Handbuch philosophischer Grundbegriffe* (München: Kösel-Verlag, 1973), I, 386ff; J. B. Metz, "Erlösung und Emanzipation," *Stimme der Zeit,* 191 (1973), 171ff; J. B. Metz, "A Short Apology for Narrative," in *The Crisis of Religious Language (Concilium,* vol. 5, nr. 9) (New York: Herder & Herder, 1973), pp. 84ff; H. Weinrich, "Narrative Theology," in J. B. Metz and J.-P. Jossua, eds., *The Crisis of Religious Language,* pp. 46ff; H. Zahrnt, "Religiöse Aspekte gegenwärtiger Welt- und

hermeneutical principle has for responsible thinking about the humanity of God will now be explained by means of a reflection on its fundamentally ontological implications.

By *narrative* we do not mean any kind of talking which could express itself *"this way or another way."* This is not an issue of arbitrary possibilities. To be sure, narrative does not simply describe what happened, and thus it is to be distinguished from the mere description of some reality. And certainly narrative does not correspond to what is to be narrated in that it comprehends this event which necessarily must be expressed *"in this way and not another."* Rather, narrative fluctuates in the middle space between the arbitrary possibility of "this way and also another" on the one hand and the rigid necessity of "this way and no other way" on the other. As the telling of history, it participates in the mode of being of history itself, which as reality incorporates within itself both the past possibility out of which it emerges and the future possibilities which it contains, and thus it is what it is only within the realm of its own possibilities. "That means that the narrative can expose more aspects in an event than could be ascertained at the point in time when the event happens."[15] To narrate history means to delve into its unique and irrevocable reality by returning to its *past* possibility from which it came, with regard as well to its *future* possibilities, and thus to grant to the past reality a future.[16] In contrast with the arbitrariness of inventing stories, but also in contrast with the necessity of the concept, narrative is a powerful kind of talk which should result in past history liberating its most authentic possibilities anew. If these possibilities are not liberated, then the narrative of reality was inattentive to what was possible and missed the historicity of that reality which was narrated unhistorically; in such a case, both the historicity and the essence of narrative were missed. The historian too, so long as he is not only describing but also explaining history, has the task "of varying the event against the background of all the possibilities which do not become visible until after the fact,"[17] and thus of leading to an "understanding of the facts as one possibility among many."[18] Of course, this last possibility is to be understood as the one which became relevant and will probably remain relevant.[19] Under this presupposition of the reality of the events, historical understanding is in fact an "understanding which is more interested in the possibility than the facticity of the historical events. 'The single thing proves over and over

Lebenserfahrung; Reflexionen über die Notwendigkeit einer neuen Erfahrungstheologie," *Zeitschrift für Theologie und Kirche,* 71 (1974), 94ff; D. Mieth, "Narrative Ethik," *Freiburger Zeitschrift für Philosophie und Theologie,* 22 (1975), 297ff; G. Lohfink, "Erzählung als Theologie; Zur sprachlichen Grundstruktur der Evangelien," *Stimme der Zeit,* 192 (1974), 521ff.

15. F. Fellmann, *op. cit.,* p. 131.

16. "To grant a future" in a double sense: (a) as the representing repetition of history which has happened, (b) as the liberation of the assumptions contained in it.

17. F. Fellmann, *op. cit.,* p. 132.

18. *Ibid.,* p. 133.

19. R. Bultmann analyzed the understanding of history from the point of view of the possibility which remains relevant and which discloses itself to the one who understands as the opportunity for his own existence. See Bultmann, *Jesus and the Word,* trs. L. P. Smith and E. Huntress Lantero (New York: Scribners, 1934), pp. 3-15; "Das Problem der Hermeneutik," in *Glauben und Verstehen II* (Tübingen: J. C. B. Mohr, 1968⁵), pp. 211ff; *The Presence of Eternity; History and Eschatology* (The Gifford Lectures, 1955) (Edinburgh: University Press, 1957), pp. 110-22.

again to be unimportant, but the possibility of every single thing reveals something about the nature of the world.' Wittgenstein's statement, which applies to philosophy in general, can also be properly applied to history."[20]

Narrative is therefore an especially strict form of talk. It expresses reality in such a way that it originally unites the suppressed freedom of possibility with the driving power of the forceful. For in it history returns to that element out of which it emerged, back into language. And through this return to language that *happened* history advances as *happening* history.

If it is true of all human history that it demands narration, then the humanity of God which is to be understood only as history certainly finds its lingual correspondence in the process of narrative. The literary gospel is that form of narrative process which has become text, narratives in which the oldest Christian communities narrated the humanity of God as the story of Jesus Christ. And again, in the gospel the story of Jesus is told as a *narrator* who proclaimed, or as a proclaimer who *narrated* so that the literary genus gospel (as the narration of the humanity of God which became an event in the history of Jesus Christ) implies the story of the story-teller Jesus. At the same time, this narration insists on its being *passed along*. As such, it has kerygmatic character, and thus does not simply address one privately but rather in such a way that it can be passed on as something addressing everyone. The gospel as kerygmatic talk has, from an hermeneutical perspective as well, a fundamental missionary thrust which apparently corresponds to the universal claims of the humanity of God which is to be told.

This content was aptly described by H. Weinrich:[21] "Jesus of Nazareth is presented to us primarily as a person about whom stories are told, and frequently also as a person about whom narratable stories are told, and the disciples appear as listeners to stories, who then spread and retell, orally or in writing, the stories they have heard." The theological deficiency in Weinrich's extremely stimulating discussion on the possibility of narrative theology consists of a neglect of the unique characteristic of the story (or stories) to be told. Thus he can deal with Jesus' narration of parables and the story of this narrator in the gospel as hermeneutically identical, so that the uniqueness of Jesus as the parable of God remains untouched, even though for a narrative theology the question would have to be raised as to how the one who told of the kingdom of God could himself become the narrator who was the theme of the narrative. Weinrich does note that the "Easter event formula . . ." became "simply an event about which a story is told, and one which sums up all the other events about which stories have been or could be told."[22] Here the *kerygmatic* character of the entire christological context of narration becomes unavoidably urgent. But Weinrich draws only the one conclusion (which is potentially quite correct): "But this central event can also produce a situation in which those who have accepted the story of the Easter event as hearers and in this quality acknowledge themselves as

20. F. Fellmann, *op. cit.*, p. 133. See also L. Wittgenstein, *Tractatus Logico-philosophicus*, tr. F. P. Ramsey (New York: The Humanities Press, 1951), nr. 3.3421, p. 59; see also E. Jüngel, "Die Welt als Möglichkeit und Wirklichkeit," in *Unterwegs zur Sache*, pp. 206ff.

21. See H. Weinrich, *op. cit.*, p. 48.

22. *Ibid.*, p. 51.

members of the Christian storytelling community in the Easter greeting 'Christ is risen,' are thereby dispensed from accepting or retelling any other stories. The Christian now needs only to retell the story of the Easter event, and no other, an important dispensation in a post-narrative age."[23]

But that this was possible in an age which was by no means post-narrative can be illustrated in the apostle Paul's dispute with those Christian enthusiasts who identified themselves with the telling of the Easter event in such a way that they believed they could dispense with the passion history of the resurrected one. And against them Paul pointedly proclaimed the Resurrected One *as the Crucified One*. In hermeneutical correspondence with this, the christological tradition turned from its enthusiastically usurpable and isolatable christological-eschatological hymns—and *with* them!—to the narratable story of the earthly Jesus and thus back to the Old Testament tradition, which now made the resurrection and death of Jesus narratable as events "according to the scriptures" (I Cor. 15:3ff; I Cor. 11:23ff). If the telling of the Easter event really would *dispense* "with the passing on of all other narratives," then the literary genre gospel would scarcely have emerged.[24] The one gospel of the resurrection of the Crucified One calls for a narrative which proclaims the Resurrected One as the Crucified One, a narrative of the life and suffering of the one who told about God's kingdom.[25] "The Gospel cannot maintain its identity without the Gospels."[26] There is an interest in truth, irrevocable for the telling of the Easter event, which is seen in the kerygmatically necessary return to the tradition of Jesus. On the one hand it relates to the *real happening* of the resurrection Jesus, which means, the event character which does not set aside the earthly context but rather involves itself in it and thus defines it anew. The truth interest of faith in Jesus Christ expresses itself in the statement "The Lord has risen indeed!" (Luke 24:34)—which can scarcely be understood as directed against doubt in the resurrection, as Weinrich suggests.[27] On the other hand, the same truth interest relates to the correct *explication* of the Easter event, which takes place *christologically* in the narrative of the Gospels, and *anthropologically* in the doctrine of justification. To be sure, this is another kind of interest than that of the historical scientist looking for the "truth-content of its stories," with regard to which Weinrich says[28] that the literature has "lost its narrative innocence" with this interest.[29] But in view of a theologically so reflectively proceeding tradition like that of the synoptic materials, there can be no talk of "narrative

23. *Ibid.*

24. See on this my essay "Jesu Wort und Jesus als Wort Gottes; Ein hermeneutischer Beitrag zum christologischen Problem," in *Unterwegs zur Sache*, pp. 126ff, and the works listed there on this problem, authored by E. Fuchs and E. Käsemann.

25. On the logical and theological problematic, see H. G. Geyer's penetrating "Rohgedanken über das Problem der Identität Jesu Christi," *Evangelische Theologie*, 33 (1973), 385ff.

26. Ernst Käsemann, "The Beginnings of Christian Theology," in *New Testament Questions of Today*, tr. W. J. Montague (Philadelphia: Fortress Press, 1969), p. 97; see also Martin Hengel, "Die Ursprünge der christlichen Mission," *New Testament Studies*, 18 (1971/72), 34f, n. 63.

27. Weinrich, *op. cit.*, p. 53.

28. *Ibid.*, p. 53.

29. *Ibid.*, pp. 51, 54.

innocence."[30] Rather, the *soteriological* interest in the *extra nos* ('outside of us') character of the salvation event was at least a latent motivation of the circumstance that very early a vehement interest can be seen on the part of Christian faith for the way in which the story of Jesus Christ, which was to be narrated, really did happen—that is, an interest in its truth-content. Of course, as historical questions began to assert themselves explicitly, that soteriological source of the Christian interest in truth also became the source of the danger *of asserting* that to be true, based on the question of salvation, which could not well be verified historically or even had to be falsified. But those kinds of processes are still, in their intellectual dubiosity, a negative documentation of the fact that the faith could certainly not be disinterested in the truth question. And certainly they are to be distinguished from the constant changes which took place with the narrative tradition in the history of the synoptic tradition—a process which documents the general historical insight "that the past event can be described not just from one but from several points of view in sequence. In every narrated story varying temporal aspects of the same event are realized successively."[31]

Weinrich had to overlook this genuine truth interest on the part of narrating faith, probably because he relates the way in which the hearers are "touched" by the narrative to man *as the actor,* and thus interprets it *imperativistically.* He writes, "The stories did not try to produce a clear yes or no as to truth, but more or less relevance. The most relevant stories are directed at faith: they want the hearer himself to imitate the actions of the story."[32] He is interested in "a simple pre-told or retold story which produced an effect on its hearers which made them 'doers of the word' and retellers in their turn."[33] But this analysis only partially describes the function of Christian narrative. It is, to be sure, true of narrative in the Bible and, based on the Bible, of the general hermeneutical structure that every true narrative, as W. Benjamin puts it,[34] "contains, openly or covertly, something useful," that therefore "the storyteller . . . has counsel for his readers." But the "practical interest" on which the narrator focuses does not lead *directly* to action; rather, it wants to make experienceable what otherwise would not be understood on its own, apart from the narrative word, for whatever reason that may be; yet, on the basis of the narrative word, it then appears to be the most understandable thing there is. It is not practical reason but the power of judgment which is primarily provoked into action. That is the reason that the hearer (Mary) chose the better part over the zealously busy person (Martha; Luke 10:42). Even those exemplary narratives of Jesus which are oriented toward action, which end with "go and do likewise," only formulate with this imperative a newly discovered indicative, that is, something which the listener must say to himself. They make something self-understandable *in a new way* which ought always to have been self-understandable but was not. But in order for this to

30. D. Mieth, *op. cit.,* p. 301, correctly finds "that the narrative . . . innocence of Christendom is more likely a legend."

31. F. Fellmann, *op. cit.,* p. 132.

32. H. Weinrich, *op. cit.,* p. 49.

33. *Ibid.,* p. 56.

34. W. Benjamin, "The Storyteller; Reflections on the Works of Nikolai Leskov," in *Illuminations,* tr. H. Zahn, ed. H. Arendt (New York: Harcourt, Brace & World, Inc., 1968), p. 86.

happen anew, man must apparently first be *liberated* from the pressure to concentrate on himself. It is for that reason that man first becomes a *"hearer* of the
word," who cannot do anything at all as long as he is listening, and then on the
basis of his hearing he can act out of the *newly gained freedom* so that his action,
precisely as activity, remains a doing of the *word.*

This is especially true with regard to the telling of the christological story,
which bursts apart everything which is obvious and matter of course, in that in
this story God identifies himself with a crucified person so that there is a story
to be told about a crucified God and a man who has been awakened to a new
life. The hearer must be drawn existentially into this story through the word,
precisely because it is also his story, and this must happen before he can *do*
what corresponds to this story. The story of Jesus Christ, through the word
which emerges from it and tells it, becomes a 'sacrament' (to speak along the
lines of Augustine and Luther) before it can function as an 'example' (*sacra-
mentum, exemplum*). It is the sacramental function of the telling of the christological story to let the hearer win freedom from himself.[35] For that very reason,
the narration depends on the *truth* of what is told—even if primarily from the
truth of the point of the story and only secondarily from the truth of the factual
situation out of which the point emerges. But one must distinguish here between
the parable narratives on the one hand and the narrated story of Jesus Christ on
the other hand to the degree that the story of Jesus Christ cannot arrive at the
"truth of the point" apart from the "truth of the factual," while the parable can
be indifferent to the "truth of the factual."

In any event, as far as the narration of the story of Jesus Christ is concerned, it is the *truth* which sets free, and then out of that gained *freedom* which
derives from *hearing* there follows the *deed* which moves history further.

In his gripping essay entitled "Das Ende des Laplaceschen Dämons,"
F. Fellmann disputes that the ego telling stories can desire to advance history as
the reality of life through narration. That may be true of the historian—perhaps!—that as an ego who tells stories he resembles the phenomenologically
oriented ego of E. Husserl so that we can apply to the historian what Husserl
writes about the phenomenological ego: "If the Ego, as naturally immersed in
the world, experiencingly and otherwise, is called 'interested' in the world, then
the phenomenologically altered—and, as so altered, continually maintained—
attitude consists in a *splitting of the Ego*: in that the phenomenological Ego
establishes himself as 'disinterested onlooker,' above the naively interested Ego."[36]
And yet the epic poet, as distinct from the dramatic poet, who according to
Friedrich Schiller[37] moves around the plot which is said to be standing still,
cannot really be understood as a disinterested spectator, as Fellmann suggests[38]—

35. On the so-called sacramental function of the text, see E. Fuchs, *Jesus; Wort
und Tat* (Tübingen: J. C. B. Mohr [Siebeck], 1971), p. 40; further, the valuable essay by
G. Schunack, "Textverständnis, Textbegriff und Texttheorie," in *Festschrift für Ernst
Fuchs* (Tübingen: J. C. B. Mohr, 1973), pp. 299ff.
36. Fellmann, *op. cit.,* pp. 137f. See E. Husserl, *Cartesian Meditations,* tr.
D. Cairns (The Hague: Martinus Nijhoff, 1960), 2nd Meditation, par. 15, p. 35.
37. Letter of December 26, 1797, to Goethe, *Correspondence Between Schiller
and Goethe,* tr. L. D. Schmitz (London: G. Bell & Sons, 1877), I (1794-97), pp. 451-56;
see also F. Fellmann, *op. cit.,* p. 131.
38. F. Fellmann, *op. cit.,* p. 138.

unless it is meant in the sense of Kant's "disinterested pleasure." But that certainly would not apply for the believer's ego who narrates the stories. Rather he is, to use W. Schapp's image, "entangled in stories," namely in the stories of Yahweh with Israel and then in the stories of God with his *newly* called people of Jews and Gentiles (Rom. 1:16; Gal. 3:28; I Cor. 9:20; 12:13; Eph. 2:12-22) and thus in the story of God's humanity which reveals and fulfills itself definitively in the identification of God with the man Jesus. Fellmann's principle does not apply to the believing ego: "Whoever is entangled in 'stories' cannot tell them, and whoever can tell them is no longer entangled in them."[39] Following the Psalmist's statement, later quoted by Paul (Ps. 116:10; II Cor. 4:13), "I believed, and so I spoke," we will have to come to precisely the opposite conclusion and say, "For out of the abundance of the heart the mouth speaks" (Matt. 12:34 par. Luke 6:45; compare Acts 4:20 and I Cor. 9:16). Entangled in the story of the humanity of God, the Christian storytelling community is much concerned that other people become entangled in the same story.

The antithesis of the hermeneutical structure of Christian narrative to Fellmann's principle becomes *understandable* only in the fact that biblical narration and Christian proclamation are by no means a telling after the fact but also always a "pre-telling." "The question Danto asks at the beginning of his poem (and answers negatively), whether it is possible to tell the story of an event that has not yet happened, must be answered by theologians with a firm yes. The prophecies in the biblical corpus can be regarded as rough sketches in story form of actions which have not yet taken place, as a pretelling. The fulfillment (or filling out) of the prophecy enriches the outline story with elements of action which are then themselves re-told together with the pre-told prophecy."[40] The reason for this is that trust in the God who speaks out of himself assigns to possibility an ontological priority over reality, so that reality stands totally at the service of the possibilities which condition it and which are also conditioned by it. What is impossible for men is *possible* for God according to the judgment of faith (Mark 10:27). And faith participates in the possibilities of God, that faith which by no means leaps over reality but which can be asserted by God (or Jesus) alone against unbelief (Mark 9:23f). The *critical potential* which is added to historical reality by the God who speaks out of himself, and out of which every word which speaks in the name of God emerges, has been expressly recognized and confessed by the oldest Christian theology. Paul calls the word of the cross (I Cor. 1:18, 24) or the gospel (Rom. 1:16) a 'power of God' (*dynamis theou*), a mighty capacity which surpasses all reality, but does so *within* this reality, which has not only the critical-differentiating function (I Cor. 1:18-25) but also the critical-transvaluing function (I Cor. 1:26-28). The *telling* of the passion story of Jesus Christ, summarized in Paul in the kerygma of the new life of the Crucified One (which according to II Cor. 13:4 is life "by the power of God"!), can for its part certainly lead to death (II Cor. 1:8). But this story

39. *Ibid.*, pp. 136f.
40. H. Weinrich, *op. cit.*, p. 52. Weinrich refers for this to the work of E. Auerbach, whose theological significance was already pointed out by F. Gogarten ("Das abendländische Geschichtsdenken; Bemerkungen zu dem Buch von Erich Auerbach 'Mimesis'," *Zeitschrift für Theologie und Kirche*, 51 [1954], 270ff) and by E. Fuchs (*Hermeneutik* [Tübingen: J. C. B. Mohr, 1970⁴], pp. 102, 134ff, 192ff).

also asserts about death that it has already been conquered (II Cor. 1:9f). This story is thus *dangerous*—perhaps because the power of death considers it a joke which insults its fatal majesty when there is talk about victory over death.[41] The critical potential of the word of the cross creates for itself, as a precise possibility which surpasses reality, a remembrance which entangles one in the history of freedom. J. B. Metz coined for this the apt category of the "dangerous memory,"[42] which actualizes "dangerous tradition,"[43] in that it tells "dangerous stories," "in which the interest in freedom introduces itself as narrative and identifies itself,"[44] because "what is new and has never yet been can only be introduced in narrative."[45] The gospel of the humanity of God has been introduced as the word of the cross narratively into the world—and immediately led back to itself, identified through theological argumentation. Since then, the dangerous story of Jesus Christ has entered as *critical* potential into the thesaurus of historical reason and is thus indirectly present today in world history. It can emerge from this indirect presence only when the story is told.

This, of course, appears to be opposed by the fact that historical reason in the modern age threatens to lose more and more of its narrative depth structure. In a society which "has adopted (finally?) post-narrative habits of communication,"[46] "reason is closed to the narrative exchange of experiences of what is new," and threatens to "exhaust itself in reconstructions. . . ." It "remains finally a piece of technique, as Th. W. Adorno noted in the concluding passage of his *Minima Moralia*."[47] To be sure, history as narrative construction with an emancipative intention is still held to be possible today.[48] And to be sure, conversely, the end of "naive" unreflected narrative (when was there ever "unreflected" narrative?) is to be welcomed as the liberation from "narrative

41. Dictators customarily revenge themselves for jokes which have to do with them on those who told them.

42. See J. B. Metz, "The Future in the Memory of Suffering," *op. cit.*, p. 14.

43. See J. B. Metz, "Erinnerung," *op. cit.*, p. 394.

44. *Ibid.* Metz takes up the late phenomenology of W. Schapp, which F. Fellmann had opposed. In that he follows H. Lübbe, who praised in Schapp's later work the restoration of the connection (this was made into a problem in Husserl's phenomenology) of the world of life and the ego through the retro-connection of the historicity of consciousness to a "consciousness in stories"; "The unity of the subject and his world has in the final instance no other content than this, that it is entangled in stories" (" 'Sprachspiele' und 'Geschichten'; Neopositivismus und Phänomenologie im Spätstadium," *Kant-Studien*, 52 [1960/61], 236).

45. Metz, "A Short Apology for Narrative," *op. cit.*, p. 86; but see also Metz, "Erlösung und Emanzipation," *op. cit.*

46. Weinrich, *op. cit.*, p. 54. See Th. W. Adorno, *Noten zur Literatur* (Berlin: Suhrkamp, 1965), I, 63, and, above all, W. Benjamin's definition of the end of narrative: "Familiar though his name may be to us, the storyteller in his living immediacy is by no means a present force. He has already become something remote from us and something that is getting even more distant" (*op. cit.*, p. 83, also pp. 88f). For theology, see H. W. Frei, *The Eclipse of Biblical Narrative; A Study in Eighteenth and Nineteenth Century Hermeneutics* (New Haven and London: Yale University Press, 1974).

47. Metz, "A Short Apology for Narrative," *op. cit.*, p. 86. See also Th. W. Adorno, *Minima Moralia; Reflections from Damaged Life*, tr. E. F. N. Jephcott (London: NLB, 1974), p. 247: "Knowledge has no light but that shed on the world by redemption: all else is reconstruction, mere technique."

48. See J. Habermas, "Zur Logik der Sozialwissenschaften," *Philosophische Rundschau*, Beiheft 5 (1967), 166ff.

surrogates" and from narration as the surrogate for decisions which are relevant to today.[49] To be sure, there is something like the "theologically competent interruption of narrative surrogates," which can be observed in, of all places, the narrator Jesus (Matt. 22:23-33).[50] But that must not lead us away from the fact that even in a post-narrative age the humanity of God can be told appropriately only as a story. One can therefore not estimate highly enough the fact that in the *Christian church*, as 'the creature of the word' and as 'the congregation of the saints in which the gospel is purely taught,' an *institution of narration* exists which is maintained only by the fact that it continues to retell that dangerous story of God. The church is preserved only in that it preserves that retelling. It will have to take seriously in its hermeneutics the post-narrative situation of the technical age and will have to find new and effective ways of telling the story. But it will not take the situation seriously if it breaks off that retelling. Instead, the church as an institution of narration will do justice to its task only if it reflects on the narrating, in order then, in a kind of "second naiveté," to return to the 'proper intention' of the narrative. But before that comes the necessary reflection of dogmatic thought, which has "to emancipate story-telling from being the trade of children's nurses."[51] For argumentative theology to become narrative theology, a dialectical discursive theology needs to have been developed which will reflect on narrative and what is to be narrated.[52] If "discursive theology is to become narrative again," it "needs for that purpose a discursive theory of narrative."[53] Such a theory of narrative in theology would have to present, on the one hand, the linguistic characteristics and structures *of narrative* in contrast to other modes of speech with their linguistic characteristics.[54] On the other hand, it would have to reflect on *that which is to be narrated* in its special characteristic which demands that it be narrated.

49. See D. Mieth, "Narrative Ethik," *op. cit.*, p. 302.

50. *Ibid.*, p. 303. The anti-apocalyptic thrust of Jesus' eschatological proclamation is comparable.

51. R. Musil, *Tagebücher, Aphorismen, Essays und Reden*, ed. A. Frisé (Hamburg: Rowohlt, 1955), p. 778, quoted in this context by D. Mieth, who (*op. cit.*, p. 304) "calls for the inwardly critical self-enlightenment of narrative."

52. F. Schleiermacher certainly knew about the narrative peculiarity of religious discourse which one must be able to adopt and also knew about the necessity of that peculiarity. But he looked on the dogmatic propositions of the faith, in their distinctiveness from the more poetic and rhetorical faith propositions, as necessary and proved himself a master of "dogmatic proposition . . . of the descriptively didactic type, in which the highest possible degree of definiteness is aimed at" (*The Christian Faith*, trs. Mackintosh and Stewart [Edinburgh: T. & T. Clark, 1928; New York: Harper & Row, 1963], I, 78). It was the special genius of Karl Barth which made possible a genuine combination of argumentative and narrative theology, whereby Barth himself understood how to emphasize the argumentative power of narrative: 'true narration is demonstration' (*vera narratio est demonstratio*).

53. D. Mieth, *op. cit.*, p. 304. When J. B. Metz presented his draft of a narrative theology in October 1972 to the editorial board of *Evangelische Theologie*, reference was made to the differentiation between different approaches to the same content, based on the historical situation itself: "After all, there is a time for story-telling and a time for argument. There is a difference between the two which has to be recognized" ("A Short Apology for Narrative," *op. cit.*, p. 88); see also H. G. Link, "Gegenwärtige Probleme einer Kreuzestheologie; Ein Bericht," *Evangelische Theologie*, 33 [1973], 337ff).

54. See on this H. Weinrich, *Tempus; Besprochene und erzählte Welt* (Stuttgart: W. Kohlhammer, 1971²).

3. The task still before us, which is to bring our considerations of the thinkability and speakability of God further so that the 'reason for being' (*ratio essendi*) which defines totality is comprehended in the 'reason for knowing' (*ratio cognoscendi*), makes the humanity of God the actual theme of what is to be narrated in theology. But it is not our intent to investigate further the linguistic characteristics and structures of narrative. It would be preferable for that to be done in the prolegomena to a narrative dogmatics or narrative homiletics, since narrative is hermeneutically dependent on what is to be narrated, even with regard to its structures.[55] Rather, we shall reflect now only on the basic processes which must be understood if the humanity of God is to be narrated as history. The argumentation must be carried out at the conceptual level so that then the narrative of the story can argue for itself.

Such discursive reflection is all the more necessary since, from the outset, faith, as the Bible shows, not only demonstrates and grounds through narrative, but also argues discursively using the content of the story. This happens so that, for instance, an apocryphal degeneration of the narrative does not take place, a danger which early on threatened the christological tradition. *God's being as history* can be implied through *stories* but not totally comprehended by them. As a passion story, it has its own intrinsic perception. And no stories can nor should be permitted to usurp this perception *sui generis,* which concretely is realized in the story of the crucified God, just because such stories present themselves as exemplifications or illustrations of this uniquely perceived story. *Quod non!* Precisely because God has let himself be perceived in the Crucified One so that the crucified Christ is the true 'image of God' (*imago dei*), the commandment against graven images gains its most profound meaning and its total focus. It is quite correct when the oldest texts which deal with this story are apostolic epistles of a very discursive character, and when in them the assertion is made that God is exclusively perceived in the Crucified One (compare Gal. 3:1 with I Cor. 2:2). This instructional fixation, if you will, on the Crucified One lends the narratives of the story of Jesus Christ as gospel their narrative uniformity, in that they are all oriented toward the passion story which reaches its climax in the Easter event. The *definitiveness* of divine revelation and the *uniqueness* of the God who reveals himself make it impossible for God's story to be totally dissolved in stories.[56] God does not have stories, he is history. To

55. Not everything is told in the same narrative way, not every narrative signal is significant for every story, not every tense (*tempus*) is always timely, etc. It is especially the eschatological characteristic of the story to be told which requires its own theological hermeneutic and a linguistics of narrative.

56. D. Mieth (*op. cit.,* p. 307) expressly referred to this: "God appears as ahistorical because he is unique in his kind." This statement recapitulates a remarkable passage from Thomas Mann's novel *Joseph and His Brothers* (pt. II, *Young Joseph,* tr. H. T. Lowe-Porter [New York: Alfred A. Knopf, 1935], pp. 48f). It is taken from the chapter entitled "How Abraham Found God," in which, according to G. von Rad (*Biblische Josephserzählung und Josephroman* [München: C. Kaiser, Sonderdruck, 1965], p. 25), "the old content seems to have overcome the poet." Thomas Mann wrote: "Much besides did Forefather know of God—but not in the sense in which others knew of their gods. There were no stories about God. That was indeed perhaps the most remarkable thing: the courage with which Abram represented and expressed God's essence from the first, without much ado, simply in that he said "God." God had not proceeded, had not been born, from any woman, no Ishtar, Baalat, mother of God. How could there be? One had

emphasize that is the function of the eschatological narrative tenses of the New Testament, which for their part are established in the concept of "once and for all" (*ephapax*) and had to be exposited in homological formulae if one was to be able to narrate the humanity of God as history in a language which corresponds to it.

The uniqueness, definitiveness, and the "once and for all" nature of the humanity of God are expressed most stringently in the confession "God is love." To tell about God's being can and may mean nothing else than to tell about God's love. The statement "God is love" must accompany all talk about God, even about the anger and judgment of God(!), if such talk is to correspond to God. In this sense, then, our task is to think the statement "God is love" in such a way that his truth remains narratable (sects. 20f below). But since God can be thought as love only on the basis of his identity with the man Jesus, and since, moreover, the essence of love implies the polarity of lover and loved, the discussion of the statement "God is love" must necessarily lead to the understanding of God's self-distinction from God and ultimately to the concept of the triune God, whose only 'vestige' (*vestigium*) can be the being of man with whom God has identified himself (sect. 22). When we have expounded the staurological approach of a doctrine of the triune God (sects. 23 to 25), then this study will have arrived at its hermeneutical goal and its theological ground, in that then the statement can be responsibly made that God's being is in coming. As the one who is coming, God turns being toward salvation. Thus he is the mystery of the world of man.

SECTION 20. The God Who Is Love; On the Identity of God and Love

1. Christian theology has given many answers to the question of the being of God. But among all those answers, it has always assigned unconditional primacy to this one: God is love. To do so, one could not only appeal to a New Testament *statement* but also to *the event* apart from which the entire New Testament would never have been written: to Jesus' death and God's resurrection of Jesus from the dead. The New Testament statement "God is love" (I John

---

only to use one's common sense to understand that, considering the nature of God, it was not a possible conception. God had planted the tree of knowledge and of death in Eden, and man had eaten of it. Birth and death were of man, but not of God; He saw no divine female at His side, because He needed not to know woman, but was Baal and Baalat at one and the same time. Neither had He children. For the angels were not so, nor Sabaoth who served Him, nor yet those giants whom some angels had begotten upon the daughters of men, led astray by sight of their lewdness. He was alone; such was the mark of His greatness. The wifeless and childless condition of God might perhaps explain His great jealousy concerning His bond with man; however that may be, it certainly explains the fact that He has no history and that there is nothing to tell of Him.

"Yet even so, one may only take all this in a qualified sense; referring it to the past, but not to the future—if indeed we may speak of the future in this sense at all. For God did after all have a story; but it referred to the future, a future so glorious for Him that His present, splendid as it always was, could not compare with it. And that very discrepancy between the present and the future lent to God's sacred majesty and greatness a shadow of strain and suspense, of suffering and unfulfilled promise, which we must frankly recognize in order to understand the jealous nature of His covenant with man."

4:8) is thus only possible—to the extent that people are defined in their entire existence by this event—in that they receive the spirit of love who is the spirit of this very God. They are speaking about it when they confess Jesus Christ as God's Son and Savior of the world (I John 4:12-15; see also 4:2 and I Cor. 12:3). "God is love" is then a true human statement only if God as love is an event among mankind: "If we love one another, God abides in us and his love is perfected in us" (I John 4:12).

The statement "God is love" is formulated truth. If it is not to be diluted into a formula, then it must be both lived and thought. To think God as love is the task of theology. And in doing so, it must accomplish two things. It must, on the one hand, do justice to the essence of love, which as a predicate of God may not contradict what people experience as love. And on the other hand, it must do justice to the being of God which remains so distinctive from the event of *human* love that "God" does not become a superfluous word. In order to clarify this double task, the problematic with which our thinking is challenged will be explicated by reference again to Ludwig Feuerbach.

Feuerbach understood the statement "God is love" as the interpretation of the dogma of the incarnation of God. But the anthropology he advanced distinguishes itself from the theological intention of the dogma in that it views the statement of this dogma as the announcement of the overcoming of deity by love: ". . . it criticizes the dogma and reduces it to . . . love. . . . The dogma presents us two things—*God and love*. God is love: but what does that mean?"[1] According to Feuerbach, the error made by theology and by speculative philosophy along with it is that in the statement "God is love" they assign to love ". . . the rank simply of a predicate, not that of a subject. . . ." "Here love recedes and sinks into insignificance in the dark background—God."[2] Against that Feuerbach asserts with his "anthropological" interpretation of Christianity: "Not because of his Godhead as such, according to which he is the *subject* in the proposition, God is love, but because of his love, of the *predicate*, is it that he renounced his Godhead; thus love is a higher power and truth than deity. *Love conquers God*. . . . Who then is our Saviour and Redeemer? God or love? Love; for God as God has not saved us, but Love, which transcends the difference between the divine and human personality. As God has renounced himself out of love, so we, out of love, should renounce God; *for if we do not sacrifice God to love, we sacrifice love to God*. . . ."[3]

We can leave aside the adventuresome logic of Feuerbach's argumentation. We are interested in the basic premise of this argumentation. Feuerbach certainly put it plainly enough. The dogma of the incarnation of God is interpreted from the presupposition that God cannot *become* man at all because he *has always been* man: ". . . the incarnate God is only the apparent (viz. visible) manifestation of *deified* man."[4] We shall also not have to delve into the problematic of this premise here. What is interesting in our context is the critical question which a self-critical Christian theology must direct to itself, a question which emerges

1. L. Feuerbach, *The Essence of Christianity*, tr. G. Eliot (New York: Harper & Brothers, 1957), p. 52.
2. *Ibid.*
3. *Ibid.*, p. 53.
4. *Ibid.*, p. 50.

from Feuerbach's argument. We must bluntly ask whether the logical distinction of subject and predicate in the statement "God is love" is not generally interpreted by theology in the sense of an ontological difference between God and love, so that love certainly "recedes and sinks" into what is truly a "dark background—God." In spite of all its exaggeration, does not Feuerbach's caricature hit the mark when it can view the God who is differentiated from love only as a loveless monster? Is not Feuerbach right when he fears that theology is more interested in the 'absolute power of God' and in the 'hidden God' (*potentia dei absoluta, deus absconditus*) than it is in the truth that God *is* love? We should not lightly evade this diagnosis of an inappropriate theological distinction between God and love: "So long as love is not exalted into a substance, into an essence, so long there lurks in the background of love a subject who *even without love is something by himself*, an *unloving monster*, a *diabolical being*, whose *personality, separable and actually separated from love*, delights in the blood of heretics and unbelievers—the *phantom of religious fanaticism!*"[5]

The positive intention of this polemical diagnosis is the challenge to take seriously that God's being is irrevocably defined as love. If one does not want to deprive the statement "God is love" of its theological stringency, then one must be careful (this is what we learn from Feuerbach's polemics) not to differentiate God and love ontologically in the sense that God's being is not *defined* by love. It will be difficult for a theology which is so practiced in making distinctions between subject and predicate to give up the common ontological differentiation between God and love in the sense of the "bearer" (subject) of love on the one side and love on the other as the mode of being of a person. And the "Lutheran" argument that one must distinguish between the revealed God who is love and the concealed God who possibly is something completely other comes to mind. But it should then be understood that the statement "God is love" has been devalued into a statement like "God has love," and then the difference between God and man would have been abrogated. Christian theology, however, is not primarily concerned with a God who has love but with a God who is love. An unimpeachable witness like Regin Prenter has emphatically stated this: "One can . . . say of a person that he or she has and exercises love, or that he receives love, but not that she is love. For every love which is the mode of being of a person must have a personal bearer, who has it, but who is not it. . . . To give up one's life for one's brothers, *is* love. To forgive the prodigal son, *is* love. But the one who gives his life for others is not love, he *has* it."[6]

Prenter concludes "that the love of God can only be expressed in the conceptuality of the trinitarian dogma. For to love God as he himself loves can be done only by God himself."[7] That is true. Obviously the being of the triune God is not to be deduced from the logic of the essence of love. Rather, the full understanding of the statement "God is love" will become understandable only on the basis of the history of the being of God, in which and as which he realizes his being as subject in a trinitarian way. But even the understanding of the trinitarian history as the history of love presupposes a pre-understanding of love.

5. *Ibid.*, pp. 52f.
6. R. Prenter, "Der Gott, der Liebe ist; Das Verhältnis der Gotteslehre zur Christologie," *Theologische Literaturzeitung*, 96 (1971), 401.
7. *Ibid.*, p. 406.

This pre-understanding may well be corrected or made more precise if the task is to identify God and love—just as in any love story, what love is will be articulated in a new and special way in spite of the "general similarity" of the experience.[8] That our provisional understanding of love can be corrected and made more precise, and that our understanding of love will always remain a pre- or post-understanding over against an understanding in the experience of love, only confirms that one can know something about love even outside the *event* of love. Even the statement "God is love," by using the term "love," shows that. We are certainly not moving away from the christological context of this state- ment in First John, but rather are providing help for better understanding, when we first ask generally what love is. This is not in order then to identify love as we understand it with God and then to read the result of this identification in the statement "love is God." Karl Barth was right: "If we say with I Jn. 4 that God is love, the converse that love is God is forbidden until it is mediated and clarified from God's being and therefore from God's act what *the* love is which can and must be legitimately identified with God."[9] Now this does not mean that the hermeneutical nonsense may be adopted that the word "love" could just as well be replaced by any other word because this word which functions as the predicate of the subject God receives its meaning through God's being and act. Rather, it is a case at most of a *change* in meaning which presupposes a very definite meaning. Although certainly we must understand the *statement* "God is love" (I John 4:8, 16) in terms of its christological context (and with a view to anal- ogous New Testament contexts such as John 3:14-16; Rom. 8:35-39; Gal. 2:20), still we cannot regard ourselves as released from the task of first asking about the essential meaning of the *word* "love" as it is used in this statement. Love— what is it?[10]

2. In the preceding sections we arrived at an understanding of love which emerged, of course, in a theological context but which claimed to refer to generally valid evidence. Formally judged, love appeared to us as the event of a still greater selflessness within a great, and justifiably very great self-related- ness. Judged materially, love was understood as the event of the unity of life and death for the sake of life. We shall now analyze the phenomenon love more exactly, using these already established definitions. We shall proceed on that basis of the full form of love (this is by no means self-evident) in which a loving I is loved back by the beloved Thou.[11]

If love is the event of a still greater selflessness within such great self-

8. To that extent, love is always defined by the way the lovers are. But it is also true in a fundamental sense that those who love are like their love. ". . . such is each one as is his love" (Augustine, "The Homilies on the Epistles of John, to the Parthians," *NPNF*, 1st ser., VII, Homily II/14, p. 475; see also J. Pieper, *About Love*, trs. R. and C. Winston [Chicago: Franciscan Herald Press, 1974], p. 21). Tell me how you love and I will tell you who you are.

9. Karl Barth, *CD*, II/1, p. 276.

10. On what follows, see the impressive monograph by J. Pieper, *op. cit.* The careful student will easily recognize where the following considerations are especially indebted to Pieper.

11. Clearly one cannot exclude the possibility that the essence of love will emerge with greater hermeneutic sharpness where the beloved Thou does *not* love the loving I. The New Testament deals frequently with this situation (see, e.g., John 3:19; Rom. 5:8, etc.).

relatedness, then the loving ego experiences both an extreme distancing of himself from himself and an entirely new kind of nearness to himself. For in love the I gives himself to the loving Thou in such a way that it no longer wants to be that I without this Thou. I do not want to have myself anymore without the beloved Thou. In order to be close to the beloved Thou, he risks every distance. The relationship he has had to himself until now is profoundly disturbed, and the relationships he has had to the world are alienated in a remarkable way. The I is suddenly a stranger in the world. But it also becomes alien to itself. Yet that is only one side. For when love is fulfilled, then that peculiar alienation is transformed into an intensity of self-relation and world-relationship which was never there before. Lovers are aliens in the world and yet are more at home in it than others. Lovers are always alien to themselves and yet, in coming close to each other, they come close to themselves in a new way. In that the loving I has won the beloved Thou, it has also won itself anew. To be sure, I want to *have* the beloved Thou. It is a major part of every form of love that I want to have you. And only in that way do I also "have" myself. This means, obviously, that "having" is transformed utterly. The entire phenomenon of "having" becomes different.

Before we pursue this further, it must be candidly noted that love is not identical with absolute selflessness. Love is oriented toward a specific Thou. It desires *this* Thou and not anyone. It looks with pleasure on the beloved Thou and is by no means blind. Rather, "where love is, there is vision" (*ubi amor, ibi oculus*).[12] And the way in which love looks is a very intensive form of the desire to take possession, for which reason that look can be equated with adultery (Matt. 5:28). In short, love includes the desire or lust of love.

One might call this the eros-structure of love, or 'concupiscent love' (*amor concupiscentiae*), or need-love, in order to distinguish between it and gift-love, or 'benevolent love' (*amor benevolentiae*), or the agape-structure of love. This is an entirely proper distinction. We shall have to return to it. But one should be very careful that one does not establish these different forms as opposing alternatives! The corresponding endeavors of Protestant theology chiefly,[13] which

---

12. Richard of St. Victor, *Selected Writings on Contemplation (Benjamin Minor — Of the Preparation of the Soul for Contemplation)*, tr. C. Kirchberger (New York: Harper & Bros., 1957), ch. 13, p. 91; see also Thomas Aquinas, *In III. Sent.*, dist. 35, q. 1, a. 2, qa. 1, sol. (nr. 32); Pieper, *op. cit.*, p. 34.

13. The opposition of eros and agape is old and is found in the confrontation between self-love and love of God in, for example, Augustine (*The City of God, NPNF*, 1st ser., II, bk. XIV, ch. 28, p. 282): "Accordingly, two cities have been formed by two loves: the earthly by the love of self, even to the contempt of God; the heavenly by the love of God, even to the contempt of self." In more recent theology, it has been mainly Protestant authors who have sought to make a strong contrast between eros and agape. I will mention as representative: H. Scholz, *Eros und Caritas; Die platonische Liebe und die Liebe im Sinne des Christentums* (1929); Anders Nygren, *Agape and Eros*, tr. P. S. Watson (London: S.P.C.K., 1953; Philadelphia: Westminster Press, 1953); Emil Brunner, *Eros und Liebe (Furche-Bücherei, 32)* (Berlin: Furche-Verlag, 1937). Mention must also be made of Karl Barth, *CD*, IV/2, pp. 727ff; Barth, *Evangelical Theology: An Introduction*, tr. G. Foley (New York: Holt, Rinehart & Winston, 1963), pp. 196ff. To be sure, Barth still "whispers" his preference for the more loving treatment of eros by H. Scholz over Nygren's theological critique of eros with "eyes sharpened (perhaps over-sharpened) by the controversial theology of Sweden" (*CD*, IV/2, p. 738). And in spite

then try to develop controversial theological fruit from this little root, may have
been motivated by holy zeal for the difference between divine and human love.
Let their zeal be honored! "I bear them witness that they have a zeal for God,
but it is not enlightened" (Rom. 10:2). An ingenious remark betrays it: "Agape
is related to Eros, as Mozart to Beethoven. How could they possibly be confused?"[14] We won't ask what Mozart would say about that. Rather, bearing its
tones in our ears, we want to lead this false alternative *ad absurdum* with reference to the phenomenon itself, without failing to see that there is a certain
truth to the distinction between eros and agape which should be emphasized in
the proper place.[15] We shall orient ourselves to the indisputable insight that love
opens the eyes. Not for everything, but for the beloved Thou. "Where love is,
there is vision." That means that love desires to see the beloved because it is
desirable. The look hastens to that one to whom the one looking is drawn. The
loving I wants to be with the beloved Thou in order to have it. Its moving close
has the purpose of bringing about another kind of "being with another one" than
that of being next to each other or in each other's vicinity. The I wants to *be*
with the Thou in such a way that it *has* the Thou, and only in that way does it
have itself or is it with itself.

What is then of great significance ontologically and theologically is that
the fact that the loving I wants to have the beloved Thou and only then wants
to have itself transforms the structure of having. For the beloved Thou is desired
by the loving I only as one to whom it may *surrender* itself. Love is mutual
surrender, and the desire of love is the most extreme enemy of violent assault.
The exchange of mutual surrender means then, with regard to the element of
having in love, that the loving I wants to have itself only in the form of being
had by someone else. And it means at the same time that it wants to have the
beloved Thou only as an I which also wants to be had. It can be put this way:

---

of all opposition between eros and agape, he still knows of a "*common* place from which
they both come" (*CD*, IV/2, p. 740). It is also comforting to experience that "Christian
love lives in this antithesis, but not by it" (*ibid.*, p. 746), and that "our final word can
and must be conciliatory" with regard to the relation of agape and eros (*ibid.*, p. 849).
Yet this is to consist of the statement that agape "conquers eros by making it pointless
and superfluous" (*ibid.*, p. 751). 'May God turn it to the good!' (*Quod deus bene vertat!*)
    14. Karl Barth, *Evangelical Theology: An Introduction*, p. 201.
    15. What is normally distinguished as eros and agape can be led back to the
common structure of love which was described as "the still greater selflessness in the
midst of such justifiably great self-relatedness." Love without some kind of self-relatedness
would be, both in theory and in practice, an enormous abstraction and at the same time
a falsification of the love from above. Conversely, love without the greater selflessness
within the self-relationship—and this is true also of both the understanding and the
practice of love—would be the opposing abstraction, what one might call the falsification
of love from below. If in the first case there is a threat of the moral castration of the
essence of love (whereby one fails to see that love does not belong primarily to the
dimension of "should" but rather is a phenomenon of being), there is in the second case
the danger of what might be called the sexual raping of the essence of love (whereby one
fails to see that love dialectically alters the dimension of willing in that the loving I must
be willing to submit its will to the being of the beloved Thou). It need only be noted that
obviously the moral abstraction from above cannot be remedied through mere sexuality,
nor can the sexual abstraction from below be remedied by means of a moral imperative.
Only the event of genuine love, only the phenomenon itself, possesses the power to
overcome its falsifications.

in love one I and another I encounter each other in such a way that they become for each other beloved Thou's. I must always become a Thou to the other person if I am not to be had by the other I in such a way that I become an It. In love there is no having which does not arise out of surrender. Anything else would be assault. In the event of love, then, the self-having which constitutes the I is transformed into a structurally different phenomenon. The loving I has itself only as though it did not have itself. It wants to be had by that very Thou that it wants to have. In order to have this Thou, it must surrender to it, that is, cease to have itself. This content is decisive for the understanding of love.

To have oneself (self-having) is an old expression of being.[16] The issue is in fact one of being or nonbeing when love is at stake. And the dispute about the alternative between eros and agape possesses its particle of truth (which still must be emphasized) and has its ultimate ground in the insight that in the event of love the being of the lovers can be both gained and lost, both forfeited and preserved—preserved by the beloved Thou and not by the loving I. But absolutely nothing can ever be gained without at the same time having lost not only everything which one has but even one's having of oneself! If there is such a thing as a dialectic of being, then it reigns in the essence of love. But it reigns not as an irrational dialectical, nor as a paradoxical one, but as an ontological dialectical defined by an unsurpassable inner rationality. We have always had this in mind whenever we have spoken of the unity of life and death for the sake of life. Now we are in a position to understand this expression more accurately in that we seek to move step by step closer to the dialectic of being and nonbeing which reigns in the essence of love.

3. Love implies or presupposes *affection* (*Zuneigung* — 'inclination'). Disaffection contradicts love. In affection an intention of the I is carried out with reference to another, an intention from the I to the Thou. But in affection, the I remains with itself. I want to move toward the other, but I have not yet arrived there with that one. The I does not take leave of itself. In affection, the self-relatedness in which every I naturally and innocently (seen ontologically) turns toward itself is confronted by an emergent selflessness which favors the Thou who is the object of affection. But the self-relatedness has not yet been surpassed by the selflessness.

But if, after earlier processes and situations which by no means are necessarily the source of what now might happen, the I now has the experience that it finds itself entangled in a still greater selflessness in the midst of such great self-relatedness, then the affection has become serious. Affection becomes a *turning to* that person, whereby the I senses itself to be passive: it turns itself in *irresistible freedom* or in *free irresistibility* to the other. The beloved Thou, who is not yet taken as an I but only as a desired Thou, demands without knowing it that this turning about take place.

In this process, in which affection advances to a turning to the other, there is also a turning of the loving I away from itself. Yet this turning of the I away from itself as it turns to the beloved Thou is still a completely ambivalent state. There are ways of turning away from oneself which have no other intent than to increase the pleasure of self-gratification when one has turned back to oneself.

16. On the problem of the category of self-having, see below, p. 390.

As a sublimated form of self-turning, the turning to another person and turning away from oneself would not be radical at all. The reason it happens is that I promise myself something out of it. We speak of flirtation. It may be a posture of eros but is not really that. Eros is more passionate. It is distinguished from mere flirtation by more seriousness and more joy at the same time. The same is true of agape.

In contrast with flirtation, the I in love promises itself *nothing*, or at least not *something*. But love itself promises it *everything*, or more precisely, more than everything. For the I who truly loves promises itself nothing at all but turns itself (not in the form of some exertion) with the greatest of ease to the beloved Thou in such a way that it is turned completely away from itself. The turning away from oneself and the turning to someone else are now radical. We are now speaking of *surrender*.

In such surrender, I don't promise myself anything; rather, I promise myself nothing at all because I do not want to have anything from anyone, not even myself; I don't even want to have and to hold myself. Rather, I want to be had. Self-possession, self-having, is replaced by being possessed. But the same is true of the beloved I. Thus the structure of having is changed as the active side of being had. For the beloved Thou can "have" the loving I only to the extent that it is had by it as well. The Thou to which the loving I surrenders itself promises thus a totally new being. *For that reason* the loving I does not have to promise itself anything for its love. Love itself promises a new being, which relates the I to the Thou out of this being and the Thou to the I from that being, and that indicates that "relates" means "receives." Thus, the statement addressed to God is true of every genuine love relationship: "Whom have I in heaven but thee? And there is nothing upon earth that I desire besides thee" (Ps. 73:25). Heaven and earth—that would be too little, much too little, in comparison with the beloved Thou. Yes, the beloved Thou is more to the loving I than its own existence. And since the beloved Thou is more to it than its own existence, since I do not want absolutely anything more for myself, the beloved Thou becomes the source of a totally new being, so that the loving and loved I can then say, *mutatis mutandis*(!), "My flesh and my heart may fail, but God is the strength of my heart and my portion for ever" (Ps. 73:26).

In the event of loving surrender, then, a radical self-distancing takes place *in favor* of a new nearness to oneself—a nearness, to be sure, in which the beloved Thou is closer to me than I am to myself.[17] "In favor" is not understood

17. It is thus understandable that great theologians could risk the assertion that the eros of God is in a certain sense more divine than agape: "love is more Godlike than dilection" [a more literal translation conveys Jüngel's intentions better—TR: "erotic love is more divine than self-giving love"]; ". . . some of our writers about holy things have thought the title of 'yearning' diviner than that of 'love' " (see Thomas Aquinas, *STh* [in *Great Books of the Western World* (Chicago: Encyclopaedia Britannica, 1952), vol. 19], First Part of the Second Part, q. 26, art. 3, reply to obj. 4, p. 737; and Dionysius the Areopagite, *On the Divine Names and the Mystical Theology,* in *Translations of Christian Literature,* ser. 1, tr. C. E. Rolt [New York: Macmillan, 1920], p. 104). Behind this formulation and its reception by Aquinas there is a history with a different orientation, to which H. Scholz (*op. cit.,* pp. 114ff) has drawn attention by taking up the results of research done by A. von Harnack ("Der 'Eros' in der alten christlichen Literatur," *Sitzungsberichte der preussischen Akademie der Wissenschaften* [1918], I, 81-94). Accord-

in the sense of an *ut finale* (a subjunctive of purpose). What is desired is not one's own being, but rather the beloved Thou and only for its own sake. "That which is not loved for itself is not loved" (Aristotle). But the beloved Thou *gives* me myself in that it has me, so that I have myself again, but in a completely new way.

As an I who is had by the beloved Thou, I do not *have* myself at all anymore, but rather I have lost myself, surrendered myself. But altogether there is no claim on this: the beloved Thou gives to the loving I a new being which *anticipates* the loss of self in the event of surrender. There can be no trace here of an *ut finale*. If there is any *ut* at all, then the only one which applies here is the "radiant *ut consecutivum*."[18] But the actual sequence here is much quicker and earlier than the sequence of one thing after another which is allowed by the 'sequence of tenses' (*consecutio temporum*). It is a prevenient consequence in which the self-loss in the event of love is already surpassed by the new being which the loving I receives from the beloved Thou in the act of surrender. In this anticipative exchange of being between the self-surrendering I and the Thou who gives me myself anew consists *the true desire* or *lust* of love, which cannot be made to happen.

One would, however, not only have denied but never have seen the true seriousness of every genuine love if one felt one could ignore the self-surrender and the self-loss it contains because of the prevenient character of the new being

---

ing to him, Ignatius (Rom. 7:2), perhaps with reference to Paul (Gal. 5:24; 6:14), informed the Romans that he was indeed writing as a living person but that he loved death. His love (for life?) had been crucified and any kind of love for the material was now no longer present in him: "Rather heed what I am now writing to you. For though alive, it is with a passion for death that I am writing to you. My Desire has been crucified and there burns in me no passion for material things" (Ignatius, *Epistle to the Romans*, in *Early Christian Fathers*, ed. C. C. Richardson [*Library of Christian Classics*, vol. 1] [London: S.C.M. Press, 1953], p. 105). Whereas Ignatius means the crucified love of self with his reference to "crucified desire," this statement was referred by Origen (in "Prologue," *The Song of Songs; Commentary and Homilies* [*Ancient Christian Writers*, vol. 26], tr. and anno. R. P. Lawson [Westminster, MD: Newman Press, 1957], pp. 35f) to the object of eros so that "my crucified eros" now means the same thing as "my crucified Christ": "He who hangs upon the cross is my love," is the way "it has been put in a hymn for more than 1500 years" (Scholz, *op. cit.*, p. 115). "Through this exposition of Ignatius, Origen" not only created the basis "for the emergence of Christ-eroticism which became one of the most remarkable chapters in the history of Christianity," but he also "declared that the Johannine equation 'God = love' could correctly, or at least not incorrectly, be replaced with the pseudo-platonic identification of 'God=eros': "I don't think that it would be wrong if anybody called God love [*amorem, erōta*] as John called him *caritatem* [*agapē*]. Then I remember that one of the saints, Ignatius, said of Christ, 'My love is crucified,' and I don't judge that this was reprehensible . . ." (H. Scholz, *op. cit.*, pp. 115f, with reference to A. Harnack, *op. cit.*, p. 81). Scholz then quotes, as "later effects of this Origenistic combination" (*op. cit.*, pp. 116f), the corresponding utterance in Dionysius the pseudo-Areopagite, where one can see the "replaceability of agape with eros" and the identification of God and eros; the latter happens "with the reasoning that God is called eros because he is the one who in the whole world attracts eros to himself." Transplanted by John Scotus Erigena to western Europe, it now is declared to be legitimate in Latin Christian usage to speak of God as *amor*, "because he is the cause of all *amor*."

18. Karl Barth, *CD*, IV/2, p. 750: "An *ut finale* necessarily means a relapse into eros-love. The only valid *ut* is the radiant *ut consecutivum*." Thus, Karl Barth reserves this "radiant *ut consecutivum*" for the agape which makes eros superfluous and irrelevant.

which arises out of love. Every despair of love is an indirect reference to how very seriously in successful love the lovers are subjected to nothingness (this is much more serious than unsuccessful love, for which reason the despair of love can be considered only an indirect reference). It is not the fact that they are lovers, but only the fact that they are beloved and thus receive themselves from the Thou which makes them people who *are existing ex nihilo*. The loving I *may* not be without the beloved Thou. But it is only through the love of the beloved Thou which he experiences that his being-nothing-for-himself in his self-surrender becomes real, and this happens in such a way that the loving I is given an existence which does not derive from it. In that sense, love makes new or, with a very apt metaphor, young again: The lover does not *exist* on the basis of what he has been until now or has made of himself. Instead, in receiving himself from another, the lover *exists*. Thus he *exists* only because of the existence which is *given* to him, and apart from that he is nothing. The loving and beloved I is then totally related to the beloved Thou, and thus to his own nonbeing: without Thee I am nothing.[19]

This then is the *positive aspect* of love (that I am only what I am out of Thee), which gives love its peculiar nearness to death which poetry has always recognized. Love conceals within itself the dimension of death in that it grants new being. Augustine put it soberly: in that love makes us new and young, it also causes death in us: "Love createth a sort of death in us."[20] "For where love awakens, there dies / The ego, the sinister despot."[21]

The death dimension of love is already implied in the selective character of love. To select means first of all to *differentiate*: it is this person and no other. But selection is not made on the basis of comparison. The *look* of love is not there before the lover is seen; rather, that look is ignited by the sight of the beloved person. It comes to be when the eye is directed to the beloved person as one who is loved. "Where love is, there is vision!" The beloved Thou is differentiated totally on its own merits, and not on the basis of comparisons made with all the other daughters in the country. This Thou raises itself up for

19. See J. Pieper (*op. cit.*, p. 29), and the authors cited there: R. O. Johann (*Building the Human* [New York: Herder & Herder, 1968], p. 161) and F. D. Wilhelmsen (*The Metaphysics of Love* [New York: Sheed and Ward, 1962], p. 139). According to Pieper, "what has been said about the creativity of human love also suddenly acquires a wholly new-founded meaning" in that in it "the creative act of the Deity in establishing existence is continued—so that one who is consciously experiencing love can say, 'I need you in order to be myself. . . . In loving me you give me myself, you let me be.' Put differently, 'What being-loved makes being do is precisely: be.' " Whether one ought to speak of a continuation or even of a perfection of the divinely creative act would appear to be at least doubtful to the degree that love on earth is totally weak over against everything which is not love. I would prefer to speak of an analogy to the divinely creative act which for its part is an act of creative love. In that God himself *is* this love, his creativity needs neither continuation nor perfecting, but it does need human correspondence.

20. Augustine, *Expositions on the Book of Psalms, NPNF*, 1st ser., VIII, 596 (Ps. cxxii:12).

21. F. Rückert, "Wohl endet Tod des Lebens Not," *Gedichte*, ed. J. Pfeiffer (Stuttgart: P. Reclam, 1969), p. 24. See also F. Gogarten, *Die Verkündigung Jesu Christi; Grundlagen und Aufgabe* (Tübingen: J. C. B. Mohr, 1965²), p. 481: "This being nothing, as it is experienced in love, encloses within itself all the blessedness of loving and all the fullness of being loved."

the selecting I out of the numbers of others and is then lifted out and up by the I in such a way that from the view of love there are no others anymore. This differentness based on selection is such an elevating experience for the selected Thou that the hypothetic negation of that selection can no longer mean mere return to the situation as it was, back to the numbers of those who were not selected. Rather, it would mean *rejection*, which is *entry into the horizon of death*. What was true in a certain sense of the relationship of the lovers to the many others who were not selected is all the more radically true of the relationship of the two lovers to each other. If one of them must involuntarily return to the numbers of those others, then "the brightness of Paradise is exchanged for dark and hideous night."

But the selective character of love implies only negatively to what extent death is present in the event of happy love. The event of happy love goes beyond mutual selection and is to be evaluated as a phenomenon *sui generis*. There are two people who have chosen each other. They turn to each other and thus each one away from him- or herself. They surrender to each other and forget themselves. The I is freed of its self and becomes a selfless I. In such selflessness, the lovers receive their selves anew, each from the other and only from that one. In that they receive themselves from each other, they now relate *to* themselves in a new way. But they no longer derive their existence from *out* of themselves. The existence from the other is an existence which is burdened with *the potential of their own nonbeing*. That is what invests their mutual closeness with the incomparable ontological ardor which far surpasses the *old* closeness in which I was closest to myself, and thus makes it impossible. Now the beloved Thou comes closer to me than I have ever been able to be to myself, and brings me to myself in a completely new way, so that I come to myself from the furthermost distance, or better, am brought to myself. The incomparable ardor of love which conceals the most radical distance of a person from himself within it leads to an event of nearness which is quite rightly called union (*unio* or *unitio*). I am united with myself in a new way in that—but only in that!—the beloved Thou, coming closer to me than I am able to be to myself, brings me close to myself in a new way. The union of Thou and I leads to a new and highly differentiated unity of the I with itself, a unity which has been *opened* up from inside.

In that sense, the union of I and Thou constitutes a new self-relationship which emerges out of the radically understood selflessness of the loving I. And the love, which began as the event of a still greater selflessness in the midst of such great self-relatedness perfects itself now as the event of a new self-relatedness coming out of still greater selflessness which continues as such. As the event of unsurpassable nearness between I and Thou, the union of love constitutes a new I. Thus, the strength of love consists of its union. It is as strong as death (Song of Sol. 8:6) because it bears death within it as conquered when the beloved Thou, without doing anything at all, gives existence to the loving I.

4. For that same reason, the strength of love is limited to the event of love.[22] If love ceases to happen, it ceases to be. The metaphysical principle

---

22. Event is more than a momentary happening. Events can have their history and can make it. The accusation of "existentialistic punctualism" would simply miss entirely what is being presented here.

"unity is stronger than union" is completely wrong here. There is no such thing as a standstill in love. Thus being with the beloved Thou is always a process of being taken along. And since that happens *from both sides* (alternately), the event of love always implies a *common path*. Love is strong on the pathway of love. But this path is crossed by other paths which confront the lovers with what is not love. Love is not afraid of this confrontation. For it does not lead the lovers in their new being out of the world but constantly more deeply into it. In the process, love experiences its unique weakness and frailty. Insight into the strength of love implies at the same time the knowledge of the weakness which inheres in love over against everything which is not love. With this knowledge of the weakness of love, derived from insight into the strength of love as an I-Thou relationship, the understanding of the phenomenon love leads beyond the I-Thou relationship, although of course not in the sense that this relationship may be left behind as though it had received enough consideration. Rather, the I-Thou relationship itself leads beyond itself. Love wants to radiate. As love, it presses to move beyond the lovers themselves. For that reason, love does not lead into an idyllic retreat from the world, nor into a realm beyond, away from all lovelessness, hate, or even inattentiveness and boredom. Rather, it leads into all of these, engages in struggle with them, and moves more deeply into them. True love squanders itself. It wants to radiate out into the realm of lovelessness. As a personal relation, it also has a worldly dimension. As a "matter of the heart," it is also turned outward. And so it does not fear lovelessness but rather drives out fear (I John 4:18).

In view of its own weakness, it does this over against everything which is not love. Thus one could say that love does not even fear its own weakness. The one who does *not* want to share in the weakness of love is basically incapable of love. For the strength of love consists of the certainty that love can be helped to victory only by love. To be sure, when opposed by everything which is not love, it is totally unprotected and vulnerable. And thus love produces not only joy but also "sadness and heart-suffering"—*"tristesse"*: "joy and sorrow both proceed from love."[23] But it is the very *power* of love which implies its weakness against everything which is not love. For love does not assert itself in any other way than through love. And that is both its strength and its weakness. Since love asserts itself only lovingly, it is highly vulnerable from outside, but inwardly it is profoundly indestructible. It remains within its element, and it radiates in order to draw into itself. It cannot destroy what opposes it, but can only *transform* it. Where that happens, there is a turning away from one's own I, an event which surpasses destruction in its radicality. There a dialectic of being and nonbeing takes place which belongs to the essence of love.

That confirms how much love carries death within itself. Since love is absolutely weak over against everything which it is not, and since it can resort to itself only in struggle, one can *share* in love only when one shares in this its weakness. How helpless the loving I becomes! And yet it is so strong. Between love and nonlove there is a yawning chasm, in comparison with which the con-

---

23. Thomas Aquinas, *STh* (in *Great Books of the Western World* [Chicago: Encyclopaedia Britannica, Inc., 1952], vol. 20), Second Part of the Second Part, q. 28, art. 1, p. 527.

trast between heaven and earth threatens to lose its significance. Whoever is not "in love" can share in it only through a 'transformation into another kind' (*metabasis eis allo genos*). For that reason, the lover senses nothing less than death *between* nonlove and "being in love." And for that reason, one thinks that one has death behind one when one loves. In that sense it is indeed true of the event of love that "it makes a kind of death in us" (*facit in nobis quandam mortem*). It unites life and death in favor of life.

The unity of life and death in favor of life, as we have understood love, is expressed with one word and pregnantly in the old metaphor which speaks of the *fire of love*. Both H. Scholz[24] at the climax of his austere study on *Eros and Caritas* and J. Pieper[25] at the conclusion of his impressive book *Über die Liebe* resort to this metaphor in that both of them recall the old Pentecostal prayer for the coming of the Holy Spirit, which is "more and other than a piously harmless matter": "Come, Holy Spirit, fill the hearts of thy believers and ignite in them the fire of thy love!"

5. Our consideration of the essence of love brings us back to our insight that God is love. On the basis of this consideration, we have gained a pre-understanding of the identification of God and love just as in our discussion of the thinkability and speakability of God we were constrained by the content itself to anticipate the statement "God is love." Now it is our task to think through this identification of God and love in such a way that the subject and predicate in the statement "God is love" interpret each other. We are to read the statement "God is love" as an exposition of the self-identification of God with the crucified man Jesus. Quite unmistakably the New Testament context, from which our statement becomes understandable, requires that we do this. We shall now take up the problem of the unity of Jesus with God, to which we shall have to return later when we discuss the identification of God with Jesus as an act of God in order to understand more exactly in what way God is love. In the second section after this, the same event of God's identification with the crucified Jesus will be thought through and expounded from the perspective of the being of this man.

The First Epistle of John (ch. 4) speaks of the identity of God and love in the context of an argument. The argument is about the being of believers *out of God*. The people who are regarded as believers are pointedly called "beloved" here (vv. 1, 7, 11). That address contains the entire dispute. For the beloved is already participating in love in such a way that he is then able to love. And thus he can be called on to love. In that he does that, *he is of God*. For, after all, the love which is possible for men is *of God* (v. 7). In significant parallelism, the statement was made just before this that every spirit "which confesses that Jesus Christ has come in the flesh" is also *of God* (v. 2). The opponents in the argument are the proponents of the view that the man Jesus was not the Christ, or that the heavenly Christ was not identical with the earthly man Jesus (see 2:22 and II John 7). But that must result in doubting God. And "as 1:2f already indicated, Father and Son belong together as a unity. . . . Whoever then has a perverted view of Jesus, by that very fact also thinks wrongly of God. . . . The denial

24. Scholz, *op. cit.*, p. 67.
25. Pieper, *op. cit.*, p. 122.

that Jesus is the Christ is thus nothing more or less than a denial of God."[26] Therefore, whoever denies the identification of God with the man Jesus cannot be *of God,* which identification expresses itself in that this man merits being called the *Son of God.* For in this identification, the being of God realizes itself as love. And that makes plain why both the one who disputes this identification and the one who does not love *cannot* be of God. In that he does not love, he disputes that christological identification. And in that he disputes the identification of God with Jesus, he excludes himself from the love which is of God.

Apparently the presupposition here is that love is love only when it is of God. If it is of God, then no one can love without first being loved by God. To that extent, the issue is the correct understanding of the term of address "Beloved," which the author uses so pointedly. For one learns to love by being loved and by letting oneself be loved. Thus one can love neither God nor the other if one has not *already* been loved by God and let oneself be loved by him. "He first loved us" (v. 19). "In this is love, not that we loved God but that he loved us" (v. 10), so that we then, *as a result,* can and should love (v. 11).

Love is based on God, because apparently he alone can start the event of love, initiate it, because he alone can *begin* to love without any reason, and always has begun to love. In that God comes from God, he has always been the one who loves. God is the one who loves out of himself, who does not have to be loved by man in order to love. That he is so is revealed in the sending and the surrender of "his Son" (v. 10). In this sending, God reveals himself as the one who loves in freedom. In Johannine language, we are speaking of *God the Father* when we recognize God as the one who loves out of himself.

But First John says more than that God is the one who loved first. In his identification with the man Jesus which is presented as his sending his *only* Son into the world (". . . that he sent his only-begotten Son into the world . . ."), God demonstrates that he is love itself. That becomes understandable only if God is both lover and beloved at the same time. And, in fact, the term "only-begotten" does designate "the unique one as beloved at the same time."[27] God is thus one who loves himself. But this love cannot be misunderstood as the self-love of an I. God *differentiates* himself in that he loves himself. In an irremovable differentiation within himself, he is *lover and beloved.* In John's language, he is God the Father *and God the Son.*

But even in this oppositeness of loving Father and beloved Son, God is still not *love itself.* The identifying statement "God is love" can be made only on the basis of the fact that God as the loving one sends this his beloved Son into the world, which means to a certain death; that the loving one separates himself from his Son; that as the loving one he subjects himself to lovelessness in the beloved—who is as the beloved one closer to him than he is to himself! God is not only *in* love just as two people who love each other are *in* love. God is not only a loving I and a beloved Thou. God is rather the radiant event of love itself. And so, formulating the last necessary refinement of our theme in this context, he is that event in that he, as the one who loves and who separates

26. R. Bultmann, *The Johannine Epistles,* tr. R. Philip O'Hara, ed. R. W. Funk (Philadelphia: Fortress Press, 1973), p. 38.
27. *Ibid.,* p. 67.

himself from his beloved, not only loves himself but (in the midst of such great self-relatedness still more selfless) loves another one and *thus* is and remains himself. God has himself only in that he gives himself away. But, in giving himself away, he has himself. That is how he *is*. His self-having is the event, is the history of giving himself away and thus is the end of all mere self-having. As this *history*, he is God, and in fact, this *history of love* is "God himself."[28] Again with John, we speak of *God as Spirit* when we have to interpret the death-accepting separation of loving one and beloved one so that the loving one and the beloved have to *let each one participate* in their mutual love. And we are also speaking of *God as Spirit* when we have to interpret the death-accepting separation of loving one and beloved one in such a way that God in the midst of this most painful separation does not cease to be the *one and living* God, but rather is supremely God as such. God is the one and living God *in that he* as the loving Father gives up his beloved Son and thus turns to those others, those people who are marked by death, and draws the death of these people into his eternal life.[29] Thus, in the midst of his separation from him, the loving Father remains in relationship to his beloved Son. Pointedly and yet expressing the heart of the matter, the Johannine Christ says, "For this reason the Father loves me, because I lay down my life, that I may take it again." And thus he is the beloved Son who, in the midst of his separation from the Father, relates to him. In that way God is Spirit, establishing the link between Father and Son in such a way that man is drawn into this love relationship. And in that sense the perfected

28. It is simply an act of logical violence and a theological short circuit when F. Mildenberger (*Gotteslehre; Eine dogmatische Untersuchung* [Tübingen: J. C. B. Mohr, 1975], pp. 161f) feels that he must refuse to permit the question to be raised "about God himself, beyond the history of God." The issue is to think the history in which God is as his history in such a way that this history is "God himself." To put it in Karl Barth's words (*CD*, IV/1, p. 205), against whom Mildenberger is arguing, "His being as God is His being in His own history." Such an understanding of God has as little to do with a presupposed identity of thought and being, which Mildenberger cannot "go along with," as it does with the disputation of such an identity. But the issue certainly is to *understand* what we are saying when we call God *Father* and then *Son* and also *Holy Spirit*. It is then a rather remarkable assertion to say that thus the "knowability of God" is sought "in a contradictionless intellectual construction which is built up over the facticity of the revelation of God in Jesus Christ." "We seek the knowability of the being of God" with Mildenberger "more in the understandability of the history of God." But we are *seeking* it in order to *find* it.

29. Karl Barth (*CD*, IV/2, 757f) paraphrases the Johannine thinking accordingly: "The equation of I Jn. 4:8, 16: 'God is love,' is a peculiarity of the Johannine witness. So, too, is that of Jn. 4:24: 'God is Spirit.' The two explain one another. To say 'love' in the Johannine sense is to say 'Spirit'—the Spirit in whom God is wholly the Father of the Son and wholly the Son of the Father and as such the One who first loves us. And to say 'Spirit' in the Johannine sense is to say 'love'—the love which as and even before God loves us is the love in which as the Father He loves the Son and as the Son the Father. It is again in John's Gospel that this eternity of the basis of Christian love in the Trinity is expressly indicated: 'The Father loveth the Son, and hath given (this is His eternal love, His fatherly and divine self-giving) all things (no less than His whole divine worth, His whole divine sovereignty and power over all things) into his hand' (Jn. 3:35, cf. 5:20). He has given Him His glory (Jn. 17:24) as and because He loved Him from the foundation of the world. But this love of the Father for the Son is described (Jn. 10:17) as an answer to the fact that the Son (this is His eternal love, His self-giving) staked Himself, His life, in obedience to the Father, to receive it again in so doing."

identification of God with the crucified man Jesus is the mutual work of the Father, the Son, and the Holy Spirit. Or to put it in terms of the 'rationality of knowing' (*ratio cognoscendi*): The identification of God with the crucified Jesus requires the differentiation of God the Father, God the Son, and God the Holy Spirit![30] Only in this threefold differentiation of the being of God does the statement that God is love become understandable.

Now, we have definitely taken the preceding analysis of love in a new direction. We had understood love in terms of the relationship between the loving I and the beloved Thou. I and Thou had been simply assumed to be *lovable* by each other. "Where love is, there is vision"—we had expounded that in terms of the phenomenological situation in such a way that one I among many emerges for a specific I as its beloved Thou. It attracts that I. And thus love does consist of that "process of attraction" on the part of a figure who appears worthy of loving, put platonically, "by the *eidos* ['sight'] of the beautiful."[31] The loving I is attracted by the loveworthy Thou in such a way that the loving one is "transformed in a radical sense." "He becomes a completely different person."[32] We did also say of this love that it *radiates* and thus leads beyond the I-Thou relationship. That insight now is refined in a special way in that God is not only the loving one and the beloved one, but as the Holy Spirit goes out beyond himself and thus determines the relationship of the loving I to the beloved Thou. God does not want to love himself without loving the other, the man. Thus the "Son of God" in New Testament usage is always the one sent into the world, the one who has been given to the world. If God were only the one who loves himself eternally, then the differentiation between God and God would be pointless, and God would actually not love at all in his absolute identity. Spinoza would then have been right: "God does not love or hate anyone."[33]

But we have seen that God is love precisely in that he loves his Son in his identity with man, that is, with the scandalously murdered man Jesus. Love here is not directed toward a loveworthy Thou. That is emphasized in the Johannine scriptures with the statement that God loves *the world* in which sin and death dominate. The love which God is cannot be understood as only a love which *radiates* into lovelessness. It *involves itself* with that lovelessness. That counterpart which it finds is not worthy of love. Rather, it makes what is totally unloveworthy into something worthy of love. And it does that *by* loving it. To speak of the transforming power of the fire of love, which is requested together with the prayer for the coming of the Holy Spirit, is both the critical and soteriological point of the statement "God is love."

It should now be perfectly understandable, on the basis of that point, why one can, in fact, say of humans that they are loving I and beloved Thou, but one could never say that they are as such love. The human love relationship takes

---

30. It is not really possible to understand the Christian doctrine of the Trinity without affirming *the sense* of the ancient churchly doctrine of the two natures: in the 'hypostatic union' to think the perfected identity, in the difference of the two natures at the same time to think the unprejudiced *event* of the identification of God and Jesus.

31. H. Scholz, *op. cit.*, p. 11.

32. *Ibid.*

33. B. Spinoza, *Ethics,* in *Chief Works*, 2 vols., tr. R. H. M. Elwes (New York: Dover Publications, 1955), II, pt. V, prop. 17, cor., p. 262.

place between two subjects who are loveworthy to each other. As such, it *radiates* beyond them into the realm of those relationships which are not love. But more than that cannot be said of it. Its definition remains determined by the relationship between two people who are loveworthy to each other. "The love of man is created by the object of its love," says Luther[34] aptly, and explains with Aristotle, ". . . the object of love is the cause of love." But God, by contrast, loves the *lost* sheep (Matt. 15:24), the *unlovable and the sick* (Luke 5:31f), the totally unrighteous *sinners* (Luke 19:10 pars.). He selects what is foolish, weak, ignoble, and contemned by the world, that is, everything which amounts to *nothing* (I Cor. 1:27f). In contrast to the 'love of man,' God's love, according to Luther, first makes the 'object of love' loveworthy: "The love of God does not find but creates the object of its love." Luther explains this with the justification of the sinner: ". . . the love of God living in a man loves sinners, evil men, foolish men, weak men, so that the love of God makes them righteous, good, wise, and strong."

But man, who as a sinner is so totally despicable, becomes beautiful as the "object" of God's love. If human love already *makes* a person beautiful in a certain way, then it is certainly true that God's love, in a qualitatively superior sense, makes the ugly person beautiful and worthy of love. "Thus sinners are lovely because they are loved: they are not loved because they are lovely. . . . And that is what love of the cross means. It is a love born of the cross, which betakes itself not to where it can find something good to enjoy, but where it may confer good to the wicked and the needy." This 'love of the cross' is meant when God and love are posited as identical.

To establish that identity must, however, also mean that "the converse that love is God" is an allowable statement. And it was, after all, Karl Barth who pointedly took the position that, as far as the author of First John is concerned, "the context shows that this was the mind of the author."[35] The "context shows" this indeed as the point of the admonition that there is to be love for each other (vv. 7, 11, 19f). That leads all the more to the old question whether, ultimately, God is destined to be the predicate of human life and accordingly the humanity of God is to be stated as the co-humanity of man and nothing more.

34. M. Luther, "Heidelberg Disputation," in *Early Theological Works* (*Library of Christian Classics*, vol. 16), ed. and tr. J. Atkinson (Philadelphia: Westminster Press, 1962), thesis 28, p. 295. Luther's distinction between the 'love of man' and the 'love of God' with regard to the 'object of love' was apparently either not illuminating or unknown to early Protestant Orthodoxy. Polanus, for instance (*Syntagma theologiae christianae* [Hannover, 1624], 542 E; II, cap. 12), gives this definition: "The love of God is an essential property and essence of God through which God delights in himself in that which he approves and wishes well." And Quenstedt (*Theologia didacticopolemica sive systema theologicum* [Wittenberg, 1696], 291; I, cap. 8, sect. I, thesis 30) appears to contradict Luther: "The love of God is that in which he unites himself sweetly with a lovable object." Karl Barth (*CD*, II/1, pp. 278f) asserted against this and similar definitions that "God's loving is concerned with a seeking and creation of fellowship *without any reference* to an existing *aptitude* or *worthiness* on the part of the loved. God's love is not . . . conditioned by any worthiness to be loved on the part of the loved. . . ." In fact, ". . . the idea of an *objectum amabile* cannot be normative when we are concerned with the relationship of the love of the Father for the Son, with which 'thou hast loved me before the foundation of the world' (Jn. 17:23-26)." It is rather remarkable that Barth did *not* then turn to Luther's parallel definition of the 'love of God.'
35. Karl Barth, *CD*, IV/2, p. 756.

SECTION 21. Faith in the Humanity of God;
On the Distinction between Faith and Love

1. The identification of God and love leads necessarily to the question as to how the apparently unavoidable reversal of the statement "God is love" into "love is God" can be protected from the grave misunderstanding that the loving person as such is divine, and so God is a fundamentally replaceable word. We have already noted that First John puts stress on the reversal of the statement. But it would also be illogical to dispute the reversibility of the statement "God is love." It is, after all, consequent, "as long as there is European logic. . . ," that "from x=y for every value of x and y: y=x, where x and y are signs for any two individuals and the identity relationship asserted for x and y is so defined that every characteristic of x is also a characteristic of y, and vice versa."[1] Then the theological question becomes all the more urgent: Is this not an endorsement of the deification of human love relationships?

The question becomes even more pointed when we turn to the love of man toward God. If it is true that loving persons give existence to each other, then the consequence must emerge that not only does God give man, but also man gives God existence. The loving person would then become the origin of his love and that love would become the *creatrix divinitatis* ('creatoress of divinity'), which would be tantamount to the most ingenious de-deification of God. In this context, one is reminded of the Alexandrines of Angelus Silesius' *Cherubinischer Wandersmann*. It is not only that they recall thoughts which are reminiscent of Augustine:

"That which you love enough can render you rebirth:
Love God and become God, love earth and become earth."[2]

And it is not only that for, moreover, the demand is expressly uttered that the man who loves God should be defied:

"If you would to God, then become a God; for God does not lower
  himself to
Him who does not want to be God, and what he is, with him."[3]

"Man, be not ever man! the summit must be gained!
In God's house Gods and Gods alone are entertained."[4]

The consequences of equality between God and the I are then drawn:

"I am as great as God, he is as small as I;
He is not over me, not under him am I."[5]

1. H. Scholz, *Eros und Caritas; Die platonische Liebe und die Liebe im Sinne des Christentums* (1929), p. 54, n. 1.
2. Angelus Silesius, *Cherubinischer Wandersmann (Geistreiche Sinn- und Schlussreime)*, ed. G. Ellinger (*Neudrucke deutscher Litteraturwerke des XVI. und XVII. Jahrhunderts,* nr. 135-38) (Halle: M. Niemeyer, 1895), p. 130 (V, 200). [Quotations from an English edition will be given where possible; not all of the German edition has appeared in an English edition; my translations of the German edition do not attempt to be metric—TR.] Angelus Silesius, *Alexandrines; translated from the "Cherubinischer Wandersmann"* (1657), tr. J. Bilger (North Montpelier, VT: Driftwind Press, 1944), p. 43 (V, 200).
3. German edition, *op. cit.,* p. 162 (VI, 128).
4. Angelus Silesius, *Selections from "The Cherubinic Wanderer,"* tr. J. E. Crawford Flitch (Westport, Connecticut: Hyperion Press, Inc., 1932), p. 135 (V, 219).
5. Bilger edition, *op. cit.,* p. 77 (I, 10).

For:

"God loves beyond himself; loved I him more than me,
I would then give as much as he, of charity." [6]

This mutual giving of love must then produce, with the strictest logic, the result that God and I give each other our existence and essence, our life:

"God nothing is at all; and if he something be,
Only in me it is, he having chosen me." [7]

"I mean as much to God as he can mean to me;
Each helps the other cherish his own identity." [8]

"I know that God no hour without myself can live.
If I die, God himself his precious life must give." [9]

Accordingly, God and I experience in this mutuality the entire anxiety and blessedness of love:

"God loves only me, and he is so concerned about me,
That he will die of fear if I do not remain true to him." [10]

"That God so blissful is and lives without desire,
No less did he from me than I from him acquire." [11]

Before one dismisses these and similar sayings as "pious effrontery,"[12] one should give that statement by the *"Cherubinischer Wandersmann"* its due in which he declares expressly that God is the sole source of salvation, and thus understands the I which is becoming God solely in terms of God's grace:

"It is out of love that God becomes I, and out of grace I He,
Thus comes all my salvation solely from him." [13]

One should also bear in mind the preface to the 1657 edition of the *"Geist-reiche Sinn- und Schlussreime"* according to which "it was never the author's opinion that the human soul should or could lose its created nature and through

6. Bilger edition, *op. cit.*, p. 59 (I, 18). [This is perhaps too free a translation to get the entire point; here is a prose translation which is more literal: "God loves me beyond himself. . . . If I love him beyond myself, / Then I give to him as much as he gives to me of himself"—TR.]

7. Angelus Silesius, *The Cherubinic Wanderer Selections,* tr. W. R. Trask (New York: Pantheon Books, Inc., 1953), p. 28 (I, 200).

8. Bilger edition, *op. cit.*, p. 79 (I, 100).

9. Bilger edition, *op. cit.*, p. 25 (I, 8).

10. German edition, *op. cit.*, p. 68 (III, 37).

11. Trask edition, *op. cit.*, p. 14 (I, 9).

12. Karl Barth (*CD*, II/1, p. 282) comments: "The '*Cherubinischer Wandersmann*,' in which these pious blasphemies are to be read (Rainer Maria Rilke has the same sort of thing on his conscience) is published with the imprimatur of a Roman Catholic bishop, and we may well ask whether this bishop was an imbecile or whether he had a secret understanding with the modern rogue. What is beyond question is that this is *the* impossible way of talking about the relations of God and man, and yet it is incontestably possible, and even necessary, in a train of logic in which—in view of the indispensable requirement of all human love, a beloved object different from the one who loves—we try to tie the love of God to the existence of an object of this kind, and to exhaust it in the relationship to this other."

13. German edition, *op. cit.*, p. 136 (V, 270).

deification be transformed into God or his uncreated essence: that cannot happen in all eternity. . . . For that reason Tauler says in his *Spiritual Instructions,* ch. 9, that because the Almighty could not create us as gods by nature (for only he can be that), he then worked it that we would be gods out of grace."[14]

The question remains whether in such thinking God's deity threatens to be identified with love in the sense that ultimately there still is necessarily talk of the love relationship between the loving I and the beloved Thou, but there is really no more talk about God. It is expressly asserted, however, that God's deity stands and falls with the I-Thou love relationship:

"*Naught is but I and Thou. Were there no Thou nor I,*
Then God is no more God, and Heaven falls from the sky."[15]

Of course one may not read even this syllogism without the warning:

"*It is not thou, who live; for creatures all are dead;*
The life that lives in thee, and makes thee live, is God."[16]

"*Did not God love Himself through thee and in thee, Man,*
Thy love for Him would ever fail of its full span."[17]

But such warnings do not lead out of the deep and yet intended ambiguity which spreads itself like a diffuse light over the aphorisms of Angelus Silesius. For insensitive love is declared to be divine, and, in true Spinozan form, passionate love for God is declared to be inappropriate:

"*Whoever lives without sensitivity and without knowledge*
Is called quite rightly more God than man."[18]

"*Man, when both joy and grief leave thee unmoved and free,*
Then art thou seated firm in God, and God in thee."[19]

And so we must ask whether the identification of God and love which is presupposed here ultimately results in a God who cannot love, who cannot initiate love. What should the following mean?

"*God doth become what now I am, assumes my manhood; what He*
is,
The same aforetime I have been: therefore it is He doeth this."[20]

Further we must ask how it should be possible to maintain the difference between God and man, if this is true:

"*To me, God is God and man; to him, I am man and God;*
I soothe and quench his thirst; he helps me in my need."[21]

"*I am God's other self. He findeth but in me*
That which resembleth him eternally."[22]

14. German edition, *op. cit.,* p. 5.
15. Flitch edition, *op. cit.,* p. 128 (II, 178).
16. Trask edition, *op. cit.,* p. 47 (II, 207).
17. Flitch edition, *op. cit.,* p. 176 (V, 297).
18. German edition, *op. cit.,* p. 46 (II, 59).
19. Trask edition, *op. cit.,* p. 40 (I, 293).
20. Flitch edition, *op. cit.,* p. 132 (V, 259).
21. Trask edition, *op. cit.,* p. 31 (I, 224). Is this a result of the Lutheran understanding of the *communicatio idiomatum*?
22. Bilger edition, *op. cit.,* p. 33 (I, 278).

The author of First John also was saying that "God is God and man to me" with his identification of God and love. But he certainly did not think that "I am man and God to him," for that is a conclusion which could never be drawn from his identification, but rather a view which is totally excluded by that identification. And so the final and most pointed counterquestion to be addressed to Johannes Scheffler, who like Luther appealed to Tauler—*and* converted to the Roman Catholic Church [Angelus Silesius is his pseudonym]—is this: Was he not singing the praises of a monstrous lovelessness, when he continued the christological identity of God and man in a soteriological and anthropological identity of man and God ("out of grace"!). For nothing is worse for man than for him to cease to be a mere man. A much deeper understanding of the relationship between God and man is revealed when the human existence of that one man with whom God identified himself was interpreted with the category of sacrifice. Only then is the statement "God is love" protected from being distorted to be the expression of a loveless monstrosity and a monstrous lovelessness when it helps to make the differentiation between God and man as concrete as possible. Thus Karl Barth's warning against the wrong view of the reversibility of the statement "God is love" must be expanded: Not only the "robbing God of His deity," as Barth thought, but also the dehumanization of man, even the distortion of love into ultimate lovelessness, would be the unavoidable result "if we are not careful at this point."[23]

2. Through this discussion, we have now returned to the question raised by Ludwig Feuerbach.[24] The well-known theological concern that the identification of God and love must necessarily lead to Feuerbach's conclusion that God must be sacrificed to love is, in fact, not without grounds. It has a legitimate claim to be taken seriously. This is because both God's deity and the very essence of love both threaten to be misunderstood here. Responsible theology resolutely confronts the question, then, as to how such a consequence could be avoided without weakening the identity of God and love in the process. In our attempt to answer this question, we shall again direct our discussion along the lines of a few of Feuerbach's statements. They relate to the differentiation between faith and love, which he opposed so passionately and instructively.

Feuerbach reasons that God must be sacrificed to love because of the singularity of love. There is no plural to love. He concludes that the highest utterance of the Christian faith, "God is love," is to be expounded critically in

23. Karl Barth, *CD*, II/1, p. 281.
24. Just as Feuerbach stands historically within the realm of influence of the aphorisms of Angelus Silesius. It certainly was no mistake when, over two centuries later, Gottfried Keller puts the following words in the mouth of the Count in *Grüner Heinrich*, who speaks them as he peruses "with pleasure" the *Cherubinischer Wandersmann*: "How the extremes meet each other and can suddenly shift from the one to the other. Doesn't one think one is hearing our Ludwig Feuerbach when we read this verse: 'I am as great as God, he is as small as I; He is not over me, not under him am I?' . . . All of this leaves the virtually perfect impression that the good Angelus could live today and would only need to change a few outer circumstances, and the mighty seer of God would have been just as mighty and energetic a philosopher of our age!" (Keller, *Der Grüne Heinrich*, zweite Fassung, IV/12, *Sämtliche Werke und ausgewählte Briefe*, ed. C. Heselhaus [München: C. Hanser, 1963²], I, 1064f; in the erste Fassung, IV/12, *op. cit.*, p. 727).

such a way that *faith* in God is disclosed to be a contradiction to the essence of love. "In the proposition 'God is love,' the subject is the *darkness* in which faith shrouds itself; the predicate is the *light* which first illuminates the intrinsically dark subject. . . . Faith clings to the *self-subsistence* of God; love does away with it. . . . Faith advances with its pretensions, and allows only just so much to love as belongs to a predicate in the ordinary sense. It does not permit love freely to unfold itself; it makes love the abstract, and *itself the concrete [or: essence], the fact, the basis*."[25] And for that reason, Feuerbach thinks that faith contradicts the essence of love. For "love identifies man with God and God with man, consequently it identifies man with man; faith separates God from man, consequently it separates man from man. . . ."[26]

For Feuerbach, the essence of love is "identifying" or "universalizing," whereas the essence of faith is "individualizing" or "separating." "Faith isolates God, it makes him a *particular, distinct* being; love universalizes; it makes God a *common* being, the love of whom is one with the love of man."[27] According to the Feuerbachian premise that anthropology is the mystery of theology, the polarity between God and man caused by faith is then obviously and ultimately a division of man within himself and also within the human race. "Faith produces in man an *inward disunion*, a *disunion with himself*, and by consequence an outward disunion also; but love heals the wounds which are made by faith in the heart of man."[28] But once one has seen that ". . . the consciousness of God is nothing else than the consciousness of the species . . . ,"[29] then faith has been revealed to be the arrogance of Christianity which must now be conquered in the name of love. True love drives out faith. Since faith prevents the sacrificing of God to love, then appropriately *faith* must be sacrificed to *love*. God and faith are combined in their negation.

Feuerbach's argumentation is particularly characterized by a special sensibility for the essence of Reformation Christianity.[30] That is his enormous advantage over against the frequent (theological!) attempts made today to identify faith and love as phenomena and thus sacrifice faith to love. Statements like "faith and love are in the interim of waiting," or even "we turn now from the problems of faith to the reality of love,"[31] impress one as very naive theological program propositions when compared with the theologically critical statements of Feuerbach. Feuerbach knew how to strike Christian theology a fatal blow. And he demonstrated a precise sense for the actual function of Christian *theology* in contrast to the phenomenon *religion* in that he made theology, and not religion, responsible for the penetrating distinction between faith and love. For he under-

25. Ludwig Feuerbach, *The Essence of Christianity*, tr. G. Eliot (New York: Harper & Brothers, 1957), p. 264.

26. *Ibid.*, p. 247.

27. *Ibid.*

28. *Ibid.*

29. *Ibid.*, p. 270.

30. See on this J. Wallmann, "Ludwig Feuerbach und die theologische Tradition," *Zeitschrift für Theologie und Kirche*, 67 (1970), 56ff, and O. Bayer, "Gegen Gott für den Menschen; Zu Feuerbachs Lutherrezeption," *loc. cit.*, 69 (1972), 34ff.

31. See W. Hamilton, " 'Death-of-God-Theology' in den Vereinigten Staaten; Bericht über einen Trend theologischen Denkens," *Pastoraltheologie, Wissenschaft und Praxis*, 56 (1967), 429 and 433.

stands theology as that "reflection about religion" which "awakens . . . within religion," but prevents religion, through its reflective process, from seeing through its own innocent disorientation. Instead, this disorientation is stabilized by theology, so that the true essence of religion is distorted into a theological nuisance.

Feuerbach, with his polemical opposition of love and faith, doubtlessly understood the essence of Christianity as its critic better than its apologists with their unreflected identification of faith and love. For the indisputably close relation of faith and love can be seen only when one has understood the peculiar characteristic of faith in contrast with love. What Feuerbach called the arrogance of faith is entirely true of the peculiar characteristic of faith in contrast with love. Faith senses that it has been well understood. Luther even asserted that this arrogance of faith was what made faith distinctively Christian: "Therefore let every Christian follow the example of Paul's pride here. Let love bear all things, believe all things, hope all things (I Cor. 13:7). Let faith, by contrast, bear absolutely nothing; but let it rule, command, triumph, and do everything. For love and faith are exact opposites in their intentions, their tasks, and their values. Love yields even in trifles and says: 'I bear everything and yield to everyone.' But faith says: 'I yield to no one; but everything must yield to me.' "[32]

Why does faith merit this unusual special position? Certainly not in order to distinguish God, with the help of faith, from love in such a way that he can be thought of as an unloving monster lurking behind the love which he predicates. Feuerbach's objections in this direction cannot receive enough attention from Christian theology. The argumentative insistence on the concealment of God, which ultimately does not take seriously the knowledge of the God who reveals himself as love, but rather makes him a problem again by speaking of *deus absconditus* ('concealed God'), should at long last become impossible on the basis of these objections. Concealment is a mode of the revelation of God but not its problematization which would put the definitive event character of revelation as love at general disposal once more. To that extent, Feuerbach takes the position that God is irrevocably love, a position which should be the basic diet of every Christian theology. Whatever else is to be said about God can serve only to make this elementary equation more precisely understood.

The identification of God and love would, however, fully lose its theological significance and become totally meaningless if it were only the expression of an obvious tautology. The statement "God is love" is a different kind of statement from the tautology "a=a." More is being said here than merely that love is love, or that God is God. Feuerbach did indeed recognize the special character of the Johannine identification of God and love when in this context he ascribes to faith the function of making God "a particular, distinct being." Of course, to be precise, one will have to say that faith alone preserves the special character of the divine being as an unmistakably special being. For that reason, faith itself demands that the absolutely necessary distinction between faith and love be made. But it demands this distinction as a difference which ultimately serves the proper understanding of love. To explain that, we must return again

32. Martin Luther, *Lectures on Galatians, 1535, Chapters 1–4,* in *Luther's Works,* ed. J. Pelikan (St. Louis: Concordia, 1963), XXVI, 119.

to the analysis of the essence of love and now emphasize the aspects of truth in the contrast made between eros and agape.

3. Love is an event which does not only occur in relation to God. Love does not only take place between man and God. Love is no less an interhuman event. It has therefore been found necessary to speak of a "paradox of the Johannine equation": "For it is obvious that it is totally out of the question that an *individual* of the type, deity, can ever be identified with a *characteristic* of the type, love."[33] Scholz concludes that it is necessary "to interpret the Johannine identity in such a way . . . that we retain the statement, God is the being which satisfies the condition: there is a love which can be predicated *only* of this being. Or more briefly: God is the being for which a love exists which can be articulated *only* of this being."[34] That would mean that God himself is the subject of the love which applies to him and which has its effect between man and man. We would be dealing with a "concept of God's love for which God himself is the subject."[35] And such a concept of God's love could, in fact, not be harmonized with what has been understood as eros in the tradition of Platonic-Aristotelian metaphysics, whereby we may at this point presuppose that *all* eros ultimately rises up to the love of God, or at least has the tendency toward that love within it. "In every metaphysic of this kind the love of God can only function as love *of* deity. A love whose subject is God himself is totally ruled out in *this* metaphysic."[36]

We can follow the argumentation of Heinrich Scholz to the extent that the love to be articulated of God must in fact have God as its subject. We also agree with the view that this is the very point at which the differentiation between eros and agape becomes relevant. It would be advisable, however, to derive this distinction from the fact that within the phenomenon of love eros attempts to make itself absolute as a partial phenomenon, and thus enters into opposition with love as agape. Eros is to be understood as the process of attraction to another person without which a person knows that he is not complete. That beauty which is lacking for one's own completion appears worthy of love and desirable. And so one wants to have it. Eros is thus—we are reminded here of Plato's *Symposium*—a phenomenon which arises *out of a deficiency*. That *lacking*

33. H. Scholz, *op. cit.*, p. 54, n. 1.
34. *Ibid.*, pp. 55f.
35. *Ibid.*, p. 56.
36. *Ibid.* Scholz, appealing to Aristotle ("De Caelo," in *The Works of Aristotle*, tr. J. L. Stocks, ed. W. D. Ross [Oxford: Clarendon Press, 1953], II, i, 9, 297a a, 33f), argues persuasively: "If such a love existed, it could only exist as a striving of the godhead towards a higher form of existence; for this is the form and the only form in which *eros* manifests itself. But then deity would have to be the being for which there is a still more perfect being so that it can strive after it. And that is absurd; for God himself is the most perfect being . . ." (*ibid.*). " 'For there is nothing else stronger than it to move it—since that would mean more divine—and it has no defect . . .', so that it would be required to resist actively, '. . . and it lacks none of its proper excellences,' so that a movement to appropriate such a 'lacking excellence' could follow. For this reason and only this reason, the Aristotelian deity is 'unchangeable' or 'immovable' (*ibid.*, pp. 56f, n.1). As a striking commentary, Scholz (*ibid.*) quotes Maurus (*Aristotelis opera III*, 298 a): All that moves or is changed is either moved in order to escape some evil, or is moved in order to acquire some good; but the first being neither has evil to flee nor needs good to acquire; *ergo.*"

good seen in another leads one to fall in love and moves one toward that other. What is lacking is what is attractive, in order to enhance myself. In that one loves erotically and only erotically, the loving person does not have everything which he needs in order to have himself. "I am. But I do not have myself. Therefore we first become."[37] This becoming is the expression of an elementary deficiency and of its overcoming, at the same time. Deity, on the other hand, which has always had everything and thus has itself, does not *love*. It cannot at all. And it does not *become*. It is not permitted to. It is by no means inactive as a result. "Not in the least! . . . In that it thinks without interruption, and in such a way that the content of its thinking is the most elevated conceivable"— namely, itself!—it exists "in the uninterrupted exercise of the highest activity at its highest level"[38] and thus leads its incomparably blessed life. The only thing is that this blessed life consists of uninterrupted preoccupation with itself! And that is the goal of the emancipated eros: self-realization as an end in itself. This *abstract* eros then steps antithetically into opposition against agape understood as surrender.

Then! For it must be contested that eros must make itself particular and emancipate itself in this sense. Heinrich Scholz, Anders Nygren, and others are correct that no bridge can be built from a metaphysic which erects itself on the foundation of an eros which is so independent and seeks only to make itself more independent, to the so-called metaphysic of the Johannine agape. Emancipated, abstract eros does not love selfless surrender. This eros does not *love* agape. That is how it reveals itself as abstract. For it excludes an essential, even the essential element of love, out of itself and still wants to be love itself. It is not total, pure love. But conversely it must be emphasized that love which is fully understood will not exclude eros from itself. Here we cannot follow the careful argumentation of Heinrich Scholz "that absolutely no bridge exists which could lead us from this love of God [*scil*. whose subject is God] back to Platonic love."[39] If "Platonic love" is supposed to be understood as that emancipated eros, then it should be stated that even agape understood as selfless surrender behaves in relation to eros as does the father to the son in the parable, but not like his brother who is no less prodigal. Agape *loves* eros. And that is what distinguishes the one from the other. It is nothing other than love, totally, purely love.

Based on this understanding of love according to which agape is a power which integrates eros, we shall now have to direct a critical question to Feuerbach's demand that God be sacrificed to love. We shall have to ask if this demand is not also guided by a concept of abstract eros. It is, after all, supposed to realize the perfection of man as a race, that perfection which it is alleged is

37. Ernst Bloch, *Tübinger Einleitung in die Philosophie, Gesamtausgabe* (Frankfurt/Main: Suhrkamp, 1970), XIII, 13.

38. H. Scholz, *op. cit.*, pp. 57f.

39. *Ibid.*, p. 56. And yet the Pentecost invocation, "Come, Holy Spirit," and Augustine's *Confessions* (bk. III, ch. VII/11, *NPNF*, 1st ser., I, 63: "Too late did I love Thee, O Fairness, so ancient, and yet so new!") do lead him to the admission that there is "in fact a place in *caritas* . . . where it moves over into the Platonic" (*ibid.*, p. 67). "In a way wonderful for the one who feels it, eroticism presses at the tenderest point into the harsh metaphysic of *caritas*" (*ibid.*, p. 66). One can speak here of a happy inconsequence which is coerced out of this thought, an inconsequence which serves only to honor the consequent thinker!

separated from man and regarded as God by faith. In that God, as the utmost of man, is claimed by him and is to be "universalized" into the human race through love, love becomes the epitome of human self-realization. But in this concept of God, the utmost and highest of what is possible for man is attained so that the possibilities of human existence are exhausted by the love which universalizes God.[40] The result is the ontologically and ethically most significant consequence that God so understood, as the goal of man so understood, has *no possibilities* anymore. In him, everything is completed, in accordance with the metaphysical concept of deity whose essence is simple (*haplē*), "because it is activity without potency."[41] Of course, in a deity conceived of as *reality without possibility, the possibility* of *surrendering oneself* to another is excluded. That God who is captured by man through the "universalizing of love" is himself the end of love. For love without possibilities is no love. Rather, love is full of creative possibilities. It is this as the unity of life and death for the sake of life which the loving ones can never exhaust, a unity which God revealed in his identification with the Crucified One. This *surrender* is the precise opposite of that self-realization which exhausts all the possibilities worthy of striving after. It opens up constantly new, inexhaustible possibilities. This love, which does not exclude but integrates eros, does not exhaust itself. Rather, it is the epitome of the creative. And for that very reason, the equation "God is love" is a statement which preserves the deity of God. Every creative act of divine power is as such an act of divine love in action, which not only establishes reality as realized possibility but also creates still more possibilities with every reality. If, by contrast, God is sacrificed to love, then love itself is deprived of its essence. But only faith identifies God and love in such a way that *neither* God is sacrificed to love and thus love is deprived of its true essence, *nor* is love sacrificed to a God who is lurking behind it ("God above God") somewhere, thus depriving this God of his true deity. Faith alone experiences and knows God as the event, the subject, and the object of love at once, that is, as one who loves, is loved, and is the process of love in indissoluble unity.

To say "only faith" means not even the human love which corresponds to the love of God. The erotic and caritative activities of love done by men are, for their part, correspondences of the divine being which is love. But they correspond to it on the basis of faith. Even in First John it must first of all be *said* that the love with which we love one another is of God (I John 4:7). That every loving person *knows* God means that he *believes* that Jesus is the Christ (I John 5:1), the beloved Son of God whom God gave up to death out of love for us (I John 4:9f). It is not only the love which radiates erotically into lovelessness but the love which submits to it, the love which surrenders itself to the unloved which alone promises to gain the victory. But one can *only believe* in this victory

40. God then signifies the boundary at which man can do no more. He cannot *do* any more, because he cannot do any *more*. He is exhausted. This accords with the principle that *thought*, too, arrives at its farthest boundary with the thought of God and has fully realized itself only when it has thought God (see above, pp. 141-46). God is always the boundary of the possible.

41. H. Scholz, *op. cit.*, p. 58; see Aristotle, *Ethica Nicomachea*, tr. W. D. Ross, *The Works of Aristotle*, ed. W. D. Ross (Oxford: Oxford University Press, 1954), IX, vii.14, 1154b, 25ff.

of love, in view of its weakness over against everything which is not love, and in view of the superior power of lovelessness.

Loving people will, of course, become active for the victory of love, in that they not only radiate their love erotically, but also devote themselves caritatively, through love to the unlovely, to the spreading of love in the midst of so much lovelessness, as it is described by the Johannine concept of cosmos. When love wins, then it wins in fact only through love. But those who love cannot *guarantee* the *victory* of love. One can believe in the victory of love only in the sense that one believes in the identity of God and love.

Faith here is not to be understood as a problematical regarding something as true. That would mean merely to *hope* for the victory of love *without certainty*. But faith is the reliable ground of a certain hope in that it is a certainty disclosed by God himself, the certainty that this God is nothing other than love. Faith is not only a theoretical certainty, but rather a certainty which arises out of the *experience* of divine love. But as such experience, faith is pure passivity, unalloyed inactivity, in distinction from the active love which emerges out of it. For one cannot do anything for the experience of being loved. Thus the author of First John emphasizes to those who are loved by God that God loved them first (I John 4:10, 19; see also John 15:12). One can only submit to the experience of being loved and thus to the love of God, just as one can only submit to election—unless, of course, one wanted to reject one's own election. But in that one submits to it, the *certainty* of being loved and thus the best-founded trust is present, that God is love and nothing but love. Faith is therefore the primary correspondence to the love of God, in order then to become "faith working through love" (Gal. 5:6). Therefore, faith alone *guarantees* the *victory* of love. whereas love wins solely through loving.[42]

According to Feuerbach, faith is ultimately to be distinguished from love in that it alienates man from himself by leading man to transpose his *own* perfection out of himself and positing it *as God,* instead of attaining that perfection by grasping himself as a human generic being. If the mystery of theology

---

42. Note may be taken here of what is really a philosophical argument. It begins with the practical impossibility of making a consequent distinction between love and lovelessness in the so-called realm of nature, as far as this is distinguished from that of history, with relative justification. One will not deny that there is a certain form of (erotic) love in this realm, just as nature presents a certain analogy to the unity of life and death for the sake of life, which was the way we understood God who is love. But in this unity of drive to love and loveless drives there is *killing for the sake of life,* so that in the greater affinity of the unity of life and death for life, death paradoxically triumphs. In the realm of nature, love always is engaged with a kind of lovelessness which makes it difficult to speak unambiguously of love. Man, then, as an historical being, does belong to the realm of nature, but is also distinguished from it, one of the reasons for which is his *unique* determination for love. Thus, together with the being of man, love enters clearly into opposition with everything which is not love. But man endures within this opposition, he remains entangled in the side-by-side struggle of love and lovelessness—which can certainly be distinguished. And thus in his being (understood here in an exclusively philosophical sense) he is what might be called a sigh for another being, which is clearly *and* totally love. This sigh could be understood in a *philosophical* sense as faith, as a philosophical faith in the God who is love. But it is to be contrasted with theologically understood faith by virtue of its exclusively postulatory character.

is anthropology, then this is logical. For Feuerbach, anthropology is that doctrine of man which understands the essence of man only in the encounter with man and nature. But under the entirely different presupposition that anthropology is that doctrine of man which sees man defined by God's encounter with the human race through the person Jesus Christ, anthropology could be the mystery of theology in a radically different sense from that of Feuerbach. Then it would be so that faith does *transpose man* out of himself, but not as God, but as a *new man,* who still is distinct from God—all the more so. Faith would then be a kind of self-alienation (II Cor. 5:17). But in contrast to Feuerbach's presupposition, God would not be the highest possibility of man but rather, although he is 'superior to me,' he is even more so 'more intimate to me than I am to myself.' God would not be the uttermost of man's possibilities; rather, *because he is beyond that extreme boundary,* he is *all the more on this side* of the boundaries of human existence, present in the weaknesses of human existence. For the majesty and power of God, considered in the name of Jesus Christ, are perfected in weakness (II Cor. 12:9).

The essence of faith understood this way does not only benefit zeal for God but, for that reason, also benefits the understanding of man. For the essence of faith, thus understood, gives anthropology decidedly more dignity than the demand to sacrifice faith to love ever could. For the person whose faith lets God come as the one who is 'superior to me' and yet is the God 'who is more intimate to me than I am to myself' is never fixed on a "no more" or "no further" as is implied by the Feuerbachian postulate that God is to be claimed as my uttermost possibility and to be universalized into the human race through love. If God, because he is superior to me, is yet totally near to me, then God is the love for which man cannot *do* anything at all. But this total inability to *do* anything, which is the way in which faith must be understood, is characterized by a fundamental superiority of human activity and possibilities of progress, compared to the inability to do anything *more* at the point where the human exhausts its possibilities.[43] Not to be able to do anything as far as God is concerned by no means excludes, but rather includes, the fact that man can do more, and ever more, for the welfare of mankind: "Because God has done enough for our

43. Karl Marx and Friedrich Engels objected quite rightly to Feuerbach that he was criticizing only heaven but not earth: ". . . but as a philosopher, too, he stopped halfway; the lower half of him was a materialist, the upper half idealist . . . [he] achieved nothing positive beyond a grandiloquent religion of love and a meager, impotent system of morals" (F. Engels, *Ludwig Feuerbach and the Outcome of Classical German Philosophy,* ed. C. P. Dutt [New York: International Publishers, 1941], p. 42; see also Karl Marx, "Contribution to the Critique of Hegel's Philosophy of Right," in K. Marx and F. Engels, *On Religion* [Moscow: Foreign Languages Publishing House, 1957], pp. 41-58; Karl Marx, "Theses on Feuerbach," *op. cit.,* pp. 69ff; K. Marx and F. Engels, *The German Ideology,* ed. C. J. Arthur [New York: International Publishers, 1970], pp. 39ff). The Marxist critique of religion could much more easily be accepted by theology than that of Feuerbach, if the latter were not presupposed by the former. Certainly one can integrate critically the specific interest of Marx's critique of religion into theology—and in some ways it must be done. But that is the current fashion anyway, so that there is scarcely too little being done along these lines theologically. *Videant consules!* ('Let the consuls take action!')

salvation, we can not do enough for the welfare of the world."[44] "To do nothing
at all" does not have to be less than "to do nothing more," and "to be able to
do nothing at all" can be much more than "to be able to do nothing *more.*"

Faith alone which engenders activity by doing nothing at the right time is
then the anthropological expression of the fact that God and love are identical.
One can, in fact, do nothing at all *for* love, although one can do everything *out*
of love. That I am loved can "only" be believed. But the evidence of faith cannot
be surpassed by anything else. Only believe—that is the evidence which belongs
to love itself.

4. The result of our discussion with Ludwig Feuerbach's critique of Christianity for our problem would be that the theologically necessary *identification
of God and love* can be protected from the impetus toward letting the word
"God" degenerate into a concept expressing the superlatives of human existence
only when *as strict a distinction as possible is made between faith and love.*
Although love is a strong uniting force, it still preserves the distinctiveness of
those who are united in love and remains itself distinct from those who love each
other. This distinction is maintained by the faith that believes that God *is* love.
Faith is not a competitor of love. It does not set aside the union of those who
are in love. This is also true of the union of God and man, as well as of the
degree that God and man do in fact *love* each other. But faith preserves the
union of man and man, as well as the union of God and man, from confusion
and a failure to distinguish between the human God and the human man. Such
a confusion would ultimately be the death of love. Faith resists it by interpreting
the statement "God loves" with the statement "God is love."

No man *is* love. Two people who love each other *are* not love. Those who
love know that best, in that they constantly experience the weakness of love,
because they are not love. When God and man love each other, then they also
experience between themselves the weakness of love. But *faith* is trust in the fact
that the loving God *is* also love itself. Thus faith distinguishes between God and
man. It does so for the sake of the union of God and man which never abolishes
the distinction, and which one thus best should not call a 'mystical union.' Faith
is trust in God, because in view of the weakness of love it trusts that this love
will never cease (I Cor. 13:8).[45] For this, it appeals to Jesus Christ, to whom

44. The sentence is found in a similar form in the Declaration of the Theological
Committee of the Evangelische Kirche der Union: F. Viering, ed., *Zum Verstandnis des
Todes Jesu; Stellungnahme des Theologischen Ausschusses und Beschluss der Synode der
EKU* (Gütersloh: Gütersloher Verlagshaus, 1968), p. 22.

45. See E. Fuchs, *Jesus; Wort und Tat* (Tübingen: J. C. B. Mohr [Siebeck],
1971), p. 121: "Love is love because it speaks, in that it speaks itself, is future-oriented
in itself, and thus as such irreversible so that it opens up the future." In that sense, one
can join Ernst Fuchs (*Marburger Hermeneutik* [Tübingen: J. C. B. Mohr (Siebeck),
1968], p. 197) in "calling faith the interim definition of love," without becoming Catholic
in the process. But this interim definition does not automatically work. Fuchs emphasizes
that "faith stands in a firm relation to the 'Word' (Rom. 10:8ff)" (*ibid.*). One should take
care not to seek to make a proof of God out of the dependence of those who love on a
trust which refers to the future of life and thus of the distinction between faith and love.
Dependence on trust and the event of trusting are two different things. That is also true
of righteousness, as it is of love. The beatitude of those who hunger and thirst after
righteousness (Matt. 5:6) is a word spoken in the name of God, a word which grants
faith. The passion story of the world is in fact the time within which faith in God becomes

the statement "God is love" is obligated for its truth. For Jesus Christ is that man in whom God has defined himself as a human God. It is then faith in the humanity of God which preserves the identity of God and love. Faith in the humanity of God is *the evidence* of the identity of God and love. It expounds this evidence in that, in the power of God the Holy Spirit, it knows that it is *related* to God the loving and almighty Father through the death and resurrection of the true man and true Son of God, Jesus Christ, and thus knows that the believer is *concretely distinct* from the triune God. Faith in the humanity of God expounds the evidence of the identity of God and love in that it believes: in God the Father, who gave up his beloved Son for man's sake, and thus is truly the Father who loves this his Son. It believes in the love of the Father in that it believes in God the Son, who was given over to death and who surrendered himself in simultaneous love for the heavenly Father and for earthly man. And it believes in God, Father and Son, because it believes in the power of God the Holy Spirit, who is as the event of the love of the triune God the power which unites the opposition of life and death for the sake of the possibility of new being. A theology which emphasizes the identity of God and love by virtue of the distinction between faith and love will, then, devote special and thoughtful attention to faith in the triune God. It may not shy away from explicating the identity of God and love in a trinitarian fashion.

SECTION 22. The Crucified Jesus Christ as 'Vestige of the Trinity'

1. The doctrine of the Trinity is the indispensable, and indispensably difficult, expression of the simple truth that God lives. The expression of this simple truth is indispensably difficult because the certainty that "God lives" must prove itself in the reality of the man Jesus of Nazareth who is proclaimed, believed, and confessed as God. And that certainly means that the certainty that "God lives" must prove itself in the *death* of this man who belongs to God. That is not only because the life of this man includes the fatal end of a human life; rather, because in the fatal end of this human life the beginning of a new relationship to God for all people is grounded! The death of Jesus opens a new relationship to God because it discloses the *being of God* in its *divine* vitality, on the basis of the death of Jesus. The deity of the living God—the divinity of his life and thus the vitality of God—is compatible in a very precise sense with the death of this human life. God's life is compatible with the death of Jesus in

---

possible. But it is not the reason for it. The morally unquenchable longing that the murderer should not triumph over his innocent victim may articulate itself as the "longing for the Other." But it has something to do with God only on the basis of the presupposition of God. To construct a God for that is unworthy of a God. That God is righteous and creates righteousness (but how!) is something we should be permitted to demand of a God if we believe that there is a God. But that there must be a God because unrighteousness should not ultimately triumph is a reason for the existence of this God which is probably rather irritating for that God. God is not God because he is a judge, but he is judge because he is God. And his justice is defined as the justification of the sinner. A Christian theology which takes its lead from the morally indispensable longing that the murderer should not triumph over his innocent victim will not be permitted to exclude that murderer from the grace which justifies, if it does not want to rob Christianity of its identity.

that it *bears* it. And by taking death on himself, he conquers it. As the victor over death, God discloses himself as God. In that the living God in his deity bears the death of Jesus, in that he burdens the eternity of his being with the crucifixion of Jesus, he demonstrates his divine being as a *living* unity of life and death. The faith, which is obligated to the living God for the certainty which was proven in the death of Jesus, proclaims and tells the tension which defines the being of God itself, the tension between eternal life and temporal death, as the story of Jesus Christ. And it thinks and confesses this story in the concept of the triune God.[1] Therefore, in the doctrine of the Trinity, the issue in special concentration and ultimate concreteness is that of God himself. And since the issue here is God in special concentration and ultimate concreteness, the doctrine of the Trinity is the dogma of soteriology in an absolute sense—and it certainly is anything other than a speculation which has little to do with the question of man's salvation. Ancient dogmatics was correct when it asserted the necessity of God for salvation as that of the triune God, even if it perhaps went too far in expanding the category of salvation necessity to *belief in the dogma* of the Trinity of God: "The necessity of believing this dogma is so great that it is not only not possible not to deny it but even impossible for anyone to ignore it without losing salvation, John 17:3; I John 5:11, 12; I John 2:23; John 5:23; 2 Thess. 1:8."[2]

The Christian doctrine of the triune God is the epitome of the story of Jesus Christ, because the reality of God's history with man comes to its truth in the differentiation of the one God into the three persons of the Father, the Son, and the Holy Spirit. The doctrine of the Trinity basically has no other function than to make the story of God so true that it can be told in a responsible way. In the doctrine of the Trinity, God's historicity is thought as truth. In the power of this truth, God can be spoken of in a Christian way, God's being can be told as history. Apart from this truth, conversely, *God's* history is not told. Or else, it is not God's *story* that is *being told*. Apart from this truth, the story of someone else is told in the name of God, or at best stories *about* God are narrated. Or else God's being is postulated and proven. But whichever way, the talk will completely miss God and thus also man. The trinitarian dogma has the function of keeping talk about God from being at cross-purposes with man because it is at cross-purposes with God. Thus the doctrine of the Trinity belongs to the properly understood concept of the word of God.

2. The category of the word of God then leads to still another necessary differentiation of the *being* of God, which in more recent days has frequently tended to replace the trinitarian differentiation of the being of God. The truth of talk about God is not measured in terms of the differentiation of the one being of God as Father, Son, and Spirit, but rather of the differentiation of God, who expresses himself in the word and reveals himself as the word, the 'preached

1. I am pleased to note that this thesis, which I find important and have often propounded, regarding the relationship of the story of Jesus Christ which is to be told and the doctrine of the Trinity which articulates it, has made its literary mark in the books of other authors and thus has been affirmed.

2. J. F. König, *Theologia positiva acroamatica.* (Rostock, 1699[2]), Pars prima, par. 80; quoted after C. H. Ratschow, *Lutherische Dogmatik zwischen Reformation und Aufklärung,* Teil II (Gütersloh: Gütersloher Verlagshaus G. Mohn, 1966), p. 82.

God' (*deus praedicatus*), from God "as he is in his own nature and majesty."[3] With this latter God we have nothing to do because he does not want to deal with us, being without the word. We are speaking here of the distinction between 'revealed God' (*deus revelatus*) and 'concealed God' (*deus absconditus*)—a distinction especially emphasized in the theology of Luther. It applies the distinction between law and gospel to the very concept of God itself, although clearly in a highly refined way. Thus it makes evident that there is a contradictoriness in the concept of God which spans all of human existence, and thus it is evaluating talk about God in terms of man's experience of the encounter with God's word and thus in terms of the failure to have that encounter. The distinction between concealed and revealed God appears to be theologically necessary, an appearance created by the way it is interwoven with the distinction between law and gospel. By contrast, the differentiation of the one being of God into the three modes of being, Father, Son, and Spirit, appears to be existentially irrelevant and thus theologically less necessary. In the distinction and tension between the killing 'pure God' (*deus nudus*) and the enlivening 'preached God' (*deus praedicatus*) there resides that necessity of faith which deals with all distress and thus confronts all human existence. By contrast, there appears to be only a logical or speculative necessity in the distinctions of the trinitarian doctrine, and the experience of faith can do without that. That is approximately the situation of contemporary discussion. Luther certainly did teach the doctrine of the Trinity, but it was not a matter of controversy and thus did not occupy so central a place.[4] Moreover, formulations of the trinitarian doctrine like this, "That Father, Son, and Holy Spirit, three distinct persons in one divine essence and nature[!], are one God. . . ," and Luther's title which says that in the doctrine of the Trinity one is dealing with the "High Article of the Divine Majesty,"[5] all lead one to identify the triune God with God "as he is in his own nature and majesty." Then, within the distinction between 'revealed God' and 'concealed God' the triune God would be considered under the concept of the 'concealed God.' What Luther says about the 'concealed God,' "that God hides himself and wills to be unknown to us, it is no business of ours . . . God must therefore be left to himself in his own majesty,"[6] would be taken to apply to God precisely in his threefold self-differentiation.

Now the whole matter is much more differentiated in Luther, and the entire problem cannot be reduced to the alternative of the differentiation between the three persons of the one God and the differentiation between revealed and concealed God. The distinction between the 'concealed God' and the 'revealed God' is a theologically legitimate one and, in fact, is necessary. But it becomes illegitimate and one-sided if it is supposed to replace the doctrine of the Trinity.

3. Martin Luther, "De Servo Arbitrio," in *Luther and Erasmus: Free Will and Salvation* (*Library of Christian Classics*, vol. 17), trs. and eds. E. G. Rupp, P. Watson, and B. Drewery (Philadelphia: Westminster, 1969), p. 201.
4. See the Smalcald Articles, in *The Book of Concord; The Confessions of the Evangelical Lutheran Church*, tr. T. G. Tappert (Philadelphia: Fortress Press, 1959), pt. I, p. 292: "These articles are not matters of dispute or contention, for both parties confess them. Therefore, it is not necessary to treat them at greater length."
5. *Ibid.*, p. 291.
6. Luther, "De Servo Arbitrio," *op. cit.*, p. 201.

The distinction between 'the concealed God' and 'the revealed God' is a differentiation which maintains the coming of God in motion between its Whence and Where-to. The trinitarian differentiation between God the Father, the Son, and the Spirit, on the other hand, is the critical expression of the fact that the Whence and the Where-to of God's coming, in which God's being is, is nothing other than God himself. To put it positively, this implies that God himself is both origin and goal. The distinction between 'the concealed God' and the 'revealed God' means in its final consequences that even in the situation of God-forsakenness we are dealing with God, that even the reality of lacking knowledge of God is a form of the reality of God, the reality of his law and judgment, that then really 'no one can be against God' 'except God himself' (*nemo contra deum; nisi deus ipse*). If that is the import of that distinction, then the doctrine of the Trinity, with its distinctions (which as such are always relationships), means that the God who reveals himself to us is really *God himself,* that he cannot be relativized by any other "god," that he does not put his own revelation in question, and that his concealment is really a definition of his revelation. Briefly, the differentiation between God and God can never be understood as a contradiction in God. There is a threat of such a contradiction in God in Lutheran dogmatics, to the extent that it does not gauge the distinction between the revealed and concealed God expressly by the self-differentiation of the triune God. God does not contradict himself. God corresponds to himself. For that reason we need the doctrine of the Trinity, through the whole sweep of theology.

But clearly it cannot be denied that the traditional doctrine of the Trinity has its weakness. And that is that the dialectic given with the distinction between 'revealed God' and 'concealed God' has remained curiously irrelevant for the doctrine of the Trinity. This means on the one hand that the tension between law and gospel has remained ultimately meaningless for talk about God himself and on the other hand that the trinitarian doctrine evolves into a dangerous abstraction of the history in which God wants to be and is the God of man. The danger is evoked by the traditional distinction between the immanent and economic Trinity. The immanent trinitarian doctrine understands God himself with no regard for his relationship to man; the economic trinitarian doctrine, by contrast, understands God's being in its relationship to man and his world. This distinction within the doctrine of the Trinity corresponds then to the old distinction between 'theology' (*theologia*) and 'economy' (*oikonomia*). But it is legitimate only when the economic doctrine of the Trinity deals with God's history with man, and the immanent doctrine of the Trinity is *its* summarizing concept. Here careful corrections of the traditional form of trinitarian doctrine are absolutely called for. These corrections must do justice to the dialectic of law and gospel with regard to "God himself."

In the economic doctrine of the Trinity, which considers God's history with man, the dialectic of law and gospel is emphasized in the distinction of 'revealed God' and 'concealed God.' But this dialectic must also be made fruitful for the immanent doctrine of the Trinity if these forms of the word of God are to be based in God himself, and if the 'word of God' (*verbum dei*) is really to be 'the person of God speaking' (*dei loquentis persona*). For one must speak about God the way God speaks about himself—through gospel and law (Elert). Where the economic doctrine of the Trinity speaks of God's *history* with man, the immanent doctrine of the Trinity must speak of God's *historicity*. God's history is his coming to man. God's historicity is God's being as it comes (being in coming). We must ponder this if we want to take God's history with man seriously as an event in which God is God. In the process, of course, the immanent doctrine of the Trinity, which considers the historicity of God, must take seriously that God is *our* God. In that the doctrine of the Trinity maintains the deity of God and yet lets God in his self-being be our God— "in advance, so to speak" (Barth)— and no one else's God, it draws the distinction between law and gospel into the unity of God's being and gives it its proper weight. By giving its proper weight to the distinction of law and gospel in the unity of God's being, the doctrine of the Trinity demonstrates its own necessity.

3. Any theology, however, which appeals exclusively to the Bible to substantiate the necessity and the possibility of its statements must submit to the following question: To what extent does Holy Scripture provide a basis for the doctrine of the Trinity of God? The Reformation theology formulated in the Augsburg Confession was confronted with this question just as soon as it established the doctrine of the Trinity in Augsburg, Article I, with reference back to the Nicaeno-Constantinopolitan Creed. The assertion was made in Augsburg I that "we unanimously hold and teach, in accordance with the decree of the Council of Nicaea, that there is one divine essence, which is called and which is truly God, and that there are three persons in this one divine essence. . . ."[7] The Roman Confutation then immediately asked whether "the Reformation principle of *sola scriptura* would allow the faith model of the Trinity, which is foreign to Scripture." Melanchthon then emphasizes in the Apology to Article I that "we believe that the Holy Scriptures testify to it firmly, surely, and irrefutably." But he does not cite the scriptural texts. "This little prelude reveals the inner difficulty of the doctrine of the Trinity in Lutheran dogmatics."[8] Only later would the scriptural proof be presented extensively. And there is clearly the obvious contrast between the simple biblical phrases and names on the one hand and the noticeably subtle conceptual distinctions of the churchly doctrine on the other hand. These subtleties have been explained by referring to the function of the church's doctrine of the Trinity as a doctrine which protects against heresies. The content which is expressed in these unbiblical concepts is, moreover, clearly grounded in the Bible and has always been believed since the beginning of the church. "Neither is it something new, devised by the Council of Nice[a] (as some blasphemously assert that the doctrine of the Trinity was first framed in the Councils of Nice[a] and Constantinople), while, before that, the Church piously believed that there was one God. But we solemnly declare that it is the most ancient and constant harmonious testimony of the Church from the very beginning."[9]

7. The Augsburg Confession, Article I, in *The Book of Concord; The Confessions of the Evangelical Lutheran Church*, tr. T. G. Tappert (Philadelphia: Fortress Press, 1959), p. 27.

8. C. H. Ratschow, *op. cit.*, p. 88.

9. M. Chemnitz, *Loci theologici*, I, 33, quoted in H. Schmid, *The Doctrinal Theology of the Evangelical Lutheran Church, verified from the original sources*, trs. C. A. Hay and H. E. Jacobs (Philadelphia: United Lutheran Publication House, 1889), p. 140, n. 9.

In Reformation and early Protestant theology, the doctrine of the Trinity was understood as a product of the church's doctrinal development solely with regard to its form. Its content was felt to be grounded in Scripture, and over the years increasing attention was given to providing a scriptural foundation for the trinitarian doctrine. Related to that is the fact that in the early stages of the development (for example, in Melanchthon) the so-called 'vestiges of the Trinity' (*vestigia trinitatis*) were referred to as significant for the foundation of the doctrine of the Trinity—that is, those structures of creation which are allegedly trinitarian in their order and thus refer to the divine Trinity. But later on, much less reference was made to them,[10] whereas the equally important statement by Melanchthon gradually established itself as authoritative, "One must think of God as he has revealed himself"[11]—also as a foundation for the necessity of the trinitarian dogma.

4. The old assertion that there are certain 'vestiges of the Trinity' confronts us with a dogmatic problem of the first rank which cannot simply be evaded. For this assertion is an attempt to represent revelatory knowledge, which is expressly designated a 'mystery of faith' (*mysterium fidei*) and strictly distinguished from all 'natural knowledge of God' (*notitia dei naturalis*), by comparing it to expressly natural phenomena. Worldly phenomena which exist in a threeness but are still one were understood in their trinitarian disposition as traces of the triune God within existence, which either allowed one to deduce the Trinity of God (that was seldom) or were able to make the presupposed Trinity of God evident by referral to the being of the world. Although the examples cited in the early church and frequently by Scholasticism, but also by the Reformers and in more recent theology, are amusing,[12] the fundamental dogmatic problem they raise is sobering. Is a mystery of faith which can be illustrated in that fashion really a mystery of faith? Quite rightly, Karl Barth insisted that with the "assertion of the presence and knowability of those 'vestiges of the Trinity' . . ." the decisive question is placed "not only for the question of the root of the *doctrine of the Trinity* but for the question of *revelation generally.*"[13] Nevertheless, there is a moment of truth in the assertion that there are 'vestiges of the Trinity.'

Barth sees the relative rightness in the assertion of 'vestiges of the Trinity,' the 'particles of truth' which are present in spite of the fundamental questionableness of the idea, in that we must *talk* about God, that revelation must be stated in worldly language, and that in fact it has been expressed in that way. But this human talk about God cannot be illustration but may only be and certainly must be interpretation of the revelation. However, a conceptual objection to Barth's thesis is unavoidable. Revelation cannot first gain worldly speech through interpretation. Revelation has as such worldly speech as a part of itself—else it could

10. See Ratschow, *op. cit.*, p. 89.
11. *Ibid.*, p. 91.
12. Examples: spring, river, and estuary (Anselm of Canterbury); essence, form, and power (Luther); grammar, dialectic, and rhetoric (Luther); memory, mind, and will (Augustine); but also the three ages of man (Joachim of Fiore), etc.
13. Karl Barth, *CD*, I/1, p. 385. See E. Jüngel, *The Doctrine of the Trinity; God's Being Is in Becoming*, tr. H. Harris (Grand Rapids: Wm. B. Eerdmans, 1976), pp. 6ff [the subtitle of the German original is emphasized by the author: "Responsible Talk about the Being of God in Karl Barth; A Paraphrase"—TR].

not reveal. The world must be conceived within the concept of revelation. And to the degree that language is the epitome of human historicity, we must speak of human history when we use the concept of revelation. Barth's concern that human history may not become the subject of revelation and revelation not become the predicate of history is by no means a lost cause in this understanding of revelation. The human history with its worldly language which is already conceived together with and within the concept of revelation is a *special* human history, special because it is *defined* by the event of revelation and thus special *de facto* but not in and of itself.[14] I emphasize: it is special, but not in and of itself. It is so by the power of a process of becoming which is not founded in its own historicity. *Such* a history speaks then, by virtue of the revelation taking place within it, of the God who reveals himself. And then it is necessary to say of that history that it is the trace of the triune God, the 'vestige of the Trinity.'

The man Jesus and his death on the cross would basically not affect faith in God if God himself had not come to the world in this human life and death. Conversely, if there were no man Jesus and his history, there would be no Christian faith at all. Christian faith stands and falls, both historically and systematically, with the fact that it sees God coming to the world in the life and death of this man. For that reason, it is virtually an axiom of the Christian faith that God has come to the world in the being of the man Jesus. This assertion is, to be sure, an Easter confession. It presupposes both the *end* of this man's life and a new way in which he is present. It is the end of the direct presence of Jesus, his death and his removal from us, which then first make it possible to understand his coming as the coming of God. Without his going away, there would be no revelation, if, as was presented above, revelation is the becoming present of an absent one as absent.[15] That God as the Absent One is all the more present is the basic structure of revelation in the world. For that reason, faith corresponds anthropologically to the event of revelation. Because the absent Jesus Christ is present as the Absent One solely in faith, it is possible to believe, in fact, that God has come to the world only in the being of the man Jesus. But faith does, certainly, perceive the trace of the coming of God in Jesus' being as human.[16] It understands the man Jesus as a 'vestige of the Trinity.'[17]

14. A history that was special in and of itself would then be a history which *determines* and *defines* revelation by virtue of its own quality. Such an understanding of the relationship of revelation and history leads with logical necessity to the construction of a "history of salvation" made up of "salvific facts," which it is not our purpose to endorse here.

15. Rudolf Bultmann worked this through thoroughly for the Gospel according to St. John. The systematic-hermeneutical structure according to which what is absent is present as absent is of decisive importance for G. Ebeling's understanding of language. See G. Ebeling, *Introduction to the Theological Theory of Language,* tr. R. A. Wilson (Philadelphia: Fortress Press, 1973), pp. 54ff, 202.

16. The christological wealth of the resurrection discovers its own origin in the christological poverty of the earthly existence of Jesus. The so-called theory of the Marcan secret is a theological means of dealing with this content germanely in the form of a literary Gospel. See, on this, H. Conzelmann, "Gegenwart und Zukunft in der synoptischen Tradition." *Theologie als Schriftauslegung; Aufsätze zum Neuen Testament* (München: C. Kaiser, 1974), pp. 42ff.

17. The methodological consequence of this fact is that one can ask relevantly about the historical Jesus only when faith in Jesus Christ has been acknowledged as at least a *factual* result of the fact that Jesus the man did exist on earth. But then it is

However, in that sense, *the man Jesus alone* can be exclusively asserted to be the 'vestige of the Trinity.' Apart from the humanness of this man, apart from his life-history and his suffering, talk about the triune God would be at best a 'mystery of logic' (*mysterium logicum*), a pointless and groundless speculation. But the opposite is true: if it is possible to speak of the revelation of God at all, then the man Jesus must be asserted to be the *'vestige of the Trinity.'* Apart from that, neither faith in Jesus *as* God's Son nor faith in God who *is* love can be grounded. The New Testament kerygma which proclaims and tells the identity of the ascended Christ with the earthly Jesus calls for the concept of the triune God, if it is to be protected beyond its historical origin from being confused with mythological god stories. It is theologically meaningful to question the life history and passion of the earthly Jesus only on the basis of the proclamation of the resurrected and crucified Christ as the Lord of the world, and in a similar way the man Jesus must be seen as a 'vestige of the Trinity' if biblical talk about God the Father, about the Son of God, and about the Holy Spirit is not to appear arbitrary, and further, if the doctrine of the justification which is necessarily implied by such talk is not to appear totally unfounded. A consequent interpretation of the New Testament tradition about Jesus as the Christ leads necessarily to the recognition of the triune God. It is already implied when, on the one hand, the "absolute character of the salvation promise" of the earthly Jesus as asserted in "the representation of God as the Father,"[18] and, on the other hand, the identification of God with the crucified Jesus, are to be combined in our thinking and the two together are to be understood as that eschatological event in which the promises of Scripture are fulfilled—and that means, in which the God of the Old Testament, who *speaks of himself, has defined himself.* One must understand the *fact of the biblical history of promise* not merely as a witness (or only as documentation) but *as a phenomenon which belongs to the concept of God,*[19] if one wants to understand in what respect in

already a statement made by faith to say that faith in Jesus Christ is the *relevant* result of the man Jesus' having been on earth, and anything but a misunderstanding. There is no historical mediation between the two. If there is no revelation without Jesus' going away, then it is quite true that "There is no question that all this is not an event which takes place visibly and demonstrably like the historical events with which the historian deals. . . . it is accessible only to faith" (F. Gogarten, *Christ the Crisis,* tr. R. A. Wilson [Richmond: John Knox Press, 1970], p. 71). [The translation is rather free; here is a literal rendering as Jüngel quotes it: ". . . that this event cannot, in terms of its essence, be historically visible. . . . it is accessible only to faith"—TR.]

18. See H. Conzelmann, art. "Jesus Christus," in *Religion in Geschichte und Gegenwart,* 3rd ed., III, 633.

19. E. Lohse (*Grundriss der neutestamentlichen Theologie* [*Theologische Wissenschaft,* 5] [Stuttgart: W. Kohlhammer, 1974], pp. 14f) dealt with this content by emphasizing, as what one might call a primitive Christian phenomenon, the obvious sense in which the unmistakably *special* meaning of the story of Jesus Christ appears to be understandable "only with the aid of Scripture." However, the relationship of the biblical history of tradition and the being of Jesus Christ is not to be understood as something external, which would mean that the promises are taken as a help in interpreting the passion and death of Jesus Christ. Rather, based on the being of Jesus Christ, the necessity of these now fulfilled promises is first fully seen. To put it hypothetically and in a somewhat exaggerated way (in full knowledge that this may provoke some misunderstanding): if there had been no Old Testament promises, they would have had to be invented because of the being of Jesus Christ.

Jesus God himself came to the world and yet for that reason God the Father must be distinguished from God the Son. This distinction is successful only when one simultaneously understands the fact of the history of promise as an expression of a God who not only *speaks of himself* but also *speaks with eschatological purpose*. The noncontradictory differentiation of God from God implies the event of God as the Holy Spirit.

It is not adequate, then, simply to collate the biblical statements about God as the Father, God as the Son, and God as the Spirit, and then to derive from this material the coercive necessity of the doctrine of the Trinity. The "biblical material" as such offers only a possibility for the doctrine of the Trinity, but not its necessity. To put it in terms of a statement by Bernhard Steffen which recently has been quoted often:[20] "The scriptural basis for Christian belief in the triune God is not the scanty trinitarian formulas of the New Testament, but the throughgoing, unitary testimony of the cross, and the shortest expression of the Trinity is the divine act of the cross. . . ."[21]

5. Our research has led us several times to the conclusion that God's being requires that it be understood as the being of the triune God. Coming from many and varying points of view, the necessity of distinguishing God from God, on the one hand, and the assertion of the relatedness of these differentiated modes of being of God from God, on the other hand, have become understandable. The guiding motif was, however, always faith in the identification of God with the man Jesus. The material understanding was also what guided our formal discussion of the thinkability and speakability of God. Our illumination of the christological origin of the dark talk about the death of God was in fact a constant hermeneutical anticipation of material which is still to be explicated. Now we must present explicitly what has up to now materially determined the character of our research. If in what was just discussed we stated *that* the crucified man Jesus of Nazareth is to be understood as the 'vestige of the Trinity,' then we must now show *in what respect* his history, in what respect the human existence of Jesus, is the trace which leads to the foundation of faith in the triune God.[22]

20. See H. Mühlen, *Die Veränderlichkeit Gottes als Horizont einer zukünftigen Christologie; Auf dem Wege zu einer Kreuzestheologie in Auseinandersetzung mit der altkirchlichen Christologie* (Münster: Aschendorff, 1969), p. 33; J. Moltmann, *The Crucified God; The Cross of Christ as the Foundation and Criticism of Christian Theology*, trs. R. A. Wilson and J. Bowden (New York: Harper & Row, 1974), p. 241.

21. B. Steffen, *Das Dogma vom Kreuz; Beitrag zu einer staurozentrischen Theologie* (1920), p. 152 [English quotation from Moltmann, *op. cit.*, p. 241]. Steffen interprets "the divine act of the cross" as an act "in which the Father allows the Son to sacrifice himself through the Spirit" (*loc. cit.*; Moltmann, *loc. cit.*). H. Mühlen (*op. cit.*, p. 33) refers to this interpretation in relation to Hebrews 9:14, in order in this way to present the cross event as an event of divine love and this love as the being of the triune God. This comes very close to the thoughts which now follow, although we shall not speak of sacrifice, in spite of the corresponding biblical passages, because of the misunderstandings which are associated with the phrase—they appear to be stubbornly resistant to correction.

22. One of the weaknesses of the marvelous trinitarian architecture which defines Karl Barth's *Church Dogmatics* in both its dogmatic structure and its individual systematic arguments is that the *foundation* of the doctrine of the Trinity in the Prolegomena can lead to the misunderstanding that the knowledge of the Trinity of God was deduced from the axiomatically presupposed proposition "God reveals himself as the Lord" with the

In what respect is the story of Jesus' life and passion the trace which leads to the foundation of faith in the triune God? We can best answer this question by means of an exegetical recapitulation. We point to what can be said dogmatically about Jesus' being as a human, based on more recent exegetical insight. The dogmatic statement differs here from the historical in only one regard: it takes seriously Jesus' unique *relationship to God*, which is characteristic of Jesus' self-understanding, not only as a category for an historical report on the way the earthly Jesus saw himself but as an objective expression of *God's relationship to Jesus*. Whereas historical analysis as such neither can ask nor decide the question of the existence of a God, but only leads up to a report about what was apparently a possible way for a person to understand himself, which included a *unique relationship to God*, in a dogmatic statement this relationship is referred back to *God's relationship to Jesus*, on the basis of our belief in the identity of God with Jesus. In that *God* is not only the word of an historical report but rather a word which refers to a reality *sui generis* through a very particular event, the Easter kerygma remains the theological dimension within which the question about Jesus' being as human is raised. This theologically reflexive presupposition of faith in the exegetical question has no influence on the historical analysis, but takes over the word *God*, which for historical analysis can of necessity be used only to designate an empty place, as a word which is justified by the existence of a God. The existence of that God, for its part, can be experienced only through the revelation of his essence, that is, only in the direct identity with the divine essence.

We shall attempt, first of all, to formulate the basic features of the human existence of Jesus as they can be seen in the kerygmatically and christologically molded tradition of the New Testament.[23] We shall then identify the results we found, with the theologically requisite dispatch, as statements about the being of God, working within the dimension of the basic Easter knowledge of that kerygmatic and christological tradition.

Jesus' highly individual announcement of the kingdom of God must be mentioned as a characteristic basic feature of Jesus' humanity. For the coming kingdom of God was so proclaimed by Jesus that its eschatological future appeared to be combined with the present in the person of Jesus himself. He announced that the kingdom of God was coming now, and he claimed that the time of his presence was the period of decision which God himself had introduced. Mark 1:15 summarizes what Jesus was saying: the decisive hour was there, and thus the time of God's kingdom had now come. This proclamation of the kingdom of God determined not only the authority of his words, which let them appear as effective deed-words (Mark 1:22 par.; 1:27a par.; 2:10 par.), but

---

help of formal differentiation of subject, object, and predicate in the revelatory event. Such a misunderstanding is avoided when the humanity of Jesus is not only interpreted dogmatically within the context of faith in the triune God (see chiefly *CD*, IV/2), but faith in the triune God is first presented as dogmatically founded in the context of the humanity of Jesus.

23. The hermeneutical legitimacy of this query has been carefully researched most recently by F. Hahn, "Methodologische Überlegungen zur Rückfrage nach Jesus," in K. Kertelge, ed., *Rückfrage nach Jesus; Zur Methodik und Bedeutung der Frage nach dem historischen Jesus* (Freiburg/Breslau/Basel/Wien: Herder, 1974), pp. 11ff.

the authority of his behavior as well (Mark 1:27b, 34 par.; 2:16f par.; Luke 9:41-43; 11:20-22 par., etc.). And through both his words and his behavior he determined his story himself in the way in which it then became his destiny. For it may be assumed that Jesus, on the basis of his claims, had to count on his violent death and did count on it.[24] One can say that Jesus' entire humanity was so unlimitedly molded by his proclamation of the kingdom of God that his humanity is virtually defined by it. His human life was a being in the act of the word of the kingdom of God, whose time he proclaimed as coming now.[25] He totally was claimed by the coming of the kingdom of God and for that reason he was a proclaimer who made such an incomparable claim.

This basic feature of Jesus' humanity must, however, be immediately explained more concretely. From what we have just said it is by no means obvious to what extent Jesus' proclamation could come across as a message of joy, for example, and thus ultimately could result in hostility and suffering for him. The announcement of the kingdom of God must be understood as the inauguration of a qualitatively new fellowship with God, if one wants to understand that Jesus made that announcement as the promise of salvation and blessing: "Blessed are you poor, for yours is the kingdom of God!" In this salvific fellowship with God, the man to whom it is promised is supposed to attain to his blessedness: "Blessed are you that hunger now, for you shall be satisfied. Blessed are you that weep now, for you shall laugh" (Luke 6:20f). The salvation of the kingdom of God is accompanied by the blessedness of those who are suffering distress.

This significant content reveals to us a more exact understanding of what Jesus announced when he declared that the age of the kingdom of God had come. The kingdom of God is an expression for God himself; more precisely, for God's being as it is active within the world, transforming it from the roots up. The kingdom of God is the majestic act of God with which he asserts himself over the world. Now, absolutely everything depends on how this happens. Thus it is not sufficient if the individual character of Jesus' proclamation is defined only as his announcing that the kingdom of God was coming *now*. It is no less important to demonstrate *how* this is happening and what kind of age this presence of Christ, which has been qualified as the age of decision, is shown to be. There is a time for sorrowing, a time for joy, a time for fasting, a time to celebrate, and so on. For what can and should Jesus' hearer decide when the time of God's kingdom is announced to him as having come? In order to answer such questions, we are directed back to Jesus' proclamation and his behavior, which was a commentary on his proclamation.

And here, in terms of content, we find a confirmation of what we had already recognized to be the formally hermeneutical special characteristic of Jesus' parabolic discourse: Jesus' proclamation and his behavior have an expressly

24. See E. Fuchs, "The Quest of the Historical Jesus," in *Studies in the Historical Jesus*, tr. A. Scobie (Naperville, IL: A. R. Allenson, 1964), pp. 25-31; Martin Hengel, *Gewalt und Gewaltlosigkeit; Zur 'politischen Theologie' in neutestamentlicher Zeit (Calwer Hefte, 118)* (Stuttgart: Calwer Verlag, 1971), pp. 43f; E. Lohse, *op. cit.*, p. 49; F. Hahn, *op. cit.*, pp. 41ff.
25. See my essay "Jesu Wort und Jesus als Wort Gottes; Ein hermeneutischer Beitrag zum christologischen Problem," in *Unterwegs zur Sache; Theologische Bemerkungen* (München: C. Kaiser, 1972), p. 129.

societal structure. It is not that he had a low view of the individual or simply
passed over him in favor of the collective! Precisely the opposite—his proclamation of the kingdom of God confronted each individual so directly[26] that he
has been ascribed "an eminently individualizing tendency."[27] And how could
this be any different if the kingdom of God is an act of God's majesty with
which he asserts himself over against the world so that no worldly institution,
no worldly bond or community, not even father and mother (see Mark 10:29f)
can intervene between God and the individual, but rather each person is addressed directly as an individual! On every person whom Jesus addresses there
falls the reflected splendor—or should one say, a shadow?—of the individual
existence which characterized him, so that the proclaimer of the kingdom of
God appears as the individual in an absolute sense. But that is not said of him
on the basis of an *a priori* "infinite value of the human soul"[28] or because of the
truth that "the highest happiness of earth's children is . . . the personality."[29]
Jesus was encouraged to be himself on the basis of the *relationship* to God in
which he found himself. It is this *fellowship* with God which made Jesus, in an
incomparable way, an individual, a special, unmistakable person in his individual
existence and thus, in a certain way, the loneliest of all men. And thus it is the
new *fellowship* with God which he inaugurated which gives his proclamation
that "eminently individualizing tendency."[30] The hearer is addressed about this
new fellowship with God in such a way that he gains a new understanding of
himself, a new self-understanding. The new self-understanding consists not only
of the fellowship with God, but also of an indestructible dependence on my
neighbor who needs me, and thus on the neighbor whom I need. The other
person who is there for me, and the one who may expect that I am there for him
are discovered to be my neighbors at the very same time that I discover this new
fellowship with God, and they belong to that same fellowship. In that new self-
understanding which Jesus' proclamation inaugurated, the one who hears it will
discover the relationship to his neighbor already present. And thus he first becomes an individual self as a nature who is destined for fellowship with God
and with other people.

Going beyond this *societal structure*, Jesus' announcement of the kingdom
of God is characterized more exactly by the fact that it inaugurates a *very specific*
fellowship. We can best describe the special nature of this fellowship inaugurated
by Jesus as paradoxical when we describe it as a matter of course which is by

26. See H. Conzelmann, art. "Reich Gottes. I. Im Judentum und NT," *Religion
in Geschichte und Gegenwart*, 3rd ed., V, 915.

27. E. Grässer, "Jesus und das Heil Gottes; Bemerkungen zur sogenannten 'In-
dividualisierung des Heils'," in *Jesus Christus in Historie und Theologie; Neutestament-
liche Festschrift für H. Conzelmann zum 60. Geburtstag* (Tübingen: J. C. B. Mohr,
1975), p. 172.

28. We are reminded of the respectable view of A. von Harnack, that in the gospel
the concern is God and the infinite value of the human soul (*What is Christianity?*, tr.
T. B. Saunders [New York: Harper & Row, 1957], p. 63, title of sect. II).

29. We are reminded of the no less respectable view of Goethe ("West-östlicher
Divan; Buch Suleika," in *Goethes Werke* [Weimarer Ausgabe] [Weimar: Hermann Böhlau, 1888], VI, 162).

30. E. Grässer then emphasizes that "the universality of salvation" (*op. cit.*, p. 183)
corresponds to that individualizing, so that the "question of 'individualization or collec-
tivization of salvation' " so often posed in reference to Bultmann's theology is shown to
be "a pseudo-problem" (*op. cit.*, p. 184).

no means matter of course. Paradox should not delude us into thinking that there is no such thing. Every genuine greeting fulfills the conditions of this paradox. It can be demonstrated that this is characteristic of Jesus' proclamation. It is certainly not a matter of course that one should fall into the hands of robbers, a fact illustrated by the behavior of the priest and the Levite as they pass that victim by, but also illustrated by the presence in today's lawbook of a law making it a punishable crime not to provide help where needed. But that it is at the same time the most obvious and matter-of-course thing that could happen on earth is shown by the actual point of this story (Luke 10:30ff). Something which is obviously a matter of course is communicated in such a way that it now really becomes evident how obvious it is. And that is characteristic of Jesus' entire proclamation and of his entire behavior as well. That in heaven there is more rejoicing over one repentant sinner than over ninety-nine righteous men who do not need to repent (Luke 15:7, 9) *is* totally other than obvious and a matter of course, but it *becomes* immediately obvious when it is made evident in the parable about joy over a lost and then found sheep (Luke 15:1-6) or in the parable of the lost and then found coin (Luke 15:8f). It is no accident that these parables are recorded as arguments for the defense of Jesus' behavior which angered the Pharisees and scribes: they "murmured saying, 'This man receives sinners and eats with them' " (Luke 15:2). Even the behavior of Jesus had to become evident in its obviousness. And that means that it had to assert itself as a *new* kind of obvious and matter-of-course behavior, *over against* the dominantly obvious and matter of course. When that happens, a new attitude results in which what is totally other than matter of course becomes identical with what is most obvious and matter of course of all: joy. For in joy, the event which finds its anthropological expression is that event in which the *obvious and matter of course* happens as *surprise*. It must be remembered that joy is a community phenomenon. It is no coincidence that the Jesus who speaks of the joy of God is the one who causes the joy to take place through his proclamation. Whoever responds to his speaking and his behavior is supposed to experience that God will act in the world in the same way that Jesus sits down at table with the lost of this world.[31] This majestic act of God, in which he asserts himself over against the world, thus becomes evident as an event which provides joy, and for that reason it calls forth anger from the representatives of the dominantly obvious and matter of course. The terror which could certainly be bound up with the proclamation of the God who asserts himself over against the world appears now as the terror of those who deny themselves the joy which the kingdom of God brings. It is the terror of the *law* which refuses to experience joy at the fact that Jesus coexists with "those who were excluded from this world on the basis of its law"[32] and in that claims to be a human parable of God. Jesus established the new fellowship with God against the dominantly obvious and matter-of-course character of the law. This contrast lent the inaugurating of this fellowship the character of a newly self-evident matter of course which must first become evident and thus

31. See Gunther Bornkamm, *Jesus of Nazareth,* trs. I. and F. McLuskey (New York: Harper, 1960), pp. 75ff.

32. F. Gogarten, *op. cit.,* p. 128.

releases rejoicing. We may summarize this with an appropriate concept when we speak of the *obviousness of reconciliation*.

Reconciliation is, as long as it does not take place, never obvious and yet, when it really does happen, gains immediately the character of a new obviousness, which remains new and never ages. The obviousness of reconciliation found probably its most impressive sign in the eschatological peace greeting with which the Resurrected One salutes, in a few appearance legends, those who have been called into the fellowship of reconciliation (Luke 24:36; John 20:19, 21). The peace greeting reflects Jesus' earthly appearance. But even when one limits oneself critically to the historical minimum of an authentic tradition of Jesus, "when one proceeds only from Jesus' proclamation of God the Father as summarized in the Lord's Prayer, and when one sees how this proclamation of God finds its new and independent expression in his striking parables of the prodigal son (Luke 15:11ff), the workers in the vineyard (Matt. 20:1ff), the good Samaritan (Luke 10:30ff), the Pharisee and the publican (Luke 18:10ff), or the wicked servant (Matt. 18:23ff); when further this new proclamation is accompanied by the incredible assertion that in his own authority he can forgive sins (Mark 2:5; Luke 18:10f), and then this forgiveness is made concrete in the symbolic act of table fellowship with sinners in anticipation of the eschatological banquet fellowship; further, when the healing of the sick, those who are excluded from the temple ceremonial, is placed above the Sabbath law, and the cultic Torah is broken in favor of the direct encounter with those who are lost and lawless (Mark 1:21ff; 3:1ff; 7:14f), and even the wording of the Torah together with its Pharisaic interpretation is questioned and the love of the enemy is declared to be the original will of God (Matt. 5:43ff)—when all of this is taken together, the result is the picture of a proclaimer of the kingdom of God 'who breaks apart all patterns' (E. Schweizer)." *Against* what was dominantly obvious, he now vouchsafes a new obviousness of love which one can certainly call "a manifestation of the messianic reconciliation disclosed to men by God."[33]

In order to understand fully this new fellowship inaugurated by Jesus, we must give greater attention to the fact, already mentioned, that the present tense of the world's time and the future of the coming kingdom of God are combined in his own person. We shall have to take a decisive step further and consider that Jesus not only announced the coming kingdom of God but as its proclaimer carried out in his own person the majestic act with which God asserted himself within the world. Thus Jesus is not only a member of the new fellowship with God, but rather the person who brings about this fellowship. In and through his person, this new fellowship with God comes about, the new obviousness of reconciliation takes place. But that means that the opposition to the new and dominant obviousness is carried out on his person. The basic feature of the humanity of Jesus, which we described as his being in the act of the word of the kingdom of God, can be properly understood only when this opposition is emphasized as its constitutive factor. We shall, then, have to perceive the new

33. Peter Stuhlmacher, "Jesus als Versöhner; Überlegungen zum Problem der Darstellung Jesu im Rahmen einer Biblischen Theologie des Neuen Testaments," in G. Strecker, ed., *Jesus Christus in Historie und Theologie; Festschrift für H. Conzelmann, zum 60. Geburtstag* (Tübingen: J. C. B. Mohr, 1975), p. 97.

obviousness of reconciliation and the opposition to the dominant obviousness which accompanies it *in the being of the man Jesus*.

For this purpose, it is best to proceed from the unique relationship to God which Jesus has, in which according to Jesus' own understanding a unique relationship of God to him is expressed. Man can virtually say that Jesus' relationship to himself and thus his being as a person is consummated *as* relationship to God based on the preceding relationship of God to him. Earlier, one tried to express this with the unfortunate category of the messianic self-consciousness. But this category is inappropriate because it says too much anthropologically and too little theologically. The category of anthropological expansion is not adequate to the task of expressing that Jesus belongs to God in an incomparable way and thus can be understood as a "royal man."[34] Jesus existed as a strangely human human, and not as a person who surpassed humanity and came as close as possible to the "divine," or was even a "divine man." Just as the kingdom of God he proclaims is "not coming with signs to be observed," so that it can be pointed at as people say, "Lo, here it is!" or "There!" (Luke 17:20f), so his unique relationship to God can be demonstrated in no other way than in an outspokenly human humanity. In contrast to the foxes who have holes and the birds who have nests, he has no place to lay his head (Luke 9:59 par.). And how did his claim to inaugurate a new fellowship with God harmonize with the kind of behavior which led to the accusation that he was a glutton and a drunkard (Matt. 11:19)? It was indeed the grotesque-appearing contrast between his theologically demanding proclamation and his totally earthly mode of existence which made him appear crazy to his family (Mark 3:21) and as in league with the devil to the scribes who were less cordial to him (Mark 3:22). In fact, he was completely contemned by his hometown, by his relatives, and by his own household (Mark 6:4). These notations in Mark's Gospel are certainly historical reminiscences of the tension which characterized the earthly existence of Jesus. The special thing about this person who promises salvation to those who do not take offense at him (Matt. 11:6) is the simultaneity of his high claim with regard to God, and his total unpretentiousness with regard to himself. Each of these taken for itself, or even expanded by what appears to be complementary: the claim by the appearance of the son of man coming on the clouds, or the unpretentiousness by a life in accordance with his situation as a modest carpenter's son—that would have been suitable. But when speaking of the kingdom of God, whose arrival he appeared to have brought about, driving out demons with God's finger (Luke 11:20), he could only tell the parable of the mustard seed which is smaller than all other seeds although it will later produce great branches in which the birds of the heaven will build their nests (Matt. 13:31f). He who wants to see deeds to legitimize the claims being made hears instead a parable of growing seed for whose growth man can do nothing at all (Mark 4:26-29).

And yet this composed deliberateness corresponds most appropriately to Jesus' high claims. It expresses the intensity with which Jesus knew that he was defined by the nearness of God. The self-relationship of this man consisted basically of this, that he let God be the God who prevailed in every act of his

34. See Karl Barth's presentation of the humanity of Christ under this title: *CD*, IV/2, pp. 154-264.

life. Jesus *permitted* himself to come closer to God than he was close to himself. In that he was a person, he was—he himself. That God *is* 'more intimate to me than I am to myself' is not the only component of his self-being. That would not distinguish him from other people. What characterized Jesus' self-relationship was this unique *openness* for this divine activity which corresponds to the 'God who is more intimate to me than I am to myself' in the performance of his own human existence. He relied so totally on God that he could not really be a person without God's existence turned toward him. And because of his total dependence on God he was able, as one who was without pretension in regard to himself, to be completely there for others. It was the openness for the unsurpassable nearness of God which, with his absolutely new and yet great sense of the obviousness of God, let Jesus be completely there for other people. His humanity consisted of the freedom to want to be nothing at all *for himself.* A royal freedom! And the precise opposite of moral exertion! To love God and one's neighbor was so obvious to this man that he loved himself only to the extent that he loved God and the neighbor, rather than loving his neighbor *as himself.* There is nothing here of balance between selflessness and self-relatedness. The *being* of this man was rather the *event* of a selflessness which surpasses all self-relatedness. Thus it was a humanity which was not concerned with its own preservation, but rather a humanity which *placed its own life on the line* in every act of life. As such, it was the being of a man who corresponded to God, and it was the human parable of the God who is love.

With that, Jesus is now recognized as the human consummation of new fellowship with God. What Jesus inaugurated to the people whom he addressed is now consummated in him. And at that point he puts himself into the most pointed opposition to the dominant obviousness whose representative is the law. According to the Jewish faith, only the law made fellowship with God possible. However, the necessity of the law consists of the very fact that what is commanded by it has to be commanded even though it ought to be clearly understood in and of itself.[35] The law, then, is the representative of that obviousness of force to which human exertion and human achievement correspond. The law commands that one should love. To love God and one's neighbor, in fact, is the very epitome of the law's demands (Mark 12:29ff). But this demand is fulfilled by one's *exertions.* And for that reason, Paul, whose statements in this regard are also significant for the pre-Easter situation, calls the law a law of works (Rom. 3:27). These achievements correspond to the law, so that 'works of the law' (*erga nomou*) is an established terminological designation of categorical rank

---

35. My colleague H. P. Rüger has drawn my attention to the fact that in ancient Judaism the view was held that the law would be most appropriately fulfilled if one were to do what corresponds to it *before* the law itself were given. Thus, for instance, the example is cited from *Seder Eliahu Zuta* 4 Gen. 35:2-4 where "our Father Jacob fulfilled the entire law before the law was given." And *Num. Rab.* 14:2 says, "The Holy, may he be praised, said: Joseph, thou hast observed the Sabbath before the law was given." It is then interesting that Joseph, in what might be called an answer to God's unrealistic question in Job 41:11, "Who has given to me that I should repay him?", receives the instruction, "That refers to Joseph, who did something for him previously and observed the Sabbath, before it was commanded, or given in the law." The aniticipative fulfillment of the law is expanded here to the meritorious character of the act. In both texts, the point is the reward which the act deserves.

(Rom. 3:20-28; 9:32; Gal. 2:16 and often). Man, through the exertion of his works, endeavors to be righteous before God and the world. In that he does what should be done, he is more interested in himself than in what is to be done. Paul calls that seeking to establish one's own righteousness (Rom. 10:3; Phil. 3:9). The law forces one to do this. And by forcing that, the law forces man as doer *under* the law (Rom. 6:14). Man *under* the law is the man who does what is to be done, not out of himself, and certainly not without interest in himself. He is the one who is chained to himself and is thus the unfree man. In his ultimately infinite interest in himself he is, as Paul can say, under the power of sin (Rom. 3:9). For sin is nothing other than the compulsion toward oneself into which man places himself.

The characteristic thing about Jesus, however, is that he *forgives* sin with God's authority and thus breaks the human compulsion toward itself. He battles against sin by being merciful to the sinner. He *breaks* the power of sin by *pitying* the misery of the sinners who are people chained to themselves because they have chained themselves to themselves. As the merciful one, he is the one who acts without compulsion because he does what has to be done out of himself and without interest in himself. Thus Jesus clearly understood his own behavior not as exertion, and not as a work. That is illustrated by the parable of the good Samaritan (Luke 10:25-37), which is coupled with the double commandment of love as the essence of the law, certainly not by accident. What distinguishes the Samaritan from the priest and the Levite in regard to the same situation is not to be understood in terms of the priest and Levite who refuse to exert themselves to help, but is solely to be understood in terms of the Samaritan's behavior. When he saw the needy man, he *had pity* (*esplanchnisthē*) on the man who had fallen among thieves. It was not the law which evoked that response from him, but rather his love for the distressed man led him to an act which is obvious for love, but which as such was the fulfillment of the law. A conclusion may be drawn here with regard to Jesus' own existence. The statement made in all the Gospels that Jesus, as he taught, proclaimed, and healed, was simultaneously a man who experienced *pity* when he saw the suffering people, captures the basic feature of his humanity. Jesus was the man who anticipated the law out of the obviousness of love and thus more than satisfied the law with a great, although new, obviousness. And he thereby made plain that one could fulfill the law only by *preceding* it, anticipating it in its fulfillment. That is the only way in which man can show himself to be absolutely *free*.

Jesus was this absolutely free man. He was able to be there for others in freedom and absolutely not for himself because he existed solely out of God's fatherly act of majesty, so that God could prevail in this man against the world *under* the law. In that Jesus existed completely from the kingdom of God, deriving his own being entirely from God's fatherly act of majesty, his life and then his death were emphatic insistence on God's coming. *As the man who existed entirely from God, Jesus enabled faith in God's fatherly nearness, faith in the nearness of God as the Father.*

Inherent in this existence from God and the insistence on God's coming which corresponds with it was the fact that the works of the law had to mobilize themselves against it. There is an intolerable opposition between this man who, because he does it obviously, fulfills the law, and the world of men who, in order to fulfill the law, must do these things and not do those things. The dispute about the Sabbath (Mark 3:1-6; Matt. 12:1-15 par.) is symptomatic of this intolerable opposition into which the law necessarily must be drawn. Jesus, by fulfilling the law through the love which precedes the law, *brought the law into conflict with the law*—the harsh statement is unavoidable. And in opposition, the world had to assert the law. A world under the compulsion of the law can battle against the freedom to precede the law only through love, battle it as the destruction of the law and as a questioning of the world's right to set up its own righteousness. That is what it did. And although Jesus apparently endured the fear of death (Luke 22:44; a statement which later Orthodoxy apparently found particularly irritating), he was prepared to endure in his own person the conflict into which he had brought the law with himself. The execution of Jesus, even if it was a misunderstanding of the Roman rulers who regarded Jesus as a political rebel, was, in any event, the external confirmation of his freedom to be able to be nothing for himself. That violent death is, in a certain way, the consequence of his original mystery, which one can certainly call the mystery of an implicit Christology. For no other person is able to be nothing for himself. That is what Jesus was from the very beginning. The death which was forced on him was integral to his existence. It was unavoidable that this death was understood as the death appropriate to this life, *post festum* ('after the feast').[36]

36. Methodologically we will have to limit ourselves to this statement. It would be better not to say that Jesus had to die the death imposed on him because of his actions and their effect. But the objective situation is certainly there that this death would have to appear as the result of his life, *after* the execution of Jesus had been carried out. More recent exegetical research is coming to such or similar conclusions. As one representative of the Bultmann school, E. Fuchs expressed the view that Jesus' violent death was a result of his activity and was even affirmed by Jesus as the appropriate ending to his life. But Bultmann rejected that position ("Das Verhältnis der urchristlichen Christusbotschaft zum historischen Jesus," *Sitzungsberichte der Heidelberger Akademie der Wissenschaften; Philosophisch-historische Klasse* [Heidelberg: Carl Winter, 1960], III, 11f; also in *Exegetica; Aufsätze zur Erforschung des Neuen Testaments* [Tübingen: J. C. B. Mohr, 1967], pp. 445-69). More recent critical research has affirmed once more a material relationship between Jesus' activity and his violent death. So, for instance, E. Lohse (*op. cit.*, p. 49) concludes: "Jesus' preaching and his activity, which placed in question the universally obligatory nature of the law, brought him into sharp opposition to the authoritative representatives of the Judaism of that day. . . . The authority which he claimed was either acknowledged or evoked resolute hostility, so that Jesus' cross stands in an indissoluble connection with his message." And Peter Stuhlmacher (*op. cit.*, pp. 98f), in agreement with analogous evaluations by Martin Hengel (*Was Jesus a Revolutionist?*, tr. W. Klassen [Philadelphia: Fortress Press, 1971], p. 15; *Gewalt und Gewaltlosigkeit. . .*, pp. 43f) and F. Hahn (*op. cit.*, pp. 41ff), goes even further when he states that Jesus could not be tolerated by any of the Jewish groupings of that day for any length of time so that his violent end was "unavoidable": "For the Pharisees, Jesus' free way of dealing with the Torah and his lack of concern with regard to the Levite ideal of purity had to be intolerable. For the Zealots, his command to love one's enemy which had to include the religious opponent, his lack of prejudice even in relationship to the Roman military (Luke 7:1ff pars.), and his statement about imperial taxation (Mark 12:33f) were all more than a provocation. The Sadducees and the high-priestly nobility had to feel extremely challenged by Jesus' freely exercised forgiving of sins, separated from the cultic acts of atonement, his (dark) statement about the destruction of the temple (Mark 14:58 par.; John 2:18ff), and then his position against the trade in sacrificial animals and the money changers in his cleansing of the temple (many find this incident nonhistorical, of course). The great response which Jesus received from the people would have led the political

The death of Jesus was integral to his existence in that in this death the conflict of the law with the law which Jesus summoned went its full course, especially with regard to his relationship to God. The meaning of this can be evaluated when one remembers that the crucifixion of a criminal was the event of total God-forsakenness according to the law's understanding. But Jesus had brought the law into conflict with the law by preceding the law with love on the basis of his openness for God's unsurpassable nearness. Because he depended totally on God, he not only initiated this conflict of the law with itself, but he submitted himself to this conflict which then ended in God-forsakenness. By depending totally on God, his life ended in the event of God-forsakenness. The special severity of Jesus' God-forsakenness on the cross is the experience of that God-forsakenness by an existence which derived solely from God. The Marcan cry of the dying Christ, interpreted with Psalm 22:1, can express that God-forsakenness as vividly as it does only because its precondition is God-relatedness. Jesus' fatal God-forsakenness is not lessened by that but rather intensified to an extreme degree because it occurs within the context of a unique certainty of God. The God whose coming was proclaimed by Jesus has now forsaken him on the cross. That Jesus, according to Mark, cries out to the God who is forsaking him, "My God, my God, why hast thou forsaken me?" (Mark 15:34), is the experience of a distance of God which is not his fault, which was caused by the law, and which exceeds the hell of godlessness in that Jesus' lifelong insistence on the coming of God is compressed into this cry. Paul's interpretation is harsh but precise: he became "a curse" (Gal. 3:13).

6. But Paul goes further and says that Christ became a curse *for us*. These two words are decisive. For they ascribe a significance to the death of Jesus on the basis of which his humanity is interpreted within the context of the identification of God with his death. That this man died *for us*, that he became a curse *for us* on the gallows, can be asserted only on the basis of an event which interprets the God-forsakenness of this death *positively*. If Jesus is the parable of God, then one will have to say that God is no longer to be understood on the basis of this parable, but rather this his parable is to be understood in terms of God. It is not obvious in looking at the cross of Jesus that he became a curse *for us*. The words "for us" are a *confession*. In order to be able to add "for us" to "curse," the cross of Jesus must already be interpreted as the cross of Christ, the cross of the Son of God. For, through this *for us*, the being of Jesus Christ itself is expressed as the *new fellowship with God* which Jesus had announced

---

powers in the land—the Herodians, the Sanhedrin, and of course the Romans—to be suspicious of him. That then a catastrophe came when Jesus decided to go up to Jerusalem . . . is both historically unavoidable and easily understandable. Jesus' death is to be seen as a result of his mission mandate (his 'sending') and his messianic ministry. Jesus apparently accepted this death with his eyes open and without trying to flee or to resist."

In our *historical* judgment we will not go quite so far, bearing in mind the fundamental principle which also holds true for historical logic: 'the possibility that something is does not require those consequences' (*a posse ad esse non valet consequentia*). At the same time, we will decisively go one step further, in that we see in Jesus' violent death on the cross the external consummation of what Jesus had lived, which was a life of anticipative, active love which brought the law into conflict with itself and then bore this conflict in itself.

and inaugurated.[37] In that sense, even the oldest primitive Christian creeds represent the death of Jesus not as an event merely among men, but rather as an event between this one man and God, so that Jesus' God-forsakenness is now seen as God's most authentic work. In Mark, too, the death-cry of the Crucified One is followed by a *confession* which interprets the death of Jesus. As the Gentile centurion who faced him saw "that he thus breathed his last," he said, "Truly this man was the Son of God" (Mark 15:39). That confession responds to Jesus' death-cry, which apparently *was understood* by this Gentile as a cry inspired in the dying man by God. At least that is how it is to be understood in Mark. For Jesus died crying out; he cried with a "loud voice." This 'loud voice' (*phonē megalē*; Mark 15:34, 37) is to be taken as the 'voice of God' (*phonē theou*).[38] But then the voice with which Jesus cried out as he died would be God's own voice. Jesus' last words and his human death-cry would have been *the word of God.* That is how Easter faith interprets it when it tells the passion story. But this faith is itself the result of the conclusion of the story which it is narrating. As Easter faith, it is no other than faith in the Crucified One *as* God's Son, or more precisely, faith in God's Son *as* the crucified Jesus of Nazareth. The identification of God with Jesus which permits this one to be confessed *as* God's Son is simultaneously the origination of the Christian faith. Faith sees its origin in that christological *as.* Therefore, we must probe beyond the mere observation that Jesus' death was understood that way and ask about the inner possibility of such an understanding.

Jesus as God's Son—how does that coincide with the God-forsakenness of Jesus on the cross? To what extent did the Crucified One not only become a curse, but become a curse *for us*? What happened on the cross between God and Jesus if the response to the God-forsakenness of this dying man is the confession that this dead man is the Son of God?

The answer to this question will also answer the question of the essence, or, in today's language, the identity of Christianity—a question raised with special urgency in this age. For it not only states *what* the Christian faith believes, but also gives the reason for the fact *that* one believes. The theology of the Crucified One answers the question about the content and origin of the Christian faith. *Formally,* it is the agreement of the faith with itself about itself. Of course, one of the *material* results of this self-agreement of faith is that the faith points beyond itself in every way.

The kerygma of the Resurrected One irrefutably has the first word. It says first of all that something did happen in the death of Jesus. But death is the very

37. See P. Stuhlmacher, *op. cit.,* p. 92: "Whereas in the creed of I Cor. 15:3b-5 Jesus' entire being is drawn together in his atoning death and his resurrection, the tradition of Acts 10:34ff, which seems to be almost an outline of the Marcan Gospel, presents the work of Jesus in general as a salvific work which brings about the eschatological peace promised by God. This salvific work ends with the crucifixion, but God has elevated it through the resurrection to make it the enabling factor of faith, that faith which experiences the forgiveness of sins and thus can participate in the eschatological salvation as fellowship with God."

38. See, for example, Ignatius, Philadelphians 7:1: "When I was with you I cried out, raising my voice—it was God's voice . . ." (in C. C. Richardson, ed., *Early Christian Fathers* [*Library of Christian Classics,* vol. 1] [London: SCM Press Ltd., 1953], pp. 109f).

opposite of a happening. It can be ascertained only after it has already taken place. When death happens, the happening ends which we call human life. Death is not really an event. It is eventless, a non-event.

But in contrast to that, the kerygma of the resurrection of Jesus states that something took place in the death of Jesus. But if being dead is the precise opposite of an event, then what we are saying is that in this death God himself was the event which happened. That is a difficult thought, as Hegel emphasized. It is a thought which Christian theology has constantly evaded. But it is a necessary thought. The resurrection of Jesus from the dead means that God has identified himself with this dead man. And that immediately means that God identified himself with Jesus' God-forsakenness. And that means further that God identified himself with the life lived by this dead man.[39] Now what does all of that mean?

To identify oneself with another, foreign essence implies the capacity to differentiate oneself. That is already true in the very limited sense of one person's identifying with another person. If I assert that I identify with another person, then that is actually hyperbole. But even that hyperbolically described process is possible only under the presupposition of a limited capacity for self-differentiation. Such self-differentiation belongs to human existence, and thus is not self-destruction although it can turn into that. But one does not have to be in disunity with oneself in order to be quite unified with another person. Self-differentiation as the implication of identification with another is, however, the expression of the fact that that other profoundly defines my own being from outside of myself. That other one steps between me and me, so to speak.

In this sense, God's identification with the dead Jesus implies a self-differentiation on God's part. The being of this dead man defines God's own being in such a way that one must speak of a differentiation between God and God. But it must immediately be added that it is an act of God himself who effects his identity with the dead Jesus and as its precondition the differentiation of God and God. In view of the understanding of death as God-forsakenness, this is an especially important aspect which calls for more explanation. The differentiation of God from God may not be understood as an opposition which is coerced on the being of God. Goethe's mysterious statement is relevant here: "No one is against God unless it is God Himself."[40] Only a divine motive can differentiate God from God. And for that reason it must be said that *God defines himself*

39. As far as I can see, Wolfhart Pannenberg is the only one beyond Ernst Fuchs who has seriously discussed the ontological possibility of an event having retroactive ontic effects. I strongly concur with his remarks on this (in *Jesus—God and Man*, trs. L. L. Wilkins and D. A. Priebe [Philadelphia: Westminster Press, 1968²], p. 321): "What is true in God's eternity is decided with retroactive validity only from the perspective of what occurs temporally with the importance of the ultimate. Thus, Jesus' unity with God—and thus the truth of the incarnation—is also decided only retroactively from the perspective of Jesus' resurrection for the whole of Jesus' human existence on the one hand . . . and thus also for God's eternity, on the other." See also my "Thesen zur Grundlegung der Christologie," in *Unterwegs zur Sache*, pp. 274ff.

40. J. W. von Goethe, *The Autobiography of Goethe, Truth and Poetry: From My Life*, ed. P. Godwin (New York: Wiley & Putnam, 1846), pt. IV, bk. XX, p. 107; for further elucidation, see Carl Schmitt, *Politische Theologie II; Die Legende von der Erledigung jeder Politischen Theologie* (Berlin: Duncker & Humblot, 1970), pp. 122f.

when he identifies himself with the dead Jesus. At the same time he defines the man Jesus as the Son of God, as an old New Testament formulation puts it (Rom. 1:4). The kerygma of the Resurrected One proclaims the Crucified One as the self-definition of God.

Only when the truth of this assertion is affirmed is it at all meaningful to speak of the Resurrected One, that is, to say of one who is dead that he is alive. Jesus' resurrection is not an "intervention" of God into the world's structures, which then leaves behind a new fact within this world, but does not affect the being of God. In the resurrection of Jesus, the issue is not only one of a divine action, but of the divine being itself. For that reason this event is *sui generis* not a worldly event among others, but rather the "turning point of the world."[41] For the statement "he lives," justifiably asserted about one dead man, turns the relationship of death and life around.[42] Resurrection means the overcoming of death. But death will cease to be only when it no longer consumes the life which excludes it, but when life has absorbed death into itself. The victory over death, which is the object of faith's hope on the basis of God's identification with the dead Jesus which took place in the death of Jesus, is the transformation of death through its reception into that life which is called eternal life. For that reason the death which was turned around on the cross of Christ is called a "Phenomenon of God."[43] It is only short-circuited criticism which wants to see here a final triumph of death. Rather, what happens here is that turning around of death into life which is the very essence of *love*. The issue here is the truth in the profound statement (I John 3:14): "He who does not love abides in death." Death is not turned around apart from love, because love alone is able to involve itself in the complete harshness of death. In the death of Jesus, love itself was at work and revealed God as the one who is love. For "by this we know love, that he laid down his life for us" (I John 3:16). And "in this the love of God was made manifest among [on, with?] us, that God sent his only Son into the world, so that we might live through him" (I John 4:9).

To be "sent into the world" is tantamount to being "given up to death."[44] The "only" about whom this is said is, as we discussed above, the expression for "the beloved one."[45] The love of God reveals itself remarkably in the giving up to death of the beloved one. Does love sacrifice the loved one? What apparently is to be expressed here is that God loves himself. But God's love for himself, which is expressed with the term "only," is understood pointedly as selflessness. God would then be love in that he does not desire to love himself without loving his creature, that absolutely other who is his counterpart. That is the eternal and

41. Gogarten's expression "Jesus Christ—The Turning Point of the World" [this is the literal translation of his book title, which was rendered *Christ the Crisis* in the English edition—TR] is in my opinion especially apt as an interpretation of the old term "Savior of the World." The Savior is the Turning Point of the world.

42. See the result of this turning point, which happened 'once and for all' (*ephapax*), for those who involve themselves in it in faith (John 5:24; I John 3:14).

43. See E. Jüngel, "Vom Tod des lebendigen Gottes," in *Unterwegs zur Sache*, pp. 123f.

44. Bultmann points out that "although *edōken* (gave) appears instead of *apesteilen* (sent) in Jn. 3:16, the meaning is of course identical" (Bultmann, *The Johannine Epistles*, p. 67).

45. *Ibid.*

divine motivation of God's self-differentiation, apart from which his identity with the man Jesus would not be conceivable.

7. Before we can further discuss the relationship between the divine self-differentiation and the self-identification of God with Jesus, we must return to the aspect of God-forsakenness in the death of Jesus, without which the differentiation between God and God would only be understood inadequately. We shall take up again here the problem of the law. For the law curses everyone who hangs on the tree (Deut. 21:23; Gal. 3:13). It does this because the person who is hanged under the law is cursed by God. For every legal execution avenges the injured order of creation, according to the view of that day. We saw that the fact that Jesus was subjected to the curse of the law was the result of his bringing the law into conflict with the law through his *anticipative* fulfillment of the law, his *freedom*. We interpret this conflict now within the framework of the insight that Jesus died *for us*, because and to the extent that God identified himself with this death.

Jesus' proclamation and behavior made the law a problem because he changed the role of the person who is subjected to the demands of the law: the role of the person who is *active* is changed into the role of the one who *first receives*. The love which the law requires of man was already provided by Jesus in advance. In that he not only announced God's coming but also realized it in his own behavior and proclamation, God's kindness was communicated to his fellowmen so that love for God and for the neighbor, as the closest object to them, was disclosed to them. The well-known antitheses, which heightened the demands of the law, are the *a posteriori* focusing of what was already disclosed by Jesus as man's possibility. But that meant that the law was fundamentally put into question as a path to salvation. For if what the law demands is already *given*, then no new gift was to be expected from the law. Where "give what you command, and command what you wish" is the principle, there "I give that you might give" is no longer valid. The law could not grant salvation if one were to fulfill it because, before one even became active, the salvation of fellowship with God would already have been received. The law thus became pure demand. It was "de-soteriologized." In other words, Jesus' freedom with the law[46] was completely defined by the way in which the nearness of God laid claim on him, a nearness which admits of no competition.

But it was precisely this claim to be totally under the claim of God's nearness which made him the object of accusation on the part of those whose piety was based on the law. They countered Jesus' free approach to the law with their legalistic approach to the law. That piety submitted to the law's demands in order then to demand of the law what it could not give at all: the salvation of fellowship with God. For the law does not give anything. It demands and it ascertains. The legalistic approach to the law, with the help of the law, makes God the one who really is the object of demands in that such an approach promises the salvation of fellowship with God as a result of the law's fulfillment. But only God can grant that fellowship. Thus he is required to fulfill the law on

---

46. To deal "freely" with the law is obviously something else than dealing with it "arbitrarily" or "generously." In contrast with the legalistic way of dealing with the law, this could be called the evangelical approach to the law.

his part in case man should fulfill it too. But that reduces God to the principle
of human self-confirmation. The legalistic approach to the law is thus ultimately
nothing other than the disputation of God's deity, which God himself defends
when he asks in Job 41:11: "Who has given to me, that I should repay him?"
Basically, the granting of salvation through the law is a challenge to God in the
form of a reclamation of one's own works. Thus, nothing really new is expected
of God. For whoever willingly submits to the law's demands in order then to
demand salvation of God *can* really not expect anything new of God: "Scorn
not the law—permit its iron band/The sense (it cannot chain the soul) to thrall,/Let
man no more the will of Jove withstand,/And Jove the bolt lets fall!"[47] Where
God is understood only as one who *demands,* he is no longer expected as the
one who originally *gives.* But where God is no longer expected as the one who
originally gives, but is considered only as the one who gives back, there his
deity is put in question. For he cannot then combine with the gift of himself the
further gift that the *old* man is made *new.* Since the law knows God only as the
one who gives back, but not as the one who originally gives, the old man is
fixed in his state by the law: "For the flesh or the old man must be coupled with
the law and works."[48]

The profound paradox dominant here is that at the very point where it is
expected of the law that it will give something, the affirmation is made that it
does not give anything at all but rather only gives back (Rom. 2:9-11). The
salvation which is demanded on the basis of the law is then "one's own righteousness": ". . . so too we become just by doing just acts. . . ."[49] Jesus opposed
that in the same way that Luther, with Paul, formulated it against Aristotle: "For
we are not, as Aristotle believes, made righteous by the doing of just deeds,
unless we deceive ourselves; but rather—if I may say so—in becoming and
being righteous people we do just deeds."[50] Thus the law was consigned back
"within its bounds."[51] The God who only makes demands reveals the legalistic
approach to the law as a blasphemy which makes the world absolute.[52] The
proclamation of the kingdom of God with its claim of the nearness of God makes
the law pure demand in which the legalistic approach to the law is recognized
as the *sin* which will *not* let God be the giver, the one who is coming, the one
who makes everything new—in short, which won't let God be God. But Jesus
had to die for this evangelical insight. The legalistic approach to the law mo-
bilized the law against the free approach to the law. And thus the godlessness

47. Friedrich Schiller, "The Ideal and the Actual Life," in *Poetical Works of
Friedrich Schiller,* tr. P. E. Pinkerton (London: Robertson, Ashford & Bentley, 1902),
I, 85-89.
48. Martin Luther, *A Commentary on St. Paul's Epistle to the Galatians,* ed. P. S.
Watson (Westwood, NJ: F. H. Revell, 1964), p. 24.
49. Aristotle, *Ethica Nicomachea,* tr. W. D. Ross, *The Works of Aristotle,* ed.
W. D. Ross (Oxford: Oxford University Press, 1954), IX, ii.1, 1103a, 34f.
50. Martin Luther, Letter to Spalatin, October 19, 1516, *Letters I,* in *Luther's
Works,* vol. 48, ed. and tr. G. G. Krodel (Philadelphia: Fortress Press, 1963), p. 25.
51. Martin Luther, *Commentary on Galatians,* p. 24.
52. It would be worthwhile to enter into debate with Immanuel Kant's understanding of religion, proceeding from this premise; in a rather peculiar combination, his understanding of religion is both the heir and the radical disputation of the Reformation's
understanding of God.

of a self-justifying world nailed him to the cross. For a world which looks on the results of its own reality as the only thing possible is objectively godless.[53]

The death of Jesus, however, is not only the *consequence* of that godlessness but at the same time his *bearing* of that godlessness. In that Jesus suffers the godlessness of the world, the conflict with the law which he provoked is decided in his own person. For the godlessness which will not let God be God leads to death, according to the law. This cursed death is the fate of a godless world. That Jesus suffers the death which the law foresees for the godless, *because* he identified this godlessness as such, is the conflict of the law with the law which is decided in his own person. And that is what constitutes the God-forsakenness of the cross. The theological tradition has quite rightly used the category of substitution for this.[54] It is, to be sure, a category which presupposes the identity of God with Jesus.[55] It is only on the basis of this identity that one can call Jesus Christ our substitute in the sense that "Jesus Christ is in Himself 'for us'—without our being with Him, without any fulfilment of our being either with or after Him—on the contrary (Rom. 5:6f), even when we were without strength, godless, and enemies."[56]

God has then identified himself with the Jesus who made himself sin for us as our substitute. We have recognized this identification of divine life with the dead Jesus as the event of divine love. As such, it is the turning point of the world, because God has interposed himself in the midst of fatal God-forsakenness in order to create a new relationship with God. This is a relationship which

53. On this ontological problematic of the doctrine of justification I refer to my essay "Die Welt als Möglichkeit und Wirklichkeit; Zum ontologischen Ansatz der Rechtfertigungslehre," in *Unterwegs zur Sache*, pp. 206ff.

54. The category of substitution has to be used christologically in a dual fashion: it serves to signify the man Jesus who acts in God's place as well as to designate the Son of God who dies in our place. If Jesus dared to speak and to act in God's place while alive (see Ernst Fuchs, "Die biblische Auffassung vom Menschen," in *Zum hermeneutischen Problem in der Theologie; Die existentiale Interpretation, Gesammelte Aufsätze* [Tübingen: J. C. B. Mohr (Siebeck), 1965²], p. 270), then the Christ had to suffer and be silent in our place as he died. If actively he was the living substitute for God on earth, then passively he became the dying substitute for the human race. What makes the death of Jesus Christ on the cross the salvation event in an absolute sense is this: The man Jesus was not only the *one who worked in God's place, but that same person was the one who suffered in our place,* suffering the death of God-forsakenness; Jesus Christ as man is simultaneously the person in whom God himself bears the God-forsakenness of the human race. The early church, using the philosophical language of its day, properly expounded this salvation event by saying that the person who lived and died in that way was totally man and totally God. But over against the metaphysics of substance which permeates the christological doctrine of two natures, and based on the existence of Jesus Christ in its double substitutionary role, his humanity and deity should not be understood so much as two sides of one person as two poles of an ultimate differentiation and tension which defines the one godly-human person. The *oppositeness* of God and man is what constitutes the unity of the person of the God who became man. On the basis of that oppositeness, then, all of the christological definitions of the being of this person are to be understood and to be developed further.

55. Apart from God's identity with Jesus, the most of which one could speak would be of the human tragedy which is always there when people suffer for the freedom of those whose unfreedom resists freedom and thus lets the freedom fighter suffer for freedom. There is greatness in such "substitutions," but no salvation.

56. Karl Barth, *CD*, IV/1, p. 229.

does not arise out of man's being, but rather emerges out of annihilating death out of which the world receives that future which it cannot make itself. In the death of Jesus Christ, God shows himself to be the one who calls into existence things that do not exist (Rom. 4:17), as the God who is the Creator *because* he is the Reconciler.

Thus we return to the trinitarian meaning of the statement "God is love." For the God who identifies himself with the dead Jesus encounters himself in the death of Jesus in such a way that he participates in Jesus' God-forsakenness. But that is a meaningful assertion only if it is possible to make a real differentiation between God and God. In that God differentiates himself and *thus*, in unity with the crucified Jesus, suffers as God the Son being forsaken by God the Father, he is God the Reconciler. God reconciles the world with himself in that in the death of Jesus he encounters himself as *God the Father* and *God the Son* without becoming disunited in himself. On the contrary, in the encounter of God and God, of Father and Son, God reveals himself as the one who he is. He is God the Spirit, who lets Father and Son be one in the death of Jesus, in true distinction, in this encounter. The 'chain of love' (*vinculum caritatis*) emphasizes God's eternal being in the death of Jesus. Thus God is differentiated in a threefold way in his unity: in the encounter of Father and Son, related to each other as Spirit. But in the fatal encounter, God remains *one* God. For he remains as Father and Son in the Spirit the one "event God."

Whereas the Jesus who exists totally from the Father made it possible to believe in God as the Father, the God who identifies with Jesus in his death makes it possible to believe in God the Son. To believe *with* Jesus *in* God (the Father) means, with all the necessity of Easter, to believe *in* Jesus *as* God (the Son). But this faith is not derived from man; it is possible only in the power of the Spirit who comes to man. To believe *in* God with Jesus, and to believe in Jesus as God, means thus to believe *in* the Holy Spirit. Since it is solely the Holy Spirit who makes faith in God the Father *and* in God the Son possible as *one* faith, faith *in* the Spirit is necessarily faith in God the Father, the Son, and the Spirit: faith in a triune God. But faith in the triune God can identify God and love without having anxiety about God's existence. Anxiety about God is to be forbidden for faith.[57]

SECTION 23. God's Being in the Differentiation between Father and Son

The theology of the Crucified One is talk about God as the love which took place in the death of the man Jesus. Love is essentially the heightening and expansion of being. It is this particularly in its unique selflessness. For that reason, the one who gives up his life will gain it, according to a statement of Jesus (Matt. 10:39). This is also true about God. The theology of the Crucified One is speaking, then, of a heightening, an expansion, even an overflowing of the divine being, when it considers God as the total surrender of himself for all men in the death of Jesus. In that God *is* that total self-surrender, that is, not

57. Ernst Steinbach, verbally.

only the one who surrenders or what is surrendered, but the event of self-surrender itself, the New Testament statement is true: God is love.

But this statement immediately makes certain distinctions necessary. For love does not take place without those who love. The statement "God is love" implies another assertion: God loves. A loving person is not possible without the preceding gift of love. No person could love if he had not experienced love before, either directly or indirectly. Man is as little able to love in and of himself as he is to speak in and of himself.[1] But if the statement "God is love" is supposed to a valid one, then it must be asserted of God that he loves out of himself, in and of himself. But that can be said only when one says at the same time that God loves *himself.* But that is to say that God as love is differentiated equally, and originally, from himself and thus related to himself, that is, that he exists in three modes of the same being: as the Father, the Son, and the Spirit, as the formulation has been from the very beginning, proceeding from the biblical names. God loves himself in the differentiation between the one who loves (and thus who is loved), the beloved (and thus again the lover), and the 'chain of love' (*vinculum caritatis*; the event of love).

The theological tradition has constantly spoken in this or a similar fashion. It has thus understood God as the absolutely self-related essence. The so-called "immanent" doctrine of the Trinity was accordingly understood as a statement of divine self-relatedness. But this statement collides with the word of the cross which states that God gave up his beloved Son for us all (Rom. 8:32; see also 3:16), or that the Son of God gave himself for me (Gal. 2:20). This giving up of oneself is always expressly stated as an act of love. It would appear then, based on the theology of the Crucified One, that God who is love is better understood as the absolutely selfless essence.

But the very essence of love would be mistaken if one were to play off the self-relatedness and the selflessness of God against each other. That is as little possible as the (often attempted) opposition of "immanent" and "economic" Trinity. The essence of love would also be mistaken if the attempt were made to think of God's self-relatedness and selflessness, or God's inner-divine love and his love of man, or of the "immanent" and the "economic" Trinity as *paradox.* In love, selflessness and self-relatedness do not contradict each other. Every lover knows that. Rather, self-relatedness and selflessness *correspond* to each other in such a way that here, as we have already shown, the basic structure of evangelical talk about God is to be applied *mutatis mutandis;* we must speak of a still greater selflessness in a very great, a properly great self-relatedness. A "still greater selflessness in the midst of a very great, and justifiably great self-relatedness" is nothing other than a self-relationship which in freedom goes beyond itself, overflows itself, and gives itself away. It is pure overflow, overflowing being for the sake of another and only then for the sake of itself. That is love. And that is the God who is love: the one who always heightens and expands his own being in such great self-relatedness still more selfless and *thus* overflowing. Based on that insight, Karl Rahner's thesis should be given unqualified agree-

1. See G. Ebeling, "Gott und Wort," in *Wort und Glaube II; Beiträge zur Fundamentaltheologie und zur Lehre von Gott* (Tübingen: J. C. B. Mohr [Siebeck], 1969), p. 418.

ment: *"The 'economic' Trinity is the 'immanent' Trinity and the 'immanent' Trinity is the 'economic' Trinity."* [2] This statement is correct because God himself takes place in Jesus' God-forsakenness and death (Mark 15:34-37). What the passion story narrates is the actual conceptualization of the doctrine of the Trinity (see sect. 22).

The thesis that the "economic" Trinity is the "immanent" Trinity, and vice versa, opens up the possibility of a new foundation for the doctrine of the Trinity, in that it makes the express constitution of the trinitarian concept of God possible through a theology of the Crucified One, and thus does greater justice to the exegetical problem than was possible for the classical form of trinitarian doctrine—although it did arise implicitly to do justice to the cross of Christ. But the explicit theoretical grounding then took a different shape than could have been expected from its factual ground. This led to the forcible separation of the "immanent" and "economic" Trinity with the overemphasis on "absolute unity of divine activity outwardly."[3] But as Seeberg aptly observes, the "concept that in concrete reality one can perceive an absolutely unified work of God only because that which is actually trinitarian takes place in the immanent life of the deity doubtlessly contributed to a practical unitarianism and to the designation of the trinitarian concept as a more or less obsolete school formula." Seeberg concludes correctly that the doctrine of the Trinity "needs another theoretical foundation than the old one."[4] The foundation attempted here does, however, differ significantly from the one Seeberg offered. The great Schleiermacher was of the opinion and declared it to be "important" that "the main pivots of the ecclesiastical doctrine—the being of God in Christ and in the Christian Church— are independent of the doctrine of the Trinity."[5] But no one would dare to assert that "the orthodox doctrine of the Trinity is to be regarded as an immediate or even a necessary combination of utterances concerning the Christian self-consciousness."[6] Thus Schleiermacher's observation about the factual role of the traditional doctrine of the Trinity within the total realm of theology pretty much hits the mark. I would not want to object that "our Christian self-consciousness" may not be any kind of criterion for "ecclesiastical doctrine." Quite the contrary! But a distinction must be drawn between a criterion and a principle. That Schleiermacher can do relatively little with the doctrine of the Trinity is related to his obstinacy with regard to the possibility of a 'theology of the cross' (*theologia crucis*). Werner Schultz[7] has demonstrated this with a reference to the ancient interpretation of pain as the interpretive scheme of the suffering Christ in Schleiermacher. That is the revenge of the axiom of apathy upheld by the Moravian of a higher order, who was still a Reformed theologian. But instead of criticizing Schleiermacher, our attention here should be directed to the con-

2. Karl Rahner, *The Trinity*, tr. J. Donceel (New York: Seabury Press, 1974), p. 22.

3. R. Seeberg, *Zum dogmatischen Verständnis der Trinitätslehre* (1908), p. 5.

4. *Ibid.*

5. F. Schleiermacher, *The Christian Faith*, trs. Mackintosh and Stewart (Edinburgh: T. & T. Clark, 1928; New York: Harper & Row, 1963), II, par. 170, 3, p. 741.

6. *Ibid.*, p. 740.

7. W. Schultz, "Die Transformierung der theologia crucis bei Hegel und Schleiermacher," *Neue Zeitschrift für systematische Theologie*, 6 (1964), 314f.

dition which Schleiermacher did correctly sense and which Karl Rahner has recently asserted of Catholic Christendom and regretted: the "doctrine of the Trinity" leads its own respected life in the church's liturgies, but scarcely influences our Christian self-consciousness, if at all. Perhaps the end of theism had to begin to dawn in order to disclose the existential relevance of a doctrine of the Trinity which must be grounded and explicated anew. Schleiermacher would gain our agreement when he says that "We have the less reason to regard this doctrine as finally settled since it did not receive any fresh treatment when the Evangelical (Protestant) Church was set up; and so there must still be in store for it a transformation which will go back to its very beginnings."[8] Perhaps no one did more for that than Schleiermacher's great antipode and admirer, Karl Barth, chiefly in the last volumes of his *Church Dogmatics*.

Before we can begin to formulate how the doctrine of the Trinity conceptualizes the passion history of God, a reminder of the aporia of the traditional doctrine of God is necessary in order to make plain both that and how it can be overcome. The aporia was revealed in Descartes to be the separation from each other of the essence and the existence of God, which was against the Cartesian intention. The God who is understood as love does not permit this distinction between the divine essence and the divine existence as a mere 'rational distinction.' Love, as the *essence* of something which exists, cannot be separated from its *existence* at all. The God who is love is totally identical with his essence in his existence. His existence is his essence. That is precisely what the doctrine of the Trinity formulates. It does this by thinking of the essence of God, which is love, as an essence constituted by relations and by thinking of the relations which constitute God's essence as the divine existence.[9]

The distinction must be made: God is the one who loves out of himself in that he relates himself to himself in such a way that he derives his being from himself. This mode of his being is called by the theological tradition *God the Father,* following the biblical pattern. But the one who loves out of himself must always be related to a beloved one, since it is not possible to love without reference to that beloved one who always receives this love: *God the Son.*

But the New Testament always speaks of the love of God with stringent reference to man and his world. The inner-divine self-relatedness which is love takes place as the radical relatedness of God to an other which is absolutely

8. F. Schleiermacher, *op. cit.*, II, par. 172, p. 747.
9. In what follows, I am presupposing what I already stated in my paraphrase of Barth's doctrine of the Trinity, with regard to the problem of relationality (*The Doctrine of the Trinity; God's Being Is in Becoming*, tr. H. Harris [Grand Rapids: Wm. B. Eerdmans, 1976]). The concept of the relations which constitute the essence of God is identical with the trinitarian "persons," which as such in their absolute distinctness make up the unsurpassable intensity of their relations, and in their absolute relatedness to each other make up the unsurpassable radicality of this differentiation from each other. Or to put it in Heribert Mühlen's words (*Die Veränderlichkeit Gottes als Horizont einer zukünftigen Christologie; Auf dem Wege zu einer Kreuzestheologie in Auseinandersetzung mit der altkirchlichen Christologie* [Münster: Aschendorff, 1969], p. 25): "The differentness of the divine persons, to the extent that they are persons . . . is so great, that it cannot be conceived as any greater, whereas their unity . . . is so intensive that it cannot be conceived of as any more intensive."

opposite to him, that is, to the human essence which he creates for that reason.[10] This radical relatedness of God to man is revealed in the giving up of what is most particularly his own,[11] the sending of his Son to death. In this selflessness of the divine being the self-relatedness of that same being does not end but is rather implemented and confirmed to the highest degree. This is seen first of all in the fact that, according to the New Testament view, it is not the Father who gives up the Son, but the Son who gives himself.[12] The Son is not only the object but also the subject of that giving.[13] In that the Son carries out this self-giving through the Father as his self-surrender, he is "obedient unto death, even death on a cross" (Phil. 2:8), related to the Father in the most intensive fashion.

The self-relatedness of the deity of God takes place in an unsurpassable way in the very selflessness of the incarnation of God. That is the meaning of talk about the humanity of God. It is not a second thing next to the eternal God but rather the event of the deity of God. For that reason, the "economic" Trinity is the "immanent" Trinity, and vice versa. And thus the Crucified One belongs to the concept of God. For the giving up of the eternal Son of God takes place in the temporal existence of one, that is, of this crucified man Jesus. In him, the love of God has appeared (I John 4:9), because that love has happened in him. The crucified Jesus belongs to the Christian concept of God in that he makes it necessary that a distinction between God and God be made. Therefore, the incarnation of God is to be taken seriously to the very depths of the harshness of God's abandonment of the Son who was made sin and the curse for us.[14]

10. The objective precedence of the love-relatedness of God toward man before the creator will of God was expressed by Karl Barth in that he interpreted the covenant as the inner ground of creation, and creation as the outer ground of the covenant. On the understanding of this, see my study "Die Möglichkeit theologischer Anthropologie auf dem Grunde der Analogie; Eine Untersuchung zum Analogieverständnis Karl Barths," *Evangelische Theologie*, 22 (1962), 535ff.

11. For this reason, Heribert Mühlen asserts: *"The being of God, the essence of his essence, is his giving away that which is particularly his own"* (*op. cit.*, p. 31). If this formulation is interpreted in the sense of that ever greater selflessness *in very great self-relatedness*, then we may agree with it. This is supported by the view of the crucifixion which is understood as the "historical self-assertion of the Trinitarian We-Act . . . in such a way that in the most radical antithesis between Father and Son their most radical nearness and unity appear" (*ibid.*, p. 33).

12. Older theology spoke of an 'active and passive mission of the Son of God' (*missio filii dei activa et passiva*). It must be emphasized that the Father, as the one who sends, participates indirectly in the passivity of that sending as he surrenders what is most authentically his when he surrenders his Son. Conversely, the Son participates in the activity of sending as he surrenders himself in *free* obedience. On the parallelism of the Johannine concept of self-surrender with the concept of sending, see the Zürich dissertation by W. Popkes, *Christus Traditus; Eine Untersuchung zum Begriff der Dahingabe im Neuen Testament* (1967).

13. It should be noted that exegetically God's giving of his Son and the Son's giving of himself are not connected (see Popkes, *op. cit.*, p. 193). Apparently both formulations express the same thing, as far as the content is concerned. This would provide even more support for the systematic interpretation which is given above.

14. Adolf Schlatter (*Jesu Gottheit und das Kreuz* [*Beiträge zur Förderung christlicher Theologie*, 5. Jg., 5. Heft] [Gütersloh: Bertelsmann, 1901, 1919²], p. 78 n.) comments, "The curse is wrath becoming an action, the word which abrogates fellowship and separates from God; 'sin' implies the total deprivation of divine pleasure, total God-forsakenness."

There is no gospel here apart from the hardness of the law which emphasizes the difference between God and God as the *wrath* of God over the sinner. This hardness of the law, of course, is there only for the sake of the joy of the gospel, the wrath of God is only for the sake of his love which is present in the distinction between God and God, even when it is concealed, as it "surrenders itself to lovelessness in all its malformities, without retreating one step."[15]

By orienting this distinction between God and God to the Crucified One, we have significantly corrected the classical doctrine of God. For this distinction between God and God based on the cross of Jesus Christ has destroyed the axiom of absoluteness,[16] the axiom of apathy,[17] and the axiom of immutability,[18] all of which are unsuitable axioms for the Christian concept of God.[19] The distinction between law and gospel makes this necessary.[20] That the God who is love must be able to suffer and does suffer beyond all limits in the giving up of what is most authentically his for the sake of mortal man, is an indispensable insight of the newer theology schooled by Luther's Christology and Hegel's philosophy. Only the God who is identical with the Crucified One makes us certain of his love and thus of himself.[21]

15. Martin Kähler, *Das Kreuz; Grund und Mass für die Christologie (Beiträge zur Förderung christlicher Theologie*, 15. Jg., 1. Heft) (Gütersloh: Bertelsmann, 1911), p. 70.

16. See especially E. Biser, *Theologie und Atheismus; Anstösse zu einer theologischen Aporetik* (München: Kösel, 1972).

17. See W. Elert, *Der Ausgang der altkirchlichen Christologie; Eine Untersuchung über Theodor von Pharan und seine Zeit als Einführung in die alte Dogmengeschichte*, eds. W. Maurer and E. Bergsträsser (Berlin: Lutherisches Verlagshaus, 1957).

18. See especially H. Mühlen, *op. cit.* (see p. 371, n. 9).

19. Theology is indebted to the philosophical work of Hegel for this decisive breakthrough, and it should not be embarrassed to express that debt. I refer to the two books on Hegel: H. Küng, *Menschwerdung Gottes; Eine Einführung in Hegels theologisches Denken als Prolegomena zu einer künftigen Christologie* (Freiburg/Basel/Vienna: Herder, 1970); M. Theunissen, *Hegels Lehre vom absoluten Geist als theologisch-politischer Traktat* (Berlin: de Gruyter, 1970).

20. Because it is oriented to the Trinity, it is understood in a different way here from that of Gerhard Ebeling, "Existenz zwischen Gott und Gott; Ein Beitrag zur Frage nach der Existenz Gottes," in *Wort und Glaube II; Beiträge zur Fundamentaltheologie und zur Lehre von Gott* (Tübingen: J. C. B. Mohr [Siebeck], 1969), pp. 257ff.

21. Basically, the proposition of the apathy of God is the expression of an understanding of God which is not certain of its God. The axiom of apathy is ultimately a vote of no confidence in God's deity. It concedes to atheism. For if an *apathetic God must still suffer*, then he is dead as God before he dies. He cannot really be *God* in suffering and in death and thus also not be victor but instead remain God because of his immortality, in spite of his suffering—like the "old god" Prometheus, who was crucified by Zeus, the father of the gods, and who while suffering comforted himself that as an immortal he would ultimately be freed and rehabilitated as a god (see Lucian of Samosata, "Prometheus," *Selected Satires of Lucian*, ed. and tr. L. Casson [Chicago: Aldine Publishing Company, 1962], pp. 125-35; M. Hengel, "Mors turpissima crucis; Die Kreuzigung in der antiken Welt und die 'Torheit' des 'Wortes vom Kreuz'," in *Rechtfertigung; Festschrift für Ernst Käsemann zum 70. Geburtstag* [Tübingen: J. C. B. Mohr, 1976], pp. 131f). A "crucified god can," according to this understanding, "at best suffer for a while but never die" (Hengel, *loc. cit.*, p. 132). But the word of the cross makes plain that the true God is not apathetic. His capacity for suffering is already witnessed to in the passion of God documented in the Old Testament.

SECTION 24. God as Event of the Spirit

That we *become certain* of the God who is love because of the crucified Jesus now implies a problem which directly concerns the Christian concept of God. It is a twofold concern. If love is that still greater selflessness within such great self-relatedness, then, with reference to the God who gives up what is most authentic for him in the person of the Crucified One, the urgent question arises: Has God not been deprived of what is most authentically his and thus ceased to be God? Is God dead in that sense?

The question which goes along with that is this: How can we become certain of a God who empties himself? If the selflessness of God threatens to put God himself in question, then his surrender for us threatens to put into question man's relationship to God. Based on the cross of Jesus Christ, must we not speak of the God who *was* love rather than of the God who *is* love? Should we not quote again Jean Paul's "The Dead Christ Proclaims That There Is No God," and lament, "How lonely is every man in the broad crypt of the universe?"

If that *were* the case, then everything we have discussed until now would have certainly been both pointless and unnecessarily trying, something attempted only, it would appear, in order to be led *ad absurdum*. Feuerbach would have been proven right, although at a higher order of things. But would we really have spoken of God? And of love?

A love story which is only a story of suffering and wants to be only that would contradict the essence of love; what Nietzsche said about the nature of lust is probably truer of the essence of love: It desires eternity. Part of love, in any case, is the joy of love.[1] And part of the experience of the weakness of love is faith in the power of love.

The New Testament does not tell the passion story of Jesus Christ, the story of divine self-surrender, as a lamentation. The appropriate response to the cross of Jesus Christ is the hymn of praise and thanks, not the lament; it is hope, not resignation. This hope, praise, and thanksgiving are directed toward God. The death of Jesus Christ, which forced a differentiation between God and God, has been properly understood only when one experiences, on the basis of the resurrection of Jesus Christ, that the divines modes of being, Father and Son, which in this death separated into such a great differentiation than which nothing greater can be imagined, now so differentiated relate to each other anew *in the Holy Spirit*. Next to the Father and the Son, the Holy Spirit is a third divine relationship, namely, the relationship between the relationships of the Father and the Son, that is, the relationship of the relationships and thus an eternally new relationship of God to God. This eternally new relationship of God to God is called, christologically, resurrection from the dead, and is ontologically the being of love itself. Only in the *unity* of the giving Father and the given Son is God the *event* of giving up which *is* love itself in the relation of lover and beloved. The *Spirit* who proceeds from the Father and the Son constitutes the unity of the divine being as that event which is love itself by preserving the differentiation.

1. In the debate regarding Rudolf Bultmann's exposition of St. John's Gospel, Ernst Fuchs concluded that the issue in the Gospel is the wonders "which are worked by the joy of love which derives from love" (*Marburger Hermeneutik* [Tübingen: J. C. B. Mohr, 1968], p. 157).

We are dealing here with the most fundamental difference between God and man. Certainly there is love between persons. But these persons are never love itself, as has been said. The person who is love is not possible. It is solely the Spirit of God as the relation of the relations who constitutes the being of love as event.

This love as event is what makes up the essence of deity, so that the full identity of the divine essence and divine existence has been thought in these three divine relations: the Father, who loves of himself; the Son, who has always been loved and has loved; and the constantly new event of love between the Father and the Son which is the Spirit. The concept of the trinitarian God who is love implies then the eternal newness according to which the eternal God is always his own future.[2] God and love never grow old. Their being is and remains one that is coming.

But is that not to speak of a still greater self-relatedness in so very great a selflessness? Is God then the most sublime egoist? That would be a justified suspicion were it not for the 'chain of love' (vinculum caritatis) which first defines God as the one who is love, were it not for the Holy Spirit who is simultaneously the gift in which and as which God relates himself to mankind in such a way that humanity is drawn effectively into the event of divine love. One can speak of God as an eternally new relationship between God and God only on the basis of the selfless differentiation of Father and Son for the sake of another. The eternal God is, as such, concerned with humanity. In the Holy Spirit, the selfless God and totally self-centered man meet each other in such a way that the eternally new relationship of love between God and God effectively draws man into itself. It is true here as well that the "immanent" Trinity is the "economic" Trinity. The eternally new relationship between the Father and the Son, which is the Spirit, does not revise the selflessness of God, but rather implements it for us.[3] It is therefore true of the man who is drawn by the eternally new relationship of the Spirit into the oppositeness of Father and Son that he is made new: "If any one is in Christ, he is a new creation" (II Cor. 5:17). Only in this way, only when one is drawn into God's love, can one become certain of God. Certainty of God is not a normal characteristic of the human consciousness, but is rather the event of renewal of all human relationships, including the consciousness, through the fire of love with which God desires to grasp us and in which every person is totally grasped by God. For that to happen,

2. One could say, with approximate reference to Schelling (Philosophie der Offenbarung, in Sämmtliche Werke, ed. K. F. A. Schelling [Stuttgart and Augsburg: J. G. Cotta, 1858], II/4, p. 353), that God does not empty himself without elevating himself within himself.

3. Quoting Mühlen (H. Mühlen, Die Veränderlichkeit Gottes als Horizont einer zukünftigen Christologie; Auf dem Wege zu einer Kreuzestheologie in Auseinandersetzung mit der altkirchlichen Christologie [Münster: Aschendorff, 1969], p. 27), we might say "that absolute identity and just as absolute distinctiveness of the divine persons do not mutually exclude each other, but rather increase each other mutually"—in the Spirit's power, who, if it is a new relationship, does not abolish the difference between the Father and the Son, even when it reaches God-forsakenness, but which is this relationship between those so differentiated. This is the only way to speak with good reason of the justification of the godless by God.

the human *word* is needed which allows the triune God to be expressed in language in that it tells the story of Jesus Christ as God's history with all people.

SECTION 25. The Triune God as the Mystery of the World

1. No one has ever seen God. That is not only a biblical assertion (John 1:18; 6:46; I Tim. 6:16; I John 4:12). Everyone knows that personally: God is invisible.

However, there is certainly a difference between the person who *experiences* the invisibility of God and the one who is content with the *nonexperiential* statement that something like a God cannot be seen (that is probably the way that must be expressed). In the second instance, the invisibility of God becomes the abstract assertion of his nonexperienceability, whereas in the first instance the invisibility of God is part and parcel of the basic structure of the experience of God. That no one has seen God can be stated as a correct assertion which in its triviality lends itself as an introduction to atheism. But this indisputable truth can also become the actual testing stone of faith in God. The statement is certainly true. But the spirits are tested and separated in terms of its correctness. As a statement about the absolute unknownness of God it can be made into an argument against God—which always betrays a certain disquiet about the possibility that there might be a God. If he were not seriously and profoundly disquieted by the possibility of something like God, would the speaker say in his heart, "There is no God" (Ps. 14:1; 53:1)? That doubtless correct statement can also be the sharpest expression of a truth without which the being of God is neither thinkable nor experienceable. That no one has ever seen God would then not be the statement of his unknownness but rather the basic characteristic of his being known under the conditions of the world. Then we would not be dealing with the problem of God's revelation and knownness, but rather with the concrete form of that revelation. That no one has ever seen God would then be the negative expression of a positive truth which is most appropriately described with the term "mystery." Our studies began with this understanding of the invisibility of God. The intended purpose of these studies has been to illumine this understanding, to demonstrate that it is well founded. Our purpose has been to encourage the thinking of God as the mystery of the world.

Such an understanding of the invisibility of God cannot interpret this invisibility as God's unknownness in principle. It is not even possible to explain it as God's knownness among Christians over against his unknownness among non-Christians. One reason that cannot be done is that one then could be easily fascinated by the world's nonknowledge of God and become fixated on it so that ultimately it defines the tasks which are to be done by Christian talk about God in such situations.[1] The invisibility of God is rather to be interpreted on the basis

---

1. In his last lectures in the *Church Dogmatics*, Karl Barth, with good reason, stated that he had to "part company with a whole trend in Christian and even theological thought and utterance that has most unfortunately prevailed for some decades. Enough of the sorry futility [or] futile sorrow which constantly assures us that in this century— as though the nineteenth and sixteenth centuries and the Middle Ages were golden ages in this regard—we have to do with a world which is alienated from God in a distinctively radical and refined way, having become totally secular, autonomous, adult, and profane!

of the experience of acquaintance with God. Within the context of that experience, the truth that no one has ever seen God gains its ultimate precision.

It is then characteristic that the New Testament statements about the unknownness and concealment of God all bear the function of defining more precisely the knownness of God. The Johannine-sounding logion in Matthew 11:27 makes the undoubtedly true point that no one knows God the Father except as a way to define more precisely the truth that the Son alone knows the Father, and so only through the Son can one know the Father. For that reason, Matthew 11:28 follows with the great invitation of the Son (originally it was probably an isolated statement) to all who are weary and heavy laden. For, to come to know the Father through the Son means to find healing rest. In John 1:18 and 6:46f, this same dialectic between the general unknownness of the divine Father and his still greater, concrete, precise knownness in and through the Son is underlined. In I Timothy 6:13-16, finally, God is said "to dwell in unapproachable light" (v. 16). The function of this statement is, however, to emphasize the historical (v. 13) and more importantly the eschatological (v. 14) appearance of Jesus Christ as God's own work, in order to intensify the bonds of the believer to the teachings of Jesus Christ. Generally this is true of other statements which are similar to the basic assertion that no one has ever seen God.

The negative experience of God's invisibility is thus to be understood as increasing the positive experience of God's self-communication. That certainly does not exclude the fact that this negative experience can *de facto* take place, as well, as a problematizing of this positive experience. For, on the basis of every experience of God, we are dealing with the experience of possible nonbeing,[2] which is not always abstractly present as the experience of *vanquished* nonbeing, although it is concrete in the event as the experience of definitively vanquished nonbeing. Even the unequivocality and irreversibility of such a positive basic experience has its appointed time and can be replaced by another time in which we are threatened by the experience of possible nonbeing, without being in the least encroached on in its truthfulness. The existential ambivalence of our basic experiences does not make the decision about the truth of what we experience. And even, and especially(!), the experience with experience, which

---

Enough of the impenitence that will not even inquire into the serious ignorance of God in Christianity itself but at most will only chide it for being so insensitive, old-fashioned, and clumsy in dealing with the children of the world who today have supposedly become so terribly ungodly! Enough of the critical psychological and sociological analyses of the age with which it is hoped to understand and reach the children of the world, but with which they are not in truth understood or reached, because the problem of their ignorance of God certainly cannot be exposed in this way, and all the delight and love lavished on the problem can only detract from the joy in the knowledge of God with which alone the children of the world can be effectively and victoriously met! And enough especially of thinking and speaking with an order of priorities that is wrong because in the light of the center of Christian faith it is impossible; it is an order according to which people are, even if only temporarily, more strongly stimulated and claimed by the undeniable ignorance of God in the world than by the knowledge of God in the world, as though the former were not from the very outset of a far lower rank than the latter!" (Karl Barth, *The Christian Life; Church Dogmatics, IV/4; Lecture Fragments,* tr. G. W. Bromiley [Grand Rapids: Wm. B. Eerdmans, 1981], pp. 126f).

2. See above, pp. 30-35.

claims to possess *absolute* significance, has its own time.[3] For that reason, the experience of God's invisibility which *tests* man does not abolish the certainty of God, in which the invisibility of God appears as the powerful increasing of the experience of his self-communication, so that it must be understood as such. In this sense, God's invisibility is the negative side of the positive content which we were describing when we called God the mystery of the world.

God is then grasped as the mystery of the world as he *comes* to the world. That God comes to the world means for the latter that it can never *have* itself. For, as long as, for example, any person still needs to have something added to himself, even if he is quite perfect and has everything, that person is not in possession of himself. He does not have himself. The world, too, does not have itself, does not possess itself. That certainly need not be a deficiency. If the impossibility of self-possession were interpreted as a deficiency, then it would be misunderstood. If the reason that an I does not possess itself is that another I *belongs* to him in such a way that it can only be *added to him,* then that is certainly not a deficiency. Rather, the possibility of having oneself so that no other I could be added on and could belong to the I would have to be regarded as a deficiency. Thus, with regard to the world, it is not a deficiency when it cannot have or possess itself *because* God is the one who is coming to the world in his humanity. We should speak here not of a deficiency but of a distinction of the world and its people, if God comes to the world and is thus its mystery. In that God comes to the world, it is as little encroached on in its abilities and possibilities as would God become necessary because the world does not have itself. In both directions the basic insight stands that God is more than necessary.

But, given the conditions of the world, God's coming to the world cannot be seen. If this were to be made visible, then, as one option, the end of the world would have to be postulated. For God's divine way of appearing would surpass the world's possibilities, which are divided into space and time and thus within time into the various tenses of time,[4] and consequently cannot facilitate the appearance of the eternal God in an eternal or divine way. If such an appearance were thinkable, then it would only be as an appearance which abolished the world.[5] The other option would be, if the world is not to be ended by the

3. It is wrong to conclude from the lack of continuity of this unequivocality and irreversibility, and therefore the experience of the grace of God which claims absolute validity, that this claim is falsified. It is not accidental that the praise of God and thanksgiving correspond verbally to that experience, and no one would assert that praise and thanksgiving, even the admonition to praise and thank God at all times, would have to take place at all times. Such an abstract assertion deprives praise and thanksgiving of their character as praise and thanksgiving. It is characteristic of the faith that it expresses each truth at its time, but they are not all experienceable at every time, while they are certainly true at every time. And it is characteristic of the experience of the irreversibility of God's grace (which saves from nonbeing) that this experience knows how to distinguish between the act of experience which has its particular time and what is experienced. That person who has reason to praise and to give thanks knows that there are possible tests and challenges ahead.

4. See E. Jüngel, "Grenzen des Menschseins," in *Probleme biblischer Theologie; Gerhard von Rad zum 70. Geburtstag* (München: C. Kaiser, 1971), pp. 199ff.

5. The apocalyptic texts of the Bible possess, with their narrative language, a clearer concept of this ontological content than do many systematic attempts to present

visible coming of God, to degenerate God's coming to the world into a phantom-like appearance. The phantom enters the scene but does not belong to it. It is there without belonging—an addition without any structure or relationship, lacking any correspondence with the world. But God, by contrast, comes to the world in such a way that he belongs there, namely, by claiming the world as his property, as "his own" (John 1:11). But the world becomes experienceable as a world which belongs to him only when it is defined anew from its ground up—just as the light which shines in the darkness claims that darkness as "its own" by illuminating it. Darkness can as darkness grasp the light shining into it as little as the world can make God visible. For the light which illumines the darkness is the end of the darkness, just as the God who appears as God would be the end of the world. If God did not appear in a divine fashion, if his coming to the world was *invisible,* then that means positively that he brought the world to its turning point rather than to its end.

We are, then, to understand as the actual point of all talk about the invisibility of God the fact that the world is not at its end, but rather that God claims it as his creation anew and rights it. That point is the invisibility of the God who comes to the world, whereby we should take the expression "comes to the world" precisely in its normal and common sense: God came to the world *as man.* As that man, he was visible. As that man he belonged to the world, which for that reason belonged to him. Jesus Christ is that reason, which distinguishes the world, for the fact that it does not possess itself and that we do not have ourselves. To be without having oneself, without possessing oneself, and yet not to not be but rather to be there—that is the material content of the mystery of creaturely existence. In his identity with Jesus Christ, God is the actual mystery of the world.

When the experience of the invisibility of God is understood as the powerful increasing of the experience of his self-communication, then it leads to the mystery of the triune God. The identification of God with the Crucified One implied the trinitarian self-differentiation of God, so that the doctrine of the unity of God with the crucified man Jesus revealed itself to be the grounding of the doctrine of the Trinity. The Trinity of God implies, within the horizons of the world, the self-differentiation of the *invisible* Father in heaven from the Son on earth, *visible* as man, and from the Spirit who reigns as the bond of unity and love between the invisible Father in heaven and the visible Son on earth and who produces in an *invisible* way *visible* results in us. The Holy Spirit is thus both the relationship between Father and Son which constitutes the life of God and their powerful turning to man who is drawn in this way into the relationship of the Son to the Father. As Holy Spirit, God is the mystery of the world. This he is in that this Spirit is the invisible but powerful relationship in which, on the one hand, the Son of God, visible as man, relates himself to the invisible Father in heaven, and in which, on the other hand, that same Son of God, who was visible as man, relates himself to us in order to draw all men to himself (John

---

this problem conceptually. They tell the story of the end of the world in advance, so to speak, when they speak of the divine appearance of God or of the appearance of the Son of Man in power and glory.

12:32). In this regard as well, the invisibility of God cannot be understood as his unknownness, but rather as the invisible communication of his knownness.

It is the task of material dogmatics to unfold this understanding of God's invisibility as the understanding which preserves God as the mystery of the world. Without neglecting the stringency of concepts, it ought to tell the story of God as the mystery of the world. At the end of these studies, whose sole purpose was to serve the founding of a material dogmatics, the attempt will now be made to explicate how God, as the one who is coming to the world, is its mystery. This will be done with reference, on the one hand, to the trinitarian understanding of the being of God, and on the other, to the special human acts and modes of being which are related to the being of God. Our purpose is to explain theologically and anthropologically, in a final phase of our argumentation, how God is more than necessary so that man learns to understand, not as a lack (which God must correct) but as a distinction which establishes his autonomy and freedom, that his being, and the being of his world, is something other than the capacity to possess itself. The negatively formulated fact that we do not have ourselves and cannot have ourselves is to be expounded in its positive phenomenality—that is the task before us. We begin with the insight that God has come to the world and is as such the one who is coming.

2. This insight that God has come to the world and is as such the one who is coming implies a fundamental distinction between God and the world. This difference is understood theologically only when it is seen, not as a deficit of the world grounded in the world's being, but rather as a distinction of the world based in God. We are to understand the difference between God and the world on the basis of God's being, and that means that we are to understand God's being in such a way that this difference becomes comprehensible as a positive relationship. The insight that God has come to the world and is as such the one who is coming is comprehended as an insight based on God himself only when we understand God as being intrinsically the one who is coming, and not only because of the existence of the world. We did that in our previous studies when we said that God's being is in coming. We shall address ourselves again to this statement by asking about its trinitarian structure and meaning. In this, we are querying the self-differentiation of God, presented in the preceding paragraphs as trinitarian and soteriological, about its trinitarian and ontological implications.

The statement *God's being is in coming* implies first of all that God's being is the event of his coming to himself. This event, this coming of God's being to itself, is what the tradition has meant when it spoke of eternity. But eternity is not something distinct from God. God himself is eternity. God is eternally coming to himself.

That statement is more than a tautology when it expresses that God comes out of himself when he comes to himself. God always derives or comes from God. He is his own absolute origin. But, coming from himself, God really does come to himself. God comes to God. He is his own goal. But he does not strive to reach himself as goal in order to move away from his origin. God does not leave himself as origin behind. He always comes as God from God to God. God is his own mediation. We have said this on the basis of the trace of the coming of God which is revealed in the humanity of Jesus. God came in the event of self-identification with the man Jesus from God the Father. And God came to Jesus as his beloved Son, and thus came to himself, to God the Son, along the path which led into the far country. And yet God remained totally in the process of coming, as God the Holy Spirit. That is the mystery that God is already in himself, the 'mystery of the Trinity' (*mysterium trinitatis*), the mystery of his triune nature: that God is in that he comes to himself—from God to God as God.

(a) *God comes from God*. Nothing other than God himself can be regarded as God's origin. Neither being, nor nothingness. God is his own origin. God lives, and he lives totally out of himself.

The statement that even being cannot be regarded as the origin of God might appear initially to be somewhat suspect logically. All the more so because nothingness is not supposed to be considered as the origin of God. The tradition provided help in this difficulty by identifying God and being, or else God and nothingness, or took refuge in the thesis of the Beyondness of God's Being (*epekeina tēs ousias*). The advantage of this thesis is that it distinguishes between God and being in favor of God. But we found it to be deficient because it rendered it impossible to speak *positively* of God and instead only expressed God as the one who is actually unspeakable and unthinkable. In contrast to that, we must think God as the one who is coming from himself as well as speaking of himself. We think this "of himself" properly when we subordinate the concept of being to the concept of God so that, in the statement *God is,* the predicate is understood in terms of the subject. That means that only to the extent that God comes from God does being result. Only in that God is his own origin is there being at all. But if something like being is the result of the absolute originality of God, then something like nothingness is a result of the fact that God comes from himself. If God's absolute originality constitutes being, then it also and simultaneously constitutes nothingness. Because and in that God comes from himself, there is being at all, and also nothingness.

We express the absolute originality of God, speaking with the tradition, when we speak of God the Father. As God comes from God, he is called the *Father*. As God the Father, God is the origin of himself. As the origin of himself God is, at the same time, the Father of everything living and the Father of all fathers (Eph. 3:15). Since God, as the origin of himself, is earlier than being and nonbeing, he is as eternal Father eternally distinct from everything which emerges under the presupposition of the difference between being and nonbeing. God is, therefore, not the Father of what exists—unless he wants to become that. And if he becomes that, then he is believed in first as the God who is the eternal Father in himself.

To believe in the eternal Father means then to acknowledge God as the sovereign of being. To believe in the eternal Father means to accept God as the Lord who is distinct from all that exists, not only like being and also not only like nothingness. The eternal Father is, as sovereign of being, as distinct from everything which is as is his Yes from what he affirms. This qualitatively infinite and yet positive distinction is respected and acknowledged in faith in God the eternal Father. God the eternal Father is differentiated from what exists as the one who calls into being. The encounter with the sovereign superiority of the God who is absolutely original in himself is an experience of faith in God. It makes the consent possible which Paul apparently presupposes when he asks, "Who are you, a man, to answer back to God? Will what is molded say to its molder, 'Why have you made me thus?' Has the potter no right over the clay, to make out of the same lump one vessel for beauty and another for menial use?" (Rom. 9:20f). Briefly, to believe in the eternal Father means, first of all, to believe in God the Creator.

But the concept of the Father is not to be thought as the concept of a 'solitary thing' (*solitarium*). "Father" always is stated as "Father and. . . ." To believe in the eternal Father means, further and more precisely, to acknowledge God as a social essence, namely, as an essence who *vouchsafes* fellowship, as the sovereign of being who permits *participation* in being. God is thus asserted to be the one who is related both eternally and graciously to everything which is and who in his sovereign superiority both unconditionally concerns and unconditionally maintains everything that exists. As the eternal Father, God is the *gracious* sovereign of being and time. To believe in the eternal Father means, thus, to *find delight* in God as the Lord. The encounter with the God who permits participation in being takes place as the experience of the God who does kill but in order to make alive, who does strike down but in order to heal, from whose hand no one can be saved but only because he is the only savior (Deut. 32:39; see also Job 5:18 and Hos. 6:1). If God is eternally distinctive from all that is, as the Sovereign over being, then the eternal Father who permits participation in being does allow his sun to rise over both wicked and good and graciously permits his rain to fall on the just and the unjust (Matt. 5:45). If the *eternal* Creator is distinct from his creatures as is his Yes from what he affirms, then he as the eternal Father bears the vessels of wrath which were made for corruption in order thus(!) to proclaim the riches of his glory on the vessels of mercy which he prepared for glory. As eternal *Father* he calls forth believers not only from among the Jews but also from the Gentiles, and calls the people which is not his people, "my people," and the unloved, "beloved." It accords with his being as Father that even those who did not have to be called his people may be called sons of the living God (Rom. 9:22-26; see also Hos. 2:1).

This gracious fatherhood of God is profoundly demonstrated in the justification of the rejected ones which took place in the death of the eternal Son of God. In him, God made the one who knew no sin into sin for us, so that we might become God's righteousness in him (II Cor. 5:21; see also Rom. 8:2f). The eternal God shows himself as the *Father* in the sending of the *Son* (Gal. 4:4; Rom. 8:3). As eternal Father, God exists in eternity with this Son. God is, as eternal Father, his own origin. And he remains his own origin. But he is not only his own origin. God encounters himself out of this origin in such a way that he becomes his own partner. God is also his own goal. God does come from God. But just as he comes to himself, God comes to God. A father is not a father without a child. God is God the Father as the Father of the *Son*. To believe in God as the eternal Father thus means to believe simultaneously in God as the eternal Son.

(b) *God comes to God.* We already have provided the foundation for this statement when, on the basis of the humanity of Jesus Christ, we had to speak of the deity of Christ. The statement *God comes to God* was the result of the insight that God has come to man. We can thus not simply assert in parallelism to the statement that *God comes from God* that God, just as he is exclusively his own origin, is now also his own goal. God does come from God and only from God. But God does not only come to God. God also comes to *man*. He *has come* to man in the person of Jesus Christ. This is where all Christian knowledge of God must begin. The result of this knowledge that God has come to man in the person of Jesus Christ was, first, the constituting of the Christian concept of God and thus the knowledge of the truth that God comes from God. But God comes in that he comes to man, not as something other but as the same one who always is, in and for himself. God goes into the far country when he goes to the death of Jesus. But even in death, he involves himself in nothingness, but he is not conquered by nothingness. Even in the far country of death, God comes to himself. Thus he is the victor over death! God comes to himself even in the death of Jesus Christ, the Father to the Son. And thus he comes to man as his eschatological goal. In the death of Jesus, God comes in one and the same event as God to God and as God (definitively) to man, as the Father to the Son, and as the Son to Jesus. This death is the seal of that event in which God comes both to God and to man, of that event then in which God as man is his own goal.

Therefore, God shows himself in death to be the living one, the eternal one, the eternal God. And thus it is true that God is eternally his own goal, that wherever he goes, he always comes to God.[6] God does not come to himself only when he comes from himself. He is his own goal because he is his own origin. But he is as goal distinct from himself as origin. He really *comes* to himself. He is not only origin. He does not only beget. He is also the eternally begotten Son and as such completely like God the Father: the same once more and yet as the goal of himself distinct from the origin of himself— 'repetition of eternity in eternity' (*repetitio aeternitatis in aeternitate*).

This must be said on the basis of the 'repetition of eternity in time' (*repetitio aeternitatis in tempore*) which is revealed in the death of Jesus (in the 'annihilation of time'—*annihilatio temporis!*). To believe with Jesus in God means to believe in Jesus as God 'under the category of the death of Jesus Christ' (*sub specie mortis Jesu Christi*). Whoever believes with Jesus in God believes with him in God the eternal Father. Whoever believes in Jesus as God believes in God the eternal Son.

To believe in the *eternal* Son means, first of all, to acknowledge God as the original image and the end of being. In faith in the eternal Son, God is asserted to be the one through whom all things are and toward whom all things are. Following the New Testament texts, the Nicaeno-Constantinopolitan Creed confesses of Jesus Christ expressly that "through him all things were made" in that it confesses him as the only begotten Son of God. In that the eternal Son is eternally from the Father, God is aiming in him as well toward a becoming

6. God's eternity may not be thought of as "another space" in abstract contrast with time. God is becoming all in all (I Cor. 15:28). And all (*panta*) is only in that God is in all (*en pasin*). To the extent that God is in all (God!), he obviously is distinct from all. And although God is in all, he is not yet *all* in all. But in all, God is the eternal one, and as the eternal one, he is in all. And if he is not yet *all* in all, still in all he is *God*. Wherever God comes, he always comes to God. For in that God *is*, he comes from himself to himself.

in which God not only comes from God, but, beyond that, man with his world is made, caused, created by God. But God *aims* in himself at what is other. God aims in his divine eternal becoming toward the incarnation of man, toward the becoming of the world. God aims in his eternal begetting toward creation. If one wants to escape the fatal proposition "God is in and of himself," then one must confess (against the Arians) that God in his own becoming is aiming at the becoming of creation, that Jesus Christ is not (only) the *creative* instrument of the Creator-God, but that Jesus Christ as eternal God is himself the *original image,* the divine original image of the creation which is eternally distinct from him. He is the original image of the creation in that God the Father aims at creation in him.

But God's aiming toward the world is understandable only as the expression of his grace which is revealed in the being of God. God is his own goal. And only because he is his own goal, he aims toward that being which is to be made, the creation. God by no means first becomes his goal when he aims toward man. He is adequate to himself. But precisely in that he is adequate to himself, he is overflowing being, and his overflowing being is the expression of his grace, the original image of his covenant with a partner who is not God, who at first does not exist at all but must first be created as God's partner: man. In the eternal Son of God, who himself was not created, but comes eternally from God the Father, in this Son of God coming *eternally* from God God aims at the man who *temporally* comes from God.

A strict distinction must be maintained between the eternal derivation of God from God and the temporal derivation of man from God in order to recognize the factual relationship which obtains between the two, the factual grace relation between God's eternal becoming and our temporal becoming in faith. Because the eternal Son of God is in fact the original image of the divine turning to created being, because in God's eternal being God's grace is already expressed so that God *de facto* can never be thought "per se," there must be both a distinction and a confession made with regard to the Son: "begotten, not made." And thus, the being of Jesus Christ is itself creative being: "Through him were all things made" (see John 1:3, 10; I Cor. 8:6; Col. 1:15f; Heb. 1:2). The statement *God comes to God* cannot be made as a true statement apart from the statement *God comes from God.* In that God comes to God, he does not cease to come from God. There must be a strict distinction made between God, to the extent that he is his own origin, and God, to the extent that he is his own goal. These are two different modes of existence (*tropoi hyparxeōs*) of God. The goal is not the same thing as the origin. But in God the goal is as original as the origin. Not himself the origin, not himself the 'source of divinity' (*fons divinitatis*), yet God the Son is as original as the essence of God the Father. The goal which God himself is, is not the same as the origin. But it is equal to the origin. The Son is "of one being with the Father." Thus he himself is also creative being.

In this creative being of God the Son as the aim of God the Father, God is aiming at man. In that God the Father loves the Son, in the event of this divine self-love, God is aiming selflessly at his creation. To believe in God the eternal Son thus means to take delight in God as the Lord in such a way that we take delight in ourselves, that we take delight in ourselves in the difference between us and him (as those who "are made, not begotten"). Whoever takes absolutely no delight in himself as God's good creation does not believe in the eternal Son of God in whom God is his own purpose in order to aim at us in love. Whoever does not take delight in himself, whoever raises his hand gently or violently against himself, is raising his hand against God, and in particular against the God who turns to us in love, freely and selflessly, in the event of his divine self-love. For we understood God's self-love as that event which was consummated in the selflessness of the death of the eternal Son of God. Just as in the death of Jesus Christ the Father comes to the Son, to the Son of God who is identical with the dead man Jesus, God's eternal self-love is the origin of his selflessness which saves us.

At the same time, God is the *end* of our temporal being in the death of Jesus Christ. The original image of being implies the end of being and time. As the alpha, the eternal Son of God is also the omega. Time ends in death. In death, being ceases. In his identity with the dead man Jesus, the eternal Son of God is the end of all time and is the cessation of all being. For in this one death, all dying is collected together and all perishing is integrated. In him, all that is old has passed away (II Cor. 5:17). And with him, everything that is perishing has passed away. As the one, he died for all so that in him all have died (II Cor. 5:14b). The Easter hymn thus does not speak in an unreal sense when it says, "If he were not risen, the world would have passed away." In him, it has passed away. It is really true that "O great distress, God himself lies dead!" The world truly sees there its own "life hovering on the stem of the cross," *its* "salvation sinks into death."

But those are all statements which benefit the world. It is the love of Christ which forces us, together with the apostle (II Cor. 5:14), to such a conclusion. All of this can be said only because the God who is love also comes to God in the death of Jesus Christ, because God is his own purpose in this death, and because it is precisely in the selflessness of the identification of the Son of God with the man Jesus that God's self-love is demonstrated. For that reason, we can and must say that the divine self-love in the eternal relation of the Father to the Son aims at this act of God's selflessness for man's benefit. But in this selflessness for man's benefit, God does not give up himself as the aim of himself, nor does he do so in the death of Jesus Christ. Rather, in that he affirms the Crucified One as his beloved Son, he truly demonstrates that he is the eternal Father, remaining his own origin even when the crucified Son of God surrenders his deity to the grasp of death. To put it in the language of older dogmatics, he does not permit 'eternal generation' (*aeterna generatio*) to end in death, but rather perfects it in the killing of death. In eternal originality, he affirms his own deity in the crucified Jesus Christ in that he confirms the being of the man Jesus. And thus he is the Father who awakens from the dead. God's self-affirmation is thus forever identical with his Yes to the world which is judged in the Crucified Christ and confronts its own end. Affirmed by the fatherly love of God, which as absolute originality preserves him from the annihilating power of death, Jesus Christ is as the end of the old also the beginning and ground of the new being. "Therefore, if any one is in Christ, he is a new creation; the old has passed away, behold, the new has come" (II Cor. 5:17).

Through his action toward God the Son, in which he affirms and seals the identity of the eternal Son of God with the crucified man Jesus, the eternal Father of the eternal Son now reveals himself to be simultaneously the heavenly Father of his human creatures. In that he affirms and seals the identity of his eternal Son with the temporal man Jesus, he makes these people, who for their part affirm this identity, his earthly children. Therefore, to believe in God the eternal Son means to believe in the love of God the Father and thus to affirm ourselves as his beloved children. When we confess Jesus Christ as the true Son of God and true man, then we may understand ourselves as God's temporal daughters and sons, in the analogy of faith which maintains the difference between time and eternity, and between God and man. For, "when the time had fully come, God sent forth his Son, born of woman [not only coming eternally from God the Father but now also coming temporally], born under the law, to redeem those who were under the law [the condemned], so that we might receive adoption as sons" (Gal. 4:4f).

What happens here is, in fact, a genuine correspondence between God and man. An analogy results in which the relation of God the eternal Father to God the Son finds its correspondence in the relation of God the heavenly Father to us humans as his earthly children. It must be noted that this analogy *results*; we *come* to it. Man is not of himself analogous with God. God is as such without analogy in all that exists. But through the death of the Son of God and his resurrection from the dead, the analogy comes, and we become analogous to him, the Son of God. For in him, God comes to man as God comes to God. In that we are renewed in our being through the being of the crucified and resurrected Son of God, we gain the position of children of God who correspond to him, in order as such to be humans who correspond to the triune God.

The person who corresponds to God then is entirely different from an I which has itself, possesses itself. The first reason for that is that he corresponds to the triune God only in the fellowship of at least two people who say "we." What distinguishes him is that he, instead of having himself, has the Holy Spirit who relates him through and through to God the Father. "And because you are sons, God has sent the Spirit of his Son into our hearts, crying, 'Abba! Father!' " (Gal. 4:6; see also Rom. 8:15f).

Here, once again, God must be differentiated from God. The God who has no analogy in all that exists has become accessible to us as God in his Son. He, the Son, is the image of God (II Cor. 4:4), and that means the image of the invisible God (Col. 1:15), the reflection of his glory and the imprint of his being (Heb. 1:3). As such, he is God's self-communication: the Son through whom God has ultimately spoken (Heb. 1:2). In God the Son, God has now expressed himself in such a way that he has become speakable for us. For that reason, he is called, as the eternal Son, also the eternal word of God (John 1:1). In this word God is knowable, speakable, perceivable, as God. For whoever hears the word hears the Father, and whoever sees him who is the eternal word of God sees the Father (see John 14:9; 12:45).

But one can hear and see the eternal word of God only because it was present in the personal union with the man Jesus and is, in this having been present, both *the image of God* and the *original image of the world*. One must decisively refer all of the related statements of the tradition[7] to the humanity of the Son of God in order to risk this proposition with regard to his identity with the man Jesus: "The Son has in Himself not only the image of the Divine Majesty but also the image of all created things."[8]

This identity with the man Jesus which brings God into language is, however, not directly present to every man and to every historical reality, in its historical uniqueness. That which in meaningfulness directly affects us to the highest degree must be reached by our historical reality on its own. The significance of that event must become an event itself. For, although God has become speakable, addressable, perceivable, and knowable as God in his Son, that is not reason alone for us to know, perceive, address, and call him God. We cannot do it without God the Holy Spirit relating to us once more in order to establish himself with us. We do not press through to God; rather, the Holy Spirit presses through to us. And when that happens, our language gains the power which enables us to express ourselves fully and thus to bring ourselves before God. In the Holy Spirit we can express ourselves before God the way God expressed himself in Jesus Christ. In the power of the Spirit, man shares himself rather than possessing himself, shares himself with another. And only there where man expresses himself in that way, where thus his entire being *de facto* attains to the dimension where he calls on God, do his words no longer simply speak about God, but really speak of God. In Jesus Christ, indeed, God has become *addressable as* God and we have become *addressable as* his earthly children. But in the Holy Spirit, God has become *expressible* as God. To express God as God always means to present one's own humanity in such a way that the entire person is drawn out of itself. This happens in the power of the Spirit. Through Jesus Christ we have indeed gained the indisputable and irrevocable *right* to call God our Father. But only in the Holy Spirit do we have both the *need* and the *strength* to call on God as our Father and to live our life as an act of calling on God.[9] Thus, faith in God the eternal Son is simultaneously faith in God the Holy Spirit.

(c) *God comes as God.* We said that God went into the far country when he went to the death of Jesus. For in the death of Jesus, the eternal God is, in fact, perishing. But God does not become alien to himself in that far country. God does not alienate himself from himself. Even in perishing, he does not alienate himself. Rather, God alienates death and perishing. Because he did not fear perishing, God's being continues to come while in the midst of perishing. That God's being *remains* in the process of coming, that God is indestructibly his own origin and irrevocably his own goal, that God thus remains related to himself as origin and goal, as Father and as Son, and thus does not cease to

7. See Thomas Aquinas, *STh*, I, q. 34, art. 3, vol. I, pp. 337f.

8. Martin Luther, *Lectures on Genesis, Chapters 1–5*, in *Luther's Works*, ed. J. Pelikan (St. Louis: Concordia, 1958), p. 58, on Genesis 1:20. Karl Barth addresses this problem extensively in *CD*, I/1, pp. 501-12.

9. See, on this, Karl Barth, who in the fragmentary ethic of his doctrine of reconciliation defined the situation of the Christian life as that of calling on God, and based on that sought to expound the imperatives which define the Christian life, using the Lord's Prayer as his outline (Karl Barth, *The Christian Life*, pp. 41ff and 49ff).

come from God to God—in short, that God himself is mediation—that is the third mode of being of God, God the Holy Spirit.

To speak of God as Spirit means, first, that when God is at the origin which he is, he is not already at his goal, which he is himself in another way. There is a real movement from the origin to the goal, although of course this goal does not become an end point. God's being as such is in coming. In the relatedness of goal and origin, and in the backward relatedness of the goal to the origin, God's coming takes place. But this event is not an alien fate which confronts God, but is God himself once more. We could also say that in that God comes from himself to himself, he is his own future. That is the meaning of the statement "God comes as God."

The coming in which God's being is, is God himself. But this coming has been thought in its completion only when it is grasped as source, arrival, and future. God is his own source in that he is origin itself. God's source is not his past which is passing away. God is arrival himself, in that he is his own goal. But God's arrival is his present which is not passing away. God is his own future in that he is mediation itself. But God's future is the imperishability of his past and present and yet his continuation, God's going on: as the origin of himself and as the goal of himself God goes on, God advances and precedes. And thus, in the unity of origin and goal, God is the one who is coming. But if God, in that he is coming to himself from his origin and goal, is the God who is coming, then he is in this mode of being the Spirit who proceeds from the Father *and* the Son (*filioque!*). In the Spirit, the Father and the Son affirm each other mutually. It is the Spirit of love which lets God advance in the union of origin and goal. As love, God's being is in coming. As the Spirit of love, God gives himself eternal future, in which God is eternally his own origin and his own goal. For that reason, this third mode of being of God has been understood as the 'bond of love' (*vinculum caritatis*) from early on. This "bond of love" does not chain one tightly, but rather moves those who are bound eternally "toward something new." As the 'bond of love,' the Holy Spirit is simultaneously the 'vehicle of eternity' (*vehiculum aeternitatis*). As the Spirit of love, God is *from* eternity *to* eternity, from age to age. As Spirit, God is eternally not only the one "who is" and "who was," but also "who is to *come*."

All of this we say on the basis of the revelation of God which took place in the humanity of Jesus. We saw that whoever believes with Jesus in God believes in God as the eternal Father. Whoever believes in God the eternal Father must necessarily believe at the same time in God the eternal Son, who is made identical with the man Jesus by the judgment of the Father in the death of Jesus. This judgment of identity made by the Father can only be recapitulated by man; the statement "Jesus is Lord" can be believed only "in the Holy Spirit" (I Cor. 12:3). According to I John 4:2, the Spirit of God may be recognized where he confesses the identity of the Son of God with the flesh of Jesus Christ, whereas conversely every Spirit which does not confess the Son of God as the man Jesus is not only not of God but is in fact the spirit of the Antichrist. That means that apart from the Spirit of God, God's identity with Jesus remains a past tense which never embraces the present tense of man. Apart from the Spirit of God, we cannot *believe* in Jesus as our Lord and thus as the eternal Son, because "I believe that by my own reason or strength I cannot believe in Jesus Christ my

Lord, or come to him."[10] Apart from the Spirit, one cannot state that God is his own goal and yet does not want to be his own goal without having us as his goal. In the Spirit, the judgment of God the Father which unites God and man *reaches* us. In the Spirit, God binds himself to us and us to himself. Therefore, "unless one is born of water and the Spirit, he cannot enter the kingdom of God" (John 3:5). For "any one who does not have the Spirit of Christ does not belong to him" (Rom. 8:9), in whom the love of God has been revealed (Rom. 8:39). It is the Spirit who first makes us alive to love (II Cor. 3:6; John 6:63), which means, he draws us into the life of God which is love.

We have thus understood the Spirit as the giving of a share in God's own life. But this giving of a share in God's own life is itself not merely something like the structure of a relationship with God, but rather a personal power which directly confronts us in an unmistakable fashion in that it comes to us as the power which opens up the future. The future opened up by the Holy Spirit is not empty but instead concretely and sharply contoured by the person of Jesus Christ. According to Paul, the Spirit is the *arrabōn*, the 'down payment,' 'deposit,' 'pledge' for the "future of him who has come."[11] By relating us to this personal future, he validates in us that God does not want to be his goal alone without our becoming his goal as well. The Spirit of God, powerfully present in proclamation and confession, implements the fact that God in Jesus Christ has *reached* this his goal. The Spirit of God, through his inexpressible groanings, makes us understand that we have not yet reached that goal, that God then will still come with his goal. Thus the Spirit with his gifts enters into the moved and moving state of anticipation of faith, in which we for our part are oriented to the future out of which God is coming. The spiritual giving of a share in God's own life means, then, the giving of a share in a future which God desires to have together with us and toward which we are going because we are already defined by it.

To believe in God the Holy Spirit means then to acknowledge Jesus Christ as our future and to rejoice in anticipation of it. God and man will have love as their mutual future. Faith in the Holy Spirit takes us along into this future by leading us now along the way of love. Whoever goes the way of love, however, exists in the paradox of intensively expectant wanderers. They advance with God the Spirit in this world and yet await hopefully their salvation out of this world in God's eternal love. For that is what faith in the Holy Spirit means, taken to its ultimate consequence: that God allows the negation suffered in the death of Jesus Christ to be perfected in our mortal bodies, our earthly life, as the victorious power of love, in that he makes a place for us to live within his own being. The Spirit provides us certainty that we shall be saved and kept alive in God, so that our life, too, is in the process of coming with God's being.

In that sense, faith in the triune God leads to a common life with the triune God.

3. For the understanding of the invisibility of God which preserves God

10. Martin Luther, Shorter Catechism, in *The Book of Concord; The Confessions of the Evangelical Lutheran Church*, tr. T. G. Tappert (Philadelphia: Fortress Press, 1959), p. 345.
11. On this term, see W. Kreck, *Die Zukunft des Gekommenen; Grundprobleme der Eschatologie* (München: C. Kaiser, 1966).

as the mystery of the world, the trinitarian explication of the statement *God's being is in coming* has provided only the basic terminology which exposes the self-movements of the divine being and with whose help a material dogmatics has to narrate the being of God as history and this history as the mystery of the world. To unfold these basic concepts of divine being is the task of a narrative theology. We have been occupied in these studies with the foundations for that. We shall conclude the laying of that foundation for a theology which narrates the being of God as the mystery of the world by asking about the human acts and modes of being which correspond to the divine self-movements. We shall give no more than a reference to the fact that God as the mystery of the world has his anthropological correspondences. To develop these correspondences also is a part of the task of a theology which narrates the divine mystery of the world. We shall point out here only that there are such human acts and modes of being in which man involves himself with God as the mystery of the world. Those are the human acts and modes of being which express, in that specific quality which characterizes them, that they are concerned with something completely other than an unknown Invisible. In them, man enters into the fact that God is coming to the world and that therefore man is not destined to possess himself. We speak of faith, love, and hope.

Faith, love, and hope, when one believes, loves, and hopes, express as acts and modes of being of man that we do not have ourselves. In all three acts man is so related to the God who is coming into the world that his invisibility becomes concrete as the focusing of his knownness. For in faith, love, and hope, man is so *addressed*, the God who speaks of himself comes so close to him, that man is defined by God's Holy Spirit " 'in, with, and beneath' the phenomena of reality,"[12] defined in a way that is both totally invisible and yet totally concrete.

(a) This is true, first, of *faith*. Whoever possesses himself does not believe. He certainly does not believe that he can only receive himself and thus cannot have himself. And he first of all believes that the receiving of oneself is an event in which one also experiences the deprivation of oneself, a deprivation which creates a totally new relationship not only to what one has, but also to the act and condition of having itself. In its formal structure, by contrast, which obviously is completely defined by the so-called content of what is believed, faith is the existential expression of the fact that man does not have himself. At the same time, it makes plain that this is not a deficiency. Even in the act of hope we do not hope that we shall finally possess ourselves sometime. And in the event of love we certainly do not experience ourselves as those who possess themselves. It is not the case that hope and love compensate for the alleged deficiency of faith which does not permit man to possess himself. Since faith experiences not having oneself as an anthropological benefit, it expresses the fact that the self-relatedness of having is derived from a wrong anthropological attitude which is oriented to traffic with things which can be had. Self-possession, self-having, is a category oriented ontologically to the metaphysic of things, and is thus intrinsically wrong in its orientation. It is, however, a category which derives not only from a theoretical but also from an eminently practical false

12. See G. Ebeling, *Introduction to the Theological Theory of Language*, tr. R. A. Wilson (Philadelphia: Fortress Press, 1973), p. 202.

attitude of man about his humanity. But where God is experienced as the one coming to the world and thus coming nearer and nearer to man (as individual and genus!), nearer than man can be to himself, there the experience of not having oneself becomes an experience of anthropological expansion. The being of that person who is always related to himself is expanded into freedom from itself. In this freedom, man truly comes to himself, and that means not alone but together with God, but he does so without possessing himself. When man, addressed by God, permits himself to be interrupted in order to move further with God (rather than constantly returning to himself) and thus to advance the world of all men—that is the expansion which man experiences when he believes. And in *that* sense the believing person is the one liberated from fixation on himself, and believers are "the first released captives of creation."[13] To be able to let go of oneself—that is the *liberating* experience of God as the mystery of the world which makes man himself a mystery. Freed from himself, man *is* then on pathways which he must first prepare in the power of his freedom. But that is no deficiency but rather an advantage. In contrast with the theological tradition which follows Luther and the philosophical tradition up to Ernst Bloch, the insight that man's being is a becoming is to be understood as man's distinction. In faith, this distinction is affirmed to the extent that the believer preserves man as the mystery which corresponds to God. This he does in that he permits himself to be taken along by the God who is coming to the world in such a way that within the world new ways for humanity to come to itself become possible. These are ways which are not there before they are trod on. Thus one can predict and predetermine them only in a very limited way. Whether they will become human ways is something which the believing man, as he is letting himself go, can judge on the basis of two criteria apart from which faith cannot happen: love and hope.

(b) It is also true of *love* in its formal structure that it demonstrates man to be an essence which does not possess itself and therein is really human. Whoever possesses himself does not love. He does not desire to give himself away in order to win the beloved person. In love the transformation of having as man's basic attitude about himself takes place. But it is notable that it does not take place merely as the denunciation of having as a wrong attitude of man's in relation to his being, but rather it takes place when the loving I does not want to have itself apart from the beloved Thou. One could interpret that as an intensification of the possessive structure of human existence. There are certain depraved forms of love which suggest this. But in truth, having transforms itself in the event of love. It loses its analogy to the relation of possession in which man has things. In love, *having*, because it is inherently also a *being had*, becomes a *being*. We have already discussed this in detail and can now refer back to that discussion.[14] It should suffice to recall that the event of love is the most intensive event of self-withdrawal and of new and creative self-relatedness. It may be adequate to articulate love as that event in which an I no longer can exist for itself, so that it exists in connection with a Thou to become a We, and

13. On this term, see J. G. Herder, *Ideen zur Philosophie der Geschichte der Menschheit*, in *Sämmtliche Werke*, ed. B. Suphan (Berlin: Weidmannsche Buchhandlung, 1887 [=1967]), 1. Teil, 4. Buch, XIII, 146.
14. See above, pp. 318ff.

thus is really and properly an I in an unsurpassable sense. For that reason, the love relation radiates out beyond itself and penetrates society not only to create its own institutions and orders within it (such as the family) but also to question critically all the existing orders and institutions in favor of the conquest of love in all the areas and objectifications of human existence. In the event of love, man corresponds to the God who has come to the world in both the most intensive and most extensive ways. For this God is love. In the event of love man is at his most mysterious, not because he is most ununderstandable when he loves and is loved (that is always true, in a certain sense), but because he, as lover and beloved, corresponds to the God who reveals himself as love and who as love works invisibly. In the event of love, God and man share the same mystery.

In the event of love, the believer has the decisive criterion to judge whether humanity's ways to itself are humane ways—for the man liberated to freedom has been set into motion by his faith to find and to walk those ways. What serves love is human. Everything which serves love makes man more human, brings man further along the way of becoming a humanity which corresponds to God. But what hinders love is inhuman. It might be the most tested traditions and the holiest of orders—if they oppose the victory of love, they are hopelessly antiquated and reveal themselves to be institutions of that death which destroys all relations. Great steps of progress may be taken, and revolutions may take place— if they are opposed to the victory of love, then they may indeed influence the reality of the world but in all their influence they are merely processes which maneuver into cul-de-sacs, and in reality they are completely reactionary, because at the end of it all they simply promote death. Finally, life itself may be highly glorified and death may be battled against with every available means— if the struggle for life and against death does not serve love, its conclusion will be only the abstract glorification of a loveless life, and that is really the involuntary glorification of death. Because only that love which submits to death is as strong as death and thus stronger, love itself decides whether humanity will prepare its roadways in agreement with God's ways in order to advance the world on human ways. Love makes the decision whether man is a being of hope.

(c) Now it is also true of *hope,* as far as its formal structure is concerned, that it protects man from possessing himself. Whoever possesses himself, whoever has himself, does not hope. In the act of hope as well, as in this human mode of being, man lives out of the mystery that God has come to the world and as such remains the one who is coming into the world. Basically, every hope, even if it is directed existentially toward something entirely different, lives from the fact that man does not have himself and the being of his world is not self-having, self-possession. And the reason for that is that man and his world receive far more with the God who is coming into the world than the most perfect self-possession, the most perfect self-having, could ever offer.

Hope, when it is based on God's having come and thus is oriented to his future coming, is something other than the processing of the situation of deficiency connoted by something "not yet" being there. Obviously that is also a kind of hope, but one does not know whether it is something good or evil, like the 'hope' (*elpis*) which remained in Pandora's box. Hope can function as an opiate which provides diverting comfort over against the intolerability of present deficiencies, without giving any substance to what is hoped for. It is possible that even that kind of hope is valuable, although it is only an empty illusion. But the hope which corresponds to the God who is coming into the world is not any empty illusion. It does not happen as a result of one's own decision and thus is fundamentally different from the therapeutic function which is generally ascribed to hope when it is said, correctly, that it is inhuman to rob a man of hope. There is, to be sure, an affinity, a well-founded neighbor relationship between Christian hope and that respectable hope found on earth. But this affinity and neighborhood become comprehensible only on the basis of the fundamental difference of Christian hope from the therapeutic function of hope in that form.

The reason that Christian hope does not happen as a result of one's own decision, haphazardly made, is that it is a *result of love*. Whoever loves hopes for the future of love. For that reason, Christians who have experienced the love revealed in Jesus Christ in such a way that they believe the promise of that love and love without bounds hope for the future, hope for the return of Jesus Christ. That faith which is directed to the fact that Jesus Christ has come, that faith which is actively present in love, is directed at the same time as hope toward the future. It does that because it is hoping for God's coming and has good reason for that hope on the basis of his having come to the world. The future is for faith not a form of time which is before us anyway, and in which perhaps God could come once more. The reverse is true: the hope for the coming of God is what opens up the future for Christians. To put it anthropologically, this does not mean that in a future which is coming anyway love might assert itself as an exception (even as the absolute exception) and might possibly gain the victory, and so there is hope that this might really happen. Rather, the well-founded trust in love's universal victory emerges from that love in the present, which always establishes itself as an absolute exception. Calvin said correctly that he who does not hope does not believe.[15] It will be even more correct to have to say that whoever does not love also does not hope. Briefly, whoever loves has a reason to hope. Perhaps it is only the one who loves who has a reason for hope. He has it only because God himself is love.

Resting on that foundation, Christian hope does then approach a critical nearness to all the respectable hopes on earth. Because it emerges out of love, which when properly understood is identical with God, Christian hope is justified in seeing in every hope which hopes for the sake of love, an orientation of human existence toward what is coming to us, an orientation which is not in vain. Because it counts on the possibility of totally unfounded hopes and addresses these as to their emptiness, Christian hope is itself a hope for all whose well-founded hope is based on the fact that they love. It is in this critical solidarity with the hopes of the world that the man who hopes in God pursues his way through the world, in which he has a future because God is coming. And because of this critical solidarity of the hope which is directed to the God who is coming

15. Calvin, *Institutes of the Christian Religion,* ed. J. T. McNeill, tr. F. L. Battles, 2 vols. (*Library of Christian Classics,* vols. 20, 21) (Philadelphia: Westminster, 1960), III, ii, 42, p. 590: "Yet, wherever this faith is alive, it must have along with it the hope of eternal salvation as its inseparable companion. Or rather, it engenders and brings forth hope from itself. When this hope is taken away, however eloquently or elegantly we discourse concerning faith, we are convicted of having none."

with the hopes of the world, hope becomes the general criterion for the humanity of those ways on which humanity comes to itself and advances its world. But on these ways to itself, humanity can move further only if it recognizes, affirms, and processes its own *limitedness*. Ways without boundaries do not lead any farther.

It is with hope that man struggles with the anthropological truth that he and thus his world have limits. Man can also evade this struggle with this truth. Man can also give up over against the hard fact of his own limitedness, which is especially painful in view of the boundary of death and its finality, its *non plus ultra*. But then one would be giving up as a consequence of the humanity of man; one could be giving up in view of oneself. Man would then be understood apart from his call to faith and apart from his definition to love. The particular humanity of that man who is giving up is a humanity which is being catapulted into inhumanity. By contrast, hope is man's serious acknowledgment of and yet the no less serious struggle with his own limitedness. To relate oneself in hope to one's own limits means to affirm the limitedness of human existence and the limitedness of the world. In hope man takes seriously that there are boundaries drawn for him. But he struggles with this truth positively in the act of hope, in that first of all he learns to distinguish between those boundaries which represent finality and thus are set immovably, and those very different boundaries which man must set for himself if he wants to achieve something, but which as such are constantly to be broadened, changed, and if necessary even drawn more narrowly.[16] One can observe whether hope is present in the way in which man deals with the boundaries which are set by man for himself and those which men set for other men. Whoever wants to exist here without boundaries or who regards the standing boundaries as of value intrinsically and thus seeks to maintain them as immovable has no hope. To be without boundaries would mean to be hopeless. Whoever wants everything at once, and thus desires to be unlimited and boundariless, desires as one who has himself, possesses himself, and thus is a totally hopeless being. In the posture of the revolutionary Titan, he negates the mystery of the God who is coming just as much as does the reactionary who regards the boundaries set by man as eternal limitations. What hopeless figures! The invisible hope in the coming God becomes visible in the constantly new processing of the boundaries which man must constantly set anew, if his ways into the future are to be hopeful and thus also human.

But the hope of man is not limited to the ways which are to be followed in this world. Even those boundaries which are immovably set for man are by no means removed from the sphere of his hope. Quite the contrary, Christian hope applies especially to them to the extent that this hope knows man to be definitively limited solely by the God who is coming. The end of being, the end of the world age, and also of one's own period of life, all of which are seen here again as especially painful boundaries, are the objects of the most intensive hope as that end of being and time which is set by the God who is coming. For when God sets the end, then he, God, is there. And that means that the end is not followed by nothingness but rather the *transformation* of that earthly exis-

16. See E. Jüngel, "Grenzen des Menschseins," in *Probleme biblischer Theologie; Gerhard von Rad zum 70. Geburtstag* (München: C. Kaiser, 1971, 1973³), pp. 148-54.

tence, so limited and now ended, by the God who has limited and ended us with himself.[17] There is only a beginning and an end where being and time separate from each other. The end which is set by the God who is coming will be not an end only within being and time, but will be the end of that difference. God, as the end of being and time, is their absolute identity and thus also the transformation of human existence, limited by being and time, into an eternal life, a life in unsurpassable fellowship with God.

But with the end of being and time, the distinction between visible and invisible will also be moot. The God whom no one has ever seen will then—because "then" there will no more be a past, present, and future—become visible in his knownness as love "face to face" (I Cor. 13:12).

Looking toward that end, one can and may "rejoice in hope" (Rom. 12:12). Whereas man, resigned to his definitive boundaries and above all his end, is with his resignation (in what might be called the mode of renunciation) still fixated on the ontologically false ideal of humanity as self-having and self-possession, the man who is hoping for the God who is coming as the end can release himself. In a very precise sense, he can *let himself go*—toward the God who is coming.

Returning in faith to the God who is coming from himself to the world, taken along in the love of the human God who is coming to himself even in death, and in hope going toward the God who is coming and who is helping love to its victory, man preserves God as the mystery of the world. For that reason, faith, love, and hope *remain* (I Cor. 13:13). Joined together, they express in human form that God's being is in coming. And so they belong as human acts and modes of being to God as the mystery of the world. But since, in the event of love God and man already share the same mystery, love is the greatest of them (I Cor. 13:13). That is not because love is something than which nothing greater can be thought! Love—that is, rather, God as he cannot be thought and hoped for in any more human fashion. Love—that is therefore also the power which makes man human and still more human. In faith in *this* power and in the hope for its victory man never ceases to become *man*. Even in utterly clear distinction from that love, in a state of confusion, that man who is human without God will share more in the event of love, in faith in its power, and in hope for its victory, than an I which has itself would ever be able to have, and more than we would gain if we were ever able to have ourselves. The man who is human without God remains *one who has*, whether it is much or little, himself and everything. In love, we become *those who are*, who cannot cease *becoming*. In the dimension of having, becoming remains a process between too much and too little. But out of the being which corresponds to love arises a freer becoming which does not censure what it has surpassed, rejecting it as a deficiency, but which preserves it as something which was obviously earlier: an advance whose comparative honors what has been surpassed. To be sure, in this process of becoming we *have* a world without which we would neither be nor could be human. In the world which is characterized far too much by too much and too little, we remain those who have because we are not capable of being anything without having. To have enough remains a goal to be fought for in the world

---

17. See E. Jüngel, *Death, the Riddle and the Mystery*, trs. I. and U. Nicol (Edinburgh: St. Andrew Press, 1975), pp. 115-22.

where possession belongs to the basic structures. But love transforms those who
have into those who are, who understand how to become, as though they did
not have anything—namely, in the relationally rich differentiation from the God
who is that love which can neither be surreptitiously gained nor coerced, which
is entirely unnecessary and thus is more than necessary, becoming peculiarly
human and ever more human people.

Index of Names

Index of Subjects

—as 'Chain of love' (*vinculum ca-ritatis*) 388
—Trinitarian Structure of the Propositions
— "God is love" 368
— "God is coming" 380
—see also Coming
—Vestige of the Trinity 348f
Trust 170, 191, 196f, 251, 278
Trust in God 180f, 191
Truth viii, 106, 108, 113, 117, 180, 229, 307f, 309, 344, 377f
—of the Factual 308f
—Interest in 307f
—of Life 216
—of the Point 309
—Question of 112
—of What Is Told 309
Turning Away from Oneself 320
—see also Distance
—see also Freedom
Turning (to) 278, 320f, 328

Unbelief 102
—see also Faith
Unconditionalness 35f
Understanding 69f, 134, 278
Understanding of God 176, 205
Unity
—see Christology
—see Identity
—see Life and Death
—see Love
Univocality 144, 268-270, 272
Unknowability of God 283
—see also Knowing
Unspeakability of God 231f, 233f, 235f, 244f, 252, 255, 257, 260f, 277, 381
—see also Speakability
Unthinkability of God vii, 4, 8f, 139, 152, 207, 252, 381
—see also Thinkability
Usage 95, 294
'Used' (*uti*) 5f
ut consecutivum 322
ut finale 322f

Vernacular Language 10
viae ('Ways'), see Knowledge of God
Vulnerability of God 123

Way
—God's Way (of Life) 159f
—of Man 159
Weakness, Deficiency 113f, 116, 119, 121, 186, 216f, 337f, 378, 380

—of God 60, 101, 123
—Ontological 186
—see also Powerlessness
Wealth, see Abundance
Will
—Creative Human Will 148f, 372
—(Un)free 36
—of God 278
Wonder 33
Word 9f, 155, 164-166, 189f, 300f
—as Acts of Inclusion 10
—as Address (*kēryssein*) 301
—As Confession (*homologein*) 301
—as Eschatological Declaration of Time 301
—Event of 10, 12, 165, 213
—Ont(olog)ic Combination or Sequence of Past, Present, and Future 189f, 215
—as 'Note of the presence of a thing' (*nota praesentis rei*) 11
—as 'Sign' (*signum datum*) 4f, 6, 9ff
—as Signal 9f
—Structure of 171
Word of God 161-164, 165f, 170, 174, 176f, 198, 201, 226, 231, 288 344f, 386f
—see also Definitiveness of the Word of God
—as Image of God 386f
—as Original Image of the World 386f
— 'Word of God is the person of God speaking' (*verbum Dei est dei loquentis persona*) 346
Work 358f, 365
—Person and Work 196f
World 45, 52f, 57, 105, 228, 259, 276f, 301f, 349
—End of the World 301f, 379
—Experience of 52
—Infinity of 58
—as Man's Object 178f
—Maturity of 59f, 61
—in the Modern Age 52f
—see also Overimportance of
—Production of 52, 178
—see also Production
—Secular Interpretation 61
—Secularity 57f, 62
—Spirit of 56
—Turning Point of 301, 304, 364, 379
—Without God 57, 61f
—World-contradictions 53
—World-relationship 285
—World-understanding 176
—Secular World-understanding 58f
—see also Overimportance of

Yes of God 287f, 385

CPSIA information can be obtained
at www.ICGtesting.com
Printed in the USA
LVOW10s1724051217
558747LV00007B/31/P